LEARN, THINK AND
PREDICT THROUGH
ASTROLOGY

Professor C. P. Arora, PhD, is a former dean, head of department and professor of IIT. He has been involved in spiritual practices for many years now, including pranic healing, reiki, counselling and astrology. He also specializes in personality development.

LEARN, THINK AND PREDICT THROUGH
ASTROLOGY

*A Text on Vedic/Hindu/Indian Astrology with
Interface of Western Astrology*

C.P. ARORA

RUPA

Published by
Rupa Publications India Pvt. Ltd 2005
7/16, Ansari Road, Daryaganj
New Delhi 110002

Sales centres:
Allahabad Bengaluru Chennai
Hyderabad Jaipur Kathmandu
Kolkata Mumbai

ISBN: 978-81-291-0821-0

10 9 8 7 6

The moral right of the author has been asserted.

Typeset in Mindways Design, New Delhi

Printed at Anubha Printers, Greater Noida

Contents

APPENDIX

Preface

The interest of the common man in astrology has greatly increased in recent years. This is evident from the host of fortune forecast columns published by almost every newspaper, magazine or journal of importance. Everyone goes through them because of inherent interest. However, these do not help the reader much.

At the same time, there is a need for a book of substance on astrology for the common man from which one can learn on one's own. This book aims at fulfilling that need. The work is an effort to lay the subject of astrology on a logical basis. At first, the basic principles are enunciated, and then the reader is encouraged to derive results using those principles.

The salient features of the book are:

(i)   Common Sanskrit/Indian technical words with which the Indian reader is generally conversant, have been used liberally.
(ii) The soul of the subject is based on Vedic/Hindu/Indian astrology. However, the similarities and differences with Western astrology have been clearly explained.

(iii) Although this book is meant to be a text on predictions of astrology, a chapter has nevertheless, been devoted to calculation not only to make the work comprehensive, but also to bring out the basics about the movement of signs and planets in the heaven.

(iv) As and when required, illustrations, figures and tables have been given liberally to help the reader in the understanding of the subject.

(v) A sample horoscope has been constructed and analysed. It has been taken up as a case study so that the reader learns to cast a horoscope, and at the same time analyse and interpret it independently.

(vi) All topics of importance have been included. Hence, both *Lagna* and *Navansha* charts have been cast and discussed.

(vi) The last two chapters are an exclusive feature of the book. One on 'Special Topics' covers matters of common interest in detail. Another on 'Remedies' will guide the reader

    (a) to accept destiny, which is nothing but the result of one's own *Karmas* of present and innumerable previous births, and as a divine prescription for happiness in life after exhausting the effects of those Karmas;

    (b) to undertake rituals and spiritual practices to alleviate suffering while at the same time following virtuous conduct and reciting prayers;

    (c) and to wait for divine grace.

Thanks are due to my son Amitabh for developing the birth-chart on the computer, to my daughter Sangeeta for inspiration and help in preparing the manuscript and to my brother Ajaya for suggesting the name for the book.

C.P. Arora

Chapter 1

The Signs (*Rashis*)

Our destiny (*bhagya*) is nothing but the result of our own actions (*karmas*) of innumerable previous lives, as well as the present one. The birth-chart (*Janma-Kundali*) with which a person is born is simply an imprint of the same. The chart relates, at the time of birth of a person, the positions of various signs (*rashis*), planets (*grahas*) and constellations (*Nakshatras*) with respect to the houses (*ghar* or *bhavas*) signifying different aspects of an individual's life. Astrology is the science of predicting destiny with the help of birth-chart. We begin with the signs or *rashis* in this chapter.

1.1 INTRODUCTION TO SIGNS (*RASHIS*)

With the Earth at the centre of the universe as the reference point, the zodiac is a belt around the Earth as shown in Fig. 1.1. The Sun, the Moon and various other planets move among the stars along this belt within a certain width on either side of the centreline of motion. This circular belt involves

360 degrees of longitude. The zodiac is divided into twelve equal parts called signs (*rashis*). Thus, each sign or *rashis* comprises 30 degrees of the zodiac as also shown in Fig. 1.1.

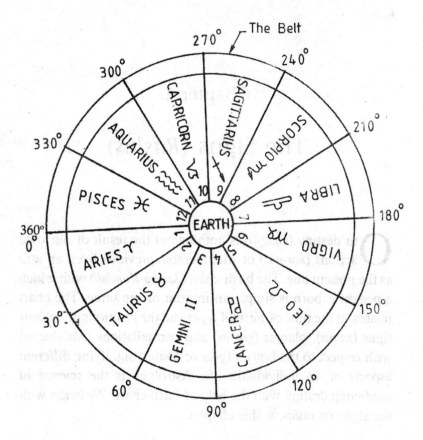

Fig. 1.1 The Signs of the Zodiac

The first of the twelve signs is Aries (*Mesh*). The starting point of the zodiac is at the beginning of this sign where the Sun enters on or about 15th April according to Vedic/Hindu astrology, and on 21st March according to Western astrology. The difference between the two systems has been explained later in this book. The counting of degrees of longitude begins from this point, which is assigned zero degree. Each sign is represented by an imaginary figure formed by prominent stars located in that sign. For example, a ram, denoted by the symbol ♈ for convenience, represents Aries. The names of the twelve signs, their degrees, symbols representing them and planets ruling over them are given in Table 1.1.

Table 1.1
Numbers, Degrees, Names, Symbols, Figures and Ruling Planets of Astrological Signs

Sign No.	Long. Deg.	Sign Name Western	Vedic/Hindu	Symbol	Figure	Ruling Planet
1	0–30	Aries	Mesha	♈	The Ram	Mars
2	30–60	Taurus	Vrishabha	♉	The Bull	Venus
3	60–90	Gemini	Mithuna	♊	The Twins	Mercury
4	90–120	Cancer	Karka	♋	The Crab	Moon
5	120–150	Leo	Simha	♌	The Lion	Sun
6	150–180	Virgo	Kanya	♍	The Virgin	Mercury
7	180–210	Libra	Tula	♎	The Balance	Venus
8	210–240	Scorpio	Vrishchika	♏	The Scorpion	Mars/Pluto
9	240–270	Sagittarius	Dhanu	♐	The Archer	Jupiter
10	270–300	Capricorn	Makara	♑	The Goat	Saturn
11	300–330	Aquarius	Kumbha	♒	The Pitcher	Saturn/Uranus
12	330–360	Pisces	Meena	♓	The Fish	Jupiter/Neptune

All the twelve signs have their intrinsic qualities. Their qualities are similar to those of the planets that rule over the signs. The keywords that summarise those qualities are given in Table 1.2.

Table 1.2
Characteristics of Astrological Signs

Sign	Keywords
Aries	head, energetic, dynamic, commander, assertive, aggressive,
Taurus	sincere, honest, simple, earthly, sensual, possessive, connoisseur of food.
Gemini	sociable, airy, talkative, communication, singing/reading/writing, sexual pleasure.
Cancer	masses, home loving, heart dominated, Emotional.
Leo	classes, status, regal, leader, protective, proud, valorous,
Virgo	precision, perfection, computation, earthly, calculative, feminine, sweet, amorous.
Libra	balance, harmony, diplomacy, sophistication, love.
Scorpio	passion, intense emotions, sexuality, secretive, drugs, chemicals.
Sagittarius	outdoor life, freedom, brave deeds, jovial, pious, magnanimous, expansive, travels.
Capricorn	earthly, prudent, slow but steady, perseverance, disciplinarian, just.
Aquarius	unconventional, values own freedom.
Pisces	idealist, saintly, intuitive, learned, spiritual, grateful, loving, compassionate, solitary, emotional, foreign lands.

1.2 RULERSHIP/LORDSHIP OF SIGNS

Although planets will be discussed in detail in Chapter 4, it is necessary to point out here itself that each sign has a planet which rules over the sign. This Ruling Planet is named the Lord (*swami*) of the sign. A planet is most comfortable if it is placed in the sign ruled by it, that is, in its own sign (*swarashi*). Its potential to do good is optimum when in its own sign. It also enhances the positive qualities of the sign. The names of ruling planets, viz., Lords of all twelve signs are also given in Table 1.1.

The Sun and the Moon are the two luminaries or royals of the zodiac. After assigning Sun to Leo and Moon to Cancer, the basic principle is to assign Mercury, the planet nearest to the Sun, to Virgo next to Leo in regular order and to Gemini next to Cancer in reverse order. Similarly, Mars, Jupiter and Saturn are assigned two signs each as shown in the chart below:

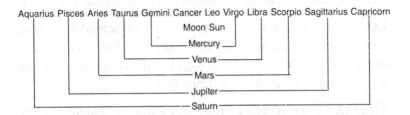

In Vedic astrology, it is very important to remember which planet is the Lord of which sign.

Note: The outer planets, Uranus, Neptune and Pluto were discovered only in the 20th century. They are slow moving planets and are far away from the Earth. They have very little effect on the day-to-day lives of individuals. These planets are additionally assigned to Aquarius, Pisces and Scorpio, respectively.

1.3 THE BASIC NATURE AND CHARACTERISTICS OF SIGNS

See Table 1.2 also.

Aries (*Mesha*) resembles a ram. Ram is a fighter that roams among the sheep and the goats. The sign is ruled by the planet Mars. Hence, it has all the characteristics of Mars.

Taurus (*Vrishabha*) is strong but calm like a bull. It resides in farmlands and cow-houses. It has the characteristics of physical love derived from its ruling planet Venus.

The amorous twins, viz., a man and a woman represent **Gemini (*Mithuna*)**. The couch and the pleasure-houses are the places where it likes to reside. It circulates among the speakers, talkative people, singers, dancers, sculptors and sports lovers. The sign has the characteristics of its Lord Mercury.

Cancer (*Karka*) is watery, implying fluidic/emotional, represented by a crab, which lives in water, garden beds, riverbanks, etc. It has waxing and waning moods like the Moon.

Leo (*Simha*) is brave, dominating and represented by a lion, which lives in forests, mountains and caves. Leo is referred to as the king of the zodiac. The sign has the characteristics and regal status attributed to its Lord Sun.

Virgo (*Kanya*) is represented by very feminine maiden/virgin, that is, *Kanya* in Sanskrit. Women's pleasure rooms are its favourite places of residence. This sign also has the characteristics of its Lord Mercury.

Tula, meaning weighing balance, represents the characteristics of the **Libra (*Tula*)**. Accordingly, the sign implies the balancing act in all respects. Its places of residence are in bazaars and marketplaces. It has the characteristics of sophistication of its Lord Venus.

A scorpion truly represents the **Scorpio (*Vrishchika*)**. It moves in dark secretive places. It resides in areas with poisonous substances, insects, excreta of animals, etc. The sign has the dynamism and aggressiveness of its Lords Mars and Pluto.

Sagittarius (*Dhanu*) is represented by a radiant and cheerful charioteer or archer, riding on a horse and holding a bow and arrow in hands. It is well versed in handling arms and doing risky and daredevil deeds. It likes outdoor life and activities. The sign has the characteristics of expansion of its Lord Jupiter.

Capricorn (*Makara*) is represented by a slow but steady and serious looking creature resembling a goat with small but sharp eyes like those of an elephant, shoulders like those of a bull and the mouth of a deer. It prefers to reside in rivers. The sign has the earthly characteristics of discipline and perseverance of its Lord Saturn.

Aquarius (*Kumbha*) is freedom loving and is represented by a man holding a pitcher. Its favourite places of residence are drinking dens and gambling houses. The sign has the characteristics of a person who loves common people, and is signified by its Lord Saturn. It also has the freedom loving nature of Uranus.

Finally, **Pisces (*Meena*)** is watery in nature and represented by a pair of fish with the head of one beside the tail of the other. Its favourite places of residence and circulation are the oceans, rivers, pilgrim centres, religious places, temples, etc. It moves among saintly people. The sign is characterised by the spirituality and idealism of its Lord Jupiter and the emotionalism and vision of its Lord Neptune.

A person's total personality is determined by a combination of characteristics of signs of all the planets, and essentially by the ascendant, viz., *lagna* and the Sun and Moon signs:

Ascendant Sign or *Lagna Rashi*

Ascendant or *lagna* is the sign rising on the eastern horizon at the time of birth. It determines the overall personality and physical body of the person.

Sun Sign or *Surya Rashi*

It is the sign in which Sun is placed at the time of birth. This governs the native's spirit/soul.

Moon Sign or *Chandra Rashi*, also called *Janma-Rashi*

It is the sign in which Moon is placed at the time of birth. This determines the mind (*Mana*). When we say *Janma-Rashi* in Vedic/Hindu astrology, it implies Moon Sign.

Similarly, Mercury Sign determines the person's intelligence, Mars Sign stamina, Jupiter Sign spiritual qualities and prosperity, Venus Sign one's sex and love life, Saturn Sign one's steadfastness, etc.

There are no 'good' or 'bad' signs. Each sign has both positive and negative characteristics.

Male and Female Signs

The signs are assigned numbers, starting from 1 for Aries and ending with 12 for Pisces. The signs with odd numbers, viz., odd signs are male signs. These are:

1.Aries 3.Gemini 5.Leo 7.Libra 9.Sagittarius 11.Aquarius

Odd or male signs have some malefic tendencies and masculine attributes. Out of the above, signs 3, 7 and 9 are comparatively softer since their Lords Mercury, Venus and Jupiter are benefics.

And the signs with even numbers, viz., even signs are female signs. These are:

2.Taurus 4.Cancer 6.Virgo 8.Scorpio 10.Capricorn 12.Pisces

Even or female signs have benefic tendencies and feminine attributes. Out of the above, signs 8 and 10 are not so soft since their Lords Mars and Saturn are malefic.

Note: If the Ascendant, the Sun and the Moon, are all in male signs in the horoscope, then the person will be aggressive. On the other hand, if these are in female signs, then s/he will be passive and mild. More planets in male signs in a birth-chart endow one with vigour, stamina, courage, etc. More planets in female signs make one soft-natured.

The Triplicities of Signs and Four Elements (*Tattvas*) and their Qualities

Signs are divided into four categories, called triplicities, based on the four elements or *Tattvas,* viz., Fire (*Agni*), Earth (*Prithvi*), Air (*Vayu*) and Water (*Jala*). The elements impart the signs with their basic nature. The signs also signify directions as follows:

Element	Signs	Nature	Direction
Fire	Aries/Leo/Sagittarius	**FIERY.** Energetic, accident prone	East
Earth	Taurus/Virgo/Capricorn	**EARTHLY.** Practical, static	South
Air	Gemini/Libra/Aquarius	**AIRY.** Intellectual, communicative	West
Water	Cancer/Scorpio/Pisces	**WATERY.** Emotional, sensitive	North

Note: (i) Signs in the same triplicity are at 120 degrees to each other, forming a trine.

(ii) Fiery signs are accident-prone. But they have the best ability to recover from ill-health. Earthly signs are the next best in this respect. Airy signs are weaker in respect of resistance to disease. Watery signs have poor resistance to disease.

The Quadruplicities of Signs and their Qualities

Signs are also divided into categories of four signs each called quadruplicities, as follows:

Category	Signs	Dominant Quality
MOVABLE (Cardinal)	Capricorn Aries Libra Cancer	Fond of change/movement.
FIXED	Aquarius Taurus Scorpio Leo	Not amenable to change, cautious, reserved, sedentary habits.
COMMON (Dual/Mixed)	Pisces Gemini Sagittarius	Adaptable.

Common or dual signs, also called mixed or mutable, have the qualities of both fixed and movable signs. Generally, the first 15 degrees of these signs have the characteristics nearer to those of the fixed, and the next 15 degrees nearer to those of the movable.

Note: Signs in the same quadruplicity are at 90 degrees to each other, forming a square.

Signs and Parts of Human Body

The zodiac is conceived as representing the body of the Eternal Being (*Kaal-Purush*). The twelve signs represent different parts of body beginning with Aries representing the Head to Pisces for the Feet in that order as follows, and as indicated in Fig. 1.2:

1	Aries	Head
2	Taurus	Face (up to Tongue), mouth
3	Gemini	Throat, neck, shoulders, arms, upper chest
4	Cancer	Breasts, lungs, heart (according to Varahamira)
5	Leo	Stomach, portion above navel, heart (according to *Vaman-Purana*)
6	Virgo	Navel, portion below navel/above *basti*, digestive system
7	Libra	*Basti*, lower abdomen, urinary tract, uterus
8	Scorpio	External genitals, anus
9	Sagittarius	Hips, thighs
10	Capricorn	Back, knees
11	Aquarius	Legs, calves
12	Pisces	Feet

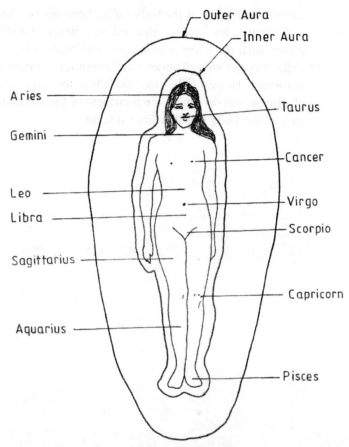

Fig. 1.2 Aura and Signs Representing Parts of the Human Body

Note: (i) Both Cancer and Leo and their Lords Moon and Sun are attributed to the heart. Cancer signifies the heart more prominently while Leo signifies the stomach.

(ii) The part of the body from the navel to the genitals is divided into two equal parts. The upper half, the navel region and below, is assigned to Virgo, and the lower half up to the external genitals, called *basti,* is assigned to Libra.

(iii) If any sign in an individual's horoscope is tenanted by a malefic (*ashubha*) planet or is aspected by it, then the corresponding part of the body suffers from disease. And, if the sign is tenanted or aspected by a benefic (*shubha*) planet, then the corresponding part will be healthy.

(iv) Different signs will fall under different houses of a person's horoscope. However, the sign that falls in the sixth house of disease will determine the proneness of the associated part of the body to suffer from disease.

Chapter 2

The Houses (*Ghar/Bhavas*)

2.1 THE BIRTH-CHART/HOROSCOPE (*JANMA-KUNDALI*)

The Birth-Chart or Horoscope (*Janma-Kundali*) is a diagram showing the sign rising on the eastern horizon and the placement of planets in different signs at the time of birth.

In a horoscope, just as there are 12 signs, there are also 12 houses (*Ghar*) signifying matters or aspects of life (*bhavas*), also called places (*Sthan*) or sections (*Khanas*). House, *Ghar*, *Bhava*, *Sthan* and *Khana*—all mean the same thing. Each of the twelve houses occupies 30 degrees of longitude, thus completing 360 degrees of the zodiac.

The sign rising on the eastern horizon at the time of birth is named the ascendant, the *lagna rashi* or simply the *lagna*. It becomes the sign of the First House in the birth chart. The first house represents the physical body and overall personality of the native, viz., the individual self. The signs of the 12 houses follow the Ascendant Sign in sequential order in an anticlockwise manner. Thus, if Taurus is the sign of the first house, then Gemini is the sign of the Second House, Cancer is the sign of the Third House, and so on, so that the sign falling in the twelfth house is Aries. Then after placing the planets in the houses according to their signs at the time of birth, we obtain the birth chart or *Janma-Kundali*.

We can say that the planets describe 'what' happens, the signs describe 'how' it happens, and the houses tell in 'which area or aspect' of a person's life it happens.

Lord of the House (*Bhavesh*)

Each house or *bhava* has a sign. The ruling planet of the sign is named the Lord of the house/*bhava*, viz., *bhavesh*. Thus, Lord of the sign in first (*Pratham*) house is referred to as *Prathamesh*, Lord of the sign in second (*Dwitiya*) house as *Dwitiyesh*, and so on. Also, since the first house is *lagna* and second house pertains to wealth (*Dhana*), hence the two are called respectively *Lagnesh* and *Dhanesh* as well. Similarly, Lords of other houses are named as follows:

Third House	*Tritiyesh, Parakramesh, Bhratra Bhavesh*
Fourth House	*Chaturthesh, Sukhesh, Matri Bhavesh*
Fifth House	*Panchamesh, Vidya Bhavesh, Putra Bhavesh*
Sixth House	*Shashtesh, Shatru Bhavesh, Rog Bhavesh* or *Rogesh*
Seventh House	*Saptamesh, Kalatra Bhavesh*
Eighth House	*Ashtamesh, Ayurbhavesh*
Ninth House	*Navamesh, Bhagyesh, Dharma Bhavesh* or *Dharmesh*
Tenth House	*Dashamesh, Karma Bhavesh* or *Karmesh, Pitra Bhavesh* or *Pitresh*
Eleventh House	*Ekadashesh, Labhesh, Aayesh*
Twelfth House	*Dwadashesh, Vyaya Bhavesh* or *Vyayesh*

2.2 FORMAT OF THE BIRTH-CHART

Fig. 2.1 shows the format of the birth-chart according to Vedic/ Hindu Astrology as followed in the northern part of India. In this chart, 1 degree 53 minutes 35 seconds of the sign Taurus was rising on the eastern horizon at the time of birth. So, the first house of the native becomes Taurus. The sign number is 2. The cusp of the first house is at 1 degree 53 minutes 35 seconds Taurus. Note that the line at the beginning of each house is known as its cusp. The cusps of other houses can also be found. However, most astrologers are content with finding the cusp of the first house, and correspondingly that of the seventh house, which is exactly 180 degrees away, and then assigning different signs to different houses. Thus in this case, the second house is Gemini (3), third Cancer (4), fourth Leo (5), fifth Virgo (6), sixth Libra (7), seventh Scorpio (8) with its cusp at 1 degree 53 minutes 35 seconds, eighth Sagittarius (9), ninth Capricorn (10), tenth Aquarius (11), eleventh Pisces (12) and twelfth Aries (1).

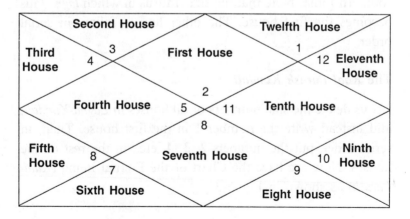

Fig. 2.1 Format of the Birth-Chart

The only thing missing in the chart in Fig. 2.1 are the placement of planets. So, after having found the Ascendant, the cusps and the signs of the houses, we have to find the positions of planets from an Ephemeris, and place them in different houses according to their respective signs in which they are located on the date and time of birth.

Note that the numbers 1, 2, 3, etc., represent the signs Aries, Taurus, Gemini and so on. And, the numerals I, II, III, IV, etc., represent the First, Second, Third, houses and so on.

Pisces	Aries	Taurus	Gemini
Aquarius			Cancer
Capricorn			Leo
Sagittarius	Scorpio	Libra	Virgo

Fig. 2.2 Format of the Birth-Chart as Prevalent in Southern India

Fig. 2.2 shows the format of the chart as prevalent in southern India. Note that the sign Taurus in which *lagna* falls becomes the first house. The other houses follow in serial order.

The *Kaal Purush Kundali*

Let us delete the sign numbers of all houses in *Lagna-Kundali*, and instead write the number 1 in the first house. Then, in serial order, put the numbers 2, 3, 4, etc., in the rest of the houses. Now, we have the Chart of the Eternal Being (*Kaal-Purush*) as shown in Fig. 2.3.

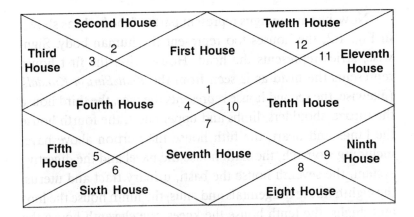

Fig. 2.3 the Kaal Purush Kundali

Now, let the placement of planets remain the same in the *Kaal Purush Kundali* as in the actual *Lagna-Kundali*. Such a horoscope will be based on the principles of *Laal Kitaab*.

There is greater emphasis in the *Laal Kitaab* on houses rather than on their signs. Thus, the **natural sign of the first house is Aries**. Similarly, the natural signs of the houses second, third, fourth, etc., are Taurus, Gemini, Cancer, and so on. Then, if Mars is placed in anyone's horoscope in the first house, it is considered good even if it is placed in an unfavourable sign, as it is the Lord of Aries, the natural sign of the first house.

2.3 MATTERS JUDGED FROM HOUSES (*BHAVAS*)

Let us now see 'what matters' are judged from each house. It will be seen that more than one matter falls under each house. We shall also see that certain matters fall under more than one house. For example, marital happiness will depend on many departments of life such as health, wealth, nature, family, compatibility, destiny, etc., of the two persons.

Now, just as the signs represent parts of the body as shown in Fig. 1.2, the houses too represent the human body. Sign-wise, Aries represents the head. House-wise, the first house represents the head as is seen from the *Kaal Purush Kundali*. Likewise, the second house represents the face, the third house the throat, shoulders, limbs and upper chest, the fourth house the lungs and heart, the fifth house the portion above navel including stomach, the sixth house the navel and the digestive system, the seventh house the basti, urinary tract and uterus, the eighth house the genitals and anus, the ninth house the hips and thighs, the tenth house the knees, the eleventh house the calves of legs, and the twelfth house the feet. Whichever *bhava* is tenanted/aspected by benefic/*shubha* planets, and if the Lord of that *bhava* is strong, then part of the body associated with that *bhava* will be healthy.

A brief list of matters judged from various houses is given in Table 2.1. The guiding principles are described below. Note that the principle of *Bhavat-bhava* as described in Sec. 2.5 is very important in assigning matters of consideration for each house.

The First House or Ascendant (*Lagna*)

The first house/*lagna* represents the 'self', the native him/herself, his/her physical body, features, complexion, personality, characteristics, nature, temperament, health and longevity. It is the natural house of Aries sign. Hence, it represents the head in the body. The ruling planet of Aries is Mars. The first house, therefore, represents vitality in the person.

The Second House

The house closest to the first house is the second house. It represents matters closest to the native, viz., family, wealth, food, and speech and expression. The second house is for movable assets, accumulated wealth, etc. It is the natural house of Taurus. Hence, it governs the face and the tongue. Its ruling planet is Venus. Taurus and Venus tie the native to the family, possessions, accumulated wealth, etc. In short, the second is the house of wealth (*Dhana bhava*). It also represents the right eye.

The Third House

This is the house of the native's immediate environment, viz., brothers and sisters, particularly younger ones, close relatives and servants. It also represents the native's physical and mental stamina, effort, valour and prowess, power, motivation. The natural sign of the. third house is Gemini, which controls shoulder, arms, and throat, neck, upper chest. It covers the ear nose throat, viz., ENT area. Parts of the lungs can be considered to fall under the third house. Note the throat. One is made a singer only by this house. It also represents outdoor activities such as sports. Mercury rules this sign, hence, it governs speaking, reading and writing ability, short journeys and communications and nervous system. It represents singing ability also since the melody arises from the throat. In short, the third house is the house of siblings (*Bhratra bhava*) and valour/stamina (*Parakram bhava*).

The Fourth House

The fourth house is that of the mother, home, happiness, friends and private life and character of the native, as well as vehicles owned by the native. While the second is for movable assets, the fourth is for immovable assets such as house, property, land, agricultural fields, etc. It is the heredity house, the one where the native is born.

It is the natural house of Cancer and its Lord, the Moon. Hence it governs one's emotions, attachment to home, mother, lungs and emotional as well as physical heart. Basically, the fourth is the house of home and happiness (*Sukha bhava*) and mother (*Matri bhava*).

The Fifth House

This is the house of creativity. It is the house of the native's intelligence and discretion, education, conception leading to birth of a child, sons and daughters and happiness from them, love-life, romance, etc. It is the natural house of Leo and its Lord, the Sun. Hence, it governs the soul/spirit/enthusiasm in the person.

It also represents gains arising from the spouse, as fifth is eleventh from seventh house of spouse. In short, it is the house of education (*Vidya bhava*) and children (*Putra bhava*). It also represents the upper abdomen/stomach.

The Sixth House

The sixth house is one of the three evil/inauspicious houses known as *trik,* the other two being the eighth and twelfth. They represent largely negative matters. But some positive matters are also covered under these houses.

Sixth is the house of diseases (*Rog bhava*) and enemies (*Shatru bhava*), disease being the worst enemy of any person.

Apart from the above negative matters, there are some positive matters under this house as well. For example, it represents health matters. It is the natural house of Virgo and its Lord, Mercury. It represents the navel region, waist and digestive system. It represents maternal uncle/s and aunt/s, or maternal relations and cousins in general. It hints about competition and success in those respects. Thus, one is made a sportsperson by this house.

The sixth house being ninth from tenth and tenth from ninth also represents success in career, service to others, etc.

Note: (i) Houses from the first to the sixth are related to the native's inner life. More planets here would indicate that the native is primarily concerned with his/her inner world.

(ii) Houses from the seventh to the twelfth are related to native's interaction with others. More planets therein would show that the native's interest is in the outside world.

(iii) The two groups of houses seem to pair off, for example, first with the seventh, second with eighth, third with ninth, and so on, i.e., with the 'opposites'.

The Seventh House

This house pairs off with the first house. As a counterpart to *lagna* the self, it is the house of the partner of the native. It is the natural house of Libra and its Lord, Venus. The house, therefore, represents partnerships. The greatest partner in life is one's spouse. Hence, it is the house of husband or wife in particular and the opposite sex in general. It also represents the Basti region, viz., the lower abdomen and internal organs of the sexual and urinary system. It is also the house of business partnerships, joint ventures and foreign travel.

It also indicates the nature/personality of the marriage partner and quality of relationships. For example, Mars in seventh implies a dominating spouse. Uranus in seventh implies upheavals in married life since such a native would care more for his or her own freedom than for deep attachment. Saturn in the seventh house indicates a stable but dull and lukewarm married life.

The Eighth House

Like the sixth, the eighth too is an evil/inauspicious house. It is the house of death, accidents, chronic diseases, thefts and sudden losses, etc. It represents some positive matters also such as longevity as a counterpart to death, sudden gains and legacies as a counterpart to sudden losses, destruction, and so on. It is primarily the house of longevity (*Ayur-bhava*). The natural sign of the house is Scorpio. Therefore, it represents external genitals, uterus, sexuality, etc. On a profound level, signifying the intensity of Scorpio sign, it has connections with the occult and spiritual wisdom (*Gyan-Tattva*). The eighth house is second from the seventh. Hence, it represents wealth of spouse as well.

The Ninth House

It pairs off with the third house of one's efforts, prowess and stamina. The ninth house, therefore, deals with the outcome of the same, which is one's 'fate'. It is primarily the house of destiny (*Bhagya bhava*). It also represents water reservoirs, wells and lakes. While the third house deals with short journeys, the ninth house deals with long journeys. The natural sign of the house is Sagittarius. Sagittarius stands for possibilities of living abroad, dealings with foreigners, etc. Its Lord is Jupiter. Hence, it is the house of spirituality and religious acts (*Dharma bhava*). A strong Jupiter in the ninth will make the native religious and pious. A strong Saturn herein will make one more philosophical than religious. Mars and Ketu in the ninth will lead one to unorthodox behaviour. It is also the house of one's preceptor or Guru. In southern India, the ninth house is taken for father as well since father is held in high esteem like a Guru.

The third house stands for brothers/sisters. Hence, the ninth, seventh from third, is for their spouses. Again, since the ninth is also third from the seventh, it represents brothers and sisters of spouse. Accordingly, the ninth house represents all brothers- and sisters-in-law.

As the ninth is fifth from the fifth, it also represents children's children, viz., grandchildren.

The Tenth House

The fourth house stands for one's mother. Opposite the fourth, the tenth is for father (*Pitra bhava*). The fourth house deals with matters of home, happiness, etc. As opposed to this, the tenth deals with matters pertaining to public life, the nature of one's job, career, skill, achievements, success, recognition, status, name and fame, etc. Thus, it is the house of one's deeds (*Karma bhava*).

It is the natural house of the sign Capricorn and its Lord Saturn that governs service. Planets in the fourth house show the native's standing as a private person. Planets in the tenth house show his/her standing in the outside world.

The Eleventh House

It pairs off with the fifth house. As the fifth house stands for education or training, the eleventh is for gains (*Labha sthan*) accruing as a result of the same. It is the house of recurring income (*Aaya bhava*) or earnings (*Artha bhava*).

As the fifth stands for love life, the eleventh stands for intimate friendship, hopes, aspirations, impulses and fulfilment of desires (*Kaam bhava*). Venus herein will show that the native develops relationships in a very easy manner. While the fifth is for children, the eleventh is for children's spouses as also for elder brother/sister because the first house would be third from the eleventh house. Legs also come under this house.

A strong eleventh house is essential for the fulfilment of desires. And unless the desires are fulfilled, one cannot hope for detachment, and ultimately liberation from the cycle of birth and death.

The Twelfth House

The twelfth house represents all kinds of expenditure and losses (*Vyaya bhava*), even waste of energy, wanderings far away from home, etc. It is an inauspicious house like the sixth and the eighth. It includes positive aspects like pleasures of the bed, sleep, left eye, enlightenment, foreign visits, stay abroad and gains thereof.

It is the natural house of Pisces, ruled by Jupiter and Neptune. Both Jupiter and Neptune signify self-denial and service to others. Hence, it represents a kind of retreat or withdrawal from worldly life in the mental sense. A good twelfth house indicates the pursuit of liberation/salvation (*Moksha*). Jupiter herein, however, indicates religious fanaticism, or belief in a cult. Mercury herein may make one interested in meditation.

Table 2.1
Matters Judged from Houses (*Bhavas*)

House	Part/s of Body	Relation/s	Other Matters
I	Head, physical body	Self	Ascendent/*Lagna*, personality, features, complexion, temperament, health, longevity
II	Face, right eye, tongue, mouth	Family	*Dhana bhava*, wealth, family, food, speech, accumulated wealth
III	Shoulders, arms, ENT area, right ear	Brothers/ sisters, relatives, servants	*Bhratra-bhava, Parakrama/Purushartha-bhava*, valour, stamina, prowess, voice, reading/writing/speaking/singing ability, sports, short journeys, communication
IV	Chest, lungs, heart	Mother, friends	*Matri-bhava, Sukha-bhava*, home, residence, birth place, happiness, mental peace, moral values, character, property, water reservoirs, conveyance, vehicles
V	Stomach	Children	*Putra/Santaan-bhava. Vidya-bhava*, education, intelligence, astrology, love life, devotion to God, speculation gains
VI	Navel, digestive system	Maternal relations, cousins	*Shatru bhava, Rog-bhava*, enemies diseases, illness, fear, vices, debts, litigation, suffering, sports, success in competitions, gain from service, Career

contd.

House	Part/s of Body	Relation/s	Other Matters
VII	Urinary tract	Spouse	*Kalatra-bhava,* spouse, marriage, sexual relations, partnership, foreign travel
VIII	Genitals, anus		*Aayu-Sthan,* longevity, death, accidents, spiritual wisdom (*Gyan Tattva*), occult, windfall gains/losses, inheritances
IX	Thighs, hips	Brothers-sisters-in-law, grand-children	*Bhagya-sthan, Dharma-Sthan,* destiny. religion, dharma, spirituality, preceptor, higher education long journeys.
X	Back, knees	Father	*Pitra-bhava, Karma-bhava,* career, deeds, status, name/fame, government/authorities
XI	Legs, left ear	Elder siblings intimate friends	*Aaya-sthan. Kaam bhava,* income Gains, fulfilment of desires
XII	Feet, left eye	Paternal relations	*Vyaya-sthan,* expenditure/losses scandals, hospitalisation, pleasures of the bed, sleep, gains from foreign lands pilgrimages

2.4 CLASSIFICATION OF HOUSES

Houses I, II, IV, V, VII, IX, X and XI are considered good (*shubha*). Their Lords, except the Lord of the eleventh house, are also *shubha*. Houses III, VI, VIII and XII are considered evil (*ashubha*). Their Lords are also *ashubha*. The following are some of the classifications adopted to designate the houses.

Angles or Quadrants (*Kendras*)

The four houses I, IV, VII and X are called Angles or Quadrants (*kendras*). These form the central quadrants of the horoscope. The midpoints of these houses are at 90 degrees to each other forming a square. These and their Lords are *shubha*.

Trines (*Trikonas*)

The three houses I, V and IX are called Trines (*trikonas*). The midpoints of these houses are at 120 degrees to each other, forming an equilateral triangle. These and their Lords are great benefics/*shubha*.

Note: The *lagna* is both an angle as well as a trine. It is the most important and powerful house. Its Lord is always *shubha*. Astrologers consider the ninth as the next most powerful house in any chart after the Ascendent. Its Lord is also always the *shubha*. Ninth is the strongest *trikona*, and the tenth is the strongest *kendra*. Ninth is for *Dharma*, and tenth is for Dharma. Both are intimately connected. Dharma is one's religious philosophy. *Karmas* or actions without Dharma would be devoid of any significance. The two together will make the basic difference between good and evil.

Evil *Trik* Houses

The houses VI, VIII and XII are the three inauspicious or the evil *trik* houses. These and their Lords are *ashubha*. The eighth house and eighth Lord are the most malefic.

Upchaya Houses

The houses III, VI, X and XI are called *Upchaya* houses. The two houses III and XI are considered as Lean or Weak Houses. The third and its Lord are mildly *ashubha*. The eleventh Lord is *ashubha*, but the eleventh house is *shubha* for placement of any planet. It is best for the malefic/*ashubha* planets to be in houses III, VI and XI.

Note: The only remaining house is the second which is considered as *shubha sthan*.

Houses of Longevity (*Aayu-Sthanas*)

The eighth house is the house of longevity. The eighth from eighth is the third house. The third house also becomes the house of longevity.

Maraka-Sthanas

A house, which is twelfth from a house, denotes its loss. Thus, the seventh house, being twelfth from eighth, and second house being twelfth from third become houses of loss of longevity. They are named as *Maraka-Sthanas*. The Lords of these houses are called *Marakas*. During the period of their influence, they can inflict death or death-like situations on the native.

2.5 MATTERS JUDGED FROM HOUSES RELATIVE TO EACH HOUSE (*BHAVAT-BHAVA*)

The principle that works is that of *Bhavat-bhava.* This is applied in two ways.

First, we judge the matter not only from the *bhava,* viz., the house, but also from the the same number of houses away from the house under consideration. For example, we judge children from the fifth house, and also fifth from the fifth, i.e. from the ninth house. As stated earlier we judge longevity from eighth house as well as from third house, which is eighth from eighth.

Second, we can judge matters related to each house considering the house under consideration as the first house. For example, consider the seventh house. The eighth house being second from seventh represents spouse's wealth, the ninth house being third from seventh represents spouse's brothers/ sisters, and so on. The sixth house, which is twelfth from seventh, represents loss or ill-health or unhappiness to/from the spouse.

Note: (i) The twelfth house from every house represents expenditure/
loss/waste of potential and significations of that house.
Placement of the Lord or ruling planet of the house in the
house preceding it, which is twelfth from itself, implies, the
denial of significations of that house. For example, Seventh
Lord in sixth denies marriage, fourth Lord in third denies
happiness, and so on.

(ii) The house-Lord (*Bhavesh*) should not be in the evil *trik*
houses, viz., sixth, eighth or twelfth from *lagna*. In addition,
according to the principle of *Bhavat-Bhava*, it should also
not be in the sixth, eighth and twelfth positions counted
from the house itself.

Chapter 3

Casting the Horoscope/Birth-Chart (*Janma-Kundali*)

The subject of astrology has two parts: *Ganit*, the calculation part and *Phalit*, the predictive part.

Astrologers are mainly interested in the predictive part. However, it is not possible to predict with accuracy without knowing the intricacies of the calculation part. It is therefore necessary to know how the calculations are done. The basics of calculation procedure are given in this chapter.

3.1 REQUIREMENTS AND PROCEDURE

For casting the birth-chart (*Janma-Kundali*) of any person, the following data are needed:

(i) Date of birth;
(ii) Local mean time of birth;
(iii) Place of birth with its latitude and longitude.

The procedure involves the following steps:

(i)   Finding the ascendant sign rising on the eastern horizon at the time of birth along with the longitude of its cusp. Likewise, the longitudes of the cusps and the signs of the other houses are found.

(ii) Planets are then placed in the chart in different houses according to their positions in different signs at the date and time of birth.

(iii) Finally, periods of influence (*Dashas*) of various planets in the native's life are determined.

In this chapter we will deal with the first two parts, viz., making the chart.

Why is the time of birth required? We know that the Earth revolves about its axis. In one rotation of 360 degrees, which takes 24 hours, all the 12 signs appear on the horizon. Thus, different signs appear on the eastern horizon every 24/12 or 2 hours. And each sign stays on the horizon until the next sign appears after 360/12 or 30 degrees. This rising sign at the time of birth becomes the ascendant or *lagna,* viz., the first house in the native's horoscope. Once the ascendant sign is decided, the signs of the rest of the houses also get fixed. Accordingly, even if two persons are born on the same day their *lagnas* and hence their characteristics and destinies will be different.

The aids required in casting the horoscope consist of:

(i)   Raphael's Table of Houses that gives the duration of each sign rising for different latitudes.

(ii) Ephemeris for the year of birth, which is a table showing the date-wise position of each planet at a certain fixed time, usually Greenwich Mean Time or

GMT Noon which is the same as Indian Standard Time, IST 5:30 p.m.

Note: Needless to say, one must know the difference between Local Standard Time/LST and GMT. This difference between IST, LST of India, and GMT is 5H 30M.

At the outset, let us use the following notations:

For longitude angles: S D M S for signs, degrees, minutes and seconds, respectively. Note that one sign means 30 degrees, two signs 60 degrees and so on.

For time: H M S for hours, minutes and seconds, respectively.

3.2 SAMPLE HOROSCOPE

Let us make a sample horoscope for a male child with birth details as follows:

Date of Birth (DOB)	8 August 1934
Time of BIRTH (TOB)	11:50 pm, Indian Standard Time (IST)
Place of Birth (POB)	Lucknow, India.
	Latitude 26 D 50 M North
	Longitude 80 D 54 M East of Greenwich

This indicates that we need the table of houses for 26 D 50 M latitude. The same for Delhi, Latitude 28 D 40 M is reproduced in Appendix A in abridged form.

Secondly, we need the ephemeris for the year 1934.

IST is the same throughout India, from the far northeast to the far west. However, at 11:50 pm IST, the solar time and hence the rising sign and its degrees will be different for different places from east to west.

3.3 LOCAL MEAN TIME OR LMT OF BIRTH

The ascending degree of the rising sign, viz., the cusp of the first house/*lagna* will have to be determined on the basis of actual solar time called the Local Mean Time LMT at Lucknow. Hence, the first step is to convert the IST into LMT.

For the purpose, we have to ascertain the central meridian of the country/state on the basis of which the Standard Time, ST, has been fixed. For example, the IST is fixed for Allahabad in India, which is 82 D 30 M East of Greenwich. During its rotation, the Earth takes 4 minutes of time for each degree of longitude adding up to 24 hours for full 360 degrees of rotation. Accordingly, difference between IST and GMT is:

(82.5 D East) x 4 minutes/degree = 330 minutes = 5 H 30 M.

Thus, IST is ahead of GMT by 5 H 30 M. West of Greenwich, ST is behind GMT. Note that it is not necessary to know the central meridian on which the standard time is based if one knows the time difference itself between ST and GMT.

Now, the longitude of POB in the present example is 82 D 54 M East of Greenwich. The difference between LMT at Lucknow and GMT is, therefore,

(82 D 54 M) x 4 minutes/degree = 331.6 minutes = 5 H 31 M 36 S.

The LMT is then calculated as follows:

		H	M	S
ST at POB		23	50	0
Difference between GMT and ST at POB	(−)	5	30	0
GMT at TOB		18	20	0
Difference between LMT and GMT	(+)	5	31	36
LMT at TOB		23	51	36

Thus, the local mean time for the present example is 23 H 51 M 36 S.

3.4 TIME ELAPSED SINCE NOON

Now we find the time elapsed since noon at POB, to be used latter in calculations.

	H	M	S
LMT at TOB	23	51	36
Noon Time	− 12	0	0
Time elapsed since noon	11	51	36

3.5 SIDEREAL TIME OR SRT

The Sidereal Time/SRT or Star Time of a given locality is the time that has elapsed since the most recent entering of the Sun into the spring Equinoctial Point.

What is meant by the sidereal time/SRT? It can be understood from the difference between Mean Solar Day that depends on the rotation of the Earth around its own axis, and Sidereal Day that depends on the revolution of the Earth around the Sun.

The Earth spins around its axis relative to Sun in 24 hours. Thus, a Mean Solar Day comprises of 24 hours. All watches and clocks register time according to the mean solar day.

However, the Earth also goes round the Sun in an orbit, which takes very nearly 365.25 days, a quarter day more than 365 days. The Sidereal Day is, thus, less than 24 hours. It is 3 M 55.91 S shorter than the Mean Solar Day.

The sidereal clock is, therefore, faster than the ordinary clock. It accelerates by 3 M 55.91 S, viz., approximately 4 minutes per day. In the period of orbit of 365.25 days, this difference adds up to 24 hours. The sidereal time at noon, therefore, provides the information as to how far the Sun and the planets have travelled from the initial Spring Equinoctial Point. The daily sidereal time at noon is furnished in all ephemerides. For the convenience of the reader, it is given in Tables 3.1 and 3.2 for Greenwich.

Table 3.1
Sidereal Time on January 1 Each Year at 12 Noon GMT

Year	Sidereal Time			Year	Sidereal Time		
	H	M	S		H	M	S
1990	18	43	26	2000	18	41	44
1991	18	42	29	2001	18	44	43
1992	18	41	32	2002	18	43	46
1993	18	44	31	2003	18	42	49
1994	18	43	33	2004	18	41	51
1995	18	42	36	2005	18	44	51
1996	18	41	38	2006	18	43	54
1997	18	43	39	2007	18	42	47
1998	18	42	42	2008	18	41	59
1999	18	43	03	2009	18	44	58
				2010	18	44	01

Note: The values repeat every fourth year but with a precession of a few seconds.

Table 3.2
Date-wise Motions in Sidereal Time in H M S

Date	January	February	March	April	May	June
1	0 0 0	2 2 13	3 52 37	5 54 50	7 53 7	9 55 21
2	0 3 57	2 6 9	3 56 33	5 58 47	7 57 4	9 59 17
3	0 7 53	2 10 6	4 0 0	6 2 43	8 1 0	10 3 14
4	0 11 50	2 14 2	4 4 26	6 6 40	8 4 57	10 7 10
5	0 15 46	2 17 59	4 8 23	6 10 36	8 8 53	10 11 7
6	0 19 43	2 21 55	4 12 19	6 14 33	8 12 50	10 15 8

contd.

Date	January	February	March	April	May	June
7	0 23 39	2 25 52	4 16 16	6 18 29	8 16 46	10 19 0
8	0 27 36	2 29 48	4 20 12	6 22 26	8 20 43	10 22 56
9	0 31 32	2 33 45	4 24 9	6 26 22	8 24 39	10 26 53
10	0 35 29	2 37 42	4 28 5	6 30 19	8 28 36	10 30 49
11	0 39 25	2 41 39	4 32 2	6 34 16	8 32 32	10 34 46
12	0 43 22	2 45 35	4 35 59	6 38 13	8 36 29	10 38 42
13	0 47 18	2 49 32	4 39 56	6 42 9	8 40 25	10 42 30
14	0 51 18	2 53 28	4 43 52	6 46 6	8 44 22	10 46 35
15	0 55 12	2 57 25	4 47 49	6 50 2	8 48 18	10 50 32
16	0 59 8	3 1 21	4 51 45	6 53 59	8 52 15	10 54 28
17	1 3 4	3 5 18	4 55 42	6 57 55	8 56 11	10 58 25
18	1 7 1	3 9 14	4 59 38	7 1 52	9 0 8	11 2 21
19	1 10 57	3 13 11	5 3 35	7 5 48	9 4 4	11 6 18
20	1 14 54	3 17 8	5 7 31	7 9 45	9 8 1	11 10 15
21	1 18 51	3 21 5	5 11 28	7 13 41	9 11 58	11 14 12
22	1 22 48	3 25 1	5 15 25	7 17 38	9 15 55	11 18 8
23	1 26 44	3 28 58	5 19 22	7 21 34	9 19 51	11 22 5
24	1 30 41	3 32 54	5 23 18	7 25 31	9 23 48	11 26 1
25	1 34 37	3 36 51	5 27 15	7 29 28	9 27 44	11 29 58
26	1 38 34	3 40 47	5 31 11	7 33 24	9 31 41	11 33 54
27	1 42 30	3 44 44	5 35 8	7 37 20	9 35 37	11 37 51
28	1 46 27	3 48 40	5 39 5	7 41 17	9 39 34	11 41 47
29	1 50 23		5 43 1	7 45 13	9 43 30	11 45 44
30	1 54 20		5 46 58	7 49 10	9 47 27	11 49 41

Date	July	August	Sept.	Oct.	Nov.	Dec.
1	11 53 38	13 55 50	15 58 4	17 56 21	19 58 34	21 56 50
2	11 57 34	13 59 47	16 2 0	18 0 17	20 2 31	22 0 47
3	12 1 31	14 3 44	16 5 57	18 4 14	20 6 27	22 4 43
4	12 5 27	14 7 40	16 9 53	18 8 10	20 10 24	22 8 40
5	12 9 24	14 11 36	16 13 50	18 12 7	20 14 20	22 12 36
6	12 13 21	14 15 33	16 17 46	18 10 3	20 18 17	22 10 33
7	12 17 17	14 19 29	16 21 43	18 20 0	20 22 13	22 20 30
8	12 21 14	14 23 26	16 25 40	18 23 57	20 26 10	22 24 27
9	12 25 10	14 27 23	16 29 37	18 27 54	20 30 6	22 28 23
10	12 29 6	14 31 20	16 33 33	18 31 50	20 34 3	22 32 20
11	12 33 3	14 35 16	16 37 30	18 35 47	20 38 0	22 36 16
12	12 36 59	14 39 13	16 41 20	18 39 43	20 41 56	22 40 13
13	12 40 56	14 43 9	16 45 23	18 43 40	20 45 52	22 44 9
14	12 44 52	14 47 6	16 49 19	18 47 37	20 49 49	22 48 6
15	12 48 49	14 51 2	16 53 16	18 51 33	20 53 45	22 52 2

contd.

Date	July	August	Sept.	Oct.	Nov.	Dec.
16	12 52 45	14 54 59	16 57 12	18 55 30	20 57 42	22 55 59
17	12 56 42	14 58 55	17 1 9	18 59 26	21 1 39	22 59 56
18	13 0 38	15 2 52	17 5 5	19 3 22	21 5 36	23 3 53
19	13 4 35	15 6 48	17 9 2	19 7 10	21 9 32	23 7 49
20	13 8 32	15 10 45	17 12 58	19 11 15	21 13 29	23 11 46
21	13 12 29	15 14 41	17 16 55	19 15 12	21 17 25	23 15 42
22	13 16 25	15 18 38	17 20 51	19 19 8	21 21 22	23 19 39
23	13 20 22	15 22 34	17 24 48	19 23 5	21 25 18	23 23 35
24	13 24 18	15 26 31	17 28 44	19 27 1	21 29 15	23 27 32
25	13 28 15	15 30 27	17 32 41	19 30 58	21 33 11	23 31 0
26	13 32 11	15 34 24	17 36 37	19 34 54	21 37 8	23 35 25
27	13 36 8	15 38 20	17 40 34	19 38 51	21 41 4	23 39 21
28	13 40 4	15 42 17	17 44 31	19 42 48	21 45 1	23 43 18
29	13 44 1	15 46 14	17 48 28	19 46 45	21 48 57	23 47 14
30	13 48 57	15 50 11	17 52 24	19 50 41	21 52 57	23 51 11
31	13 51 54	15 54 7		19 54 38		23 55 7

Note: In the case of a leap year, the sidereal motion for the date next to the date under consideration should be taken after 28 February.

3.6 SIDEREAL TIME AT PRECEDING NOON

The SRT at preceding noon, viz., on 8 August 1934 is first found for Greenwich as below:

		H	M	S
SRT at Noon at Greenwich on 1.1.1934		18	40	54
Motion up to 8.8.1934	+	14	23	26
SRT at Noon at Greenwich on 8.8.1934		33	04	20
Subtract 24 hours to normalise	−	24	0	0
Actual SRT at Noon at Greenwich on 8.8.1934		9	04	20

Note: Whenever the time is more than 24 hours, we subtract 24 hours to normalise.

However, we have to find the SRT at noon at Lucknow. We know that SRT accelerates by 3 M 55.91 S per day, that is, by 9.8 seconds per hour. It comes to about 2/3 second per degree of longitude. Now, since the noon at Lucknow occurs 5 H 31 M 36 S earlier, the difference in SRT between Greenwich and Lucknow is:

(5 H 31 M 36 S) x 9.8 seconds/hour = 55 S

So, we have to deduct 55 seconds from SRT at Greenwich to get SRT at Lucknow. Thus:

	H	M	S
SRT at Noon at Greenwich	9	4	20
Difference in SRT −	0	0	55
SRT at Noon at Lucknow	9	5	15

Note: For calculating LMT, we add the difference to GMT if POB is East of Greenwich, and subtract from GMT if POB is West of Greenwich. For calculating SRT, it is the opposite. We subtract the difference if POB is East of Greenwich, and add if POB is West of Greenwich.

3.7 SIDEREAL TIME OF BIRTH

We have found SRT at noon on 8 August 1934 at Lucknow. We now need to find SRT at TOB. For the purpose, we add to this SRT the time elapsed since noon found earlier. In addition, we add acceleration at 9.8 seconds per hour corresponding to the time elapsed since noon. Thus we, have:

		H	M	S
SRT at Noon at POB		9	5	15
Time elapsed since noon	+	11	51	36
Acceleration at 9.8 seconds/hour for 9 H 5 M 15 S	+	0	1	30
SRT at TOB at POB		20	58	21

3.8 TROPICAL (*SAYANA*) ZODIAC

We see by adding values from Tables 3.1 and 3.2 that SRT at noon at the Spring Equinoctial Point, viz., on 21 March approaches zero or 24 hours every year. In the Tropical (*sayana*) Zodiac, followed in Western astrology, this point is taken as 0 D Aries. This assumes that 0 D Aries appears at sunrise on 21 March every year followed by 0 D Taurus on 19 April, 0 D Gemini on 21 May, and so on. Raphael's Table of Houses is based on this Tropical Zodiac.

In the sample horoscope, 20 H 58 M 51 S is the SRT at TOB and POB of the native. This information will now be employed to determine the degrees of the ascendant rising, and cusps of the other houses using Raphael's Table of Houses for the given SRT.

3.9 ASCENDENT CUSP AND CUSPS OF HOUSES IN SAMPLE HOROSCOPE IN TROPICAL/*SAYANA* ZODIAC

Thus, from the Table of Houses for the latitude of POB, we read the signs and longitudes of cusps of ascendant and other houses for our SRT as shown in Table 3.3.

Table 3.3

Signs and Longitudes of Cusps of Houses in Sample Horoscope in Tropical/*Sayana* Zodiac

House	X	XI	XII	I(ASC.)	II	III
Sign	Aquarius	Pisces	Aries	Taurus	Gemini	Cancer
Longitude in D M	10 7	9 38	15 55	24 56	21 39	15 19

Note: The longitudes in the Table of Houses are given only for certain values of SRT. One is required to interpolate for the exact SRT.

3.10 PRECESSION OF EQUINOXES (*AYANSHA*) AND SIDEREAL (*NIRAYANA*) ZODIAC

On equinox days, 21 March, Spring Equinox and 23 September, Autumnal Equinox, the projection of the Sun's path is exactly along the Equator.

On the day of spring equinox on 21 March, at a certain time in Earth's life, Aries used to appear at sunrise. Had the stars in the heaven been fixed with respect to the solar system alone, there would have been no complication! But they are shifting backwards, preceding at the rate of 50.25 seconds of arc per year. This comes to 1 degree in 72 years and full 360 degrees in 25,920 years. This Precession stands at 23 D 52 M 25 S on 1 January, in the year 2001. This is known as the Precession of Equinoxes (*Ayansha*). Table 3.4 gives the values of *Lahiri Ayanshas* for the current period.

Accordingly, on 21 March, Aries, represented by a group of stars in the shape of a ram, does not appear at sunrise on the eastern horizon although the equinox does take place as it depends on the solar system only, viz., on the rotation of the Earth around the sun. Instead, on that day, 30 D – Precession 23 D 53 M = 6 D 7 M of Pisces, formed by a group of stars in the configuration of The Fish, appears. And, Pisces continues to appear until 13 April when the full 30 degrees of Pisces are covered. The sign Aries actually starts appearing from April 14.

Table 3.4
Precession of Equinoxes/*Ayanshas*

Year	Ayansha			Year	Ayansha		
	D	M	S		D	M	S
1951	23	10	31	1981	23	36	37
1961	23	18	50	1991	23	44	10
1971	23	27	52	2001	23	53	33

Sidereal (*Nirayana*) Zodiac

Western astrologers follow the Tropical/*Sayana* Zodiac, assigning a longitude of 0 D Aries or 360 D Pisces to the spring equinox position of the Sun on 21 March. The corresponding longitudes of the cusps of houses and those of the Sun and other planets are called the Tropical/*Sayana* longitudes.

This does not take into account the precession of equinoxes. The zodiac that takes care of the precession of equinoxes (*Ayansha*) is called the Sidereal (*Nirayana*) Zodiac. The longitudes therein are named as Sidereal/*Nirayana* longitudes. These longitudes are equal to the tropical longitudes minus the *ayanshas*.

Vedic/Indian/Hindu Astrology gives great importance to the stars/constellations. Accordingly, it follows the Sidereal/ *Nirayana* Zodiac.

Note: (i) We subtract the *Ayanshas* from the *Sayana* longitudes of the cusps of houses as well as of planets to get their *Nirayana* longitudes.

(ii) Signs of houses and planets may change when we convert from *Sayana* to *Nirayana*. Thus, they may not be same in western and Vedic/Indian horoscopes. For example, western astrologers will call a person born on 8 August a Leo, considering the Sun is in Leo. But, according to Vedic astrologers, the Sun will actually be in Cancer on that day.

3.11 ASCENDANT CUSP AND CUSPS OF HOUSES IN SAMPLE HOROSCOPE IN SIDEREAL/ *NIRAYANA* ZODIAC

The precession of equinoxes, viz., *Ayansha* for the year 1934 was 22 D 56 M 25 S. Hence, subtracting this from the values

of Tropical/*Sayana* longitudes in Table 3.4, we get the Sidereal/
Nirayana longitudes of cusps as given in Table 3.5.

Table 3.5
Signs and Longitudes of Cusps of Houses in Sample Horoscope in Sidereal/*Nirayana* Zodiac

House	X	XI	XII	I (ASC.)	II	III
Sign	Capricorn	Aquarius	Pisces	Taurus	Taurus	Gemini
Longitude in D M S	17 10 13	16 41 39	22 58 31	1 59 35	28 42 20	22 22 4

Now, the signs and longitudes of the cusps of the opposite
houses are obtained by simply adding 180 degrees to the values
in Table 3.5. The same are given in Table 3.6.

Table 3.6
Signs and Longitudes of Cusps of Opposite Houses in Sample Horoscope in Sidereal/*Nirayana* Zodiac

House	IV	V	VI	VII	VIII	IX
Sign	Cancer	Leo	Virgo	Scorpio	Scorpio	Sagittarius
Longitude in D M S	17 10 13	16 41 39	22 58 31	1 59 45	28 42 20	22 22 4

Note that the ascendant cusp and the cusp of the second
house are both Taurus. Similarly, the cusps of both the seventh
and eighth houses are Scorpio being 180 degrees apart from
the cusps of first and second houses. Some of the houses are
occupying less than 30 degrees here. However, the sixth house
occupies more than 30 degrees so that its cusp starts with Virgo
sign, covers Libra completely, and then ends with Scorpio.
Similarly, the twelfth house opposite the sixth is occupying

more than 30 degrees with the cusp starting with Pisces sign, covering Aries completely, and ending with Taurus.

However, the practice in Hindu astrology is to establish the sign of the ascendant and then assign the signs to the other houses in sequential order. The chart drawn in this manner is called a *Rashi*-Chart as shown in Fig. 3.1 for the sample horoscope. Note that it is possible to show the cusps also of houses in the South Indian format.

Rectification of *Lagna*

Predictions can go completely wrong if there is a mistake in the determination of *lagna* cusp. This can happen when time of birth is not exactly known, and when *lagna* seems to be changing from one *rashi* to another. It is then necessary to rectify *lagna*.

There are many methods for the purpose. But the simplest one is the 3-Chart (*Trikundali*) method. In this method, two additional *kundalis* are made, one for the former and the other for latter *lagna*. And the past events are matched with the predictions of the three. Whichever gives the correct results is supposed to be the correct one.

3.12 POSITION OF MOON AND OTHER PLANETS AT TOB IN SAMPLE HOROSCOPE

After assigning the signs to the houses, the planets are placed in respective houses according to their signs and longitudes at the time of birth as shown in Fig. 3.1.

Ephemerides give longitudes of planets for each day at 12 noon GMT, viz., 5:30 pm IST. They give *Sayana* longitudes while some in India give *Nirayana*.

The method involves taking *Sayana* longitudes of planets from any ephemeris for 12 noon GMT for two consecutive days, say, 8 and 9 August of 1934 for the sample horoscope. The same for Moon are 115 D 1 M and 126 D 49 M, respectively. The movement of Moon over a period of 24 hours, viz., 1440 minutes is by difference equal to 11 D 48 M, viz., 708 minutes. Now, the TOB is 11:50 pm or 6 H 20 M = 380 minutes after 5:30 pm IST or GMT Noon. The movement at TOB by interpolation is therefore:

(708/1440) x 380 = 187minutes = 3 D 7 M

Hence the tropical/*Sayana* longitude of Moon at TOB on August 8 of 1934 is:

115 D 1 M + 3 D 7 M = 118 D 8 M

Since, one sign covers 30 degrees, the above longitude corresponds to:

3 S 28 D 8 M 0 S

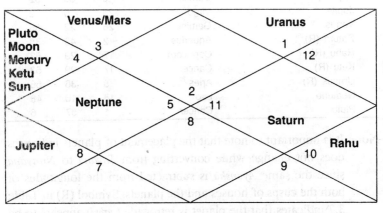

Fig. 3.1 Sample Horoscope in Nirayana Longitudes

Hence, Moon is at 28 D 8 M 0 S in the fourth sign of Cancer in Tropical/*Sayana* zodiac.

Now, just like the cusps of houses, the longitudes of planets in the sidereal/*Nirayana* zodiac are also obtained by subtracting the *Ayansha.* So, subtracting 22 D 56 M 25 S from the *Sayana* longitude, the sidereal/*Nirayana* longitude of Moon at TOB is:

3 S 28 D 8 M 0 S – 22 D 56 M 25 S =3 S 5 D 11 M 35 S

Likewise, the sidereal/*Nirayana* longitudes of all planets can be determined as given in Table 3.7. Planets are shown accordingly in their respective signs and houses in Fig. 3.1.

Table 3.7
Nirayana Longitudes of Planets in Example Horoscope

Planet	Sign	Longitude		
		D	M	S
Sun	Cancer	22	38	50
Moon	Cancer	5	11	35
Mars	Gemini	23	2	12
Mercury	Cancer	5	50	32
Jupiter	Virgo	25	9	2
Venus	Gemini	26	22	56
Saturn (R)	Aquarius	2	43	38
Rahu (R)	Capricorn	17	29	53
Ketu (R)	Cancer	17	29	53
Uranus (R)	Aries	8	36	56
Neptune	Leo	18	16	48
Pluto	Cancer	1	57	6

Note: It is important to note that the placement of planets in houses does not change while converting from *Sayana* to *Nirayana* since the same *Ayansha* is subtracted from the longitudes of both the cusps of houses and the planets. Symbol (R) in Table 3.7 indicates that the planet is retrogade (*vakri*) appears to be moving in a backward direction. Since it does not have forward motion, it is not Direct (*margi*).

Yoga at Birth

Yogas are combinations of planets, signs and houses that bring particularly good or bad results. However, the *yogas* at birth that are being referred to here are formed by the combined position of the Sun and the Moon. There are 27 such *yogas* in total. If we add the longitudes of Sun and the Moon, and then divide the sum by 13 D 20 M, then we get a whole number, and some remainder. The whole number represents the number of *yogas* elapsed at the time of birth. The *yoga* at birth is the next one pertaining to the remainder. Thus, in the sample horoscope:

	S	D	M
Longitude of Sun	3	22	39
Longitude of Moon	3	5	12
Sum	6	27	51

This is equal to (6 x 30 + 27) D and 51 M = 207 D 51 M. Dividing this by 13 D 20 M, we get the whole number of 15, and a remainder. Thus, *yoga* formed is the sixteenth one. So, now, we have to go to the list of *yogas*, and see which is the sixteenth one. The sixteenth *yoga* is *Siddhi*.

By the way, this is a very good *yoga* to be born in. Some *yogas* are good and some are bad. The list of all the 27 *yogas* is given below:

1. *Vishwakambha*	10. *Ganda*	19. *Paridh*
2. *Priti*	11. *Vriddhi*	20. *Shiva*
3. *Aayushman*	12. *Dhruva*	21. *Siddhi*
4. *Saubhagya*	13. *Vyaghat*	22. *Sadhya*
5. *Shobhan*	14. *Harshad*	23. *Shubha*
6. *Atiganda*	15. *Vajra*	24. *Shukla*
7. *Sukarma*	16. *Siddhi*	25. *Brahma*
8. *Ghriti*	17. *Vyatipat*	26. *Aindra*
9. *Shoola*	18. *Variyan*	27. *Vaidhrati*

Priti, Aayushman, Saubhagya, Shobhan, Sukarma, Vriddhi, Dhruva, Siddhi, and *Shubha yogas* are auspicious. *Vishkambha, Atiganda, Shoola, Ganda, Vyaghat, Vajra, Vyatipat, Paridh* and *Vaidhrati* are inauspicious. Their names are suggestive of their nature.

3.13 *NAVANSHA* CHART

Nav means nine, and *ansha* means division. If each sign of 30 degrees is divided into nine divisions then each division will correspond to an arc of

$$30/9 = 3 \text{ D } 20 \text{ M}$$

Such an arc is named *Navansha*. Each sign can therefore be divided into nine *Navanshas*. The degrees of each *Navansha* from the first to the ninth are given in Table 3.8.

Table 3.8
Navansha Degrees in Each Sign

Navansha	From		To	
	D	M	D	M
First	0	0	3	20
Second	3	20	6	40
Third	6	40	10	0
Fourth	10	0	13	20
Fifth	13	20	16	40
Sixth	16	40	20	0
Seventh	20	0	23	20
Eighth	23	20	26	40
Ninth	26	40	30	0

Table 3.9 gives the sign numbers of *Navanshas* corresponding to each sign from 1 to 12. The *Navansha* cycle can also be expressed in terms of the names of signs as in Table 3.10.

The following rule makes it simple to remember Tables 3.9 and 3.10.

The first *Navansha* in movable signs (Aries, Cancer, Libra, Capricorn), the middle *Navansha* in fixed signs (Taurus, Leo, Scorpio, Pisces), and the last *Navansha* in dual signs (Gemini, Virgo, Sagittarius, Pisces) is *Vargottama*.

Vargottama Navansha

What is *Vargottama*? If the *lagna* or any planet has the same sign both in the *lagna* as well as in the *Navansha*-Chart, then it is deemed as *Vargottama*. For example, in Aries sign since the first *Navansha* is Aries itself it is called *Vargottama Navansha*. Hence, the cusp of a *lagna* or a planet in 0 to 3 D 20 M Aries is deemed as *Vargottama*. *Vargottama lagna* is very strong. *Vargottama* planet is considered as good as in its own sign.

Note: That does not mean that a *Vargottama* planet that is exalted in both charts has the same quality as the one that is debilitated in both charts. Obviously, the quality varies from excellent to poor. An astrologer must take this gradation into account.

How to Construct the *Navansha* Chart?

We first find the *Navansha lagna*. In whichever *Navansha*, the cusp of the *lagna* falls, that sign becomes the *lagna* of the *Navansha*-Chart.

Table 3.9
Navansha Cycle: Sign Numbers of *Navanshas*

Navanshas	1	2	3	4	5	6	7	8	9	10	11	12
First	1	10	7	4	1	10	7	4	1	10	7	4
Second	2	11	8	5	2	11	8	5	2	11	8	5
Third	3	12	9	6	3	12	9	6	3	12	9	6

contd.

Navanshas	1	2	3	4	5	6	7	8	9	10	11	12
Fourth	4	1	10	7	4	1	10	7	4	1	10	7
Fifth	5	2	11	8	5	2	11	8	5	2	11	8
Sixth	6	3	12	9	6	3	12	9	6	3	12	9
Seventh	7	4	1	10	7	4	1	10	8	4	1	10
Eighth	8	5	2	11	8	5	2	11	9	5	2	11
Ninth	9	6	3	12	9	6	3	12	10	6	3	12

Table 3.10
Navansha Cycle: Sign Names

Signs	Navanshas
Aries	Aries, Taurus, Gemini, Cancer, Leo, Virgo, Libra, Scorpio, Sagittarius
Taurus	Capricorn, Aquarius, Pisces, Aries, Taurus, Gemini, Cancer, Leo, Virgo
Gemini	Libra, Scorpio, Sagittarius, Capricorn, Aquarius, Pisces, Aries, Taurus, Gemini
Cancer	Cancer, Leo, Virgo, Libra, Scorpio, Sagittarius, Capricorn, Aquarius, Pisces
Leo	Aries, Taurus, Gemini, Cancer, Leo, Virgo, Libra, Scorpio, Sagittarius
Virgo	Capricorn, Aquarius, Pisces, Aries, Taurus, Gemini, Cancer, Leo, Virgo
Libra	Libra, Scorpio, Sagittarius, Capricorn, Aquarius, Pisces, Aries, Taurus, Gemini
Scorpio	Cancer, Leo, Virgo, Libra, Scorpio, Sagittarius, Capricorn, Aquarius, Pisces
Sagittarius	Aries, Taurus, Gemini, Cancer, Leo, Virgo, Libra, Scorpio, Sagittarius
Capricorn	Capricorn, Aquarius, Pisces, Aries, Taurus, Gemini, Cancer, Leo, Virgo
Aquarius	Libra, Scorpio, Sagittarius, Capricorn, Aquarius, Pisces, Aries, Taurus, Gemini
Pisces	Cancer, Leo, Virgo, Libra, Scorpio, Sagittarius, Capricorn, Aquarius, Pisces

Thus, in the example horoscope, the ascendant is 1 D 59 M 35 S Taurus. It falls in the first *Navansha*. The first *Navansha* of Taurus sign is Capricorn. Hence the *lagna* of the *Navansha* Chart is Capricorn, the second house is Aquarius, and so on. Likewise, the *Navansha* sign of each planet can also be found and the planet placed in the chart. *Navansha* Chart thus determined for the sample horoscope is shown in Fig. 3.2.

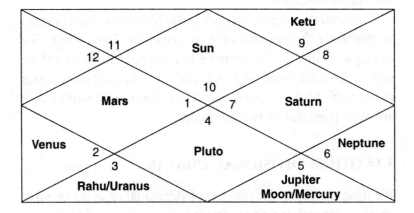

Fig. 3.2 Navansha Chart of Sample Horoscope

Importance of *Navansha* Chart

The *Navansha*-Chart may be considered as an additional or supplementary horoscope.

Indian astrologers give equal weightage to the *lagna* chart and the *Navansha*-Chart. Basically if *lagna* chart is considered the body then *Navansha*-Chart is its heart. So, even when the body is weak but the heart is strong, the native leads a good life. On the other hand, if the body is strong but the heart is weak, it may not take much time for the heart to fail and the body to collapse.

Another analogy of *lagna* chart is that of a tree with *Navansha*-Chart as its fruit. Thus the tree may be huge and tall, but the fruit may be small, sour and few. Conversely, the tree may appear to be small, but the fruit may be large in size, sweet and in plenty.

How to use the *Navansha*-Chart?

Firstly, the native's destiny is examined house by house and planet by planet by examining not only the *lagna* but also the *Navansha*-Chart.

Secondly, seeing its strength in the *Navansha*-Chart one has to moderate the strength of a planet in the *lagna* chart. For example, Saturn in the example horoscope is in *moola-trikona* sign in the tenth house in *lagna*. Then, it is in exaltation, again in the tenth house, in *Navansha*. Thus, Saturn and tenth house are very powerful in the horoscope.

3.14 OTHER DIVISIONAL CHARTS

We now, introduce the concept of divisional or *ansha* or *varga* charts in general. If a sign is divided into two parts of 15 degrees each then each half part is called a *hora*. Similarly, if a sign is divided into three equal parts then each part is called a *Drekkana*, if in seven parts *Saptamansha*, if in nine parts *Navansha*, if in ten parts *Dashamansha*, if in twelve parts *Dwadashamansha*, if in sixteen parts *Shodashamsha*, and so on.

Matters judged more specifically from each of these charts are given in Table 3.11. All the divisional charts are finer sub-divisions of *lagna*. The overall benefic or malefic nature of each planet and all house matters are judged from all charts.

Table 3.11
Matters Judged from Divisional Charts

Chart	Matter/s
Lagna	(*Deh-Vichar*) Body, health, medical astrology
Hora	(*Sampada-Vichar*) wealth
Drekkana	(*Bhratri-Soukhyam*) Siblings, medical astrology
Saptamansha	(*Putra-Poutri-Gyanam*) Children/grandchildren
Navansha	(*Kalatra-Soukhyam*) Spouse,

contd.

Chart	Matter/s
Dashamansha	(*Rajya-Vichar*) Livelihood, position, success, power,
Dwadashmansha	(*Pitra-Soukhyam*) Parents
Shodashamansha	(*Vaahan-Sukh Vichar*) Conveyance

However, the *lagna* and *Navansha*-Charts are the most important. But, for medical astrology, one must see both *Drekkana* and *lagna* charts. Similarly, for happiness from children, the *Saptamansha* chart and *Dwadashansha* chart for happiness from parents have additional significance. For example, if the Lord of *lagna* in *Dwadashansha* chart is a benefic (*shubha*) planet, the parents of the native will have good conduct but if it is a malefic (*ashubha*) planet their conduct will not be worthy. Further, if this planet is placed in a good sign and a good house the native will have full happiness to/from parents but if it is placed in an unfavourable sign and an evil house the same will be denied. Likewise, other charts may be referred to.

Note: It must be kept in mind that the *Chandra Kundali* with Moon Sign as the first house, and *Surya Kundali* with Sun Sign as the first house have also to be considered as supplementary charts, the *Chandra Kundali* for emotional well-being, and *Surya Kundali* for soul power. Note that the *Chandra Kundali* is given importance like *Lagna-Kundali* in Hindu astrology.

Chapter 4

Planets (*Grahas*)

4.1 PLANETS IN ASTROLOGY

Large masses orbiting the Sun are called planets while the masses orbiting the planets are called satellites. Although the Sun is not a planet as such, and the Moon is a satellite of the Earth, for the sake of convenience, both are referred to as planets or *grahas* along with others in astrology. The Sun (*Surya* or *Ravi*) and the Moon (*Chandra*), of course, have the status of luminaries or royals of the zodiac among the whole group of planets.

Fig. 4.1 gives an idea about the relative sizes of planets and the length of their orbits. The Earth itself is a planet of the sun. We note that Mercury (*Budha*) is the smallest planet, and is closest to the Sun, so close that it cannot be seen in the sky with the naked eye. Otherwise, it is the hottest and the brightest planet. Venus (*Shukra*) is next to Mercury. It is slightly smaller in size than the Earth. It is the brightest planet that can be easily seen in the sky either just before sunrise or just after sunset.

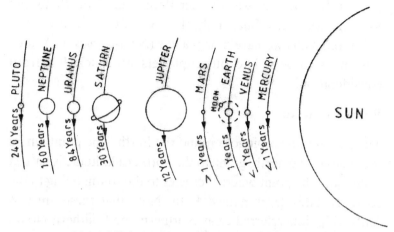

Fig. 4.1 Relative Sizes of Planets and Their Orbits

After Mercury and Venus on one side, we have Mars (*Mangal* or *Kuja*), Jupiter (*Brihaspati* or *Guru*) and Saturn (*Shani*) on the other side of the Earth. Mars, Jupiter and Saturn can be seen when they are in signs that appear in the night sky.

Mars looks like a reddish planet. Jupiter, yellowish in hue, is the largest planet. Saturn is next to Jupiter in size. It appears to carry a ring around it. Both Jupiter and Saturn exert great influence on the lives of people.

Then, we have the outer planets Uranus (*Arun*), Neptune (*Varun*) and Pluto (*Yama*) discovered in the twentieth century only. In effect, Uranus is like Saturn, Neptune like Jupiter, and Pluto like Mars only. Their sizes are very small. And, they are far away from the Earth. Due to these reasons, they are not considered to exert their influence separately on the day-to-day lives of individuals. They, however, affect the destiny of large groups of peoples like nations, civilisations, etc. Out of these, Pluto is far too small. It is just about 1/8th the mass of Moon.

In Vedic/Hindu astrology, only these seven—Sun, Moon, Mars, Mercury, Jupiter, Venus and Saturn—are considered as planets. In addition, we consider Rahu and Ketu. Rahu and Ketu are not planets but simply, shadows of two sensitive parts of Moon. Thus we have nine planets (*Nava-Grahas*) in Vedic/ Hindu astrology. The outer planets are excluded from consideration.

Rahu and Ketu

The Moon in its orbit goes round the Earth. The point where it crosses to the north, going to the northern latitude, is named Rahu, and the point where it crosses to the south, going to the southern latitude, is named Ketu. Note that these are two sensitive points referred to as Northern and Southern Nodes of the Moon. They are mathematically determined and inserted in the birth-chart as shadowy planets. Also, note that there will always be a difference of 180 degrees of longitude between Rahu and Ketu. Thus, they form an axis in the birth-chart. The two houses opposite each other on this axis are immensely affected for better or for worse.

The Rahu-Ketu axis is likened to a snake or dragon, Rahu representing the head named as Dragon's Head, seen as cunning, scheming and cruel, and Ketu representing its tail named as Dragon's Tail, epitomic of courage, but at the same time of obstinacy as well.

4.2 PERIODS OF STAY OF PLANETS IN SIGNS

The Moon takes about 30 days to go round the Earth. Hence, it stays for about 2.5 days in each sign. The Earth takes 12 months to go round the sun. Thus the Sun stays in each sign for one month as seen from the Earth. Accordingly, Sun moves very nearly by 1 degree every day covering 360 degrees of longitude in 365 days. Mercury and Venus take less than one year to complete their orbits round the sun. Hence, they stay in each sign for less than a month, say, fewer than 30 days on an average. Mars takes less than 2 years to complete the orbit. Hence, it stays in each sign for 45 days on an average.

Jupiter and Saturn are slower moving planets. They take 12 and 30 years respectively to complete their orbits. Accordingly, Jupiter stays in each sign for 1 year while Saturn stays for 2.5 years. As this period is long and they are huge planets, their effects on the sign and the house in horoscope they occupy is very prominent.

Jupiter's orbit is almost completely circular. The orbits of other planets are elliptical. Hence, Jupiter stays in a sign for close to one year while the periods for others are variable.

The outer planets are far away from the Sun and the Earth. Their orbits are also very long. So, they take many years to complete their orbits. Accordingly, the periods of orbits of Uranus, Neptune and Pluto are 84, 165 and 312 years, respectively. They stay in each sign for 7, 13(3/4) and 26 years, respectively. The average lifespan of a human being is, say, 80 years. These planets are far too small, and they cannot move through all the twelve signs and hence all the twelve houses in a horoscope during the lifetime of a person. Therefore, they do not significantly affect the life of an individual. However, they do leave a marked overall affect on one's life particularly on the sign and house they occupy in the birth chart. And, they do affect the destiny of collective groups such as nations, cultures and societies as they move from one sign to the other spanning over centuries.

Now, the two nodes Rahu and Ketu are ever-receding in their positions. Unlike the other planets which have direct motion, i.e. from Aries to Taurus, Taurus to Gemini and so on (unless they become retrograde for some time in the course of their orbit), the nodes Rahu and Ketu are always in retrograde motion. Thus, Rahu moves from Aries to Pisces, Pisces to

Aquarius, and so on. Ketu correspondingly moves from Libra to Virgo, etc. The Rahu-Ketu axis takes about 18 years to complete its rotation. Hence, Rahu and Ketu stay in their respective signs opposite each other for a 1.5 year-period.

4.3 SIGNS PLANETS RULE AND SIGNS OF DETRIMENT OF PLANETS

Table 4.1 and Fig. 4.2 show the signs ruled by planets. The figure also shows the symbols representing planets along with the symbols representing signs. Note that the Sun and the Moon rule only on one sign each, that is, Leo and Cancer respectively. The other planets are Lords/Rulers (*Swami/ Adhipati*) of two signs each. Thus, Mercury rules over Gemini and Virgo, Venus over Taurus and Libra, Mars over Aries and Scorpio, Jupiter over Pisces and Sagittarius and Saturn over Capricorn and Aquarius.

The outer planets Uranus, Neptune and Pluto are assigned the lordships of Aquarius, Pisces and Scorpio respectively jointly with Saturn, Jupiter and Mars.

Planets are beneficial to the houses they tenant if they are in the signs they rule. They are not beneficial in the opposite signs. They are said to be in detriment in the opposite signs. Thus, the Sun is in detriment in Aquarius, Moon in Capricorn, Mars in Libra and Taurus, Mercury in Sagittarius and Pisces, Jupiter in Gemini and Virgo and Saturn in Cancer and Leo. Similarly, Uranus is in detriment in Leo, Neptune in Virgo and Pluto in Taurus.

Rahu is considered to be in its own sign in Virgo, and hence in detriment in Pisces. Ketu similarly is considered in its own sign in Pisces and hence in detriment in Virgo.

Table 4.1
Exaltation, Debilitation and *Moola-Trikona* Signs of Planets with Degrees of Highest Exaltation, Deepest Debilitation and *Moola-Trikona*

Planet	Exaltation	Debilitation	Mool-Trikona
Sun	Aries (10)	Libra (10)	Leo (0 – 20)
Moon	Taurus (3)	Scorpio (3)	Taurus (4 – 30)
Mars	Capricorn (28)	Cancer (28)	Aries (1 – 12)
Mercury	Virgo (15)	Pisces (15)	Virgo (16 – 20)
Jupiter	Cancer (5)	Capricorn (5)	Sagittarius (1- 10)
Venus	Pisces (27)	Virgo (27)	Libra (0 – 5)
Saturn	Libra (20)	Aries (20)	Aquarius (1 – 20)

4.4 EXALTATION (*UCHCHA*), DEBILITATION (*NEECHA*), AND *MOOLA-TRIKONA* SIGNS OF PLANETS

A planet is called 'exalted' (*Uchcha*) when it is in its sign of exaltation (*Uchcha rashi*). And it is called 'debilitated' (*Neecha*) when it is in its sign of debilitation (*Neecha rashi*). An exalted planet is deemed stronger than itself in its own sign. It is very beneficial to the house it occupies and the house/s it is Lord of in the birth-chart. It is also beneficial to its significations, for example the Sun for father, the Moon for mother, and so on. A debilitated planet is deemed very weak. It is very harmful to the house it occupies, and the house/s it is Lord of, and the significations it represents. Table 4.1 gives the signs of exaltation and debilitation of planets along with their degrees of Highest Exaltation and Deepest Debilitation in brackets.

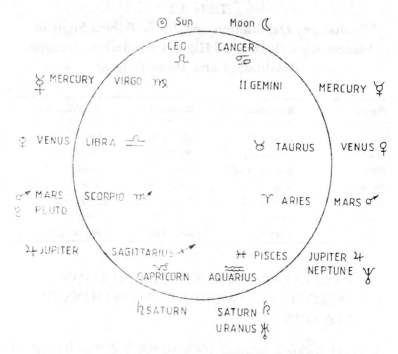

Fig. 4.2 Planets, their Symbols and the Signs they Rule

The table also gives the *moola-trikona* signs of planets along with the degrees in which they are actually considered to be so. A planet in *moola-trikona* is also considered good and stronger than in its own sign.

Now, Rahu is considered to be in its sign of exaltation in Taurus according to some, and in Gemini according to some others. Correspondingly, it is in debilitation in Scorpio and Sagittarius. Thus, Rahu is best in signs owned by Mercury and worst in signs owned by Jupiter. Similarly, Ketu, is considered to be in its signs of exaltation in Scorpio and Sagittarius, and in signs of debilitation in Taurus and Gemini. Thus Ketu is best in signs owned by Jupiter and worst in signs owned by

Mercury. Further, Aquarius is considered as the *moola-trikona* sign of Rahu, and Leo of Ketu.

4.5 RELATIONSHIP BETWEEN PLANETS

Apart from being well-placed if in own sign or in signs of exaltation and *moola-trikona*, a planet remains well placed if it occupies a sign of its friendly planet. On the contrary, a planet is ill-placed if it is in detriment or if it occupies its sign of debilitation or the sign of its enemy planet.

Thus a planet may be a friend (*mitra*) or an enemy (*shatru*) of another planet. The planets that are neither friends nor enemies are considered neutral (*sam*) in astrology.

The planets fall generally in two groups of natural friends. In the first group are the Sun, the Moon, Mars and Jupiter. These four are friendly with each other. In the second group are Mercury, Venus and Saturn. These three are again friendly with each other. The two groups are mutually inimical. There are, however, some exceptions as follows:

(i) The Moon has no enemies except Rahu and Ketu. Thus, Venus and Saturn are not Moon's enemies. They are neutral towards Moon while Mercury is a great friend of Moon. The Moon itself, however, is inimical to the three.

(ii) Jupiter is not an enemy of any planet. It is neutral towards Mercury, Venus and Saturn. But only Saturn reciprocates with neutrality towards Jupiter whereas Mercury and Venus remain Jupiter's enemies.

(iii) Mars and Venus are neutral towards each other.

A planet may not be just a friend or *mitra* but a great friend (*param/adhi mitra*) of another planet. For example, the Moon is a great friend of the Sun, Mercury is a great friend of the Moon, the Sun is a great friend of Mercury, and Mars and the Moon are both great friends of Jupiter. The reverse, however, may not be true. Thus, the Moon offers enmity in return for the great friendship of Mercury. And Mercury exhibits neutrality towards the Sun in spite of the latter's great love for Mercury whom it considers as a child planet (*bal-graha*). Venus and Saturn are, however, great mutual friends of each other.

Similarly, a planet may not be just an enemy or *shatru* but a great enemy (*param/adhi shatru*) to another planet. Thus, the Sun and Saturn who are considered father and son respectively are great enemies of each other. Further, Mars is a great enemy of Saturn while Saturn is just neutral towards Mars. Table 4.2 presents this information in a concise form. Note that Rahu more or less behaves like Saturn and Ketu like Mars.

4.6 NATURAL BENEFICS (*SHUBHA GRAHAS*) AND MALEFICS (*ASHUBHA GRAHAS*)

Benefic planets (*shubha grahas*) give favourable results whereas malefic planets (*ashubha grahas*) give unfavourable and even evil results. The natural benefics in order of increasing beneficence are the following:

Waxing Moon, Mercury, Jupiter, Venus

And the natural malefics in order of increasing maleficence are:

Waning Moon, Sun, Mars, Saturn, Rahu/Ketu

Table 4.2
Natural Relationships of Planets

Planet	Friend (*Mitra*)	Enemy (*Shatru*)	Neutral (*Sam*)
Sun	Moon Mars Jupiter	Venus Saturn Rahu/Ketu	Mercury
Moon	Sun Mercury	Rahu Ketu	Mars Jupiter Venus Saturn
Mars	Sun Moon Jupiter	Mercury	Venus Saturn
Mercury	Sun Venus	Moon	Mars Jupiter Saturn
Jupiter	Sun Moon Mars	Mercury Venus	Saturn
Venus	Mercury Saturn	Sun Moon	Mars Jupiter
Saturn	Mercury Venus	Sun Moon Mars	Jupiter
Rahu	Mercury Venus Saturn	Sun Moon Jupiter	Mars
Ketu	Mercury Venus Saturn	Sun Moon Jupiter	Mars

The Sun is the least malefic of all. The Moon, particularly on the 14th and 15th of waning Moon period and on the 1st of waxing Moon period acquires maleficence. Mercury acts differently when it is conjoined with other planets. Conjoined with other benefics, it becomes more benefic. But conjoined with malefics, it starts behaving like a malefic.

Note: (i) There are more malefics than benefics.
(ii) Even a malefic may bring good results if well-placed, and a benefic may bring bad results if ill-placed in respect of certain houses.
(iii) In addition to being a natural benefic or malefic, a planet may acquire benevolence or malevolence as a result of ownership of a good or a bad house.

4.7 COMBUST (*ASTA*) PLANETS

The beneficence of a planet is damaged and maleficence is increased due to its nearness to the Sun. Such a planet, within a few degrees of the Sun, is called combust (*Asta*) implying 'burnt' or 'set'. A combust planet loses its capacity to do any good. Instead, it produces evil effects. Even a natural benefic becomes a great malefic. Note that the combustion of a planet is simply its conjunction with the Sun. The closer the planet is to the Sun, the more the evil effect. Conjunction of a planet within a degree or two of the Sun is called 'deep combustion'. A planet in deep combustion is capable of causing death-like inflictions.

The Moon is combust if it is within 12 degrees from the Sun. Thus, on the 15th day of the Waning Moon period (*Krishna Paksha*), the Moon becomes a malefic. In such a case, Sun and Moon may fall in the same house in the birth-chart. When the Sun and the Moon fall in the same house and in the same sign, and in addition if they fall in the same *Navansha* also, it implies then that the Moon is within 3 degrees and 20 minutes of the Sun, viz., it is in deep combustion. Such a Moon, significator/ *karaka* for mother, becomes her destroyer. Mercury and Venus are always close to the Sun. Mercury is never more than 28 degrees away from the Sun. Its combustion is, therefore, not considered very evil. Venus is never more than 48 degrees away from the sun. It becomes combust when within 10 degrees if direct and within 8 degrees if retrogade.

Jupiter becomes combust when within 11 degrees of the Sun. Mars is combust if it is within 17 degrees and Saturn becomes combust if it is within 15 degrees of the Sun.

Benefics, Venus and Jupiter, if combust, behave like malefics. Malefics, Mars and Saturn, if combust, become all the more evil.

4.8 INTENSITY OF FAVOURABLE/UNFAVOURABLE EFFECTS OF A PLANET

The intensity of effects of a planet depends on its sign placement, and its combustion, in the following order:

Sign of Exaltation (*Uchcha rashi*)
Moola-trikona Sign (*Moola-Trikona rashi*)
Own Sign (*Swa-rashi*)
Friend's Sign (*Mitra rashi*)
Neutral's Sign (*Sam rashi*)
Fall/Detriment Sign
Enemy's Sign (*Shatru rashi*)
Sign of Debilitation (*Neecha rashi*)
Combust (*Asta*)

In the first five, it gives favourable effects provided it is not combust. It is most benefic in sign of exaltation. In the next four, it gives unfavourable effects. It is most malefic if it is deep combust, and if it is in the sign of debilitation also.

Even if one planet is exalted or is in its own sign in the birth-chart it brings fortune to the native.

Thus, two things are obvious in the sample horoscope.

Firstly, Saturn as Lord of two most powerful houses, the ninth house of fortune/*bhagya* and the tenth house of career, profession, name, fame, recognition, *karmas*, etc., placed in *kendra* in the tenth house itself in its *moola-trikona* sign makes the native very fortunate in general and very successful in matters of career and recognition.

Secondly, the Moon as Lord of the third house of effort, valour/*parakram,* physical and mental stamina and siblings placed in the third house itself in its own sign Cancer should make the native very hard working and successful in his undertakings, and should give good brother/s and sister/s. However, since the Moon is waning and is within 17 degrees of the Sun, it is close to combustion. Hence, even though it is in its own sign, it does not give native happiness in full measure in these respects, and in respect of mother, its signification.

Vargottama **Planet**

It was earlier stated that a *Vargottama* planet is as good as a planet in own sign. It may be clarified here that there are grades of beneficence of a *Vargottama* planet ranging from excellent to harmless. For example, if a planet is in its sign of exaltation in both the *lagna* and the *Navansha*-Charts it gives excellent results, but if it is in its sign of debilitation in both the charts the ill-effects will only be mitigated to some extent.

Cancellation of Debility

It has been seen very often that even a debilitated planet gives very good results. This happens when its debility gets cancelled. The three important ways in which debility of a planet is cancelled are the following:

(i) If the debilitated planet is retrograde, then it becomes a strong benefic. This applies to Mars, Mercury, Jupiter, Venus and Saturn. For retrogression of planets, see next section.

(ii) If aspected by its Dispositor, it becomes *Raja-Yoga karaka.* The dispositor is the Lord of the sign tenanted by the planet.

(iii) If it is conjoined/aspected by the planet that would be exalted in the sign tenanted by the debilitated planet.

Thus, debility of the Sun tenanting Libra is cancelled if it is aspected or conjoined by Venus. It could be considered as cancelled also according to rule 3 if it is conjoined or aspected by Saturn. However, since Saturn is a great enemy of the Sun, the debility is *not* cancelled, in this case, by conjunction with or aspect of Saturn. The debility of the Moon in Scorpio is cancelled if it is aspected by Mars. Note that no planet is exalted in the sign Scorpio.

The debility of Mars in Cancer gets cancelled if aspected by the Moon and if conjoined/aspected by Jupiter.

The debility of Mercury in Pisces gets cancelled if conjoined/aspected by Jupiter and Venus. The debility of Jupiter in Capricorn is cancelled if conjoined/aspected by Saturn and Mars.

Mercury cancels debility of Venus in Virgo if it is aspects Venus.

The debility of Saturn in Aries is *not* cancelled if conjoined/aspected by Mars or Sun because both are its great enemies. Thus, *the debility of Saturn never gets cancelled.*

4.9 DIRECT (*MARGI*) AND RETROGRADE (*VAKRI*) PLANETS

Planets have forward motion. They proceed from, say, 1 degree Taurus to 2, 3, 4, etc., degrees Taurus and so on. However, due to the elliptic nature of their orbits and their relative speeds at certain points in the orbits as seen from Earth, a planet may appear stationary or as having backward motion, say, from 5 degrees Taurus to 4, 3, 2 degrees Taurus, etc. It may even enter Aries and remain there for some time and then re-enter Taurus.

Thus, we have planets having forward motion referred to as direct or *margi*. And, when the planets have backward motion, they are referred to as retrograde or *vakri*. When a planet becomes retrograde, it stays for a longer time in a sign and house. Its effect is, therefore, more intense and long lasting.

Note: (i) A retrograde planet has greater propensity to do good if it is benefic, and evil if it is malefic.

(ii) A retrograde planet is generally adverse for health even though it may be a natural benefic.

(iii) The Sun and the Moon never become retrograde, whereas Rahu and Ketu always have retrograde motion.

4.10 BENEFICENCE AND MALEFICENCE OF PLANETS BASED ON LORDSHIPS OF HOUSES FOR EACH *LAGNA*

Besides being natural benefics or malefics, the planets acquire benevolence or malevolence depending on the houses they own. Thus, for a given *lagna*, certain planets behave as benefics/*shubha*, and certain others as malefics/*ashubha* as seen from Table 4.3. Sage Parashar lays the following principles in this regard:

(i) Lords of *kendras* (*Kendradhipatis*) are benefics.
Lord IV is more powerful than Lord I.
Lord VII is more powerful than Lord IV.
Lord X is more powerful than Lord VII.

(ii) Lords of *trikonas* (*Trikonadhipatis*) are great benefics:
Lord V is more powerful than Lord I.
Lord IX is more powerful than Lord V.

(iii) Lord of *lagna* (*Lagnadhipati*) being both a *Kendradhipati* as well as a *Trikonadhipati* is very great benefic.

(iv) Lords of houses III, VI and XI are malefics:
Lord III is the least powerful. III is considered a lean house.
Lord VI is more powerful than Lord III.
Lord XI is more powerful than Lord VI.

(v) Lords of houses II and VII are *marakas*.

(vi) Lords of the three evil *trik* houses VI, VIII and XII are great malefics. Lord VIII is the most malefic. The Sun and Moon as Lords of VIII are not so evil. If Lord VIII happens to be *lagna* or Trine Lord also, it is not inauspicious. On the contrary, if VIIIth Lord is also Lord of either IIIrd or XIth, it becomes a great malefic. In the sample horoscope Jupiter, though a great natural benefic, is in fact great malefic to the native being Lord of both VIII and XI.

Table 4.3
Benefic and Malefic Nature of Planets for Various
Lagnas—Number in Brackets Indicate Houses Owned

Lagna	Yoga-Karaka	Benefics	Malefics	Great Malefic	Marakas
Aries		Moon (IV) Mars (I) Sun (V) Jupiter (IX)	Saturn (XI)	Mercury (III, VI)	Venus
Taurus	Saturn (IX, X)	Sun (IV) Venus (I) Mercury (V)	Moon (III) Jupiter (VIII, XI)		Mars Mercury
Gemini		Mercury (I) Venus (V) Saturn IX)	Sun (III) Mars (VI, XI)		Moon Jupiter
Cancer	Mars (V, X)	Moon (I) Jupiter (IX)	Mercury (III) Venus (XI) Saturn (VIII)		Sun Saturn
Leo	Mars (IV, IX)	Sun (I)	Mercury (XI) Saturn (VI) Venus (III)		Mercury Saturn
Virgo		Mercury (I) Venus (IX)	Mars (III) Moon (XI)		Venus Jupiter
Libra	Saturn (IV, V)	Mars (VII) Mercury (IX) Venus (I) Moon (X)	Sun (XI)	Jupiter (III, VI)	Mars
Scorpio		Sun (X) Moon (IX) Mars (I) Jupiter (V)	Saturn (III)	Mercury (VIII,XI)	Jupiter Venus
Sagittarius		Sun (IX) Mars (V) Jupiter (I)	Saturn (III)	Venus (VI, XI)	Mercury Saturn
Capricorn	Venus (V, X)	Mercury (IX) Saturn (I)	Jupiter (III) Mars (XI)		Moon
Aquarius	Venus (IV, IX)	Mercury (V) Saturn (I)	Moon (VI) Mercury (VIII) Jupiter (XI)	Mars (III, VIII)	Sun Jupiter
Pisces		Moon (V) Mars (IX) Jupiter (I)	Sun (VI) Saturn (XI)	Venus (III, VIII)	Mercury

Trik Lords

Lords of evil *trik* houses, Sixth representing diseases, enemies, etc., eighth representing death, accidents, suddenness, chronic and incurable diseases, etc., and twelfth indicating expenditure/ losses, suffering, hospitalisation, etc., are evil and particularly adverse for health. Their periods (*Dashas*) must be watched for illnesses, accidents, sudden losses, etc. eighth house Lord has special propensity to kill.

Maraka Lords

Houses eight, and three, which is eighth from eighth, represent longevity. The seventh house which is twelfth from eighth and second house that is twelfth from third, therefore, represent loss of longevity, hence death. Accordingly, Lords of the second and seventh have death-inflicting potential. They are therefore called *marakas* or killers. Their periods/*Dashas* must also be watched for such eventualities. Note that a planet simultaneously owning both houses II and VII becomes a strong *maraka*. But luminaries the Sun and the Moon are never *marakas*.

Great Benefic (*Yoga-Karak*) and Great Malefic

A planet which is doubly benefic may be considered a great benefic or *yoga-karak*. Similarly a planet, which is doubly malefic, is considered a great malefic. A planet, which is Lord of both a *kendra* and a *trikona*, becomes a very powerful benefic and hence a *yoga-karaka*. It becomes stronger if it is also placed in the *kendra* or in the *trikona*, and most strong if it is in its sign of exaltation, or *mool-trikona* or own sign, etc., in that order. In the sample horoscope, Saturn as Lord of IX and X, and also placed in *kendra* in *moola-trikona* sign is a very great *yoga-karaka* for the native. If a planet owns two houses from amongst III, VI, VIII and XI, it becomes a great malefic.

The categorisation of planets in this manner for each *lagna* is given in Table 4.3. The table gives the numbers of houses owned by the planet in brackets. Numbers of houses two and seven of *maraka* Lords are not indicated though. Note that Venus is doubly *maraka* for Aries *lagna*, and Mars is doubly *maraka* for Libra *lagna* as the two own both houses Two and Seven.

Note: In case if a planet owns both a good house and a bad house, such as Saturn for Gemini *lagna*, one should make judgment based on the extent of beneficence and/or maleficence and the strength of the planet and houses involved.

4.11 BASIC CHARACTERISTICS/NATURE OF PLANETS

It is clear that whatever is judged about the characteristics of the native from the *lagna rashi* should also be judged from the Lord of *lagna* and also planets tenanting and aspecting *lagna*. This applies to the other houses as well.

For example, if Leo is the *lagna*, then along with the characteristics of Leo *rashi*, *lagna* Lord Sun will have its affect on the personality of the person according to its own nature. But if the *lagna* is Aquarius, the personality of the native's spouse, and not the native's, will be determined by the Sun, as it will then be Lord of the seventh house.

Further, if there is a planet in the *lagna*, then the nature and characteristics of the native will bear the imprint of that planet. For example, if anyone has Mars in *lagna*, s/he will have the qualities of aggressiveness, dynamism and courage. And the position of Mars will also affect greatly one's nature. Thus, if Mars is strong, say, in Aries, Scorpio or Capricorn in *lagna* the native will be very brave and ready to accept any challenge, and may be fighting a war like an army commander, but if Mars is weak, say, in Cancer then s/he may simply be quarrelsome.

Take another example. The Sun in Leo or Aries in *lagna* will give a regal personality to the native, but the same Sun in Libra will make one opt for superficial pomp and show.

Similarly, the Moon in *lagna* in own sign Cancer or exalted in Taurus will make a person very affectionate and confident, but in debilitation in Scorpio will make him/her lack in confidence. S/he will ever remain depressed.

The Moon, Jupiter and Venus in the first house bestow fair complexion. The Sun and Mars would give coppery tinge while Saturn, Rahu and Ketu would make one dark complexioned.

The planets aspecting *lagna* also affect native's characteristics.

Even diseases are governed by the nature of planets. For example, the Sun will cause *pitta rogas*, diseases due to heat, high blood pressure, fever, etc.

The same principles apply to every other house. For example, we see the characteristics of the spouse from the sign, its Lord and planets tenanting and aspecting the seventh house, those of the children from the fifth house, and so on.

Some of the basic characteristics endowed by planets are given below:

The Sun gives strong bones. Complexion is coppery. Pupils in the eyes are brown with reddishness. The native has scanty hair, wears red coloured clothes and is fierce and chivalrous.

The Moon gives slender body, young looks. The native has fair complexion and fine dark hair. The eyes are beautiful and the voice is sweet. The native is soft by nature as well as physique, and prefers white clothes.

Mars gives thin waist, curly and shining hair and strong muscles. Complexion is reddish. The native looks younger than one's age. S/he wears red coloured clothes. Though liberal, Martian is militant by nature, and strongly sexed.

Mercury gives a well-proportioned body and radiant skin. A Mercurian is fun loving, intelligent, witty and diplomatic in speech. His/her favourite colour is green.

Jupiter gives yellowish complexion and brownish eyes and hair. Jupiter gives wisdom as against intelligence of Mercury. One is learned, sober, magnanimous and spiritually inclined. Jupiter bestows wealth and prosperity. Jupiter is the Guru or religious preceptor. A Jupiter born person likes yellow/saffron colour clothes.

Venus makes one handsome/beautiful. A Venus-governed person has beautiful face, large thighs, chest/and breasts, and very fair complexion. S/he is strongly sexed. The favourite colour is white. Venus in the eighth house may cause sex/semen-related diseases.

Saturn causes weak legs and sunken eyes. The body is long but lean. One looks old, has swollen veins and clumsy teeth and nails. For a person governed by Saturn complexion is dark. The native is lazy by nature and generally hard-hearted. S/he wears purple, black, dark blue or simply dark coloured clothes. But if Saturn is strong, then the native is a disciplinarian, sober, deep, serious, sagacious, fond of occult sciences, philosophy, etc.

Rahu is somewhat like Saturn. The native has a large body, bluish complexion and dirty skin. S/he is irreligious, hypocritical, cunning, Always talks ill of others and wears old/tattered clothes. If anyone has a misfortune or suffers a loss during the *Dasha* of Rahu, one can safely say that it must be due to his/her own faults/habits. But, if Rahu is strong it endows one with extraordinary intelligence and discrimination. Rahu is 'discontent incarnate'. It is never satisfied. Nothing is good enough for Rahu.

Ketu is somewhat like Mars. The native has a tall, aggressive and lean body with eyes that look red with anger. The complexion is dark. One has scars on body, and is cruel by nature. S/he wears clothes with spots. A strong Ketu bestows courage and spirituality on the native.

Ketu is 'fanatic incarnate'. It is unreasonable and irrational.

While Rahu will listen to logic in self-interest, Ketu will remain adamant like a child.

Rahu and Ketu are the Sun's enemies. Hence they torment the soul when ill-placed.

Note that a planet endows its positive qualities if it is strongly placed, but the same qualities turn negative if the planet is weak.

Colours, Jewels, Metals and Tastes of Planets

Table 4.4 below gives the colours, jewels, metals and tastes favoured by each planet.

Table 4.4
Colors, Jewels, Metals and Tastes of Planets

	Sun	Moon	Mars	Mercury	Jupiter
Color	Coppery Crimson	White	Blood Red	Green	Yellow Saffron
Jewel	Ruby	Pear	Coral	Emerald	Topaz
Metal	Copper	Silver	Copper	Alloys	Gold
Taste	Bitter	Salty	Hot	Mixed	Sweet

	Venus	Saturn	Rahu	Ketu
Colour	White	Black Purple	Dark	Spotted
Jewel	Diamond	Sapphire	*Gomed*	Cat's Eye
Metal	Silver	Iron	lead	Alloys
Taste	Sour	Astringent		

The intensity of characteristics, vibrations, energy fields, etc., pertaining to a planet increase if one wears a gem corresponding to that planet. The jewel is worn on the finger above the mount of the planet on the palm of the hand as follows:

Little finger	Emerald, Pearl
Ring finger	Ruby, Coral
Middle finger	Blue Sapphire, *Gomed*, Cat's Eye
Index finger	Yellow Topaz, Diamond

Temperament of Planets

The Sun and Mars give hot temperament. The Moon and Venus make one soft. Mercury gives a happy-go-lucky temperament. Jupiter makes one sagacious. Saturn makes one stern. Other key words in relation to the temperament of planets are as follows:

Sun: Fiery, steady, vitality, power, regal, status, dignified, nurturing like father

Moon: Emotional, waxing and waning, fickle, home-loving, sensitive, nurturing like mother

Mars: Fiery, aggressive, energy, stamina, drive, decisive, passionate

Mercury: Communicative, volatile, adept, clever, intelligent, fun-loving

Jupiter: Wisdom, amiable, magnanimous, broad minded, soft hearted, spiritually inclined, optimistic, expansion, fortunate, wealthy

Venus: Harmony, easy going, artistic, graceful, compassionate, lover

Saturn: Harsh, hard hearted, responsible, disciplinarian, just, practical

Rahu: Material destiny, discontented, clever

Ketu: Humility, fanatic, obstinate, illogical, irrational, courageous

Uranus: Violent change, freedom loving, unconventional, original, inventive

Neptune: Gradual change, idealistic, spiritual transformation

Pluto: Change, but first elimination/destruction followed by reconstruction

Other related words can be found under the description of signs ruled by the planets.

The Three Qualities (*Gunas*)

The three intrinsic qualities (*gunas*) are stated as purity and simplicity (*satva*), pleasure-seeking (*raja*), and dullness (*tama*).

The Sun, the Moon and Jupiter have *satvic gunas*. These planets are basically pious in intent. Those governed by these planets will sacrifice their own interests, but will not harm anybody. Although Sun is a malefic, it is not evil. It is a symbol of highest purity.

Mercury and Venus have *rajasic gunas*. These are neither godly nor devilish. Their main aim is to seek pleasures and enjoy life. They will not sacrifice their interests although to fulfil the same they will not harm anybody.

Mars, Saturn, Rahu and Ketu have *tamasic gunas*. These planets are not supposed to represent pious intensions. They may turn selfish, and may even harm others to fulfil their needs.

Sex of Planets

The Sun, Mars and Jupiter are male, Moon and Venus are female, and Mercury and Saturn are treated as eunches. The planet, during the *Dasha* of which a child is born, particularly determines the sex of the child. The influence of male planets on the fifth house gives more sons. The influence of female planets gives more daughters. Eunuch planets give daughters rather than sons.

Among the nodes, Rahu is feminine while Ketu is a eunuch.

The Sun, Mars and Jupiter endow manly qualities. The Moon and Venus endow womanly qualities. Mercury and Saturn cause deficiency of these two qualities. If Mercury and Saturn influence the seventh house, the native may be weak in sex.

Humours of the Body

Planets related to the three humours of the body are as follows:

Vat/wind/gas   Moon, Mercury, Venus, Saturn
Pitta/heat/bile   Sun, Mars, Mercury
Kapha/phlegm   Moon, Mercury, Jupiter, Venus

Thus, we see that Sun and Mars cause diseases due to *Pitta*/heat/bile in the body, Moon and Venus cause *Vat* and *Kapha* implying Gas/wind and phlegm, Mercury gives illnesses governed by all the three humours of the body, Jupiter causes *Kapha*/phlegm and Saturn suffers from *Vat*/wind/gas related problems.

4.12 PORTFOLIOS/SIGNIFICATIONS (*KARAKATVAS*) OF PLANETS

Various matters of life fall within the portfolios of the planets. In other words, each planet is a significator or *karaka* for certain matters. For example, the Sun represents the soul, bones, father, enthusiasm, etc., of the native. Hence, the Sun is the *karaka* for these. Similarly, the Moon is *karaka* for mind, emotional as well as the physical heart, mother, home, happiness, etc. Mars represents one's valour, physical as well as mental stamina, muscles, brothers and sisters, masculinity, sexual prowess, etc. Mercury is *karaka* for skin, speech, intelligence, friends, adopted son, maternal uncle, etc. Jupiter confers wealth, prosperity, happiness, wisdom, spirituality, and so on, and happiness from the husband in the case of a woman. Here, Jupiter has been considered as *karaka* for husband. Venus governs semen and potency. It is also the *karaka* for spouse, wife, love, marriage, passion, sex, comforts, luxury, prosperity, all conveyances, art, dance, music, acting, etc., and happiness from wife in the case of a man. Here, Venus has been considered as *karaka* for spouse, and particularly for wife. The three key words associated with Venus are beauty, cleanliness and fragrance. Unlike Jupiter, Venus is not magnanimous. It looks after its own interests. But in the process, it benefits others too. Both Jupiter and Venus are the greatest benefics. Saturn, on the other hand, indicates grief. It is the *karaka* for nerves, sorrow, service, servants, etc. It also represents poverty, penury, hardships, the company of the ignoble, laziness, loss of reputation, means of agriculture, iron, etc.

Note that a single planet is *karaka* for more than one matter.

Now, if a *karaka* planet is strong in a person's horoscope, the person is bestowed with the portfolios of that planet. But if the planet is weak, the person misses the bounties due to that planet. For example, the Moon in Cancer or Taurus would bestow a strong mind, a confident nature and happiness whereas the Moon in Scorpio would indicate a weak mind, lack of confidence, lack of happiness, etc.

In the case of Saturn, it is the opposite. A strong Saturn does not indicate too much sorrow. Rather, it means less grief. A weak Saturn means too much suffering.

Planets not only affect the matters of their significations, they also endow the native with their nature and characteristics for good or for bad depending on whether the planet is strong or weak. If a planet is placed in a favourable sign and a favourable house and is Lord of a good house and is not combust, it is considered as strong, but if it is placed in an unfavourable sign and an evil house and is Lord of an evil house and/or it is combust, it is considered weak.

Primary Significations of Planets

The planets signify the following for the *Kaal-Purush:*

Planet	Sun	Moon	Mars	Mercury	Jupiter
Signification	Soul	Mind	Stamina Prowess	Skin Speech Intelligence	Wisdom Happiness

Planet	Venus	Saturn	Rahu	Ketu
Signification	Love Comforts Pleasures	Sorrow Hard work	Sorrow	Sorrow

A weak Sun will indicate depleted soul, enthusiasm, etc. A weak Moon indicates lack of confidence, emotional problems, and so on.

Ingredients of Body

The following table shows the body ingredients that are judged from each planet.

Sun	Moon	Mars	Mercury	Jupiter	Venus	Saturn
Bones	Blood	Marrow	Skin	Fat	Semen in Males	Nerves
	Heart				Ovaries in Females	Teeth

Thus, a weak/afflicted Sun will indicate bone problems, and the Moon the problems of heart and blood circulation, and so on. On the other hand, a strong, well placed, unafflicted and well-aspected planet will indicate the corresponding ingredient as strong and healthy.

Relations Planets Signify

Planets signify relations as follows:

Sun	Moon	Mars	Mercury	Jupiter	Venus	Saturn
Father	Mother	Husband	Maternal	Sons,	Spouse	Servant/s
		Brother/s	Uncle	Daughters	Wife	Paternal
		Sister/s	Friends	Guru		Uncle
			Adopted son			

Thus, happiness to/from father is judged not only from the tenth house and its Lord but also from *karaka* Sun. An exalted Sun in Aries shows exalted status of father.

Similarly, happiness to/from mother is seen not only from the fourth house and its Lord but also more importantly from *karaka* Moon. An exalted Moon in Taurus indicates a very affectionate and kindly mother.

Happiness from spouse, and more importantly from wife, is judged not only from seventh house and its Lord but also from Venus. Venus in Taurus or Libra or Pisces means great happiness of a beautiful and loving life partner.

Similarly, happiness to/from children is judged not only from fifth house and its Lord, but also from Jupiter.

Directions Planets Signify

Planets signify directions as follows:

East	South-East	South	South-West	West	North-West	North	North-East
Sun	Venus	Mars	Rahu/Ketu	Saturn	Moon	Mercury	Jupiter

It implies from the above that the native will gain and prosper from activities/work undertaken in these directions from birthplace during the period/*Dasha* of the planet provided the planet is strong. But if the planet is weak, there will be loss in that direction.

Abodes/Places Planets Signify

Let us now look at the places presided over by planets.

Open well-lit spaces, forests, mountains, places of worship belong to the Sun.

Places where women reside, and where honey, herbs and wine flow, and which are near water suit the Moon.

War-torn zones suit Mars. Mars also governs kitchens, furnaces, etc., where fire is used.

Mercury likes gatherings of intelligent people and places of fun, entertainment and sports, also places where mathematical/astrological calculations are done.

Jupiter's favourites are prosperous lands and gatherings of learned and pious people. Jupiter also governs banks and treasure houses.

Venus likes bedrooms, women's quarters, places of enjoyment, dance, lustful actions, etc.

Saturn resides where the ignoble live. It has lordship over farm houses and dirty places.

Preferred places of Rahu and Ketu are narrow dark areas such as those inhabited by snakes.

This is to imply that the native feels most comfortable in such surroundings particularly during the *Dasha* of the planet if the same is well-placed in the horoscope. If the planet is not well-placed, then the native may be living in those places during the *Dasha* of the planet under compulsion remaining dissatisfied.

Listing of Significations of Planets

Fulfilment of significations of planets is judged from their placement in houses and signs, whether favourable or unfavourable, and whether they are direct or retrograde or combust or otherwise.

Table 4.5 is an attempt to list important matters of significations of planets.

Table 4.5
Significations (*Karakattvas*) of Planets

SUN	Soul, bones, father, protective, happiness to/from father, health, brilliance, enthusiasm, success, prestige, power, administrator, authority, status, royalty, name/fame, recognition, people of classes, government, favour from government/authorities, ruby, gold.
MOON	Heart, blood, mind, mother, nurturing, happiness to/from mother, woman, breasts, beauty, company/love of a woman, conceiving, menses, phlegm, watery places, imagination, sensitivity, emotions, happiness, mental peace, sleep, travel, masses/common people, grains, fruits, flowers, soft/white objects, cow, milk, pearl, silver.
MARS	Physical/mental stamina, husband for females, marrow/muscles, younger brothers/sisters, excitement, adventure, youth, fearlessness, valour, warrior, anger, land/property/house, sweets, kitchen, fire, weapons, accidents, wounds, coral, copper, blood red.
MERCURY	Skin, speech, tongue, expression, education, intelligence, memory, communications, reading, writing, knowledge of scriptures, maternal uncle, nephew, cousins, friends, adopted son, mathematics, occult

emotional and may have the temperament resembling to the waxing and waning of the Moon.

Likewise, Jupiter rules over number 3. Number three persons are rich, magnanimous and pious. Mercury rules over 5. Number 5 people can adjust with everybody. Venus rules over 6. Number 6 people enjoy the comforts of life. They are charming too. Saturn rules over 8. Number 8 people are fatalistic but hard working. They stick to principles. Mars rules over 9. Number 9 people are energetic but dominating. And they are prone to accidents.

Further, Uranus rules over 4, and Neptune over 7. Number 4 people value their own freedom only, not others. They are also fatalistic. Number 7 people are idealistic.

To find if the native's name suits his/her lucky number, we can use the numbers allotted to each alphabet as follows:

A=1, B=2, C=3, D=4, E=5, F=8, G=3, H=5, I=J=1, K=2, L=3, M=4, N=5, O=7, P=8, Q=1, R=2, S=3, T=4, U=V=W=6, X=5, Y=1, Z=7

4.13 PLANETS AS *KARAKAS* FOR HOUSES/*BHAVAS*

Just as planets are *karakas* for different matters, they are *karakas* also for houses representing those matters. Thus, the Sun is *karaka* not only for father but also for all tenth house matters. Similarly, the Moon is *karaka* for mother as well as *karaka* for fourth house. Fig. 4.3 places the planets in the houses of which they are *karakas*.

Note that some planets are *karakas* for more than one house. Also, houses IV, VI, IX and X have more than one *karaka* planet.

Note: While judging matters pertaining to houses, it is important that we take note also of the planet that is *karaka* for the house.

Hence, while judging the first house, take into consideration how the Sun is placed in the chart. Then, we must take note of Jupiter in the judgments of the second, fifth, ninth, tenth and eleventh houses. While judging the third and sixth, take note of Mars also. In matters pertaining to the fourth, do not fail to consider how the Moon is placed in the chart. In the judgment of the seventh house, importance must be given to Venus in the chart. While examining the eighth and twelfth, we must see how Saturn is placed. In judging the tenth house, take into consideration all four *karakas*, Jupiter signifying fortune, the Sun power and position, Saturn service and livelihood and Mercury communication.

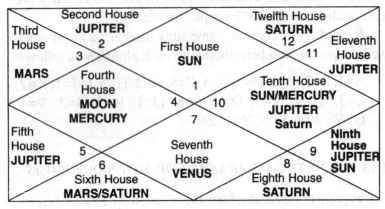

Fig. 4.3 Houses and their karaka Planets

To clarify further, let us consider the first house representing body, health, vigour, etc. It is not enough to see that the first house is strong. For the native to have good health, we must also see the Sun. Despite strong first house and its Lord, if the health is not good it implies a weak sun.

But if we want to know about father, then also we have to see how well the Sun is placed, but then we have to see the tenth house and its Lord and not the first house.

4.14 STRENGTH OF PLANETS

Earlier, we discussed the strength of a planet depending on its sign. At the same time, a planet is considered weak if it is combust even though it may be in its sign of exaltation or in own sign or in a friend's sign. The following are some other ways in which the strength of planets is determined.

Directional Strength

The Sun and Mars have maximum strength, say 100 percent, in the tenth house. They have zero strength in the fourth house. Progressively, the strength decreases from 100 to zero as they move from the tenth to the fourth house, and increases from zero to 100 as they move from the fourth to the tenth house. This is to say that the best house for the Sun and Mars to tenant in a birth-chart is the tenth house. This gives success to the native in dealing with the outside world, and in matters of his/ her career. The strength of these planets in *lagna* and seventh house is 50 percent. Likewise, the Moon and Venus have maximum strength in fourth house, Mercury and Jupiter in the first house and Saturn in seventh house.

Strength of Degrees

Then we have *ansha bal* or strength due to the degrees of the planet within a sign. A planet within the first 1–2 and the last 29–30 degrees in a sign is considered as good as dead. Within the first 3–9 degrees in a sign it is supposed to be in its childhood, while within the last 23–28 degrees, the planet is in old age.

That between 10–22 degrees is considered in its youth exerting maximum influence.

4.15 IDEAL PLACEMENT OF PLANETS IN HOUSES

Some general guidelines are given here based on *karakattvas* of planets, their directional strength, and the *Kaal Purush Kundali*. But first we make two definitions.

One is about the fixed/permanent house (*pucca ghar*) of a planet. The house of signification/*karakattva* of a planet is its *pucca ghar*. A planet in its *pucca ghar* brings fulfilment of those significations, though some people feel otherwise.

The other is about the natural house of a planet. This is on the basis of the *Kaal Purush Kundali*. The house of lordship of a planet in the *Kaal Purush Kundali* is its natural house. For example, Aries and Scorpio are the signs of the first and eighth houses in the *Kaal Purush Kundali*. Accordingly, natural houses of lordships of Mars are the first and the eighth. The placement of a planet in its house of lordship in the *Kaal Purush Kundali* is good in general irrespective of the sign it is placed in. If in a favourable sign, it is all the more beneficial.

Accordingly, let us see which is the best house for each planet:

The Sun is good in the first, ninth and tenth houses, as it is their *karaka*. It is particularly good in the tenth in which it has maximum directional strength. It is best in the first and the fifth where it will be in its sign of exaltation Aries and in its own sign Leo in the *Kaal Purush Kundali*.

The Moon is *karaka* for the fourth house. It also has directional strength in this house. The fourth is also the Moon's natural house having Cancer sign in the *Kaal Purush Kundali*. It is, therefore, the best house for the Moon. It is also very good in the second where it is in its sign of exaltation, Taurus in the *Kaal Purush Kundali*.

Mars is good in the third and sixth houses being their *karaka*. Even as a malefic, it is good in these houses. It is good in the first and the eighth where it would be in its own signs in the *Kaal Purush Kundali*, but it will have *mangalik dosha*. It is best in the tenth house where it is in its sign of exaltation in the

Kaal Purush Kundali, and where it has maximum directional strength also.

Mercury: Mercury is good in the fourth and tenth houses of which it is *karaka*. According to the *Laal-Kitaab*, Mercury is *karaka* for the seventh house also. Hence, it is good in the seventh house as well. In the *Kaal Purush Kundali*, the third and sixth houses are Gemini and Virgo respectively. Hence, Mercury is good in third and sixth as well. But sixth will be a *trik*.

Jupiter is good in the second, fifth, ninth, tenth and eleventh houses of which it is *karaka*. In the *Kaal Purush Kundali*, the fourth, ninth and twelfth houses are Cancer, Sagittarius and Pisces respectively. Hence Jupiter is good in ninth and twelfth houses. But twelfth is *trik*. Thus it is doubly beneficial in the ninth. It is *karaka* as well as Lord of the ninth in the *Kaal Purush Kundali*. From the ninth house, the great benefic Jupiter aspects *lagna*, and third and fifth houses.

Venus is *karaka* for the seventh house. In the *Kaal Purush Kundali*, Venus's own signs Taurus and Libra fall in the second and seventh houses respectively, and Pisces, its sign of exaltation, falls in the twelfth house. Hence, Venus is good in second, seventh and twelfth also. It has directional strength in the fourth. For this reason, it is good in the fourth as well.

Saturn is good in the sixth, eighth, and tenth houses for which it is *karaka*. As a malefic, it is good in the third and sixth houses as well. It is in its sign of exaltation, Libra, own sign Capricorn and own and *moola-trikona* sign Aquarius in the *Kaal Purush Kundali* in the seventh, tenth and eleventh houses respectively. Hence, it is good in these houses, and best in eleventh house.

Rahu is best in the third and sixth houses. These will have Mercury's signs Gemini and Virgo in the *Kaal Purush Kundali*, which are Rahu's own too. As a malefic also it is good here.

Ketu, correspondingly, is best in ninth and twelfth having Jupiter's signs Sagittarius and Pisces in the *Kaal Purush Kundali*. As a malefic, it is good in third and sixth.

(i)   In addition, if the planet is placed in a favourable sign, it is all the more better.

(ii)   It not good for any of the seven planets, in general, to be in the evil *trik* houses, sixth, eighth and twelfth. However, an exception can be made for the sixth house in which malefics are well placed.

Hence, in summary, we can recommend the best houses for planets as follows:

- Sun in I, V, IX and X.
- Moon in II and IV.
- Mars in III, VI and X.
- Mercury in III, IV, VII and X.
- Jupiter in II, IV, V, IX, X and XI.
- Venus in II, IV, VII and XII. It is good for XII even though it is a *trik*.
- Saturn in III, VI, VIII, X and XI.
- Rahu in III and VI.
- Ketu in III, VI, IX and XII. Ketu in VI, means Rahu in XII, which is not good.

Chapter 5

Planetary Aspects (*Drishti*)

Planets cast their glances on other houses as well as the planets posited in those houses. This is called planetary aspect or *drishti*. The effect of this aspect/*drishti* is two-fold:

(i) If the planet is benefic, it has a beneficial effect on the aspected house/*bhava* and the aspected planet. And if the planet is malefic it has adverse effect. A malefic spoils not only the good effects of the house tenanted by it, but also the good effects of the houses and planets aspected.

(ii) Again, if a planet aspects its house of exaltation, *moola-trikona* or own sign or its friend's house, even if it is a natural malefic, it promotes the good affects of the house aspected. But, if it aspects its house of debilitation or its enemy's house, etc., it spoils the house.

Note: The effects of aspect are felt more intensely during the *Dasha* of the planet.

5.1 ASPECTS IN HINDU ASTROLOGY

In Hindu astrology, aspect is counted from sign to sign. Every planet has full aspect on the house seventh from itself. Mars, Jupiter, Saturn and Rahu have aspects as follows:

Mars	4th, 7th and 8th
Jupiter	5th, 7th and 9th
Saturn	3rd, 7th and 10th
Rahu	5th, 7th, 9th and 12th

Ketu, which represents the dragon's tail, is not supposed to have any aspect.

While counting for the aspect, we begin with the house tenanted by the planet. As an illustration, consider the various aspects in the example horoscope that are as follows:

Sun and Moon have inimical aspects on the ninth house, since both are enemies of Saturn.

Mars has 4th neutral aspect on the fifth house, friendly 7th aspect on the eighth house and 8th exalted aspect (*uchcha drishti*) on the ninth house. Mars's aspect on the ninth house is excellent for the native's fortune.

Mercury aspects the ninth house also as a great friend.

Jupiter has 5th debilitated aspect (*neecha drishti*) on the ninth house. Though a great benefic, it does not help the native's fortune. It has 7th aspect on its own sign in the eleventh house, which is very good for native's income/gains. It has 9th benefic aspect on *lagna*. By its aspect on *lagna*, Jupiter imparts its qualities of piety, magnanimity, wealth, prosperity, etc., to the native. Venus has inimical aspect on the eighth house. Saturn has 3rd, 7th and 10th aspects on the twelfth, fourth and seventh houses respectively as their great enemy. Though Saturn is in its *moola-trikona* sign in tenth house which is very good for the native's career, name and fame, it does not give him/her pleasures of the bed of the twelfth house, happiness in general and in particular from mother of the fourth house, and marital happiness of the seventh house.

Finally, Rahu has 5th aspect on its exaltation sign, Taurus, in *lagna*. It provides material well-being to the native. It has 7th inimical aspect on third house of siblings, and 9th favourable aspect in its own sign Virgo on the 5th house of children and education.

Interplanetary Aspects

The aspect of a planet on another planet may be for better if the aspecting planet is benefic and/or friendly, or for worse if it is malefic and/or inimical. In general, a benefic aspecting a malefic reduces the maleficence of the malefic planet, and a malefic aspecting a benefic reduces the beneficence of the benefic planet.

Planets aspecting a house simultaneously aspect the planets placed in that house.

Thus, in the example horoscope, Rahu not only aspects the third house, it also aspects the Sun, the Moon and Mercury placed in the third house. Thus it makes the Sun and the Moon weaker.

Mutual Aspect and *Sambandh*

When two planets mutually aspect each other they form a special relationship called *'sambandha'* in Sanskrit. This brings about the fusion of their influences on each other.

All planets have 7th aspect. Hence planets in the opposite houses aspect and affect each other and have a *sambandh*. Such planets placed in houses 1–7 relative to each other are said to be in *opposition*. Planets in the same house similarly affect each other. Such planets placed in houses 1–1 relative to each other are said to be in conjunction. Conjunction and opposition are called mutual aspects.

Another example of mutual aspect is between Mars casting its 4th aspect on Saturn, and Saturn in turn casting its 10th aspect on Mars when Saturn is 90 degrees away or in the fourth house counted from Mars, and Mars is 270 degrees away or in the tenth house counted from Saturn. This is one of the worst aspects since Mars and Saturn both are malefics, and Mars happens to be Saturn's great enemy. This mutual aspect makes the two planets even more malefic spoiling the houses tenanted and owned by them, and also the matters and houses of which they are *karakas*.

A *sambandha* is also formed when Lords of two houses are placed in each other's houses resulting in mutual exchange, a kind of *yoga*. This mutual exchange between Lord of any house with Lord of a good house is good for the house, but with the Lord of a bad house is bad for the house. For *yogas*, see Chapter 11.

Conjunction of Planets

Conjunction refers to the placement of two planets in the same sign within a few degrees of each other. It affects the conjuncting planets either favourably or unfavourably.

For example, the conjunction of the Sun with the Moon makes the Moon combust. It indicates weakness of both the soul, body as well as the mind, since the Sun is *karaka* for the soul and body and the Moon is for the mind. It may lead to depression. This happens to those born around *Amavasya*.

The conjunction of the Sun and Mars, since both planets have hot temperament, increases anger and makes one proud and haughty.

The conjunction of the Sun and Mercury gives *Budhaditya-Yoga*. It makes one scholarly.

The conjunction of the Sun and Jupiter makes one highly spiritual but very dominating.

The conjunction of the Sun with Venus makes one artistic.

Affliction of the Sun, *karaka* for father, by aspect or conjunction by great enemy and malefic Saturn or Rahu or Ketu may cause illness or loss of happiness or even death to father. Similarly, the Moon, *karaka* for mother, if aspected by or in conjunction with Saturn/Rahu/Ketu may result in illness or loss of happiness or death to mother. The Sun and Saturn, great mutual enemies, together in any house, destroy that house.

The placement of the Moon and Saturn together in any house in a birth-chart is evil. It shows that the native's birth took place during *Sadhe-Saati*. It means that Saturn was transiting over the Moon at the time of birth. This kind of conjunction is equivalent to sitting on the back of a blind horse, or living in a house floating on river. Such a person lacks aim and direction and finds difficult to achieve his/her objectives and reach goals. It also indicates loss of mother or suffering to her.

The conjunction of Moon with Mars makes one short tempered and angry. Such a person may even dislike his/her mother. It makes one daring though. The native is fond of opposite sex. S/he has wealth, but no mental happiness.

The conjunction of the Moon with Mercury, the Moon being Mercury's enemy, may lead to problems of nervous system, sleep, etc. But the native is kind, and speaks softly since Mercury is a great friend of the Moon. Thus the Moon's significations improve while Mercury's are hampered.

The conjunction of the Moon with Jupiter, or any aspect of Jupiter on the Moon, gives rise to *Guru-Chandra-Yoga*. The mind of such a person is very peaceful, pious and unselfish.

The Moon-Venus conjunction makes one very cheerful, optimistic and romantic. One is fond of luxury, pleasures and opposite sex.

The Moon-Rahu and Moon-Ketu conjunctions are bad like the Moon-Saturn ones.

The Mars-Jupiter conjunction makes one an officer/ administrator.

The Mars-Venus conjunction makes one immoral in man-woman relations.

The conjunction of Mars-Saturn, the two great malefics and Mars a great enemy of Saturn, makes one jealous, untruthful and sorrowful.

The Mercury-Jupiter conjunction makes one a poet/ composer/journalist.

The Mercury-Venus together make one an orator with lovable speech.

The Mercury-Saturn together gives a shady deceptive character.

The Jupiter-Venus conjunction gives an ideal spouse, and happiness from spouse.

The Jupiter-Saturn conjunction, Jupiter being *karaka* for children and liver, gives liver trouble and problems to/from children. Thus, Jupiter becomes weak. It robs Jupiter of some of its beneficence. However, in conjunction with or aspected by Jupiter, Saturn becomes benign (*dharmi*). The nature of Saturn gets changed.

Finally, the Venus-Saturn conjunction may result in illness/ suffering to wife. Saturn either in conjunction with or aspecting Venus will make the native unfaithful in lovemaking.

5.2 ASPECTS IN WESTERN ASTROLOGY

Some of the important aspects according to Western astrology are as follows:

Conjunction	Conjunction is 1–1 position house-wise in the same sign when two planets are close together, say, within 8 degrees orb of each other.
Opposition	Here the two planets are in opposite signs. They are in 1–7 positions counted from each other, e.g. Aries-Libra, etc. Exact opposition occurs when they are 180 degrees apart. But an orb of 8 degrees is allowed.
Trine	Here the two planets are on the vertices of an equilateral triangle if we join them, viz., in 5–9 positions counted from each other. Thus, they are four signs or 120 degrees apart. The orb allowed is 6 degrees.
Sextile	This is the 3-11 position. The planets are two signs or 60 degrees apart. An orb of only 4 degrees is allowed.
Square	The planets are in 4–10 positions counted from each other. This occurs when they are three signs apart or there is difference of 90 degrees in their longitudes. An orb of only 4 degrees is allowed.
Quincunx	The planets are in 6–8 positions. This occurs when one is at 150 degrees and the other at 210 degrees from the other. For example, a planet in Aries is in quincunx aspect with planets in Virgo and Scorpio. An orb of only 2 degrees is allowed.
Semi-Sextile	This is 2–12 position. The two planets are in adjacent signs, meaning they are 30 degrees apart. Thus, a planet in Aries is in semi-sextile with a planet in Pisces or Taurus.

Some of these aspects are considered good or easy, others as evil or difficult while some as neutral as indicated below:

Neutral	Good/Easy	Evil/Difficult
Conjunction (1–1)	Trine (5–9)	Square (4–10)
Opposition (1–7)	Sextile (3–11)	Quincunx (6–8),
		Semi-Sextile (2–12)

In fact, conjunction and opposition aspects, whether good or bad, depend very much on the planets forming the aspects. Both the trine and sextile aspects are very good. While the square aspect is a difficult one, the semi-sextile is evil and the quincunx is the worst.

5.3 COMPARISON OF ASPECTS IN HINDU AND WESTERN ASTROLOGY

In Hindu astrology, aspects are counted from sign to sign whereas in Western astrology they are counted from degrees to degrees.

Experience shows that interplanetary aspects according to Western astrology have profound effect on the person. But, it often happens that, because of the orb allowed, a *dissociated aspect* is formed. This happens when one planet is at the end of a sign and the other is near the beginning of another sign. Though they are within the orb, they are actually in different signs and houses. This weakens the aspect.

That is why in Hindu astrology importance is given to aspects formed from sign to sign between planets and not so much by their degrees. But this may also result in another anomaly when, say, one planet has 0.5 degree in a sign and the other planet has 29.5 degrees (i) in the preceding sign or (ii) in the same sign. In case (i), though the two planets appear to be in 2-12 positions sign-wise, there is only 1-degree difference in their longitudes, which makes them conjunct. And in case (ii), though the two planets appear to be in conjunction sign-wise, they are actually 29 degrees apart. This makes the aspects virtually ineffective. Similar anomalies appear in opposition and other aspects too. One must, therefore, make predictions keeping these in mind.

Another slight difference exists in the interpretation of the nature of these aspects. Trine and sextile aspects are considered good both in Hindu as well as Western astrology. The square aspect is interpreted differently. It is not much discussed in Hindu astrology. And whenever it is discussed it is not considered bad. Sometimes, it is even considered good also such as in the Moon signs of the bride and bridegroom for matching.

A word must be said about the quincunx and semi-sextile aspects. These are considered evil in both systems. That is why in Hindu astrology marriage is *never recommended* between persons having their Moon Signs (*rashis*) in 2–12 or 6–8 positions.

In 2–12 positions, it will cause *daridra yoga*. Such a partnership will never flourish. One's Moon is in second house of wealth from the other's, and the other's Moon is in the twelfth house of loss/expenditure of wealth, physical energy, etc., from the former's. The two persons, instead of helping, will only be consuming each other.

In 6–8 positions, it will cause *shatru yoga*. Such couples will always be fighting each other. One's Moon is in the sixth house of enemy, and the other's is in the eighth house of death with respect to each other.

Temporary Relationships between Planets

Natural relationships between planets described in Chapter 4 apply to all charts. But the temporary relationships are unique to each chart such as the following:

Planets in 6–8 Positions: Planets placed in 6–8 positions in a chart will always be inimical to each other irrespective of them being natural friends or enemies. In the minor period of one during the major period of the other, the results will be unfavourable.

Planets in 5–9 Positions: Planets placed in trine, viz., 5–9 positions in chart help each other irrespective of them being natural friends or enemies. In the minor period of one during the major period of the other, the results will be good in general.

5.4 SOME ASPECTS IN WESTERN ASTROLOGY

Some interplanetary aspects according to Western astrology are described below:

Conjunction, Opposition and Square Aspects of Mars/ Venus with Saturn

Saturn and Rahu are notorious for causing perversions and disharmony in marital life if they form difficult aspects to Venus and Mars. These give rise to either of the following:

(i)   Frigidity or impotence due to fear.

(ii) Lack of passion due to lack of respect for spouse.

Note that in a woman's chart Venus represents the woman herself and Mars represents the husband, and in a man's chart Venus represents wife and Mars his own self.

In a Woman's Horoscope

Venus-Saturn/Rahu conjunction, opposition or square in a woman's horoscope means:

Venus + Saturn or Rahu = Fear

This fear causes frigidity. It may cause the feelings to be frozen. The woman's body does not respond to sexual urges. She requires a degree of maturity on her part before entering into marriage. She is like an insecure child, unsure of being loved, and withholds until she obtains a proof that entering into marriage will be safe. She remains cold, as she does not acknowledge her own femininity. She has no self-confidence, and may even consider herself inferior.

Mars-Saturn/Rahu conjunction, opposition or square in a woman's horoscope means:

Mars + Saturn or Rahu = Lack of Respect for Husband

This aspect in a woman's chart colours the image about man. She thinks the man inferior and somewhat lesser than herself. She loses respect for him. Her sexual frigidity in this case will actually be a means to keeping the man away. She remains cold towards her man, as she does not trust him and his masculinity.

In a Man's Horoscope

Similar results follow in a man's chart except that Mars and Venus exchange their positions. Thus we have:

Mars + Saturn or Rahu = Fear. Psychological impotence. Man considers himself inferior.
Venus + Saturn or Rahu = Lack of Respect for Wife. Man considers wife inferior.

Conjunction, Opposition and Square Aspects of Outer Planets with Venus or Moon and Mars or Sun

Until the discovery of Uranus, Neptune and Pluto, the sexual aberrations were ascribed only to Saturn and Rahu. But the outer planets are found to be equally great culprits.

In a Woman's Chart

In a woman's chart, the aspecting culprit is Uranus.

The affected planets are Venus and the Moon both of which represent femininity while Mars and Sun represent masculinity. The picture appears like this:

Venus or the Moon + Uranus = Woman afraid of losing her independence in the relationship.

Sun or Mars + Uranus = Image of man is that of a shatterer/destroyer of relationship.

In a Man's Chart

In a man's chart, Neptune and Pluto are considered as the culprits. Neptune distorts the image of a woman as that of an unfathomably sacrificing mother while Pluto distorts it to the contradictory image of a powerful possessive ruthless mother. The result is:

Mars or Sun + Neptune or Pluto = Man wonders if he is doing justice to his woman.
Venus or the Moon + Neptune = Expects woman to make unlimited sacrifices.
Venus or the Moon + Pluto = Considers woman to be too possessive/cruel.

Saturn-Jupiter Aspects

With conjunction, opposition and square of Saturn and Jupiter, the native alternates between the benign expansive characteristics of Jupiter, and the restrictive characteristics of Saturn, that is between hope and despair, magnanimity and meanness, and so on. Though Saturn becomes less malefic due to Jupiter's aspect, Jupiter itself loses some of its beneficence on account of Saturn's influence.

Hard Aspects of Saturn and Outer Planets

Outer planets are basically malefic in nature though they make silent notes. Uranus rules the ideas, and Neptune the oceanic depths of feelings, while Pluto rules the underworld. Accordingly, when we have their hard aspects with Saturn, the results are as follows:

Saturn + Uranus = Sudden catastrophes.

Saturn + Neptune = Deceit. Drugs/Alcohol.

Saturn + Pluto = Self-destruction. Obsessive nature. Melancholy. Suicidal thoughts.

5.5 SUN-MOON ASPECTS AND LUNAR DATES (*TITHIS*)

For most of the 'lunation period', we can see only some part of the Moon as it merely reflects the light of the Sun back to us. The Moon takes about 29.6 days to complete 360 degrees orbit round the Earth. It stays in a sign, covering 30 degrees of longitude, for about 2.5 days. Therefore it covers about 12 degrees of longitude in one solar day.

Dark Moon (*Amavasya*)

On the lunar date, that is popularly known as *Amavasya*, the Moon is exactly between the Earth and the Sun as shown in Fig. 5.1. The Sun's light is then completely reflected back to itself. The side of the Moon facing the Earth, therefore, appears completely dark. Thus we have *Dark Moon* at night. This occurs when the difference in longitudes of the Sun and the Moon is zero, i.e. there is the Sun–Moon conjunction.

Waxing Moon Period (*Shukla Paksha*)

On the 2nd day after the *Amavasya*, the position of the Moon shifts in the course of its monthly orbit around the Earth to the extent that a Crescent Moon appears. The crescent increases in size and then Full Moon appears after about 15 days. This period of Waxing Moon is called *Shukla Paksha*. *Shukla* means bright. *Paksha* means fortnight.

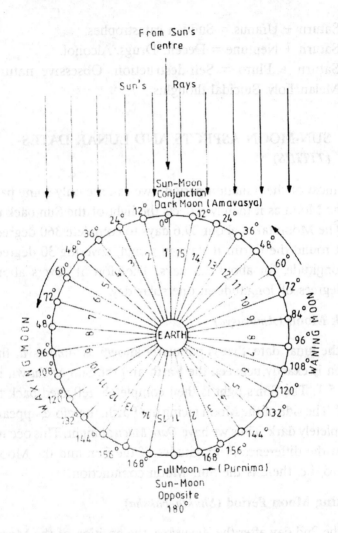

Fig. 5.1 Longitudes of the Moon and the Sun According to the Lunar Dates

Full Moon (*Purnima*)

At Full Moon, the Moon is exactly in opposition to the Sun. The difference in longitudes of the two is exactly 180 degrees. Although the Earth is in between the Sun and the Moon, the

Moon is fully visible as its orbit is tilted with respect to that of the Earth. The lunar date in this Full Moon position is named *Purnima* or *Purna-Masi* meaning end of the lunar month. In Hindu calendar, this is the day on which the lunar month ends.

Waning Moon Period (*Krishna Paksha*)

The Moon starts slowly waning from the Full Moon position to the Dark Moon position. This is called the Waning Moon Period or *Krishna Paksha*. *Krishna* means dark.

The total lunation period of the Moon is 29.6 solar days. Accordingly, *Shukla Paksha* and *Krishna Paksha* are of 14.8 solar days each.

Lunar Date (*Tithi*)

The *tithi* is determined from the difference in longitudes of the Moon and the Sun. This difference on *Amavasya* is zero, and on *Purnima* it is 180 degrees. The period from *Amavasya* to *Purnima* is divided into 15 lunar *tithis*. Similarly, from *Purnima* back to *Amavasya* it is another 15 *tithis*. In one full lunar month, from *Amavasya* to *Purnima* and then back to *Amavasya* it becomes 360 degrees change in longitude after 30 *tithis*. One lunar day or *tithi* is thus exactly equal to the change in the difference in longitudes of the Moon and the Sun of 12 degrees.

There are names for *tithis*. They are the same in both fortnights. After *Purnima*, starting from the first *tithi* called *Padva* or *Pratipada* to *Amavasya*, the *tithis* belong to the *Krishna Paksha*. And after *Amavasya*, again starting from *Padva* up to *Purnima* the *tithis* belong to the *Shukla Paksha*. Fig. 5.1 shows the difference in longitudes of Moon and Sun according to *tithis*. The same are listed in Table 5.1. Note that *Purnima Tithi* begins when the Moon is 168 degrees away from Sun and ends when it is 180 degrees from it.

There are three triads of 5 *tithis* in each *Paksha*. In each triad, the first *tithi* is *Nanda*, second is *Bhadra*, third is *Jaya*, fourth is *Rikta* and fifth is *Purna*. Thus *Nanda tithis* are 1, 6, and 11, *Bhadra* are 2, 7 and 12, *Jaya* are 3, 8 and 13, *Rikta* are 4, 9 and 14, and *Purna* are 5, 10 and 15. *Rikta tithis* are considered inauspicious.

Table 5.1
Lunar Dates or *Tithis* and Difference in Longitudes of Moon and Sun

Tithi	Shukla Paksha Long. Difference In Degrees	Krishna Paksha Long. Difference In Degrees	Tithi
			(Amavasya)
1	0 – 12	12 – 0	15
2	12 – 24	24 – 12	14
3	24 – 36	36 – 24	13
4	36 – 48	48 – 36	12
5	48 – 60	60 – 48	11
6	60 – 72	72 – 60	10
7	72 – 84	84 – 72	9
8	84 – 96	96 – 84	8
9	96 – 108	108 – 96	7
10	108 – 120	120 – 108	6
11	120 – 132	132 – 120	5
12	132 – 144	144 – 132	4
13	144 – 156	156 – 144	3
14	156 – 168	168 – 156	2
15	168 – 180 (**Purnima**)	180 _ 168	1

5.6 CHARACTERISTICS OF EACH *JANMA-TITHI*

The *Janma-tithi*, viz., lunar date of birth actually implies the Moon–Sun aspect. According to Hindu astrology, this has great influence on the nature and personality of the native as described in Table 5.2. It will be seen from Table 5.2 that *Purnima* is the best *tithi* to be born. On the day of *Purnima*, both luminaries, the Sun and the Moon, fully aspect each other. This position gives high-spirited soul, an elevated mind and noble parents. No doubt, many great saints like Gautam Buddha and Guru Nanak were born on *Purnima*. *Amavasya* also is not a bad day to be born. However, persons born on *Amavasya* may remain depressed and pessimistic since Moon is in deep combustion. But such people possess a reflecting mind, and a spirit of renunciation. Many saints have been born on *Amavasya* also.

By far, thirteenth and fourteenth are not desirable *tithis* to be born. On *tithis* 13 and 14 before *Purnima*, the Sun and the Moon move close to the inimical 6–8 positions. And on the 13 and 14 before *Amavasya*, they are close to the 2–12 positions, and the Moon approaches combustion.

Table 5.2
Characteristics Based on *Janma-Tithis*

Tithi	Characteristics
1	First *tithi* signifies *vriddhi,* meaning increase, large family, well-educated, discretion, active, persevering.
2	Signifies auspicious happenings, native is kind, generous, wealthy, thoughtful, noble, personable.
3	It is power giving, more than normally sexed, educated, travels frequently, proud, good conversationalist, always apprehensive.
4	Much stamina, fighting spirit, miserly, over-sexed litigations, frequent traveller.
5	Signifies Lakshmi meaning wealth, likes spouse/children, lustful, lean, kind to animals, studious, respected by authorities, fond of walking/ travelling.
6	It is fame giving, native makes promises and fulfils them, is intelligent, has wealth and children, not much strength.

contd.

Tithi	Characteristics
7	Friendly, connoisseur of arts, prominent eyes, inclined to religious rites, has more daughters than sons, occupies good position, phlegmatic diseases.
8	Signifies conflict, wealthy, kind, occupies a position of authority, conjugal happiness, fond of spouse and children, no fixity of mind, phlegmatic diseases.
9	Signifies aggressiveness, famous, intelligent but uses harsh language, averse to doing a good turn to relations, conduct is not good, over sexed, good physique, no happiness from spouse and children.
10	Sober *tithi*, highly religious, learned, generous, courteous, clever in speech, rich, over-sexed, adorable personality, happiness from spouse and children.
11	Eleventh is *Ekadashi*, a day of fasting, to pay homage to gods and saints, Signifies enjoyments, has riches/servants, not physically strong, fiery temper.
12	Signifies fame/great qualities, has spirit of renunciation, generous in giving, scholar, earns money from government, has good house to live in.
13	Signifies victory, pleasing personality, valour, clever, prominent neck, greedy, over-sexed.
14	It is a bad *tithi*, signifies aggressiveness mirthful, angry temperament. very brave, little forbearance, tendency to contradict, much inclination for sex, inclined to liaison with others' spouses.
15	One fifteenth is *Amavasya*, it is considered a bad *tithi*, Devoted to parents, recluse, fond of travelling, not a strong body, will earn with difficulty, not much lustre. Depressed, always apprehensive, pessimistic. The other fifteenth is *Purnima*, a *shubha tithi*, brings name and fame to family, good heart, cheerful mind, soft adorable body, earns through rightful means, has riches, enjoys life well, inclined to charity, benevolent.

Note: *Tithis* are chosen in day-to-day life for fixing days for ceremonies, fasting, etc., and to find auspicious time (*muhurta*) to undertake any new work. For *muhurta*, See Sec. 14.11 in Chapter 14.

Chapter 6

Judging from Ascendant

In the *Lagna-Kundali*, the ascendant or *lagna* sign represents the characteristics of the person. The nature of the signs was briefly mentioned in Chapter 1.

Once the ascendant is known, the signs of the other houses and hence general characteristics of relations and affairs pertaining to those houses are also possible to predict. The same are briefly given below for each *lagna*.

6.1 ASCENDANT ARIES/MESH *LAGNA*

In the *Kaal Purush Kundali*, Aries ruled by Mars is the natural sign of the first house. The ascendent sign of the person as also the signs of all the houses in this case, therefore, remain exactly the same as in the *Kaal Purush Kundali*.

The person with Aries *lagna* is full of vigour, dynamic and assertive.

The second house of family is Taurus. Taurus is for sincerity. S/he is sincere towards family. The third house of travels is

Gemini, a movable sign. Hence, the person will enjoy short travels/changes. The fourth house of home is Cancer. A Cancerian is anyway fond of home. The fifth house of children is Leo. Leo being like a lion/lioness protects his/her children. The sixth house of disease is Virgo representing navel/stomach region. Hence, s/he is prone to stomach disorders.

The seventh house of spouse is Libra. Libra stands for sophistication in love. In addition to sophistication, a Libran spouse is reasonable, compromising and cooperative. S/he has higher-class upbringing with the desired luxury and refinement in life. The eighth house of genitals is Scorpio. Scorpio is passionate about sex. The ninth house of *Dharma* is Sagittarius ruled by Jupiter and imparts a religious outlook. The tenth house of *karma* is Capricorn. Capricorn is hardworking and sincere in work. But s/he is self-centered, and may favour own kith and kin. The eleventh house of gains and friendship is Aquarius. An Aquarian prefers own personal freedom in friendship. The twelfth house is Pisces ruled by Jupiter. Likes to go on pilgrimages and spends on worthy causes.

6.2 ASCENDENT TAURUS/*VRISHABHA LAGNA*

Taurus ruled by Venus is the natural sign of the second house. Hence the native with Taurus *lagna* is fond of good food. S/he is also sincere, earthly, practical and sensual.

The third house is Cancer, representing homeliness. Any travel, therefore, is only to visit family and friends. The fourth house is Leo. Leo is for royalty. Likes royal atmosphere in home. The fifth house is Virgo. Virgo is for perfection. Children are hard working and perfect. The sixth house is Libra. Likes pleasant work conditions. Libra represents *Basti*. The weak point of health is, therefore, kidneys and urinary system.

The seventh house is Scorpio. Spouse should be a passionate lover. The eighth house of death is Sagittarius ruled by Jupiter. Sagittarius governs foreign lands. Therefore, peaceful/easy death in a foreign land or on a journey at mature age is predicted. The ninth house is Capricorn ruled by Saturn. Likes justice to all and is philosophical in religious matters. The tenth house is Aquarius. Suitable professions are teaching and research. But one is devoid of sincerity. The eleventh house of friends is Pisces ruled by Jupiter. Has few but noble friends.

6.3 ASCENDANT GEMINI/*MITHUNA LAGNA*

Gemini ruled by Mercury is the natural sign of the third house of throat, short travels communication, valour, etc. Hence, the native is sociable, gossipy and fond of conversation, singing, reading, writing, not fond of outdoor life, preferring to stay indoors. *Mithuna* means sexual intercourse. Geminians are therefore fond of sexual pleasures.

The fourth house is Virgo. S/he is a perfectionist at home. The fifth house of love is Libra. Prefers stable and sophisticated love life. The sixth house is Scorpio. Likes passionate involvement in work. Weak points of health are lower abdominal, genital and anus areas.

The seventh house is Sagittarius. Has noble partner of outgoing nature. The eighth house is Capricorn ruled by Saturn. Natural death in very old age is predicted. The ninth house is Aquarius and hence the native is not much inclined towards religion. The tenth house is Pisces, which signifies success in solitary professions. The eleventh house is Aries. Likes friends full of vigour.

6.4 ASCENDANT CANCER/*KARKA LAGNA*

Cancer ruled by the Moon is the natural sign of the fourth house of mother, home, happiness and heart. Native with

Cancer *lagna* is, therefore, basically a heart dominated home loving person. The sun governs classes while the Moon governs masses. Hence, s/he is a man/woman of masses/people.

The second house is Leo representing royalty. Gets wealth/ financial success as a result of support of influential people. The third house is Virgo. Seeks perfection in whatever s/he does. The fourth house is Libra. Likes sophistication and luxury in home. The fifth house of love is Scorpio. Is a passionate lover. Love may, however, result in quarrels. The sixth house of work is Sagittarius. Likes to work where travel or outdoor life is involved. Weak point of health is blood circulation and thighs.

The seventh house is Capricorn ruled by Saturn. Likes a sober person as spouse. The ninth house of long travel and *Dharma* is Pisces, a watery sign ruled by Jupiter. Likes cruises on sea/rivers. Is religiously inclined. The tenth house is Aries. Provides dynamism in work. May act foolishly. Should try to maintain amiable atmosphere. The eleventh house is Taurus. Likes good hearted, sincere and informal friends.

6.5 ASCENDANT LEO/ *SIMHA LAGNA*

Leo ruled by Sun is the natural sign of fifth house of mind, education, children and love life. A Leo is a man/woman of class and royal nature. Has a steady mind. Is proud and valorous. Loves in style. Dotes over and protects his/her children.

The fourth house is Scorpio. Is emotional and irascible at home. The fifth house is Sagittarius, a movable sign, but ruled by Jupiter. May have lot of love affairs. But settles down after finding a suitable partner. The sixth house is Capricorn ruled by Saturn. Unceasingly and patiently devotes to work. Weak point of health is gas trouble, and knees. May suffer from arthritis.

The seventh house is Aquarius. Spouse is unconventional and is of independent nature. The eighth house of death is

Pisces. Should be careful of water. The ninth house is Aries. Likes adventure travels. The tenth house is Taurus signifying honesty, simplicity and sincerity in work. Person is liked by all. The eleventh house is Gemini. Likes talkative friends. The twelfth house is Cancer. Native may have problems from the home front.

6.6 ASCENDANT VIRGO/*KANYA LAGNA*

Virgo ruled by Mercury is the natural sign of sixth house of diseases, enemies, and work. A Virgoan is predisposed to illness. Is suitable for medical and social service. Always seeks precision and perfection. Is sweet and feminine in nature.

The fourth house is Sagittarius. Sagittarius stands for foreigners. Hence, may set up home abroad. The fifth house is Capricorn. Takes care to have unproblematic love affairs. The sixth house is Aquarius. Will be a professional. May opt for teaching and research. Is good for medical profession.

The seventh house is Pisces. Seeks a loving, tender and compassionate partner. The eighth house is Aries ruled by Mars. Haste could prove dangerous to life. The ninth house is Taurus. Has fixed ideas of philosophy. Never changes principles. The tenth house is Gemini. There are frequent changes in profession/place of work. Person adheres to rules. Loves all. The eleventh house is Cancer. Has sincere friends. But family comes first. The twelfth house is Leo. Problems with authority/superiors are predicted.

6.7 ASCENDANT LIBRA/*TULA LAGNA*

Libra is the natural sign of the seventh house of partnership. One is good as a business partner. Lives with a degree of luxury and sophistication. Is rational, reasonable, compromising and cooperative. Balance is the rule of life. But in trying to do so, may fall between two stools.

The fourth house is Capricorn. Prefers to settle down in home in contemplation. The fifth house is Aquarius. Does not like routine style love affair. The sixth house is Pisces. Weak point is emotional health.

The seventh house is Aries. Spouse will be active and dynamic. The eighth house is Taurus. Hence natural death after happy old age is predicted. The ninth house of long travels is Gemini, natural sign of third house of travels. Hence, one is very fond of travelling. The tenth house is Cancer ruled by Moon that represents masses. Likes a career that involves dealing with common people. Person is lenient and merciful. The eleventh house is Leo that represents classes. Friends are people of class/status.

6.8 ASCENDANT SCORPIO/VRISHCHIKA LAGNA

Scorpio is the natural sign of the eighth house of genitals. Sexuality is most important in his/her life. Is dominated by passions and intense emotions. Scorpio is secretive. S/he is a born detective.

The second house is Sagittarius. Wealth from foreign sources is predicted. The third house is Capricorn. Is methodical in activities. The fourth house is Aquarius. Prefers own freedom. Does not like to conform to the rules of homely life. The fifth house is Pisces. Idealist in love. The sixth house is Aries. Has ability to command in work. Aries represents heard. Hence, headache, fevers, etc.

The seventh house is Taurus. Seeks amorous, attractive and sincere spouse. The eighth house is Gemini, natural sign of third house of throat/lungs. Hence, chronic lungs problem. So one must not smoke. It can cause death. The ninth house is watery sign Cancer. Likes sea voyage. The tenth house is

Leo. Shows leadership qualities in profession. Expects high standards from others also. The eleventh house is Virgo. Likes friends who are intelligent and perfect.

6.9 ASCENDANT SAGITTARIUS/*DHANU LAGNA*

Sagittarius ruled by Jupiter is the natural sign of the ninth house of long travels and spirituality. A Sagittarian enjoys outdoor life, foreign lands and travel. Does not like restricted atmosphere. Is outgoing, jovial, magnanimous and broad-minded.

The second house is Capricorn ruled by Saturn. Wealth comes only by hard labour. The fourth house is Pisces. Likes ideal home life. The fifth house is Aries. Children are healthy and strong. Has vigorous love life. The sixth house is Taurus. Is honest and trust-worthy at work. Weak point is face/mouth.

The seventh house is Gemini. Early marriage. Wife is good in conversation, and is fond of sex life. The eighth house is Cancer natural sign of fourth house of heart. Heart trouble can be fatal. The tenth house of *karma* is Virgo ruled by Mercury. Medical, social work, business, computational work are suitable. The eleventh house is Libra. Likes sophisticated balanced friends.

6.10 ASCENDANT CAPRICORN/*MAKARA LAGNA*

A Capricornian ruled by Saturn has lot of mental stamina. S/he is slow but steady. Is a disciplined, justice loving and no-nonsense person. Spends life all the time instructing self on a right path. Usually, lives up to a mature old age. May suffer from gas trouble.

The fourth house is Aries. Wields authority in the family. The fifth house is Taurus. Is sincere in love. Has sweet loving children. The sixth house is Gemini ruled by Mercury. Likes a job that requires lot of conversation and travels. Weak points of health are throat and nervous system.

The seventh house is Cancer. Spouse is emotional. However, the native with Capricorn *lagna* is usually attached to an older man/woman. The tenth house is Libra. Diplomatic and popular in work. Judicial service is suitable. The twelfth house is Sagittarius. One may have problems with foreigners or matters pertaining to foreign countries.

6.11 ASCENDANT AQUARIUS/*KUMBHA LAGNA*

Aquarius is ruled by malefics Saturn and Uranus. It is the natural sign of the eleventh house of income, gains and friends. Aquarian is, therefore, a group conscious person having many friends. Is a good teacher, researcher and/or professional. Most of all, s/he loves own freedom and does not like routine way of living. Is unconventional. And is peevish in nature, greedy of others' wealth and may be a stealthy sinner.

The third house is Aries. Is, therefore, always ready to take initiative. The fourth house is Taurus. Is sincere in taking care of home and possessions. The fifth house is Gemini. Changeable in love. The sixth house is Cancer. Likes jobs that bring contact with people. Weak point of health is heart.

The seventh house is Leo. Partner is of regal nature and personality. The eighth house is Virgo. Death is natural after a happy old age. The tenth house is Scorpio. Is curious and suspecting by nature in work. Professions involving investigations are suitable. The eleventh house is Sagittarius. Friends are decent, jovial people.

6.12 ASCENDANT PISCES/*MEENA LAGNA*

Pisces ruled by benefics Jupiter and Neptune is the natural sign of twelfth house of expenditure, loss, renunciation and abroad.

Pisceans have attractive fish-like eyes. They are learned, grateful and always content with their spouse. They hardly have any extra-marital relation. They gain from water-borne and foreign products. A Piscean is highly righteous, sincere, noble, compassionate, idealistic, tender, loving, understanding and imaginative person. S/he respects orthodox principles and looks for love of the pure and perfect kind that is though difficult to get.

The Second house is Aries. Financial success is through initiative and energy. The third house is Taurus, a fixed sign. Is not much fond of travel. The fourth house is Gemini. Hence, frequently changes home. The fifth house is Cancer. Very often in love until s/he finds a suitable partner. After that, no more flirting. Would like to raise a family and have loving children. The sixth house is Leo. Will command authority at work. Weak point of health is stomach.

The seventh house is Virgo. Spouse should be perfect in all respects. The eighth house is Libra. Natural death after happy old age. The ninth house is Scorpio. Likes sea voyages. The tenth house is Sagittarius. Professions involving teaching, outdoor life, and foreign countries are suitable. One is basically engaged in benevolent profession. The eleventh house is Capricorn. Prefers stable friendships with wise and composed people.

Note: The planets tenanting and aspecting the houses and placement of Lords of the houses must also be considered. For example, for a *Meena lagna*, fifth house is Cancer. The native is supposed to have loving children. But if Mars is tenanting the fifth house in debility in Cancer, or if the Lord of the house the Moon is placed in the evil *trik* houses, then the happiness to/from children will be curtailed.

Chapter 7

Results of Planets in Signs
(*Grah-rashi-phal*)

7.1 GENERAL PRINCIPLES

The nature and personality of the native are attributed to the *lagna rashi*, as was described in Chapter 6. The same characteristics are more or less applicable if the Sun and/or the Moon are in that *rashi*. The additional difference is in respect of the following principles which are applicable to all planets.

(i) The house of *karakattva* of a planet is its stronghold, and is named as its *pucca ghar*. The sign occupied by the planet affects the *karakattvas* of the planet, and matters pertaining to the houses of which it is *karaka*. For example, the Sun in exaltation in Aries or in own sign Leo will bestow not only happiness to/from father, but will also be good for the first and tenth houses that are its *pucca ghars*. Similarly, the Moon in Taurus or Cancer will bestow happiness to/from mother. In addition, it will also be good for the fourth house, its *pucca ghar*. On the contrary, the Sun in Libra and Moon in Scorpio have opposite effects.

(ii) As per the *Kaal Purush Kundali*, for many purposes, the natural sign of the first house is Aries; the natural sign of the second house is Taurus, and so on. Thus, a malefic in Aries, the first house in the *Kaal Purush Kundali*, would adversely affect the head, a malefic in Scorpio, the eighth house in the *Kaal Purush Kundali*, would cause problems of the genitals, and so on. On the other hand, a benefic in Taurus, the second house in the *Kaal Purush Kundali*, would be favourable for increase in wealth, a benefic in Libra, the seventh house in the the *Kaal Purush Kundali*, would endow conjugal happiness, and so on.

Also, since the Lord of the the first house in the *Kaal Purush Kundali* is Mars, a good Mars indicates strong body. Lord of the fifth house is the Sun. A good Sun indicates good children. The Lord of seventh house is Venus. A good Venus means a good spouse/wife. Likewise we can analyse.

(iii) Signs also represent directions. How can we use this knowledge? For example, if the Lords of *lagna*, ninth and tenth are placed in Scorpio, a watery sign in anyone's chart, then we can say that the person will have a rise in fortune in the north direction.

The more the number of planets in exaltation, friend's sign, etc., the more the person feels elevated and happy. The more the planets in debility, enemy's sign, etc., the more the person has a negative nature and the more s/he suffers in life. Note that prime source of energy is the Sun. All others get their brilliance from the Sun only. So if the Sun is weak in a chart, full benefit cannot be obtained even if some other planets are strong.

Described below are the good and bad effects of each planet placed in different signs.

7.2 SUN IN DIFFERENT SIGNS

A well-placed Sun ameliorates matters of its *karakattvas*, soul, father, bones, name, fame, status, personality, etc. It promotes matters of the first and the tenth houses of which it is *karaka*, and the fifth house of children that it owns in the *Kaal Purush Kundali*.

GOOD EFFECTS	BAD EFFECTS
Exalted in Aries Ruled by Mars	
Leadership. Strong bones. Name, fame and status. Lucky in respect of father/children.	Sun and Mars both have *Pitta*/bile nature. Native suffers from excessive heat/bile.
In Enemy Venus's Sign Taurus	
Fond of music and singing. Relates to physical love and earthly world of Taurus.	Inimical to wife signified by Venus. Likes pleasures though.
In Neutral Mercury's Sign Gemini	
Courteous. Intelligent. Has discrimination.	Gemini is changeable. Lacks persistence.
In Great Friend Moon's Sign Cancer	
Tender. Thoughtful. Sensitive. Calm.	Humble. Timid. Indecisive.
In Own Sign Leo	
Proud. Famous. Has status. Courageous. Likes authority. Commanding manners.	Pride, vanity, and arrogance. May be a little pretentious. Likes pomp and show.
In Neutral Mercury's Sign Virgo	
Shy. Feminine. Seeks perfection. Good in arts/mathematics. Subtle. Diplomatic.	May be fussy, petty and over-critical.
Debilitated in Libra Ruled by Venus	
Likes and respects justice. Learns to recognise opposites within own nature. Tries to be level headed.	The first and tenth houses and Sun's significations suffer. Resorts to low acts. Suffers in status. Disharmony with father. Promiscuous, Libra being natural sign of the seventh house.

contd.

GOOD EFFECTS	BAD EFFECTS

In Friend Mars's Sign Scorpio

Daring. Chivalrous. Sexually strong. Good in professions connected with chemicals, drugs, investigation, etc.,	Suspicious. Vindictive. Fiery temper. Scorpio being natural sign of the eighth house indicates living in danger

In Friend Jupiter's Sign Sagittarius

Developed body. Likes outdoor life. Free style. Cheerful. Pious. Respected. Wealthy.	May be stubborn.

In Great Enemy Saturn's Sign Capricorn

Is reserved.	No status. Uses unfair means. Jealous.

In Great Enemy Saturn's Sign Aquarius

Native has collective consciousness. Likes group activities.	Resorts to lowly acts. May be a backbiter. Is not straightforward.

In Friend Jupiter's Sign Pisces

Compassionate. Idealistic. Offers self as a gift to larger life. Gains from love/ favour of ladies, trade across waters, etc. Likes administration.	Over-sensitive. Emotional. Liable to scandal, Pisces being natural sign of the twelfth house.

7.3 MOON IN DIFFERENT SIGNS

A well-placed Moon ensures good heart and mind, and good luck in respect of mother, home, happiness, blood, beauty, enjoyment of life, etc., and the fourth house matters.

GOOD EFFECTS	BAD EFFECTS

In Friend Mars's Sign Aries

Over-sexed. Active. Bold.	Aggressive and impulsive.

Exalted In Taurus Ruled by Venus

Broad chest. Forgiving. Has forbearance. Artistic. Amorous. Fond of pleasures/food, Taurus being natural sign of IInd house of food. Happy in respect of mother/home.	Suffers from phlegm, and excesses in pleasures.

contd.

GOOD EFFECTS	BAD EFFECTS

In Great Friend Mercury's Sign Gemini

Gemini represents copulation and IIIrd house of reading, writing, communications. Well up in these and amorous arts.	Gemini is a dual sign. Not sincere.

In Own Sign Cancer

Amorous. Significations of Moon and IVth house, home, happiness, mother, etc., prosper.	Too much imagination.

In Great Friend Sun's Sign Leo

Dignified personality. Taste for splendour.	Too much pride.

In Great Friend Mercury's Sign Virgo

Slender body. Intelligent. Sweet speech. Good in mathematics, science, medicine.	Too shy. Servile nature.

In Neutral Venus's Sign Libra

Sophistication in love. Balanced. Dutiful. Good citizen.	Under the influence of wife/women, Libra being natural sign of the seventh house.

Debilitated in Scorpio Ruled by Mars

Very attractive to opposite sex. Fond of sex.	Thievish nature. Hard hearted. Lacks confidence. Has liaisons.

In Friend Jupiter's Sign Sagittarius

Fond of adventure/travels. Generous.	Audacious. Rebellious. Takes great risks.

In Neutral Saturn's Sign Capricorn

Reserved nature.	Liaison with elderly woman. Cruel hearted.

In Neutral Saturn's Sign Aquarius

Progressive. Original. Non-conformist.	Sharp mood swings. Inimical. Covets others' spouses, Aquarius being natural sign of the eleventh house of desire.

contd.

In Friend Jupiter's Sign Pisces

Beautiful eyes. Religious. Idealistic. Fond of spending and interested in foreign lands, Pisces being natural sign of the twelfth house.

Too sentimental. Worried. Nervous.

7.4 MARS IN DIFFERENT SIGNS

Mars in favourable signs ensures stamina, valour, healthy marrow, happiness to/from brothers/sisters, qualities as a man/ husband, conquering of enemies, etc., and matters of the third and sixth houses. It can also cause violence, anger, cruelty, lack of character, etc. In the *Kaal Purush Kundali*, Mars rules over the first and eighth houses, and is exalted in the tenth house.

All significations of Mars flourish in Capricorn, Aries and Scorpio, and suffer in Cancer. The native occupies a kingly position with exalted Mars in Capricorn, the natural sign of tenth house. S/he is active, courageous and victorious. Similar results follow with Mars in Aries and Scorpio. Debilitated Mars in Cancer makes one wicked and prone to domestic quarrels and dislike of home, mother, etc., Cancer being natural sign of the fourth house.

With Mars in Taurus and Libra ruled by Venus the native is under the influence of women. In Taurus, the natural sign of the third house, Mars makes one domineering in speech.

In the Libra, natural sign of the seventh house, it may result in liaisons with other peoples' wives.

In Gemini and Virgo it makes one fond of music and dancing if in Gemini, natural sign of the third house, and fearless and courageous if in Virgo, natural sign of the sixth house of enemy.

In Leo, ruled by friend Sun, it makes one fearless and strong with great stamina. The danger is too much aggressiveness and *pitta,* resulting in harm.

In Sagittarius and Pisces ruled by friend and great benefic Jupiter the native occupies an eminent position. S/he fights for principles. But may however go to extremes in fighting.

In Aquarius, ruled by Saturn the native is cruel, resorts to untruth, and suffers distress and losses, Aquarius being the natural sign of the eleventh house of gains and desires, and Mars being Saturn's enemy.

7.5 MERCURY IN DIFFERENT SIGNS

Well-placed Mercury indicates good skin and speech, wit, fun-loving nature, friends, relations, knowledge, communication, mathematics, intelligence, understanding, etc., and the affairs of the fourth and tenth houses. In the *Kaal Purush Kundali*, Mercury owns third and sixth houses. All significations prosper with exalted Mercury in Virgo and in own sign in Gemini.

If in Gemini, the natural sign of the third house, the native will like reading, writing and speaking. S/he is amorous, may have more than one love, and has endearing speech.

If in Virgo, the native is good in mathematics, research, etc. S/he seeks perfection, is logical, critical, analytical, practical and orderly in nature. Sexual vigour is below normal.

In Taurus and Libra ruled by great friend Venus, native is good in speech, likes all pleasures of life, is a happy-go-lucky type, and remains engaged in acquisition of wealth.

Although Leo, the sign of the Sun and the fifth house of love, since Mercury is neutral towards the Sun, the native has a flirting tendency and will not be liked by the opposite sex.

In Capricorn and Aquarius, signs of friend Saturn, Mercury makes one dutiful. However, one occupies only subordinate positions and the native is not truthful.

With debilitated Mercury in Pisces, the native is good only in work that does not require much dexterity. In Sagittarius, also ruled by benefic Jupiter, one is intelligent and courteous in speech. The native will be liked by superiors, and can be a good teacher or preacher.

In Cancer ruled by enemy Moon, with Mercury being a great friend of the Moon, the significations of Cancer and the Moon prosper but those of Mercury suffer. Thus, the native is fond of home, peaceful life, etc., but may be inimical in speech to his/her own people.

In Aries and Scorpio, as Mercury is the enemy of Mars, the native is argumentative, ironical and harsh in speech. S/he mocks at others and criticises. His/her conduct is hypocritical and s/he has unworthy friends.

7.6 JUPITER IN DIFFERENT SIGNS

The Sun, the Moon, Mars, Mercury and Venus are personal planets as they symbolise personal urges. Jupiter and Saturn, on the other hand, take the individual outside the sphere of personal ego/consciousness. Thus, they both have two influences, one going within, and the other going without. Jupiter represents rewards of good *karmas*, and Saturn stick represents punishment for the bad ones.

Jupiter is *karaka* for wisdom, wealth, banking, happiness, prosperity, spirituality, teaching, generosity, children, liver, body fat, etc., and affairs of as many as five houses, viz., the second, fifth, ninth, tenth and eleventh. In the *Kaal Purush Kundali*, Jupiter owns the ninth and twelfth houses, and is exalted in the fourth house. No wonder, a well-placed Jupiter in a horoscope bestows the native with many virtues and gifts of life.

Jupiter is best in exaltation in Cancer, and in own signs in Sagittarius and Pisces. It makes one both religious and a good administrator. One may become a religious preceptor. The native will hold a high position among people. Happiness to/from children is assured. Cancer being the fourth house of home and happiness, Jupiter in Cancer means a happy home life. The native will be amorous. The adverse effect is that the native likes to eat too much and may gain weight, fat being the signification of Jupiter. And, one may become a stay-at-home type.

Jupiter in Leo also has effects similar to those in Cancer.

In friend Mars's signs Aries and Scorpio, the native occupies an eminent position. S/he is chivalrous, and has a forgiving nature at the same time.

In the enemies' signs of Taurus, Libra, Gemini and Virgo, the significations of Jupiter suffer. Benefic Jupiter, however, improves the significations of these signs. In Venus's signs Taurus and Libra, the native has a comely appearance, company of women, paraphernalia of luxuries, etc. In Mercury's signs Gemini and Virgo, the native receives good education, is intelligent, has friends, and may be a counsellor or advisor.

With debilitated Jupiter in Capricorn ruled by Saturn, the religious conduct of the native is below merit. S/he is inclined to lowly acts. One has little happiness.

With Jupiter in Aquarius also, the native has an ambivalent attitude.

7.7 VENUS IN DIFFERENT SIGNS

Venus is *karaka* for comforts, pleasures, love, romance, passion, wife, spouse, enjoyment of sex, semen, ovaries, etc., and the affairs of the seventh house. In the *Kaal Purush Kundali*, Venus owns the second and seventh houses.

Exalted Venus in Pisces gives the native a host of good qualities. S/he is amorous and a generous lover with a charming personality, enjoys pleasures of life, loves music and gets riches, comforts and happiness from spouse/opposite sex.

Similar results follow in own signs of Taurus and Libra as well. Venus in Taurus prefers more earthly physical/sensual relationships in love. Venus in Libra prefers relationship with flowers, aesthetics, gentleness, grace, sophistication, candlelight dinners, dance, etc.

Venus in Sagittarius too is good. The native likes foreigners and may find love abroad.

In Capricorn and Aquarius, the native may be attached to an older/unworthy person.

In friend Mercury's sign Gemini, the native always finds the right words to express love. Though s/he may be flirtatious and inconsistent in love.

In Virgo, Venus is debilitated. The native has no success in love and sex life. In the chart of male nativity, it makes one resort to lowly acts, always longing for love, running after unworthy women, and not getting much happiness in return.

In enemy Sun's sign Leo, one marries into a status family.

In enemy Moon's sign Cancer, the native is very romantic, pleasant and comfortable in relationships. S/he is amorous, may have more than one relationship simultaneously with the opposite sex.

In Aries and Scorpio, the native is strongly sexed. Men may have liaisons with others' wives.

7.8 SATURN IN DIFFERENT SIGNS

Saturn is *karaka* for sorrow, longevity, nerves, servants, etc., and the affairs of the three *trik* houses—sixth, eighth and twelfth—and the tenth house. As such, Saturn in a favourable sign is a must to have a life without sorrow. In the *Kaal Purush Kundali*, Saturn owns the tenth and eleventh. A well-placed Saturn makes one dutiful and just. An ill-placed one, cruel and hardhearted.

Saturn is best in Libra, its sign of exaltation. The native has minimum sorrows. Significations of the tenth and eleventh houses prosper. Thus, the native occupies a high position in his/her job and has high income. The native is endearing to opposite sex with whom s/he has intense emotional involvement, Libra being the natural sign of seventh house. S/he enjoys long life Saturn being *karaka* for longevity.

Similar results follow in own signs of Capricorn and Aquarius.

In Taurus, another sign of great friend Venus, native may have several women in life.

In Gemini and Virgo, signs of great friend Mercury, one occupies a good position.

In Sagittarius and Pisces, signs ruled by neutral and pious Jupiter, the native is religious and learned. S/he is happy and prosperous. S/he is a leader, and occupies a high position.

Saturn is worst in debilitation in Aries. The native will suffer great sorrow. S/he is cruel and deceitful. Similar results follow in Scorpio. The native may also suffer from accidents Scorpio being the natural sign of the eighth house and Saturn being malefic.

In Leo, sign of great enemy Sun, the native will feel unloved, Leo being the natural sign of the fifth house of love. The native's conduct is low. S/he has no happiness and will lead a life of drudgery.

In Cancer, the natural sign of the fourth house of mother, home and happiness, Saturn destroys mother. The native has no happiness and may suffer emotional isolation.

7.9 RAHU AND KETU IN DIFFERENT SIGNS

Rahu and Ketu always form an axis. Rahu is *karaka* for cruelty, intrigue, wickedness, hypocrisy, greed, material gains, etc. Ketu is *karaka* for ambition, courage, obstinacy, surgery, religion, *moksha*, etc.

A well-placed Rahu such as in Taurus, and Mercury's signs Gemini and Virgo gives success, riches and material gains. Its bad effects are mitigated. The native is clever. S/he is not honest, though. Rahu is favourable in Saturn's signs, Capricorn and Aquarius. The native is able to overcome problems by dint of hard work, secret methods, patience and resilience, and put up an exterior show of success.

An ill-placed Rahu such as in Scorpio, Sagittarius and Pisces makes one untruthful and cruel in speech and deeds.

A well-placed Ketu such as in Scorpio, and Jupiter's signs Sagittarius and Pisces gives courage and religiousness, and minimises ill-effects. Ketu is favourable in Aries and Leo too.

An ill-placed Ketu makes one obstinate and quarrelsome.

Note: It is very important that malefics in a horoscope be strong. They should preferably be placed in own or exaltation or *moola-trikona* signs in order for life to be free from suffering. In addition, if they are in the *Upchaya* houses—the third, sixth tenth and eleventh—it is all the more better. This will ensure success. Hence, along with the sign one has to see the house in which a planet is placed whether good or bad, as described in the next chapter.

7.10 GOOD AND BAD DEGREES OF PLANETS

A planet may be strong and in a very good sign in the *lagna* chart but if it is weak and in an unfavourable sign in the *Navansha*-Chart then all the good effects are devalued or minimised while the bad effects become prominent and maximised.

For example, the Sun in exaltation in Aries in *lagna* is devalued if it is placed from 20D to 23D 20M when it would be in Libra *Navansha* in which it would be debilitated.

On the other hand, if a planet is weak in *lagna*, but strong in *Navansha*, its evil influences will be mitigated, and some good results will be felt. For example, the evil effects of the Sun in Libra in *lagna* will be mitigated to a great extent if it occupies 0D to 3D 20M when it would be in Aries *Navansha* in which it would be exalted.

One must, however, be cautious in predictions keeping the gradation in the quality of the planet in mind. For example, Saturn is *Vargottama* in exaltation from 0D to 3D 20M in Libra. Again, Saturn is *Vargottama* but in debilitation from 0D to 3D 20M Aries. Though both are *Vargottama*, there is a vast difference between the two.

The Table in Appendix B gives the good and bad degrees for the seven planets occupying different signs in *lagna* chart. It includes only exaltation, own sign, *Vargottama* and debilitation degrees in *Navansha*-Chart. It does not include *Navanshas* of friends, enemies and neutrals.

Chapter 8

Results of Planets in Houses (*Grah-Bhavashraya-Phal*) and Judging Each House/*Bhava*

Since the same *Ayansha* is subtracted from the *Sayana* longitudes of cusps of houses as well as of planets to get the *Nirayana* longitudes, there is no effect of *Ayansha* as far as the placement of planets in houses is concerned. They remain in the same houses in the birth-chart both in Western as well as in Vedic/Hindu systems. Hence, predictions based on the placement of planets, house-wise, are the same in both. But since the signs may change, the qualitative effect may be different.

8.1 GOVERNING PRINCIPLES

It must be noted that a planet functions in the following three different ways:

(i) As a natural benefic or malefic placed in a house/ *bhava*.

(ii) As significator or *karaka* for certain matters and houses/*bhavas*.

(ii) As Lord of a house/*bhava* (*Bhavadhipati*).

As a natural benefic, it promotes, and as a natural malefic, it spoils the *bhava* it occupies. This is the simple rule.

As a significator and/or Lord of a house, the planet promotes the matters of its significations and those of the house of lordship if placed in a good house (*shubha sthana*) and a favourable sign, and spoils the same if placed in an evil house (*ashubha sthana*) and an unfavourable sign.

We know that the *kendras*, *trikonas* and second and eleventh in a horoscope together form the group of 8 *shubha sthanas*.

The *trik* are the three *ashubha* Sthanas and the third is a lean/mildly *ashubha* Sthan.

The four *kendra* houses—the first, fourth, seventh and ninth—are complementary to the ninth, tenth eleventh and twelfth houses. *Lagna* and ninth both represent spirituality or *dharma*; the tenth common between the two groups, represents accrual of wealth or *artha* through profession/*karma*; seventh representing spouse/opposite sex/*kaama* is complementary to the ninth representing fulfilment of desire/*kaama*; and the fourth representing mental peace is complementary to the twelfth, which stands for liberation/renunciation/*Moksha* implying eternal peace. *Dharma, artha, kaama* and *moksha* are the four objectives of life.

The following general rules apply for the placement of planets in different houses.

(i) It is best for benefics to be in *kendras*, *trikonas*, and the second and eleventh houses. This way the beneficence is fully realised.

(ii) It is best for malefics to be in the third, sixth and eleventh houses. This way the malefics do minimum harm. Rather, they become helpful in warding off evils and giving worldly success. For the Sun, the tenth house is also good. Note that the sun, though malefic, is not an evil planet.

(iii) It is best not to have any planets in the evil *trik* houses the sixth, eighth and twelfth houses. This way the significations of the planets and the houses of their lordships are not damaged. The sixth house is good for malefics though.

It may be noted that the eleventh house is good for both benefics and malefics. Ascendent/*lagna* being both a *kendra* and a *trikona*, and the ninth house are the two best houses. Their Lords are considered strongest benefics.

Some familiar points about the effects of placements are as follows:

- Planets in *kendras* and *trikonas* are powerful.
- Planets in the 8 *shubha-sthanas* generally give favourable results.
- Planets in the third house enhance stamina/valour in accordance with their nature/sign.
- Planets in the *trik* give unfavourable results. Even malefics should not be placed in the *trik* except the sixth house.
- Saturn is best in the third, sixth and eleventh houses. Sixth has its sign of exaltation and eleventh the *moola-trikona* sign in the *Kaal Purush Kundali*.
- Saturn in the eighth house, though a *trik,* nevertheless gives long life. It is *karaka* for this house.
- One experiences *shubha* effects of the *bhava* tenanted or aspected by its Lord irrespective of it being a benefic or malefic.
- Whichever *bhava* is tenanted or aspected by benefics, the native experiences *shubha* effects in that *bhava*. *Ashubha* effects if malefics tenant or aspect.
- Whichever *bhava* lord is aspected by benefics, the native experiences *shubha* effects in that *bhava*. *Ashubha* effects if *bhava* Lord is aspected by malefics.

- Placement of *bhava* Lord in any of the *trik*, or in the sixth, eighth and twelfth from the *bhava* is *ashubha* for the *bhava*. Placement of *bhava* Lord in the 8 *shubha-sthanas*, or in the first, second, fourth, fifth, seventh, ninth, tenth and eleventh from the *bhava* is *shubha* for the *bhava*.
- Placement of *trik* Lord in any *bhava* is *ashubha* for the *bhava* but *shubha* for the positive matters of the *trik bhava*.
- The effects of Rahu and Ketu are opposite. In any horoscope if Rahu is *ashubha* then Ketu will be *shubha*, and if Ketu is *ashubha* then Rahu will be *shubha*. Overall, in whichever *bhavas* Rahu and Ketu are placed they damage the two *bhavas*. The intensity depends on the signs in which they are placed.
- Though malefic by nature, Ketu is considered a *shubha* planet.
- Moon, Mercury, Venus and Jupiter, though benefic, get their effects reduced to half if placed in the signs of malefics.
- Jupiter in first, fourth, fifth, ninth and tenth is able to compensate for 1,00,000 ill-effects. In the same *bhavas*, Mercury is able for 100 and Venus for 1,000.
- A strong *lagna* and strong *lagna* Lord is antidote to most evils.
- Eighth Lord, whether benefic or malefic, always gives *ashubha* results. But if the same planet rules over *lagna* as well as eighth, or if the Sun or Moon rule over eighth, or if eighth Lord is in own house then it gives *shubha* results.

The effects must be qualified on the basis of the signs planets are placed in, and whether they are combust or retrograde or not. For example, the malefic Rahu in *lagna* in Taurus or Gemini or Virgo will not be bad. It will rather make the native emotionally strong and bring material gains. The same Rahu in *lagna* in Scorpio, Sagittarius or Pisces will make the native cruel, deceitful and mean.

Jupiter is the greatest benefic. Aspects of Jupiter are very good for the houses. But the house tenanted by Jupiter itself remains at low ebb. Jupiter does not spoil the house, but does not promote it very much either. For example, Jupiter in the twelfth house will not increase expenditure. It will rather make the native miserly. It also makes the native fanatical in his/her beliefs.

On the other hand, the aspects of Saturn are very bad. But it promotes the house tenanted by it under all circumstances provided it is in a favourable sign. In fact, all malefics are good for the houses they tenant provided they are in their own, or exaltation or *moola-trikona* signs. This is on the basis of the axiom that even a scoundrel does good to and does not harm its own house.

It must, however, be stated that even though a malefic in a favourable sign promotes the significations of the house tenanted, it does not promote the relationship signified by that house. For example, Saturn in its *moola-trikona* sign Aquarius in the tenth house is very good for one's career, recognition, etc. But it is not good for the relationship with the father.

Needless to say that any single planet cannot predict the results of a chart by itself. One has to consider the positions of all planets, their signs, strengths and lordships, whether combust or not, their placement in *Navansha Kundali*, and so on.

One also has to see the *Dashas* and transits of planets current at the time of prediction.

8.2 RESULTS OF PLACEMENT OF PLANETS IN HOUSES (*BHAVASHRAYA-PHALA*)

Now, we describe the effects of placement of all the nine planets (*nava grahas*) in different houses. In the final analysis, however, one must, take note of the sign occupied by the planet, and whether it is combust or not, its conjunction or aspects with other planets, etc.

The Sun in the Twelve Houses

The Sun falls in *lagna* in a horoscope if a person is born at sunrise. It is the time for offering prayers. It makes the native devoted to God.

The Sun falls in the tenth house if birth takes place at noon. With the Sun in the tenth house, the native works to serve society and mankind at large.

The Sun in the seventh house indicates birth at sunset. It makes the native relax in the company of spouse and friends.

The Sun in the fourth house means birth at midnight, the time for deep sleep. The native gets real happiness only by forgetting the body completely, attaining detachment from everybody and renunciation.

The Sun is the soul, king, ruler, administrator and father. It is best in the first and fifth houses where it would be in exaltation and own signs in the *Kaal Purush Kundali*. It is worst in the seventh house in which it would be in debilitation in the *Kaal Purush Kundali*.

In the first house it makes one a 'Benign Ruler or Administrator'. The Sun in Leo and Aries in *lagna* will make the native strong and independent, commanding status, but in Libra *lagna* it is very inauspicious. The native suffers from indigent circumstances.

With the Sun in *lagna* the native has a high forehead and thin hair on his/her head. S/he is fierce, and chivalrous but hot-tempered, cruel in nature, unforgiving and proud.

In the fifth house it is the 'Harbinger of Progress of Family'. From the day of the birth of a child, there is all round progress in all aspects of life. This is a good position for happiness to/from father, the Sun being the significator for father and placed in a trine.

The Sun as a malefic has adverse effects on things associated with the house in which it is placed. For example, in *lagna* the native may suffer from *pitta*/bile/heat and some eye disease. In the second house it adversely affects family. The native suffers from diseases of right eye, face and mouth. His/her speech is harsh. May have stammering. If the Sun is in the fourth house, the native is cruel, and is devoid of home and happiness. Suffers from heart trouble, lacks happiness to/from mother. In the seventh house, it is very bad. One has no marital happiness as the Sun in its natural sign of debilitation in the *Kaal Purush Kundali*. Government, authorities or those who matter ignore the native. In male nativities, it implies humiliation from women.

But as a malefic, the Sun is good in the third, sixth, tenth and eleventh houses. In the third, it imparts valour/*parakram*/*purusharth*. It makes the native hard working and self-reliant. S/he is like a fearless lion but pure of heart. But the servants and subordinates would be wicked. The native may be without siblings or his/her relationship with them may suffer.

In the sixth house, it makes the native strong. S/he destroys enemies, and overcomes obstacles. But, the sixth being an evil *trik* house, this placement is not good for Sun's significations.

In the tenth, the native commands position, name, fame, status and recognition. It is good for one's career. The Sun in the eleventh gives high income. One has friends of status.

In the ninth house, the best trine, the Sun raises the native's status. Its significations shine here in full glory. The native gains from Government/authorities. It gives happiness to/from children, being the Lord of fifth house in the *Kaal Purush Kundali* placed in the very auspicious ninth, which is also the fifth from fifth. Such a person respects the pious and learned people.

If the Sun is placed in the evil *trik* houses—the sixth, eighth and twelfth—all its significations suffer. Since the Sun is the *karaka* for the father, the native has no happiness to/from the father. In favourable signs and favourable *Navanshas*, the evil effects are mitigated to some extent.

Malefic Sun in the sixth, otherwise, is very good as stated above. Expenditure is heavy as the Sun aspects the twelfth house from here.

The Sun in the eighth house is bad for longevity. One suffers from *pitta*. One's soul remains tormented and discontented. It also affects the right eye, wealth, family, etc., since it aspects the second from the eighth. The native, however, gains wisdom (*gyan tattva*).

The Sun in the twelfth house destroys sleep. One falls from good conduct/grace. There is antipathy to the father. Expenditure is heavy, but it is on benefic activities/objects. The native is troubled by enemies but wins over them. S/he suffers in the left eye. Childlessness is indicated, as the twelfth is eighth from fifth.

Note that the Sun is a 'Separator'. In whichever house it is placed, it will cause separation from the relationship signified by that house. Thus in the seventh house, it results in disharmony from spouse, in the third from siblings, subordinates, etc., in the fifth from children, and so on. Even in *lagna*, it results in separation from one's own self.

The Moon in the Twelve Houses

The Moon is the mind, queen, mother, milk, nourisher, etc. It is best in the second and fourth houses where it would be in exaltation in Taurus and *swa-rashi* in Cancer in the *Kaal Purush Kundali*.

As a benefic, it is good in most houses except the *trik*.

With the Moon in the first, the native gains from the mother. A waxing Moon, particularly in Taurus and Cancer in *lagna* gives a strong comely body. It makes the native cheerful, fearless, amorous and fond of aesthetic pleasures.

The Moon in the second house, viz., *dhana-sthan*, is greatly benefic for wealth. It is like 'Goddess of Wealth Earned by Self'. The native is peace loving and sweet in speech.

The Moon in the third house, the natural house of great friend Mercury, is the 'Native's Protector'. It implies that even death is afraid of such a person. The native will always receive divine protection. Even though leading a worldly life, the native remains contented and detached like King Janak. But if such a person renounces the world and becomes a mendicant (*saadhu*), s/he will be the repository of mystic powers (*siddhis*). The native is loving, compassionate and respectful towards women. There is happiness to/from siblings.

The Moon in the fourth house is best. The native is endowed with peace of mind, happiness (*sukha*), mother's love, home, conveyance and enjoyments of life.

In the fifth house representing children and great friend Sun's natural house, the Moon is like a 'Doting Mother' for the native's children with continuously flowing river of milk. It gives good children and happiness to/from them. One has more daughters than sons. The native is intelligent. S/he is inclined to religious prayers.

In the seventh house, the Moon is like the 'Goddess of Wealth, Lakshmi'. One gains in business. The native is pure in love. Does not indulge in extra-marital relations. Both the native and his/her spouse are comely in appearance and are attached to each other.

The Moon in the ninth house is like an 'Ocean of Merits'. The native is very fortunate and pious. S/he is 'Protector of the Deprived', has good conduct, and is fond of travel.

With the Moon in the tenth house, the native does good deeds, is devoted to work and successful in whatever s/he does. S/he has positive thinking mind, and happiness to/from mother.

The Moon in the eleventh house is one of the best placements for income/gains. One has friends, especially females. It leads to fulfilment of desires. But it gives worries of the mind and about the mother, as the eleventh is eighth from the fourth.

The Moon is bad in the evil *trik* houses. There is no happiness to/from mother.

The native has many enemies if the Moon is in the sixth house. S/he may suffer from cough, stomach problems, weak digestion and appetite and lack of sexual vigour.

In the eighth house, Moon is debilitated in the *Kaal Purush Kundali*, the natural sign of the house being Scorpio. It is like 'Death for Mother' unless the Moon is aspected by Jupiter. As in the sixth, here also, native suffers from poor health. S/he sleeps a lot.

The native with the Moon in the twelfth house undergoes suffering after suffering. With one episode after another, there may be no happiness in his/her life. So much so that the native's sleep is disturbed, and the mind remains unsteady. One may, however, settle abroad if other factors support the same.

Mars in the Twelve Houses

According to the *Kaal Purush Kundali*, Mars is good in the first, eighth and tenth houses and worst in the fourth. But, we may eliminate eighth as it is a *trik* house. It causes *mangalik dosha* as well in the eighth as explained latter. Mars, as a malefic, is good in the third, sixth and eleventh houses.

In *lagna*, Mars is *swa-rashi* in the *Kaal Purush Kundali*. It makes one very active, bold and ambitious but cruel hearted. The native may get injured in the body especially in the head. S/he appears young even in old age. Mars herein in Aries, Leo, Scorpio, Sagittarius and Capricorn gives good results though the native may suffer from bile/*pitta*.

Mars is very good in the third house wherein it is like the 'Celestial Tree of Fruits' for the benefit of everybody. The malefic planet becomes totally harmless in third. It endows the native with great physical and mental stamina.

In the sixth house also Mars is harmless. The nature of the native resembles that of a saint. For helping others, s/he may even allow self to suffer. Often however, such a person does not have brothers/sisters or is not happy in respect of them since Mars, their *karaka*, is placed in an evil *trik* house. Mars in the sixth house gives success in ventures/career, and makes one a conqueror of enemies or an army or police officer. It makes the native strongly sexed. But s/he is prone to problems due to high blood pressure. As the sixth house represents maternal relations, due to malefic Mars, native does not have good relations with them. Also, expenditure is heavy as Mars aspects the twelfth from the sixth.

The best position of Mars is in the tenth house. It is like a 'King in a Poor Ant's House' thereby implying that even an ordinary person having Mars in such a position rises high in life. The native is a leader in his/her profession. S/he gets name, fame and recognition. Careers suitable are those concerned with activity, fire and red-hot things such as engineering, military or police service. But since Mars is a malefic, this position is not good for father's health, longevity, and relations with him.

In the eleventh house also Mars is *shubha*. One has high income and powerful friends. But its adverse aspect on the fifth house will mean abortion, miscarriages, difficulties with children, disturbed love life, etc.

In the fifth, the natural house of friend Sun, Mars makes the native's children basically strong. But happiness to/from children is curtailed. One will have stomach problems. The native's education may suffer. If in a favourable sign, one will receive good education.

In the ninth house, the natural house of friend Jupiter, Mars is good for material success.

Mars is bad in the second, fourth, seventh eighth and twelfth houses.

If Mars is in the second house, the native may suffer from eye/ear disease. The native is harsh in speech. This position is not conducive for family happiness and wealth. It is not good for happiness from children as malefic Mars aspects the fifth house.

In the fourth house, Mars is like 'Fire in Home'. The native is robbed of happiness particularly from mother. It affects the seventh house also by its fourth aspect. The native's character is suspect.

In the seventh house, it mars marital happiness anyway. There may be separation from the spouse. From the seventh, its eighth aspect on the second house makes one harsh in speech.

In the eighth house, it affects longevity. One is prone to accidents/sudden losses. One may have diseases in anus and genitalia. The aspect on the second house makes one worried about wealth.

The Twelfth house is the worst position of Mars for marital happiness. It takes away any possibility of enjoying pleasures of the bed. One may suffer in the eye. The native is a spendthrift.

Mars Defect (*Mangalik Dosha*)

Let us see now what is *Mangalik Dosha*, the Mars factor that becomes an impediment to matrimonial happiness. This happens when Mars is placed in the first, second, fourth, seventh, eighth or twelfth house. In fact, all malefics in these houses, but more particularly Mars, affect conjugal happiness.

Mars in the first makes the native aggressive and dominating over his/her spouse, while Mars in the seventh makes the spouse more dominating over the native.

The second house represents family. The spouse is the pillar of the family. Mars in the second is destructive of family life, wealth, and speech.

The fourth house represents home, happiness/*sukha,* mental peace, character, etc. The native's character will be questionable. From here, Mars aspects the seventh house also. Without the character and the spouse, there is no home or happiness.

If Mars is in the seventh house, the native indulges in immoral acts. It is equivalent to having a spouse as good or as bad as not having.

The eighth house is the house of genitals. The native may suffer from genito-urinary problems. It also affects longevity of both self and spouse. In a woman's chart Mars and Saturn are considered very bad in the seventh and eighth houses. Mars in the eighth house is indicative of widowhood.

Finally, the twelfth house represents pleasures of the bed. Mars in the twelfth house results in loss of this pleasure. In fact, this is the worst position of Mars. From here, Mars spoils the seventh house also by its eighth aspect. With Mars in the twelfth, the native is cruel, irreligious and effectively without a spouse.

Mangalik dosha is considered not only from *lagna* but also from the Moon, and Venus the significator for seventh house.

It is necessary that marriage should be solemnised between two persons who are both *mangalik*, and more importantly *mangalik* in a similar manner.

Note: We must keep the *Kaal Purush Kundali* in mind while examining a chart. For example, if Mars is in first and Saturn is in seventh house then *mangalik dosha* will be feeble. The reason is that Mars, in the first house is in its own sign Aries, and Saturn in the seventh is in exaltation in Libra in the *Kaal Purush Kundali*. On the other hand, if Mars is in the seventh and Saturn is in the first then this *dosha* will certainly be more severe since Mars would be in fall, and Saturn would be debilitated.

Mercury in the Twelve Houses

Mercury is mostly benefic. Its significations, though, suffer if it is placed in the evil *trik* houses. Even among the *trik*, it is actually supposed to be well placed in the sixth, the natural sign of the house being its sign of exaltation, Virgo.

Mercury in *lagna* makes one intelligent, learned, a mathematician, fun loving and clever in speech, but to an extent promiscuous and selfish. It endows one with a comely body. One is fond of friends and relatives.

Mercury is very strong in the second house. The native is endowed with a sweet voice. S/he gets to enjoy good food, and earns wealth by using intelligence/*buddhi* and business acumen. Mercury in the third house is in its own natural sign, Gemini, in the *Kaal Purush Kundali*. It gives good brothers and sisters. The native is well versed in arts, reading, writing, etc. One may become a poet, author, editor, or interested in travelling, shipping, etc.

The natural sign of the fourth house is Cancer. Mercury, a great friend of the Moon, is very strong in this house. It is also the *karaka* for the fourth. It endows one with the comforts of home, happiness, property, friends, conveyance, etc., the native is devoted to his/her mother.

Mercury in the fifth house also is very strong. The natural sign of the house is Leo ruled by great friend Sun. It gives education, and happiness to/from children. The native is well versed in scriptures. S/he may become a counsellor or advisor. Words spoken by him/her carry weight. They are like blessings. Even if s/he says anything at random, it will come true.

If Mercury is in the sixth house, the native has no enemies. Mercury here, like a faithful *Djinn*, serves the native well. But s/he speaks harsh words and gets angrily involved in arguments.

If Mercury is in the seventh house, the native as well as spouse are both intelligent and comely in appearance. The native gets success in business and trade. S/he helps near and dear ones. S/he is well versed in arts, artisanship, etc. If a writer, has great power with his/her pen.

Mercury in the ninth house gives good speech, learning, and commendable conduct.

Mercury in the tenth house, the house of its *karakattva*, gives success right from the beginning in whatever the native undertakes including career. S/he gains favours in work and trading by virtue of pleasing speech. The native's deeds are good. S/he is devoted to parents.

One earns much with Mercury in the eleventh house. His/her desires are fulfilled. One has intelligent and refined friends.

Evil places for Mercury are the eighth and twelfth.

The natural sign of the eighth is Scorpio. Mercury is inimical to its Lord, Mars. With Mercury, Lord of the sixth in the *Kaal Purush Kundali* placed in the eighth, the native may encounter sudden difficulties in work/service. It indicates a 'hard life'. It is, however, good for the of the second house as it aspects it from the eighth, the natural sign of the second being Taurus ruled by friend Venus.

Mercury in the twelfth is in debility in the *Kaal Purush Kundali*. It destroys one's sleep. The native is devoid of intelligence, goes through indigent circumstances, and is inimical to relations.

Jupiter in the Twelve Houses

Jupiter, the great benefic, is not inimical to any planet. Hence it is good in every house, including *lagna*, except the *trik* in which its significations suffer. Even among the *trik*, it is considered well placed in the twelfth, the natural sign of the house being Pisces. It is very strong in the fourth house, the natural sign of the house being Cancer, its sign of exaltation. Jupiter is the *karaka* for as many as five houses, the second, the fifth, the ninth, the tenth and the eleventh. Hence, it is very good in the second, fifth, and eleventh. But it is very weak in the tenth, the natural sign of the tenth being Capricorn in which Jupiter is debilitated.

It is very strong in the ninth. The natural sign of the ninth is Sagittarius, Jupiter's own.

Jupiter is 'Guru/Preceptor'. With Jupiter in *lagna*, the native is like a 'Rajguru'. S/he is learned, prosperous, pious and spiritually inclined. S/he has pleasing personality, and enormous life force (*jeevan shakti*). The native has happiness from children.

Jupiter in the second is like a Guru for the world, say, 'Jagatguru'. It gives the native a charming face, eloquence in speech, wealth, and enjoyment of good food.

With Jupiter in the third, the native is bold but miserly. S/he enjoys the confidence of his/her brothers/sisters. Due to the fifth, seventh and ninth aspects from here on seventh, ninth and eleventh houses respectively, the native remains fond of his/her spouse, is religious and has good income.

Jupiter in the fourth house is exalted in the *Kaal Purush Kundali*. It is like 'Indra Devata'. The native has heavenly comforts and happiness in respect of home, property, mother, etc. S/he has long life, happiness to/from a noble father and success in career, and spends on good causes as it aspects the eighth, tenth and twelfth from here.

Jupiter in the fifth house gives good children. From the day of the birth of a child, the native's prosperity starts increasing. The native is religiously inclined due to its aspects on the ninth house and *lagna*. S/he has high income, paraphernalia of luxuries, and fulfilment of reasonable desires due to its aspect on the eleventh house.

Jupiter in the seventh makes one handsome and magnanimous. The native's spouse is equally handsome and pious. But it makes the spouse dominating. Such a person should marry someone who also has an equally strong planet such as the Sun in the seventh house. From the seventh, its aspect on the eleventh gives high income to the native.

In addition to the fourth, the ninth is the best position for Jupiter. It is the house of its *karakattva* as well as its own in the *Kaal Purush Kundali*. The native is extremely fortunate, prosperous, pious, religious and magnanimous. S/he is endowed with good children and brothers/sisters. Although the native has everything, s/he is not craving for the same.

The placement of Jupiter in the tenth, a *kendra*, is good for happiness from children. The native is devoted to parents. S/he does good deeds, gets success in his/her career, undertakings, etc., and enjoys name, fame and recognition.

Jupiter in the eleventh house gives sober friends, good children and high education. It is a fine placement for love and romance.

Jupiter in the evil *trik* houses robs it off most of its benefits. The native does not have happiness of children. His/her actions are not commendable. However, the positive significations of the *trik* flourish. For example, in the sixth house the native does not suffer becouse of enemies. In the eighth the native has a long life and is fond of occult. In the twelfth the native travels a lot and is inclined to austerity. One does not spend much on oneself. One may, however, be a fanatic in his/her beliefs.

Venus in the Twelve Houses

Venus, another great benefic, is generally good except when it is in two of the *trik* houses, the sixth and eighth. In the *Kaal Purush Kundali*, the second house is Taurus and the seventh is Libra, both ruled by Venus, and the twelfth is Pisces, the sign of its exaltation. Hence, Venus is best placed in these houses. The sixth is Virgo, sign of its debilitation, and a *trik*. Venus is worst in the sixth house.

If Venus is in *lagna*, the native has a beautiful body and attractive personality. This position bestows company of the opposite sex. The native is amorous and follows the dictates of his/her own desires and passions to the extreme limit. An example is Razia Sultana who fell in love with one of her slaves.

In the second house, Venus is in its own sign in the *Kaal Purush Kundali*. It gives sweet speech. One may become a poet. The native enjoys wealth, family and sumptuous foods.

With Venus in the third the native is not very hardworking.

If Venus is in the fourth house, the native leads a happy and rich life.

Venus in the fifth gives good education, riches, loving children, love affairs, etc.

If Venus is in the seventh house, the native and spouse both have good personality. The spouse is very affectionate as well as beautiful. The native is, however, over-sexed and may have liaisons with others.

Venus in the ninth makes one very fortunate in general and in respect of spouse in particular. Venus in the tenth house gives success in ventures/career, and name and fame.

If Venus is in the eleventh, the native is very fortunate in fulfilling desires, goals and ambitions. S/he has very high income and leads a luxurious life. S/she has many friends, especially females.

Venus in the twelfth is like a 'Wish-Yielding Cow'. The planet here is in exaltation in the *Kaal Purush Kundali*. It gives pleasures of the bed. The spouse is a great support to the native. The native may have extra-marital relations.

Venus in the sixth house is very bad. The native has no happiness from wife or husband. It is worst for Aries and Scorpio *lagnas* since the seventh Lord would then be in the twelfth from the seventh. The seventh Lord in the sixth denies marriage. The native lacks wealth and happiness. S/he indulges in love fantasies and may develop impotence or frigidity. One, however, does not have enemies.

Venus in the eighth gives long life, sudden gains, inheritances and wealth. But the love planet is like a 'Witch'. The native's spouse is hard-hearted. The spouse never has anything good to say. the surprising thing is that curses due to Venus in eighth, more often than not, do materialise. It is worst for Aries/Scorpio *lagnas* again since the seventh Lord would be in the eighth.

Saturn in the Twelve Houses

The natural sign of the first house is Aries in which Saturn is debilitated. Hence, if Saturn is in *lagna*, the native is lazy, hard-hearted and cunning. S/he has an unclean body, goes through sufferings in life, and is always hankering after sexual pleasure. But if Saturn here were in Libra or Capricorn, the native is very wise. S/he holds a kingly position and upholds justice. Similar results follow, though to a lesser degree, if Saturn is in Jupiter's signs, Sagittarius and Pisces, and the other Venus sign of Taurus. It is good in Aquarius also. Saturn in the first is either thrice as good or thrice as bad. It depends upon the sign in which it is placed.

If Saturn is in the second house, the native is not good looking. S/he is not truthful, loses wealth and may suffer separation from family. Saturn aspects the fourth house from here. This will make the native leave home and move to some other place.

Saturn, as a malefic, is very good in the third, sixth and eleventh houses. It is also good in the tenth house.

With Saturn in the third, the native is chivalrous and fond of travelling. But, s/he is not happy in respect of brothers/sisters, and children also due to its third aspect on the fifth house.

The propensity of Saturn to do harm gets blunted if it is placed in the sixth house. Though the native has constant apprehensions from enemies but s/he triumphs over them.

In the tenth, Saturn's own house in the *Kaal Purush Kundali* as well as its house of *karakatava*, it gives very good results. Such a person is close to the authorities, and achieves success in service or occupations dealing in iron, oil, petrol, minerals or agriculture. Saturn's placement in the tenth house is like a blank paper on which the native can write his/her destiny by his/her own deeds. The native is just and compassionate. S/he earns name and fame. But this is not a good position in respect of happiness from mother and father, and also spouse as it aspects the fourth and the seventh houses from here.

Saturn is best in the eleventh house. It brings handsome gains. It is in its *moola-trikona* sign Aquarius in the *Kaal Purush Kundali*. But this is not a good position for eldest sibling. It is also not good for love relationships and children as Saturn aspects the fifth house from here.

With Saturn in the fourth house, the native is devoid of happiness. There is trouble to the mother. The native has to suffer much mental anguish. S/he is bereft of home, property, etc.

The fifth, the natural house of great enemy Sun, is a very unfavourable position for Saturn in respect of happiness from children and family, and love matters.

Saturn in the seventh gives results of exaltation though the native is attached to unworthy men/women. Marriage is usually stable, but there is no real charm in married life.

Saturn is the *karaka* for eighth. It is like its headquarters. It gives long life. The native suffers from piles. It is not a good position for wealth, family, etc., as Saturn aspects the second house from here.

If Saturn is in the ninth house, the native is more philosophical than religious.

Finally, Saturn in the twelfth will lead to the premature decay of teeth, eyesight, etc. The native spends a lot, loses wealth, family happiness, etc., due to Saturn's aspect on the second house. There is no enjoyment of sexual pleasures.

Rahu and Ketu in the Twelve Houses

Since Rahu and Ketu are malefics, the best houses for them to be placed individually are the third, sixth and eleventh houses. But Rahu and Ketu form an axis; and there is hardly any axis for both to be simultaneously in good positions. Thus, they will always spoil a good house as is clear from the table below.

From the *Kaal Purush Kundali* we know that the best houses for Rahu are third and sixth falling under Mercury's signs, Gemini and Virgo. Corresponding houses for Ketu are the ninth and the twelfth, falling under Jupiter's signs, Sagittarius and Pisces. We can see that Rahu in the third with Ketu in the ninth, or Rahu in the sixth with Ketu in the twelfth are the best combinations for the Rahu–Ketu axis. Note that Rahu is 'discontent incarnate', 'ever dissatisfied' and 'attachment'. Ketu is 'fanaticism incarnate', 'obstinate', 'courageous' and 'detachment'.

Rahu in Lagna	*Shubha* Rahu gives intelligence, riches,sex, success. *Ashubha* makes secretive, serpent-like, cruel, merciless, irreligious, deceitful.
Ketu in Seventh	One is attached to unworthy persons of the opposite sex. The spouse may be sickly, may suffer from sexual/urinary troubles.
Rahu in Second	Untruthful in speech. Diseases of mouth, face. Loss of family happiness/wealth.
Ketu in Eighth	Longevity suffers. Chances of injury, surgery, accident. Piles/ anal diseases.
Rahu in Third	Best position. The native is bold, hardworking, firm, intelligent, valorous. Possesses clairvoyance. Opposes brothers/sisters.

Ketu in Ninth	The native is unorthodox in religion, marriage, etc. May possess supernatural powers of blessing people.
Rahu in Fourth	No happiness. Ever discontented. No happiness from parents.
Ketu in Tenth	Success in career. Relations with father may be strained.
Rahu in Fifth	Devoid of children. The native is hard-hearted and not dependable in love. Diseases of abdomen, stomach and uterus.
Ketu in Eleventh	Gain of money. Matters in respect of children, love relationships suffer since Rahu is in fifth.
Rahu in Sixth	Best position. In favourable sign it is all the more *shubha*. Oppressed by enemies, but wins over them. May suffer from kidney problems, ulcers, etc.
Ketu in Twelfth	Very good since in Jupiter's house. Twelfth Ketu gives *moksha*. The native is voluptuous. May indulge in sinful acts secretly. Spends much. Suffers from eye disease.
Rahu in Seventh	No conjugal happiness. Sickly partner. May be widowed, impotent or weak. Losses in business and partnerships.
Ketu in *lagna*	The native is avaricious, sickly, backbiter, ungrateful. Has an imaginary worry.
Rahu in Eighth	Worst position. Even a favourable sign will not help. Not long-lived. Sexually weak but much inclined. Diseases of private parts.
Ketu in Second	No accumulation of wealth. Uses foul language. Depends on food doled by others. Diseases of mouth.
Rahu in Ninth	Success in ventures but the native is not pious.
Ketu in Third	Great stamina. Receives divine help.
Rahu in Tenth	Fearless and famous. Rich but devoid of good deeds. Not good for parents.
Ketu in Fourth	Loses property, land, mother, happiness, etc. May have to leave one's birthplace.
Rahu in Eleventh	Excellent for material gains. Gains from foreign sources. Trouble in ears. Desires unfulfilled. Children, love life suffer.
Ketu in Fifth	Worried mind. Happiness to/from children curtailed. Stomach problems.
Rahu in Twelfth	Indulges in secret/sinful acts. Wanders in lonely places. Expenditure. No pleasures of bed. No happiness. Eyes and teeth weak.
Ketu in Sixth	Overcomes enemies. Achieves objectives. Occupies high position. Enjoys good health. May have some powers/ *siddhis*.

Note: The only way to get benefit from Rahu/Ketu is by having them in favourable signs. Note that Rahu is worse than Saturn in spoiling relationships pertaining to houses it tenants and aspects.

8.3 PARS FORTUNA

Pars Fortuna represents the overall factor in a horoscope. It is found to exercise great influence on one's life. What is Pars Fortuna? It is the resultant force determined by the longitudes of the *lagna*, the Moon and the Sun. To determine the longitude of Pars Fortuna, add the longitudes of the *lagna* and the Moon, and then subtract the longitude of the Sun from the sum. In the sample horoscope:

		S	D	M
Longitude of *lagna*		1	1	53
Longitude of Moon	(+)	3	5	11
Sum		4	7	4
Longitude of Sun	(minus sign −)	3	22	33
Longitude of Pars Fortuna		0	14	31

Thus, Pars Fortuna is in 0 S 14 D 31 M. So, it falls in Aries, viz., in the twelfth house in native's chart. Like any benefic, it should better be placed in any of the good houses. It is unfortunate to have it in the *trik*.

In whichever house Pars Fortuna is placed that becomes the prominent feature of the native's life. Now, we describe the salient features of Pars Fortuna in the twelve houses:

In *lagna*: Desire for self-expression and recognition.

In the second house: Desire for power. Native dotes over the family.

In the third house: One is hardworking. S/he is a thinker/evangelist/author.

In the fourth house: Pleasant home conditions. Native is happy. Happiness from mother.

In the fifth house:	Creditable children. High education. Love dominates one's life.
In the sixth house:	Impatient. Wanting in self-control. Health impaired.
In the seventh house:	Ideally married. Great interest in marriage partner/opposite sex.
In the eighth house:	Accident-prone. Strained finances. One is always short of money.
In the ninth house:	Spiritually inclined. Generally lucky. Fond of travels/pilgrimages.
In the tenth house:	Occupies high office. Lacks home comforts. Happiness from father.
In the eleventh house:	Good income. Good friends. Leads to fulfilment of desires.
In the twelfth house:	Inferiority complex.

8.4 PLACEMENT OF LORD OF A HOUSE/*BHAVESH* IN THE TWELVE HOUSES

In Section 8.2, we discussed the effects of placement of different planets, as natural benefics and malefics and as significators for certain matters and houses, in the twelve houses. In the tables below, we give, briefly, the effects of placement of a planet as Lord of a particular house in any of the twelve houses. It may be reiterated that matters pertaining to the *bhavas* are enhanced if their Lords are placed in good houses. The *bhava* matters suffer if its Lord is placed in any of the evil *trik* houses, or if the *trik* Lords are placed in the *bhava*. For example, if the fourth Lord is placed in the sixth house or the sixth Lord is placed in the fourth, domestic happiness will be disturbed by animosity, quarrels and illnesses.

Lagna Lord/*Lagnesh* in the Twelve Houses

House	Results
First	Great Man or *Maha-Purush-Yoga*. One has strong positive characteristics of sign and its Lord. Lives by own efforts. Has self-confidence. Good health.
Second	Accumulates wealth. Dotes on family.
Third	Has perseverance/stamina. Singer/writer. Likes siblings. Amorous since natural sign of the house is Gemini.
Fourth	Has home/property/conveyance/happiness/peace of mind. Fond of mother.
Fifth	*Yoga-karaka* for significations of both first and fifth houses. Educated. Fond of children. Falls in love. Religious. Propitiates deities.
Sixth	Suffers from diseases. Is one's own enemy. Suitable for army/medicine.
Seventh	Fond of spouse/opposite sex. Engages in business. Foreign travel.
Eighth	Poor health. Sufferings. Accident-prone. Sudden gains/losses. Has wisdom.
Ninth	Is fortunate, noble and religious. Blessed with divine grace. Fond of travel.
Tenth	Interested in career. Gets success/recognition/respect. Fond of father.
Eleventh	Income/gains by own efforts. Desires are fulfilled. Likes friends.
Twelfth	Poor health. Possible hospitalisation. Expenses. May become non-resident.

Second Lord/*Dhanesh* in the Twelve Houses

House	Results
First	Loved by family. Wealth by own effort.
Second	Endowed with wealth/family/good speech. May marry more than once.
Third	Fond of travel/reading/writing/music. Much wealth as second Lord is in second from second. If malefic, one is strong, but opposes brothers/sisters.
Fourth	*Dhanesh* in *kendra* gives wealth/family happiness. Evil for mother if malefic.
Fifth	Speculation gains. Wealth. Family happiness. Evil for children if malefic.
Sixth	No family happiness. Gains from enemies or by questionable means.

contd.

House	Results
Seventh	Wealth from marriage/opposite sex. Gains from journeys to foreign countries. Laxity of morals of both husband and wife.
Eighth	No family happiness. Loss of wealth. Always short of money.
Ninth	Philanthropic. Happy family life. Fortunate in wealth. Gains from voyages.
Tenth	Accumulates wealth from profession/undertakings, and government favours.
Eleventh	Earns considerable wealth by different means, or through elder sibling/s.
Twelfth	Unhappy family life. Loss of wealth. Harsh speech.

Third Lord/*Parakramesh* in the Twelve Houses

Note: Third house and third Lord are mildly malefic.

House	Results
First	Hardworking. Interest in sports, reading, writing, fine arts, music, dancing.
Second	Lack of success in efforts/loss of siblings, second being twelfth from third.
Third	Very hardworking. Successful. Happiness to/from brothers/sisters if benefic.
Fourth	Loved by siblings. Inimical to parents. Homemaker. Work gives happiness.
Fifth	Happiness from children curtailed. Education suffers a bit. Success in efforts, and benefit from brothers/sisters since fifth is a trine, and third from third.
Sixth	Opposes brothers/sisters. Becomes an athlete, sportsman/woman.
Seventh	Cordial relations between brothers/sisters.
Eighth	Hardwork does not bring returns. Sufferings to brothers/sisters. Chronic problems of throat, thyroid, etc. Longevity suffers if malefic.
Ninth	Handsome returns from hardwork. Loves brothers/sisters. Long journeys.
Tenth	Puts all efforts in one's career. Journeys connected with profession.
Eleventh	Income/gains possible by dint of hardwork. Success in financial matters.
Twelfth	Lazy. Brings sorrow to brothers/sisters. Spendthrift. May leave homeland for work.

Fourth Lord/ *Sukhesh/ Matri-Bhavesh* in the Twelve Houses

House	Results
First	Loved by mother. Happy home life. Owns house, conveyance, etc.
Second	Happiness from family.
Third	Loss of mother, happiness, etc., third being twelfth from fourth. May suffer from stepmother, stepbrothers/sisters.
Fourth	*Maha-Purush-Yoga*. Great happiness from mother, home, property, etc.
Fifth	*Yoga-Karaka* for significations of both fourth and fifth houses. Devoted to mother. Happiness to/from children. Native is learned/ religious.
Sixth	Devoid of home, happiness, property, etc. Illness to or inharmonious relations with mother.
Seventh	Seventh is fourth from fourth. Great happiness of home, mother, spouse, etc.
Eighth	Unhappy miserable life. May suffer from chronic lungs/heart trouble.
Ninth	*Raja-Yoga karaka* for significations of both fourth and ninth houses, mother, home, happiness, conveyances, religiousness, virtues, pilgrimages, etc.
Tenth	Home/happiness since aspecting own house. Devoted to parents if benefic.
Eleventh	Eleventh is eighth from the fourth. Tendency for depression. Unhappiness.
Twelfth	Deprived of happiness. May lose mother early in life. Miserable existence.

Fifth Lord *Vidya/ Putra-Bhavesh* in the Twelve Houses

House	Results
First	*Yoga-karaka* for significations of both first and fifth houses. Loved by and blessed with noble children. Good education. Knowledge of scriptures.
Second	Trine Lord in second. Good family life. Endowed with wealth.
Third	Valorous. Success in undertakings.
Fourth	Trine Lord in fourth. Happiness from mother, home, etc., if benefic. Problems to/from children since fourth is twelfth from fifth.
Fifth	High education. Knowledge of scriptures. Good children. Happy love life.

contd.

House	Results
Sixth	Significations of fifth suffer. Good for positive matters of sixth such as health, career, etc.
Seventh	Children attain distinction and may live abroad. Native is educated.
Eighth	Obstacles in education. Happiness to/from children curtailed. Difficult childbirth. Stomach problems. Good for positive matters of eighth, windfall gains, wisdom, etc.
Ninth	Ninth is fifth from fifth. Very fortunate and noble children. Native is highly educated, religious and fortunate. Gains from travels. Fortunate in love life.
Tenth	*Raja-Yoga* is foretold in respect of significations of fifth and tenth houses.
Eleventh	Good education/children/income. Finds love. Desires fulfilled. Many friends.
Twelfth	Education suffers. No *sukha* to/from children. No love life. Good for positive matters of twelfth. One seeks non-attachment, ultimate reality, and renunciation.

Seventh Lord/*Kalatra-Bhavesh* in the Twelve Houses

House	Results
First	Spouse very fond of native. Native is liked by opposite sex.
Second	Problems in married life since second is eighth from seventh.
Third	Spouse is lucky since third is ninth from seventh. Success in partnership business.
Fourth	Happiness, property, etc., if benefic; loss of the same if malefic.
Fifth	Spouse has high income since fifth is eleventh from seventh.
Sixth	Denies marriage, sixth being twelfth from seventh. Inimical to spouse. Evil effects mitigated if one marries a cousin or a known person. Spouse may still be sickly.
Seventh	*Maha-Purush-Yoga*. Spouse is a great person. Very happy married life. More than one attachment simultaneously possible.
Eighth	Devoid of marital happiness. Ill-tempered sickly spouse.
Ninth	Spouse very fortunate, and righteous. Rise after marriage. Happy marriage.
Tenth	Working spouse. S/he may be coworker. Job may involve travelling abroad.
Eleventh	Spouse is beautiful, good natured, devoted and from a rich background. Rise in luck after marriage. Gains from women and/or foreign connection.
Twelfth	Unloved by spouse. Separation. Or spouse may be living far away/abroad.

Ninth Lord/*Bhagyesh*/*Dharma-Bhavesh* in the Twelve Houses

House	Results
First	Native is pious. Makes fortune by own effort. Marital happiness if benefic.
Second	Trine Lord in second. Family happiness. Riches. Truthful in speech.
Third	Sudden turns in life. But Lord aspects own ninth house always. Makes destiny by dint of hardwork. May make fortune by writing, speaking, teaching, etc.
Fourth	*Kendra-Trikona-Yoga*. Significations of fourth, ninth and tenth prosper. Devoted to parents. Bestowed with happiness/property. Pious. Noble.
Fifth	*Yoga-karaka*. Ninth Lord in the ninth from the ninth. Both native and children well educated, fortunate, and pious. Abundance. Faithful/idealistic in romance.
Sixth	Troubled by enemies. Devoid of religious merit.
Seventh	Noble spouse. Fortune after marriage. Success in business and partnership.
Eighth	Destiny eludes. Devoid of religious merit. Eighth is *trik*/twelfth from ninth.
Ninth	Very fortunate, pious, virtuous, philanthropic. Indicates abundance, happiness, and easy success in all matters. Loves Guru, and brothers/sisters.
Tenth	*Raja-Yoga karaka* for significations of ninth, tenth and fourth. Fortunate in respect of parents. Ethical. Moralistic. Gets success, name, fame, respect, etc.
Eleventh	High income. Good children. Good intimate friends. Desires are fulfilled.
Twelfth	Inauspicious. Has to work hard to make fortune. May flourish abroad.

Tenth Lord/*Karmesh*/*Rajyesh*/*Pitra-Bhavesh* in the Twelve Houses

House	Results
First	Success in career by own effort. May be self-employed. Pioneer in own field. Loved by father if benefic.
Second	Fortunate in career and second house affairs. May engage in family business.
Third	Valorous. Journeys in connection with work. Success in writing, speaking, computing, communications, etc.
Fourth	Good for father/career/name/fame. Happiness/mother's *sukha*, if benefic.

contd.

House	Results
Fifth	*Raja-yoga karaka* in respect of both tenth and fifth house affairs. May have career in educational field. Success in speculation.
Sixth	Generally lucky in profession, even though the sixth is a *trik*, sixth being ninth from the tenth. Career as doctor, judge, soldier, jailor, etc., likely.
Seventh	Helped by spouse/partners in career/business. Very successful/lucky in respect of career, father, etc., seventh being tenth from tenth. Travels abroad.
Eighth	Derailments in career. Evil for father. May become a mystic. Fond of occult.
Ninth	Though the ninth is twelfth from tenth, it is the most powerful house. Native becomes a spiritual stalwart, preacher, teacher, or healer. Royal status.
Tenth	*Maha-Purush-Yoga*. Immensely successful in profession. Has name, fame, recognition and status. Gets support of government/authorities. Fortunate in respect of father.
Eleventh	Earns immensely from work. Meritorious career. Has many friends.
Twelfth	Losses/difficulties in work. Work in far-off places. No support of authorities.

Eleventh Lord/*Laabhesh*/*Aayesh* in the Twelve Houses

House	Results
First	Born rich. Has high income also from own efforts. Endowed with gains.
Second	Accumulates wealth. May earn from family business, finance, banking, etc.
Third	May earn by writing, speaking, singing or computing, communications, etc.
Fourth	Mother very cultured. Gains from mother's support/property/real estate.
Fifth	May earn in educational field. Gains from speculation. Derives happiness and gains from children. High income as eleventh Lord aspects own house.
Sixth	Gains from running nursing homes, army/police, disputes/litigations.
Seventh	Gains from spouse/opposite sex. Liaisons. Dual marriage possible. Prospers abroad.
Eighth	Life full of sudden losses. Possible gains from inheritance.
Ninth	Has high income and gets many opportunities in life since ninth is strongest trine and eleventh from eleventh. Hopes and desires are materialised.

contd.

House	Results
Tenth	Earns sufficiently from his/her profession. Gains from government. Brings under control his/her senses. Latter develops tendency to asceticism.
Eleventh	High income. Fulfilment of desires. Wide friends circle. Elder sibling lucky.
Twelfth	Much expenditure. Low income. Suffers losses. Elder sibling may suffer.

Evil *Trik* Lords in the Twelve Houses

Placement of a *trik* Lord in a house is detrimental to the affairs of that house and the house opposite to it. Lord of the sixth house of disease and enemy in any house implies enmity with or illness to relations signified by that house, and disease in the part of the body signified by that house. The Lord of the eighth house of death, accidents, suddenness, etc., in a house will lead to accidents, sudden losses/harms/chronic diseases to relations and parts of body signified by that house. Lord of the twelfth house of loss, expenditure, and hospitalisation will similarly affect the house. In addition, it will indicate on whom and/or on what matters the native will spend away his/her money and energy. For example, the twelfth Lord in the second house indicates expenditure on family, in the third on siblings, in fourth on home and mother, in the fifth on children, in the sixth on enemies and litigations, in the seventh on spouse or opposite sex, in the ninth on religious purposes, in the tenth on father, promoting own career, etc.

Placement of a *trik* Lord in another *trik* house is *yoga-karaka*. See Section 8.5.2.

8.5 A STUDY OF THE *TRIK* HOUSES

As we have seen above, the *trik* houses and the *trik* Lords effect in two ways:

(i)   Either a *trik* Lord tenants a house.

(ii) Or a house Lord is placed in any of the *trik* houses.

The extent of the maleficence caused to a house by its being tenanted by a *trik* Lord depends on the following:

(i)   Whether the *trik* Lord is natural benefic or malefic.

(ii) Whether the *trik* Lord is friendly or inimical to the Lord of the house.

For example, a benefic like Jupiter owning a *trik* house is not very adverse to the house tenanted by it. But a natural malefic like Saturn, if simultaneously Lord of a *trik* house, becomes doubly malefic. Even benefic Jupiter will, however, show evil effects of the *trik* house owned by it during its *Dashas* and transits.

Secondly, matters of the houses get adversely affected when their Lords are placed in the evil *trik* houses. Not only the matters of houses but also the significations/ *karakattvas* of the planets are also greatly affected.

Placement of Benefics and Malefics in *Trik* Houses

We know that benefics promote the *bhavas* and malefics demote them. But in the case of the *trik* houses the reverse is true. It implies that malefics promote the *trik bhavas* and benefics demote them. Note that the sixth, eighth and twelfth *trik bhavas* represent disease/enemy, death and expenditure/loss respectively. Thus we have as follows:

If a benefic like Jupiter or Venus occupies the sixth there will be no enemies, if the eighth there will be no danger of early death, and if the twelfth there will be no expenditure/ losses; Jupiter here makes one rather miserly.

But if a malefic like the Sun or Mars occupies the sixth, the enemies will increase though s/he will overpower them, if the eighth then dangers to life will increase, and if the twelfth then there will be losses.

Negative and Positive Matters under *Trik* Houses

We note that even though the *trik* houses denote essentially negative matters, they also rule over some positive matters of life, as indicated in Table 8.2.

So when we say that the malefics in a *trik* promote the *bhava*, it actually means that malefics promote the negative matters of the *trik bhava*, and when we say that benefics in a *trik* demote the *bhava*, it only implies that they mitigate the evil effects of negative matters of the *bhava*. We may now add further that benefics in the *trik* not only demote the negative matters, they also promote the positive matters of the *bhava*.

So, a malefic in the sixth will increase enemies, diseases especially of the digestive system, etc., in the eighth it may cause sudden accidents, losses, death, etc., and in the twelfth it may lead to expenditure, losses, scandals, evil deeds, etc. A benefic, on the other hand, in the sixth will give good results in work, service, maternal relations, health of the digestive system, etc., in the eighth a long life, peaceful death, wisdom, windfall gains, etc., and in the twelfth pleasures of the bed, residence abroad, pilgrimages, and even renunciation and liberation (*moksha*).

Further, when a *trik* Lord is in its own house, the positive matters get a great boost.

Table 8.2
Negative and Positive Matters under *Trik* Houses

Trik Bhava	Negative Matters	Positive Matters
Sixth	Enemies. Vices. Diseases. Injuries. Suffering. Debts. Litigations. Disappointments.	Health. Digestive System. Sports. Success in Competitions. Gain in Work. Service to Others. Maternal Relations.
Eighth	Death. Accidents. Dangers to life. Sudden Losses.	Longevity. Sexual Organs. Wisdom (*gyan tattva*). Occult. Windfall Gains. Inheritance. Spouse's Wealth.
Twelfth	Expenditure. Losses. Sins. Wanderings.	Pleasures of the bed. Residence Abroad. Renunciation. Pilgrimages.

But when a *trik* Lord is placed in any of the other two *trik* houses, the positive matters of the house of lordship suffer, though the negative matters get mitigated. Simultaneously, the positive matters of the house tenanted get a setback, whereas the negative matters will meet their ruin. Thus, the negative matters of both the house of lordship as well as the house tenanted are mitigated. Hence, this is considered a good *yoga*. In addition, if two *trik* Lords are placed in each other's houses in mutual exchange, it is a still better combination named as *Vipareet Raja-Yoga*. This *yoga* mitigates the evil effects of the two evil houses involved.

8.6 JUDGING EACH HOUSE/*BHAVA*

Effects of each individual planet placed in the twelve signs and the twelve houses have been described in the eight chapters. It is now time to summarise the essence of the same and synthesise the steps involved in judging each house/*bhava*.

For good effects pertaining to the affairs of a house/*bhava*, we should have the following conditions fulfilled:

(i)   The Lord of the house should be strong.
(ii) The house itself should be strong.
(iii) The significator/*karaka* for the house and for the matter should be strong.

When all the three factors are strong, then the house gets fortified. Expanding further, we can say that each house is to be judged from the following:

(i)   The nature of the sign of that house.
(ii) The Lord of the sign of the house, its nature, in which sign and in which house it is placed, if it is combust or retrograde, planets conjuncting or aspecting the Lord, and the sign and house of the planet in *Navansha Kundali*, and whether it is *Vargottama*.
(iii) Planets tenanting the house.
(iv) Planets aspecting the house.
(v)   *Karaka* for the house. Its placement in the sign and the house, whether combust or retrograde, its conjunction and aspect with other planets, in *lagna* as well as in *Navansha Kundali*, and whether it is *Vargottama*.
(vi) From *Bhavat-Bhava*, viz., from other houses relative to the house.

These principles are applied for predicting from *Janma Lagna Kundali*, the *Chandra Kundali* and *Navansha Kundali*. Predictions are made based on planetary periods and transits. Predictions by transits are, however, gross.

Planetary periods are explained in Chapter 10, while transits are discussed in Chapter 11.

Chapter 9

Nakshatras

9.1 *NAKSHATRAS* AND SIGNS

The zodiac constitutes 360 degrees. Just as it is divided into 12 signs each extending over 30 degrees, it is also divided into 27 equal sectors each constituting 13 degrees and 20 minutes. Each of these sectors is formed by a multitude of millions of stars in space forming a constellation. If we look towards the sky, then we will notice prominent stars in these constellations forming conglomerations in the shape of creatures such as horse, lion, deer, elephant, cow, snake, etc. Each constellation is presided over by a primary star and is called by the name of that star. Both the constellation and the primary star are referred to as *Nakshatra* or Asterism. The list of all the 27 *Nakshatras* starting from the first *Ashwini* in Aries/*Mesh*, second *Bharani* again in *Mesh*, etc., and ending with Revati in Pisces/*Meena* is given in Table 9.1. *Nakshatras* are one of the most powerful aspects of Vedic astrology. As these are not considered in Western astrology, only ancient Sanskrit names have been used here. Note that each *Nakshatra* is ruled over by a planet.

In Vedic astronomy, distances in space are measured in terms of these *Nakshatras*. Note that each sign covers 27/12 = 2.25 *Nakshatras* in space. Thus, if we divide each *Nakshatra*-space comprising of 13 D 20 M into 4 equal parts of 3 D 20 M each called a *Charana* or *Pada* then each Sign-space would overlap over 9 *Charanas/Padas* of *Nakshatras*, each *Charana/Pada*-space occupying a quarter or 0.25 of *Nakshatra*-space, so that each Sign-space is equal to 9(0.25) = 27/12 = 2.25 of *Nakshatra*-space.

Table 9.1
Longitudes of *Nakshtras*, and Ruling Planets of *Nakshatras*

No.	Longitude Range		Nakshatra	Ruling Planet
	From S D M	To S D M		
1	0-0-0	0-13-20	Ashwini	Ketu
2	0-13-20	0-26-40	Bharani	Venus
3	0-26-40	1-10-0	Krittika	Sun
4	1-10-0	1-23-20	Rohini	Moon
5	1-23-20	2-6-40	Mrigashira	Mars
6	2-6-40	2-20-0	Ardra	Rahu
7	2-20-0	3-3-20	Punarvasu	Jupiter
8	3-3-20	3-16-40	Pushya	Saturn
9	3-16-40	4-0-0	Ashlesha	Mercury
10	4-0-0	4-13-20	Makha	Ketu
11	4-13-20	4-26-40	P. Phalguni	Venus
12	4-26-40	5-10-0	U. Phalguni	Sun
13	5-10-0	5-23-20	Hasta	Moon
14	5-23-20	6-6-40	Chitra	Mars
15	6-6-40	6-20-0	Swati	Rahu
16	6-20-0	7-3-20	Vishakha	Jupiter
17	7-3-20	7-16-40	Anuradha	Saturn
18	7-16-40	8-0-0	Jyeshtha	Mercury
19	8-0-0	8-13-20	Moola	Ketu
20	8-13-20	8-26-40	P. Ashadh	Venus
21	8-26-40	9-10-0	U. Ashadh	Sun

contd.

No.	Longitude Range		Nakshatra	Ruling Planet
	From S D M	To S D M		
22	9-10-0	9-23-20	Shravana	Moon
23	9-23-20	10-6-40	Dhanishtha	Mars
24	10-6-40	10-20-0	Shatabhisha	Rahu
25	10-20-0	11-3-20	P. Bhadra	Jupiter
26	11-3-20	11-16-40	U. Bhadra	Saturn
27	11-16-40	12-0-0	Revati	Mercury

Fig. 9.1 is a chart showing distribution of *Nakshatras* and their *Charanas* over signs. Thus, *Mesh rashi* comprises of 4 *Charanas* of *Ashwini*, 4 of *Bharani* and one of *Krittika*. Next 3 *Charanas* of *Krittika* fall in *Vrishabha rashi*. The remaining 6 *Charanas* in *Vrishabha* are 4 of *Rohini* and 2 of *Mrigashira*. The balance of 2 *Charanas* of *Mrigashira* fall in *Mithuna rashi*. The rest of the *Nakshatras* follow in their order.

Thus, we see that *Krittika* falls in Aries and Taurus, *Mrigashira* in Taurus and Gemini, *Punarvasu* in Gemini and Cancer, *U. Phalguni* in Leo and Virgo, *Chitra* in Virgo and Libra, *Vishakha* in Libra and Scorpio, *U. Ashadh* in Sagittarius and Capricorn, *Dhanishtha* in Capricorn and Aquarius, and finally *P. Bhadra* in Aquarius and Pisces. The remaining 18 *Nakshatras* fall in one *rashi* only.

Note that *Krittika* extends from 0 S 26 D 40 M to 1 S 10 D 0 M of the zodiac. Likewise signs, degrees and minutes of all *Nakshatras* are given in Table 9.1. The table also names planets ruling over the *Nakshatras*.

ARIES (Mesh)			TAURUS (Vrishabha)		
Ashwini	Bharani	Krittika	Krittika	Rohini	Mrigashira
1 2 3 4	1 2 3 4	1	2 3 4	1 2 3 4	1 2

GEMINI (Mithuna)			CANCER (Karka)		
Mrigashira	Ardra	Punarvasu	Punarvasu	Pushya	Ashlesha
3 4	1 2 3 4	1 2 3	4	1 2 3 4	1 2 3 4

LEO (*Simha*)			VIRGO (*Kanya*)		
Makha	P. Phalguni	P. Phalguni	U. Phalguni	Hasta	Chitra
1 2 3 4	1 2 3 4	1	2 3 4	1 2 3 4	1 2

LIBRA (*Tula*)			SCORPIO (*Vrishchika*)		
Chitra	Swati	Vishakha	Vishakha	Anuradha	Jyeshtha
3 4	1 2 3 4	1 2 3	4	1 2 3 4	1 2 3 4

SAGITTARIUS (*Dhanu*)			CAPRICORN (*Makara*)		
Moola	P. Ashadh	U. Ashadh	U. Ashadh	Shravana	Dhanishtha
1 2 3 4	1 2 3 4	1	2 3 4	1 2 3 4	1 2

AQUARIUS (*Kumbha*)			PISCES (*Meena*)		
Dhanishtha	Shatabhisha	P. Bhadra	P. Bhadra	U. Bhadra	Revati
3 4	1 2 3 4	1 2 3	4	1 2 3 4	1 2 3 4

Fig. 9.1 Distribution of Nakshatras and their Charanas over Signs
(rashis)

9.2 BIRTH STAR OR *JANMA NAKSHATRA*

In a person's horoscope, various planets are placed in different signs occupying different degrees. The planets are accordingly placed in different *Nakshatras* also. We have already seen the significance of placement of planets in *rashis*. In addition to *rashi* there is significance attached to the placement of the planet in a *Nakshatra* within the *rashi*. Great significance is attached not only to the *rashi* but also to the *Nakshatra* within the *rashi* in which the Moon is placed at the time of birth. The term *Janma-Rashi* is used for the Moon-Sign at the time of birth. Similarly, the *Nakshatra* within the Janma *rashi* in which the Moon is placed at the time of birth is named *Janma-Nakshatra* or Birth-Star.

Janma-Nakshatra has definite well-proven influence upon the nature and personality of the native so much so that, for the purpose of marriage, the *Janma-Nakshatras* of the boy and the girl are matched. One important aspect is the Birth-Womb or *Janma-Yoni*, which refers to the name of the creature with which the shape of the constellation forming the *Nakshatra* resembles. Thus, *Ashwini*-born is horse or *Ashwa-Yoni*, *Bharani* is elephant or *Gaja-Yoni*, *U. Phalguni* is cow, *Chitra* is tiger and so on. Some *yonis* are not compatible with others. For example, there cannot be any compatibility between a cow and a tiger. Accordingly, for marriage, *U. Phalguni* and *Chitra* cannot be matched.

Further, the 27 *Nakshatras* are divided into three broad categories of 9 each as follows:

   (i)   *Dev-Gana*
   (ii) *Manushya-Gana*
   (iii) *Rakshas-Gana*

Dev means Angel. *Dev-Gana* natives are supposed to be angel-like. They may not be so totally as such because that will depend on many other factors as well, but they are certainly subtle and refined. *Manushya* means human. Natives born under *Manushya-Gana Nakshatras* are just human. And *Rakshasa* means demon. Natives born under these are really not demons. But, they may basically be gross and crude to some extent.

The important characteristics of natives of each *Nakshatra* from 1 to 27 are given below. In bracket is also given the category to which it belongs.

Ashwini (Dev)

In this *Nakshatra* there are groups of three stars each shining together making the shape of the mouth of a horse. *Ashwini* born is considered as born in the *Ashwa-yoni*.

Ashwini natives are beautiful. They like to dress up well. Females like to be adorned with jewellery. They possess calm temperament, and are usually fond of astrology and medicine.

Bharani (Manushya)

The shape of this *Nakshatra* is that of a womb. There are three prominent stars in it. *Bharani* natives have a great zest for life. They enjoy good health and prosperity. They seldom tell lies.

Note: In the following three *Nakshatras*, the Moon is exalted in the Taurus sign in the last three *Padas* of *Krittika*, whole of *Rohini*, and the first two *Padas* of *Mrigashira*. This gives the natives born in those *Padas* great mental and emotional strength.

Krittika (Rakshasa)

In this *Nakshatra*, seven stars are clearly visible. They form the shape of a horseshoe.

Krittika extends over the two *rashis* of *Mesh* and *Vrishabha* having qualities of either depending on the *rashi*. In addition, it has its own qualities like any other *Nakshatras*.

Krittika born are proud. They have great thirst for power, strong physique and good health. They are good eaters. They have excessive anger, and are easily driven to indulge in litigations. They may be cunning and deceitful. But they enjoy fame. Usually they have insatiable lust. Socially they move in high circles. They love astrology.

Rohini (Manushya)

Stars in *Rohini Nakshatra* are in the shape of a bullock-cart with narrow front and wide rear. *Rohini* natives are very beautiful. They have attractive personality. They are honest, truthful, generous and charitable. Females are full breasted. They have large eyes.

The Moon, representing the mind is not only in exaltation in *Rohini* but it is also in its own *Nakshatra*. Hence, *Rohini* natives have an unperturbed mind. They are interested in music, arts and crafts. They are cultured and sweet in speech.

Mrigashira (Dev)

It has three prominent stars. Its shape is that of the face of a deer with deer-like eyes.

It extends over *Vrishabha* and *Mithuna rashis*.

Mrigashira born are persevering in nature, even though they love easy life. Money comes to them easily. But, generally, they are timid, and suffer from inferiority complex.

They have tender feelings and enjoy the company of the opposite sex.

Ardra (Rakshasa)

There is one very bright star in *Ardra* shining like a gem. *Ardra* born are full of emotions. But they are usually not sincere or trustworthy. They are proud, quick-tempered and often self-centreed. They may be cruel, quarrelsome and deceitful, but sweet tongued. Basically, they are wanderers and cannot stay at one place.

Punarvasu (Dev)

There are four prominent stars in *Punarvasu* in the shape of a hermitage. It was the birth star of Lord Rama. 'Punah' means 'again', and 'Vasu' means 'abode'. Lord Rama was already established in the heart of the hermit Bharadwaj. But when Lord Rama in his incarnation appeared before the hermit, the Lord was established again in his heart rather in earthly physical form. The *Nakshatra* extends over *Mithuna* and *Karka rashis*.

Punarvasu natives are polite and tactful. They are clever in business dealings.

Pushya (Dev)

Pushya has three prominent stars forming the shape of an arrow. It is considered to be the most pious star. Natives of *Pushya* are basically *sadhakas*/seekers of the Supreme Truth. They are devoted to God. They have a balanced and calm mind. They are intellectually inclined, ascetic, righteous, dutiful, law abiding, noble and philanthropic.

They are, however, timid and cautious in their approach.

Ashlesha (Rakshasa)

This is the ninth *Nakshatra*. Stars in this *Nakshatra* are in the shape of 'Sudarshan Chakra', the divine wheel.

Ashlesha natives are, however, like villains. They enjoy torturing others. They may be insincere, cunning, ungrateful, selfish and licentious. They ignore others.

But they have a cheerful temperament. They are prominent eaters.

Makha (Rakshasa)

There are five stars in *Makha*. They form the shape of a house.

Makha natives are proud. They are usually not hard working. However, prosperity comes to them easily, and they live a long life of luxury. They love beautiful things and flowers. They are highly sexed.

Purva Phalguni (Manushya)

This *Nakshatra* has two stars. *Purva Phalguni* natives are artistic, sincere, philanthropic and noble hearted. They have pleasant disposition. They make good businessmen since they are tactful in speech, and also since they can foresee the outcome.

However, they have an unsteady mind, and they love seclusion.

Uttar Phalguni (Manushya)

This *Nakshatra* also has two stars. It extends over *Simha* and *Kanya rashis*.

Uttar Phalguni natives are proud, and a little short tempered. They are, otherwise, sincere, truthful and noble hearted. However, they suffer from poor appetite.

Hasta (Dev)

There are five stars in *Hasta* making the shape of a human hand. *Hasta* in Sanskrit means hand. With the Moon in its own *Nakshatra*, *Hasta* natives are noble, grateful and charitable.

They are sexual, and may be covetous. They may be fond of alcohol and music.

At times, however, they can be stealthy.

Chitra (Rakshasa)

There is one very bright star in *Chitra* looking like a pearl. The *Nakshatra* extends over *Kanya* and *Tula rashis*. *Chitra* born have a good physique, sexy and shapely figure and attractive features and eyes. They are fond of wearing good clothes and adorning themselves with ornaments. In general, they are good-natured.

They can, however, be stingy. Also they may be covetous of others' wives or husbands.

Swati (Dev)

There is just one star in *Swati*. It looks like a coral.

Swati natives are well known for their refined, dignified and polished manners. They are law abiding, and make very good citizens. They are dutiful and devoted to their parents and preceptors. They are logical and self-confident and make able administrators.

They are quite shy and possess great self-control. They may, however, be stubborn.

Note: In the next three *Nakshatras* the Moon is debilitated in Scorpio sign in the last *Pada* of *Vishakha* and all the *Padas* of Anuradha and *Jyeshtha*. This makes these natives emotionally weak and lacking in self-confidence.

Vishakha (*Rakshasa*)

It is constituted of five main stars forming an arch of a gate. It extends over *Tula* and *Vrishchika rashis*. *Vishakha* natives are god-fearing and honest.

At the same time, they may be aggressive, jealous, stingy, and a little short tempered.

Anuradha (*Dev*)

There are four stars in Anuradha. Its shape looks like that of 'Bali', devotee of God.

Moon here is in debility but in *Dev-Gana Nakshatra*. Anuradha natives are therefore patient, persevering, dutiful and god-fearing.

They have distinguishingly beautiful hair and eyelashes and great attraction for the opposite sex. They will find themselves luckier in foreign lands.

Jyeshtha (*Rakshasa*)

There are three prominent stars in *Jyeshtha* appearing like an earring.

Jyeshtha born are amorous and attractive to the opposite sex. They are quite charitable.

The Moon here is in debilitation, and in *Rakshasa-Gana Nakshatra* as well. As such, they have bad temper. They are generally cruel and secretive. They have few friends.

Moola (Rakshasa)

It consists of eleven stars forming the appearance of a lion.

Moola natives are firm and fixed in their own ideas and opinions. They are shrewd, clever and haughty. They keep away from their close relatives.

They are also very lazy and want to enjoy the fruits of others' labour.

Poorva Ashadh (Manushya)

There are four stars representing a stage. They are just like the four supports of any stage.

Though *Poorva Ashadha* natives are proud but at the same time they are generous, noble, kind hearted and charitable.

In any crowd, they will stand out. They are distinguished by their tall stature. They are sexual and they love opposite sex.

Though they are loyal friends but, at the same time, they can be dangerous enemies.

Uttar Ashadh (Manushya)

It has three prominent stars resembling an elephant's tooth. It extends over *Dhanu* and *Makara rashis*. *Uttar Ashadh* natives have strong muscular body with long nose, chiselled features and majestic appearance. They are fond of good food.

They have a pleasant disposition, and a gentle and kind nature.

Shravana (Dev)

There are three stars in *Shravana*. The shape is that of 'Trivikram, Vaman Bhagwan'.

With the Moon in its own *Nakshatra* here, *Shravana* natives have high intellect and noble heart. They are distinguished by their polite manners and dignified behaviour.

They have great zest for life. They may, however, be fond of drinking.

Dhanishtha (*Rakshasa*)

With four stars its shape is that of 'Mardal' a drum. It extends over *Makara* and *Kumbha rashis*.

Dhanishtha natives are ambitious and distinguished for their valour, courage and independent nature.

Shatabhisha (*Rakshasa*)

There are hundred stars in *Shatabhisha* but only one can be seen.

Shatabhisha natives are virtuous and truthful. They are generally loved by all.

However, they are uncompromising and self-serving.

Poorva Bhadra (*Manushya*)

There are two stars in *Poorva Bhadra*. It extends over *Kumbha* and *Meena rashis*.

Poorva Bhadra natives generally think less of themselves than their real worth. They are given to melancholy.

They are also prone to jealousy and greed.

Uttar Bhadra (*Manushya*)

There are two stars in *Uttar Bhadra*.

Uttar Bhadra natives are fond of arts and sciences. They are generally charitable and kind.

However, they are easily given to arguments and gossip, though they are tactful and diplomatic.

Revati (Dev)

There are thirty-two stars forming the shape of 'Mridang', an elongated drum.

Revati born have great attraction for the opposite sex. They have a well built figure and robust body.

Tactful and diplomatic, they have good manners, learning and riches.

Naming the Child

A child is often given such a name that the first syllable of the name conveys the *Nakshatra* and its *Charana* in which s/he is born. For example, a child born in *Charana* 1 of *Ashwini* may be named starting with the syllable *Chu*, and in *Charana* 2 with syllable *Che*, and so on. This information can be found in any book on Vedic astrology.

Nakshatras Designating *Panchak* Periods

Panchak means five days. In every lunar month, there is a period of five days when the Moon transits through Aquarius and Pisces passing over the five *Nakshatras*, *Dhanishtha*, *Shatabhisha*, *P. Bhadra*, *U. Bhadra* and *Revati*. This period is called *Panchak*. The period is not considered *shubha* for holding any auspicious ceremony such as marriage, etc.

Moola-Designated *Nakshatras*

Nakshatras falling at the junctions of the three groups are called *Moola* or *Ganda-Moola Nakshatras*. Thus we have *Ashlesha* and *Makha*, *Jyeshtha* and *Moola*, and *Revati* and *Ashwini*. Birth in these *Nakshatras* is quite harmful to the child or to the mother or to the family.

Most critical *Charanas* of these *Nakshatras* are *Ashlesha* 4, *Jyeshtha* 4, and *Revati* 4, and immediately next to them *Makha* 1, *Moola* 1 and *Ashwini* 1. They cause birth evil referred to as

Gand-Moolarishta. Survival of the child born under these is critical.

Of these, *Moola Nakshatra* is the most malefic. Birth under *Moola* 1 is harmful to father, and under *Moola* 2 to mother. Loss of money to parents is indicated under *Moola* 3.

Birth under *Jyeshtha* 1 is harmful to elder brother, and under *Jyeshtha* 2 and Revati 4 to younger brother.

Pacification of planets (*graha-shanti*) is usually advised at the time of birth of the child born under these *Nakshatras*.

Division of *Nakshatras* according to *Nadis*

The 27 *Nakshatras* are divided into three categories called *nadis* as shown in Fig. 9.2. The three *nadis* are:

1. *Aadya*. It means beginning. *Ashwini* is the first among *Aadya nadi Nakshatras*.
2. *Madhya*. It means middle. The first *Nakshatra* having *Madhya nadi* is *Bharani*.
3. *Antya*. It means end. The first *Nakshatra* having *Antya nadi* is *Krittika*.

AADYA	1.Ashwini 6.Ardra	7.Punarvasu	12.U. Phalguni
	13.Hasta	18.Jyeshtha	19.Moola
	24.Shatabhisha	25.P.Bhadra	
MADHYA	2.Bharni 5.Mrigashira	8.Pushya	11.P. Phalguni
	14.Chitra	17.Anuradha	20.P. Ashadh
	23.Dhanishtha	26.U.Bhadra	
ANTYA	3.Krittika 4.Rohini 9. Ashlesha 10.Makha 15.Swati		
	16.Vishakha 21.U.Ashadh 22.Shravana 27.Revati		

Fig. 9.2 Diagram showing division of Nakshatras according to nadis

9.3 MATCHING *RASHIS* FOR MARRIAGE

Marriage is not recommended at all between certain *rashis* as follows:

1. Persons belonging to adjacent Moon-Signs, viz., *rashis* in 2-12 positions, for example, between Aries and Taurus, or Taurus and Gemini, and so on. This will cause *Darridra-Yoga*. *Daridra* implies penury. The husband and wife will be constantly consuming each other. They will be draining each other's energy, finances and emotions. Even if the *Nakshatra* is the same, but *rashis* are adjacent such as *Krittika* in *Mesh* and *Krittika* in *Vrishabha*, they should not marry.

2. Person belonging to *rashis* in 6-8 positions. For example, Aries with Virgo or Scorpio, Taurus with Libra or Sagittarius, and so on should not marry. This causes *Shatru yoga*. *Shatru* means enemy. The husband and wife will remain inimical to each other. Best matches are made between *rashis* in 1-7, 3-11 and 4-10 positions subject to matching of *Nakshatras*. For example, for Aries, best *rashis* are Libra in 1-7 position, Gemini and Aquarius in 3-11 positions, and Cancer and Capricorn in 4-10 positions. Marriage between same *rashis* is also possible subject to matching of *Nakshatras*.

9.4 MATCHING NAKSHATRAS FOR MARRIAGE

For marriage, in addition to the *rashis*, the *Nakshatras* of the boy and the girl have to be matched. This is done in two respects, one is by matching the quality points (*gunas*), and the other is by avoiding *Nadi* defect (*nadi dosh*) as described in the following sections:

Matching Quality Points (*Gunas*)

Each *Nakshatra* represents certain inherent qualities of the native some of which have been described above. There are 9 quality factors to be matched each carrying 4 points aggregating to 36 points in all. If all factors match completely then there will be 36 points. For a successful marriage, it is stipulated that at least 18 points must match, the more the better.

The calculation for matching points is a one-time affair. Once the *Nakshatras* and *rashis* are known, the matching quality points or Gunas can be found by referring to a table developed from these calculations. The same are given in the table in Appendix C in which *rashis* are indicated by the first three letters of their names, and *Nakshatras* by the first two, except in the case of *Punarvasu*, *Ashlesha* and *Shatabhisha* which are indicated as PN, AL and SB to distinguish them from PU for *Pushya*, AS for *Ashwini* and SH for *Shravana*.

How to read the table? Mark the girl's *Nakshatra* on the left side. Move horizontally along the row. Mark the boy's *Nakshatra* on the top. Then move vertically down the column. Where the row and column cross, we get the matching points.

When a *Nakshatra* extends over two *rashis*, keep in mind that the *Padas/Charanas* in one *rashi* may match but those in the other *rashi* may or may not match. Note that the numbers in margins indicate as to how many *Padas* of *Nakshatra* fall under each *rashi*.

Note: (i) Table in Appendix C does not take care of 2–12 and 6–8 positions of the *rashis*.

To the matching points of the table, the following corrections must be applied.

(a) Subtract 4 points for 2–12 positions of *rashis*.

(b) Subtract 6 points for 6–8 positions of *rashis*.

(ii) *Dev-Gana Nakshatra* can adjust both with *Manushya* and *Rakshasa-Gana Nakshatras*. But *Rakshasa-Gana* and *Manushya* Gana cannot adjust at all with each other. This is called *Gana-Mahadosha*. Hence, marriage is prohibited between *Manushya* and *Rakshasa-Gana* natives. As far as points are concerned, one point for this defect/*dosha* may be subtracted from the points in table in Appendix C.

(iii) Subtract 3 points if the two *Nakshatras* belong to the same Nadi.

Although points to subtract have been specified, marriage is not recommended if any of the above defects/*dosha*s are present.

Nadi-Dosha

It is believed that even though the matching points may be high, one should not marry in the same Nadi. This will seriously affect the married life, family, progeny, etc. There is danger to the lives of the married couple. It is called *nadi dosh*.

To clarify further, if we see the table in Appendix C along its diagonal, we find that there are 28 matching points between people belonging to the same *Nakshatra* such as *Ashwini* with *Ashwini*, *Bharani* with *Bharani*, and so on. And, if we subtract 3 points as prescribed for *nadi-dosh*, even then there will be 28–3 = 25 matching points. But in spite of these high points, marriage is not recommended since they belong to the same *nadi*.

There is another reason because of which marriage between same *Nakshatras* is not recommended. Such people are likely to have the same planetary periods (See Chapter 10). Accordingly, if the planets are well-placed both will have good time, but if they are ill-placed then both will have bad time simultaneously. Good or evil effects will thus get multiplied.

Good effects are welcome though, but the ill effects may be difficult to bear.

Note: Here is a warning. High matching points are not a guarantee to happy married life. It depends on the placement of planets as well, and *Dashas* and transits at the time of marriage and the duration of married life.

Chapter 10

Planetary Periods (*Graha-Dashas*)

10.1 PREDICTING THE EVENTS

Thus far we have learnt how to interpret the birth chart of
the native and to describe his/her qualities and to tell
broadly 'what' is in store for him/her. But the question to be
answered now is 'when' the particular events will take place,
that is, when the good or bad effects of the planets will be
experienced based on their placement by sign, house, aspects,
etc., in the birth chart.

Take for example, the life of Pandit Jawaharlal Nehru.
He spent most of his youth in struggle and strife fighting for
India's freedom under the leadership of Mahatma Gandhi.
During the period of freedom struggle he could not even take
sufficient care of his wife when she was seriously ill and lost
her at a very young age. But when good times came, he
became the first Prime Minister of independent India, and
reigned over the country almost like an emperor for seventeen
years.

We all pass through such periods of misfortune and good fortune.

In Western astrology, predictions are made on the bases of transits and progressed horoscopes. But in Vedic/Hindu astrology, predictions are essentially based on planetary periods or *Graha-Dasha*. This is a very powerful tool of Vedic/Hindu astrology. There are major periods called *Maha-Dashas*, minor or sub-periods called *Antar-Dashas* and sub-minor periods called *Pratyantar-Dashas*. *Maha-Dasha* is generally referred to simply as *Dasha*, *Antar-Dasha* as simply *Antar* or *Bhukti*, and *Pratyantar-Dasha* as *Pratyantar*. **If a planet is strong and well placed, its period will be good for the houses it occupies, owns and aspects. Its period will also be good for the significations it represents. On the other hand, if it is weak and ill-placed, the same will be evil.**

Of course, the transits of planets over houses are also considered. Their results are usually superimposed on the results predicted by *Dashas*. And if transits predict the same thing/s as *Dashas* then the results are doubly confirmed.

Progressed horoscopes for a particular year, popularly called as *Varsha-Phal,* are also used in Vedic/Hindu astrology.

10.2 *VINSHOTTARI DASHAS*

There are a number of systems of planetary periods described in old texts. But only a few have survived. The ones that are still being used are the *Ashtottari* or 108 years system in Bengal and Gujarat, *Yogini* or 36 years system in Kashmir and Himachal, and *Tribhangi* in Nepal.

But the most popular system being universally followed in India is the *Vinshottari* or 120 years system. It is based on the assumption of 120 years as the expected life of man.

Out of 120, the major periods, viz., *Mahadashas* or the number of years during which each of the nine planets has sway on the life of the native are as follows:

Planet	Major Period (*Mahadasha*)	Planet	Major Period (*Mahadasha*)
1. Sun	6	6. Saturn	19
2. Moon	10	7. Mercury	17
3. Mars	7	8. Ketu	7
4. Rahu	18	9. Venus	20
5. Jupiter	16		
		Total	**120 years**

Why the planets have their periods in the above order, and why the numbers of years allotted to each planet are as above, apparently has no logic. Why should the Sun get only minimum 6 years when it is the largest around which all planets revolve, and why should Venus get the maximum 20 years when it is the second smallest merely and a satellite of the Sun is apparently not a matter of logic. As far as the order is concerned, it is in accordance with Table 9.1. It shows that the 9 planets rule over the three groups of 9 *Nakshatras* each from 1 to 9, 10 to 18, and 19 to 27 in cyclic order as given below:

	Nakshatras		Ruling Planet
1. *Ashwini*	10. *Makha*	19. *Moola*	1. Ketu
2. *Bharani*	11. *P. Phalguni*	20. *P. Ashadh*	2. Venus
3. *Krittika*	12. *U. Phalguni*	21. *U. Ashadh*	3. Sun
4. *Rohini*	13. *Hasta*	22. *Shravana*	4. Moon
5. *Mrigashira*	14. *Chitra*	23. *Dhanishtha*	5. Mars
6. *Ardra*	15. *Swati*	24. *Shatabhisha*	6. Rahu
7. *Punarvasu*	16. *Vishakha*	25. *P. Bhadra*	7. Jupiter
8. *Pushya*	17. *Anuradha*	26. *U. Bhadra*	8. Saturn
9. *Ashlesha*	18. *Jyeshtha*	27. *Revati*	9. Mercury

Thus, the *Mahadasha* at birth is that of Ketu if one is born under *Ashwini*, *Makha* or *Moola Nakshatras*, of Venus if born under *Bharani*, *P. Phalguni* or *P. Ashadh*, and so on. In spite of the absence of logic, it is a great wonder that the results predicted on the basis of *Vinshottari Dashas* are simply true and exact. This, therefore, can be treated as an occult mystery. In this matter one can only say that it is a divine revelation in Vedic astrology.

Now, each *Mahadasha* is further sub-divided into 9 *Antardasha*. For example, the 6 years *Mahadasha* of the Sun has 9 *Antardasha*, starting with the Sun's own *Antardasha* in its *Mahadasha* followed by the *Antardashas* of the Moon, Mars, Rahu, Jupiter, Saturn, Mercury, Ketu and Venus. Likewise, the Moon has 9 *Antardasha* starting with its own followed by those of Mars, Rahu, etc, in that order. The periods of other planets are sub-divided in a similar manner starting with the planets' own *Antardasha*. The calculations are done by unitary method of proportions. Calculate, for example, the period of the Moon's *Antardasha*/Bhukti in the Sun's *Mahadasha* of a total period of 6 years:

The Moon gets a total of 10 years out of 120 years.
In a period of 6 years of the Sun, the Moon gets (10/120) x 6 = 1/2 year, viz., 6 months.

Thus, *Antardasha* of the Moon in the 6 years *Mahadasha* of the Sun lasts for just 6 months. Likewise, other minor periods can be calculated as given in Table 10.1.

Table 10.1
Duration of Minor Periods/*Antardashas* in Major
Periods/*Mahadashas* of Planets

1. SUN	Y	M	D	2. MOON	Y	M	D
Sun	0	3	18	Moon	0	10	0
Moon	0	6	0	Mars	0	7	0
Mars	0	4	6	Rahu	1	6	0
Rahu	0	10	24	Jupiter	1	4	0
Jupiter	0	9	18	Saturn	1	7	0
Saturn	0	11	12	Mercury	1	5	0
Mercury	0	10	6	Ketu	0	7	0
Ketu	0	4	6	Venus	1	8	0
Venus	1	0	0	Sun	0	6	0
TOTAL	**6 Years**			**TOTAL**	**10 Years**		

3. MARS	Y	M	D	4. RAHU	Y	M	D
Mars	0	4	27	Rahu	2	8	12
Rahu	1	0	18	Jupiter	2	4	24
Jupiter	0	11	6	Saturn	2	10	6
Saturn	1	1	9	Mercury	2	6	18
Mercury	0	11	27	Ketu	1	0	18
Ketu	0	4	27	Venus	3	0	0
Venus	1	2	0	Sun	0	10	24
Sun	0	4	6	Moon	1	6	0
Moon	0	7	0	Mars	1	0	18
TOTAL	**7 Years**			**TOTAL**	**18 Years**		

5. JUPITER	Y	M	D	6. SATURN	Y	M	D
Jupiter	2	1	18	Saturn	3	0	3
Saturn	2	6	12	Mercury	2	8	9
Mercury	2	3	6	Ketu	1	1	9
Ketu	0	11	6	Venus	3	2	0
Venus	2	8	0	Sun	0	11	12
Sun	0	9	18	Moon	1	7	0

contd.

5. JUPITER	Y	M	D		6. SATURN	Y	M	D
Moon	1	4	0		Mars	1	1	9
Mars	0	11	6		Rahu	2	10	6
Rahu	2	4	24		Jupiter	2	6	12
Total	**16 Years**				**TOTAL**	**19 Years**		

7. MERCURY	Y	M	D		8. KETU	Y	M	D
Mercury	2	4	27		Ketu	0	4	27
Ketu	0	11	27		Venus	1	2	0
Venus	2	10	0		Sun	0	4	6
Sun	0	10	6		Moon	0	7	0
Moon	1	5	0		Mars	0	4	27
Mars	0	11	27		Rahu	1	0	18
Rahu	2	6	18		Jupiter	0	11	6
Jupiter	2	3	6		Saturn	1	1	9
Saturn	2	8	9		Mercury	0	11	27
Total	**17 Years**				**TOTAL**	**7 Years**		

9. VENUS	Y	M	D
Venus	3	4	0
Sun	1	0	0
Moon	1	8	0
Mars	1	2	0
Rahu	3	0	0
Jupiter	2	8	0
Saturn	3	2	0
Mercury	2	10	0
Ketu	1	2	0
Total	**20 Years**		

Note: 'Y' 'M' and 'D' in the table refer to number of years, months and days respectively. In each *Antardasha*, further sub-divisions called *Pratyantar Dashas*, and still finer sub-divisions, known as *Sukshma Dashas*, can also be made to make the predictions more precise. But, the accuracy of predictions from finer sub-divisions will depend on the accuracy with which the time of birth is known.

10.3 BALANCE OF MAJOR PERIOD/*MAHADASHA* AT BIRTH

What are the current *Dashas* a native is passing through? To know this we have to first find the periods at birth, both major and minor. The *Mahadasha* at birth depends on the *Nakshatra* in which the Moon is placed at the time of birth. It corresponds to that of the Lord of the *Nakshatra*. Thus, if a native is born when the Moon is in Aries, and its longitude is, say, 6 degrees that is in *Ashwini Nakshatra*, then the *Mahadasha* at the time of birth is that of *Ashwini* Lord Ketu. In the sample horoscope in Chapter 3, the native is born with Moon at 3 S 5 D 12 M longitude, which is in *Pushya Nakshatra*. Hence, the *Mahadasha* at birth is that of its Lord Saturn.

Note: To find the *Dashas* at birth, nothing else but only the longitude of the Moon in the sidereal/*Nirayana* zodiac is required.

Next question, therefore, is to find how much of the *Mahadasha* period had elapsed before taking birth and how much of it was in balance to be undergone by the native after birth. To do this let us again consider the example horoscope.

Now, each *Nakshatra* extends over 13 D and 20 M, that is, 13x60+20 = 800 M. If the native had been born at the commencement of *Pushya*, which is at 3 S 3 D 20 M, then there would have been a full balance of 800 minutes of the Moon's motion, and a full balance of *Mahadasha* of Saturn extending over 19 years to be undergone after birth. But the native is born with the Moon at 3 S 5 D 12 M. How much is the balance distance, we find as follows:

	S	D	M
Longitude where *Pushya* ends	3	16	40
Longitude of the Moon at birth	3	5	12
Balance distance	0	11	28

Thus, 11 D 28 M, that is, 11 x 60 + 28 = 688 M remain in balance. Now, we use the unitary method or the method of proportions again.

For 800 M balance, the period is 19 years.

For 1 M   ,,   ,,   19/800 years.

For 688 M   ,,   ,,   (19/800) x 688 = 16.34 years.

This comes to 16 Y 4 M 10 D considering 365 days in a year. Table 10.2 is an easy reckoner to find the *rashi* and balance of *Dasha* in terms of Moon's longitude at birth.

10.4 CURRENT MAJOR PERIOD/*MAHADASHA*

In the sample, starting from the date the native was born, we can find out the major periods *Mahadashas* written simply as just *Dashas* as follows:

	Y	M	D
Date of birth	1934	8	8
Saturn *Dasha* balance	16	4	10
Saturn *Dasha* ends	1950	12	18
Mercury *Dasha*	17	0	0
Mercury *Dasha* ends	1967	12	18
Ketu *Dasha*	7	0	0
Ketu *Dasha* ends	1974	12	18
Venus *Dasha*	20	0	0
Venus *Dasha* ends	1994	12	18
Sun *Dasha*	6	0	0
Sun *Dasha* ends	2000	12	18
Moon *Dasha*	10	0	0
Moon *Dasha* ends	2010	12	18
Mars *Dasha*	7	0	0
Mars *Dasha* ends	2017	12	18
Rahu *Dasha*	18	0	0

contd.

	Y	M	D
Rahu *Dasha* ends	2035	12	18
Jupiter *Dasha*	16	0	0
Jupiter *Dasha* ends	2051	12	18
Saturn *Dasha*	19	0	0

Table 10.2
Balance of *Vinshottari Dashas* at Birth

Nirayana Longitude of Moon at Birth		Mesh Simha Dhanu			Vrishabha Kanya Makara			Mithuna Tula Kumbha			Karka Vrishchika Meena		
D	M	Y	M	D	Y	M	D	Y	M	D	Y	M	D
00	00	KET 7	0	0	SUN 4	6	0	MAR 3	6	0	JUP 4	0	0
01	00	6	5	21	4	0	18	2	11	21	2	9	18
02	00	5	11	12	3	7	6	2	5	12	1	7	6
03	00	5	5	3	3	1	24	1	11	3	0	4	24
03	20	5	3	0	3	0	0	1	9	0	SAT 19	0	0
04	00	4	10	24	2	8	12	1	4	24	18	0	18
05	00	4	4	15	2	3	0	0	10	15	16	7	15
06	00	3	10	6	1	9	18	0	4	6	15	2	12
06	40	3	6	0	1	6	0	RAH 18	0	0	14	3	0
07	00	3	3	27	1	4	6	17	6	18	13	9	9
08	00	2	9	18	0	10	24	16	2	12	12	4	6
09	00	2	3	9	0	5	12	14	10	6	10	11	3
10	00	1	9	0	MOO 10	0	0	13	6	0	9	6	0
11	00	1	2	31	9	3	0	12	1	24	8	0	27
12	00	0	8	12	8	6	0	10	9	18	6	7	24
13	00	0	2	3	7	9	0	9	5	12	5	2	21
13	20	VEN 20	0	0	7	6	0	9	0	0	4	9	0
14	00	19	0	0	7	0	0	8	1	6	3	9	18
15	00	17	6	0	6	3	0	6	9	0	2	4	15
16	00	16	0	0	5	6	0	5	4	24	0	11	12
16	40	15	0	0	5	0	0	4	6	0	MER 17	0	0
17	00	14	6	0	4	9	0	4	0	18	16	6	27
18	00	13	0	0	4	0	0	2	8	12	15	3	18
19	00	11	6	0	3	3	0	1	4	6	14	0	9
20	00	10	0	0	2	6	0	JUP 16	0	0	12	9	0
21	00	8	6	0	1	9	0	14	9	18	11	5	21
22	00	7	0	0	1	0	0	13	7	6	10	2	12
23	00	5	6	0	0	3	0	12	4	24	8	11	3
23	20	5	0	0	MAR 7	0	0	12	0	0	8	6	0
24	00	4	0	0	6	7	24	11	2	12	7	7	24
25	00	2	6	0	6	1	15	10	0	0	6	4	15
26	00	1	0	0	5	7	6	8	9	12	5	1	6

contd.

Nirayana Longitude of Moon at Birth		Mesh Simha Dhanu			Vrishabha Kanya Makara			Mithuna Tula Kumbha			Karka Vrishchika Meena		
26	40	**SUN** 6	0	0	5	3	0	8	0	0	4	3	0
27	00	5	10	6	5	0	27	7	7	6	3	9	27
28	00	5	4	24	4	6	18	6	4	24	2	6	18
29	00	4	11	12	4	0	9	5	2	12	1	3	9
29	20	4	9	18	3	10	0	4	9	18	0	10	6
29	40	4	7	24	3	8	3	4	4	24	0	5	3
30	00	4	6	0	3	6	0	4	0	0	0	0	0

So, if one wants to know what would be the *Mahadasha* current during the year 2004, one can simply refer to the above calculations and say that the *Dasha* will be that of Moon.

10.5 BALANCE OF MINOR PERIOD/*ANTARDASHA*/ *BHUKTI* AT BIRTH

Let us learn this also by taking the case of sample horoscope. The period of Saturn, elapsed while native was still in the womb, can now be found as follows:

	Y	M	D
Total period of Saturn	19	0	0
Balance period of Saturn	16	4	10
Period elapsed in womb	2	7	20

As the Saturn *Antardasha* in Saturn *Mahadasha* extends over 3 years and 3 days, this shows that when the native was born Saturn *Antardasha* in Saturn *Mahadasha* was on. The balance period of Saturn *Antardasha* can be found as follows:

	Y	M	D
Period of Saturn *Antardasha*	3	0	3
Period elapsed in womb	2	7	20
Balance *Antardasha* of Saturn	0	4	13

10.6 CURRENT MINOR PERIOD/*ANTARDASHA*/ *BHUKTI*

Now, if one wants to know what would be the *Antardasha* current on 8 August 2006, one simply can do the calculations for *Antardasha* using Table 10.1 as shown below:

	Y	M	D
Moon *Dasha* begins	2000	12	18
Moon *Antar*	0	10	0
Moon *Antar* ends	2001	10	18
Mars *Antar*	0	7	0
Mars *Antar* ends	2002	5	18
Rahu *Antar*	1	6	0
Rahu *Antar* ends	2003	11	18
Jupiter *Antar*	1	4	0
Jupiter *Antar* ends	2005	3	18
Saturn *Antar*	1	7	0
Saturn *Antar* ends	2006	10	18
Mercury *Antar*	1	5	0
Mercury *Antar* ends	2008	3	18
Ketu *Antar*	0	7	0
Ketu *Antar* ends	2008	10	18
Venus *Antar*	1	8	0
Venus *Antar* ends	2010	6	18
Sun *Antar*	0	6	0
Sun *Antar* ends	2010	12	18
Moon *Mahadasha* also ends.			

It can be seen from the above calculations that on 8 August 2006 it will be Saturn *Antardasha* in the the Moon *Mahadasha*.

10.7 GENERAL PRINCIPLES OF PREDICTION FROM DASHAS

The following principles must be kept in mind while judging the events during *dashas* of planets:

A planet during its *Dasha* gives effects relating to its *karakattvas*, the houses it owns, tenants and aspects, the houses of which it is *karaka*, and those it owns in the *Kaal Purush Kundali*.

If the planet is Lord of *shubha* houses, good results will follow in its *Dasha* provided it is placed in favourable signs and good houses. And if the planet is Lord of *ashubha* houses, bad results will follow. The best periods of one's life are those of the *Dashas* of *lagna* and Trine Lords.

Natural benefics promote and natural malefics damage the house/s tenanted and aspected.

The other rules are as follows:

(i) If a planet owns two houses, one good and the other bad, it shows good effects if it tenants the good house, and bad effects if it tenants the bad house irrespective of its ownership of the other house.

(ii) If a planet is strong in *lagna* but weak or debilitated in *Navansha*, it does not show much good effects, rather it may show some evil effects. On the other hand, if a planet is weak in *lagna* but strong or exalted in *Navansha*, it may show good effects and the evil effects get mitigated.

(ii) *Dashas* of a planet that happens to be an enemy of the Lord of the *lagna* will not be generally good for the native. The overall effect will of course depend on the placement of the planet.

(iv) Planets that are placed in good positions, trine 5-9 or sextile 3-11, in the chart will act as friends even if they

194 LEARN, THINK AND PREDICT THROUGH ASTROLOGY

are natural enemies. *Antardasha* of one during the *Mahadasha* of the other will tend to be good. On the other hand, planets that are placed in evil positions such as quincunx 6-8 or semi-sextile 2-12 will act as enemies, and their mutual periods will not be good. The effects of planets that are in opposition 1-7 depend very much on their mutual relationship.

(v) *Dashas* of retrograde planets are not generally good for health.

(iv) *Dashas* of combust planets give results of death-like situations.

(vi) *Dashas* of planets in debilitation and in enemy's signs give unfavourable results.

(viii) *Dashas* of planets in exaltation, own or friend's signs give very good results.

The prominant significations that will flourish during the *Dasha* of the planet provided it is strong would be as follows:

Sun: Gain in status. Period of penance (*tapasya*). Interest in spirituality.

Moon: Happiness to/from home/mother. Enjoyment of female company.

Mars: Gain of health/stamina/courage/valour/property.

Mercury: Intelligence, education, knowledge, communication, arts and skills, speech, etc.

Jupiter: Wisdom, piousness, magnanimity, wealth and happiness, children's welfare, etc.

Venus: Good wife, female company, love, romance, comforts, conveyances, etc.

Saturn: No suffering. Success in career. Principles and discipline, strong nerves, etc.

Rahu: Cleverness, material gains, gains from foreign sources, etc.

Ketu: Courage, religiousness, gains, name/fame, etc.

The primary effects of ownership of a house during the *Dasha* of the planet would be the following:

Lagnesh: Good health and overall well-being. Period of *lagna* Lord is always good.

Dwitiyesh/Dhanesh: Acquisition of wealth. Since it is *maraka* also, may become cause of illness, even death if the *Dasha* comes at such an age.

Tritiyesh/Parakramesh: One puts in all efforts in the fulfilment of one's aims. Results average.

Chaturthesh/Sukhesh: Mental peace and happiness, happiness to/from mother, comforts of home/conveyance, acquiring of property/house, etc.

Panchamesh/Vidya/Putra Bhavesh: Good period. Higher education, happiness to/from children, love life, etc.

Shashthesh/Rog/Shatru Bhavesh: Illness. Good health if well placed. Fear of enemies. *Ashubha* results for spouse.

Saptamesh/Kalatra Bhavesh: Happiness to/from spouse. Improvement in business, foreign trade/visits. Since it is *maraka* also, illness, even death, may result in proper age.

Ashtamesh/Aayur Bhavesh: Fear of death. Sudden losses, chronic diseases. If malefic, chances of death. If well placed, may give long life, sudden gains and wisdom.

Navamesh/Bhagyesh/Dharma Bhavesh: Best period of one's life. Good fortune. Dharma grows. Children prosper and give happiness.

Dashamesh/Karmesh: Success in career. Government support, promotion, name, fame, happiness to/from father, etc.

Ekadashesh/Labhesh: Gains, increase in income, fulfillment of desires, etc.

Dwadashesh/Vyayesh: Losses, expenditure, waste of energy, scandals, physical and mental suffering, worries, etc. Takes one to pilgrimages, brings gains from foreigners and visits abroad, leads to detachment, renunciation, etc., if benefic and well placed.

10.8 PREDICTING EVENTS FROM *DASHAS*

Let us now predict or confirm events in the life of the native in sample horoscope in Fig. 3.1 on the basis of *Vinshottari Dashas* keeping in mind that it belongs to a male nativity.

We first describe the over-riding *Mahadasha* influences over the major periods, and then superimpose the *Antardasha* events on them for the durations of the minor periods.

Saturn *Mahadasha*/16 Years 4 Months 10 Days

Saturn is placed in the tenth house a *kendra* in *moola-trikona* sign. This bestows on the native the Great Man or *Maha-Purush-Yoga*. See Chapter 12 for *yogas*. Saturn is Lord of both the ninth and tenth, the most powerful *trikona* and *kendra*. Hence, Saturn is a great benefic, *Raja-Yoga karaka*. It is further placed in the most benefic house among the *kendras*. Hence, *Raja-Yoga* is confirmed. However, malefic Saturn throws its aspects as an enemy on the twelfth, fourth, and seventh houses. Accordingly, though Saturn is very good for the ninth and tenth houses and its own significations, it is bad for the three houses aspected. The native is deprived of pleasures of the bed, domestic happiness and mother's *sukha*, and marital happiness. Even for the tenth house, since it is a malefic, it is not good for happiness to/from father. The native is otherwise very very fortunate.

These effects were most pronounced during Saturn *Antar* in Saturn *Dasha* current at the time of birth when the native's mother died only a few months after his birth.

The native could not receive the love of his father either during the entire Saturn period since the father got remarried soon.

Other major events occurred towards the end of Saturn *Dasha* during Antars of Rahu and Jupiter. Rahu is very well placed in friend's sign in ninth house of destiny, long travel and spirituality. Rahu also aspects its exaltation sign Taurus in *lagna* and own sign Virgo in fifth. The planet is also significator for grandfather. It was only during Rahu *Antar* in Saturn *Dasha* that the native had good time. He left his parents, went away to another city, joined a very good school, and lived with his grandparents who loved him dearly.

Now, Jupiter, though a great natural benefic, is a great malefic in native's chart since it is Lord of the eighth and eleventh. It has death/great loss inflicting potential with suddenness. So, as destiny would have it, the native returned to his father and stepmother during Jupiter *Antar* in Saturn Dasha, and thereafter his trials and tribulations began again.

Mercury *Mahadasha*/17 Years

This was the beginning of a very good period at the age of 16 plus. Mercury, a benefic, is the Lord of two good houses, the second and fifth, a trine, and is significator for the tenth house. It is placed in the third house of valour/*Purushartha*/

Parakram. Also, as second Lord, it is placed in the second from the second. This endows wealth, good family and speech, and enjoyment of good food. It is also placed in the eleventh position of gain, with respect to the fifth house of education and children. Mercury, a great friend of Saturn, also aspects the ninth house of destiny, travels etc. Prominent features of Mercury period were, therefore, attainment of high education, starting and growth of meritotius career as professor, begetting of children and family, happiness from them, good fortune, travel, accumulation of wealth, and so on. Results during *Antars* were as follows:

Mercury *Antar:* The native's sufferings were over. He left home for higher studies. He was selected through competition for admission into a prestigious engineering university.

Ketu *Antar:* Ketu in third is best for endeavours. He successfully worked in his studies.

Venus *Antar:* Venus is benefic being *lagna* Lord. Good period. Completed studies.

Sun *Antar:* Sun in third in a great friend's sign is a very good position for efforts, valour, stamina, etc. The Sun is the *karaka* for the first and the tenth. The native got his first job.

Moon *Antar:* The Moon is a great benefic being in its own sign in the third house of endeavours, reading, writing, etc. Native got a teaching and research position in the most prestigious institute of the country. The Moon is significator for female company. He also got married.

Mars *Antar:* Mars is benefic as the Lord of seventh. It is Lord of twelfth house of foreign lands. From second, it aspects fifth house of education. It also aspects the eighth house of sudden gain in a friendly sign, and ninth of destiny, long travel, etc., in its sign of exaltation. The native got a great opportunity to go to the USA on scholarship to pursue postgraduate programme. Mars is not good for happiness from spouse as it is placed in the eighth from the seventh. As a result, during this period he remained separated from wife.

Rahu *Antar:* The native had a son and daughter born. *Dasha* Lord Mercury is a male eunuch while *Antardasha* Lord Rahu is female. Hence, the birth of a son and a daughter. Remember that Mercury is good for the second, third, fifth, and ninth, and Rahu for the first, fifth and ninth houses. Mercury and Rahu *Dashas* together led to native's promotion also.

Jupiter *Antar:* It is a great malefic for Taurus *lagna* because of its lordships of eighth and eleventh. Once again, Jupiter acted as malefic to the native. *Dasha* Lord Mercury is Lord of second house of wealth. During the Jupiter *Antar* the native suffered sudden loss of his expensive precious jewels by his own mistake.

Saturn *Antar:* As expected, matters of ninth and tenth houses prospered but the matters of twelfth, fourth and seventh suffered. The native earned a Doctorate degree, got promoted to a Professor's post, visited UK for a year on post-doctoral fellowship, and earned recognition from authorities, and name and fame in the country. But, he had no domestic happiness and remained estranged from his wife.

Ketu *Mahadasha*/7 Years

Malefic Ketu is best placed in the third house of valour, endeavours, Parakrama, Purushartha, stamina, reading, writing, etc. The prominent feature of this 7-year period was the hard work the native put in his work. He had many achievements to his credit.

Noteworthy things during some *Antardashas* were the following. During the Moon *Antar* he had pleasant female company. During the Mars *Antar* he became full Professor. Note Mars' aspect on the ninth house of fortune in its exaltation sign. During the Rahu *Antar*, his romantic affair blossomed. Note that Rahu aspects the fifth house of love and children in its own sign. He also had another daughter. A female birth is predicted during the Rahu period. During the Saturn *Antar* he became head of the department, a boost in the ninth and tenth house affairs. He was greatly respected at that time. During the Mercury *Antar*, he guided many students for Ph.D. work, a matter of higher education, intelligence, etc., represented by the fifth house and Mercury.

Venus *Mahadasha*/20 Years

Venus as *lagna* Lord in the second, its natural house, in great friend Mercury's, sign is very well placed for wealth, family, etc. The Venus *Dasha* was therefore marked by family growth, native doting on his family, and accumulation of wealth, assets, etc. However, since Venus is also the sixth Lord, the native had to deal with illnesses, and some opposition. Mars afflicts Venus, *karaka* for wife. In fact the chart suffers from *mangalik dosha* in all three respects with Mars in second with respect to *lagna*, in twelfth from Moon and in conjunction with Venus. Add to this the evil aspects of Saturn on the twelfth, fourth and seventh house. Hence, the relationship with the wife remained unhappy. It broke down completely during the Mars *Antar*. Note that Mars is placed in the eighth from the seventh. Effects during Antars were as follows:

Venus *Antar*: Native was able to accumulate some money as a result of an assignment.

Sun *Antar:* Sun being the fourth Lord, the native was able to purchase his own conveyance.

Moon *Antar:* The Moon being significator for travel in the third house of short travel aspecting the ninth house of long travel, took the native to England. He had company of female friends. Wrote and published a book, a matter of signification both of the third house and *Mahadasha* Lord Mercury.

Rahu *Antar:* Rahu represents foreigners/foreign lands. Once again, native had a foreign assignment. He was able to better his fortune and well being implying matters of ninth and first houses. A little love also flourished for a while, a matter of the fifth house.

Jupiter *Antar:* Once again, Jupiter proved to be very inauspicious. Venus as *lagna* Lord represents body, more particularly head. Native had a fatal accident suffering head injury. But he gained from Jupiter's favourable aspect on the eleventh house in its own sign. He was able to find a match for his daughter, a matter concerning eleventh house of children's spouses.

Saturn *Antar:* Matters of the fourth, seventh and twelfth houses suffered again. But matters of significations of Saturn, and the ninth and tenth houses flourished. He once again went to the USA, this time as a visiting professor. His name and fame spread further as a renowned professor and author.

Mercury and Ketu *Antars:* Engaged himself in writing another book, a third house subject.

Sun *Mahadasha*/6 Years

The Sun represents spirit/soul. This was a period of soul searching, a kind of penance/*tapa*. The native went on a number of pilgrimages during this period. The Sun is well placed in third in great friend's house. As a malefic in the third also, it is very good. It enhances valour, capacity to work, stamina, etc. However, as Lord of the fourth in the third, twelfth from fourth, it is adverse for happiness in general. The native remained mentally troubled. The fourth house and the Sun are both significators for heart. The *Dasha* affected the native's physical and emotional heart so much so that the native had a massive heart attack during Jupiter's *Antar*.

Moon *Mahadasha*/ 10 Years

The *Dasha* began on 19 December 2000. The Moon, significator for mind, love, female company, etc., is placed in its own sign in third house of valour, courage, stamina, reading, writing work, etc. This period was distinguished by optimism, facing of life with courage, sagacity of mind, the Moon's significations, taking up of some good work again after retirement such as meditation and pranic healing, pleasant relations with siblings, third house matters, female company, etc. Moon in third in own sign proved to be the divine protector.

During the Moon, Mars and Rahu *Antars*, the native mostly spent his time on foreign visits.

It is noteworthy that the native went through serious ill-health problems relating to the digestive system during eighth Lord Jupiter's *Antar*. Jupiter is also in Virgo, the sixth house of disease and digestive system in K-P kundali.

And, the Saturn *Antar* has now begun with significant professional gains.

Note: The above descriptions are not exhaustive. These are meant only to demonstrate the approach one has to adopt in analysing a horoscope and making predictions on the basis of *Dashas*.

10.9 *DASHA* SYSTEM IN *LAAL-KITAAB*

Laal-Kitaab has its own *Dasha* system. The periods of planets in this system are fixed for everyone irrespective of *Janma-Nakshatra*. The same are as follows:

Dasha of Planet	Year/s of Life
Saturn	1 to 6
Rahu	7 to 12
Ketu	13 to 15
Jupiter	16 to 21
Sun	22 to 23
Moon	24
Venus	25 to 27
Mars	28 to 33
Mercury	34 to 35

Accordingly, Saturn governs the first six years of one's life. If Saturn is placed in the eighth house of chronic illness in a chart, that is, in the natural house of Mars, Saturn's enemy, then the child may get some illness soon after birth. If Saturn is in the eleventh, the natural house of Aquarius, it will bring good luck to the child.

After Saturn, it is Rahu' period for the next six years, and Ketu's period for the next three. This is the period when children do not find it easy to concentrate. These planets, in any case, disturb our mind. If Ketu is placed in evil/*ashubha* houses, then it is just possible that the child begins to slide down in studies.

Jupiter predominates in life during 16 to 21 years of age. This is the time, one becomes adult and mature, and aims to progress in life. If Jupiter is not well placed, then the start of life and career may not be up to one's aspirations.

Years 22 and 23 have the effect of the Sun, matters of spirit, enthusiasm, etc.

Year 24 has the effect of the Moon, that is, mind, emotions, etc.

Venus has its effects during years 25 to 27, controlling matters of love and romance, Mars during 28 to 33 governing period of hard work, and Mercury during 34 and 35 implying all round progress, dealings and relationships.

Thus, this is a 35-year cycle.

After this, the next 35-year cycle begins again starting with Saturn at first as before. When the second cycle is completed, the third begins.

The important thing is that this cycle is also proven to be effectively true. The actual effects, whether favourable or unfavourable, depend on the placement of planets in the birth chart.

Chapter 11

Transits of Planets
(*Gochar Grahas*)

11.1 WHAT IS TRANSIT?

The birth chart remains fixed for the whole life. The positions of planets in the birth chart are referred to as radical or natal positions. So we have radical or natal Sun, radical or natal Moon, and so on.

But the planets in space keep moving in orbits. They keep transiting through different signs in the zodiac, and hence through different houses in the birth chart. The Sanskrit word for transit is *Gochar*. These positions of planets at any particular time in life are, therefore, referred to as their transit or *Gochar* positions in the chart. Thus we have transit or *Gochar* Sun, transit or *Gochar* Moon, and so on.

In Western astrology, predictions are based primarily on transits. In Vedic/Hindu astrology, considerations of transits are essential to confirm certain predictions based on planetary periods/*Dashas*.

Further, in Western astrology, transits are judged from the Sun-Sign. In Vedic/Hindu astrology, transits are judged from the Moon-Sign although no less important are the effects of transits with respect to *lagna*.

Suppose your *lagna* is Taurus and the Moon is in Cancer as in the sample horoscope. Then, when we say Transit or Gochar Jupiter is in the seventh, it means that Jupiter is in Capricorn with respect to the natal Moon. It is otherwise in the ninth with respect to the *lagna*. It is therefore essential to state whether the transit is with respect to the *lagna* or the Sun or the Moon.

11.2 FAVOURABLE/AUSPICIOUS AND UNFAVOURA-BLE/ INAUSPICIOUS TRANSIT POSITIONS

Transits of Jupiter and Saturn have strong and long lasting influences, as they are huge planets, and they stay in each sign for long periods, viz., 1-year and 2(1/2)-years respectively. Rahu and Ketu that stay in each sign for 1(1/2)-year period also have marked influence. The Sun, Mars, Mercury and Venus each remain in a sign close to one month. The native can easily see their influences by observing changes in life pattern every time the planet changes sign and hence the house.

As far as the Moon is concerned it is the fastest moving planet. It changes sign and house every two and a half days. Just observing one's own moods one can easily see its effect.

The two basic and simple rules about transits of planets in general are as follows:

(i) Malefics, Mars, Saturn, Rahu and Ketu show good results when they transit the third, sixth and eleventh houses.
(ii) All planets are evil when they transit the fourth, eighth and twelfth houses.

What is *Vedha*?

Vedha in Sanskrit means obstruction. Now, when a planet A is transiting a certain house, and another planet B is transiting another house sensitive to A, it is supposed to offer obstruction to the effects of A. This position of B is named as *Vedha* position. It is equivalent to obstruction of light coming from source A by object B.

The auspicious and corresponding *Vedha* positions of planets are as follows:

Sun:	Auspicious	III	VI	X	XI					
	Vedha	IX	XII	IV	V					
Moon:	Auspicious	I	III	VI	VII	X	XI			
	Vedha	V	IX	XII	II	IV	VIII			
Mars/Saturn:	Auspicious	III	VI	XI						
Rahu/Ketu:	Vedha	XII	IX	V						
Mercury:	Auspicious	II	IV	VI	VIII	X	XI			
	Vedha	V	III	IX	I	VIII	II			
Jupiter:	Auspicious	II	V	VII	IX	XI				
	Vedha	XII	IV	III	X	VIII				
Venus:	Auspicious	I	II	III	IV	V	VIII	IX	XI	XII
	Vedha	VII	VII	I	X	IX	V	XI	VI	III

Note: (i) Actual results, whether good or evil, will also depend on the sign of transit.

(ii) There is no *Vedha* between Sun and Saturn because the Sun is the father of Saturn.

(iii) There is no *Vedha* between Sun and Mars either.

(vi) There is no *Vedha* between Moon and Mercury as the Moon is Mercury's father.

Transit Jupiter/*Gochar* Brihaspati Favouring Marriage

Transits of Jupiter play the most significant role in triggering possibilities of marriage if the *Dashas* are favourable. Marriage is possible only when either the fifth house of love or the eleventh of fulfilment of desires or both are involved by transits of Jupiter. Thus, years during which Jupiter transits the fifth and eleventh houses promote marriage. Transits of Jupiter through the second, seventh and ninth houses also support marriage. Transits through the first, fourth, sixth, eighth and tenth houses rule out marriage, as the same are twelfth from marriage promoting houses.

The counting is done from the Moon or from the *lagna* whichever is stronger.

Transits of Saturn and *Saadhe-Satti*

Saadhe-Satti means 7(1/2)-years period. It refers to transit Saturn or *Gochar Shani*. When Saturn transits over the Moon sojourning for 2(1/2)-years in each of the three houses that are twelfth, first and second from the Moon, then the native is said to be undergoing a period of *Saadhe-Satti*.

This is usually a period of great hardship for the native involving losses, expenditure, ill-health, mental agony and family problems. The actual effects basically depend on the significations of the houses transited. In the sample horoscope, since the Moon is in third, *Saadhe-Satti* will mean transit of Saturn over the second, third and fourth houses. Accordingly, the native will suffer agony in matters pertaining to the second house such as family problems, loss of wealth, etc., and serious illness since aspecting the eighth house from there, third house such as differences with brothers/sisters, etc., and fourth house such as loss of domestic happiness, living away from home, problems to/from mother, etc.

However, the effects very much depend on the actual placement of Saturn in the birth chart. If it is in a favourable sign and in a good house, the evil results are mitigated. On the other hand, some benefic results may accrue. In the sample horoscope, Saturn is the *yoga-karaka*, placed in *kendra* in its *moola-trikona* sign. In this case therefore Saturn brings benefic results of ninth and tenth houses whenever it transits over Moon.

Transits of Saturn over the fourth and eighth houses are also very bad. These 2(1/2)-years periods are referred to as *Adhaiyas*.

11.3 GENERAL PRINCIPLES ON TRANSITS

Predictions from transits will be more correct if we keep the following points in mind:

(i)   If a planet is *yoga-karaka* or owner of good houses, and/ or strong by sign and *Navansha*, and also well placed house-wise and conjoined or aspected by benefics in the birth chart, then;

    (a) it does not show bad results even when it is transiting unfavourable houses,

    (b) and it gives very good results when it is transiting favourable houses.

(ii)   On the other hand, if a planet is the owner of evil houses, and/or weak by sign and *Navansha*, and also ill-placed house-wise, and conjoined or aspected by malefics in the birth chart, then;

    (a) it shows very bad results when it is transiting unfavourable houses,

    (b) and, it does not give good results even when it is transiting favourable houses.

(iii) During transit, if a planet is conjoined or aspected by malefics, or if it becomes combust, or if it transits its sign of debilitation or enemy's sign, and/or it happens to be in debilitation in *Navansha*, then its ability to do good is lessened, and its propensity to do evil is enhanced.

(iv) On the other hand, during transit, if a planet is conjoined or aspected by benefics, or if it transits its sign of exaltation or friend's sign, and/or it happens to be in exaltation in *Navansha*, then its ability to do good is enhanced, and its propensity to do evil is lessened.

(v) When a planet becomes retrogade during transit, then it becomes more powerful,

(a) to do good if it is a benefic, or

(b) to do evil if it is a malefic.

(vi) Sec. 4.2 describes the periods of stay of planets in signs, and hence in houses. But due to the elliptical nature of their orbits, and some other factors, planets sometimes appear to be moving slower or faster than average. If they become slower, then they stay for longer than average time, and when they move faster then they stay for shorter than average time in a house.

It is to be noted that the Sun's motion does not vary much. Also, Rahu and Ketu have uniform motion.

The result of slower motion is to accentuate the effects as follows:

(a) Malefics show much more malefic influence.

(b) Benefics show much more benefic influence.

(vii) If a planet transits over its natal/radical position, it intensifies its effects on the house. Malefics show greater maleficence, and benefics show greater beneficence.

(viii) (a) If a house is strong in the birth chart, viz., it is occupied by favourable planets and is beneficially aspected, and its Lord is well placed, and so on, then even malefics would not be able to damage the house during their transit through the house, while benefics will show greater beneficence.

(b) On the other hand, if a house is weak, then even benefics would not be able to do much good to the house during their transit, while malefics will do greater harm.

(ix) (a) Whatever good or bad is indicated by its placement in the birth chart, the same will come to pass when that planet transits the *lagna*.

(b) Any planet, while transiting the twelfth, whether from the Moon or from the *lagna*, will cause expenditure of money, waste of energy, etc.

(x) If a planet occupies the *lagna* in the birth chart, during its transit through various houses, it will show its effects very prominently.

(xi) Planets show their effects very prominently during transit in a house as follows:

(a) The Sun and Mars during first 0 to 10 degrees.

(b) Jupiter and Venus during the middle 10 to 20 degrees.

(c) The Moon and Saturn during the last 20 to 30 degrees.

(d) Mercury, Rahu and Ketu during the entire 0 to 30 degrees.

(xii) The nature of effects of a planet during its transit, on the whole, depends on:

(a) Its significations and ownership of house/s and placement in the birth chart.

(b) The house transited as counted not only from the *lagna* but also from the natal/radical Moon, and from its own position in the birth chart.

Chapter 12

Yogas

The Sanskrit word *yoga* means a combination that brings
results beyond the ordinary. It can be a combination of
a planet and a sign, or planet and a house, or both, or a number
of planets forming aspects. Sometimes, two or more planets
are involved in *yoga*.

A brilliant *yoga* or a number of *yogas* have the result of a
Raja-Yoga implying a combination that bestows on the native
a kingly life.

However, there are both good (*shubha*) and evil (*ashubha*)
yogas.

The possible number of *yogas* is very large. Only some of
the main and important ones are described here.

Note: The effects of *yoga* are prominently felt during the *Dashas* of
the planet/s forming the *yoga*.

12.1 *MAHA-PURUSH YOGAS*

Good *yogas* are generally formed in terms of planets in *kendras* and Trikonas and in terms of the Lords of these auspicious houses. *Maha-Purush* means a great man. There are five *Maha-Purush-Yogas*. These are formed by placement of planets, except Sun and Moon, in *kendras* in their own signs, or better in their signs of exaltation, as follows:

Ruchika Yoga

It is constituted when Mars is placed in *kendra* in Aries, Scorpio or Capricorn. The native is brave, strong and dynamic.

Bhadra Yoga

It is constituted when Mercury is placed in *kendra* in Gemini or Virgo. The native is a gentleman. S/he is very intelligent and extremely sweet in speech. S/he gets to enjoy pleasures of life.

Hansa Yoga

In this case, Jupiter is placed in *kendra* in Sagittarius, Pisces or Cancer. The native is very pious, noble and prosperous.

Maalavya Yoga

It is constituted when Venus is placed in *kendra* in Taurus, Libra or Pisces. The native is good looking, amiable, patient and cheerful. S/he is blessed with a loving spouse and all comforts of life.

Shasha Yoga

In this case, Saturn is placed in *kendra* in Capricorn, Aquarius or Libra. The native has no sorrows, has strong nervous system and occupies a high position. S/he is inclined to extra-marital relations.

Mantreshwar Maharaj states that we consider these *yogas* with respect to *lagna*. So also, they should be considered with respect to the Moon as well.

Note: (i) Best houses for these *yogas* are *lagna* for Mercury and Jupiter, fourth for Venus, seventh for Saturn and tenth for Mars.

(ii) Two or more such *yogas* simultaneously present in a horoscope give rise to a *Raja-Yoga*. In case if three planets are in exaltation or five planets are in own signs in *kendra* with one of them in *lagna*, the native is virtually a king.

(iii) If these *yogas* are formed by malefics Mars and Saturn, the native would be cruel hearted. But if the same are formed by benefics Mercury, Jupiter and Venus then the native would be soft, benevolent and kind hearted.

12.2 WEALTH-GIVING OR DHANA *YOGAS* AND PENURY OR DARIDRA *YOGAS*

Dhana Yogas

Dhana means wealth, prosperity, etc. These are formed by *sambandh* such as exchange or conjunction or mutual aspects between Lords of two or more good houses, viz., the first, second, fourth, fifth, seventh, ninth, tenth and eleventh houses and also by their being placed in one of these very auspicious houses. They will be of little value if they are formed by placement in inauspicious houses, viz., the third, sixth, eighth and twelfth houses.

Darridra-Yogas

Daridra means penury. *Sambandh* similarly between the Lord of an auspicious house with the Lord of an inauspicious house forms *Darridra-Yoga*.

12.3 EXCHANGE OF LORDS OR RASHI-PARIVARTAN YOGAS

Exchange of the Lord of a house with the Lord of another house is *Rashi-Parivartan-Yoga*. This establishes *sambandh* between two planets as mentioned above.

Some of the *Rashi-Parivartan-Yogas* are good and some are evil. On total, there are 66 such *yogas*. Of them, 34 are good/*shubha* including 28 *Maha-Bhagya* and 6 *Vipareet Raja-Yogas*, and 32 are evil/*ashubha* which include 8 *khala* and 24 *Dainya-Yogas* as described below:

Maha-Bhagya-Yogas

Rashi-Parivartan-Yoga becomes a *Maha-Bhagya Yoga*, meaning great good luck *yoga* if the Lord of any of the auspicious 8 houses exchanges place with the Lord of another of these houses. It is seen that *Maha-Bhagya-Yoga* is one of the *Dhana-Yogas*.

These *yogas* give auspicious results in regard to the houses involved and in regard to the significations of the planets forming the *yoga* particularly during the *Mahadasha* of one and the *Antardasha* of the other planet. For example, exchange of Lords between fourth and fifth means generally happy life and mental peace, pleasant home conditions, and particularly happiness to/from children, and good education.

Note must be made of the signs involved. For example, for Scorpio *lagna*, if the *lagna* Lord Mars is placed in the ninth in Cancer in debilitation and the ninth Lord, the Moon is placed in *lagna* in Scorpio, again in debilitation, such an exchange, which could otherwise have been very powerful, will actually be evil.

Khala-Yogas

The third house is a mildly evil house. Hence, if the Lord of any of the 8 auspicious houses exchanges place with the Lord of the third house, a *Khala-Yoga* is formed. *Khala* means bad. *Khala-Yogas*, which are eight in number, weaken the good house. Significations of the good house suffer. But the significations of the third are improved as its Lord is placed in a good house, and the Lord of a good house is placed in third.

Dainya Yogas

However, if the exchange of the Lord of a good house is with the Lord of any of the three evil *trik* houses then it becomes *Dainya* or 'Pitiful *yoga*'. *Dainya-Yoga* pulls down the good house involved. It is much worse than *Khala-Yoga*. The positive significations of the *trik* house involved are improved though.

Vipareet Raja-Yogas

But the mutual exchange between Lords of the evil *trik* houses and also the mildly evil third house among themselves is considered good and constitutes *vipareet*, meaning 'opposite effect', *Raja-Yogas*. These *yogas* mitigate the evil effects of these houses. But their positive effects suffer. There are 6 such *yogas*.

Birth-Chart of Indira Gandhi

In the chart of Indira Gandhi in Fig. 12.1 there are two *Maha-Bhagya-Yogas*, one between Lords of the first and the seventh and the other between Lords of the second and the fifth. The seventh house also includes opposition in politics in addition to spouse and opposite sex in personal life. The native dealt with opposition parties as also problems from her husband very deftly.

The second exchange gave her a renowned family and a very good son who also became the prime minister after her death by assassination. She, however, lost her sons, one by accident during her lifetime and the other again by assassination after her own death. The placements of the twelfth Lord Mercury, and the Sun, a 'Separator' and the Lord of *Maraka-Sthan*, in the fifth house explain this.

There is also one *Dainya-Yoga* in her chart, that between Lords of the eleventh house of gains, friends, desires, etc., and sixth house of disease and enemy. This combination was not conducive to the fulfilment of her innate personal desires.

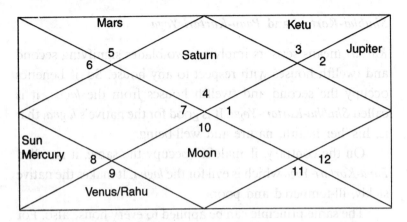

Fig. 12.1 Birth-Chart of Former Indian Prime Minister Indira Gandhi

12.4 *KENDRA-TRIKONA YOGA*

If the Lord of a *kendra* and the Lord of a *trikona* are placed together in a good house thus forming *sambandh* and Dhana *yoga* and *Maha-Bhagya-Yoga* simultaneously, it is called *Kendra-Trikona-Yoga*. When the duo is placed in *kendra* or *trikona* itself, it becomes a powerful *Raj-Yoga* named as *Shankha-Yoga*.

Such a *yoga* when formed by Lords of ninth, which is the most powerful *trikona*, and Lord of tenth, which is the most powerful *kendra*, becomes the most powerful *Raj-Yoga*.

The native with *Shankha-Yoga* is extremely fortunate and religious and occupies a very high position.

12.5 *SHUBHA-KARTARI, PAPA-KARTARI, ADHI, GAJA-KESARI, GURU-CHANDRA, GAURI, LAKSHMI* AND *SARASWATI YOGAS*

There are a large number of other *yogas*. Some of the important ones as mentioned above are described here.

Shubha-Kartari and Paap-Kartari-Yoga

Kartari means scissors implying two blades signifying second and twelfth houses with respect to any house. So, if benefics occupy the second and twelfth houses from the *lagna*, it is called *Shubha-Kartari-Yoga*. It is good for the native's *lagna*, that is, his/her health, nature and well-being.

On the contrary, if malefics occupy the same, it is called *Papa-Kartari-Yoga* which is evil for the *lagna*. It makes the native sickly, ill-tempered and poor.

The same principle can be applied to every house also. For example, if malefics occupy the sixth and eighth houses they tend to destroy one's seventh house of marriage. But benefics in the sixth and eighth save marriage in spite of afflictions caused by their own placement in the *trik* houses.

The *yoga* applies equally to the planets as well. Thus, if the Moon is hemmed between malefics, the native's happiness and particularly happiness to/from mother will be affected. But if it is hemmed between benefics, the mother will be healthy and the native will have mental peace and happiness in general and to/from mother in particular.

Adhi-Yoga

If all the three benefics, Mercury, Jupiter and Venus, occupy the sixth, seventh and eighth houses with respect to the *lagna*, it constitutes *Adhi-Yoga*. It is good for the native's as well as the spouse's well-being including their health, wealth and longevity. If only two benefics occupy these houses, it constitutes half *Adhi-Yoga*, and the benefit is partial. It becomes *Shubha-Kartari-Yoga* for the seventh house if two benefics are placed in the sixth and eighth separately.

Gaja-Kesari, Guru-Chandra **and** *Gauri Yogas*

Jupiter with Moon forms these *yogas.*

Gaja means elephant and *Kesari* means lion. A person born under *Gaja-Kesari-Yoga* has the combined power of an elephant and a lion. S/he is very brave, easily destroys enemies, has powerful voice, lives like a king and is wise and famous. The *yoga* is formed when Jupiter is in an angle, viz., in *kendra* with respect to the Moon. Accordingly, in the *Chandra-Kundali,* Jupiter would be in the fourth, seventh and tenth houses. This means Jupiter and the Moon form a square aspect. This square aspect is not considered bad in Vedic astrology. On the contrary, it is very good. However, the condition for the formation of this *yoga* is that Jupiter should not be debilitated or in enemy's sign or combust. It must also be free from malefic aspects.

Guru-Chandra-Yoga is formed when the Moon is in conjunction with or receives the fifth, seventh or ninth aspect of Jupiter. A person born with *Guru-Chandra-Yoga* is happy, pure hearted and pious in nature. S/he is fortunate in respect of mother. The *yoga* becomes a powerful *Raja-Yoga* if the full Moon occupies the *kendra* and receives Jupiter's aspect also. Note that the full Moon means the Sun in the seventh from the Moon. Thus, the Sun also aspects the Moon. If the Moon receives the aspect of Venus as well, it becomes a very powerful *yoga* for health, wealth, pleasures and happiness.

In case if the Moon is in exaltation or in own sign in the *kendra* or *trikona* and is aspected by Jupiter, it becomes a *Guru-Chandra-Yoga* and *Maha-Purush-Yoga* combined. Then it is called *Gauri-Yoga.* Gauri is Goddess Parvati, consort of Lord Shiva. Both divinities Shiva and Gauri bestow fulfilment of desires and self-control at the same time. Such a native has all the good qualities of mind, is next to the king, has good children and happiness to/from mother, and enjoys great name and fame.

Lakshmi Yoga

Lakshmi is the Goddess of Wealth. *Lakshmi yoga* is formed when Venus, the *karaka* for wealth and female company, and the ninth Lord are in exaltation or in their own signs and are placed in the *kendra* or *trikona*. A person born with *Lakshmi yoga* is bestowed with all material comforts, enjoyments and wealth. A man everlastingly enjoys the company of a good-natured woman if this *yoga* is formed in his birth-chart.

Saraswati Yoga

Saraswati is the Goddess of Education, Arts and Music. If all the three benefics Mercury, Jupiter and Venus are in good houses, and Jupiter is in exaltation, own or friend's sign, then *Saraswati yoga* is formed. Person born with this *yoga* in the birth-chart is proficient in arts, music, dance, drama, prose, poetry, scriptures, mathematics, etc. We call such a person a *Prakand Pandit* meaning a great pandit. The native is also very fortunate. S/he is blessed with a good spouse and loving children, and is respected by authorities.

12.6 *YOGA* FOR EACH HOUSE/*BHAVA*

Now, there is a separate *yoga* for each house/*bhava*. This is constituted if only benefics and *bhava* Lord tenant and aspect a house, and its Lord is not combust and is placed in a good house in its exaltation or own sign receiving only benefic aspects. The name of the *yoga* for each house along with its dominant benefits are listed below:

First House: *Chamar Yoga*: Very good personality. Long life.

Second House: *Dhenu Yoga*: Wealth. Happy family. Delicious foods. Sweet speech.

Third House: *Shourya Yoga*: Happiness from siblings. Great valour, courage, stamina.

Fourth House: *Jaladhi Yoga*: Mental peace. Happiness to/ from mother. Land, property, happy home life, comforts, conveyance, etc.

Fifth House: *Chhatra Yoga*: High education. Happiness from children. Love life.

Sixth House: *Astra Yoga*: Physically strong, proud and powerful. Torments enemies.

Seventh House: *Kaama Yoga*: Great happiness from spouse. Success in business.

Eighth House: *Asura Yoga*: Long life. Wisdom. Windfall gains.

Ninth House: *Bhagya Yoga*: Very lucky. Prosperous. Religious. Devoted to God.

Tenth House: *Khyati Yoga*: Name. Fame. Success in profession. Good *karmas*.

Eleventh House: *Suparijata Yoga*: High income through rightful means. Fulfillment of innate desires.

Twelfth House: *Musala Yoga*: Spends on worthy causes. Pilgrimages. Gains from abroad. Native is inclined towards detachment, renunciation, *Moksha*, etc,.

On the contrary, if malefics tenant and/or aspect a house, and its Lord is combust and/or conjoined or aspected by malefics and is placed in any of the evil *trik* houses, an evil *yoga* is formed for the house.

Exceptions are the third and sixth houses. For example, if the sixth house is tenanted or aspected by malefics and its

Lord is placed in any of the *trik* houses Harsha, implying joy, *yoga* is constituted. Such a native is strong-bodied, enjoys pleasures (*Bhog*), defeats enemies, and fears from committing any sin.

Malefics in third also make the native strong. They give success in all undertakings of the native.

12.7 *MALIKA-YOGA* AND *SHOOLA-YOGA*

Malika-Yoga requires arrangement of all planets including nodes in seven successive signs except when they are from sixth to twelfth house. If planets are from the the first to the the seventh house, the native occupies a kingly position, from the the second to the the eighth the native is good looking, and so on. But from the the sixth to the the twelfth the native is generally very poor.

In all these *Malika-Yogas* consideration has to be given to signs occupied. For example, if the Moon is in Cancer, the Sun in Leo, Mercury in Virgo, Venus in Libra, Mars in Scorpio, Jupiter in Sagittarius, and Saturn in Capricorn it will become a very powerful *Malika-Yoga*.

If all the planets occupy seven signs not necessarily successive ones even then it is a good *yoga*. It is called *Veena* or *Vallaki-Yoga*.

If all the seven planets occupy only six signs, then also the native occupies good position in life. With all the planets in five signs the native still enjoys life. If in four signs, it is satisfactory. But if the number of signs occupied reduces, it becomes progressively more and more evil.

If all the seven planets occupy only three signs, it constitutes *Shoola-Yoga*. A native born with this *yoga* is cruel and leads an indigent life. If the three houses occupied happen to be the sixth, eighth and twelfth then it constitutes *ashubha Malika-Yoga*. This makes the native even more cruel, ungrateful and quarrelsome but timid. S/he follows the evil path.

Further, if all the seven planets occupy only two signs or just one sign it becomes progressively more evil form of *Shoola-Yoga*.

Note: It is better for the seven planets to be distributed over seven different signs. Such placement will activate seven different houses, thus making native's life more fulsome covering seven departments of life. If they are placed in favourable signs and they make favourable aspects and *sambandh* then it is all the more better.

12.8 *KAAL-SARPA-YOGA*

Kaal-Sarpa-Yoga is constituted when all the seven planets are placed only on one side of the Rahu-Ketu axis. This is essentially an evil *yoga*. A person born with *Kaal-Sarpa-Yoga* has to struggle hard in life. S/he faces many obstacles in his/her path to progress, and has to suffer misfortunes continually such as the following:

(i)   Not having progeny.
(ii) No marital happiness.
(iii) Difficulties in achieving success in spite of great effort.
(iv) Disappointments due to mental and physical weaknesses.

In addition, the houses occupied by Rahu and Ketu are adversely affected.

Basically, the native is not able to advance his/her personal life. The intensity of the affect varies greatly depending upon the signs and houses occupied by Rahu and Ketu. If they occupy favourable signs then the evil results are somewhat mitigated particularly by taking course to selfless service. In that case, the native rises very high in life both socially and materially, and earns status, name and fame. For example, the industrialist Dhirubhai Ambani rose from rags to riches during the 18-year period of Rahu *Mahadasha* though he continued to suffer health-wise until he died of a stroke in 2002. Thus, there is a positive side to *Kaal-Sarpa-Yoga* when it is benign. The native does not live simply for one's own self. His/her life is basically dedicated to the service of others. Only by such dedication, the evil effects in personal life are partially mitigated. This kind of outcome is seen in the life of many illustrious personalities such as Abraham Lincoln, Jawaharlal Nehru, Morari Bapu and some others.

Fig.12.2 shows the birth-chart of Abraham Lincoln, the great American President and hero of that country's civil war. Mars is not shown in the chart but it is on the same side of Rahu-Ketu axis as other planets. Although Rahu is not in a favourable sign but house-wise both Rahu and Ketu are well placed. In addition, the Sun and Mercury in *lagna* are forming a powerful *Dhana-Yoga*, rather a *Raja-Yoga*. And, Jupiter and Venus in second are forming still stronger *Dhana* and *Raja-Yoga*. Though he rose to the highest position in the world, he faced poverty in childhood, had strained relations with his wife and encountered many obstacles and faced enmity in his political life. Ultimately his life ended with his assassination. But of course, he gave his entire life in the making of a great nation.

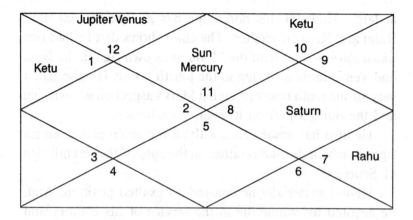

Fig.12.2 Birth-Chart of Abraham Lincoln

Fig. 12.3 shows the birth-chart of Jawaharlal Nehru, born on 14 November 1889 at 1:05 a.m. at Allahabad, the first prime minister of India who spent most of his youth fighting for the country's independence under the leadership of Mahatma Gandhi.

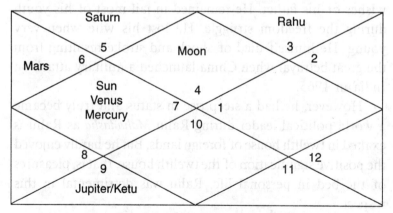

Fig. 12.3 Birth-Chart of Jawaharlal Nehru

Jawaharlal Nehru had the highest status not only in the country but also internationally, and in the hearts of Indians at large. However, his horoscope has *Kaal-Sarpa-Yoga*. But, Rahu and Ketu are exalted. The chart shows that he had two *Maha-Purush-Yogas* with the Moon in its own sign in the *lagna* and Venus in its own sign in the fourth house. He also had a very strong tenth house receiving Mars's aspect on its own sign and the Sun's aspect on its sign of exaltation.

He also has *Malika-Yoga* with all the seven planets in six signs in which the Sun is rather on the cusp of the seventh sign of Scorpio.

Hence, materially he enjoyed an exalted position. And, he devoted his whole life in the service of his country and countrymen. Nevertheless, he sacrificed his personal life renouncing all comforts that he had inherited from his father. He sacrificed his professional career as well to take part in the freedom movement. Note the Sun, significator for father, is in debility. He did not enjoy a harmonious relationship with his father. Nehru renounced his own legal practice that would have been very lucrative in those days, against the wishes of his father. He remained in jail most of his youth during the freedom struggle. He lost his wife when very young. He himself died of shock and stroke resulting from the great betrayal when China launched a military attack on India in 1965.

However, he had a steep rise in status and truly became a world political leader during Rahu *Mahadasha* as Rahu is exalted in twelfth house of foreign lands. But he hardly enjoyed the positive signification of the twelfth house, that is, pleasures of the bed in personal life. Rahu was detrimental in this respect.

Again, Fig. 12.4 shows the birth-chart of contemporary saint Morari Bapu, famous for his sweet recitations of *Rama-Katha*, the epic of Lord Rama and Sita. The chart shows that he has *Maha-Purush-Yoga* with Mercury, *karaka* for speech, in exaltation in *lagna* and powerful *Kendra-Trikona-Yoga* formed by Lords of fourth and ninth houses, Jupiter and Venus, in second house of speech.

Further, Rahu and Ketu form *Kaal-Sarpa-Yoga* but they are in exaltation. All these have made him a great saint, preacher, teacher and speaker. His life is totally devoted to singing praise in music (*sangeet*) and preaching love of God (*bhakti*). But he himself leads the life of a celebrated monk.

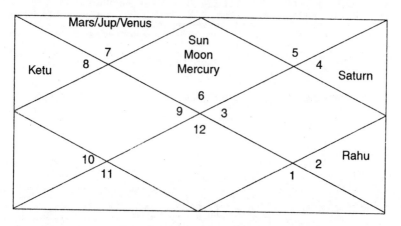

Fig. 12.4 Birth-Chart of Morari Bapu

The horoscope of India's independence at zero hour on 15 August 1947 has *Kaal-Sarpa-Yoga* with exalted Rahu in Taurus in *lagna* and Ketu in Scorpio in the seventh house. Mars is in the second in Gemini. The Sun, the Moon, Mercury, Venus and Saturn are in the third in Cancer. And Jupiter is in the sixth in Libra. This means India has to struggle hard to achieve progress. But, ultimately, this nation will work for the good of the people of the whole world.

Many notorious people also have *Kaal-Sarpa-Yoga*. But in their horoscope, Rahu and Ketu are not benign. They are not placed in favourable signs and houses. Their charts show evil *yogas* rather than auspicious *yogas*. For example, the chart of ill-famed stockbroker Harshad Mehta has *Kaal-Sarpa-Yoga* with Rahu and Ketu in debility. Accordingly, he only tried to serve his own selfish interests by fair or foul means, and had to suffer indignity.

Chapter 13

Ashtakvarga System

13.1 WHAT IS *ASHTAKVARGA*?

Vedic astrology offers variety of methods for making predictions. The main one is the *Dasha* system. The other one is from transits/*Gochar*. The *Ashtakvarga* system is a highly ingenious numerical scheme of interpretation devised by our sages to supplement the *Dashas* and the transits. Also, since the predictions from transits are only gross the *Ashtakavarga* system fine-tunes the *Gochar* system.

The *Ashtakvarga* system is based on assigning *bindus*, say, dots or zero symbols to the house for which a planet is supposed to be benefically or favourably placed with respect to itself, with respect to *lagna* and with respect to the other six planets. Thus, there can be a maximum of 8 *bindus* in any house as is evident from the name *Ashtak* that means 8. This will become even clearer when we learn to construct *Ashtakvarga* Chart.

We will soon find that the *Ashtakvarga* is employed to verify the general strength of planets with respect to houses. For example, if Venus is placed in a particular chart in the second, the natural sign of the house being Venus's own Taurus in the *Kaal Purush Kundali*, and in the *Ashtakvarga* of Venus, if *bindus* also number 6, 7 or 8 in the second house, then it can be said for sure that Venus is really very strongly placed in the house and is fully capable of conferring benefic results of the house. However, if the *bindus* number less than half of maximum 8, viz., less than 4, then the benefic affects will not be strong.

13.2 INDIVIDUAL *ASHTAKVARGA* CHARTS

How to construct *Ashtakvarga* chart for each planet? First, let us see Tables 13.1 to 13.7, which give the benefic/favourable places for each of the seven planets with respect to

(i) its own position in the birth-chart, (ii) *lagna*, and (iii) the positions of other 6 planets.

Table 13.1
Sun's Benefic Places From

Itself	1st, 2nd, 4th, 7th, 8th, 9th, 10th, 11th
Lagna	3rd, 4th, 6th, 10th, 11th, 12th
Moon	3rd, 6th, 10th, 11th
Mars	1st, 2nd, 4th, 7th, 8th, 9th, 10th, 11th
Mercury	3rd, 5th, 6th, 9th, 10th 11th, 12th
Jupiter	5th, 6th, 9th, 11th
Venus	6th, 7th, 12th
Saturn	1st, 2nd, 4th, 7th, 8th, 9th, 10th, 11th

Total Bindus or benefic places = 48

Table 13.2
Moon's Benefic Places From

Itself	1st, 3rd, 6th, 7th, 10th, 11th
Lagna	3rd, 6th, 10th, 11th
Sun	3rd, 6th, 7th, 8th, 10th, 11th
Mars	2nd, 3rd, 5th, 6th, 9th, 10th, 11th
Mercury	1st, 3rd, 4th, 5th, 7th, 8th, 10th, 11th
Jupiter	1st, 4th, 7th, 8th, 10th, 11th, 12th
Venus	3rd, 4th, 5th, 7th, 9th, 10th, 11th
Saturn	3rd, 5th, 6th, 11th

Total Bindus or benefic places = 49

Table 13.3
Mars's Benefic Places From

Itself	1st, 2nd, 4th, 7th, 8th, 10th, 11th
Lagna	1st, 3rd, 6th, 10th, 11th
Sun	5th, 6th, 9th, 11th, 12th
Moon	2nd, 4th, 6th, 8th, 10th, 11th
Mercury	3rd, 5th, 6th, 11th
Jupiter	6th, 10th, 11th, 12th
Venus	6th, 8th, 11th, 12th
Saturn	1st, 4th, 7th, 8th, 9th, 10th, 11th

Total Bindus or benefic places = 39

Table 13.4
Mercury's Benefic Places From

Itself	1st, 3rd, 5th, 6th, 9th, 10th, 11th, 12th
Lagna	1st, 2nd, 4th, 6th, 8th, 10th, 11th
Sun	5th, 6th, 9th, 11th, 12th
Moon	2nd, 4th, 6th, 8th, 10th, 11th
Mars	1st, 2nd, 4th, 7th, 8th, 9th, 10th, 11th
Jupiter	6th, 8th, 11th, 12th
Venus	1st, 2nd, 3rd, 4th, 5th, 8th, 9th, 11th
Saturn	1st, 2nd, 4th, 7th, 8th, 9th, 10th, 11th

Total Bindus or benefic places = 54

Table 13.5
Jupiter's Benefis Places From

Itself	1st, 2nd, 3rd, 4th, 7th, 8th, 10th, 11th
Lagna	1st, 2nd, 4th, 5th, 6th, 7th, 9th, 10th, 11th
Sun	1st, 2nd, 3rd, 4th, 7th, 8th, 9th, 10th, 11th
Moon	2nd, 5th, 7th, 9th, 11th
Mars	1st, 2nd, 4th, 7th, 8th, 10th, 11th
Mercury	1st, 2nd, 4th, 5th, 6th, 9th, 10th, 11th
Venus	2nd, 5th, 6th, 9th, 10th, 11th
Saturn	3rd, 5th, 6th, 12th

Total Bindus or benefic places = 56

Table 13.6
Venus's Benefic Places From

Itself	1st, 2nd, 3rd, 4th, 5th, 8th, 9th, 10th, 11th
Lagna	1st, 2nd, 3rd, 4th, 5th, 8th, 9th, 11th, 12th
Sun	8th, 11th, 12th
Moon	1st, 2nd, 3rd, 4th, 5th, 8th, 9th, 11th, 12th
Mars	3rd, 5th, 6th, 9th, 11th, 12th
Mercury	3rd, 5th, 6th, 9th, 11th
Jupiter	5th, 8th, 9th, 10th, 11th
Saturn	3rd, 4th, 5th, 8th, 9th, 10th, 11th

Total Bindus or benefic places = 52

Table 13.7
Saturn's Benefic Places From

Itself	3rd, 5th, 6th, 11th
Lagna	1st, 3rd, 4th, 6th, 10th, 11th
Sun	1st, 2nd, 4th, 7th, 8th, 10th, 11th
Moon	3rd, 6th, 11th
Mars	3rd, 5th, 6th, 10th, 11th, 12th
Mercury	6th, 8th, 9th, 10th, 11th, 12th
Jupiter	5th, 6th, 11th, 12th
Venus	6th, 11th, 12th

Total Bindus or benefic places = 39

Note: The aggregate of *bindus* or benefic places of all planets put together in any horoscope will be 48+49+39+54+56+52+39 = 337.

To demonstrate how to construct *Ashtakvarga* charts, let us do this exercise for planets in the sample horoscope. Take first the *Ashtakvarga* of the Sun. The Sun here is in Cancer. Therefore, from Table 13.1, its benefic places from itself will be Cancer 1st, Leo 2nd, Libra 4th, Capricorn 7th, Aquarius 8th, Pisces 9th, Aries 10th, and Taurus 11th. Now, place *bindus* or zeros in the respective signs in the chart as shown in Fig. 13.1.

Likewise, the Sun's benefic places can be found from the *lagna* and the other six planets. All the 8 charts thus obtained can be combined into a single chart. Then, by adding together all the *bindus* and putting a number for the sum in each sign we obtain the complete *Ashtakvarga* of the Sun as shown in Fig. 13.2. Note the total number of *bindus* or benefic places in the Sun's *Ashtakvarga* chart in Fig. 13.2 are 6+2+4+3+4+3+3+5+4+5+5+4 = 48.

What use can be made of this chart? Now, that we have obtained some numbers from the *Ashtakvarga* chart for each planet, it can be used to supplement the information to fine-tune the predictions about *Dashas* and transits as follows:

(i) *Dashas*: To know how well is the planet placed in the birth-chart to affect the *bhava* tenanted and its own *karakattva* matters particularly during its *dashas*.

(ii) *Transits*: To know how are *bhavas* affected as the planet transits through them.

Briefly, if a planet in a house is associated with 5 or more *bindus* it leads to realisation of matters pertaining to that house and those of its house/s of lordship as also its own *karakattva* matters.

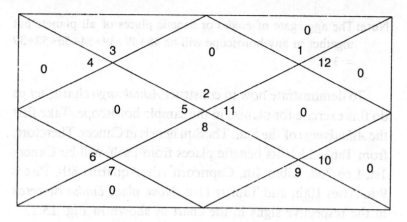

Fig. 13.1 Sun's Ashtakvarga from Itself in Sample Horoscope

So, even if a planet is well placed in the chart and even if it is in a very favourable sign it will lose its power to confer good results if it is not associated with the required number of *bindus* in its own *Ashtakvarga*.

On the other hand, if a house has 3 or fewer *bindus* for a planet then the transit of that planet through that house bodes ill for the matters of the house. If it is in debilitation or in enemy's sign or if it is combust, it becomes all the more evil.

How well is the Sun placed in the sample horoscope? From Fig. 13.2 we conclude as follows:

How does the Sun Affect during its *Dashas*?

The Sun is placed in the birth chart in the third house with 4 *bindus* only. Hence it should give only average results during its *Dasha*. But since the Sun, as a malefic, is best placed in the third house, and also since it is placed in its great friend the Moon's sign of Cancer, it should give better than average results during its *Dashas* in regard to the matters of the third house and also its own *karakattvas* matters even with 4 *bindus*.

But, note that the Sun as Lord of fourth is placed in the third, twelfth from fourth. It bodes ill for matters of the the fourth house. More *bindus* will not help fourth house matters.

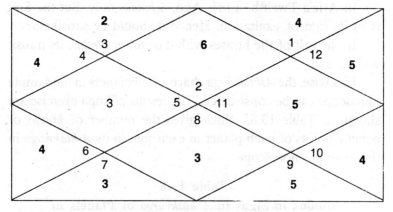

Fig. 13.2 Sun s Ashtakvarga

How does the Sun Affect during its Transits?

Since the Sun has 6 *bindus* in *lagna*, it will give best results in regard to the affairs of the first house during its transit through Taurus. That will be from the middle of May to the middle of June. The good results will, however, be somewhat watered down as the Sun is the enemy of the *lagna* Lord Venus.

Sun should also give good results when it transits over Pisces and Cancer.

In Pisces: Eleventh house. Good for a malefic. 5 *bindus*. Friend's sign.

In Cancer: Third house. Good for a malefic. 4 *bindus*. Great friend's sign.

The Sun should give satisfactory results when it transits over Sagittarius, Aquarius and Aries where it has enough *bindus*.

In Sagittarius: Eighth, a *trik*. Malefic is evil for longevity. It is evil for the Sun's own significations. But it will not be so evil because of 5 *bindus* and friend's sign.

In Aquarius: Tenth, a *kendra*. The Sun in tenth is very good for career. Also, it has 5 *bindus*. But the Sun is a great enemy of the tenth Lord Saturn. It makes its transit just satisfactory.

In Aries: Twelfth, a *trik*. And, 4 *bindus* only. But the Sun is in its sign of exaltation. Hence it should be satisfactory.

In the rest of the houses with 4 or fewer *bindus*, its transit will be evil.

Likewise, the *Ashtakvarga* charts of all planets in the sample horoscope can be constructed. The results of such exercise are shown in Table 13.8, which gives the number of *bindus* or benefic points of each planet in each sign in its *Ashtakvarga* in the example horoscope.

Table 13.8
Bindus in Signs in *Ashtakvarga* of Planets in Sample Horoscope

Sign	Sun	Moon	Mars	Mercury	Jupiter	Venus	Saturn	Total
Aries	4	7	3	5	6	4	5	34
Taurus	6	3	5	5	4	6	6	35
Gemini	2	2	2	5	4	7	2	24
Cancer	4	6	6	4	6	4	4	34
Leo	3	3	2	5	4	4	4	25
Virgo	4	5	3	4	4	5	1	26
Libra	3	4	2	4	5	4	3	25
Scorpio	3	2	4	3	5	4	2	23
Sagittarius	5	5	5	6	3	3	3	30
Capricorn	4	3	2	2	5	3	2	21
Aquarius	5	5	3	6	3	4	4	30
Pisces	5	4	2	5	7	4	3	30
Total	48	49	39	54	56	52	39	337

How Well are the other Six Planets Placed in the Chart?

The following conclusions can be drawn from Table 13.8 about the placement of the other six planets in the sample horoscope:

Moon: The Moon is well placed in the chart in the third house in own sign Cancer with 6 *bindus*. The Moon's *Dasha* should prove extra-beneficial to the native particularly in matters of the third house and those of its *karakattvas*.

Further, the Moon's transits through Aries and Cancer with 7 and 6 *bindus* respectively will be uplifting, while its transits through Gemini and Scorpio with 2 *bindus* each will be depressing. It will also be in debility in Scorpio.

Mars: Mars with just 2 *bindus* and in enemy's sign Gemini in the second house is not well placed. Even then it will show good results, during its *Dasha*, in regard to the matters of the third house in which it has 6 *bindus* and the ninth house of its sign of exaltation which it aspects.

But, its transit through the second house will be the worst particularly for matters of the second house. During its transit through the third house, even though in debilitation, it will not show bad results since it has 6 *bindus* over there and since it aspects the ninth house in its sign of exaltation. Transit through the ninth house will be rewarding anyway even though there are only 2 *bindus*.

Mercury: Mercury with 5 *bindus*, though in its enemy's sign Cancer, in the third house is well placed. It is a great benefic due to its lordship of two good houses, second and fifth, and also since the third house is its own in the *Kaal Purush Kundali*. Further, Mercury is a great friend of the house Lord Moon. In addition, in third Mercury is placed second from the second, and in the eleventh position of gain from the fifth. It is very good for fulfilment of significations of the second, third, fifth and ninth, and also Mercury's own *karakattvas*. During transits, Mercury gave best results through Aquarius, Taurus, Gemini, Leo, Sagittarius and Aquarius.

Jupiter: Jupiter is placed with 4 *bindus* in enemy's sign in fifth house. It is also the Lord of two evil houses, the eighth and the eleventh. It is, therefore, not very well placed. Further, its aspect on the ninth house is in debilitation. But it gave excellent results during its *Dashas* in regard to the affairs of the eleventh house, viz., income, gains, fulfilment of desires, friendships, etc., which it aspects in own sign and for which it is *karaka* also. However, bad results in the form of accident, sudden illness, sudden loss, etc., were foretold for the native because of its lordship of the eighth house.

Transits of Jupiter through Aries, Cancer, Scorpio and Pisces were rewarding because of the higher number of *bindus* as also the favourable signs.

Venus: Venus, the *lagna* Lord though afflicted by Mars, is excellently placed in the second house with 7 *bindus* in Gemini, a great friend's sign, which is Venus's own in the *Kaal Purush Kundali*. The native had very good life during Venus *Mahadasha* particularly doting over his family as first Lord in the second, and in regard to matters of the second house that is happiness to/from family and also career which is a sixth house matter.

Its transit through Taurus and Gemini is best.

Saturn: Although Saturn is *yoga-karaka* for the native and is placed in *kendra* in the tenth house in the *moola-trikona* sign, its quality has suffered due to mere 4 *bindus*, and because of its malefic aspects on the twelfth, fourth and seventh houses that are crucial for happy married life.

Its transit is best through Taurus, and worst through Scorpio.

13.3 SARVASHTAKAVARGA

Sarva means 'all'. In casting the *Sarvashtakvarga* chart, the Ashtakavargas of all planets are combined.

Accordingly, we add together *bindus* contained in the sign
Aries in the Ashtakavargas of all seven planets. This gives us
the total number of *bindus* in Aries in *Sarvashtakvarga*. In the
sample horoscope, it is 34 as seen from Table 13.8. Likewise,
the total number of *bindus* in each sign can be found thus giving
us the *Sarvashtakvarga* chart of the sample horoscope as shown
in Fig. 13.3.

What is the use of this chart? One could even give a
snapshot interpretation of horoscope merely on the basis of
Sarvashtakvarga chart. We note that the average number of
bindus in a house would be 337/12 = 28.1. More the number
of *bindus* than 28 associated with a *bhava*, the better it is for
the *bhava*, and less the number of *bindus* than 28, the worse
for the *bhava*.

Thus, *bhavas* associated with less than 25 *bindus* are not
auspicious. Fairly good results are indicated for the *bhava* if the
number of *bindus* exceeds 30.

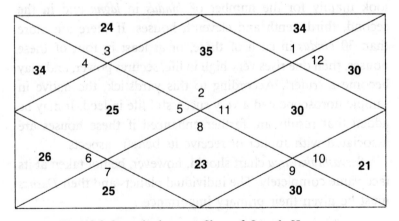

Fig. 13.3 Sarvashtakavarga Chart of Sample Horoscope:
Total Bindus 337

In the case of the sample horoscope, the first, third and
twelfth houses are found best according to *Sarvashtakavarga*

chart. The native had a very pleasant amiable personality. See that there are 35 *bindus* in *lagna*. He has been hardworking, wrote books, had good relations with brothers and sister, and was very fortunate in respect of servants as is evident from 34 *bindus* in the third house. He visited foreign countries many times over, and gained from his visits abroad. Note that there are 34 *bindus* in the twelfth house.

Next best in Fig. 13.3 are the eighth, tenth and eleventh houses with 30 *bindus* in each. Thus, the native is blessed with spiritual wisdom, status, name, and fame and good income.

The houses where he has less than 25 *bindus* are the second, fourth, fifth, sixth, seventh and ninth houses. So he lost his mother soon after birth, had no domestic happiness or marital happiness and family happiness, and remained separated from children due to their settlement abroad. He has poor digestive system and does not enjoy good health.

In judging a *Sarvashtakvarga* chart, one should essentially look mainly for the number of *bindus* in *lagna* and in the second, third, tenth and eleventh houses. If there are more than 30 *bindus* in each of these, or at least in four of these houses, then one rises very high in life, secures power, and may become a 'ruler'. According to this yardstick, the native in sample horoscope had a very successful life indeed. It may be added that results are further enhanced if these houses are associated with Jupiter or receive its benefic aspects.

Sarvashtakavarga chart should, however, be not taken at its face value completely. The individual planets and their *Dashas* must be given their primary importance.

Chapter 14

Special Topics

Let us now take up at length certain topics of common interest. We can apply the already established basic principles to every house or *bhava* as follows:

(i) Consider the house.

(ii) Consider the *bhava* Lord.

(iii) Consider the *bhava-karaka* also. Often the *karaka* is more important than the rest.

(iv) Consider the *bhavat bhava* as well. Examine if the first, second, fourth, fifth, seventh, ninth and tenth from this house are tenanted by Lord of this house and/or benefics, and if malefics are placed in third, sixth and eleventh from the house. If so then the house under judgment will prosper.

(v) Consider the position of the concerned planets and the house in the *Navansha*-Chart as well.

14.1 BODY AND TEMPERAMENT

The body as well as the temperament are to be judged from the first house.

The Sun in the first house gives coppery complexion. Mercury in first makes one agile, attractive and fun loving. Moon and Venus give fair complexion. Benefics in the first, in general, make one handsome while malefics make one bereft of good appearance. The Sun affects the eyes. Mars leaves some marks of injury on head/face. Saturn makes the complexion dark.

Body: The body takes after the sign of the first house and its Lord. It also takes after the *lagna* in *Navansha*-Chart as also its Lord.

If the *lagna* Lord is conjoined or hemmed with malefics or if it is combust or in debilitation or in enemy's sign or is placed in any of the evil *trik* houses, or if a *trik* Lord is placed in *lagna*, it deprives the native of physical and mental well-being and comforts. It also results in ill-health. But if it is conjoined/hemmed with benefics or is in exaltation or in friend's sign or is placed in *lagna* itself or in good houses or if the Lords of good houses are placed in *lagna*, it indicates that the native will enjoy healthy body and overall well-being.

In Vedic/Hindu astrology, the Moon sign is also treated as a *lagna*. Hence, the body and temperament should also be judged from the Moon-Sign or *Chandra-Lagna* in much the same way as Ascendant/*lagna*.

Temperament: As for the temperament, the Sun makes one hot tempered, the Moon gives softness and flexibility, Mars imparts anger and dynamism, Mercury makes one intelligent and mirthful, Jupiter imparts wisdom and sagaciousness, Venus inclines one to amiable and pleasure seeking nature while

Saturn makes one reserved and sober but careful and suspicious. Further, Rahu makes one clever and cruel and Ketu imparts courage and obstinacy. In addition, as stated above the Moon-Sign and aspects of other planets on the Moon also govern temperament. The Sun-Sign should also be similarly considered in this respect.

In the sample horoscope, the native's personality was ruled by earthly sign Taurus, Lord Venus, *Chandra-Lagna* Cancer, its Lord, the Moon, and to some extent by Jupiter's aspect on the *lagna*. The native is fair complexioned, slightly fleshy, very amiable and pleasant, emotional but practical at the same time, and fond of physical pleasures and comforts.

Parts of Body: Different parts of body are, however, judged from the twelve houses. A malefic in any house represents problem, wounds or sores in the part of the body represented by that house. Thus, in the sample horoscope, Mars in the second house gave scars on the forehead due to injury caused by an accident during *Antardasha* of the eighth Lord, Jupiter, in the Venus *Mahadasha*. Further, the placement of the fourth Lord, the Sun, in the third, twelfth the from fourth, inimical aspect of Saturn from the tenth house on the fourth, and also conjunction of the Sun with Ketu gave the native heart attack and angioplastic surgery. Further, the eighth Lord, Jupiter, in the fifth effects his digestive system.

14.2 WEALTH, INCOME, SPECULATION GAINS, POVERTY, PROPERTY, CONVEYANCES, WINDFALL GAINS/LOSSES, LEGACIES

Essentially, for income we examine the eleventh house and the eleventh Lord, and for wealth we examine second house and second Lord. But the fourth, fifth, ninth, tenth and first houses should also be examined. A *sambandh* between two or more of these houses forming *Dhana-Yogas* further strengthen prospects of wealth. Stronger the planets are by sign, house and benefic aspects, better the *yoga*. For both income and accumulated wealth, *karaka* Jupiter is important.

Malefics or *trik* Lords in second lead to loss of wealth.

For poverty also we consider the same houses. Their *sambandh* with the evil *trik* houses forming *Daridra Yogas* leads to extreme poverty and penury.

However, it is difficult to find a chart in which there are only good *yogas* or only evil *yogas*. Often, it happens that one has wealth during the *Dashas* of favourable planets, and faces penury and poverty when the *Dashas* of unfavourable planets are on.

Speculation Gains: The second Lord in *lagna* indicates wealth earned by own effort. The second Lord in the fifth indicates speculation gains. Speculation gains are also judged from the fifth house itself and the fifth Lord. The Moon or Rahu in the fifth incline one to indulge in speculation. Effect of placement of second Lord in other houses has already been described in Chapter 8.

Property: Immovable property is examined from the fourth house, its Lord and *karaka* Mars. These should be strong. *Sambandh* between Lords of *lagna* and fourth house is a good *yoga* for having property and owning a house. If the Lord of fourth house and Mars are strongly placed in both *lagna* and *Navansha*-Charts, one gets the comforts of owning a house and landed property. The native will lose comforts of home, property, etc., if malefics are in fourth. If Rahu and Saturn are in the fourth house, the native's house will be dilapidated.

Conveyances: These are also judged from the fourth house and its Lord, but *karaka* is Venus. If both the fourth Lord and Venus are in good signs and good houses, and are not combust, then one gets kingly chariots to ride.

Inheritances/Legacies: For these, one has to see first if the native has any circumstances to have abnormal gains. Otherwise, in the normal course, everyone gets something or the other by inheritance. Hence, for any windfall gains, legacies, etc., eighth house and its Lord have to be very strong. The eighth Lord placed in good signs and good houses, or in the eighth itself, or in the second from where it aspects the eighth, and also in the eleventh house of gains may bring sudden/windfall gains. Similarly, aspects of benefics on the eighth house and its Lord promote such gains. The influences of malefics may cause sudden losses.

14.3 HOME, HAPPINESS, MOTHER AND FATHER

Happiness and Mother: Happiness and mother come under the domain of the fourth house and its Lord. In addition, the Moon is *karaka* for both. It looks as if the two, mother and happiness are inter-connected. In fact, if any individual is not able to receive love and care of mother, the whole life is affected to a great extent. In the process, his/her attitude towards life and relationships with opposite sex may be adversely affected. It will eventually affect one's character, which also comes under fourth house. The fourth house is an indicator of long life of mother provided it is tenanted and aspected by benefics, and its Lord and *karaka*, the Moon are in the fourth house itself or in any of the good houses, and are in exaltation or in own or friend's signs, and are not combust, and both receive the aspects of benefics. However, the fourth Lord in the *trik*, the eleventh which is eighth from the fourth, and third which is twelfth from the fourth, indicates loss of mother or serious illness to her and/or unhappiness to/from her. Similarly, the conjunction of the fourth Lord and more particularly its *karaka* the Moon with Saturn, Rahu or Ketu will cause loss of mother.

Note that the natural sign of the fourth house is Cancer, the Moon's own and sign of exaltation of Jupiter. Hence, the Moon and Jupiter in fourth irrespective of the signs are great benefics. However, Mars, Saturn, Rahu and Ketu here adversely affect happiness in general and mother's health in particular. Peace of mind is strongly related to the fourth house. Malefics in fourth disturb not only happiness but also peace of mind.

For happiness, one should also see the *lagna*. The native will enjoy full happiness should the fourth Lord be in the fourth house, and *lagna* Lord also is in a favourable sign in the fourth or both have *sambandh* by exchange or conjunction in a good house.

The *lagna* Lord in the fourth house indicates native's concern for his/her mother. But if it is ill-placed, say, Mars for Aries *lagna* in the fourth in Cancer debilitated, then the native's concern for his/her mother will be negative. The native will be inimical to his/her mother trying to always find fault with her. Similarly, the fourth Lord in *lagna* indicates the mother's attachment to her son/daughter.

Venus should also be considered for happiness. If Venus is strong it gives marital happiness and enjoyments of life.

Further, a strong Jupiter in one's horoscope makes one prosperous and broad-minded. The native's heart expands for others particularly when Jupiter is aspecting the Moon. As a result, s/he remains devoid of negative thoughts and hence cheerful in general.

For fulfilment of significations of the fourth house, we should have benefics not only in the fourth house but also in the tenth house as they directly aspect the fourth house. On the same reasoning, we should have no malefics either in the fourth or in the tenth house. We know that the tenth house is for the father. Thus, planets in both, the fourth and the tenth house, equally affect happiness not only to/from the mother but also to/from the father. Often, the well being of both and happiness to/from both parents are affected simultaneously.

Happiness and Father: More concretely, however, we judge father and happiness to/from father from the tenth house and its Lord and *karaka* Sun in both the *lagna* and the *Navansha*-Charts in addition to planets in the fourth and tenth houses, and planets aspecting the tenth house, the tenth Lord and the Sun. Thus, if the Sun is well placed and the tenth house is tenanted and aspected by benefics and/or its Lord, or its Lord and Sun occupy their own or exaltation signs both in the *lagna* and *Navansha*-Charts, the native not only gets extreme happiness from the father but also enjoys fame and performs good deeds. Malefics in the tenth will curtail happiness to/from the father. The conjunction of the tenth Lord and more particularly the *karaka* Sun with Saturn, Rahu and Ketu will cause loss of father.

Heart: The fourth house in the chart represents the heart. Cancer as the fourth sign in the *Kaal Purush Kundali* and its Lord, Moon, represent the heart. The Sun is *karaka* for the heart. It governs vitality, which flows from a healthy heart. Its sign Leo therefore signifies heart. Ill-placed fourth Lord, say, in the *trik*, third and eleventh which is eighth from the fourth, and malefics in the fourth, and afflicted Sun, Moon and Cancer sign are sure indications of heart trouble and heart attack. Whether it is fatal or not can be judged from the strength of the *lagna*, and the eighth house of longevity.

Relatives: In addition to the Moon, Mercury, signifying relatives is another *karaka* for the fourth house. So, if the Lord of the fourth house and Mercury are strongly placed in both the *lagna* and the *Navansha*-Charts or Mercury occupies the *lagna*, then one is liked by relatives. One becomes very popular as the fourth house is for popularity also.

Note: To ensure happiness, or rather to ensure that there is no suffering, the malefics in the chart should be well placed, preferably in own or exaltation signs.

14.4 EDUCATION, CHILDREN AND FIFTH HOUSE

We now take up the fifth house as a whole. It covers important matters such as one's stomach, education, love life, children, next birth, etc. The fifth house also indicates our conscience and how honest we are, whether we use rightful means to earn our income. Note that planets in the fifth aspect the eleventh.

The fifth house is a precursor of our next birth as well.

Education: Education of the native is judged from the fifth house and its Lord. Further, Jupiter and Mercury are the *karaka* for education. While Jupiter imparts wisdom, Mercury confers intelligence. Both these planets must be given full consideration along with the house Lord. For good education, the fifth house should be in the sign and the *navansha* of a benefic planet, and be tenanted/aspected by its own Lord or by benefics. Further, the fifth Lord should be placed in a good house and in a favourable sign.

Children: Children are judged from the fifth house counted from both the *lagna* and the Moon. In addition, Jupiter is the *karaka* for children. Often a question is asked whether one will beget children or not. *Yoga* for having children is to have a strong fifth house, fifth Lord and Jupiter. For this one should also see the ninth house, which is fifth from the fifth, and also if there is a *sambandh* between the *lagna* Lord, the fifth house and the fifth Lord.

An unafflicted, well-placed and well-aspected fifth Lord, and that which is not combust, placed in good houses except the fourth ensures happiness to/from children. The fourth being twelfth from the *bhava* is not good. It indicates problems from children.

The nature of the children will be governed by the sign of the fifth house, its Lord and the planets tenanting and aspecting it.

Malefics and *trik* Lords tenanting/aspecting the fifth destroy children, or cause illness to or lack of happiness to/from them. In the case of women's charts, they show difficult delivery. Ketu in the fifth will result in surgical intervention.

The fifth Lord in *trik* from the *lagna* shows no happiness from children. The twelfth is eighth from the *bhava* also. It indicates separation from children.

The Lords of the first and the fifth are always friends. Take the case of Taurus *lagna*. *Lagna* Lord is Venus and the fifth Lord is Mercury. Both are great friends. Usually, therefore, there is cordiality between the native and his/her children. But if there is a *sambandh* between the two Lords formed by conjunction, mutual aspects or exchange then this cordiality is enhanced much more.

The fifth Lord in the *lagna*, without any affliction, shows children's attachment to the native. The *lagna* Lord in the fifth without any affliction, similarly, shows native's love for his/her children. If both the *lagna* Lord and the fifth Lord are in the fifth house or in *kendra* or *trikona*, the native will have abiding happiness from children.

But if the two Lords are in 6–8 positions, the children will be inimical to the native.

Jupiter is the *karaka* for children. Hence, one should examine Jupiter also in the same way as the fifth Lord.

14.5 DIAGNOSING DISEASES

The three *trik* houses are particularly involved in diagnosing disease, the sixth representing general health and disease particularly lower abdominal problems, the eighth representing chronic diseases, and the twelfth hospitalisation. The following points must be kept in mind.

(i)   *Trik* houses and their Lords are adverse for health.
(ii) Lords of the second and seventh houses are *marakas*. They are capable of inflicting death.
(iii) The eighth house represents longevity and indirectly indicates death.
(iv) Sign of the sixth: The part or organ of the body represented by the sign of the sixth house is particularly prone to disease.
(v)   Retrograde planets cause ill-health.

Nature of Diseases Caused by Planets

Now, keeping in mind the primary significations of the planets including humours of the body, as described in Sec.4.11.4, and the houses owned by them in the *Kaal Purush Kundali*, we now stipulate the diseases that could be caused by them:

Sun: *Pitta.* Fire Element (*Agni-Tattva*). A strong Sun indicates good health, a weak one poor health. It rules over fifth house of stomach. It signifies heart and bones. Hence, heart disease, bone decay, injury, stomach disorders, and fevers due to excessive heat or *pitta*, epilepsy, fire hazards, etc., could be caused by it.

Moon: *Kapha* and *vat.* Water Element (*Jala-Tattva*). Its strength or weakness reflects emotional stability and soundness of mind or otherwise. It rules over fourth house, mind, physical as well as emotional heart, fluids in the body, and blood. Cholera, oedema, pleurisy, tuberculosis, psychiatric problems, emotional disturbances, depression, lack of appetite, excessive or lack of sleep, phlegm, cold and fevers associated with it, heart problems and diseases of the breast signified by fourth house, and flow of milk, menstrual disorders, etc., could be caused by the Moon.

Mars: *Pitta.* Fire Element (*Agni-Tattva*). It reflects the health in general as also vigour, and stamina. It rules over head/first house, bone marrow, muscles, inner lining of uterus and sexual parts and eighth house. Hazards from fire/weapons, shocks, accidents, loss of blood, injuries especially of the head, surgical operations, burns, *pitta*, high blood pressure, excessive heat and associated fevers, thirst, boils, appendicitis, marrow problems, are due to Mars.

Mercury: *Vat, pitta* and *kapha.* It causes fevers from all three humors of body. Earth Element (*Prithvi-Tattva*). Hence, skin and sense of touch can be affected. Air Element (*Vaayu-Tattva*) also. It also rules over speech, throat, the third house and the sixth house. Hence, defective or abusive speech, throat problems, asthma, nervous trouble, skin diseases, leucoderma, impotence, etc., could be due to Mercury. It rules over intelligence, discrimination, and reasoning. Weak Mercury associated with a weak Moon may be cause for mental disorders and nervous break down.

Jupiter: *Kapha.* Ether Element (*Aakash-Tattva*). Hence, cough and problems of sound or hearing. A strong Jupiter protects the native from all evil effects including health problems. It rules over body fat, fever, gall bladder, spleen, pancreas, appendix, etc. Hence, cough, jaundice, liver and gall bladder problems, obesity, laziness, anemia, spleen disorder, etc., are due to a weak Jupiter.

Venus: *Vat* and some *kapha*. Water Element (*Jala-Tattva*). It rules over seventh house, urinary and sexual systems, semen, etc. Hence, urinary disorders, problems of sexual organs, ovaries, prostrate, testes, kidneys, etc., hormonal disorders, veneral diseases, diabetes, stones, etc., could be caused by Venus.

Saturn: *Vat*. Air Element (*Vaayu-Tattva*). It is the slowest moving planet. Diseases caused by it are, therefore, of chronic nature and almost incurable. It rules over legs, tenth and eleventh houses, lymphatic system, nervous system, colon and rectum. It is the *karaka* for sorrow. The Saturnian is also a loner. Wind/gas trouble, paralysis, tumours, cancers, malnutrition, fatigue, exhaustion, worries, sadness, depression, loneliness, melancholy, etc., are caused by Saturn.

Rahu: Rahu is like Saturn. It also causes chronic and incurable diseases. These include leprosy, poisoning, germs, snakebite, pain/injury in legs, insanity, phobias, chronic boils, ulcers, etc.

Ketu: It produces all illnesses signified by Rahu. It gives chronic and difficult to diagnose diseases. It is also like Mars. Hence, it can cause accidents, surgery, etc.

Note: *Vat* produces complaints of wind/gas, neurological disorders, joint pains, etc. *Pitta* produces heat, associated fevers, inflammations, liver/gall bladder disorders. *Kapha* causes cold, cough, associated fevers, respiratory ailments, asthma, etc.

Applying Basic Principles to Diagnose Disease

The basic principles that can be applied to diagnose disease are as follows:

Planets in Houses: Various houses represent different parts of the body and health factors connected with them. Malefics tenanting or aspecting any house cause disease/s in part/s of the body represented by that house according to their nature.

Weak benefics also cause disease according to their own nature. Benefics if retrograde do not protect from disease. Retrograde malefics are worse than direct malefics.

Rahu-Ketu axis falling on *lagna* is particularly adverse for health.

Note that the first house is for head, brain, body in general and appearance. The second is for face, right eye, teeth, tongue, nose and speech. The third is for right ear, throat, neck, shoulders, limbs, wind and food pipe, physical fitness and stamina. The fourth is for chest, breasts, lungs and heart. The fifth is for stomach, liver, gall bladder, spleen, pancreas, duodenum, mind, pregnancy and childbirth. The sixth is for navel region, abdomen, small and large intestines, appendix, kidneys, upper urinary tract, mental agony, tumours, ulcers and diseases in general. The seventh is for end of large intestines, rectum, lower urinary tract, uterus, ovaries, testes, prostrate, seminal vesicles and urethra. The eighth is for external genitals, anus, perineum, severe mental agony, chronic incurable diseases and death. The ninth is for hips and thighs. The tenth is for knees. The eleventh is for legs and left ear. The twelfth is for feet, left eye, sleep and hospitalisation.

Planets in Signs: Various signs represent different parts of the body. Various planets in signs cause the diseases in much the same way as in houses. For example, if Aries is tenanted or aspected by malefics, the native will have disease or injury in head or brain.

***Trik* Houses, *trik* Lords, Planets in *trik* Houses and *Maraka* Lords:** The *trik* houses, their Lords, and planets that tenant the *trik* houses are particularly adverse in relation to health. Their *Dasha* periods must be watched for determining illness.

Further, the Lords of the seventh and second houses are death inflicting or *marakas*. Their *Dasha* periods, particularly at advanced age, must also be watched.

Some Illustrations How Planets Cause Illnesses

Let us reiterate that the Sun and Mars represent the Fire Element/*Agni-Tattva* implying light and sense of vision (*Rupa*), the Moon and Venus the Water Element/*Jala-Tattva* implying body fluids, semen and sense of taste (*Rasa*), Mercury the Earth Element/*Prithvi-Tattva* implying body, skin and sense of touch (*Sparsha*), and Air Element/*Vaayu-Tattva* implying speech, throat, etc., Saturn the Air Element/*Vaayu-Tattva* affecting sense of smell (*Gandha*), and Jupiter the Ether Element/*Akash-Tattva* implying sound (*Shabda*), viz., sense of hearing.

Now, some illustrations how planets cause illnesses are given below:

(i)   The Sun represents sense of vision. In the second house of right eye or the twelfth house of left eye aspected by Mars and/or Saturn, it causes eye disease, even blindness depending on the extent of affliction.

(ii) Jupiter, representing the sound element, in the third house of the right ear or the eleventh house of the left ear, afflicted by Mars and/or Saturn causes hearing problem.

(iii) Any one of the malefics, the Sun, Mars, Saturn, Rahu or Ketu in the fifth or the eleventh house will cause stomach problems.

(iv) The sixth or eighth Lord in the seventh will cause sexual or kidney problems.

(v)   The sixth Lord in the eighth will cause problems in genitals, kidneys, etc.

(vi) The Moon in the sixth or the eighth may cause spleen problem.

(vii) The Moon in the eighth results in too much sleep and laziness.

(viii) Mars or Ketu in eighth may cause accident, injury, and danger to life.

(ix) Mars or Ketu in any other house represent injury/surgery to part of body represented by that house.

(x) Malefics in the eighth, particularly Mars, causes piles, etc.

(xi) Mars, and even other malefics, in the sixth cause *pitta*/high blood pressure.

(xii) Jupiter in *trik* may result in *kapha*, asthma, tuberculosis, etc.

(xiii) Venus in the sixth or the eighth is cause for urinary, sexual and seminal diseases.
Saturn in the sixth or the eighth causes wind.

(xiv) Affliction to Mercury gives nervous trouble.

(xv) Affliction to the Moon and Mercury causes insanity.

In the sample horoscope, Mercury afflicted by enemy Moon in the third caused constant anxiety. Ketu in third resulted in tonsillitis followed by surgery, and throat problems throughout life. Mars in second resulted in disfiguring of the forehead by accident. The fourth Lord, the Sun, in third, twelfth from fourth, conjuncted by Ketu and fourth house receiving great enemy Saturn's aspect caused not only the death of native's mother but also massive heart attack and surgery. Finally, aspect of Mars on fifth and placement of eighth Lord Jupiter in fifth caused chronic ailments of stomach.

Factors for Sound or Ill-Health

One must first make an assessment of health from the birth-chart of the native as follows:

(i) Whether the placement of planets predicts sound health or ill-health.

(ii) Whether the *Dashas* of planets affecting health are current.

The factors that would be conducive to good health in general are the following:

- Strong *lagna*, preferably *Vargottama*, occupied/aspected by benefics or its Lord.
- Strong *lagna* Lord, say, exalted, *Vargottama*, in its own sign or in friend's sign, and not combust, placed in good houses, conjuncted or aspected by natural benefics or friends or *yoga-karaka* planet/s, or forming a *Raja-Yoga*.
- *Shubha-Kartari-Yoga* for *lagna* and *lagna* Lord. Both hemmed between benefics.
- Strong and unafflicted Sun and Moon, hemmed between benefics. The Moon is very important for mental peace. Mercury is also important for mind and brain.
- Malefics confined to third, sixth and eleventh houses only. They will thus provide physical and mental stamina and resistance for annihilation of diseases.
- Benefics in good houses. Note that even benefics also, if weak or retrograde or combust cause ill-health.
- Saturn in eighth promotes longevity.
- Strong eighth Lord also promotes longevity.

Correspondingly, factors for ill-health will be a weak *lagna* and *lagna* Lord, *Papa-Kartari yoga*, weak and afflicted Sun and Moon, benefics in *trik*, malefics in houses other than third, sixth and eleventh, weak Saturn, weak eighth Lord, and so on.

Indications for Recovery from Disease

The following factors in a horoscope indicate tendency for quick recovery from disease:

(i) Strong *lagna* and *lagna* Lord.
(ii) Strong sixth Lord.
(iii) Favourable *Dasha* period operating after the disease.
(iv) Favourable transits operating after the disease.
(v) Jupiter's aspect either in chart or by transit on *lagna*, *lagna* Lord and *Dasha* Lords.

Fiery signs 1, 5 and 7 are best for recovery from disease. But they are accident-prone. Earthly signs 2, 6 and 10 also have fair amount of resistance against disease. Airy signs 3, 7 and 11 are next in order. Watery signs 4, 8 and 12 are most susceptible to disease.

Movable signs 1, 4, 7 and 10 have illnesses for short duration. They are changeable. Fixed signs 2, 5, 8 and 11 have tendency of disease becoming chronic.

Mixed or common or dual signs 3, 6, 9 and 12 have qualities of both.

14.6 LONGEVITY, BIRTH EVILS AND DEATH

For longevity, the eighth house and eighth Lord should be strong. The strength of the *lagna* and *lagna* Lord is also essential for long life. Also:

1. The Moon should be strong. If the Moon is weak and afflicted, it gives rise to birth or infancy evil (*janma/bal-arishta*). The native usually dies early in childhood.
2. Karaka Saturn, if strong, confers longevity.
3. Saturn and/or eighth Lord in eighth, or in third confer long life.

Combinations for Birth Evils

If death occurs within 12 years, it is considered as birth or infancy evil. It is not desirable to predict death within the period of infancy, as it is the consequence of sinful acts of parents, and not of the child. Hence, longevity should be judged only for natives who have crossed 24 years of age.

Janma/bal-arishta does not necessarily mean death. One may just suffer from near-death-like situation. Nevertheless, some prominent indications of the same are given here:

(i) A very weak and severely afflicted Moon receiving no aspects from benefics.

(ii) Severely afflicted *lagna*, and the *lagna* Lord in the eighth and afflicted by malefics.

(iii) Severely afflicted eighth house and eighth Lord.

(iv) Exchange between the *lagna* Lord and the eighth Lord may cause death within five years.

(v) Birth under *Ashlesha* 4, *Revati* 4, *Ashwini* 1, *Makha* 1, and particularly *Jyeshtha* 4 and *Moola* 1 and 2 is evil.

Note: Ill-health/death occurs if the *Dashas* of planets causing severe illness are current.

Antidotes To Evils

Strong *lagna* and *lagna* Lord are an insurance against any evil, ill health or death. *Lagna* Lord alone if strongly placed in *kendra* has the ability to destroy all evils.

Even if one of the benefics happens to be in *kendra*, it destroys all evils as darkness is eliminated just by the rising of the Sun.

And, a single but strong Jupiter in *lagna*, with cancellation of debility if in Capricorn, has the ability to destroy all evils just as a single reverential obeisance to the Supreme Lord can destroy all sins.

No doubt, if all planets are placed in favourable signs and/or favourable *Navanshas*, they become an antidote to any evil.

Causes of Death

According to *Phal-Deepika*, the main causes of death are the following:

Planets Tenanting or Aspecting the Eighth House: Death is caused by chronic, severe or sudden ailment governed by characteristic/s of the planet tenanting/aspecting.

Placement of the Eighth Lord: If there is no planet tenanting/ aspecting the eighth, then the death is caused by the ailment corresponding to part of the body represented by the house in which the eighth Lord is placed. In the sample horoscope, the eighth Lord, Jupiter, is placed in the fifth. Hence, the native may die of stomach ailment simultaneously suffering from *kapha* a characteristic of Jupiter.

Similarly, if the eighth Lord is in the fourth, the native may die of heart attack, and so on.

Sign of the Eighth House and the Eighth Lord: Death may be caused by the nature of the sign and Lord of the eighth house. In the sample horoscope, the eighth sign is Sagittarius, representing foreign lands. The eighth Lord is Jupiter representing liver and having *kapha* nature. Hence, the native may die abroad, and from chronic liver or cough problems.

Note: Jupiter never causes much suffering during death. One has a peaceful death.

14.7 MARRIAGE AND SPOUSE

In connection with marriage, one generally wants to know

    (i) if marriage is promised or not,

    (ii) what kind of marriage partner one would get,

(iii) when would marriage take place, and

(iv) if the married life would be happy.

Marriage is Promised or Not?

The second, seventh and eleventh houses are significators for marriage. The second stands for family. The seventh and eleventh both represent *kama*, viz., sexual desires and their fulfilment. The eleventh also represents permanent and intimate friends and ties. In addition, the fifth house of love is very important for marriage. Hence, the second, fifth, seventh and eleventh houses and their Lords give marriage.

On the contrary, the fourth, sixth and tenth houses that are twelfth from the fifth, seventh and eleventh houses respectively deny marriage. *Dashas* of Lords of the fourth, sixth and tenth houses do not favour marriage.

Thus, we see that some planets act as significators for marriage. Others deny marriage. The planets that act as significators for marriage are as follows:

(i)   Lords of the second, fifth, seventh and eleventh houses.

(ii) Planets occupying the second, fifth, seventh and eleventh houses.

(iii) Planets in the *Nakshatras* of Lords of these houses.

(iv) Planets in the *Nakshatras* of the occupants of these houses.

(v)   Planets aspecting these houses.

It is evident that planets posited in the sixth and tenth houses in addition to the Lords of these houses do not support marriage. Thus, in a horoscope in which a large number of planets and the Lords of the second, seventh and eleventh houses are placed in the sixth and tenth houses, the marriage may not take place at all.

In addition to the seventh Lord, we examine Venus for spouse. The Moon, which determines female company, is also considered for wife along with Venus.

Thus, marriage is promised usually if any of the following conditions are present:

(i)   The Moon and Venus in the chart are well placed and receive harmonious aspects.

(ii) Benefics occupy the second, fifth, seventh and eleventh houses counted from the *lagna* or the Moon.

(iii) The Moon and Venus are not aspected by Saturn. Saturn's aspect delays marriage.

(iv) The Lord of the *lagna* and the seventh Lord have mutual or favourable sextile or trine aspect with respect to each other.

(v)   Lords of the second, fifth, seventh and eleventh houses are well placed.

As stated earlier, the fifth house is a significator of love while the fourth denies love. Accordingly, there will be no love marriage if the fifth house and Lord are afflicted or if the fifth Lord is in the fourth or in any of the *trik* houses.

What Kind of Marriage Partner would One Get?

The characteristics and nature of the marriage partner are judged from the seventh house, its sign and its Lord, the nature of planets posited in the seventh house, planets aspecting the seventh house and seventh Lord and Venus. For example, Venus in Taurus indicates a wife who gives sincere love and physical pleasures to the man, Venus in Gemini indicates pleasures more from conversations, and so on. When Venus is strong, one gets a chaste wife, and great enjoyment from her.

For pleasures of the bed, we have to examine the twelfth house also. Venus in the twelfth house gives much sexual pleasure.

Pleasures from Plurality of Partners

It must be pointed out that the second house is considered for second marriage. Hence, the indications for pleasures from plurality of partners of opposite sex are the following:

- If an afflicted second house has a common sign, more than one marriage is likely.
- There is separation or more than one marriage if the seventh Lord is in the twelfth.
- Mars–Venus conjunction in a chart indicates sex pleasures from plurality of persons. Mars–Venus–Saturn combination keeps the affairs secret.
- Malefics in the fourth indicate lack of character.
- If afflicted the Moon or Venus are together in any house, the likelihood is that the native may violate the relation represented by that house.
- If both the seventh Lord and Venus are in common signs or *navanshas*, the person will have more than one marriage. The seventh Lord in the seventh shows limited pleasures with many.
- The first and seventh Lord in exchange show unlimited pleasures. If no afflictions are present, it could also mean great love between native and spouse.
- An evil aspect between Venus and Uranus indicates upheaval in married life though, in a man's horoscope, it may give pleasures from unmarried girls.
- Moon–Venus evil aspect indicates enjoyment with others' partners.
- More the number of planets in the seventh house, more the number of relationships.

Timing of Marriage

Dashas and transits decide the timing. Both must favour marriage.

Favourable *Dashas* are, primarily, those of the planets connected with the first, second, fifth, seventh, ninth and eleventh houses. The planets placed in these houses, or those that are Lords thereof, are most favourable.

As far as transits are concerned, most important factor is Jupiter, the *karaka* for marriage. The transits of Jupiter through the second, fifth, seventh, ninth and eleventh houses from the *lagna* or from the Moon, whichever is stronger, promote prospects of marriage, when the *Dashas* also support the same. Probability of marriage increases during the *Dashas* of the seventh Lord and planets aspecting the seventh, and during transit of the *lagna* Lord over the seventh house.

Contrary to the above, at the time of right age for marriage, if the *Dashas* of planets connected with the fourth, sixth and tenth houses are current then marriage will not take place.

In the case of a person in whose chart most of the planets are connected with these houses then the marriage may not take place at all.

Note: For marriage to take place, usually, the fifth house and/or the eleventh must somehow be involved, either by *Dasha* or by transit.

Will the Married Life be Happy? Will there be Separation/Divorce?

The quality of married life also is to be judged from the seventh house, its Lord and Venus. When they are strong, one has happiness and enjoyment from marriage. When they are weak, one does not have much happiness.

In addition, the second house for family, the fourth for character and inner bliss, the fifth for children and love, the second and the eighth for longevity of spouse and self, the ninth which is fifth from fifth for children and destiny, the eleventh for intimacy and the twelfth house for pleasures of the bed may also be examined.

Basically if the fifth and the seventh houses from the *lagna* and the Moon are tenanted and/or aspected by their own Lords and/or by benefics, then one gets favourable results in regard to spouse, love, children and happy married life. If it is not so, then the results are contrary.

If the seventh Lord and Venus are in debilitation or enemy's sign or combust or aspected by malefics, and if the seventh house is also tenanted/aspected by malefics, then certainly it is equivalent to the loss of marital happiness in one way or the other.

If the seventh Lord is in the sixth, which is twelfth from the seventh, then marriage is denied. And, if at all it does take place due to some other favourable factors, then the married life is not a happy one. The spouse may be suffering from some unknown illness. It is also an indication of marriage with a cousin, which can as well be considered to mean someone close or known for a long time. In fact, with the seventh Lord in the sixth, one should consider marrying only if one finds someone with whom the native is well acquainted. This way the evil effects of placement of the seventh Lord in the sixth can be mitigated.

If the seventh Lord is in the eighth then the spouse will be sickly and quarrelsome.

The seventh Lord in the twelfth implies loss of marriage partner, or separation.

If any of the *trik* Lords is placed in the seventh, then also the married life suffers.

Further, malefics particularly Mars, causing *mangalik dosha*, in the first, second, fourth, seventh, eighth and twelfth houses from the *lagna* or from the Moon are evil for marital relationship unless the evil is set off by similar placements in both charts.

Even if the two charts have similar *mangalik dosha*, the evil is not set off completely. There will be no conjugal bliss.

If malefics like Mars and/or Saturn are placed in seventh with respect to the Moon or Venus, then again one may lose one's wife. If malefics are in debilitation or in enemy's sign in the second, seventh or eighth house, then the spouse may die prematurely.

With *nadi-dosh* also, the results are very *ashubha*. The husband or wife or both may not survive if both belong to the same *nadi*.

If marriage takes place during *Dashas* of planets unfavourable for harmonious relationship, or during *Sadhe-Saati* or when Saturn is aspecting the seventh house with respect to the Moon, it bodes ill for married life. Because, when the first few years of married life are unhappy, then the rest of the life cannot be expected to be very happy.

In astrology, *lagna* represents the body and the Moon the mind. Love is the basic need and attribute of the mind. Hence, the matching of horoscopes for marriage is done in Vedic/Indian astrology on the basis of the *rashis* and *Nakshatras* of the Moon of the boy and the girl. Needless to say that if the matching points are less than 18, and/or if there is *nadi-dosh*, and/or if the *rashis* are in 6-8 or 2-12 positions, and/or if there is *mangalik-dosha*, and/or if marriage takes place between *Rakshasa* and *Manushya Ganas*, and/or if *Sadhe-Saati* prevails at the time of marriage with ill-placed Saturn in the birth horoscope, then married life will be affected. To what extent it will be affected will depend on the severity of affliction/s.

Note: Along with *Lagna-Kundali*, *Navansha Kundali* must also be examined for marriage and spouse.

Often, one asks that even when marriage was solemnised with high number of matching points, and there were no *nadi* and *mangalik doshas*, and life was going on well for quite some time after marriage, then why did it turn sour at some point of time, and why did it end in separation. The answer to this is the following. The placement of planets and the *Dashas* must also be examined. If the *Dashas* of planets unfavourable for happy married life are current during the prime of youth, such as the 7-years of Mars or18-years of Rahu or 19-years of Saturn that happen to be placed in the crucial twelfth house, or that of the seventh Lord that happens to be combust or placed in the *trik*, then in spite of the matching, results will be evil at some point of time when the evil *Dashas* are on.

14.8 LIVELIHOOD AND CAREER COUNSELLING

Primarily, livelihood is judged from the tenth house. One's life is very much dependent on the service and cooperation of others. Hence, livelihood is not only a means to regular income, but also an opportunity to serve society, and more important to earn name, fame, recognition and status, all significations of the tenth house, the house of *karmas*. One, however, earns livelihood by the application of one's knowledge and ability acquired through education. Hence, the fifth house has great influence on livelihood.

Apart from the tenth, the sixth house that is the ninth, from tenth governing fate of the work undertaken, and the seventh that is the tenth from tenth are also examined. For income the eleventh, and for accumulation of wealth, the second must also be considered simultaneously.

For agriculture, the fourth house is important. For service, the third house of effort must be taken into account. For business and partnership/s, the seventh house is examined.

Judging from Planets in Tenth House

We judge livelihood essentially from planets in the tenth in the *lagna*-chart. But, the *Chandra* and *Surya kundalis* should be considered if there is no planet in the tenth in *lagna*-chart.

The Sun in the tenth shows gain from the father and the father's support to the native's career. The Moon, similarly means gain/support from the mother, Mars from the brother/s and even enemies, Mercury from friends, Jupiter from the elder brother and from one's preceptor/Guru, Venus from women, and Saturn from servants and subordinates.

Basically, the Sun in the tenth does not merely mean gain from father alone but from all significations for which the Sun is the *karaka*. The same way, it should be understood for the other planets as well. One must also keep in mind the significations of the *rashis* and houses ruled by the planets in the *Kaal Purush Kundali*, and the houses for which it is the *karaka*.

A brief list the of kinds of work possibilities indicated by each planet are given below:

Sun: The *karaka* for the first and the tenth. Lord of Leo and fith in the *Kaal Purush Kundali*. Directional strength also in tenth. Father's support, even his wealth. Government service, or service of an eminent person. The Sun, often gives success in medical field and from medical items. The Sun is most suited for administration.

Moon: The *karaka* for the fourth. Lord of Cancer and the fourth. Exalted in the second in the *Kaal Purush Kundali*. Mother's support. Career in wealth. Money and its transactions, second house. From significations of the Moon and Cancer: Jobs including those pertaining to water such as export/import, agriculture, canals, irrigation, dams, water-works, ocean engineering, fishery, marine equipment, pearls, silver, drinks, milk, dairy, butter, oil, sugar, pilgrimages, support of women, etc.

Mars: The *karaka* for the third and the sixth. Lord of Aries in the first and Scorpio in the eighth. Exalted in the tenth in the *Kaal Purush Kundali*. The tenth house is the best position of Mars. Younger brother's support. Success through hardwork and competition. From fire and metals, welding, furnaces, metallurgy, bakery, restaurant, etc., electricity, electrical and mechanical engineering, from valour as required for army, police, technical administration.

Mercury: The *karaka* for the fourth and the tenth. Lord of Gemini in the third and Virgo in the sixth in the *Kaal Purush Kundali*, both common signs. Support of friends. Jobs that require interacting with many diverse kinds of people. From business and trade. From poetry, writing, journalism, editing, publishing, communications, rail, mail, telecommunication, linguistics, sciences, mathematics, computers, commission agency, stock brokerage, astrology, etc.

Jupiter: The *karaka* for the second, fifth, ninth, tenth and eleventh houses. Lord of Sagittarius in the ninth and Pisces in the twelfth in the *Kaal Purush Kundali*. Elder brother and Guru's support. From family business, banking, financial transactions, etc., thus promoting the second house, from jobs requiring high education/teaching signifying the fifth house, from spirituality of the ninth house, being judge, magistrate, lawyer, and as government official signifying the tenth house itself, high-income jobs leading to fulfilment of pious desires enhancing the eleventh house.

Venus: The *karaka* for the seventh. Lord of Taurus in the second and Libra in the seventh in the *Kaal Purush Kundali*. One gains from kindness and support of a rich woman/wife. From milk, dairy, and foods represented by the second house, business and partnerships promoting the seventh house and aesthetic/artistic pursuits, cosmetics, beauty aids, things of luxury, silk, garments, silver, jewellery, music, singing, cinema, TV, entertainment, conveyance and transport, etc., all significations of Venus.

Saturn: The *karaka* for the sixth, eighth, tenth and twelfth. Lord of Capricorn and Aquarius in the tenth and eleventh in the *Kaal Purush Kundali*. Greatest significator for career and income. Gains from servants, service, unreputed deeds, etc. Either one renders service or one gets service. A service job is strongly indicated. One earns by shear hard work. From jobs based in Earth's womb, land, agriculture of coarse grains, wood, furniture, stones, queries, cement, roads, construction, mining and minerals, coal, iron, railway, petrol, etc. Saturn can also make one an engineer.

Rahu: It makes one distrustful, covetous and evil in his/her work.

Ketu: Native is sincere, hardworking, compassionate, and at ease with coworkers.

Work prospects with outer planets are indicated below. They all seek change, sometimes in a violent way like Uranus and Pluto, and in a milder way like Neptune.

Uranus: Both Uranus and its sign Aquarius are independent minded and freedom loving. Uranus, in addition, is anti-establishment. It tends to enter into conflict with authorities. Careers, which permit independence and revolutionary changes, suit Uranus. It is also significator for deep and secret knowledge. Uranus may incline one towards research and invention. One seeks novel and strange ways of earning.

Neptune: Neptune is a mystical and psychic planet. Both Neptune and its sign Pisces have interest in idealistic and artistic professions. Both are *karakas* for water. Hence, one seeks professions connected with water, seas, shipping, etc. Some natives are great psychologists, psychiatrists, healers and philosophers. Cotton, cloth, textiles are connected with Neptune.

Pluto: Pluto is like Mars. It cannot sit idle and always seeks changes for progress. Hence, vocations that involve constant activity are suitable. The native also revels in defeating enemies/competitors. Jobs that require aggression suit the native.

Basically, the Sun stands for administration, leadership, medicine, Moon is for money and its transactions, music, liquids, women, Mars for fighting, competitions, army, surgery, Mercury for trade, commerce, mathematics, computers, communications, reading, writing, Jupiter for teaching, justice, religious pursuits, finance, Venus for arts, aesthetic pursuits, Saturn for diligence, service, agriculture, engineering, dentistry, and Rahu and Ketu for common jobs that do not require any special knowledge or skills.

Note that strong sixth and twelfth houses of disease and hospitalisation indicate success as a doctor. And a strong third house for stamina and sixth house for competitions indicate career as sportsman/woman.

If there are too many planets in the tenth house, it does not imply a great success in career.

If the planets are mutual enemies, they will work at cross-purposes.

Sun–Saturn together anywhere will bring trouble and sorrow to the *bhava*.

If Mars and Saturn are together, Mars will want to work to satisfy its ego while Saturn will want to work with a spirit of service. Unnecessary conflicts will result.

Saturn–Moon combination denotes depression or restlessness, which is an obstacle.

Saturn–Ketu contradiction will be dragging to the native in the pursuit of career. Ketu represents renunciation and detachment. It considers compulsion of work as bondage. Saturn, on the other hand, considers work as duty and *karma* as worship.

But if the planets are mutual friends, such as the Sun and Jupiter or the Sun and Mars, they will be complimentary to each other, and success is assured.

Judging from the Sign in Tenth House

One can get adequate hints about career from the sign of the tenth house. First note the triplicities.

Fiery Signs: Aries, Leo and Sagittarius. Aries and Leo give success in professions requiring administration, courage, valour, stamina, fire, energy, metallurgy, weapons, army, etc. Sagittarius is more influenced by its Lord Jupiter. It may lead the native into finance, teaching, and things to do with foreigners/foreign lands, outdoor activity, etc.

Earthly signs: Taurus, Virgo and Capricorn. Native engages in materially fruitful, earthly, practical, realistic and Earth-based jobs.

Airy signs: Gemini, Libra and Aquarius. Native likes jobs requiring intelligence, reading, writing, teaching, advising, and those that are air-based, such as flying, space, aircrafts, etc.

Watery signs: Cancer, Scorpio and Pisces. Native likes jobs which are water based, such as irrigation, water supply, milk, dairy, drinks, oils, chemicals, drugs, shipping, fishery, etc.

Now, consider the quadruplicities.

Movable signs: Aries, Cancer, Libra and Capricorn like jobs requiring travel, movement and change. They are basically impatient to achieve progress, wealth, name and fame.

Fixed signs: Taurus, Leo, Scorpio and Aquarius are cautious, reserved and not amenable to change. They like sedentary jobs requiring patience, self-confidence, and responsibility and working in a planned manner.

Common signs: Gemini, Virgo, Sagittarius and Pisces make one adaptable. The native recognises opportunity, exploits it and moulds situations and people s/he is working with.

Note: An important thing to note is that the signs of both the *lagna* and the tenth house belong to the same quadruplicity. Hence, basic nature of the native, and his/her preference for the nature of work whether movable, fixed or common are same.

Specific professions can be suggested for each sign keeping nature of sign and its Lord and the *Kaal Purush Kundali* in mind:

Aries: Mars/First House. Army, police, fire, metals, surgery, dentistry, self-employment.

Taurus: Venus/Second House. Money transactions. Sincere. Seeks material gains and job security. Family business. Food processing/preservation.

Beauty aids, cosmetics, garments, jewels, vehicles, music, dance, acting, entertainment, etc.

Gemini: Mercury/Third House. Reading, writing, teaching, journalism, publishing, editing, communications, travel agencies, craftsman, mathematics, computers, etc.

Cancer: Moon/Fourth House. Desire to earn name/fame. Interior designer, housewife, schoolteacher, water transport/works, irrigation, canals, manufacturing/dealing in drinks, chemicals, oil, petrol, edible oils, etc.

Leo: Sun/Fifth House: Leo leads. Earns respect. Leadership. Management. Government service. Higher education. Medical profession. Leo is related to forests, forestry, wild life sanctuaries. Leo is king of zodiac, hence as legislator/high official.

Virgo: Mercury/Sixth House: Extremely practical/perfectionist. Teacher, writer, editor, publisher, printer. Also as doctor, nurse, psychiatrist, neurosurgeon. Virgo is mathematician, computer professional, accountant, etc.

Libra: Venus/Seventh House: Business. Partnership. Foreign travel. Libra stands for justice. Lawyer, judge or constitutional expert. Careers of music, dance, arts, culture, acting, entertainment, fashion modelling/designing, cosmetics. Also as receptionist, social welfare, liaison, etc. Career in aircrafts, as pilot, airhostess.

Scorpio: Mars/Eighth House: Life insurance. Army, navy, police. Career in chemicals, drugs, medicines, pharmacy, surgery, and nursing. Scorpio is secretive. Spying/investigative agencies. Jobs reposing wisdom/philosophical knowledge.

Sagittarius: Jupiter/Ninth House: *Dharma* makes them suitable as lawyer, judge, social worker or preacher. Sagittarian takes risk. Is fond of animals. Hence, an athlete, horse rider, veterinary doctor, etc. Jupiter makes one a financial expert, banker, economist, capitalist, learned professor. Jobs of travel, outdoor life, foreign lands.

Capricorn: Saturn/Tenth House. Most realistic/practical person. Earthly. Interests in land, queries, geology, geophysics, mining, agriculture, horticulture, building construction, architecture, engineering, etc. Likes service jobs, physical labour.

Aquarius: Saturn/Eleventh House. Independent minded. Stubborn. Good mechanic whether it be cars or computers. Saturn makes one hardworking. Works that require low level of investment. Airy sign interests in teaching and research also.

Pisces: Jupiter/Twelfth House: Idealistic. Saintly. Engages in spiritual/welfare work. May become a physician/healer. Piscean is for fisheries. Twelfth is for jails, hospital service, ships, foreign lands. Watery sign makes sensitive/artistic. Career in acting, music and arts, or one dealing in fluids, liquors, chemical, oils, etc.

Judging from the Tenth Lord in Various *Bhavas*

The effects of placements of *bhava* Lords in the tenth and the tenth Lord in various *bhavas* have been discussed in Sec. 8.4. However, some specific points are being mentioned below:

In *lagna*: Usually own independent business or pursuits.

In Second: May carry on family's traditional business/profession. Since the second house governs wealth, food, and speech also, one may earn from stocks, shares, banking, etc., or from dealing in food items, or from professions that require speaking.

In Third: Reading, writing, journalism, communications, short travel, transport, etc.

In Fourth: Aspects own house from here. Very good position. The fourth house represents mother, home, land, property, vehicles, etc. It is the natural house of Cancer, a watery sign with its Lord Moon. One gets mother's support in career. May earn from jobs involving interior decoration/design, land development, housing, sale and purchase of property/vehicles, agriculture, horticulture, water supply, canals, dams, irrigation, etc.

In Fifth: Kendra-Lord in trine gives *Raja-Yoga*. Career in education, speculation, etc.

In Sixth: In *trik*. Faces problems. Can be a policeman, jailor or army officer or doctor or lawyer or judge. Since the sixth is the ninth from tenth, it is considered a good house for work.

In Seventh: Gets the help of spouse. Spouse may also be earning. Business, partnerships, work involving foreign travel or stay abroad. The seventh is tenth from the tenth, and a *kendra* also. It is a very good position for the tenth house affairs.

In Eighth: In *trik*. *Ashubha*. The native is lazy. Uses foul means. May be demoted.

In Ninth: Natural house of Sagittarius and Jupiter. Very good conduct. Truthful in work. May become a spiritual teacher. May earn from jobs involving travelling/foreign lands.

In Tenth: The tenth Lord in the tenth house is about the best placement. The significations of the sign and the Lord govern the career. The native gets recognition.

In Eleventh: Placed in the eleventh house of gains, and second from the tenth, implying wealth, it brings fortunes to the native. Financial institutions. Family business/industry.

In Twelfth: In *trik. Ashubha.* May earn from foreign lands. Work in prisons, hospitals, espionage, etc. The twelfth is third from the tenth. Constant travelling, hardwork, little return.

Note: Placement of Lords of different *bhavas* in tenth house gives similar results.

Other Methods of Judging

Saturn is one of the *karakas* for the tenth house. It is also the Lord of the tenth and eleventh houses in the *Kaal Purush Kundali.* Hence, many astrologers judge livelihood just from Saturn. In any case, the placement of Saturn should be given due importance in this respect. Basic principle is to judge from the attributes of the sign occupied by Saturn and the sign Lord.

Primarily, we judge livelihood from the *Lagna-Kundali* from planet/s in the tenth house. Next, we consider the sign in the tenth house and its Lord, and planets aspecting the tenth house.

However, *Dashamansha Kundali* may also be considered for career.

14.9 FOREIGN TRAVEL/SETTLING ABROAD

The ninth house is for long travels, and the twelfth for foreign lands. The seventh house also represents foreign travels particularly in connection with business.

The ninth and twelfth houses tenanted/aspected by benefics or their own Lords bring gains from foreign countries. The Lord of the ninth in the twelfth, though it indicates poor background and ill-luck, means foreign travel. The Lord of the twelfth in the ninth indicates residence and prosperity abroad and much property there.

The Lord of the tenth in the seventh shows travel abroad on diplomatic missions. If Lord of the seventh is in the tenth, one is involved in a career of constant travel.

The Lord of the seventh in the ninth, if fortified, will bring fortune to the native in foreign lands. Some other indications are as follows:

(i) Those born in Anuradha *Nakshatra* prosper abroad.
(ii) Those having a number of retrograde planets in their chart prosper only abroad, and not in their own country.
(iii) Rahu *Dasha* also takes one abroad.
(iv) The Moon is the *karaka* for travel. Placed in movable signs, it indicates lot of travels.
(v) The Moon in the twelfth, though evil for happiness, is a strong indicator for settlement abroad provided some other factors also favour the same.

14.10 PREDICTING FROM *PRASHNA-KUNDALI*

Often, a person comes to an astrologer with a question (*Prashna*), but s/he does not know his/her birth details. In such a situation, the astrologer usually casts a horoscope for the moment of enquiry and predicts accordingly. This horoscope is called *Prashna-Kundali*. Believe it or not, the method works very well.

Now, in the *Prashna-Kundali* we have *lagna*, and all the *bhavas*. This *lagna* represents the question of the native. Usually, only one question is answered by this *kundali*. We are concerned with the *bhava* with which the question is related. Let us call the Lord of this *bhava* as *bhavesh*, and Lord of *lagna* as *lagnesh*.

Then success in regard to the matter of the question asked is assured if we have the following:

(i) *Lagnesh* and *Bhavesh* exchange houses.

(ii) *Lagnesh* and *Bhavesh* tenant or aspect their own houses.

(iii) *Lagnesh* and *Bhavesh* are conjoined, and together they tenant or aspect *lagna* or *bhava*. Mutual aspect of the two is also to be considered in the same way.

(iv) *Lagnesh* aspects *bhava* or *Bhavesh* aspects *lagna*.

(v) If instead of *lagna* and *Lagnesh*, the ninth house and the ninth Lord are similarly placed with respect to *bhava* and *Bhavesh*, then also favourable results will follow.

(vi) If the Moon aspects any of these houses or their Lords, then success becomes very much pre-ordained. The Moon is the seed for mental strength and enthusiasm, and hence for success.

Some other combinations are as follows:

Sambandh between *Lagnesh* and the second Lord increases wealth, family fortunes, etc.

Sambandh between *Lagnesh* and the seventh Lord is conducive to marriage taking place, marital happiness, etc.

Sambandh between *Lagnesh* and/or *Bhavesh* and the *trik* are evil. With the sixth Lord, it may bring illness, enmity, litigation, etc., with the eighth Lord demotion, downfall, suffering, insult, accident, etc., with the twelfth Lord hospitalisation, scandal, excessive expenditure or loss, and so on.

We should also see the placement of the *karaka* for the *bhava*, and the great benefactor Jupiter.

General principles of prediction can also be applied to *Prashna-Kundali*. For example, good health is predicted if malefics are in the third, sixth and eleventh houses and benefics are in houses other that the *trik* and the third, in both *Janma-Kundali* and/or *Prashna-Kundali*.

14.11 AUSPICIOUS TIME (*SHUBHA MUHURTA*)

From ancient times, people have been considering auspicious (*shubha*) time (*muhurta*) for starting new activity. For the purpose we cast a chart corresponding to the date and time of commencing the activity. We call it *Muhurta-Chart*. The *lagna* of this chart is named *Muhurta-Lagna*. And the planetary positions at the time of starting of the activity in the *Muhurta-Chart* determine its progress. It is like the birth chart of the activity/event.

Other factors for successful growth of the activity are the favourable *Dashas* and positions of transiting planets in the birth-chart of the native at the time of the event, and also months, *rashis*, *tithis* and *Nakshatras*, and *yogas* that may be formed.

Shubha Muhurta for Marriage

The auspicious times are as follows:

Months:	When the Sun is in *Vrishchik*, *Makar*, *Kumbha*, *Mesha*, *Vrishabh*, *Mithun*.
Tithis:	The three *Rikta tithis* 4, 9, 14 are *ashubha*.
Nakshatras:	All fixed *Nakshatras Rohini, U. Phalguni, U. Ashadh, U. Bhadra*, are *shubha* as the event is of fixed/everlasting nature. *Mrigashira, Revati, Anuradha, Moola, Swati, Makha, Hasta* are also considered auspicious.

Muhurta lagnas:	The best *muhurta* for solemnising marriage ceremony is at the time when *lagnas* of benefics Mercury, Venus and Jupiter, viz., *Vrishabha, Mithuna, Kanya, Tula, Dhanu, Meena* are rising.
Guru-Bal:	Means strength of Jupiter. Transit Jupiter is best in the second, fifth, seventh, ninth, eleventh from the Moon-Sign. It is *ashubha* in the fourth, eighth or twelfth.
Chandra-Bal:	Transit Moon is *ashubha* in the fourth, eighth and twelfth from the Moon-Sign.
Shukra-Bal:	Venus should never be combust.
Surya-Bal:	Transit Sun should be in *Upchaya* houses from the Moon-Sign. The Sun in the first and seventh houses should be avoided.
Planets:	Benefics should be in good houses, preferably in *kendras* and Trikonas in *muhurta lagna*, and malefics should only be in the third, sixth and eleventh houses. Malefics transiting the *lagna* and the seventh house are inauspicious. Mars should not be in the first, seventh, eighth and twelfth houses. There should be no planets transiting the eighth and twelfth houses. Transit Saturn is particularly bad in the twelfth house. It is auspicious in the sixth. *muhurta lagna* Lord should not be in the sixth and the eighth in the *Muhurta-Chart*.

Likewise, auspicious times for other activities can also be decided.

The Sun in *Uttarayana* that is when it is travelling from Capricorn to Gemini is considered favourable for all auspicious *muhurtas*.

Choose a proper *lagna* and placement of planets suitable for nature of activity. Choose fixed signs (2, 5, 8, 11) for activities of fixed nature, and movable signs (1, 4, 7, 10) for activities that require mobility/change. Choose male/odd signs for activities needing dynamism, and female/even signs for activities of artistic/sobre nature.

The strength of the *lagna*, and the strength of the house pertaining to the activity must be ensured.

No auspicious activity should be undertaken when either Jupiter or Venus or both are combust, or when Jupiter is in debility.

Jupiter in Leo is also considered inauspicious. During *sankranti*, that is, when Sun is leaving a sign and entering a new sign, 6H 24M period from either sign, is to be avoided.

Further, the nature of *tithis* is as follows:

The Lord of *Nanda tithis* (1, 6, 11) is Venus. These are good for enjoyments.

The Lord of *Bhadra tithis* (2, 7, 12) is Mercury. These are good for *shubha* activities.

The Lord of *Jaya tithis* (3, 8, 13) is Mars. These endow victory. Whatever is obtained, started or done on Akshaya Tritiya, which comes twelve days before Buddha-Purnima, remains eternal source of joy. Buddha-Purnima usually falls in May.

The Lord of *Rikta tithis* (4, 9, 14) is Saturn. *Rikta* means emptiness. No auspicious activity should be undertaken on Rikta *tithis*.

The Lord of *Purna tithis* (5, 10, 15) is Jupiter. Jupiter signifies abundance. These are *shubha*.

Chapter 15

Remedies

Sant Tulsidas, in his epic *Rama-Charita-Manas* says that during Lord Rama's rule there was nobody who suffered from any of the three kinds of sufferings (*dukhas*), whether of the body (*dehik*), or proceeding from supernatural agencies (*daivik*), or those caused by living beings (*bhautik*).

Often, one classifies sufferings as of body, mind and soul.

15.1 WHY THE SUFFERING?

Everyone, naturally, wants to be happy. No one wants to be unhappy. Then, why the unhappiness, why the suffering? The root cause of suffering is 'desire' (*trishna* or *kamana*). It has two aspects:

(i) **Craving (*Raga*):** What gives us pleasure/happiness (*sukha*), we want to have it again and again. This is craving or *Raga*. And, when we do not get it we become unhappy. It is not possible to be happy simply by craving for objects (*vastu*), individuals (*vyakti*), and situations (*paristhti*). It is not in our hands. Objects, individuals and situations favouring happiness are the outcome of our past *karmas*.

(ii) **Hatred/Aversion (*Dwesha*):** What gives us pain/ unhappiness/suffering (*dukha*), we want to avoid. We start hating objects, individuals and situations we do not like. This is hatred/aversion or *dwesha*. We do not realise that the unfavourable factors also are the result of our past *karmas*.

A thing to realise is that *Raga* in something implies *Dwesh* in something else. They are two sides of the same coin.

15.2 THE WISDOM OF *GITA*

Our holy scripture the *Gita* is an infinite ocean of wisdom. Whenever we are in the midst of suffering, we go to the *Gita* for solace. But, soon after, we forget about it.

The *Gita*, essentially, preaches three paths to achieve happiness and to attain divine bliss.

One is that of Gyan, discriminating between *Sat* the soul or the 'Higher Self' that which never suffers or dies, and *Asat* the 'Body' that which suffers and dies.

The other is that of *Bhakti*, Devotion and Surrender to God leading to 'Love' and 'Bliss'.

The third is the path of *Nishkaam-Karma*, *karma* without craving or aversion that is to say without attachment to the fruits of *karmas*. Such *karmas* are devoid of any good or evil effects.

15.3 THE FIVE DELUSIONS

But how our *karmas* get deluded. The answer is the desire (*kamna*). Desire is delusion. There are five delusions, diseases of the mind, from which everyone suffers. These are:

  (i) Attachment or Infatuation (*moha*)

  (ii) Lust (*kama*)

  (iii) Anger (*krodha*)

  (iv) Greed (*lobha*)

  (v) Ego (*ahankaar*)

Tulsi Das elaborates that from these delusions arise all troubles.

Infatuation or *moha* is the root cause of all ailments and bad *karmas*.

Lust or *kama*, another name for craving/*Raga*, is counterpart of Wind or *vaat*.

Anger or *krodha*, another name for aversion/hatred/*Dwesh*, represents Bile or *pitta*.

Greed or *lobha* results in abundance of phlegm or *kapha*.

Should all these three combine, there results a derangement of all the three humours of the body causing fever which is of a dangerous type.

One may even be able to overcome *kama* and *krodha*, but *lobha* comes in many different forms.

One may possibly be able to overcome *lobha* also, but even great saints are unable to overcome *ahankaar* or ego.

Ahankaar is the feeling of 'me' and 'mine' or 'you' and 'yours'. The resulting envy and the grudging contemplation of others' happiness may result in tuberculosis. Wickedness and perversity may cause leprosy.

Egotism, in general, is the counterpart of the most painful gout.

While hypocrisy, deceit, arrogance and pride correspond to diseases caused by parasites.

There are many more types of afflictions too numerous to mention. One may die of just one disease while innumerable incurable ones are there to constantly torment the soul.

15.4 HOW TO ALLEVIATE SUFFERING (*DUKHA*)? SPIRITUAL REMEDIES

It is just not possible to have happiness ever by snatching it from others. How can then soul find peace?

The primary principle is by 'giving' rather than by always hankering for 'receiving'. Whatever you want to have for yourself, start giving the same to others. If you want more money, start giving money to your near and dear ones and also in charity to the needy. If you want to be loved, start giving love to one and all. This circulation of 'giving' and 'receiving' must go on. It is only by circulation of blood in the body that one can survive. Any attempt to stop the circulation by blocking the flow will eventually result in illness and eventual death.

Below are pointed out some basic elements of spiritual remedies to alleviate suffering and to enhance happiness.

Sacred vows (*sankalpas*).

Religious observances and practices (*dharma-karma*).

Austere penance (*tapa*).

Gyan/Spiritual wisdom or staying in equanimity (*samta*) as mentioned earlier.

Sacrifices (*tyag*).

Recitation of prayers or chanting of the names of God (*japa*).

Charity (*dana*).

Virtuous deeds (*punya*).

Compassion (*karuna*) and Service (*seva*).

Herbs and medicines (*aushadh*).

These are spiritual remedies. All these measures have the effect of either exhausting past accumulated negative evil *karmas* by self-sacrifice, or neutralising them by new positive good *karmas* of the present birth. The suffering can no doubt be eradicated if the following factors combine:

1. *Gyan*: The regimen is indifference to the pleasures of senses. That is to stay in equanimity. No craving, no aversion. When you have *sukha*, share it with others. And when you have *dukha*, consider it, as the outcome of your own *karmas* of innumerable previous births, and that this is the divine way of exhausting those *karmas*. So drop the desire for *sukha*. And suffering will be automatically gone.

2. *Bhakti*: Devotion and surrender to the Supreme Lord is the life-giving herb while a devout mind serves as the vehicle in which it is taken. In practical terms, it will mean prayer (*prarthana*), followed by efforts (*parakram*), and then wait (*pratiksha*) for divine grace. God will take care of you just like the mother who takes total care of the child on her own.

The path of *Bhakti* is very simple, but difficult to explain, while that of *Gyan* is difficult to follow though very logical and easy to explain.

The path of *Nishkaam-karma* is similar to both *Gyan* and *Bhakti*.

15.5 WHY ASTROLOGICAL REMEDIES?

If overwhelming problems are encountered in life, and if afflictions are so severe as to push a person into grave mental distress and depression such as great unhappiness in marriage and relationships, or a life threatening ailment or bankruptcy, so that one is completely incapable of undertaking corrective measures as described above on one's own, then some remedial help is required to put the person on a guided path of routine practices to eventually lead him/her to a pious and happy life.

So we find the causes and thence remedies by seeing the positions of planets in one's birth-chart and also by finding out what *Dashas* one is going through.

Malefics/*Papa-Grahas*

Note that Sun, Mars, Saturn, Rahu and Ketu are the five natural malefics. Lords of the *trik* are also *ashubha*. Planets tenanting *trik* houses also give evil results during their *Dashas*. Planets, which are weak, combust, debilitated or retrograde give *ashubha* results. If the *Dasha* or *Antardasha* Lord is the *lagna's* enemy, it causes agony to the native. Further, second and seventh Lords become *marakas* if their *Dashas* are current at proper age.

External Symptoms of Maleficence of Planets

Often, it happens that we are not able to judge as to which planet and for what reason it is acting as *ashubha*. In that case, it can be recognised from external symptoms as follows:

Sun: When the Sun is *shubha*, one is always glowing with high sprits and confidence. When the Sun is weak, its significations, happiness from father, father's health, eyesight, Government service, name/fame/status, etc., may suffer. The native encounters difficulties in inheriting parental property and wealth. His/her body may start stiffening due to bone problems. S/he may find mouth dry though always full of spit. The native loses willpower.

Moon: When the Moon is *shubha*, one is always happy, calm and simple, loves arts/music, is favoured by women, takes interest in spirituality, astrology, occult sciences, etc. In the case of an *ashubha* Moon, all the significations of the Moon suffer. The mother's health may be affected. The native's sense of taste (*rasa*) may be destroyed. Alternatively, his/her body may appear cold on touching due to cold fever.

Mars: When Mars is *ashubha*, native loses temper for nothing. Engages in unnecessary quarrels. Lacks stamina, and may find blood deficiency or some blood disorder. S/he may lose sexual vigour and may not be able to produce progeny.

Mercury: When Mercury is *shubha*, the native acts intelligently, speaks sweet and looks attractive. One has the cooperation of friends and enjoys life. Loss of sense of touch (*sparsh*) is an indication of *ashubha* Mercury. One developes skin problems. Speech defects and deterioration of relations with intimate friends are other indications.

Jupiter: When Jupiter is *shubha*, one not only has all the noble qualities, but one is also bestowed with wealth and prosperity. In the case of *ashubha* Jupiter, the native may start losing hair from head. One may lose sense of hearing (*shabda*). There will be obstacles in his/her education. Gold and wealth do not stay with the native. It may be stolen or lost.

Venus: When Venus is *shubha*, one has all the comforts and enjoyments of life. One looks beautiful, attractive, and appealing to the opposite sex. When Venus is *ashubha*, native develops diseases of the urinary/sexual systems. Also, the native's thumb,

	which extends from the mount of Venus on palm, may start paining or may become numb.
Saturn:	When Saturn is *shubha*, one is a principled and disciplined person, and is free from sufferings. When Saturn is *ashubha*, one has to face myriads of calamities. The house may fall or catch fire. Significations of Saturn suffer. For example, the body hair may start falling, particularly the hair of the eyebrows.
Rahu:	Rahu is evil in almost all cases. However, when Rahu is favourable, it removes obstacles from the life of the person and brings success and material gains. About Rahu, we should understand carefully. Mercury is significator of our intellect that helps us in understanding common things. While Rahu is significator of wisdom, not just intellect. So, when Rahu is *ashubha*, the native develops a distorted mind. One may become completely insane. One may develop phobias and fear of death, and so on.
Ketu:	Ketu is not as evil as Rahu. In fact, Ketu is considered a benefic in many respects. When Ketu is favourable, it makes a man religious. It imparts courage. When Ketu is *ashubha*, the native may have to undergo surgery.

15.6 PAST-LIFE EVIL *KARMAS* CAUSING *GRAH-DOSHAS* AND ASTROLOGICAL REMEDIES

Let us see what kind of *karmas* lead to the maleficence of each planet (*grah-dosh*), and as a result what kind of remedies could be applied to rectify the same.

As far as the remedies are concerned, they envisage consuming, wearing and giving away in charity the articles that are significations of the planet in the event of the planet being weak. In this respect, wheat, jaggery (*gur*), copper, ruby, saffron, crimson red colour objects, etc., belong to the Sun. Rice, water, milk, curds, condensed sugar (*misri*), camphor, silver, pearl, white flowers, white clothes, white articles, etc., belong to The Moon. Again wheat, sweetened bread (*roti*), sweets, *masoor dal*, deep red coral, deep red color clothes, etc., are for Mars. *moong* Dal, green objects, emerald, piercing of ears, etc., propitiate Mercury. Gold, yellow topaz, yellow clothes, yellow flowers and *laddoos*, *gram dal*, turmeric, saffron, headgear/cap/covering for head, etc., are for Jupiter. Venus is propitiated by diamond, pearls, silver, cow, milk, curds, ghee, butter, barley, rice, sugar, camphor, white clothes, white flowers, scents, perfumes, cleanliness and beautifying one's body, etc. Blue sapphire, iron, black cow/buffalo/crow, etc., coarse grains, black *urad dal*, mustard and sesame oils, black and dark blue colour clothes, etc., are in the domain of Saturn. Purple colour also propitiates Saturn. *Gomed*, coal, lead metal and radishes are for Rahu, and Cat's Eye, alloys and multi-coloured dog are for Ketu. In addition, blanket, sesame and mixed seven grains are for Rahu and Ketu both.

Some *tantrik* practices may also be used as remedies. They purify the soul.

One may also propitiate a particular deity ruling over that planet, or the planet itself.

Some of the *karmas* causing *grah-doshas*, and steps to be undertaken to rectify them are mentioned below:

Sun:

The Sun represents father. Anyone who did not respect father or showed disrespect to elders in previous lives will have a weak Sun in his/her horoscope.

For *ashubha* Sun, one can do *japa* of any *mantra* for the Sun such as *Om Suryaya Namah* 108 times every day. The *japa* should be started on any Sunday preferably on a day of *Pushya Nakshatra* or on a Sunday, which falls on any *shubha tithi*, *shubha Nakshatra* and *shubha yoga*. *Pushya Nakshatra* is the most auspicious for any *sadhana*/spiritual practice. One should rise early in the morning before sunrise. Then after morning purifications, wearing fresh clothes and sitting in a comfortable posture facing the east one should offer prayers with crimson flowers to the rising Sun every morning and do *mantra-japa* until 111 days. The *japa* should preferably end also on a Sunday. One should end it with a ceremony or *havan*, and with giving away of articles signifying the Sun in charities.

One should also pay obeisance to one's father, the main signification of the Sun.

An astrological remedy for a malefic Sun is for the native to take some sweet and then drink water before going to any place outside, or before starting any work. The logic is that if the effect of the Sun is unfavourable, we take the help of Mars, whose signification is 'sweets', and the Moon, which signifies 'water'. The two get mixed with spit in the mouth, which is produced in excess due to the unfavourable Sun.

Tantrik remedy is to take 50 grams of jaggery and immerse it every morning in a river or a stream of running water.

Moon:

Those who did not respect their mother or ill-treated her in past lives will have a weak and afflicted Moon. A person with a Moon-*Dosha* may have lot of wealth but will never have peace of mind, and may not enjoy good health.

For *ashubha* Moon, one can do *sadhana* by fasting, meagre eating, living on fruits, sleeping on ground, wearing clean white clothes, etc. This rule applies to any *sadhana* irrespective of the planet involved. As a ritual one should have a bath, adorn oneself with fresh white clothes, wear white *chandan tilak* on the forehead, place incense, light a pure *ghee* or camphor lamp (*deepak*), and offer *bel* leaves, white flowers, rice pudding, etc., to the Moon or Lord Shiva. One can do *japa* of *Om Namah Shivaya*. Other remedies are:

1. Respect and serve mother, father and elders with pure heart to receive their blessings. Give charity to widows and in old age homes.
2. Observe fast on every Monday, preferably eating no salt. Unmarried girls fast for 16 Mondays (*solah Somvar*) in continuation to get the groom of their choice.
3. Give milk, curds, rice, white articles, silver, etc., in charity. Have lots of rice. It represents energy.
4. The tree concerned with the Moon is the *palaas*. Plant and water this tree.

Mars:

Mars denotes younger brothers/sisters. It relates to Venus representing wife/women. Therefore, if you had been unkind and deceitful with your younger brothers/sisters and/or your spouse in your previous births and/or had been a meat eater, particularly of the domestic, peace loving and milk kind like cow, you are most likely to have Mars-*Dosha* in your horoscope. It will affect your stamina. Mars-*Dosha* means that your marriage will be delayed, and if you marry early then you may lose your spouse in an accident, or so on. Your relations with your spouse will be strained creating conditions for separation/divorce. You and your spouse are most likely to be quarrelsome and short tempered. Your relations with your brothers/sisters will not be amiable. A sharp weapon involving flow of blood may even kill a person with Mars-*Dosha*.

In the event of Mars acting as *ashubha*, the first thing to do is to be kind to your brothers/sisters, and when you visit them you should never go empty-handed, you should always go with gifts. Also, give respect to your spouse if married.

The other thing is to turn vegetarian, and to decide not to harm anyone including animals, birds and fish.

The native should wash his/her eyes daily and quite frequently. One can also eat sweets.

Worshiping Lord Hanuman, particularly every Tuesday, is recommended.

One should wear red colour clothes, apply red *chandan tilak* on the forehead, and offer red or pink coloured flowers and clothes to Goddess Ma Durga particularly on Fridays.

One may chant the Gayatri Mantra for 3 rosaries (*malas*) everyday.

Give wheat, *gur*, *masoor dal*, red clothes, coral, etc., in charity. Distribute sweets, *rewari* made with sesame seeds and *gur* or sugar, and buttered bread or *rotis* to children and poor. Feed *gur* to a red coloured cow.

Mercury:

Mercury represents your education, intelligence, friends, skin and power of speech, your memory and mathematics. Hence, it represents your teachers also. In the event of *ashubha* Mercury, these things are denied. One may lack good education, be devoid of intelligence, may have impaired speech, or speech that hurts. Any misdeed towards teachers, friends, etc., will cause Mercury-*Dosha*.

To mitigate this *dosha*, one should avoid bad company, be nice to one's genuine friends, show respect to teachers, and serve them.

One should consume and give away articles having greenish hue that signify Mercury. Eat *moong dal*, and lots of greens, fruits and vegetables. Feed green vegetables to a cow.

Take out 3 *rotis* from your meal everyday. Feed one to a crow, another to a cow and the third one to a dog.

Also, one can take a copper coin with a hole in it, and throw it in a river by standing in a direction facing the East. Piercing of one's ears nostrils, particularly for girls, is recommended.

Jupiter:

Jupiter or *Guru* represents noble people, sadhus, saints, etc. If one had not respected these persons in previous births, one would have afflicted Jupiter in his/her horoscope.

In the event of an *ashubha* Jupiter, one should show obeisance to and serve one's *gurus*, teachers, professors, and so on. Keep company of good people.

The head represents the Guru. You should therefore cover your head with some cloth or cap or hat to rectify *ashubha* Jupiter.

Take saffron and turmeric in food preparations, and use saffron/turmeric mark/*tilak* on your forehead, and its paste on your abdomen around navel.

Use objects signifying Jupiter such as gold, yellow or saffron colour clothes, flowers, *gram dal*, honey, saffron, turmeric, mustard, etc., and give the same in charity.

Venus:

Venus gives all the earthly pleasures and material enjoyments. Venus is significator for spouse/wife and young ladies. If you had ill-treated your spouse or divorced your partner in your previous lives, you will have Venus-*Dosh* in your birth chart. As a result, your marriage may be delayed, or you may not even get married and/or you may be without worldly pleasures in this life.

For mitigating the ill-effects of unfavourable Venus, one should be nice to wife/spouse. One should pay special attention to cleanliness of the body and clothes, and towards appearance to look charming, beautiful and aesthetic.

Give charity, such as cow, milk, butter oil, barley and pearls. Serve the weak and the poor. Whenever possible you may do all you can to help in the marriage of a poor girl.

Worship Bhagwati Lakshmi, or Devi Parvati.

Friday is the day of Venus. Unmarried girls maintain the Friday fast to please the *devi* to be blessed with a suitable groom. Others keep the fast for the fulfilment of their desires.

Saturn:

Saturn represents the poor, weak, servants, etc. If you mal-treated such people in your past lives, you will have Saturn-*Dosha* in present life. When Saturn is *ashubha*, there is no end to miseries and penury. You find that all your undertakings are getting delayed.

To correct the evil affects of *ashubha* Saturn, start treating your servant, etc., with compassion. You may feed grains, particularly coarse ones such as *bajra*, to black crows and birds, everyday until the evil is mitigated.

One may chew stems of *kikar* or *babool* trees for brushing teeth. Significations of Saturn such as blue and dark coloured clothes, leather, iron, mustard oil, *til* seeds, *til* oil, *urad*, etc., may be consumed and given in charity particularly to lepers.

Offer water to the *peepal* tree. Light an earthen lamp with mustard or sesame oil under the tree every day either before sunrise or after sunset.

Serve the elderly and earn their blessings. Saturn serves the old.

Wearing of iron or lead ring in the middle finger is suggested.

Rahu:

Rahu represents your grandparents, ancestors, *Pitras*, etc. If you did not serve them well or if you did not perform their last rites reverentially, then their unfulfilled souls will torment you. You will have Rahu-Dosh in your present life. To mitigate Rahu-Dosh it is essential to render services to your grandparents in present life. All items of Saturn can be given in charity. Protect and offer worship to peepal tree.

In-laws are significations of Rahu. To avoid the ill-effects of unfavourable Rahu, one should try to keep good relations with in-laws.

To grow a tuft of extra hair (*choti*) on the head is another method of driving off these evils. The idea is to take the help of Jupiter to drive away *ashubha* Rahu.

Ketu:

Ketu also represents grandparents. For rectifying *ashubha* Ketu, you may start respecting your elders.

Ketu signifies a dog. One may feed a dog everyday.

Rahu-Ketu *Kaal-Sarpa-Yoga*:

Deeply afflicted Rahu may appear as *Kaal-Sarpa-Yoga* in your birth-chart. Such people may never enjoy personal happiness. They may suffer from poisoning, infectious diseases, leprosy, etc.

What is the remedy for *Kaal-Sarpa-Yoga*? It can be said that a person with *Kaal-Sarpa-Yoga* should work with patience, discipline and balance. S/he should work philanthropically for the good of others and for the society at large.

If property and finance matters are involved then one should start giving charity. If health and relations with near and dear ones are involved then the best remedy is to recite *Maha-Mrityunjaya mantra* 108 times every day. If one is engulfed in some kind of fear then one could recite *Hanuman-chalisa* five times every morning and evening.

Note: To drive off evil, or as a remedy, adopt this practice. Offer a chapatti or a piece of food from own meal to cows, crows and dogs everyday.

The remedial measures mentioned above should be applied particularly during the *Dashas* of *ashubha* planets during which their effects are the most severe.

15.7 GEM THERAPY

Gems are Nature's storehouse of energy. The energy body forming an aura as shown in Fig. 1.2, envelops the physical body. The *chakras* in the energy body are energy wheels that balance the aura or the electromagnetic field around the physical body. Planetary positions in one's birth chart may cause imbalance of *chakras*. An imbalance leads to diseases and ill effects. Highly sensitive gems and crystals restore these balances and heal the body and the mind by enhancing nourishment to every cell of the body.

In general, these gems and crystals absorb the negative energies and transmit positive energies. Different colours also, similarly, allow substances to transmute from one frequency to another thus bringing balance in one's aura and well-being.

The Sun governs ruby (*manik*) and coppery and crimson colours, the Moon white pearl (*moti*) and white color, Mars coral (*Moonga*) and deep red colour, Mercury emerald (*panna*) and green colour, Jupiter yellow topaz (*pukhraj*) and yellow and saffron colours, Venus diamond (*heera*) and white and also other light colours, Saturn blue sapphire (*neelam*) and black, dark blue and purple colours, Rahu hessonite (*gomed*) and dark colours, and Ketu cat's eye (*lahsuniya*) and spotted colours.

The quality of the gem is characterised by its cut, clarity, colour and size. The cut determines its brilliance and lustre. For clarity, there should be no impurity, and there should be no damage or crack. Colour should be bright, shining and clear. Size is measured in *rattis* or carats. In terms of weight, we should know that:

One *ratti* is equal to 180 milligrams.

One carat is equal to 200 milligrams.

Prescribed weights for gems to be worn and their respective metals are as follows:

Ruby	3 to 5 carats+	in gold
Pearl	5to 7 carats+ or more	in silver
Coral	6 to 10 carats+	in silver or copper
Emerald	5 to 6 carats+	in gold
Yellow Topaz	4 to 6 carats+	in gold
Diamond	0.25 to 1 carat+	in gold or platinum
Blue Sapphire	3 to 4 carats+	in gold or five metals (*Panch Dhatu*)
Gomed	4 to 6 carats+	in silver
Cat's Eye	3 to 4 carats+	in gold

Plus sign indicates that the weight should be slightly in excess of the one mentioned.

Garnet can be worn as substitute for ruby, and moonstone or *Chandrakant Mani* for white pearl.

If the native is under the unfavourable influence of a planet, s/he is advised to wear the gem of the planet on a finger just above the mount of the planet or its friend on the palm. Thus, ruby and coral are worn on ring finger, white pearl and emerald on little finger, blue sapphire, gomed and cat's eye on middle finger, and yellow topaz and diamond on forefinger. The gem is supposed to strengthen the planet and mitigate its evil effects.

The basic principles adopted for gem selection are as follows:

(i) Strengthen the *lagna* Lord as it has the capacity to ward of all evils by enhancing the power of both the body and the soul.

(ii) Strengthen the *Mahadasha* and *Antardasha* Lords if one is experiencing difficulty during their periods.

(iii) Strengthen the house Lords that are not afflicted to enhance their capability.

Note that the strengthening of planets that are causing harm may sometimes result in more harm. There is, however, disagreement on this point, and rightly so since the evil planet, when strengthened, may actually cause increase in suffering. For example, for Gemini *lagna,* Saturn is the Lord of the eighth, an evil house, and the ninth, a good house, and for Virgo *lagna* it is Lord of the fifth and the sixth houses. So if wearing Blue Sapphire strengthens Saturn, it may increase both good and evil effects. There can be other examples. A planet may be very bad by ownership, placement and aspect in certain matters, but good in some other matters. Hence, two suggestions are made:

(i) Wrap the gem/stone in silk or cotton of the same colour as the stone and tie round the arm for a trial period of, say, three days. If it shows good effects then wear it regularly studded in a ring or pendant with the underside of the gem touching the skin and the upper side left open to catch the light rays. If it shows evil results then remove it at once.

(ii) The other alternative is to forget about the evil planet; just strengthen the good planet in your chart further by wearing its gem. Learned astrologers recommend strengthening the *lagna* Lord for all purposes since a strong *lagna* Lord alone has the capability to ward of all evils even though it may be Lord of an evil house as well.

Metals of planets can also be worn as rings/bangles/chains. For example, one can wear copper wristbands if one is suffering from high blood pressure since *pitta* planets Sun and Mars can be its cause, and they both govern copper. Jupiter primarily governs gold. Moon and Venus govern silver. Mercury governs alloys of metals. Saturn governs iron.

Gems according to each *Lagna*

It is most important to consider the native's *lagna* if a proper gem has to be selected. A gem may be harmful or beneficial for a *lagna* as described below:

Ruby: See how the Sun relates to each *lagna*. For Aries the Sun is the fifth Lord and friend of the *lagna*. For Leo the Sun is the *lagna* Lord. For Scorpio the Sun is the tenth Lord and friend of the *lagna*. For Sagittarius it is the ninth Lord. Hence Aries, Leo, Scorpio and Sagittarius *lagnas,* can wear Ruby all along life. In case of the remaining *lagnas* the Sun is either Maraka or enemy of the *lagna* or the Lord of an evil house. They should not wear ruby.

Pearl: See how the Moon relates. On the same reasoning as above Aries, Cancer, Scorpio and Pisces *lagnas* may always wear Pearl. Leo, Sagittarius, and Aquarius *lagnas* should never wear Pearl. For Virgo the Moon is the eleventh Lord, and for Libra the Moon is the tenth Lord but enemy of the *lagna* Lord. Virgo may wear Pearl for income and Libra for career provided they wear a gem of the *lagna* Lord simultaneously.

Coral: See how Mars relates to each *lagna*. Coral is *shubha* for Aries, Cancer, Leo, Scorpio and Pisces *lagnas*. It is *ashubha* for Taurus, Gemini, Virgo, Libra and Aquarius. For Sagittarius Mars is the Lord of the fifth and the twelfth and for Capricorn it is the Lord of the fourth and the eleventh. These *lagnas* may wear Coral for specific purposes with safeguards.

Emerald: See how Mercury relates. Gemini, Leo, Virgo, Libra and Capricorn *lagnas* should always wear Emerald. Aries, Cancer, Scorpio, and Aquarius *lagnas* should never wear Emerald.

Yellow Topaz: See how Jupiter relates. Yellow Topaz is *shubha* for Aries, Cancer, Sagittarius and Pisces *lagnas*. It is *ashubha* for Taurus, Gemini, Virgo, Libra, Scorpio, Capricorn and Aquarius. For Leo, Jupiter is the eighth and fifth Lord and great friend of the *lagna*. One can wear Yellow Topaz simultaneously with Ruby.

Diamond: See how Venus relates. Taurus, Libra, Capricorn and Aquarius *lagnas* should wear Diamond all along. It is *ashubha* for Sagittarius and Pisces. For Gemini, Venus is the Lord of the twelfth and the fifth and great friend of the *lagna*. One could wear Diamond simultaneously with Emerald. Same is true for Virgo *lagna*.

For Cancer *lagna* Diamond is beneficial during Venus *Dasha*.

Blue Sapphire: See the relationship of Saturn. Blue Sapphire is *shubha* for Taurus, Gemini, Libra, Capricorn and Aquarius *lagnas*. Aries, Cancer, Leo, Scorpio, Sagittarius and Pisces should never wear Blue Sapphire. For Virgo Saturn is *ashubha* as Lord of the sixth, but *shubha* as Lord of fifth and great friend of *lagna* Lord. During Saturn *Dasha* one could wear Blue Sapphire along with Emerald.

Gomed: Gomed is Rahu's gem. Rahu does not own any house. It is seen that wearing Gomed helps if Rahu is placed in *lagna*, and the third, fourth, fifth, sixth, ninth, tenth and eleventh houses. One should never wear it if Rahu is in the second, seventh, eighth and twelfth.

Cat's Eye: Cat's Eye is Ketu's gem. Ketu also does not own any house.

Wearing Cat's Eye helps if Ketu is placed in *lagna*, and the third, fourth, fifth, sixth, ninth, tenth and eleventh houses. One should never wear it if Ketu is placed in the second, seventh, eighth and twelfth.

Note: Notwithstanding what is written above, before prescribing any gem, one must see the sign and the house in which the planet is placed in the birth chart, and its aspects to check whether it will be beneficial or harmful. For example, in the sample horoscope, there is no point in strengthening Saturn by wearing Blue Sapphire since its inimical aspects on twelfth, fourth and seventh would be destructive to marital life, mental peace and happiness. Another example would be Mars, though a *yoga-karaka* for Cancer *lagna*, but placed in enemy's sign Gemini in twelfth house, wearing coral will be destructive to marital happiness as it will rather enhance the Mangalika-*Dosha* of the native.

Gem Therapy based in Ayurveda

A weak planet causes certain ailments, and whatever benefits accrue by wearing the gem of that planet; similar benefits to a much larger extent can be obtained by taking the same gem as medicine in some form such as sintered ash (*bhasma,* or *pishti)*. For example, a weak Sun causes heart trouble, impotence, weakness of bones and body, indigestion, lack of appetite, lack of immunity against diseases, etc. For that, the Ayurved recommends 1 to 2 *rattis* of *pishti* of ruby (*manik*) with honey twice daily. For weak Moon, *bhasma* of *moti* should be taken. Likewise, *bhasma* or *pishti* of other gems also is prescribed.

15.8 STRENGTHENING HOUSES/BHAVAS

Strengthening *bhava* Lords can strengthen *bhavas*.

Learned astrologers suggest other measures to strengthen each *bhava*. For the second house, they believe that to increase wealth, due attention should be paid to having loving family relationships as both wealth and family are significations of the second house.

For mental peace and happiness, mother should be respected, and mind (*Mana*) should be kept free of delusions, all these being significations of the fourth house.

The fifth house is for education, intelligence and children. Planets therein also affect eleventh house of income and intimate friends. By developing a tasteful personality, by having good friends, and by having constructive thinking, one can have the good fortune of having loving children and high income both.

The seventh house is tenth from the tenth. Mutual love and regard in marital life, along with honesty, cooperation and mutual support gives success even in one's career and profession. The seventh house is fourth from the fourth. Hence, these measures are also helpful in bringing peace and happiness in native's life.

The ninth house is for *dharma* and *bhagya*. It also represents Guru/preceptor. Further, since it is fifth from the fifth it is for children also. This house also represents brothers/sisters-in-law. Hence, for good fortune, it is necessary to earn their goodwill and goodwill of one's preceptors and elders to have love and happiness to/from children and good fortune.

The tenth house is for father, career and wife's mother too. It shows that success in career very much depends on father's support, and giving due respect to him and mother-in-law.

The eleventh house is not just for income and gains. But it also represents one's elder brothers and sisters, and intimate friends. Hence, respecting elder brother/s and sister/s and having friends of good taste strengthens the eleventh *bhava*, and brings gains.

Likewise, one can employ the principle in regard to other *bhavas* also to bring not only gains in one's life, but also to live in harmony.

15.9 STRENGTHENING *KARAKATTVAS* OF A PLANET AND HOUSE IN THE *KAAL PURUSH KUNDALI*

By strengthening a planet, we can strengthen its *karakattvas*. For example, strengthening the Sun by wearing a ruby cures all types of bone problems. It cures problems of fifth house according to the *Kaal Purush Kundali*, viz., ulcer, stomach problems, etc. It helps the father. It elevates one's soul/sprits. It enhances social status. Burma ruby is considered the best.

Wearing a white pearl for the Moon calms the mind and gives mental peace. It helps the mother. It cures insomnia, heart trouble, and respiratory problems. It promotes sexual vitality. It inspires love and affection in conjugal life. In the *Kaal Purush Kundali*, the Moon is exalted in the second house representing face. Hence, pearl increases facial lustre for ladies. Best pearls are from Basrah, Iraq.

Coral worn for Mars is useful for the first and the eighth house matters according to *Kaal Purush Kundali*. It enhances physical and mental stamina. It promotes well-being of one's younger brothers/sisters, and helps to maintain good relationship with them. In case of *mangalika dosha*, it helps to improve chances of marriage, and promotes marital harmony. Bright red Italian and Japanese corals are the best.

Emerald for Mercury is a suitable remedy for diseases of the nervous system, speech troubles, etc. It is also suitable for diseases of the digestive system represented by the sixth house in the *Kaal Purush Kundali* such as diarrhoea, dysentery, gastric problems, ulcer, bowels problems, etc. It also helps in business and trade.

Topaz for Jupiter helps cure cough, throat troubles, cold, fevers, jaundice, liver troubles, etc. It promotes matters of ninth house, good luck, religiousness and prosperity. It is good for one's children.

Diamond for Venus prevents urinary and sexual disorders, skin and uterine troubles, diabetes, etc. It promotes comforts, and happiness to/from wife/spouse.

Blue Sapphire for Saturn cures depression, nervous disorders, epilepsy, arthritis, rheumatism, cramps, gastric ulcer, deafness, baldness, etc. It wards of evils caused by a malefic Saturn. But, it should be worn only after testing it for positive effect.

Hessonite or Gomed for Rahu is helpful in treating acidity, phobias, etc. Wearing Cat's Eye for Ketu helps in chronic and terminal diseases like cancer and surgeries.

15.10 *MANTRAS, TANTRAS* AND *YANTRAS*

Other remedies are prayers in the form of words (*mantras*), practices (*tantras*) and devices (*yantras*):

The person who embarks on *mantra, tantra* and *yantra*, viz., *sadhna*, is a *sadhak*. Attainment or fulfilment of the objective is *siddhi*. The *sadhak* should embark on *sadhana* with a noble and pious mind; otherwise there will be no success. *Sadhana* must be performed in a clean, cool, pleasant and fixed place preferably under a *peepal* tree in a place of pilgrimage, on the bank of a river or canal or on a mountain or in a jungle where dead silence prevails, or otherwise in one's own home where similar environment is possible. One should preferably sleep on the ground during the period of *sadhana*. And, one day before starting the *sadhana*, one should keep a fast. One should not take any drugs or intoxicants. It will be far more effective if one takes some vows (*sankalpas*) to abstain from a few things at least during the period of the *sadhana*. If one could give up one or two cherished things as a penance for past *karmas* it would make wonders.

Mantras

Mantra-Sadhana is a spiritual remedy. *Mantras* are syllables strung together. They have great healing powers because of their vibrations. It is our good fortune that, in the present age of *Kaliyug*, the only means of deliverance is the chanting of holy names of God.

The Vedic scriptures maintain that matter evolves from subtle to the gross. The subtlest is the sound, the vibration, the energy.

First there was nothing, just the Word, the name of God (*Naam*), the vibrations. The creation came from God's *sankalpa*.

Thoughts and emotions are also vibrations. It is usually a name (*Naam*) or a form or *mantra* by which the thought can be fixed in the sole knowledge and adoration of the Lord. Repetitive chanting of God's name/s alone, or in the form of *mantras*, aloud, silently or mentally with feeling and remaining focused on their meaning, produces vibrations of immense spiritual potency that purify and harmonise the body, mind and soul of the aspirant. *Mantras* bring the suffering individual in direct communication with God in prayer, love and surrender. The only condition is that the individual him/herself should chant them unless s/he is incapacitated or bed-ridden. Chanting God's names washes away sins of the present and past lives.

The most basic *mantra* is the sound incarnation of God, viz., 'O.....M...' uttered in elongated form, or just the single name of God, 'Rama, Rama, Rama,...'. Both give great comfort to any soul who chants these names with devotion.

In Vedic psyche God has innumerable names apart from Om and Rama. Incarnations of God, Rama born as king of Ayodhya and consort Sita born as princess of Janakpuri, together are the most ideal divinity to be worshipped. Repeated chanting of the verse

'Siya Ram Jaya Ram Jaya Jaya Ram
Jaya Siya Ram Jaya Jaya Siya Ram'
gives immediate solace to the suffering.

One of the simplest *mantras* is:
'Om Namah Shivaya'
It can be uttered or sung in many different ways in adoration of Lord Shiva, Mahadev, the god of gods who is very easily pleased and grants the native of his/her wishes.

Under stress, when the mind is disturbed and when one does not know what to do, viz., there is no balance between emotions and intellect; one is advised to recite *Gayatri Maha mantra* for a fixed number of rosaries (*Malas*) everyday. The *mantra* is as follows:
'Om Bhur Bhuvah Swah
Om Tat Savitur Varenyam
Bhargo Devasya Dhimahi
Dhiyo Yo Nah Prachodayat'

The meaning of the *mantra* is the following:
'The Supreme God!
The Soul of My Soul, the Eliminator of Sorrow, the Abode of Bliss!

That One, who cannot be known by mere senses, the
Source of All Light and Energy, the Beloved Chosen One
for Me!
The Destroyer of Sins, I Take Refuge in You!
Please Awaken Our Dhi, the Sense of Discrimination, to
show us the way.'

When the mind is obsessed with fear or phobia, recitation
of *Hanuman chalisa* gives great courage. One should recite it
108 times or more every morning and at bedtime.

The *mantra* of all *mantras* is the *Maha Mrityunjaya mantra*.

When the suffering of the native has reached such a
proportion that the native feels caught between life and death
then one should chant one rosary of this *mantra*, viz., 108
times everyday for 40 days at a stretch or even more till the
evil is warded off. The *mantra* is addressed to Lord Shiva, as
the three eyed one, and is as follows:

'Om Trayambikam Yajamahe
Sugandhim Pushtivardhanam
Urvaarukamiv Bandhnaat
Mrityormukshiya Maamritaat'

The meaning of the *mantra* is the following:

O! The Three-Eyed One! The Supreme God! We Worship
You!
O! The Fragrant One! Our Nourisher!
The way the cucumber, after fully ripening, is severed
automatically from the Bondage of the Creeper!
The Same Way, Liberate Me from Death for the Sake of
Immortality!

Some *mantras* for specific objectives are the following:

For overcoming delay in marriage of a girl:

> Mitigates afflictions to the seventh house and its Lord. The girl should worship Durga, and then herself recite 5 rosaries of this *mantra* continuously for 21 days.
> 'He Gauri! Shankaraardhangini!
> Yatha Twam Shankarapriya!
> Tatha Mam Kuru Kalyani!
> Kant-Kantam Sudurlabham!'

The meaning of this verse is:

> O Gauri! Consort of Lord Shankara!
> Just as you are the Beloved of Shankara!
> Same way do good to me and bless me!
> With Husband's Sukha, so difficult to get!

> For getting rid of anger: *Krodh-Shanti mantra*
> This is a *mantra* to pacify anger; one's own or someone else's in the family.
> 'Om Shante Prashante Sarva Krodh Shamanon Swaha!'
> The *mantra* should be recited 21 times infusing water with it. After recitation, water should be sprinkled three times on the face of the self and/or the person prone to anger.

For Happiness:

> The only way to be happy is to give happiness to others.
> The following prayer is due to St. Francis of Assisi of Italy.
> One can mentally pray while meditating.
> Lord! Make me an instrument of Thy Peace.
> Where there is hatred, let me sow love.
> Where there is injury, pardon.
> Where there is doubt, faith.
> Where there is darkness, light.
> Where there is sadness, joy.

O Divine Master! Grant that I may not so much seek
to be consoled as to console;
to be understood as to understand;
to be loved as to love;
for it is in giving that we receive,
it is in pardoning that we are pardoned, and
it is in dying that we are born to Eternal Life.

Durga Saptshati

Then there are seven hundred *shlokas* or *mantras* in *Durga saptshati*. One can attain *siddhi* if one recites these Shlokas with devotion. The *saptshati* contains verses (*shlokas*) for well being and good health, cure from diseases, warding of evils, poverty, sins and fear, for getting a virtuous and good wife and children, for attaining power (*shakti*), devotion (*bhakti*) and salvation (*mukti*), and so on.

Tantras

As stated earlier one does not have to do anything else if one prays and recites the name/s of God and *mantras* with devotion and surrender. But often, people want short cuts to accomplish their desires. This can be done through *tantras* and *yantras*.

Tantra is also a kind of *sadhana*. *Tantra-Sadhana* may also involve *mantras*.

Some of the *tantra* remedies have already been described in Sec. 15.6, and some *mantras* above in Sec. 15.9.1. Sometimes, *tantrik* practices may boil down to just the use of herbs to cure diseases. Some other *tantrik* remedies are as follows:

Wearing *Rudraksh*

One does not know whether to call it spiritual or *tantrik* remedy or consider *Rudraksh* beads as having medicinal properties. *Rudraksh* drives away many ills of body and mind.

Use of *Hatha-Jori*

Hatha means hand. *Jori* means pair. *Hatha-Jori* is a herb, which looks like a pair of hands. It is 2–3 inches long. It is obtained from the roots of a plant named 'Virupa' found in the hills of Amar Kantak, a place of pilgrimage in Madhya Pradesh, and also in Lumbini valley in Nepal near India–Nepal border. *Virupa* plant, which is similar to *Dhatura* plant, has blue and white coloured flowers.

Immerse *Hatha-Jori* in sesame (*til*) oil. After it has stopped absorbing this oil until after a few days, it is taken out. Thereafter, keep it in vermilion (*sindoor*), in a silver casket along with cardamoms or cloves. Then, after performing the *pooja*, put it in the place of worship. After this, recite the following *mantra* 125,000 times to attain its *siddhi*:

'Om Kili Kili Swaha!'

This is a *tantrik mantra*. This recitation can be completed in 5 to 10 days also. Wonder of all wonders. The *Hatha-Jori* solves all the problems of its possessor. It works like *Vashi Karan mantra*. If you have it in your person while talking to someone, s/he will agree with you.

One should never try to misuse it to harm others.

Yantras

Yantra means a mystical geometrical diagram or figure or a *talisman*. Some *yantras* are worshipped. Some are simply worn on body. The most important one is the *Shri Yantra*:

Shri Yantra

This is considered to be the most sacred *yantra*. It bestows on the native wealth, favours, abundance and prosperity.

In case if the Sun is afflicted in the birth chart, this *yantra* is very beneficial. The *yantra* is made as a pendent in gold, silver or copper. First, *pooja* of the *yantra* is performed for 7 days. Then it is worn on the body on Monday morning after bath, performing *Surya-Namaskar*, offering water to the Sun and *pooja* with vermilion, incense, etc.

APPENDIX A

Table of Houses for Delhi, Latitude 28 D 40 M North

SRT H	M	S	X AR	XI TA	XII GE	ASC CA D	ASC CA M	II LE	III VI	SRT H	M	S	X LI	XI SC	XII SC	ASC SA D	ASC SA M	II CP	III AQ
0	0	0	0	5	10	12	16	5	0										
0	14	41	4	9	14	15	29	8	4	12	14	41	4	4	28	20	57	24	29
0	33	4	9	14	18	19	28	12	8	12	33	4	9	8	2SA	25	3	28	5
0	51	32	14	19	23	23	25	16	13	12	51	32	14	12	6	29	14	3AQ	10
1	10	7	19	23	27	27	23	21	17	13	10	7	19	17	11	3	32 CP	8	15
1	28	52	24	28	1CA	1	23 LE	25	22	13	28	52	24	21	15	7	57	13	21
1	51	37	30	4GE	6	6	12	30	28	13	51	37	30	27	20	13	28	20	27
2	6	59	4TA	8	10	9	29	4VI	2LI	14	6	59	4SC	0SA	23	17	19	24	2AR
2	28	26	9	12	14	13	36	8	7	14	26	25	9	5	28	22	29	0PI	8
2	46	8	14	17	19	17	49	13	12	14	46	8	14	9	2CP	27	34	6	14
3	6	9	19	22	23	22	6	17	17	15	6	9	19	14	7	3	6 AQ	13	19
3	26	29	24	27	28	26	28	22	22	15	26	29	24	18	12	8	56	19	25
3	51	15	30	2CA	3LE	1	49 VI	28	28	15	51	15	30	24	18	16	22	27	2TA
4	8	0	4GE	5	7	5	27	2LI	2SC	16	8	0	4SA	28	22	21	36	3AR	7
4	29	10	9	11	11	10	4	7	7	16	29	10	9	2CP	27	28	27	9	13
4	50	34	14	16	16	14	44	12	12	16	50	34	14	7	3AQ	5	37 PI	16	18
5	12	9	19	21	21	19	28	17	17	17	12	9	19	12	9	13	2	23	24
5	33	51	24	26	26	24	14	22	22	17	33	51	24	18	15	20	41	0TA	0GE
6	0	0	30	2LE	2VI	30	0	28	28	18	0	0	30	24	22	30	0	8	6

Table of Houses for Delhi, Latitude 28 D 40 M North

SRT H	M	S	X AR D	XI TA D	XII GE D	ASC CA D M	II LE D	III VI D	SRT H	M	S	X LI D	XI SC D	XII SC D	ASC SA D M	II CP D	III AQ D
6	17	26	4CA	6	6	3 51 LI	2SC	2SA	18	17	26	4CP	28	28	6 13AR	13	10
6	39	11	9	11	11	8 37	7	7	18	39	11	9	4AQ	4PI	13 55	19	15
7	0	50	14	16	16	13 23	12	12	19	0	50	14	9	11	21 27	25	21
7	22	18	19	21	21	18 5	17	17	19	22	18	19	15	18	28 43	1GE	26
7	43	34	24	26	26	22 43	21	22	19	43	34	24	21	25	5 42TA	6	0CA
8	8	45	30	2VI	2LI	28 11	27	28	20	8	45	30	28	3AR	13 38	12	6
8	25	19	4LE	6	6	1 40 SC	1SA	2CP	20	25	19	4AQ	2PI	8	18 38	16	10
8	45	45	9	11	11	6 10	5	6	20	45	45	9	8	15	24 37	21	15
9	5	53	14	16	15	10 29	10	11	21	5	53	14	14	21	0 15 GE	26	19
9	25	44	19	21	20	14 43	14	16	21	25	44	19	20	27	5 37	1CA	24
9	45	16	24	26	25	18 55	18	20	21	45	16	24	26	3TA	10 43	5	28
10	8	23	30	2 LI	30	23 48	24	26	22	8	23	30	3AR	10	16 32	10	3LE
10	23	35	4VI	6	3SC	27 1	27	30	22	23	35	4PI	7	15	20 14	14	7
10	42	25	9	11	8	1 1 SA	1CP	5AQ	22	42	25	9	13	20	24 43	18	11
11	1	3	14	15	12	5 0	6	9	23	1	3	14	18	25	29 4	22	16
11	19	34	19	20	16	8 57	10	14	23	19	34	19	23	0GE	3 18 Ca	26	20
11	37	58	24	25	20	12 56	14	19	23	37	58	24	29	5	7 25	0LE	25
12	0	0	30	30	25	17 44	20	25	24	0	0	30	5	10	12 18	5	30

APPENDIX B
Good and Bad Degrees of Planets in Different Signs

| Sign | Good Degrees | | | | | | Bad Degrees | |
| | Exaltation | | Own | | *Vargottama* | | Debilitation | |
	From D:M	To D:M	From D:M	To D:M	From D:M	To D:M	From D:M	To D:M
Sun								
Aries	0:0	3:20	13:20	16:40	0:0	3:20	20:0	23:20
Taurus	10:0	13:20	23:20	26:40	13:20	16:40:		
Gemini	20:0	23:20			26:40:	30:0	0:0	3:20
Cancer			3:20	6:40	0:0	3:20	10:0	13:20
Leo	0:0	3:20	13:20	16:40	13:20	16:40	20:0	23:20
Virgo	10:0	13:20	23:20	26:40				
Libra	20:0	23:20			0:0	3:20	0:0	3:20
Scorpio			3:20	6:40	13:20	16:40	10:0	13:20
Sagittarius	0:0	3:20	13:20	16:40	26:40	30:0	20:0	23:20
Capricorn	10:0	13:20	23:20	26:40	0:0	3:20		
Aquarius	20:0	23:20			13:20	16:40	0:0	3:20
Pisces			3:20	6:40	26:40	30:0	10:0	13:20

| Sign | Good Degrees | | | | | | Bad Degrees | |
| | Exaltation | | Own | | *Vargottama* | | Debilitation | |
	From D:M	To D:M	From D:M	To D:M	From D:M	To D:M	From D:M	To D:M
Moon								
Aries	3:20	6:40	10:0	13:20	10:0	13:20	23:20	26:40
Taurus	13:20	16:40	20:0	23:20	13:20	16:40		
Gemini	23:20	26:40			26:40	30:0	3:20	6:40
Cancer			0:0	3:20	0:0	3:20	13:20	16:40
Leo	3:20	6:40	10:0	13:20	13:20	16:40	23:20	26:40
Virgo	13:	16:40	20:0	23:20	26:40	30:0		
Libra	23:30	26:40			0:0	3:20	3:20	6:40
Scorpio			0:0	3:20	13:20	16:40	13:20	16:40
Sagittarius	3:20	6:40	10:0	13:20	26:40	30:0	23:20	26:40
Capricorn	13:20	16:40	20:0	23:20	0:0	3:20		
Aquarius	26:40	30:0			13:20	16:40	3:20	6:40
Pisces			0:0	3:20	26:40	30:0	13:20	16:40

Sign	Good Degrees						Bad Degrees	
	Exaltation		Own		Vargottama		Debilitation	
	From	To	From	To	From	To	From	To
	D:M	D:M	D:M	D:M	D:M	D:M	D:M	D:M
Mars								
Aries			0:0	3:20	0:0	3:20	10:0	13:20
			23:20	26:40				
Taurus	0:0	3:20	10:0	13:20	13:20	16:40	20:0	23:20
Gemini	10:0	13:20	3:20	6:40	26:40	30:0		
			20:0	23:20				
Cancer	20:0	23:20	13:20	16:40	0:0	3:20	0:0	3:20
Leo			0:0	3:20	13:20	16:40	10:0	13:20
			23:20	26:40				
Virgo	0:0	3:20	10:0	13:20	26:40	30:0	20:0	23:20
Libra	10:0	13:20	3:20	6:40				
			20:0	23:20	0:0	3:20		
Scorpio	20:0	23:20	13:20	16:40	13:20	16:40	0:0	3:20
Sagittarius			0:0	3:20	26:40	30:0	10:0	13:20
			23:20	26:40				
Capricorn	0:0	3:20	10:0	13:20	0:0	3:20	20:0	23:20
Aquarius	10:0	13:20	3:20	6:40	13:20	16:40		
			20:0	23:20				
Pisces	20:0	23:20	13:20	16:40	26:40	30:0	0:0	3:20

Sign	Good Degrees						Bad Degrees	
	Exaltation		Own		Vargottama		Debilitation	
	From	To	From	To	From	To	From	To
	D:M	D:M	D:M	D:M	D:M	D:M	D:M	D:M
Mercury								
Aries	16:40	20:0	6:40	10:0	0:0	3:20		
			16:40	20:0				
Taurus	26:40	30:0	16:40	20:0			6:40	10:0
			26:40	30:0				
Gemini			26:40	30:0	26:40	30:0	16:40	20:0
Cancer	6:40	10:0	6:40	10:0	0:0	3:20	26:40	30:0
Leo	16:40	20:0	6:40	10:0	13:20	16:40		
			16:40	20:0				
Virgo	26:40	30:0	16:40	20:0	26:40	30:0	6:40	10:0
			26:40	30:0				
Libra			26:40	30:0	0:0	3:20	16:40	20:0
Scorpio	6:40	10:0	6:40	10:0	13:20	16:40	26:40	30:0
Sagittarius	16:40	20:0	6:40	10:0	26:40	30:0		
			16:40	20:0				
Capricorn	26:40	30:0	16:40	20:0	0:0	3:20	6:40	10:0
			26:40	30:0				
Aquarius			26:40	30:0	13:20	16:40	16:40	20:0
Pisces	6:40	10:0	6:40	10:0	26:40	30:0	26:40	30:0

Sign	Good Degrees						Bad Degrees	
	Exaltation		Own		Vargottama		Debilitation	
	From D:M	To D:M	From D:M	To D:M	From D:M	To D:M	From D:M	To D:M
Jupiter								
Aries	10:0	13:20	26:40	30:0	0:0	3:20		
Taurus	20:0	23:20	6:40	10:0	13:20	16:40	0:0	3:20
Gemini			6:40	10:0			10:0	13:20
			16:40	20:0	26:40	30:0		
Cancer	0:0	3:20	16:40	20:0	0:0	3:20	20:0	23:20
			26:40	30:0				
Leo	10:0	13:20	26:40	30:0	13:20	16:40		
Virgo	20:0	23:20	6:40	10:0	26:40	30:0	0:0	3:20
Libra			6:40	10:0	0:0	3:20	10:0	13:20
			6:40	10:0	0:0	3:20	10:0	13:20
Scorpio	0:0	3:20	16:40	20:0	13:20	16:40	20:0	23:20
			26:40	30:0				
Sagittarius	10:0	13:20	26:40	30:0	26:40	30:0		
Capricorn	20:0	23:20	6:40	10:0	0:0	3:20	0:0	3:20
Aquarius			6:40	10:0	13:20	16:40	10:0	13:20
			16:40	20:0				
Pisces	0:0	3:20	16:40	20:0			20:0	23:20
			26:40	30:0	26:40	30:0		

Sign	Good Degrees						Bad Degrees	
	Exaltation		Own		Vargottama		Debilitation	
	From D:M	To D:M	From D:M	To D:M	From D:M	To D:M	From D:M	To D:M
Venus								
Aries			3:20	6:40	0:0	3:20	16:40	30:0
			20:0	23:20				
Taurus	6:40	10:0	13:20	16:40			26:40	30:0
Gemini	16:40	20:0	0:0	3:20				
			23:20	26:40				
Cancer	26:40	30:0	10:0	13:20	0:0	3:20	6:40	10:0
Leo			3:20	6:40	13:20	16:40	16:40	10:0
			20:0	23:20				
Virgo	6:40	10:0	13:20	16:40	26:40	30:0	26:40	30:0
Libra	16:40	20:0	0:0	3:20	0:0	3:20		
			23:20	26:40				
Scorpio	26:40	30:0	10:0	13:20	13:20	16:40	6:40	10:0
Sagittarius			3:20	6:40	26:40	30:0	16:40	20:0
			20:0	23:20				
Capricorn	6:40	10:0	13:20	16:40	0:0	3:20		
Aquarius	16:40	20:0	0:0	3:20	13:20	16:40		
			23:20	26:40				
Pisces			10:0	13:20			6:40	10:0
	26:40	30:0	26:40	30:0				

Sign	Good Degrees						Bad Degrees	
	Exaltation		Own		*Vargottama*		Debilitation	
	From D:M	To D:M	From D:M	To D:M	From D:M	To D:M	From D:M	To D:M
Saturn								
Aries	20:0	23:20			0:0	3:20	0:0	3:20
Taurus			0:0	3:20			10:0	13:20
			3:20	6:40				
Gemini	0:0	3:20	10:0	13:20	26:40	30:0	20:0	23:20
			13:20	16:40				
Cancer	10:0	13:20	20:0	23:20	0:0	3:20		
			23:20	26:40				
Leo	20:0	23:20					0:0	3:20
Virgo			0:0	3:20	26:40	30:0	10:0	13:20
			3:20	6:40				
Libra	0:0	3:20	10:0	13:20	0:0	3:20	20:0	23:20
			13:20	16:40				
Scorpio	10:0	13:20	20:0	23:20	13:20	16:40		
			23:20	26:40				
Sagittarius	20:0	23:20			26:40	30:0	0:0	3:20
Capricorn			0:0	3:20	0:0	3:20	10:0	13:20
			3:20	6:40				
Aquarius	0:0	3:20	10:0	13:20	13:20	16:40	20:0	23:20
			13:20	16:40				
Pisces	10:0	13:20	20:0	23:20	26:40	30:0		
			23:20	26:40				

APPENDIX C

Matching Points between Rashis and *Nakshatras* of Boy and Girl

Rashi / Pada / Nak.	ARI 4 AS	ARI 4 BH	ARI 1 KR	TAU 3 KR	TAU 4 RO	TAU 2 MR	GEM 2 MR	GEM 4 AR	GEM 3 PN	CAN 1 PN	CAN 4 PU	CAN 4 AL	LEO 4 MA	LEO 4 PP	LEO 1 UP	VIR 3 UP	VIR 4 HA	VIR 2 CH
A 4 AS	28	33	28	19	24	23	26	17	18	23	31	27	20	24	15	10	11	13
R 4 BH	33	28	28	18	27	15	18	26	26	31	23	25	19	17	24	19	19	4
I 1 KR	27	28	28	18	10	17	20	20	20	25	27	23	15	19	20	15	14	18
T 3 KR	19	28	28	28	19	27	17	17	17	21	23	19	19	22	22	20	18	23
A 4 RO	24	24	11	20	28	36	27	23	22	26	27	12	11	25	27	26	26	19
U 2 MR	24	15	19	28	35	28	19	24	23	19	19	21	20	16	25	23	24	12
G 2 MR	27	18	22	19	27	20	28	33	32	19	12	14	23	19	28	32	34	20
E 4 AR	19	18	22	19	27	20	28	24	32	19	12	14	23	19	28	32	34	25
M 3 PN	22	26	25	19	22	23	28	33	28	14	21	16	22	26	20	32	25	27
C 1 PN	22	29	25	21	24	25	32	24	13	28	34	29	17	21	15	24	18	20
A 4 PU	30	21	27	23	25	18	18	10	18	35	28	29	19	15	24	17	26	12
N 4 AL	25	23	22	18	11	19	11	19	24	28	28	28	15	16	18	26	20	25
L 4 MA	19	19	16	17	10	16	12	19	18	17	19	16	28	30	24	20	15	20
E 4 PP	25	17	19	20	24	26	19	12	26	23	26	17	27	28	34	17	21	6
O 1 UP	16	25	20	21	26	24	28	21	24	15	28	19	16	34	28	24	15	13
V 3 UP	11	21	16	21	26	25	32	27	25	18	27	21	16	23	17	16	27	25
I 4 HA	11	19	16	21	24	11	18	20	19	19	12	22	16	21	14	28	28	28
R 2 CH	13	5	19	23	19	11	12	22	27	19	11	26	21	7	14	26	27	28
2 CH	22	14	18	11	14	24	23	19	20	25	23	25	25	11	18	25	20	20
4 SW	29	28	16	15	9	17	13	26	13	21	21	13	13	24	26	18	28	21
3 VI	21	22	20	20	14	22	13	20	4	18	21	17	17	19	18	28	19	26
1 VI	17	17	20	24	28	21	11	20	12	25	18	15	25	23	22	18	18	26
4 AN	24	15	15	29	23	30	10	26	27	10	17	20	31	21	29	17	25	11
4 JY	17	18	19	20	13	13	12	13	27	8	19	25	24	24	16	24	11	24
4 MO	12	19	24	14	19	11	21	15	22	23	15	23	19	18	20	11	13	26
4 PA	26	18	25	6	10	17	19	2	15	23	23	17	9	17	25	13	27	12
1 UA	24	26	20	12	16	23	25	14	17	28	28	9	5	24	25	29	29	20
3 UA	27	29	12	12	17	26	20	26	12	28	28	14	6	20	21	24	24	16
4 SH	28	27	15	17	19	11	23	26	17	21	13	27	19	19	20	23	24	17
2 DH	20	11	12	24	26	18	8	25	18	12	4	18	25	5	11	16	17	17
2 DH	20	11	26	30	25	27	11	20	25	7	13	19	26	11	19	18	19	25
4 SB	15	21	26	27	30	31	20	16	27	12	20	12	19	20	12	18	11	18
3 PB	18	25	31	24	25	25	24	18	25	17	25	18	17	25	17	16	16	18
1 PB	15	22	20	19	18	18	17	12	18	26	19	18	18	23	15	16	16	9
4 UB	24	16	17	21	17	26	25	17	27	25	26	13	12	15	26	27	26	19
4 RE	25	24	11	13	17	26	25	18	25	25	26	13	12	23	23	24	25	19

Matching Points between *Rashis* and *Nakshatras* of Boy and Girl

		LIB			SCO			SAG		CAP					AQU		PIS		
		2 CH	4 SW	3 VI	1 VI	4 AN	4 JY	4 MO	4 PA	1 UA	3 UA	4 SH	2 DH	2 DH	2 DH	4 SB	3 PB	1 PB	4 UB	4 RE
4	AS	22	28	22	19	25	13	13	25	23	25	26	20	20	20	15	16	15	24	26
4	BH	13	28	21	19	18	20	20	18	26	28	26	10	10	10	20	23	23	17	26
4	KR	27	14	19	17	20	26	25	20	12	14	14	25	25	25	26	19	18	20	11
1	KR	22	9	14	21	25	31	22	15	7	12	11	25	29	29	30	23	20	22	13
3	RO	18	14	8	15	30	24	14	20	11	16	18	19	18	18	24	29	26	27	19
4	MR	11	25	17	24	22	25	15	11	17	22	26	12	12	12	27	28	25	18	27
2	MR	13	27	13	13	13	14	23	19	25	20	24	10	12	12	21	23	24	17	26
2	AR	13	27	13	13	13	14	23	19	25	20	24	10	19	19	21	23	19	26	26
2	PN	20	27	21	15	21	6	14	27	27	22	23	17	12	12	13	16	18	27	26
3	PN	19	27	21	19	25	11	8	21	21	26	26	21	4	4	10	10	16	25	25
1	PU	19	27	21	19	17	20	18	13	21	26	27	13	17	17	18	18	26	18	26
4	AL	24	11	16	15	19	25	23	16	8	13	13	26	24	24	25	11	18	20	12
4	MA	24	11	16	25	25	32	24	19	9	4	5	17	10	10	19	18	18	19	12
4	PP	10	25	18	24	23	25	20	17	24	19	19	6	18	18	11	24	24	17	25
1	UP	17	26	17	23	31	17	20	25	25	20	20	12	17	17	10	16	16	27	25
4	UP	17	26	17	18	26	12	14	30	30	24	24	16	19	19	21	15	17	28	26
3	HA	20	27	19	20	26	14	15	27	29	23	24	18	16	16	24	14	16	26	26
4	CH	19	21	26	27	11	25	27	13	21	16	17	15	18	18	26	17	18	9	19
2	CH	28	27	34	23	7	21	27	11	21	24	25	23	21	21	22	19	12	1	12
2	SW	28	27	20	9	22	17	23	27	19	22	23	26	24	24	26	25	19	19	11
4	VI	34	28	28	16	16	22	27	21	13	16	16	30	24	24	26	20	12	11	4
3	VI	24	19	15	28	27	32	22	16	8	11	11	25	11	11	20	20	19	18	10
1	AN	7	7	16	28	28	31	16	14	22	25	26	12	24	24	17	25	19	17	26
4	JY	20	21	16	32	30	28	14	17	17	20	20	25	29	29	22	10	24	20	20
4	MO	26	15	21	23	17	16	28	28	16	14	15	20	15	15	24	15	10	25	26
4	PA	12	11	26	17	16	18	27	35	34	22	23	6	23	23	23	29	17	23	31
1	UA	20	27	20	9	24	18	25	24	28	16	15	14	16	16	17	29	30	31	23
3	UA	23	19	12	12	27	21	15	23	17	28	27	26	17	17	18	22	30	32	23
4	SH	24	22	15	12	27	21	14	7	15	26	28	27	17	17	23	21	30	23	22
2	DH	29	22	15	25	12	26	21	16	24	17	27	28	28	28	33	18	29	15	23
2	DH	18	24	29	26	11	25	30	25	25	17	18	18	33	33	19	28	25	7	14
4	SB	26	11	26	25	20	18	23	30	30	23	18	24	17	17	7	28	17	15	16
3	PB	19	26	20	27	27	11	15	29	29	29	23	19	16	16	15	28	8	22	20
1	PB	11	19	13	21	25	10	14	22	30	30	23	19	6	6	16	15	16	33	31
4	UB	2	19	12	19	18	20	24	29	21	24	30	25	14	14	15	21	28	28	34
4	RE	11	10	4	11	26	21	26	21	21	21	22	23	21	21	16	18	33	33	28

5. Nonoperative treatment
   a. Ponseti method of serial manipulation and long-leg casting
6. Operative indications
   a. Little (or no) improvement in the severe, rigid clubfoot deformities in an infant with arthrogryposis after a long series of casts, with the presumption that it would be challenging to stretch the posterior ankle skin and align the foot in the ankle mortis even if a talectomy were performed (Figure 5-12).
      i. The *expectation* is that, following surgery, the deformities will be improved (Figure 5-13) and serial casting will be reinitiated. The deformities might then be corrected with further serial casting or improved enough with further serial casting that conventional á la carte partial-to-complete circumferential release will be successful.

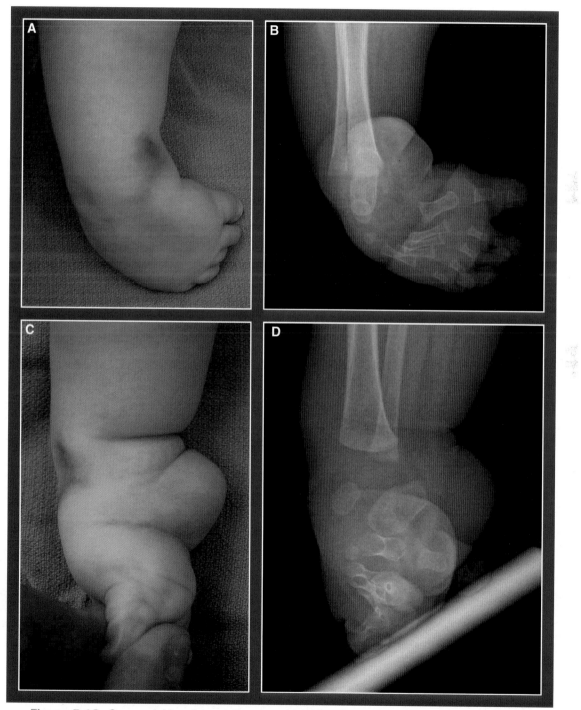

Figure 5-12. Severe, rigid, resistant arthrogrypotic clubfoot. A–D after 14 casts: A. Top photo. B. AP x-ray. C. Medial photo with maximum dorsiflexion. D. Lateral x-ray with maximum dorsiflexion.

7. <u>Operative treatment</u> with reference to the surgical techniques section of the book for each individual procedure
   a. Limited, minimally invasive soft tissue releases for clubfoot (**see Chapter 7**), as an incidental event to enable more effective ongoing serial casting (Figure 5-13)
      i. Percutaneous tendo-Achilles tenotomy
      ii. Limited open plantar fasciotomy
      iii. Limited open posterior tibialis tenotomy
      iv. Percutaneous tenotomies of FHL and FDL to toes 2-to 5
   b. Talectomy—*perform this* for failure of "a" (**see Chapter 8**)

Corrected Congenital Clubfoot (Talipes Equinovarus) with Anterior Tibialis Overpull

1. <u>Definition—**Deformity**</u>
   a. Structurally corrected clubfoot with stronger anterior tibialis than peroneus tertius and relatively weak peroneus longus resulting in a dynamic supination deformity of the foot (Figure 5-14)
2. <u>Elucidation of the segmental deformities</u>
   a. None
3. <u>Imaging</u>
   a. Standing AP and lateral of foot
      i. to confirm full correction of deformities

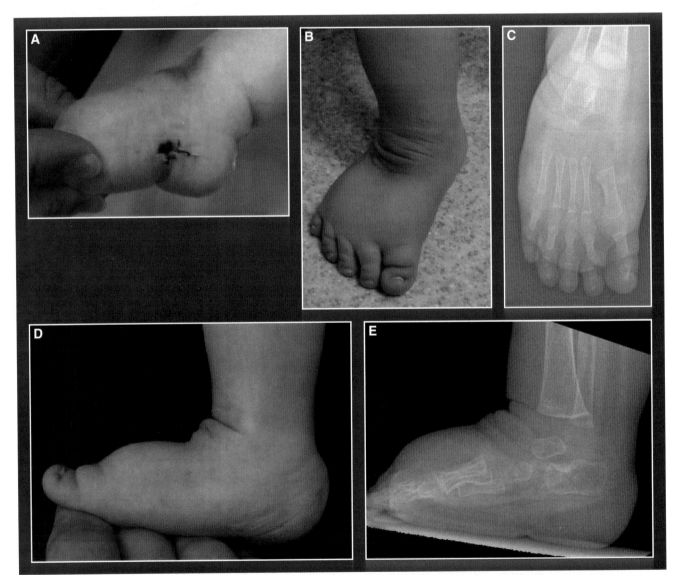

Figure 5-13. **A.** One week after percutaneous tenotomies of tendo-Achilles and long toe flexors, as well as mini-open plantar fasciotomy and posterior tibialis tenotomy in the foot in Figure 5-12. **B** to **E** after four more casts: **B.** Simulated standing top photo. **C.** Simulated standing AP x-ray. **D.** Medial photo with maximum dorsiflexion. **E.** Lateral x-ray with maximum dorsiflexion. **F** to **H** one year later, following two serial casts for minor recurrence: **F.** Standing top photo. **G.** Medial photo with maximum dorsiflexion. **H.** Lateral x-ray with maximum dorsiflexion.

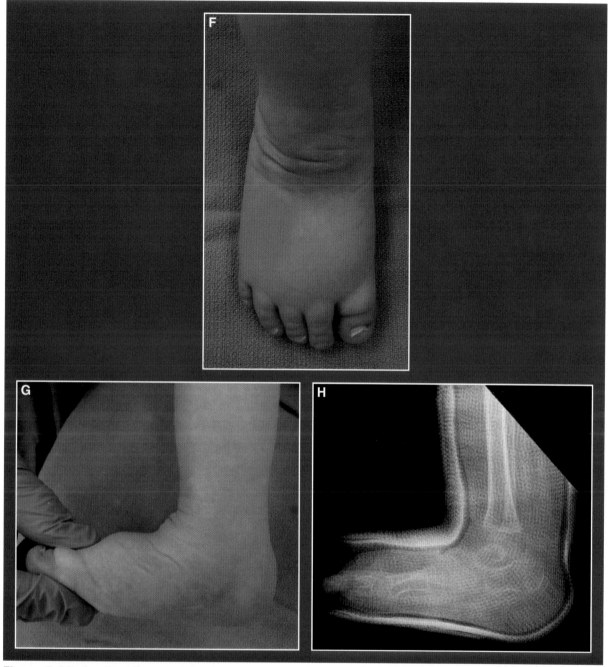

Figure 5-13. *(continued)*

ii. to ensure adequate size of the ossification center of the lateral (3rd) cuneiform to accept the anterior tibialis tendon

4. <u>Natural history</u>
   a. Instability of gait with frequent inversion injuries
   b. Pain and exaggerated callus formation along the plantar–lateral border of the foot

5. <u>Nonoperative treatment</u>
   a. Peroneus tertius strengthening exercises. Efficacy is not documented.
   b. Serial casting to correct any residual or recurrent deformities prior to tendon transfer surgery.

6. <u>Operative indications</u>
   a. Exaggerated dynamic supination of a well-corrected and flexible clubfoot during the swing phase of the gait cycle
      i. that creates instability of gait and/or excessive weight-bearing on the plantar–lateral aspect of the foot
      ii. after failure of strengthening exercises to balance the strength of the anterior tibialis and peroneus tertius muscles
      iii. in which there is a large ossification center of the lateral (3rd) cuneiform

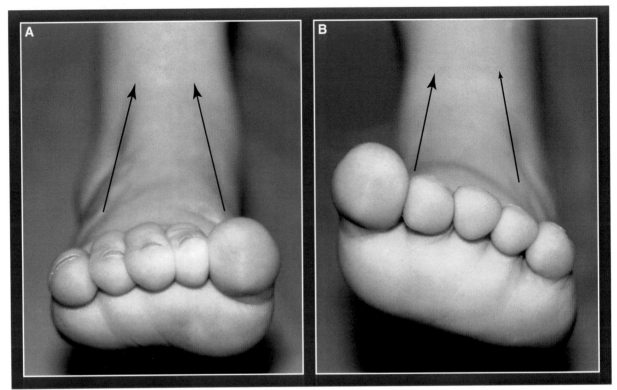

Figure 5-14. Assess muscle balance in a clubfoot by asking the child to dorsiflex the foot, or by stimulating the plantar aspect of the foot. **A.** Normal muscle balance between the anterior tibialis and the peroneus tertius. The plane of the MT heads is perpendicular to the tibial shaft. **B.** Relative overpull of normal anterior tibialis vs. weak peroneus tertius and longus in a child with a clubfoot that has excellent deformity correction and flexibility. The plane of the MT heads is supinated in relation to the tibial shaft.

7. <u>Operative treatment</u> with reference to the surgical techniques section of the book for each individual procedure
   a. Anterior tibialis tendon transfer to lateral (3rd) cuneiform (**see Chapter 7**)

Recurrent/Persistent Clubfoot Deformity

1. <u>Definition</u>—**Deformity**
   a. Recurrence or persistence of one or more of the clubfoot segmental deformities following nonoperative or operative initial treatment (Figure 5-15).
2. <u>Elucidation of the segmental deformities</u>
   a. Forefoot—*pronated*
   b. Midfoot—*adducted*
   c. Hindfoot—*varus/inverted*
   d. Ankle—*plantar flexed (equinus)*
3. <u>Imaging</u>
   a. Maximum dorsiflexion/abduction/eversion AP and lateral of foot—for younger children
   b. Standing AP and lateral of foot—for older children
   c. AP, lateral, mortis of ankle
4. <u>Natural history</u>
   a. Persistence of deformity with pain, functional disability, and inability to wear normal shoes
5. <u>Nonoperative treatment</u>
   a. Ponseti method of serial manipulation and long-leg casting, along with percutaneous Achilles tenotomy in

most cases (well described in Clubfoot: Ponseti Management, LT Staheli, editor. www.Global-HELP.org monograph), starting in children up to at least 5 to 6 years of age (and possibly older)
      i. Should be successful less often than when initiated in infants, with the rate of success inversely proportional to age at initiation
6. <u>Operative indications</u>
   a. Failure or age-inappropriateness of serial casting to correct one or more of the clubfoot segmental deformities
   b. Pain, shoe-fitting difficulties, dysfunction
7. <u>Operative treatment</u> with reference to the surgical techniques section of the book for each individual procedure
   a. Percutaneous tendo-Achilles tenotomy (**see Chapter 7**)—*perform this* when there is less than 10° of ankle dorsiflexion after the cavus, adductus, and varus have been fully corrected with serial casting in an infant or very young child
      i. This is a complete tenotomy, not a lengthening.
      ii. It should be performed when there is little (or no) expectation that a posterior ankle capsulotomy will be required, which is the assumption in most babies up to at least 2 years of age.
      • If a percutaneous tendo-Achilles tenotomy is concurrently converted to an open ankle capsulotomy, the gap in the tendon will not heal and remodel as well, and with as good preservation of excursion,

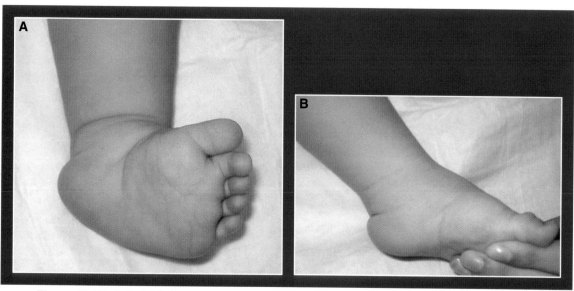

Figure 5-15. Left clubfoot in a 10-month-old boy who was treated from birth with serial casting. He apparently achieved full correction of all segmental deformities, but was lost to follow-up and returned with recurrence of all segmental deformities. **A.** Foot at rest. **B.** Maximum passive dosiflexion and eversion.

as occurs with percutaneous Achilles tenotomy alone.

iii. If the need for a posterior capsulotomy is anticipated, an open tendo-Achilles lengthening should be performed. If a capsulotomy is then deemed unnecessary, there is no measureable disability from having performed a formal tendo-Achilles lengthening.

b. Posterior release (**see Chapter 7**)—*perform this* if there are less than 10° of dorsiflexion after the cavus, adductus, and varus have been fully corrected with serial casting in an older child, particularly if there is suspicion that the posterior ankle joint capsule is contracted in addition to the tendo-Achilles

c. À la carte partial-to-complete circumferential release (**see Chapter 7**)—*perform this* if there are residual cavus, adductus, and/or varus deformities in addition to an equinus deformity

i. The McKay procedure is the surgical analog of the Ponseti method in that it embraces the pathoanatomy ascribed to by Ponseti

ii. In *non*-idiopathic clubfoot, the tendons are released rather than lengthened, because of the high recurrence rate in these feet

d. À la carte partial-to-complete circumferential release (**see Chapter 7**) *along with* one or more of the following procedures—*perform one or more of these additional procedures* if there are residual cavus, adductus, and/or varus deformities in addition to an equinus deformity, *and* structural MA, resistant hindfoot varus with a long lateral column of the foot, and/or muscle imbalance

i. Medial column lengthening for structural MA
• Medial cuneiform opening wedge osteotomy (**see Chapter 8**)

ii. Lateral column shortening for structural MA (**see Management Principle #18, Chapter 4**)

• Closing wedge osteotomy of the cuboid (**see Chapter 8**)

iii. Lateral column shortening for resistant hindfoot varus/inversion with a long lateral column of the foot (**see Management Principle #18, Chapter 4**)
• Calcaneocuboid resection/fusion (**see Chapter 8**)
• Lichtblau resection of the anterior calcaneus (**see Chapter 8**)
• Closing wedge osteotomy of the anterior calcaneus (**see Chapter 8**)

iv. Posterior calcaneus lateral displacement osteotomy (**see Chapter 8**)

v. Anterior tibialis tendon transfer to lateral (3rd) cuneiform (**see Chapter 7**)

e. Triple arthrodesis (**see Chapter 8**)—*perform this* if there are *no* other options for correcting the deformities because of severity and/or rigidity, or because of existing degenerative arthritis of the subtalar joint (**see Management Principle #13, Chapter 4**)

f. Gradual deformity correction with external fixation (not elucidated in this book)

Rotational Valgus Overcorrection of the Subtalar Joint

1. Definition—**Deformity**
a. Iatrogenically acquired flatfoot in an operatively treated clubfoot *with* excessive external rotation of the subtalar joint (Figure 5-16)
i. due to excessive release of the subtalar joint, but *without* release of the talocalcaneal interosseous ligament
ii. with all components of eversion of the subtalar joint. Essentially, an acquired "physiologic" flatfoot

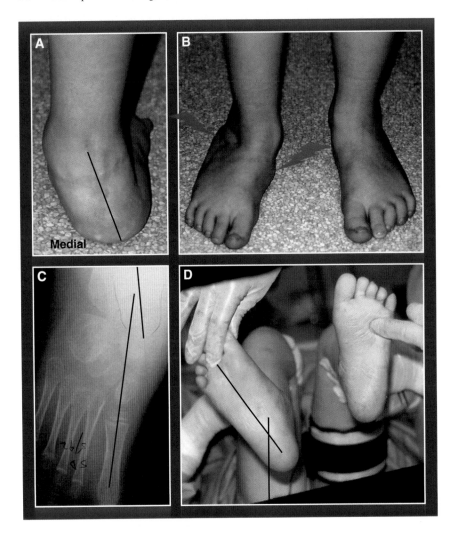

Figure 5-16. Previously operated club-foot with rotational valgus overcorrection of the subtalar joint. **A.** Posterior view of severe valgus deformity of the hindfoot, similar to that seen in translational valgus overcorrection of the subtalar joint (**see Figure 5-17A**). **B.** Standing top image showing external rotation of the foot. Pain is typically experienced under the medial midfoot (similar to a flexible flatfoot with a tight tendo-Achilles), and there is often impingement-type pain in the sinus tarsi area or between the calcaneus and the lateral malleolus. **C.** Eversion of the subtalar joint is evident, with the navicular laterally positioned on the head of the talus. The abducted foot-CORA (**see Assessment Principle #18, Figure 3-19, Chapter 3**) is in the talar head-neck, as in an idiopathic flexible flatfoot. **D.** Example of an outward (positive) thigh–foot angle, as seen in this deformity.

2. Elucidation of the segmental deformities
   a. Forefoot—*supinated*
   b. Midfoot—*neutral, abducted,* or *adducted*
   c. Hindfoot—*valgus/everted*
      i. Positive thigh–foot angle
   d. Ankle—*plantar flexed (equinus)*
   e. Looks like an idiopathic flatfoot, clinically and radiographically
3. Imaging
   a. Standing AP, lateral, Harris view of foot
   b. AP, lateral, and mortis of ankle
4. Natural history
   a. Persistence of deformity with pain under the medial midfoot and/or in the sinus tarsi area and/or in the lateral hindfoot—in some cases
5. Nonoperative treatment
   a. Over-the-counter soft arch support or gel cushion insert
   b. Accommodative shoe
6. Operative indications
   a. Activity-related pain under the medial midfoot and/or in the sinus tarsi area and/or in the lateral hindfoot that is not relieved with prolonged attempts at nonoperative treatment

7. Operative treatment with reference to the surgical techniques section of the book for each individual procedure
   a. Calcaneal lengthening osteotomy (**see Chapter 8**)
      i. with possible tendo-Achilles lengthening (**see Chapter 7**) or gastrocnemius recession (**see Chapter 7**)
      ii. with possible medial cuneiform plantar-based closing wedge (or dorsal opening wedge) osteotomy (**see Chapter 8**)
   b. If there is coexisting ankle valgus (often present), correct the ankle valgus *first* (**see Management Principle #23-6, Chapter 4**), either by guided growth (**see Medial Distal Tibia Guided Growth with Retrograde Medial Malleolus Screw, Chapter 8**) or by distal tibia and fibula osteotomies (**see Chapter 8**)

Translational Valgus Overcorrection of the Subtalar Joint

1. Definition—**Deformity**
   a. Iatrogenically acquired flatfoot in an operatively treated clubfoot *with* excessive lateral translation of the calcaneus under the talus (Figure 5-17)

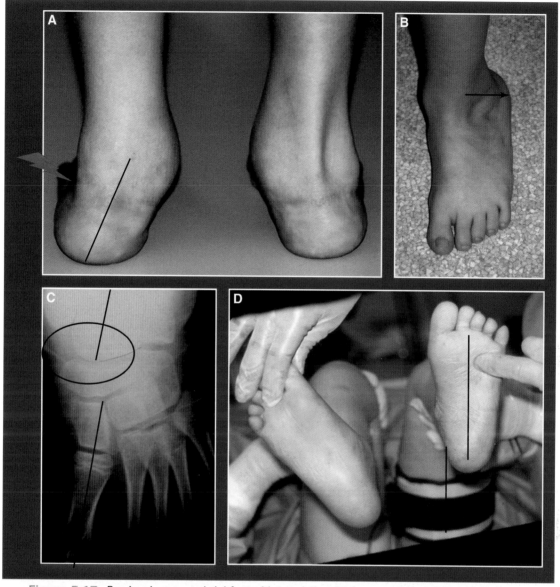

Figure 5-17. Previously operated clubfoot with translational valgus overcorrection of the subtalar joint. **A.** Posterior view of severe valgus deformity of the hindfoot, similar to that seen in rotational valgus overcorrection of the subtalar joint (**see Figure 5-16A**). Impingement-type pain is typically experienced between the calcaneus and the lateral malleolus. **B.** Standing top image of the foot showing lateral translation of the heel (*black arrow*). **C.** The talonavicular joint is well-aligned (*black oval*). The talus and 1st MT are parallel, but can have a foot-CORA (**see Assessment Principle #18, Figure 3-18, Chapter 3**) in the talar head that is usually abducted less than 12°. **D.** Example of a neutral thigh-foot angle, as seen in this deformity.

i. due to excessive release of the subtalar joint *with* release of the talocalcaneal interosseous ligament

ii. often, with acceptable alignment at the talonavicular joint

2. Elucidation of the segmental deformities

a. Forefoot—*neutral* or *supinated*

b. Midfoot—*neutral, abducted,* or *adducted*

c. Hindfoot—*valgus without eversion,* i.e., with well-aligned talonavicular joint

i. Neutral thigh–foot angle

d. Ankle—*neutral* or *plantar flexed (equinus)*

e. Looks somewhat like an idiopathic flatfoot clinically, but not radiographically

3. Imaging

a. Standing AP, lateral, Harris view of foot

b. AP, lateral, and mortis of ankle

4. Natural history

a. Persistence of deformity with pain in the lateral hindfoot and/or in the sinus tarsi and occasionally under the medial midfoot—in some cases

5. Nonoperative treatment

a. Over-the-counter soft arch support or gel cushion insert

b. Accommodative shoe

6. Operative indications

a. Activity-related pain in the lateral hindfoot and/or in the sinus tarsi and occasionally under the medial midfoot that is not relieved with prolonged attempts at nonoperative treatment

7. <u>Operative treatment</u> with reference to the surgical techniques section of the book for each individual procedure
   a. Posterior calcaneus medial displacement ± medial closing wedge osteotomy (**see Chapter 8**)
      i. with possible tendo-Achilles lengthening (**see Chapter 7**) or gastrocnemius recession (**see Chapter 7**)
      ii. with possible medial cuneiform plantar-based closing wedge (or dorsal opening wedge) osteotomy (**see Chapter 8**)
   b. If there is coexisting ankle valgus (often present), correct the ankle valgus *first* (**see Management Principle #23-6, Chapter 4**), either by guided growth (**see Medial Distal Tibia Guided Growth with Retrograde Medial Malleolus Screw, Chapter 8**) or by distal tibia and fibula osteotomies (**see Chapter 8**)

Dorsal Subluxation/Dislocation of the Talonavicular Joint

1. <u>Definition—**Deformity**</u>
   a. Iatrogenically acquired dorsal subluxation or dislocation of the navicular on the head of the talus in an operatively treated clubfoot (Figure 5-18)
      i. due to overly extensive release of the talonavicular joint, usually with failure to release a contracted plantar fascia
2. <u>Elucidation of the segmental deformities</u>
   a. Forefoot—*pronated, neutral,* or *supinated*
   b. Midfoot—dorsal, and often lateral, *subluxation* or *dislocation* of the navicular on the head of the talus with appearance of *cavus*
   c. Hindfoot—*neutral, varus,* or *valgus*

   d. Ankle—*neutral, plantar flexed (equinus),* or *dorsiflexed (calcaneus)*
3. <u>Imaging</u>
   a. Standing AP, lateral, oblique of foot
   b. Consider CT scan of the foot and ankle in all three planes and with 3D reconstruction in older children and adolescents
4. <u>Natural history</u>
   a. Persistence of deformity with pain over the dorsum of the midfoot and/or shoe-fitting problems related to the tall instep and relatively short toe-to-heel length of the foot—in some cases
5. <u>Nonoperative treatment</u>
   a. Accommodative shoe
6. <u>Operative indications</u>
   a. Pain over the dorsum of the midfoot and/or shoe-fitting problems related to the tall instep and relatively short toe-to-heel length of the foot.
   b. Painful anterior ankle impingement between the navicular and the anterior distal tibial epiphysis
7. <u>Operative treatment</u> with reference to the surgical techniques section of the book for each individual procedure
   a. 3rd street procedure (**see Chapter 7**)—*perform this* in children up to around age 6 years
   b. Talonavicular joint arthrodesis—*perform this* in older children and adolescents
   c. Resection of impinging portion of dorsally subluxated navicular (**see Chapter 8**)—*perform this* for isolated painful anterior ankle impingement in an older child or adolescent
   d. Triple arthrodesis (**see Chapter 8**)—*perform this* in an older child or adolescent if the subluxation/dislocation is associated with severe deformities and degenerative arthritis of the other joints of the subtalar complex

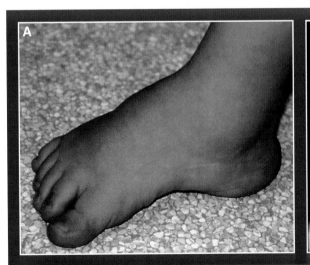
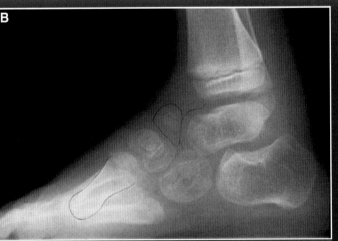

Figure 5-18. Previously operated clubfoot with dorsal subluxation of the talonavicular joint. **A.** Clinical image shows a tall instep (cavus) and short toe-to-heel length. **B.** Lateral radiograph shows dorsal subluxation of the navicular on the head of the talus and exaggerated plantar flexion of the first ray, including the MT, cuneiform, and navicular.

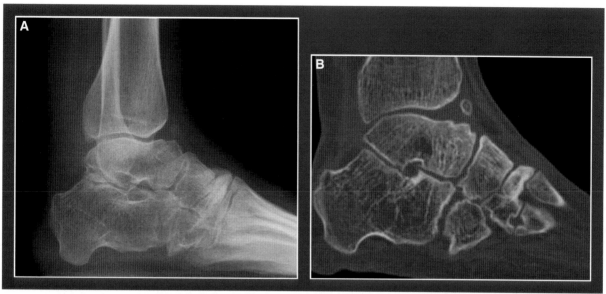

Figure 5-19. Postsurgical clubfoot in a 15-year-old girl with anterior ankle impingement pain. **A.** Flattop talus with shallow/absent dorsal talar neck concavity (and small heterotopic ossicle) causing anterior ankle impingement and pain. **B.** Sagittal CT scan image confirming the pathology.

Anterior Ankle Impingement

1. <u>Definition—**Deformity**</u>
   a. Iatrogenically acquired impingement between the dorsal talar neck (or the navicular) and the anterior distal tibial epiphysis that limits dorsiflexion
      i. Causes include:
         - iatrogenic flattop talus from casting-induced and/or surgery-related crush injury to the dome of the talus (Figure 5-19)
         - iatrogenic flattop talus from surgery-related avascular necrosis (Figure 5-20)
         - iatrogenic posterior distal tibial growth arrest with progressive procurvatum deformity and flexion mal-orientation of the ankle joint (Figure 5-21)
         - iatrogenic dorsal subluxation of the talonavicular joint (**see Dorsal Subluxation/Dislocation of the Talonavicular Joint, above**)

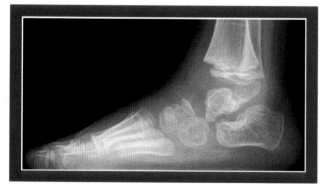

Figure 5-20. Avascular necrosis of the talus after clubfoot surgery with anterior impingement-type pain due to flattening of the dome and neck of the talus.

2. <u>Elucidation of the segmental deformities</u>
   a. Flattop talar dome with shallow or flat dorsal neck of talus
   b. *Or*, rarely, procurvatum deformity of distal tibia with flexion mal-orientation of the ankle joint
   c. *Or*, dorsal subluxation of the navicular on the head of the talus

3. <u>Imaging</u>
   a. Standing AP and lateral of foot
   b. Standing AP, lateral, and mortis of ankle
   c. CT scan of foot and ankle in all three planes and with 3D reconstruction in older children and adolescents

4. <u>Natural history</u>
   a. Persistence or progression of deformity with anterior ankle pain that is exacerbated by dorsiflexion of the ankle—in some cases

5. <u>Nonoperative treatment</u>
   a. High heel shoes
   b. Heel wedge orthotics

6. <u>Operative indications</u>
   a. Failure of nonoperative treatment to relieve the anterior ankle impingement-type pain that is exacerbated by dorsiflexion of the ankle.

7. <u>Operative treatment</u> with reference to the surgical techniques section of the book for each individual procedure
   a. Debridement/reshaping of dorsal talar neck (**see Chapter 8**)—*perform this* if there is a dorsally prominent talar neck and a relatively normally shaped talar dome in a skeletally mature adolescent (**see Figure 5-19**)
   b. Anterior distal tibia and fibula closing wedge/posterior translational dorsiflexion osteotomies (**see**

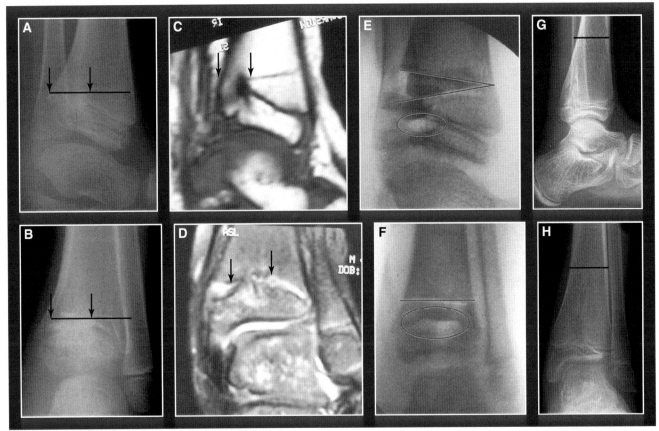

Figure 5-21. Postsurgical clubfoot in a 5-year-old boy who had progressive loss of dorsiflexion and accompanying anterior ankle impingement-type pain. **A.** Lateral radiograph shows large posterior arrest of distal tibial physis, between arrow heads. Black line is Park–Harris growth arrest line. Resultant procurvatum deformity of the distal tibia created secondary anterior ankle impingement, despite normal anatomy of the talus. **B.** AP radiograph shows the arrest, roughly between the arrow heads. **C.** Sagittal MRI scan image shows the large, solid posterior physeal bar, between arrow heads. **D.** Coronal MRI scan image of the pathology. **E.** Lateral radiograph immediately after resection and fat grafting of the physeal bar (*purple oval*) and concurrent posterior distal tibia opening wedge osteotomy (*purple wedge*). **F.** AP image of the same. **G.** and **H.** Lateral and AP images 9 years later showing black Park–Harris line parallel with, and far from, the physis. The normal sagittal 10° extension tilt of the distal tibial articular surface has been restored.

Chapter 8)—*perform this* in a skeletally mature adolescent with a flat talar dome

c. Anterior distal tibia guided growth with anterior plate–screw construct to orient the joint into recurvatum (**see Chapter 8**)—*perform this* in a skeletally immature child with a flat talar dome

d. Posterior distal tibial physeal bar resection with fat grafting and concurrent posterior distal tibial opening wedge osteotomy (**see above**)

e. *Do not* lengthen tendo-Achilles! It will only increase the impingement.

Dorsal Bunion

1. Definition—**Deformity**
   a. Dorsal prominence of the distal end of the 1st MT associated with dorsiflexion of the medial (1st) ray of the forefoot and hyperplantar flexion of the

hallux at the 1st metatarsophalangeal (MTP) joint (Figure 5-22)
   i. Iatrogenic, usually following surgical treatment of clubfoot deformity
   ii. Occasionally seen in a child with severe spastic quadriplegia as the result of primary muscle imbalance or after surgical treatment

2. Elucidation of the segmental deformities
   a. Forefoot—*supinated*
      i. *Dorsiflexed* medial (1st) ray of the forefoot—flexible or rigid
      ii. *Hyper-plantar flexed* hallux at 1st MTP joint—flexible or fixed
   b. Midfoot—*neutral, abducted,* or *adducted*
   c. Hindfoot—*neutral* or *valgus* (laterally translated)
      i. Stiff or rigid
      ii. with good or fairly good alignment at the talonavicular joint

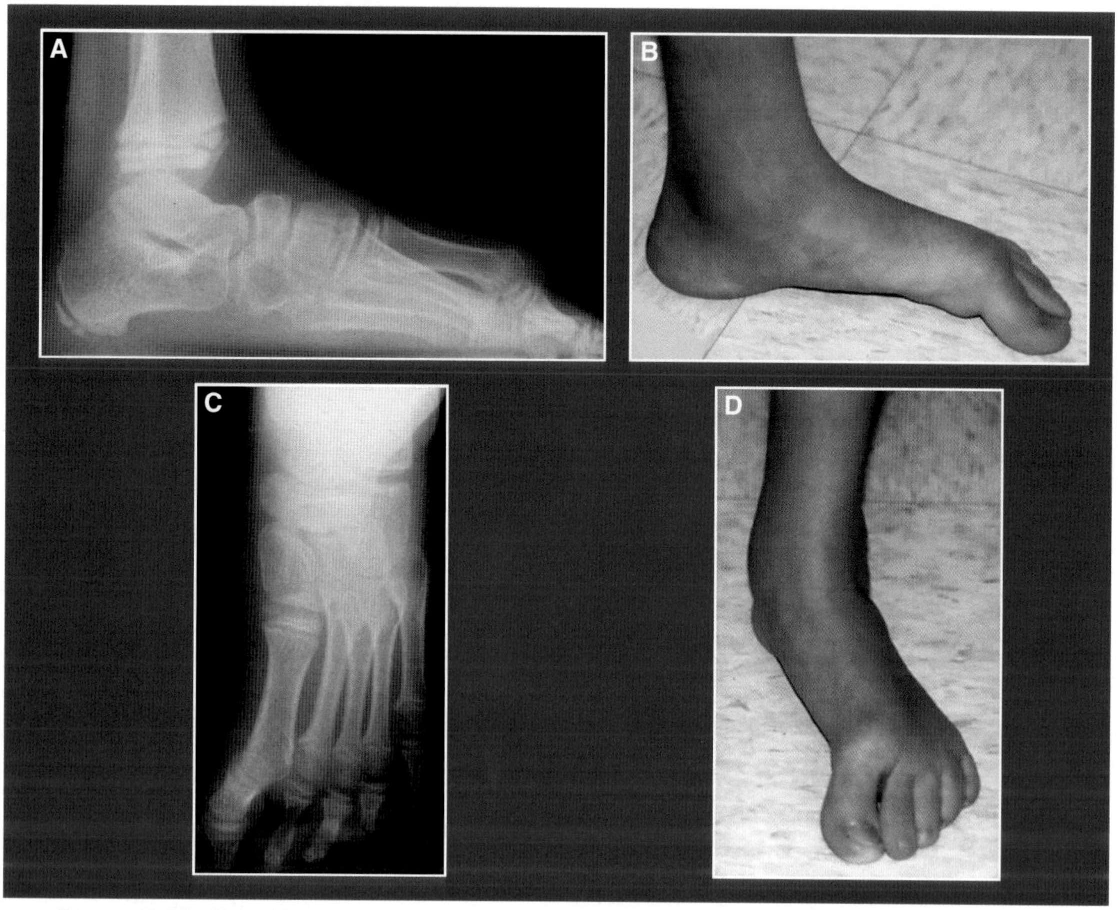

Figure 5-22. Dorsal bunion in a teenager. **A.** Standing lateral radiograph shows dorsiflexion of the 1st ray/MT and plantar flexion of the hallux at the 1st MTP joint. The hindfoot and midfoot are reasonably well-aligned. **B.** Matching clinical picture. The 1st MT head does not touch the ground in weight-bearing. There is redness, callus formation, and pain over the dorsal aspect of the 1st MT head and under the distal tip of the hallux. **C.** Standing AP radiograph shows good hindfoot/midfoot alignment, but malalignment at the 1st MTP joint with apparent plantar flexion. **D.** Matching clinical picture.

d. Muscle imbalances (*opposite* those seen in cavovarus foot deformities) (**see Cavovarus Foot, Figure 5-6, this chapter**)
   i. Strong anterior tibialis
   ii. Weak peroneus longus
   iii. Recruited and, therefore, stronger FHL than EHL
3. Imaging
   a. Standing AP and lateral of foot
   b. Standing AP, lateral, and mortis of ankle
   c. Consider CT scan of foot and ankle in all three planes and with 3D reconstruction in older children and adolescents
4. Natural history
   a. Persistence of deformity with pain and skin pressure injuries (inflammation, callus formation, blistering, ulceration) on the dorsum of the 1st MT head and/or at the tip of the hallux—in some cases
5. Nonoperative treatment
   a. Accommodative shoe wear
6. Operative indications
   a. Failure of nonoperative treatment to relieve the pain and skin pressure irritation on the dorsum of the 1st

MT head (where it contacts the shoe) and/or at the tip of the hallux (where it contacts the ground)
7. Operative treatment with reference to the surgical techniques section of the book for each individual procedure
   a. Combination of procedures (Figure 5-23):
      i. Medial cuneiform (plantar flexion) plantar-based closing wedge osteotomy, or medial cuneiform (plantar flexion) dorsal-based opening wedge osteotomy (**see Chapter 8**)—based on the coexistence of abduction or adduction of the midfoot (**see Management Principle #19, Chapter 4**)
      ii. Transfer anterior tibialis to the 2nd (middle) cuneiform (**see Chapter 7**)
      iii. Reverse Jones transfer of the FHL to the 1st MT neck (**see Chapter 7**)
      iv. Possible plantar capsulotomy of the 1st MTP joint
   b. Often, the hindfoot is stiff, but well-aligned. If not, correct the hindfoot deformity with the appropriate osteotomy (**see Chapter 8**)

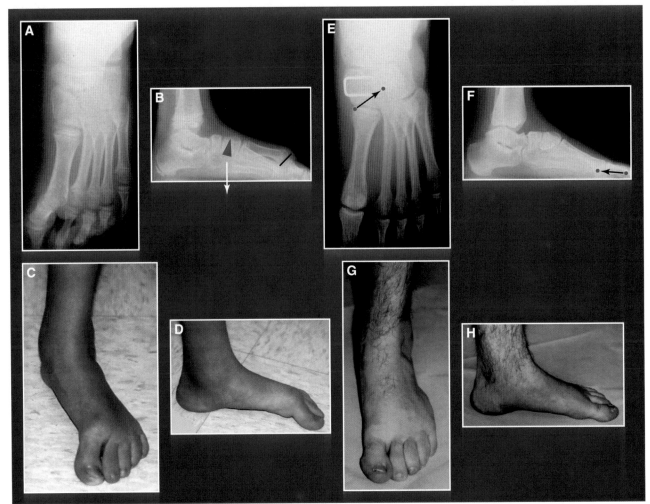

Figure 5-23. **A.** AP x-ray shows good alignment of the talonavicular joint. **B.** Lateral x-ray shows good alignment of the subtalar joint, but hyperdorsiflexion of the 1st ray. Purple triangle represents a plantar-based closing wedge osteotomy of the medial cuneiform that was used to correct the forefoot deformity. The black line represents a capsulotomy of the contracted plantar capsule of the 1st MTP joint. **C** and **D.** Matching preop clinical photos. **E.** Post-op AP x-ray shows the internal fixation staple used for the medial cuneiform osteotomy. The purple dots represent the original and transfer locations for the anterior tibialis tendon. **F.** Ten years post-op lateral x-ray shows the internal fixation staple used for the medial cuneiform osteotomy. The purple dots represent the original and transfer locations for the FHL (reverse Jones transfer). **G.** and **H.** Matching clinical photos of the foot 10 years later.

IV. CONGENITAL VERTICAL/ OBLIQUE TALUS

Congenital Vertical Talus

1. Definition—**Deformity**
   a. Congenital dorsolateral dislocation of the navicular on the talus with severe eversion of the subtalar joint and rigid plantar flexion of the talus, creating a rocker-bottom appearance of the foot. The talus is vertically aligned with the tibia (Figure 5-24).
   b. Idiopathic etiology or associated with an underlying neuromuscular or chromosomal abnormality

2. Elucidation of the segmental deformities
   a. Forefoot—*supinated*
   b. Midfoot
      i. *Abducted*
      ii. Medial column—*dislocated*
         • dorsolateral dislocation of the navicular on the talus
      iii. Lateral column—*subluxated* (or mal-oriented)
         • dorsolateral subluxation and/or mal-orientation of the calcaneocuboid joint
   c. Hindfoot—*valgus/everted*
   d. Ankle—*plantar flexed (equinus)*

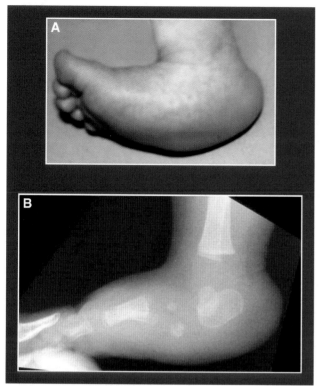

Figure 5-24. **A.** Medial-side photo of a CVT, the so-called "Persian slipper foot" deformity. **B.** Lateral radiograph shows the talus to be vertically aligned with the axis of the tibia. The calcaneus is plantar flexed. The axis of the 1st MT aligns with the dome of the talus, rather than the head.

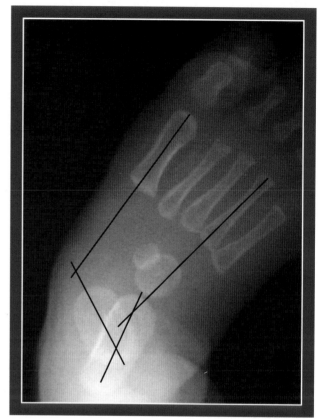

Figure 5-25. AP radiograph of a CVT. The midfoot is abducted, as indicated by the calcaneus–4th MT angle, which is straight in a normal foot and also in most flexible flatfoot deformities. The subtalar joint is severely everted, as indicated by the talus–1st MT angle. The foot-CORA (**see Assessment Principle #18, Chapter 3**) in CVT is often *not* in the talar head, whereas it is always in the talar head in a flexible flatfoot. The two possible reasons for that observation are (1) a projectional artifact created by the dorsal dislocation at the talonavicular joint and (2) a long medial column of the foot.

3. Imaging
   a. Simulated standing AP of foot (Figure 5-25)
   b. Maximum dorsiflexion lateral of foot (Figure 5-26B)
      i. The talus does not dorsiflex more than a few degrees from its colinear vertical alignment with the tibia. The calcaneus barely dorsiflexes to a right angle to the tibia. The axis of the 1st MT is dorsally translated onto the body of the talus, indicating dorsal dislocation of the navicular.
   c. Maximum plantar flexion lateral of foot (Figure 5-26D)
      i. The navicular does not align with the talus with forced plantar flexion. This is manifest by persistence of dorsal translation and angulation of the axis of the 1st MT in relation to the axis of the talus
4. Natural history
   a. Persistence of deformity with pain, functional disability, and inability to wear normal shoes
5. Nonoperative treatment
   a. Reverse Ponseti (Dobbs) casting
6. Operative indications
   a. Failure to achieve full deformity correction with nonoperative treatment
7. Operative treatment with reference to the surgical techniques section of the book for each individual procedure
   a. Tendo-Achilles tenotomy (**see Chapter 7**) and limited open talonavicular joint capsulotomy with retrograde

pinning (Dobbs method)—*perform this* if the talonavicular joint has become aligned with reverse Ponseti (Dobbs) casting, but there is persistent equinus. This is not a plication of the medial soft tissues, but merely a capsulotomy for visualization while pinning the talonavicular (TN) joint.
   b. Dorsal approach release for CVT and COT (**see Chapter 7**)—*perform this* for failure of the reverse Ponseti (Dobbs) nonoperative method to align the talonavicular joint

Congenital Oblique Talus

1. Definition—**Deformity**
   a. There is *no* consensus definition
   b. Congenital dorsolateral subluxation of the navicular on the talus with moderately severe eversion of the subtalar joint and moderately rigid plantar flexion of the talus, creating a mild rocker-bottom appearance of the foot. Complete inversion of the subtalar joint is not possible (Figure 5-27).

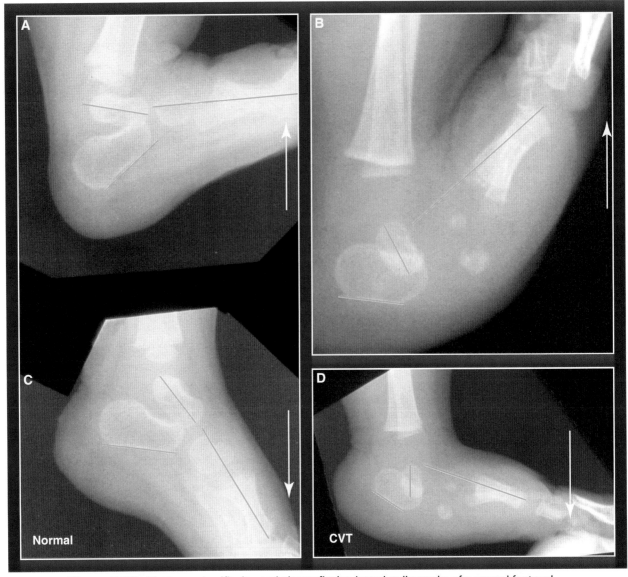

Figure 5-26. Maximum dorsiflexion and plantar flexion lateral radiographs of a normal foot and a foot with CVT. **A.** Maximum dorsiflexion lateral of a normal foot. The talus is perpendicular to the tibia. The talus–1st MT angle is 0°, though several degrees of dorsiflexion of the forefoot on the hindfoot are normal. The calcaneus is dorsiflexed well above perpendicular to the tibia. **B.** Maximum dorsiflexion lateral of a CVT. The talus rotates very slightly from its full plantar flexed position. The calcaneus is merely perpendicular to the tibia. The axis of the first MT is translated dorsally with the foot-CORA (**see Assessment Principle #18, Chapter 3**) in the body of the talus, indicating dorsal dislocation of the navicular at the talonavicular joint. **C.** Maximum plantar flexion lateral of a normal foot. The talus plantar flexes to no more than about 45°. The calcaneus plantar flexes slightly beyond perpendicular to the tibia. The axis of the 1st MT is slightly plantar flexed in relation to the axis of the talus with the foot-CORA in the talonavicular joint. **D.** Maximum plantar flexion lateral of a CVT. The talus is vertically in line with the axis of the tibia. The calcaneus is plantar flexed well beyond perpendicular to the tibia. The axis of the 1st MT remains dorsally translated with the foot-CORA in the body of the talus, confirming fixed dorsal dislocation of the navicular at the talonavicular joint.

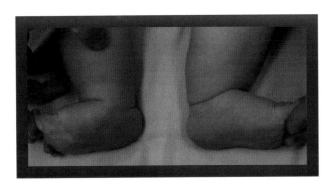

Figure 5-27. Right COT. As with CVT, there is often a single posterior heel crease. There is only one deep posterior crease on the right ankle, but a deep and multiple shallow creases on the left ankle. The right foot longitudinal arch is slightly convex plantar, i.e., rocker-bottom.

c. Idiopathic etiology or associated with an underlying neuromuscular or chromosomal abnormality
2. Elucidation of the segmental deformities
   a. Forefoot—*supinated*
   b. Midfoot
      i. *Abducted*
      ii. Medial column—*subluxated*
         • dorsolateral subluxation of the navicular on the talus
      iii. Lateral column—*subluxated* (or mal-oriented)
         • dorsolateral subluxation and/or mal-orientation of the calcaneocuboid joint

c. Hindfoot—*valgus/everted*
d. Ankle—*plantar flexed (equinus)*
3. Imaging (Figure 5-28)
   a. Simulated standing AP of foot
   b. Maximum dorsiflexion lateral of foot (Figure 5-28C)
      i. The talus dorsiflexes partially, though never completely, while the calcaneus hyper-dorsiflexes past the talus through eversion. These are also features of a flexible flatfoot with a short tendo-Achilles, but in COT, the axis of the 1st MT is dorsally translated, creating a foot-CORA (center of rotation of angulation) (**see Assessment Principle #18,**

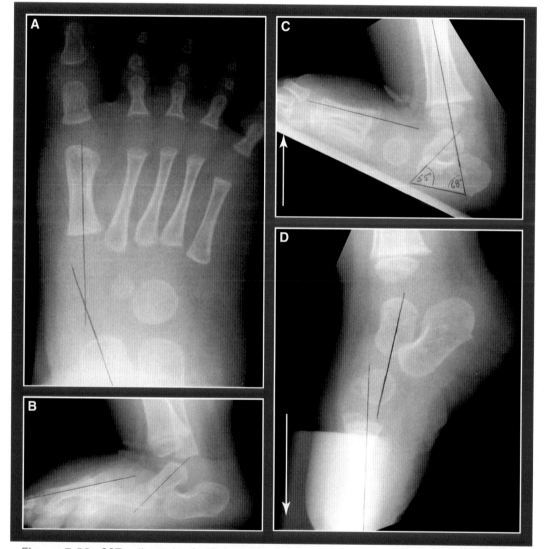

Figure 5-28. COT radiographs. **A.** AP radiograph of an apparent flatfoot, but with the foot-CORA (**see Assessment Principle #18, Chapter 3**) distal to the head of the talus. **B.** Weight-bearing lateral radiograph shows dorsal translation of the axis of the 1st MT intersecting the neck/body of the talus. This indicates dorsal subluxation at the talonavicular joint. **C.** With maximum dorsiflexion of the foot, the talus does not fully dorsiflex, while the calcaneus dorsiflexes around the talus through exaggerated eversion. The axis of the 1st MT appears to be even further dorsally translated than in the weight-bearing view. **D.** With maximum plantar flexion of the foot, the talus assumes a nearly vertical alignment with the tibia and the calcaneus plantar flexes well. However, the axis of the 1st MT remains slightly dorsally translated in relation to the talus, confirming incomplete reduction of the navicular on the head of the talus. The lateral foot-CORA should be in the head of the talus with a convex dorsal angle between the lines (**see Figure 5-26A, C**).

Chapter 3) in the neck/body of the talus rather than in the head.
  c. Maximum plantar flexion lateral of foot (Figure 5-28D)
    i. The navicular does not completely align with the talus. The axis of the 1st MT remains dorsally translated in relation to the axis of the talus
4. Natural history
  a. Persistence of deformity with pain and, possibly, functional disability (**see Basic Principle #10, Chapter 2**)
5. Nonoperative treatment
  a. Reverse Ponseti (Dobbs) casting
6. Operative indications
  a. Failure to achieve full deformity correction with nonoperative treatment
7. Operative treatment with reference to the surgical techniques section of the book for each individual procedure
  a. Tendo-Achilles tenotomy (**see Chapter 7**) and limited open talonavicular joint capsulotomy with retrograde pinning (Dobbs method)—*perform this* if the talonavicular joint has become aligned with reverse Ponseti (Dobbs) casting, but there is persistent equinus. This

is not a plication of the medial soft tissues, but merely a capsulotomy for visualization while pinning the TN joint.
  b. Deep plantar–medial plication (**see Chapter 7**), tendo-Achilles tenotomy (**see Chapter 7**), ± peroneus brevis tendon lengthening—*perform this* in an infant or young child for failure of the reverse Ponseti (Dobbs) nonoperative method to align the talonavicular joint

Neglected/Recurrent/Residual CVT

1. Definition—**Deformity**
  a. Untreated, recurrent, or residual congenital dorsolateral dislocation of the navicular on the talus with severe eversion of the subtalar joint and rigid plantar flexion of the talus, creating a rocker-bottom appearance of the foot in an older child. There is suggestive evidence that the medial column of the foot grows faster and is longer than the lateral column in neglected (untreated), recurrent, and residual CVT deformities (Figure 5-29)

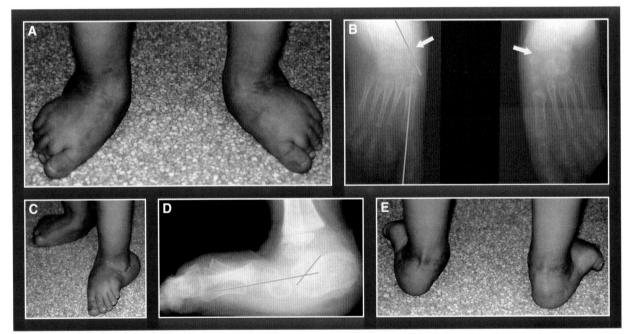

Figure 5-29. Example of a residual CVT in a recently operated 3-year-old child. **A.** Following circumferential release and realignment surgery in this older child, there is severe residual abduction/valgus deformity in both feet. **B.** Though not always the case, the talonavicular joints are well-aligned (*yellow arrows*) despite severe residual deformities. The foot-CORA is in the navicular bone (crossing of the blue axis lines of the 1st MT and talus), indicating that the deformity is not primary eversion of the subtalar joint (in which case the foot-CORA would be in the head of the talus). Instead, the foot-CORA indicates that the residual deformity is, at least in part, related to a longer medial than lateral column in each foot. This has implications for treatment, such as the possible/probable need to shorten the medial column by naviculectomy. **C.** Lateral photos show a concave, short lateral column of the left foot, and a convex, long medial column of the right foot. **D.** Standing lateral radiograph shows moderate residual hindfoot equinus with sag at the talonavicular joint. The foot-CORA is in the head of the talus, indicating no residual dorsal subluxation or dislocation at the talonavicular joint. **E.** Posterior views of the feet show severe hindfoot valgus and midfoot abduction.

b. Idiopathic etiology or associated with an underlying neuromuscular or chromosomal abnormality
2. <u>Elucidation of the segmental deformities</u>
  a. Forefoot—*supinated*
  b. Midfoot
    i. *Abducted*
    ii. Medial column—*dislocated*
      • dorsolateral dislocation of the navicular on the talus
    iii. Lateral column—subluxated (or mal-oriented)
      • dorsolateral subluxation and/or mal-orientation of the calcaneocuboid joint
  c. Hindfoot—*valgus/everted*
  d. Ankle—*plantar flexed (equinus)*
3. <u>Imaging</u>
  a. Simulated standing or standing AP of foot
  b. Maximum dorsiflexion lateral of foot
    i. The talus is vertically and rigidly aligned with the tibia in untreated cases, and dorsiflexes incompletely in recurrent and residual cases
  c. Maximum plantar flexion lateral of foot
    i. The navicular does not align with the talus
4. <u>Natural history</u>
  a. Persistence of deformity with pain, functional disability, and inability to wear normal shoes
5. <u>Nonoperative treatment</u>
  a. Reverse Ponseti (Dobbs) casting
6. <u>Operative indications</u>
  a. Failure to achieve full deformity correction with nonoperative treatment
7. <u>Operative treatment</u> with reference to the surgical techniques section of the book for each individual procedure

a. Posterolateral soft tissue release *and* plantar–medial plication (**see Chapter 7**) *and* tendo-Achilles lengthening (**see Chapter 7**) ± peroneus brevis tendon lengthening—*perform this* in an infant or young child for failure of the reverse Ponseti (Dobbs) nonoperative method to align the talonavicular joint
b. Naviculectomy (**see Chapter 8**)—*perform this*:
  i. if the talonavicular joint is well-aligned (Figure 5-29) or becomes well-aligned with serial casting or posterolateral release, yet the deformity persists
  ii. or, if the talonavicular joint cannot be aligned with a posterolateral soft tissue release because of resistance of the lateral soft tissues or too short a lateral column of the foot (too long a medial column)

V. FLATFOOT

Flexible Flatfoot

1. <u>Definition</u>—**Anatomic variation**
  a. Congenital physiologically normal foot shape with valgus alignment of the hindfoot, supination of the forefoot, a low or depressed longitudinal arch, and no contracture of either the gastrocnemius or the entire triceps surae (Figure 5-30).
  b. The arch elevates and the hindfoot valgus changes to varus with toe-standing and with the Jack toe-raise test (**see Assessment Principle #9, Figures 3-6A, B and 3-7, Chapter 3**).
  c. The ankle dorsiflexes at least 10° above neutral with the subtalar joint inverted to neutral (locked) and the knee

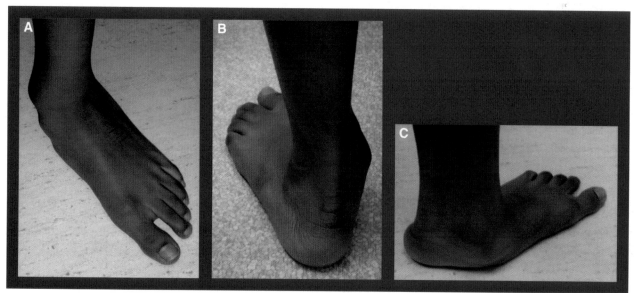

Figure 5-30. Flatfoot. **A.** Top view shows the outward (external) rotation of the foot in relation to the lower extremity that takes place in the subtalar joint (**see Basic Principle #6, Figure 2-7, Chapter 2**). The patella is facing directly forward (toward the bottom of the picture) in this image. **B.** Back view shows valgus alignment of the hindfoot and "too many toes" seen laterally. **C.** Medial view shows depression of the longitudinal arch and a convex medial border of the foot. Supination of the forefoot in relation to the hindfoot is apparent because all MT heads are on the ground despite valgus alignment of the hindfoot (**see Assessment Principle #8, Figure 3-2, Chapter 3**).

extended, based on the Silfverskiold test (**see Assessment Principle #12, Figure 3-13, Chapter 3**)

2. Elucidation of the segmental deformities
   a. Forefoot—*supinated*
   b. Midfoot—*neutral* or *abducted*
   c. Hindfoot—*valgus/everted*
   d. Ankle—*plantar flexed (equinus)*
3. Imaging
   a. None
4. Natural history
   a. Gradual elevation of the longitudinal arch in most children through normal growth and development from birth until early adolescence (**see Basic Principle #4, Figure 2-1, Chapter 2**)
   b. For those flatfeet that remain flat, comfort and function are equal to that of feet with average height longitudinal arches
5. Nonoperative treatment
   a. None indicated for the typical asymptomatic physiologic flexible flatfoot
   b. For activity-related diffuse nonspecific foot/ankle/leg pain, prescribe over-the-counter, cushioned, semirigid arch supports (Figure 5-31). These are contraindicated if the gastrocnemius or entire triceps surae is contracted (**see Flexible Flatfoot with Short (Tight) Achilles or Gastrocnemius Tendon, this chapter**).
6. Operative indications
   a. None
7. Operative treatment with reference to the surgical techniques section of the book for each individual procedure
   a. Not applicable.

Flexible Flatfoot with Short (Tight) Achilles or Gastrocnemius Tendon

1. Definition—**Deformity**
   a. Congenital physiologically normal foot shape with valgus alignment of the hindfoot, supination of the forefoot, a low or depressed longitudinal arch, and contracture of either the gastrocnemius or the entire triceps surae (**see Figure 5-30**).
   b. The arch elevates and the hindfoot valgus changes to varus with toe-standing and with the Jack toe-raise test (**see Assessment Principle #9, Figures 3-6A, B and 3-7, Chapter 3**)

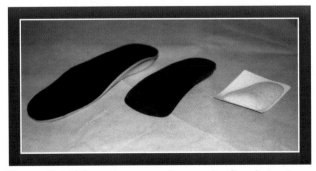

Figure 5-31. Over-the-counter inexpensive firm, but not rigid, shoe inserts/arch supports.

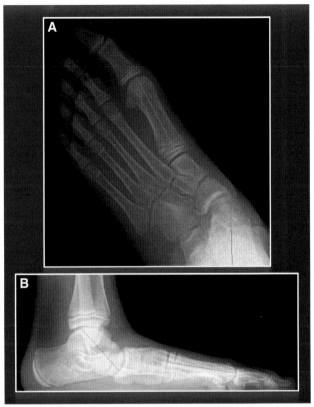

Figure 5-32. Flatfoot (with mild midfoot adductus) x-rays. **A.** Standing AP of a flatfoot with abduction at the talonavicular joint. **B.** Standing lateral of a flatfoot with a sag at the talonavicular joint and a low calcaneal pitch.

   c. The tendo-Achilles or gastrocnemius tendon is contracted, thereby limiting ankle dorsiflexion—accurately tested with the subtalar joint in neutral alignment and the knee extended (**see Assessment Principle #12, Figure 3-13, Chapter 3**).
2. Elucidation of the segmental deformities
   a. Forefoot—*supinated*
   b. Midfoot—*neutral* or *abducted*
   c. Hindfoot—*valgus/everted*
   d. Ankle—*plantar flexed (equinus)*
3. Imaging
   a. Standing AP, lateral, (and oblique) of the foot (Figure 5-32).
   b. AP, lateral, and mortis of the ankle
4. Natural history
   a. Pain under the head of the talus and/or impingement-type pain in the sinus tarsi area in many/most cases occurring with, or exacerbated by, weight-bearing (Figure 5-33)
   b. It is unknown whether the heel cord contracture is congenital or developmental
5. Nonoperative treatment
   a. Heel cord stretching exercises performed with the subtalar joint inverted to neutral and the knee extended (**see Management Principle #5, Figure 4-1, Chapter 4**)
   b. Soft, cushioned FLAT orthotics/shoe inserts (Figure 5-34)

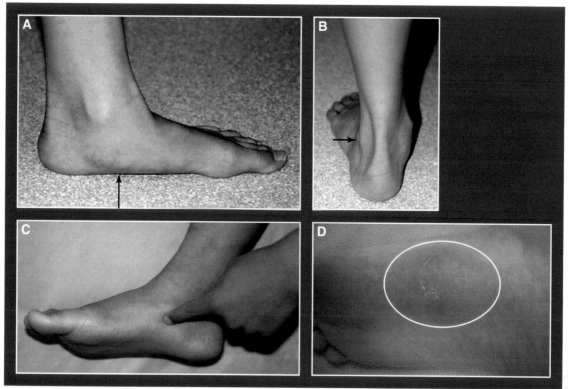

Figure 5-33. **A.** FFF-STA with most weight-bearing pain under the medial midfoot due to forced plantar flexion of the talus caused by the heel cord contracture. **B.** There may also be pain in the sinus tarsi area due to impingement of the lateral process of the talus with the beak of the calcaneus. Lateral hindfoot pain can also be caused by impingement of the soft tissues between the calcaneus and the tip of the lateral malleolus. **C.** The finger points to the focal site of pain and tenderness. **D.** Callused skin under the head of the talus (circled).

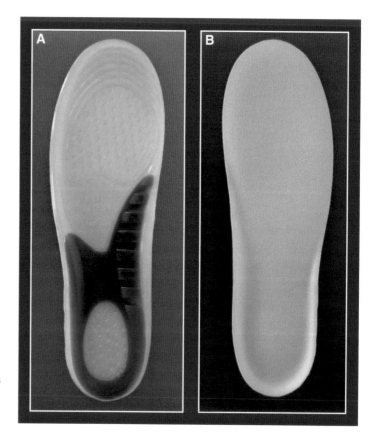

Figure 5-34. *Flat* over-the-counter gel shoe insert for a FFF-STA. This design provides extra cushioning without increasing pressure under the plantar flexed talar head. A firm or hard elevated arch support causes increased pressure under the rigidly plantar flexed talar head and amplifies the pain. That design is, therefore, contraindicated. **A.** Bottom view. **B.** Top view.

6. Operative indications
   a. Failure of prolonged nonoperative treatment to relieve the pain under the head of the talus and/or in the sinus tarsi area (Figure 5-33)
7. Operative treatment with reference to the surgical techniques section of the book for each individual procedure
   a. Combination of procedures
      i. Calcaneal lengthening osteotomy (**see Chapter 8**) with medial soft tissue plications (**see Chapter 7**)
      ii. Gastrocnemius recession (**see Chapter 7**) or tendo-Achilles lengthening (**see Chapter 7**), based on the result of the Silverskiold test (**see Assessment Principle #12, Figure 3-13, Chapter 3**), and
      iii. Possible medial cuneiform (plantar flexion) plantar-based closing wedge osteotomy (MC-PF-CWO) (**see Chapter 8**)—*perform this* if rigid forefoot supination deformity is identified intraoperatively after the hindfoot deformity is corrected
   b. Isolated gastrocnemius (**see Chapter 7**) or tendo-Achilles lengthening (**see Chapter 7**), based on the result of the Silverskiold test (**see Assessment Principle #12, Figure 3-13, Chapter 3**).
      i. *Perform this rarely*, except perhaps in very young children with FFF-STA with "mild" valgus/eversion deformity. With "moderate" and "severe" eversion deformities, this could lead to lever arm dysfunction (**see Basic Principle #7, Figure 2-10, Chapter 2**) and unacceptable weakness in push-off and jumping. Unfortunately, there are no meaningful definitions for "mild," "moderate," and "severe" valgus/eversion.

VI. METATARSUS ADDUCTUS/ SKEWFOOT

Metatarsus Adductus

1. Definition—**Anatomic variation**
   a. Congenital adductus of the forefoot on the hindfoot through the midfoot (Figure 5-35)
   b. Classification of congenital MA according to severity, using the "heel bisector method," is not prognostic, but can be used to help document initial alignment and the change in alignment that occurs both spontaneously and with intervention (Figure 5-36).
   c. Classification of congenital MA according to flexibility has been shown to have prognostic value (Figure 5-37).
2. Alternate definition—**Deformity**
   a. Congenital adductus of the forefoot on the hindfoot through the midfoot that does not spontaneously correct (Figure 5-38)
   b. Congenital adductus of the forefoot on the hindfoot through the midfoot as a residual segmental deformity of a clubfoot
   c. Congenital adductus of the forefoot on the hindfoot through the midfoot as the forefoot deformity in a skewfoot

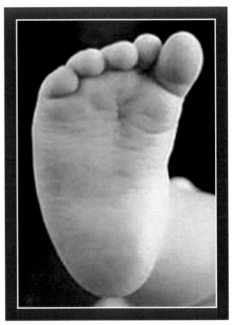

Figure 5-35. Plantar view of an infant foot with congenital MA. The lateral border of the foot is convex and the medial border is concave. There may be a vertical skin crease along the medial midfoot. The hindfoot is in neutral alignment. There is normal ankle dorsiflexion.

3. Elucidation of the segmental deformities
   a. Forefoot—*neutral* or *supinated*
   b. Midfoot—*adducted*
   c. Hindfoot—*neutral*
   d. Ankle—*neutral*
4. Imaging
   a. None initially for congenital MA
   b. Standing AP and lateral of the foot for persistent deformity when surgery is being considered in an older child (Figure 5-39)

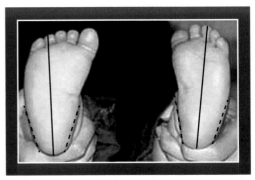

Figure 5-36. The "heel bisector method" for assessing the severity of MA assumes that, in a normal foot, the line that bisects the heel extends to the interspace between the 2nd and 3rd toes. The dashed lines represent the medial and lateral borders of the heel. The solid lines represent the heel bisectors. The heel bisector of the foot shown on the left (right foot) intersects with the 4th toe, whereas that on the right (left foot) intersects with the 3rd toe. The left foot is, therefore, less deformed.

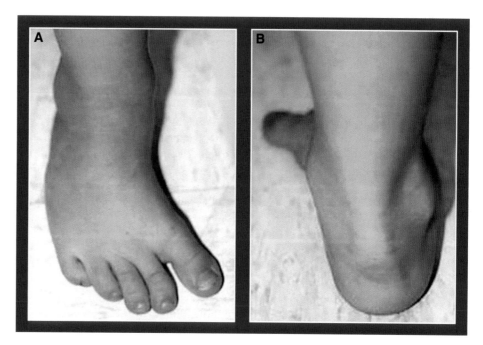

Figure 5-37. The *flexibility method* for assessing MA. **A.** MA. **B.** Rigid MA—the forefoot cannot be easily passively abducted to create a straight lateral border. **C.** Partly flexible MA—the forefoot can be easily passively abducted to create a straight lateral border. **D.** Flexible MA—the forefoot can be easily passively abducted beyond a straight lateral border. Obviously, the definition of *easy* has not been quantified.

c. There is no definitive association with hip dysplasia, so routine imaging of the hips is not indicated. A careful hip examination should be performed along with an assessment for the true risk factors for developmental dysplasia of the hip (DDH), which are a positive family history and breech presentation.

5. Natural history

a. Most congenital MA deformities (perhaps 90% to 95%) spontaneously correct in the first 1 to 3 years of life (**see Basic Principle #4, Figure 2-2, Chapter 2**).

b. For those with persistence of significant deformity, there may be pain and tenderness along the lateral midfoot and/or medial to the head of the 1st MT and the hallux.

6. Nonoperative treatment

a. None indicated—for flexible (the forefoot can be easily passively abducted beyond a straight lateral border) and partly flexible (the forefoot can be easily passively abducted to create a straight lateral border) deformities (Figure 5-37)—90% to 95% of the total

b. Serial long-leg casting for rigid (the forefoot cannot be easily passively abducted to create a straight lateral border) deformities

i. best initiated between 6 and 12 months—after persistence of deformity is confirmed and before the foot becomes too stiff

ii. cast the foot with the ankle in slight plantar flexion and the subtalar joint in slight inversion to avoid inadvertent valgus stress on the subtalar joint. Dr. Ponseti described this casting technique as well as that for clubfoot and stressed the important differences between the two methods (Figure 5-40).

Figure 5-38. Persistent MA in a toddler. **A.** Top view shows adductus of the forefoot on the hindfoot through the midfoot. **B.** Posterior view shows neutral alignment of the hindfoot and adductus of the forefoot.

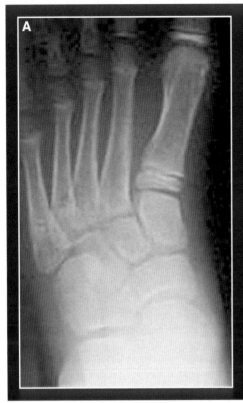
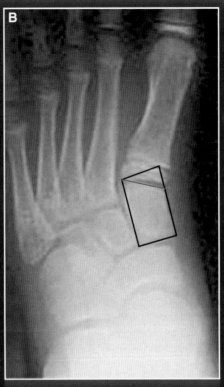

Figure 5-39. **A.** AP x-ray of a foot in an older child with persistent MA. The MTs are normally shaped, but are mal-oriented at the tarsometatarsal joints (Lisfranc joints). **B.** The medial cuneiform is rectangular in shape in a normal foot (*black rectangle*). In a foot with MA, the medial cuneiform is trapezoid-shaped (*purple line indicates distal articular surface of the bone*) which creates mal-orientation of the 1st MT–medial cuneiform joint, i.e., MA. The other cuneiform bones and the cuboid are also, no doubt, trapezoid-shaped, but it is more difficult to appreciate their shapes on plane x-rays. There is mild abduction of the navicular on the head of the talus, suggesting that this foot could, in fact, be classified as a mild skewfoot. The forefoot/midfoot deformity is the same in the two conditions.

7. Operative indications
   a. Failure of nonoperative treatment to relieve pain and tenderness located along the lateral midfoot and/or medial to the head of the 1st MT and the hallux, despite prolonged attempts to modify and adjust shoe wear (Figure 5-41)
8. Operative treatment with reference to the surgical techniques section of the book for each individual procedure
   a. Cuboid closing wedge osteotomy (**see Chapter 8**) *and* distal abductor hallucis recession (**see Chapter 7**) *and* medial capsulotomy 1st MT/medial cuneiform joint—*perform this* in young children before there is adequate ossification of the medial cuneiform (under around age 4 years)
   b. Medial cuneiform (medial) opening wedge osteotomy (**see Chapter 8**) *and* cuboid closing wedge osteotomy (**see Chapter 8**) *and* possible distal abductor hallucis recession (**see Chapter 7**)—*perform this* in older children and adolescents
   c. **NOTE:** The foot-CORA for MA (**see Assessment Principle #18, Figure 3-21, Chapter 3**) is the medial cuneiform on the medial column of the foot and the cuboid on the lateral column. Therefore, tarsometatarsal capsulotomies (the Heyman–Herndon procedure) and base MT osteotomies are distal to the foot-CORA for this deformity and are not indicated. Additionally, tarsometatarsal capsulotomies have been shown to lead to premature degenerative arthritis in those joints, and base MT osteotomies have been associated with

1st MT physeal injury and lesser MT malunions and nonunions.

Skewfoot

1. Definition—**Deformity** (some unknown percentage are **Anatomic variations**)
   a. Congenital or acquired valgus deformity of the hindfoot with adductus deformity of the forefoot (Figure 5-42)
   b. Idiopathic, iatrogenic (following clubfoot treatment), or associated with an underlying neuromuscular or chromosomal abnormality (syndromic)
2. Elucidation of the segmental deformities
   a. Forefoot—*pronated* and *plantar flexed at Lisfranc joints*
   b. Midfoot—*adducted*
   c. Hindfoot
      i. *Valgus/everted* in *older* children and adolescents
      ii. often *Neutral* in the coronal plane with *Abduction* at the talonavicular joint in *young* children, but can be *valgus/everted*
   d. Longitudinal arch
      i. *Normal* height in most *young* children with idiopathic deformity
      ii. *Flat* in many/most *older* children and adolescents with idiopathic and acquired deformity
      iii. *Normal* or *flat* in syndromic cases
   e. Ankle
      i. *Neutral* in most *young* children with idiopathic deformity

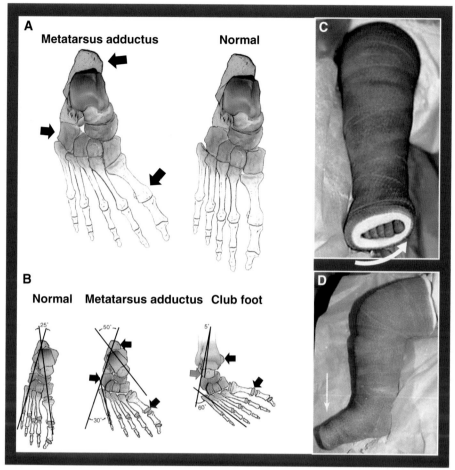

Figure 5-40. **A.** When manipulating a foot with MA, three points of pressure are applied, as if one were straightening out a bent twig. The black arrows show the three pressure points. **B.** The pressure points for MA manipulation are the medial side of the head of the 1st MT, the cuboid/lateral midfoot, and the medial side of the posterior calcaneus (*three black arrows*). Manipulation of a clubfoot is quite different, because the primary goal is to evert, or spin, the acetabulum pedis around the talus. The distal pressure point is the same for both deformities, i.e., the medial side of the 1st MT head. Importantly, the midfoot pressure point in a clubfoot is the dorsolateral aspect of the head of the talus (*blue arrow*). The 1st MT is, effectively, a handle that is used to evert the acetabulum pedis around the fulcrum that is the head of the talus. In so doing, the cavus and MA deformities in a clubfoot are concurrently corrected. The posterior calcaneus must rotate away from the lateral malleolus in a clubfoot, so the posterior pressure point is the medial malleolus, not the calcaneus. (From Ponseti IV. *Congenital Clubfoot: Fundamentals of Treatment.* Oxford: Oxford University Press; 1996:73, with permission.) **C.** During the manipulation and casting of a foot with MA, the subtalar joint is inverted to slight varus to help avoid inadvertent eversion of that joint. The latter could potentially convert MA to a skewfoot. A long-leg cast is recommended, as for clubfoot, but without the external rotation. **D.** The ankle is also slightly plantar flexed to further help avoid eversion stress on the subtalar joint.

ii. *Plantar flexed (equinus)* in many/most *older* children and adolescents with idiopathic and acquired deformity
iii. *Neutral* or *plantar flexed (equinus)* in syndromic cases
f. *In the first decade of life,*
    i. Children have the obvious skew deformity in the frontal plane, i.e., adduction of the forefoot on the midfoot and abduction of the midfoot on the hindfoot.
    ii. The longitudinal arch is often average or higher than average in height and there is full flexibility of the tendo-Achilles.

iii. The hindfoot does not appear to be in valgus.
iv. The AP and lateral x-rays do not seem to represent the same foot. On the basis of the lateral position of the navicular on the head of the talus seen on the AP x-ray, one would expect a flatfoot deformity both clinically and radiographically, but the lateral x-ray often looks normal (Figure 5-43).
g. *In the second decade of life,*
    i. The frontal plane deformities persist, i.e., adduction of the forefoot on the midfoot and abduction of the midfoot on the hindfoot.

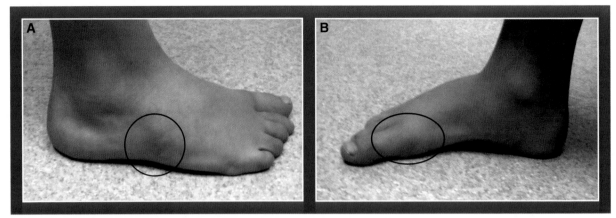

Figure 5-41. Photos of a foot from an older child with residual MA. He has pain, tenderness, callus formation, and erythema (**A**) along the lateral midfoot and (**B**) medial to the head of the 1st MT and the hallux.

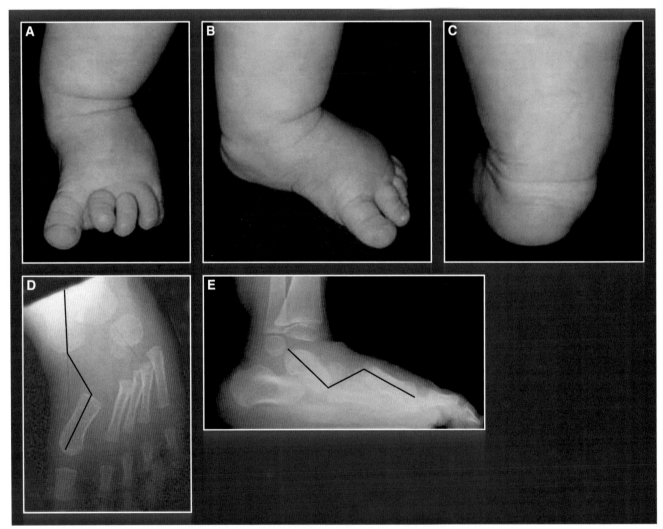

Figure 5-42. Idiopathic infant skewfoot. **A.** Forefoot adductus with a medial midfoot concavity immediately anterior to a convexity. The convexity is the head of the talus, and the concavity is the medially displaced navicular/midfoot. **B.** Medial midfoot crease at the junction of the medial concavity and convexity. **C.** Hindfoot valgus. **D.** The radiographic forefoot adductus and hindfoot valgus deformities (**see Assessment Principle #18, Figure 3-23**) match the clinical appearance of the foot. **E.** Lateral x-ray.

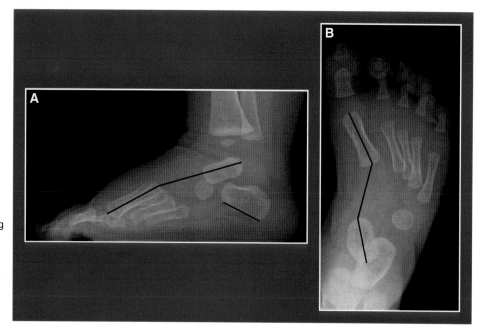

Figure 5-43. Skewfoot in a young child. **A.** The lateral x-ray looks essentially normal with a nearly straight talus–1st metatarsus angle and a normal calcaneal pitch. **B.** The AP x-ray clearly shows the skew deformities of hindfoot valgus/ eversion and forefoot adductus.

ii. But the longitudinal arch drops, the hindfoot everts to valgus, and the tendo-Achilles becomes contracted in some/all affected feet.

iii. It looks like a flatfoot.

iv. The AP x-ray looks the same as in the younger children, but the lateral x-ray shows the flatfoot appearance that one would expect to see (Figure 5-44).

3. Imaging

a. Standing AP and lateral of foot (**see Assessment Principle #18, Figure 3-23, Chapter 3**) (Figures 5-42 to 5-44)

b. There is no known association between skewfoot and hip dysplasia; so routine imaging of the hips is not indicated.

4. Natural history

a. Unknown, at least in part due to the lack of a strict definition. It is not known how much forefoot adductus is necessary to reclassify a flatfoot as a skewfoot, or how much hindfoot valgus is necessary to reclassify a MA deformity as a skewfoot. Lack of a strict definition also prevents an estimation of prevalence.

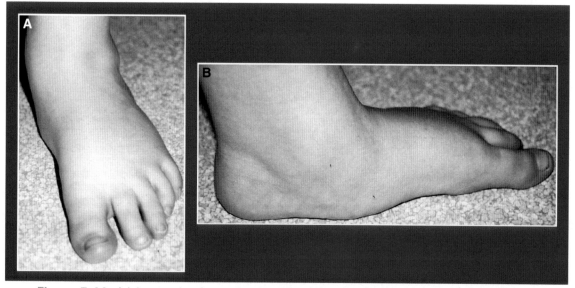

Figure 5-44. Adolescent skewfoot: valgus/eversion deformity of the hindfoot with a flat longitudinal arch and adduction of the forefoot on the midfoot. The medial cuneiform is trapezoid-shaped. **A** and **B.** Clinical photographs. **C** and **D.** Radiographs. (From Mosca VS. The Foot. In: Morrissy RT, Weinstein SL, eds. *Lovell and Winter's Pediatric Orthopaedics*, 5th ed. Philadelphia, PA: Lippincott Williams & Wilkins; 2001; page 1166, Figure 29-13, with permission.)

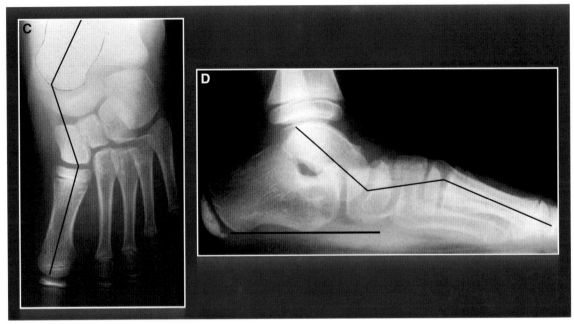

Figure 5-44. *(continued)*

b. Some *young* children develop pain, callosities, and shoe-fitting problems that are related to the forefoot adductus, with pain and tenderness along the lateral midfoot and/or medial to the head of the 1st MT and the hallux (Figures 5-41 and 5-45A).

c. Some *older* children and adolescents develop pain and callosities under the head of the plantar flexed talus or in the sinus tarsi that are related to the hindfoot valgus and contracture of the gastrocnemius or tendo-Achilles (similar to the signs and symptoms in flexible flatfoot with tight tendo-Achilles) (Figure 5-45B).

5. Nonoperative treatment
   a. Serial casting of the forefoot adductus in young children. Casting of hindfoot valgus is never indicated or successful.
      i. Best initiated between 6 and 12 months—after persistence of deformity is confirmed and before the forefoot becomes too stiff
      ii. Cast the forefoot in the same manner as in a foot with MA with the ankle in slight plantar flexion and the subtalar joint in slight inversion (to avoid inadvertent further valgus stress on the already valgus subtalar joint) (**see Figure 5-40**).
   b. Accommodative shoe wear

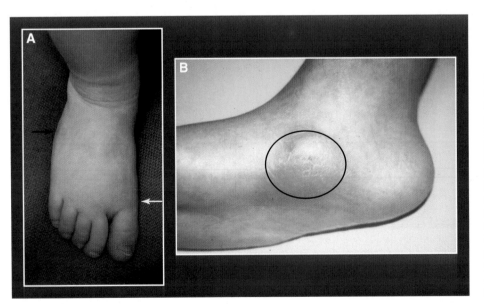

Figure 5-45. **A.** The forefoot adductus component of a skewfoot may contribute to the development of pain, tenderness, and callus formation along the lateral midfoot (*black arrow*) and/or medial to the head of the 1st MT (*yellow arrow*) and the hallux in young children. **B.** The hindfoot valgus deformity and contracture of the gastrocnemius or tendo-Achilles more commonly contribute to the development of pain, tenderness, and callus formation under the head of the plantar flexed talus (*black oval*) or in the sinus tarsi in older children and adolescents.

6. <u>Operative indications</u>
   a. Failure of nonoperative treatment to relieve:
      i. pain, callosities, and shoe-fitting problems in *young* children that are usually related to the fore-foot adductus, with pain lateral to the base of the 5th MT and/or medial to the head of the 1st MT (Figure 5-45A)
      ii. pain and callosities under the head of the plantar flexed talus or in the sinus tarsi in *older* children and adolescents that are related to the hindfoot valgus and contracture of the gastrocnemius or tendo-Achilles (similar to the signs and symptoms in flexible flat-foot with tight tendo-Achilles) (Figure 5-45B)
7. <u>Operative treatment</u> with reference to the surgical techniques section of the book for each individual procedure
   a. Medial cuneiform opening wedge osteotomy (**see Chapter 8**) with or without a cuboid closing wedge osteotomy (**see Chapter 8**)—*perform this* in *young* children with pain lateral to the base of the 5th MT and/or medial to the head of the 1st MT. If the arch has not dropped yet, it will not—at least not right away. The TN joint and posterior tibialis tendon can be plicated for partial correction of the abduction at the TN joint.

   b. Calcaneal lengthening osteotomy (**see Chapter 8**) *and* medial cuneiform opening wedge osteotomy (**see Chapter 8**) *and* gastrocnemius recession (**see Chapter 7**) or tendo-Achilles lengthening (**see Chapter 7**), as determined by the intraoperative Silfverskiold test (**see Assessment Principle #12, Figure 3-13, Chapter 3**)—*perform this* in *older* children and adolescents who have pain and callosities under the head of the plantar flexed talus or in the sinus tarsi (Figures 5-46 and 5-47)

VII. TARSAL COALITION
Talocalcaneal Tarsal Coalition

1. <u>Definition</u>—Developmental mal-deformation
   a. Autosomal dominant failure of mesenchymal differentiation and segmentation that leads to a progressive, *post-natal* synchondrosis-to-synostosis of the middle facet (usually, but can be posterior facet) of the subtalar joint
      i. with the gradual development of a *rigid* flatfoot (though neutral and varus hindfoot alignments have been reported) usually between the ages of 8 and 16 years

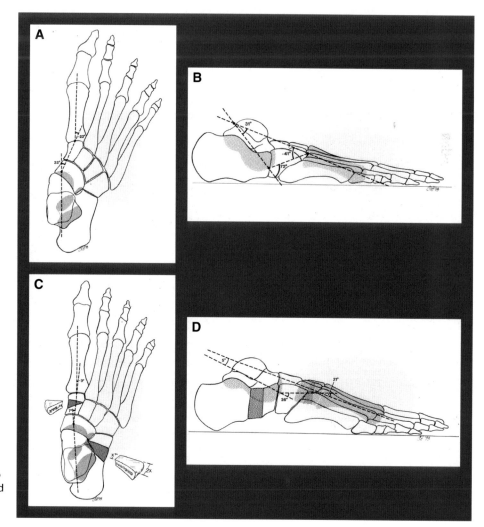

Figure 5-46. **A.** Artist sketch of an AP x-ray of an adolescent skewfoot. **B.** Sketch of the lateral x-ray of the same foot. **C.** Sketch of the actual AP x-ray taken after a calcaneal lengthening osteotomy and a medial cuneiform opening wedge osteotomy. D. Sketch of the actual lateral x-ray taken after the operation. (From Mosca VS. Calcaneal lengthening for valgus deformity of the hindfoot. Results in children who had severe, symptomatic flatfoot and skewfoot. *J Bone Joint Surg.* 1995; 77(4):500–512.)

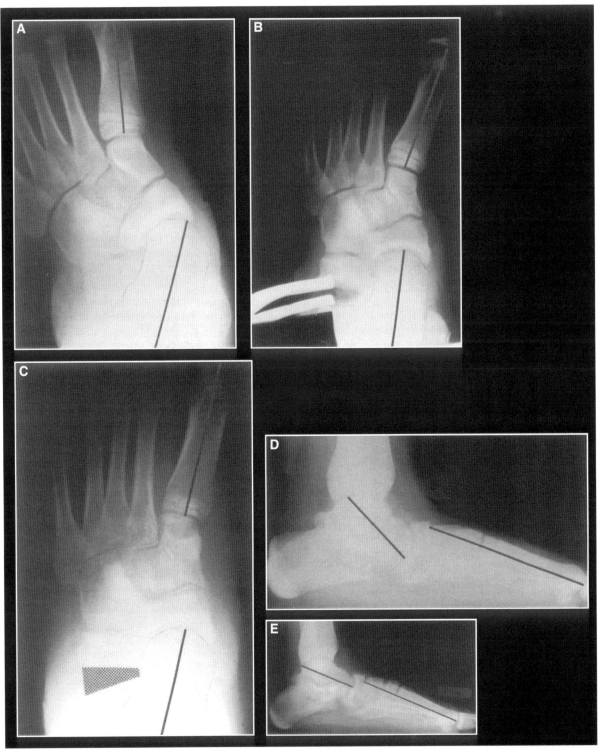

Figure 5-47. Painful skewfoot in a 13-year-old boy. **A.** AP view showing skew, or zig-zag, deformity. **B.** Laminar spreader in anterior calcaneus osteotomy showing good correction of talonavicular joint subluxation. Note apparent exaggeration of forefoot adductus. Medial cuneiform is trapezoid-shaped with proximal and distal joints converging medially. A transverse osteotomy has been made at the waist of the medial cuneiform. **C.** Hatched area highlights calcaneal graft. Medial cuneiform graft is well seen. Talus and first MT lines are now parallel. **D.** Lateral preoperative radiograph showing skew, or zig-zag, deformity in this plane as well. **E.** Postoperative correction of midfoot sag and low calcaneal pitch. Slight residual dorsal translation of MT line is due to mild midtarsal cavus. (From Mosca VS. Flexible Flatfoot and Skewfoot. In: Drennan JC, ed. *The Child's Foot and Ankle.* New York: Raven; 1992:373, Figure 17.18.) (From the private collection of Vincent S. Mosca, MD.)

ii. and, in many cases, associated with secondary hypermobility of Chopart joints that can give the false impression of subtalar joint mobility when none exists (**see Assessment Principle #10, Figures 3-10 and 3-11, Chapter 3**)

2. Elucidation of the segmental deformities
   a. Forefoot—*supinated*
   b. Midfoot—*neutral* or *abducted*
   c. Hindfoot—*valgus/everted* or *neutral* (less common) or *varus/inverted* (rarely)
   d. Ankle—*plantar flexed (equinus)* or *neutral*

3. Imaging
   a. Standing AP, lateral, oblique, and *Harris axial* of foot (Figure 5-48)
   b. CT scan in sagittal, coronal, and transverse planes, and with 3D reconstruction (**see Assessment Principle #22, Figure 3-28, Chapter 3**)
      i. The coronal image is most important (Figure 5-49).

4. Natural history
   a. Gradual development of a *rigid* flatfoot (though neutral and varus hindfoot alignments have been reported) usually between the ages of 8 and 16 years
   b. Pain, in *less* than 25% of cases, that can be located at one or more of the following locations:
      i. the site of the coalition
      ii. under the head of the talus
      iii. in the sinus tarsi area
      iv. in or around the ankle joint
      v. in Chopart joints
   c. Recurrent ankle sprains, with or without any of the above, in some cases

5. Nonoperative treatment
   a. For asymptomatic coalitions (at least 75% of cases)—None indicated
   b. For activity-related pain
      i. Activity modification, including temporary discontinuation of the pain-inducing activity
      ii. Nonsteroidal anti-inflammatory drugs (NSAIDs)
      iii. Immobilization in a CAM boot or cast for at least 6 weeks

6. Operative indications
   a. Failure of nonoperative treatment to relieve pain that can be located at one or more of the following locations:
      i. the site of the coalition
      ii. under the head of the talus
      iii. in the sinus tarsi area
      iv. in or around the ankle joint
      v. in Chopart joints
   b. Failure of nonoperative treatment to prevent recurrent ankle sprains

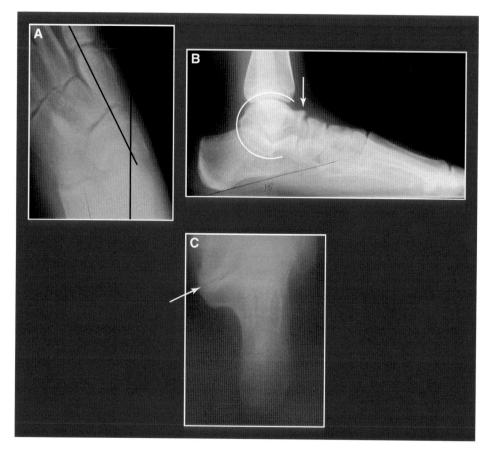

Figure 5-48. Standing radiographs of a foot with a middle facet talocalcaneal tarsal coalition. **A.** AP radiograph shows a flatfoot, indicated by lateral positioning of the navicular on the head of the talus and with the foot-CORA in the head of the talus (**see Assessment Principle #18, Figure 3-19, Chapter 3**). **B.** Lateral radiograph shows a dorsal talar beak (*white arrow*), which is often found in a foot with a talocalcaneal tarsal coalition. It represents a traction spur, not degenerative arthritis of the talonavicular or subtalar joint. The C-sign of Lateur (*white semicircular bone density just inside the yellow "C"*) is a radiographic shadow that strongly indicates a middle facet talocalcaneal tarsal coalition. It is created by the continuity of the subchondral bone of the talar dome (talus) with the posterior aspect of the middle facet coalition (talus and calcaneus) and the bony roof of the sustentaculum tali (calcaneus). **C.** Harris axial radiograph shows a narrow, down-sloping, and irregular middle facet (*white arrow*), which are characteristics of a coalition.

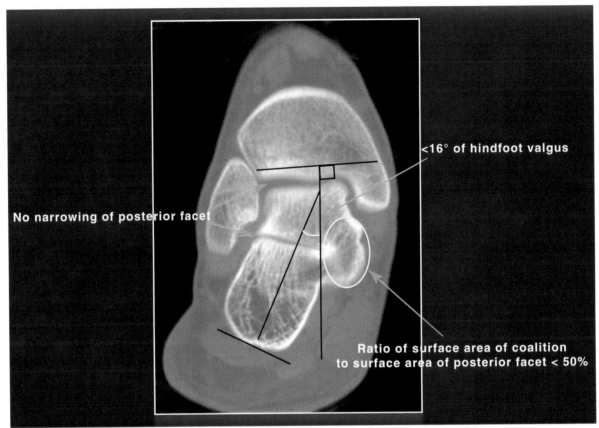

No narrowing of posterior facet

<16° of hindfoot valgus

Ratio of surface area of coalition to surface area of posterior facet < 50%

Figure 5-49. Coronal slice CT scan image shows the three criteria for resectability of a talocalcaneal tarsal coalition according to Wilde, Torode, et al. (1994): (1) the ratio of the surface area of the coalition of the middle facet (*yellow oval*) to the surface area of the posterior facet should be less than 50%; (2) there should be no narrowing of the posterior facet (*short green arrow*) when compared to the cartilage height of the ankle joint (*long green arrow*); (3) there should be less than 16° of hindfoot valgus measured between the axis of the calcaneus and the line perpendicular to the ankle joint (*indicated by the yellow arc*). *None* of the three criteria for resectability are met on this image.

7. <u>Operative treatment</u> with reference to the surgical techniques section of the book for each individual procedure (according to Mosca and Bevan, JBJS 2012)
   a. Middle facet talocalcaneal tarsal coalition resection with interposition fat grafting (**see Chapter 8**)
      i. *Perform this* for a *resectable coalition* (defined as a middle facet coalition that is *less than* 50% the surface area of the posterior facet in a foot with a *normal* posterior facet) in a foot *with less than 16° hindfoot valgus and* with pain at the site of the coalition
   b. Middle facet talocalcaneal tarsal coalition resection with interposition fat grafting (**see Chapter 8**) *and* concurrent (preferred) or staged calcaneal lengthening osteotomy (**see Chapter 8**) *and* gastrocnemius recession (**see Chapter 7**) or tendo-Achilles lengthening (**see Chapter 7**), as determined by the intraoperative Silfverskiold test (**see Figure 3-13, Chapter 3**)
      i. *Perform this* for a *resectable coalition* (defined as a middle facet coalition that is *less than* 50% the surface area of the posterior facet in a foot with a *normal* posterior facet) in a foot *with more than 16° hindfoot valgus and* with pain at the site of the coalition and/

or in the sinus tarsi (due to impingement) and/or under the talar head in the midfoot (due to the flatfoot deformity combined with a tight heel cord)
   c. Calcaneal lengthening osteotomy (**see Chapter 8**) *and* gastrocnemius recession (**see Chapter 7**) or tendo-Achilles lengthening (**see Chapter 7**), as determined by the intraoperative Silfverskiold test (**see Figure 3-13, Chapter 3**)
      i. *Perform this* for an *irresectable coalition* (defined as a middle facet coalition that is *greater than* 50% the surface area of the posterior facet and with a *narrow* posterior facet) in a foot *with more than 16° hindfoot valgus and* with pain under the talar head in the midfoot (due to the flatfoot deformity combined with a tight heel cord) and/or in the sinus tarsi (due to impingement) It does not make sense to resect a middle facet coalition if there is "significant" narrowing of the posterior facet. The histologic and radiographic manifestations of arthritis (degenerative joint disease) are thinning of the articular cartilage. Resection of a middle facet coalition will reestablish motion in a painless (because of immobility) posterior facet and, potentially, create pain.

Calcaneonavicular Tarsal Coalition

1. <u>Definition—**Developmental mal-deformation**</u>
   a. Autosomal dominant failure of mesenchymal differentiation and segmentation that leads to a progressive, *postnatal* synchondrosis-to-synostosis between the navicular and the beak of the calcaneus
      i. with the gradual development of a *stiff/rigid* flatfoot (though neutral and varus hindfoot alignments have been reported) usually between the ages of 8 and 16 years
2. <u>Elucidation of the segmental deformities</u>
   a. Forefoot—*supinated*
   b. Midfoot—*neutral* or *abducted*
   c. Hindfoot—*valgus/everted* or *neutral* (less common) or *varus/inverted* (rarely)
   d. Ankle—*plantar flexed* (equinus) or *neutral*

3. <u>Imaging</u>
   a. Standing AP, lateral, *oblique*, and Harris axial of foot (Figure 5-50)
   b. CT scan in sagittal, coronal, and transverse planes, and with 3D reconstruction (Figure 5-51)
4. <u>Natural history</u>
   a. Gradual development of a *stiff/rigid* flatfoot (though neutral and varus hindfoot alignments have been reported) usually between the ages of 8 and 16 years
   b. Pain, in *less than* 25% of cases, that can be located at one or more of the following locations:
      i. the site of the coalition
      ii. under the head of the talus
      iii. in the sinus tarsi area
      iv. in or around the ankle joint
      v. in Chopart joints
   c. Recurrent ankle sprains with or without any of the above

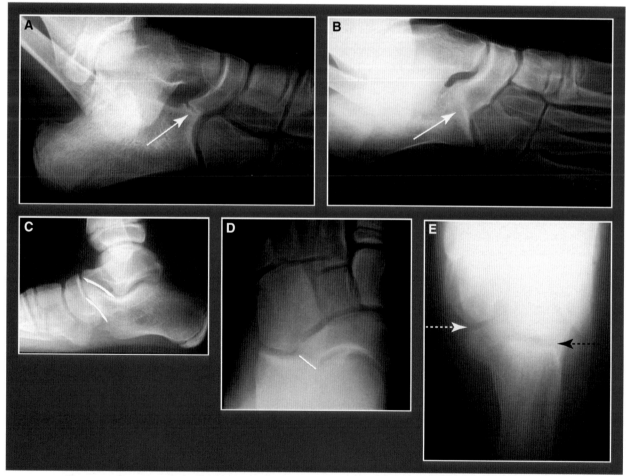

Figure 5-50. Radiographs of feet with CN tarsal coalitions. **A.** Fibrocartilaginous coalition (*yellow arrow*). **B.** Ossified coalition (*yellow arrow*). **C.** "Anteater nose" sign (*bracketed by yellow arcs*), representing radiographic appearance of the conjoined navicular and anterior calcaneus. **D.** AP view, often minimally helpful with diagnosis, because the coalition is out of the plane of the x-ray beam. **E.** Harris axial view shows normal middle facet of the talocalcaneal joint (*dashed yellow arrow*). Black dashed arrow identifies normal posterior facet. This is important information to ascertain, because both coalitions may exist in one foot. A CT scan is necessary for definitive confirmation of the preliminary x-ray evaluation of the subtalar joint.

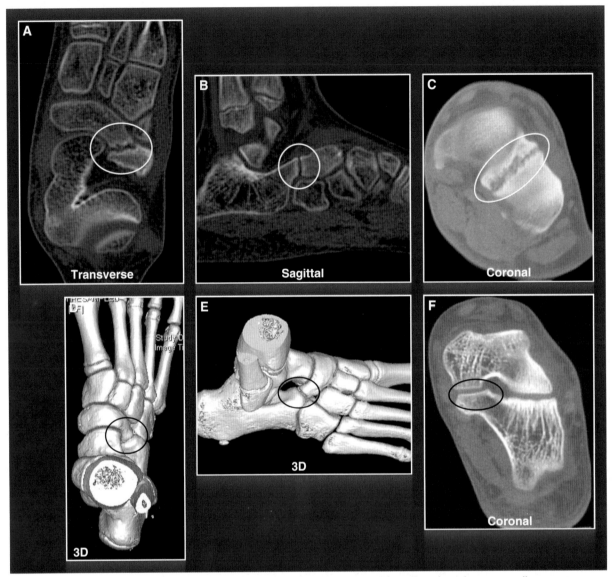

Figure 5-51. CT scan images of a CN tarsal coalition. In a normal foot, there is no bone or cartilage connection between the calcaneus and navicular. In this foot with a CN tarsal coalition, there is a narrow, sclerotic, and irregular pseudo-articulation between those bones that is composed of fibro-cartilage (*circled*). **A.** Transverse view. **B.** Sagittal view. **C.** Coronal view. **D.** and **E.** 3D reconstructions. **F.** Coronal view of subtalar joint confirming that there is not a coincident talocalcaneal middle facet coalition.

5. Nonoperative treatment
   a. For asymptomatic coalitions (at least 75% of cases)—none indicated
   b. For activity-related pain
      i. Activity modification, including temporary discontinuation of the pain-inducing activity
      ii. NSAIDs
      iii. Immobilization in CAM boot or cast for at least 6 weeks

6. Operative indications
   a. Failure of nonoperative treatment to relieve pain that can be located at one or more of the following locations:
      i. the site of the coalition
      ii. under the head of the talus
      iii. in the sinus tarsi area
      iv. in or around the ankle joint
      v. in Chopart joints
   b. Failure of nonoperative treatment to prevent recurrent ankle sprains

7. Operative treatment with reference to the surgical techniques section of the book for each individual procedure
   a. Calcaneonavicular (CN) tarsal coalition resection with interposition fat grafting (**see Chapter 8**)
      i. *Perform this* for a *resectable coalition* (defined as a fibrocartilaginous coalition) in a foot with minimal (or no) hindfoot valgus *and* with pain at the site of the coalition
   b. CN tarsal coalition resection with interposition fat grafting (**see Chapter 8**) *and* staged (or concurrent) calcaneal lengthening osteotomy (**see Chapter 8**) *and*

gastrocnemius recession (**see Chapter 7**) or tendo-Achilles lengthening (**see Chapter 7**), as determined by the intraoperative Silfverskiold test (**see Figure 3-13, Chapter 3**)

    i. *Perform this* for a *resectable coalition* (defined as a fibrocartilaginous coalition) in a foot with "significant" hindfoot valgus *and* with pain at the site of the coalition and/or in the sinus tarsi (due to impingement) and/or under the talar head in the midfoot (due to the flatfoot deformity combined with a tight heel cord)

  c. Calcaneal lengthening osteotomy (**see Chapter 8**) *and* gastrocnemius recession (**see Chapter 7**) or tendo-Achilles lengthening (**see Chapter 7**), as determined by the intraoperative Silfverskiold test (**see Figure 3-13, Chapter 3**)

    i. *Perform this* for an *irresectable coalition* (defined as an osseous coalition) in a foot with "significant" hindfoot valgus *and* with pain under the talar head in the midfoot (due to the flatfoot deformity combined with a tight heel cord) and/or in the sinus tarsi (due to impingement).

VIII. TOE DEFORMITIES

Congenital Hallux Varus

1. <u>Definition</u>—**Deformity**
   a. Congenital varus alignment of the hallux on the 1st MT (Figure 5-52)

  b. Often associated with tight cordlike structure in place of, or in addition to, the abductor hallucis (Figure 5-52B)

  c. Idiopathic or associated with an underlying chromosome abnormality—Pierre Robin syndrome, others

  d. Often associated with 1st MT longitudinal epiphyseal bracket (**see Chapter 6; and Figure 5-53**)

2. <u>Elucidation of the segmental deformities</u>
   a. Hallux and metatarsophalangeal joint
       i. *Varus* deformity of the hallux in relation to the 1st MT—i.e., hallux varus
       ii. *Varus* deformity of the distal end of the 1st MT with medial positioning of the articular cartilage creating medial deviation/mal-orientation of the 1st MTP joint—i.e., "reverse," or varus, distal MT articular angle (DMAA; **see Figure 5-56, this chapter**)
       iii. *Medial subluxation* of the hallux on the 1st MT head—i.e., 1st MTP joint incongruity
   b. Forefoot
       i. *Neutral*
       ii. Often associated with a 1st MT longitudinal epiphyseal bracket (**see Chapter 6**) with relative shortening and widening of the MT
   c. Midfoot—*neutral*
   d. Hindfoot—*neutral*
   e. Ankle—*neutral*

3. <u>Imaging</u>
   a. Simulated standing or standing AP and lateral of the foot (Figure 5-53)

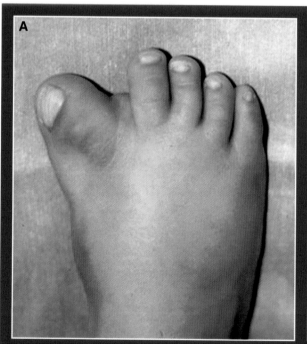
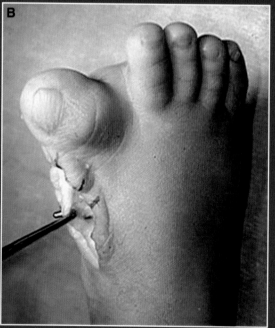

Figure 5-52. A. Clinical appearance of CHV. **B.** Fibrous band (in button hook) that is occasionally seen between the hallux and a cartilaginous duplicate tarsal anlage (From Mosca VS. The Foot. In: Morrissy RT, Weinstein SL, eds. *Lovell and Winter's Pediatric Orthopaedics*, 5th ed. Philadelphia, PA: Lippincott Williams & Wilkins; 2001:1187, Figure 29-34.)

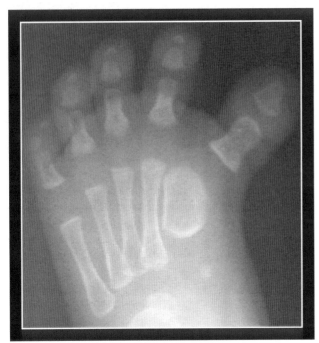

Figure 5-53. AP x-ray of an infant's foot with CHV and a 1st MT longitudinal epiphyseal bracket (**see Chapter 6**). Note the straight-to-slightly concave dense lateral diaphyseal cortex and the convex hypodense medial diaphyseal cortex of the 1st MT.

4. Natural history
  a. Increasing or persistent varus deformity of the hallux causing shoe-fitting difficulties
  b. If a 1st MT longitudinal epiphyseal bracket (**see Chapter 6**) coexists, there will be increasing length discrepancy between the 1st and 2nd MTs, resulting in stress overload and pain under the 2nd MT head (**see Longitudinal Epiphyseal Bracket**, **Figure 6-4, Chapter 6**)
5. Nonoperative treatment
  a. None
6. Operative indications
  a. The presence of this deformity
7. Operative treatment with reference to the surgical techniques section of the book for each individual procedure
  a. Distal release of abductor hallucis (**see Chapter 7**) *and* release of medial 1st MTP joint capsule *and* resection of tight cordlike medial band (if present)—*perform this* for isolated congenital hallux varus (CHV)
  b. Distal release of abductor hallucis (**see Chapter 7**) and release of medial 1st MTP joint capsule and resection of tight cordlike medial band (if present) *and* resection of 1st MT longitudinal epiphyseal bracket (**see Chapter 8**)—*perform this* if a 1st MT longitudinal epiphyseal bracket coexists
  c. Distal 1st MT opening wedge varus-correcting ± lengthening osteotomy (**see Chapter 8**)—*perform this* if varus mal-orientation of a congruous 1st MTP joint persists in an older child or adolescent
  d. Z-plasty medial skin of the forefoot (**see Longitudinal Epiphyseal Bracket Resection, Figure 8-8,**

Chapter 8)—*perform this* along with any of these procedures if the skin is under excessive stretch following deformity correction

Juvenile Hallux Valgus

1. Definition—**Deformity**
  a. Greater than 15° of valgus alignment of the hallux on the 1st MT, with medial prominence of the 1st MT head (Figure 5-54)
  b. Age at onset less than 16 years, regardless of when it is treated
  c. No arthritis of the 1st MTP joint
  d. Other features
    i. Maternal inheritance in over 70% of cases
    ii. 3:1 female: male ratio
    iii. The prevalence of juvenile hallux valgus (JHV) is unknown, but it is believed to be high.
2. Elucidation of the segmental deformities, *not all* necessarily present in every case
  a. Hallux and metatarsophalangeal joint
    i. *Valgus* deformity of the hallux in relation to the 1st MT—i.e., hallux valgus (HV)—*always* present.
    ii. *Valgus* deformity of the distal end of the 1st MT with lateral positioning of the articular cartilage creating lateral deviation/mal-orientation of the 1st MTP joint—i.e., high DMAA—see below—*not always* present, but more common in JHV than in adult onset HV.
    iii. *Lateral subluxation* of the hallux on the 1st MT head—i.e., 1st MTP joint incongruity—*not always* present. Can exist with a normal or high DMAA, but more common with a normal DMAA.
    iv. *Valgus* deformity of the distal end of the hallux proximal phalanx creating lateral deviation/mal-orientation of the interphalangeal joint—i.e., hallux valgus interphalangeus (HVIP)—*not always* present.
  b. Forefoot—*neutral*, but may be *pronated* or *supinated*, based on any coexisting hindfoot deformity

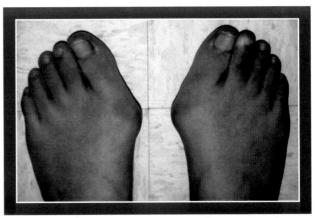

Figure 5-54. **A.** Bilateral JHV in a 15-year-old girl.

c. Midfoot
  i. *Adducted* 1st MT—i.e., metatarsus primus varus (MPV)—*always* present
  ii. *Varus/medial-deviation/mal-orientation* of 1st MT–medial cuneiform joint—*always* present
  iii. *Adduction* of all MTs—i.e., MA—*rarely* present
d. Hindfoot—*neutral, valgus/everted,* or *varus/inverted.*
e. Ankle—*neutral* or *plantar flexed (equinus)*

3. Imaging
  a. Standing AP and lateral of foot (Figures 5-55 and 5-56)

4. Natural history
  a. MPV is most likely a congenital deformity. It is unknown whether the angle between the 1st and 2nd MTs changes during growth. According to the law of triangles, the distance between the MT heads will increase as the foot grows, even if the exaggerated angle between the MTs remains the same (Figure 5-57).
  b. When the width of the forefoot at the level of the MT heads is greater than the width of the shoe, the exaggerated medial–lateral pressures experienced by the soft tissues over the 1st and 5th MT heads create pain, tenderness, and callus formation at those sites. If the 1st MT head is particularly prominent because of MPV and HV, the smaller surface area on the medial side of the 1st MT head creates even greater stresses.

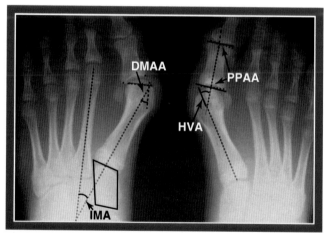

Figure 5-55. Standing AP x-ray of bilateral JHV. MPV is defined as an increased 1st to 2nd intermetatarsal angle (IMA)— normal is <9°. MPV is due to varus/medial-deviation/mal-orientation of the 1st MT–medial cuneiform joint with a trapezoid-shaped medial cuneiform (*black trapezoid*). HV is defined as a hallux valgus angle (HVA) > 15°. This can be due to valgus/lateral-deviation/mal-orientation of a congruous and stable 1st MTP joint with a high DMAA, or to lateral subluxation and incongruity of the hallux on a 1st MT with normally positioned articular cartilage. DMAA defines the position of the articular cartilage on the distal end of the 1st MT, which is variable in humans (**see Figure 5-56**). The proximal phalanx articular angle (PPAA) defines the shape of the hallux proximal phalanx, which may be rectangular or trapezoidal in shape. If the proximal and distal articular surfaces are not parallel, but instead converge laterally, the interphalangeal joint will deviate laterally, creating HVIP. The latter deformity is much easier to treat than HV.

c. The local environment of the foot, i.e., the shoe, clearly relates to the comfort of the foot with JHV
d. An unknown percentage of individuals with JHV experience unacceptable pain, tenderness, and callus formation on the medial surface of the 1st MT head

5. Nonoperative treatment
  a. Foot wear accommodations
    i. Ensure that there is adequate width of the shoe at the level of the MT heads. Apply the sole of the shoe from one foot to the plantar surface of the other. If the shoe cannot be seen extending beyond the borders of the foot, it is too narrow (Figure 5-58).
    ii. Recommend a low heel height to prevent the foot from sliding forward into the narrow toe box (Figure 5-59)
    iii. Recommend that girls wear boys' athletic shoes. They are made wider at the level of the MT heads for the equivalent length
    iv. Recommend a bunion stretcher, available at shoe repair stores (Figure 5-59)

6. Operative indications
  a. Failure of nonoperative treatment to relieve the pain:
    i. on the medial side of the 1st MT head and/or in the 1st MTP joint
    ii. and/or associated with under-overlapping of the hallux and 2nd toe that is often associated with toenail ingrowth problems and skin irritation between the toes.

7. Operative treatment with reference to the surgical techniques section of the book for each individual procedure. There are too many to show. By admission, this is not the definitive work on JHV, a frustratingly complex and poorly understood group of deformities. All JHVs are not the same. By following the principles of assessment and management, your surgical results should be good (Figures 5-60 and 5-61).
  a. Medial cuneiform medial opening wedge osteotomy (**see Chapter 8**) or 1st MT base osteotomy (**see Chapter 8**)—*perform* one of these to correct MPV
  b. Distal 1st MT osteotomy (**see Chapter 8**)—*perform this* when there is a high DMAA
  c. Resection of the exostosis on the medial aspect of 1st MT head and plication of the medial 1st MTP joint capsule (**see pertinent description in 1st Metatarsal Distal Osteotomy, Chapter 8**)—*perform this* in essentially all cases, regardless of the other procedures being performed concurrently. Create or maintain a congruous 1st MTP joint.
  d. Release the adductor hallucis and lateral 1st MTP joint capsule—*perform this* for lateral subluxation of the 1st MTP joint. *Do not perform this* concurrent with a distal 1st MT osteotomy (**see Technique "e" under 1st Metatarsal Distal Osteotomy, Chapter 8**)
  e. Possible calcaneal lengthening osteotomy (**see Chapter 8**) and gastrocnemius recession (**see Chapter 7**)—*perform these* if severe hindfoot valgus with a gastrocnemius contracture coexist

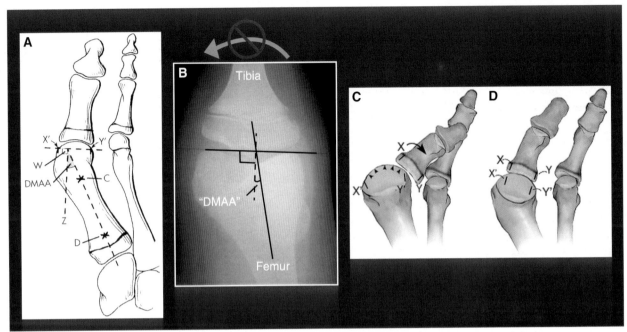

Figure 5-56. The DMAA defines the position of the articular cartilage on the distal end of the 1st MT. In most individuals, the articular cartilage is centered at the distal end of the bone. In around 50% of adolescents and 10% of adults with HV, the articular cartilage is laterally positioned on the end of the 1st MT. **A.** The DMAA is determined by measuring the angle between the shaft of the MT and the line that is perpendicular to the line representing the articular surface. The reliability of accurately drawing the line that represents the articular surface has been questioned, but it can be drawn accurately in many feet. The normal DMAA is <9°. A high DMAA means that there is valgus deformity of the distal end of the 1st MT. (From Coughlin M. Juvenile hallux valgus. In: Coughlin M, Mann R, eds. *Surgery of the Foot and Ankle.* 7th ed. St Louis, MO: Mosby; 1999:270, with permission.) **B.** The analogy to a high DMAA is valgus deformity of the distal femur, as is seen in many conditions, including fibula hemimelia. This image is the upside down AP x-ray of a knee in a child with fibula hemimelia. The anatomic distal femoral articular angle is exaggerated, creating a congrous, but malaligned, joint with genu valgum. Consider how this might be treated. One would never consider releasing the lateral joint capsule and creating joint incongruity by positioning the tibia under the medial femoral condyle. **C.** Sketch of a MT with a normal DMAA and a laterally subluxated hallux. (Redrawn from Coughlin M. Juvenile hallux valgus. In: Coughlin M, Mann R, eds. *Surgery of the Foot and Ankle.* 7th ed. St Louis, MO: Mosby; 1999:270, with permission.) **D.** Sketch of a MT with a high DMAA and a congruous 1st MTP joint. (Redrawn from Coughlin M. Juvenile hallux valgus. In: Coughlin M, Mann R, eds. *Surgery of the Foot and Ankle.* 7th ed. St Louis, MO: Mosby, 1999:270, with permission.)

Bunionette (Tailor's Bunion)

1. Definition—**Deformity**
   a. Lateral prominence of the 5th MT head with varus alignment of the 5th toe at the 5th MTP joint (Figure 5-62)
   b. The prevalence of tailor's bunions is unknown.
2. Elucidation of the segmental deformities
   a. Fifth toe
      i. *Varus* deformity of the 5th toe in relation to the 5th MT—i.e., 5th toe varus
      ii. DMAA for the 5th MT has not been reported
   b. Forefoot—*neutral*, but may be *pronated* or *supinated*, based on any coexisting hindfoot deformity
   c. Midfoot
      i. *Abducted* 5th MT—i.e., metatarsus 5th valgus
      ii. *Valgus/lateral-deviation/mal-orientation* of the 5th MT–cuboid joint (Figure 5-62)
   d. Hindfoot—*neutral*
   e. Ankle—*neutral*
3. Imaging
   a. Standing AP, lateral, and oblique of foot (Figure 5-62)
4. Natural history
   a. Abduction/valgus of the 5th MT in relation to the cuboid and the 4th MT is most likely a congenital deformity. It is unknown whether the angle between the 4th and 5th MTs changes during growth. According to the law of triangles, the distance between the MT heads will increase as the foot grows, even if the exaggerated angle between the MTs remains the same (**analogous with JHV—see Figure 5-57**).
   b. When the width of the forefoot at the level of the MT heads is greater than the width of the shoe, the exaggerated medial–lateral pressures experienced by the soft tissues over the 1st and 5th MT heads create pain, tenderness, and callus formation at those sites. If the 5th

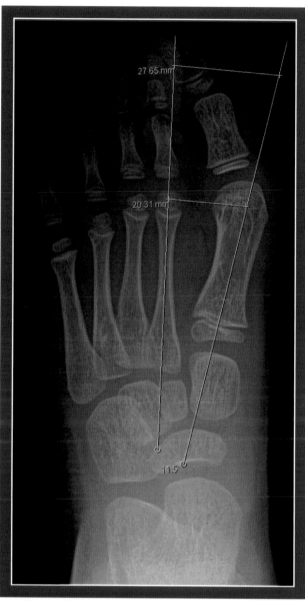

Figure 5-57. Standing AP x-ray of a foot in a 5-year-old girl with symptomatic JHV and MPV (IMA 11.5°). As her foot grows, the distance between the MT heads will increase, according to the law of triangles, even if the IMA does not increase. This geometric principle explains the reason that JHV looks worse and may cause more problems with shoe fitting as children age.

MT head is particularly prominent because of valgus deformity of the 5th MT and varus deformity of the 5th toe, the smaller surface area on the lateral side of the 5th MT head creates even greater stresses.

c. The local environment of the foot, i.e., the shoe, clearly relates to the comfort of the foot with a tailor's bunion.

d. An unknown percentage of individuals with a tailor's bunion experience unacceptable pain, tenderness, and callus formation on the lateral surface of the 5th MT head.

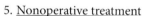

Figure 5-58. To ensure that there is adequate width of the shoe for the width of the foot at the level of the MT heads, place the shoe from one foot upside down under the other. If the shoe can be seen on both sides, it has adequate width.

5. Nonoperative treatment
 a. Foot wear accommodations (same as for JHV)
  i. Ensure that there is adequate width of the shoe at the level of the MT heads. Apply the sole of the shoe from one foot to the plantar surface of the other. If the shoe cannot be seen extending beyond the borders of the foot, it is too narrow (Figure 5-58).
  ii. Recommend a low heel height to prevent the foot from sliding forward into the narrow toe box (Figure 5-59)
  iii. Recommend that girls wear boys' athletic shoes. They are made wider at the level of the MT heads for the equivalent length
  iv. Recommend a bunion stretcher, available at shoe repair stores (Figure 5-59)
6. Operative indications
 a. Failure of nonoperative treatment to relieve the pain:
  i. on the lateral side of the 5th MT head
  ii. and/or associated with under-overlapping of the 5th and 4th toes that may be associated with toenail ingrowth problems and skin irritation between the toes.
7. Operative treatment with reference to the surgical techniques section of the book for each individual procedure
 a. Fifth MT osteotomy (see Chapter 8)
 b. Possible resection of exostosis on lateral aspect of 5th MT head and plication of lateral 5th MTP joint capsule

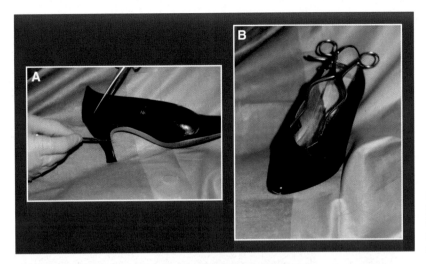

Figure 5-59. **A.** A lower heel height will prevent the foot from sliding down into the toe box of the shoe, where the width will be narrower. **B.** Shoe repair stores offer bunion stretching shoe services.

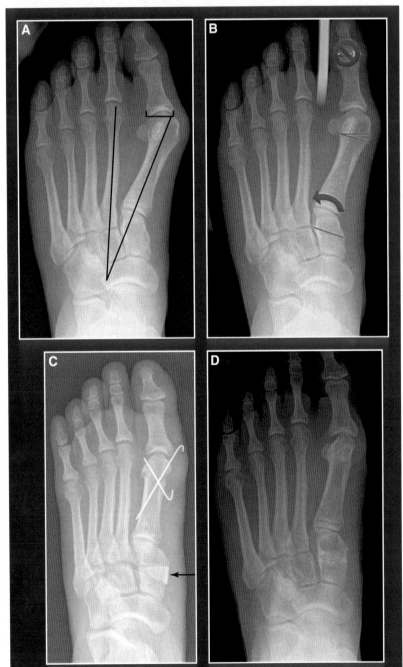

Figure 5-60. **A.** JHV with increased DMAA (valgus deformity of the distal end of the 1st MT), congruous 1st MTP joint, and increased 1st–2nd MT angle. **B.** It is not appropriate to make the 1st MTP joint incongruous by adducting the hallux on the 1st MT. Instead, a valgus-correction distal 1st MT closing wedge osteotomy (**see Chapter 8**) is performed to correct the DMAA and reorient the 1st MTP joint. The medial prominence on the 1st MT head is resected and the medial capsule of the 1st MTP joint is repaired, without creating incongruity of the already congruous joint. The vascularity to the 1st MT head could be compromised by performing a concurrent release of the adductor hallucis and lateral joint capsule. A medial cuneiform medial opening wedge osteotomy (*purple line*) is used to correct the metatarsus primus varus (**see Chapter 8**). **C.** Immediately after surgery, the deformity corrections can be appreciated. The triangular bone graft in the medial cuneiform is identified by the black arrow **D.** Deformity corrections have been maintained long term.

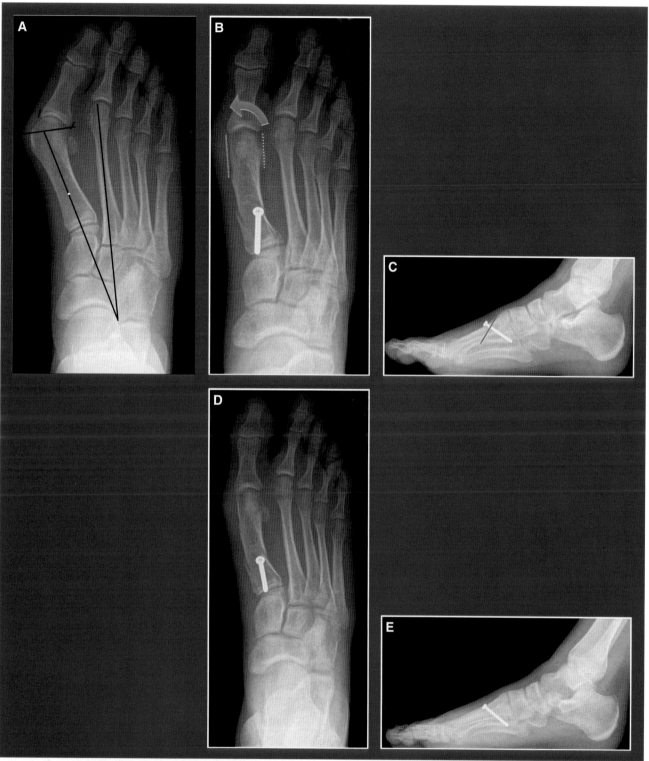

Figure 5-61. **A.** JHV with normal DMAA, incongruous/subluxated 1st MTP joint, and increased 1st–2nd MT angle. **B.** The hallux must be repositioned on the distal end of the 1st MT by release of the adductor hallucis and the lateral capsule of the 1st MTP joint (*dotted pink line*). The medial prominence on the 1st MT head is resected (*straight pink line*) and the medial capsule of the 1st MTP joint is plicated, thereby creating congruency of the joint. An oblique rotational 1st MT base osteotomy (**see Chapter 8**) is used to correct the MPV. **C.** Lateral view of the 1st MT base osteotomy (*purple line*). **D** and **E.** Long-term follow-up AP and lateral x-rays.

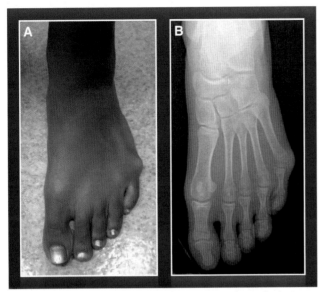

Figure 5-62. **A.** Standing top view of a foot with a prominent tailor's bunion. **B.** Standing AP x-ray of the foot. Lateral deviation of the 5th MT in relation to the cuboid and the 4th MT (metatarsus 5th valgus) and 5th toe varus deformity at the MTP joint can be seen.

Congenital Overriding 5th Toe

1. Definition—**Deformity**
   a. Congenital dorsomedial angular alignment of the 5th toe at the MTP joint. The malalignment at the MTP joint is associated with a capsular contracture as well as an extensor tendon contracture. The web space skin between the 4th and 5th toes is "malformed," as evidenced by its excessively proximal position. The toe appears to have erupted from the fetal mitten more dorsal and medial in relation to its MT than the other toes in relation to their MTs (Figure 5-63).

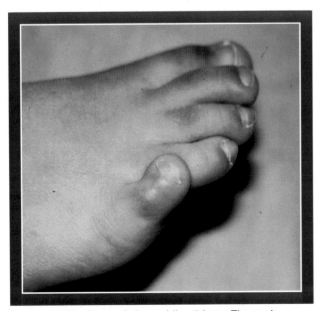

Figure 5-63. Congenital overriding 5th toe. The toe is dorsomedially angulated over the 4th toe.

b. Congenital overriding affects the 5th toe almost exclusively, though I have seen a congenital overriding 4th toe in two syndromic children.
2. Elucidation of the segmental deformities
   a. Fifth toe—*dorsiflexed* and *varus*
      i. dorsomedial angulation of the 5th toe at the MTP joint
3. Imaging
   a. None required, though AP, lateral, and oblique x-rays of the forefoot should be obtained before surgery
4. Natural history
   a. Persistence of the deformity throughout life
   b. Reportedly, approximately 50% do well with careful shoe selection and the rest experience unacceptable pain from rubbing in the shoe
5. Nonoperative treatment
   a. Accommodative shoe wear
6. Operative indications
   a. Pressure-induced pain from shoes that is not relieved by accommodative shoe wear
7. Operative treatment with reference to the surgical techniques section of the book for each individual procedure
   a. Butler procedure for congenital overriding 5th toe (**see Chapter 7**)

Curly Toe

1. Definition—**Deformity**
   a. Congenital flexion, adduction, and external rotation of one or more toes, most commonly the 4th toe (Figure 5-64)
   b. Usually, an idiopathic deformity that may be bilateral and asymmetric
2. Elucidation of the segmental deformities
   a. *Flexion, adduction,* and *external rotation* of one or more toes with contracture of the FDL, and occasionally the flexor digitorum brevis, to the affected toe

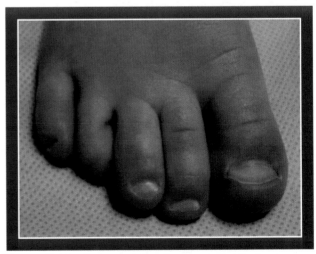

Figure 5-64. Curly toe defined as congenital flexion, adduction, and external rotation of the 4th toe.

3. Imaging
   a. None indicated in infants.
   b. In an older child with a persistent symptomatic deformity, x-rays of the toe can be obtained preoperatively, though they are not absolutely indicated
4. Natural history
   a. Most spontaneously correct either completely or sufficiently so as to avoid pain and long-term disability
      i. In many cases, the flexion deformity corrects completely, and the mild residual adduction and external rotation deformities are of no clinical significance.
   b. A very small percentage of curly toe deformities do not spontaneously correct adequately, resulting in pain and callosities on the dorsal or plantar aspect of the affected toe and/or the overlapping adjacent toe. There may also be pain associated with ingrowth or irritation of the nail plate on the curly toe.
5. Nonoperative treatment
   a. Stretching exercises for the long toe flexor tendon, although the efficacy of stretching, taping, and strapping have not been demonstrated
   b. Accommodative shoe wear

6. Operative indications
   a. Failure of the flexion/adduction/external rotation deformities to correct sufficiently through natural history and/or with stretching exercises to avoid:
      i. pain and callosities on the dorsal or plantar aspect of the affected toe and/or the overlapping adjacent toe.
      ii. pain associated with ingrowth or irritation of the nail plate on the curly toe.
7. Operative treatment with reference to the surgical techniques section of the book for each individual procedure
   a. Percutaneous tenotomy of the FDL (and possibly the flexor digitorum brevis [FDB]) to the affected toe (**see Chapter 7**)
      i. Be aware that the toe will immediately extend fully, but the adduction/varus and external rotation deformities will persist. Often, these two additional deformities will partially correct gradually over time (Figure 5-65).

Mallet Toe

1. Definition—**Deformity**
   a. Contracture of the FDL to a lesser toe creating a flexible, and eventually rigid, flexion deformity of the distal

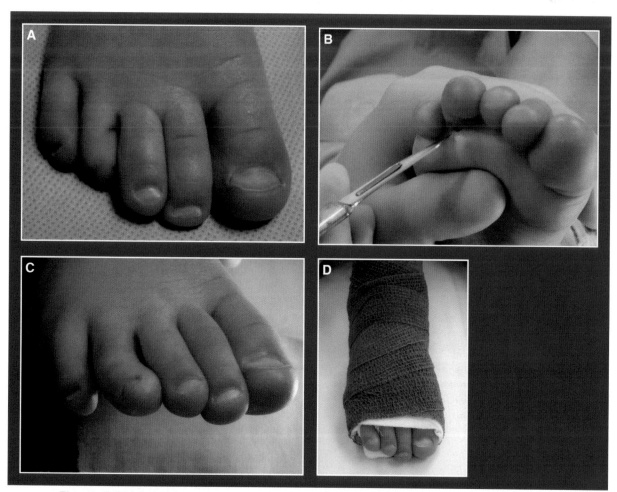

Figure 5-65. **A.** Curly 4th toe in a 4-year-old. **B.** Percutaneous FDL tenotomy was performed because of pain and irritation caused by the complete overlapping of the 3rd toe on the tip of the 4th toe. **C.** Immediately following the FDL tenotomy, the 4th toe elevated completely, but the adductus/varus and external rotation deformities remained. It is anticipated that, in time, those deformities will improve. **D.** Webril and Coban dressing.

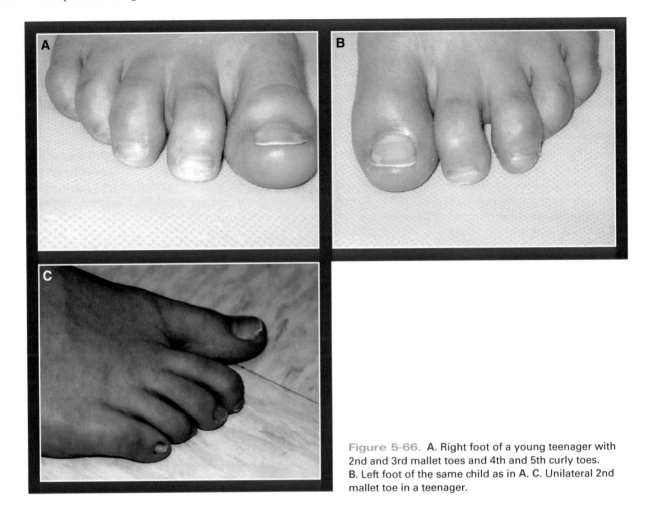

Figure 5-66. A. Right foot of a young teenager with 2nd and 3rd mallet toes and 4th and 5th curly toes. **B.** Left foot of the same child as in **A. C.** Unilateral 2nd mallet toe in a teenager.

interphalangeal (DIP) joint, without coincident extension deformity of the MTP joint (Figure 5-66)
   b. The etiology is usually unknown, but most are idiopathic and not the result of a neuromuscular disorder.
   c. One or more toes may be affected in one foot, and the deformity may be unilateral or bilateral (Figure 5-66).
2. Elucidation of the segmental deformities
   a. *Flexion* deformity of the DIP joint of a lesser toe *without* coincident extension deformity of the MTP joint
      i. The deformity is flexible at first. Plantar flexion of the ankle and toe will relax tension on the FDL and allow full extension of the DIP joint.
      ii. With time, the volar capsule of the DIP joint becomes contracted and will not allow the joint to extend fully, despite relaxing tension on the FDL by plantar flexion of the ankle and toe
3. Imaging
   a. Standing AP, lateral, and oblique of the toes/forefoot
4. Natural history
   a. Mallet toes are most common in adults (with a female predominance), increasing in prevalence almost exponentially with age

   b. Poor shoe fitting is considered a risk factor for the development of mallet and hammer toes in adults, but the risk factors for the few that develop in adolescents are unknown
   c. Pain/tenderness over the dorsum of the affected joint and/or at the tip of the plantar flexed toe, and/or toenail growth disturbances occur in many cases
   d. Flexible deformities become rigid over time
5. Nonoperative treatment
   a. Stretching exercises for the long toe flexor tendons
   b. Accommodative shoe wear
6. Operative indications
   a. Pain/tenderness over the dorsum of the affected joint and/or at the tip of the plantar flexed toe, and/or toenail growth disturbances despite attempts at nonoperative treatment
7. Operative treatment with reference to the surgical techniques section of the book for each individual procedure
   a. Percutaneous (**see Chapter 7**) or open tenotomy of the FDL to the affected toe—*perform this* when no capsular contracture exists and the DIP joint rests in the fully extended position following tenotomy

b. Percutaneous (**see Chapter 7**) or open tenotomy of the FDL to the affected toe with temporary longitudinal K-wire fixation—*perform this* when no capsular contracture exists, but the DIP joint rests in flexion immediately following tenotomy due to skin or other soft tissue contractures

c. Volar DIP joint capsulotomy along with tenotomy and temporary longitudinal wire fixation—*perform this* in cases with early DIP joint capsular contracture

d. DIP joint arthrodesis—*perform this* in long standing cases with severe deformity and/or degenerative arthritis of the joint

Hammer Toes

1. Definition—**Deformity**
   a. Contracture of the (FDB and FDL to a lesser toe creating a flexible, and eventually rigid, flexion deformity of the proximal interphalangeal (PIP) joint, with occasional flexion deformity of the DIP joint, but without coincident extension deformity of the MTP joint (Figure 5-67)
   b. The etiology is usually unknown, but most are idiopathic and not the result of a neuromuscular disorder.
   c. One or more toes may be affected in one foot and the deformity may be unilateral or bilateral (Figure 5-67)
2. Elucidation of the segmental deformities
   a. *Flexion* deformity of the PIP joint, and often the DIP joint, of a lesser toe *without* coincident extension deformity of the MTP joint
      i. The deformity is flexible at first. Plantar flexion of the ankle and toe will relax tension on the FDB and FDL and allow full extension of the PIP and DIP joints.
      ii. With time, the volar capsule of the PIP and/or DIP joints become contracted and will not allow the

joint(s) to extend fully despite relaxing tension on the FDB and FDL by plantar flexion of the ankle and toe.
3. Imaging
   a. Standing AP, lateral, and oblique of the toes/forefoot
4. Natural history
   a. Hammer toes are most common in adults (with a female predominance), increasing in prevalence almost exponentially with age.
   b. Poor shoe fitting is considered a risk factor for the development of hammer and mallet toes in adults, but the risk factors for the few that develop in adolescents are unknown.
   c. Pain/tenderness over the dorsum of the affected joint and/or at the tip of the plantar flexed toe, and/or toenail growth disturbances occur in many cases.
   d. Flexible deformities become rigid over time.
5. Nonoperative treatment
   a. Stretching exercises for the long toe flexor tendons
   b. Accommodative shoe wear
6. Operative indications
   a. Pain/tenderness over the dorsum of the affected joint and/or at the tip of the plantar flexed toe, and/or toenail growth disturbances despite attempts at nonoperative treatment
7. Operative treatment with reference to the surgical techniques section of the book for each individual procedure
   a. Percutaneous (**see Chapter 7**) or open tenotomy of the FDL and FDB to the affected toe—*perform this* when no capsular contractures exist and the IP joints rest in the fully extended position following tenotomy
   b. Percutaneous (**see Chapter 7**) or open tenotomy of the FDL and FDB to the affected toe with temporary longitudinal K-wire fixation—*perform this* when no capsular contractures exist, but one or both IP joints rest in flexion immediately following tenotomy due to skin or other soft tissue contractures

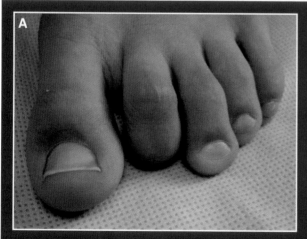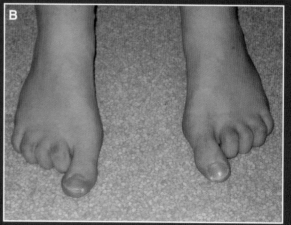

Figure 5-67. **A.** Unilateral 2nd hammer toe in a young teenager. **B.** Bilateral hammer toes 2 to 5 in a teenager.

c. Volar DIP joint capsulotomy along with tenotomy and temporary longitudinal wire fixation—*perform this* in cases with early PIP joint capsular contracture

d. PIP joint arthrodesis—*perform this* in long standing cases with severe deformity and/or degenerative arthritis of the joint

Claw Toe

1. <u>Definition—**Deformity**</u>
   a. Contracture of the flexors and extensors of a toe creating a flexible, and eventually rigid, extension (dorsiflexion) deformity of the MTP joint and flexion deformity of the interphalangeal (IP) joint(s) of a toe (Figure 5-68)
   b. Claw toes are most often associated with a cavus foot deformity, both of which are due to an underlying neuromuscular abnormality until proven otherwise. CMT disease is the most common cause.
   c. Usually all 5 toes are affected.
   d. When the underlying neuromuscular condition is systemic (CMT) or central (myelomeningocele, tethered cord), the toes of both feet are affected.
2. <u>Elucidation of the segmental deformities</u>
   a. *Extension* deformity of the *MTP joint* and *Flexion* deformity of the *IP joint(s)* of the hallux or any lesser toe
      i. The deformities are flexible at first. Plantar flexion and dorsiflexion of the ankle and toe will selectively relax tension on the flexors and extensors and allow full extension of the IP joint(s) and full flexion of the MTP joint.
      ii. With time, the dorsal capsule of the MTP joint and the volar capsule of the IP joint(s) become contracted and will not allow the joints to flex or extend fully despite relaxing tension on the extensors and flexors by dorsiflexion and plantar flexion of the ankle and toe.

b. Also, **see Cavovarus Foot—Elucidation of the segmental deformities—this chapter.**
3. <u>Imaging</u>
   a. Standing AP and lateral of foot
   b. Standing AP and lateral thoracolumbar spine
4. <u>Natural history</u>
   a. The clawing increases in severity and rigidity with time because of the progressive nature of the underlying neuromuscular disorder.
   b. Pain/tenderness over the dorsum of the IP joint(s) and/or at the tip of the plantar flexed toe, and/or toenail growth disturbances occur in many cases.
   c. Pain/tenderness under the adjacent MT head occurs in many cases due to the associated cavus deformity.
5. <u>Nonoperative treatment</u>
   a. None
6. <u>Operative indications</u>
   a. Pain/tenderness over the dorsum of the flexed IP joint(s)
   b. Pain/tenderness at the tips of the plantar flexed toe
   c. Pain/tenderness under the adjacent MT head
7. <u>Operative treatment</u> with reference to the surgical techniques section of the book for each individual procedure
   a. Jones transfer of the extensor hallucis longus to the 1st MT neck (**see Chapter 7**) with percutaneous tenotomy of the FHL (**see Chapter 7**)—*perform this* for a clawed hallux
   b. Hibbs transfer of the extensor digitorum longus to the cuboid or the peroneus tertius (**see Chapter 7**) with percutaneous tenotomy of the FDL tendons (**see Chapter 7**)—*perform this* for clawed lesser toes
   c. Correct all coincident cavovarus foot deformities (**see Cavovarus Foot—Operative Treatment, this chapter; Individual Soft Tissue Procedures, Chapter 7; and bony procedures, Chapter 8**)

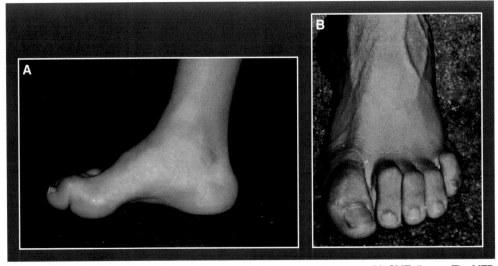

Figure 5-68. **A.** Claw toes coincident with a cavus foot in a young teenager with CMT disease. The MTP joints are extended (dorsiflexed) and the IP joints are flexed. **B.** Claw toes coincident with a cavovarus foot in another teenager with CMT disease. The MTP joints are extended (dorsiflexed) and the IP joints are flexed.

Foot Malformations

I. TOES/FOREFOOT

Cleft Foot

1. Definition—**Malformation** (most often, **Congenital mal-deformation**), "Too few" (**see Table 1-1, Chapter 1**)
   a. Congenital deficiency (failure of formation) of one or more central rays (toe or toe and metatarsal [MT]) of the foot (Figure 6-1)
   b. The most extreme form is absence of all but the lateral ray of the foot.
   c. The most subtle form is a soft tissue cleft between the 1st and 2nd MT heads, with no bone deficiency.
2. Elucidation of the segmental deformities
   a. Toes
      i. *Absence* of 0–4 toes
         • In the most subtle presentation, there is a soft tissue cleft between the 1st and 2nd MT heads, with no toe deficiency or mere deficiency of the distal phalanx of the 2nd toe.
         • 5th toe and MT are always present, or the diagnosis would be congenital transverse deficiency of the midfoot.
      ii. Hallux valgus and 5th toe varus—typically seen in feet with 3 or fewer rays (Figure 6-1)
   b. Forefoot
      i. *Dorsiflexed* (and often hypermobile) *1st ray*—typically seen in feet with 3 or fewer rays
      ii. *Absence* of 0 to 3 central rays (toes and associated MTs, and occasionally cuneiforms) of the foot, and including the 1st ray in the most extreme form
      iii. Splaying of the border rays
      iv. Soft tissues envelop the formed medial and lateral bony rays, thereby creating a central cleft (Figure 6-1).
   c. Midfoot
      i. *Abducted* lateral ray(s)
      ii. *Adducted* 1st ray
   d. Hindfoot
      i. *Neutral* or *valgus*
         • Occasionally with synchondrosis/synostosis of the hindfoot/midfoot bones
   e. Ankle
      i. Possible ball-and-socket
3. Imaging
   a. Simulated standing or standing anteroposterior (AP), lateral, and oblique of the foot
   b. AP, lateral, and mortis of the ankle
4. Natural history
   a. Comfort and function are satisfactory in most cases with the use of modified shoe wear
   b. Shoe-fitting problems and pain are experienced in the more severely deficient forms because the splaying of the MTs results in excessive width of the forefoot in relation to the length of the foot.
5. Nonoperative treatment
   a. Accommodative shoe wear, including custom shoes if necessary
6. Operative indications
   a. Inability to provide shoe-fitting comfort even with custom-made shoes and inserts/orthotics
7. Operative treatment with reference to the surgical techniques section of the book for each individual procedure
   a. Individualize treatment
      i. Be creative
      ii. Opening or closing wedge osteotomies of the midtarsal bones or MTs should be performed to narrow an excessively wide and painful forefoot. Supplement the osseous reconstruction by resecting some of the redundant

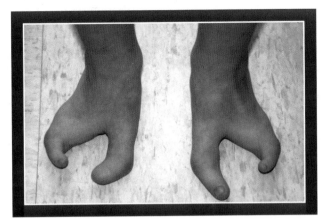

Figure 6-1. Bilateral cleft foot, class IV according to the Blauth and Borisch classification.

soft tissues in the cleft and approximating the dorsal and plantar skin edges without tension (Figure 6 2).
  b. Soft tissue procedures and even distal MT osteotomies that are used to correct hallux valgus and 5th toe varus are rarely successful.

Longitudinal Epiphyseal Bracket

1. <u>Definition—Congenital mal-deformation, "Too large"</u> (**see Table 1-1, Chapter 1**)
  a. "Delta phalanx" of a MT
  b. Almost exclusively the 1st MT, though I have seen it in the 5th MT in two syndromic children.
  c. The epiphysis and physis wrap around the medial side of the 1st MT diaphysis connecting the normal proximal epiphysis with a distal pseudoepiphysis. This leaves only the lateral side of the diaphysis without an overlying epiphysis (Figure 6-3).
  d. Longitudinal epiphyseal bracket (LEB) is always associated with either preaxial polydactyly (**see this chapter**) or congenital hallux varus (**see Chapter 5**), though both conditions may exist without an LEB.
2. <u>Elucidation of the segmental deformities</u>
  a. Short, wide 1st MT with *varus* orientation of the 1st metatarsophalangeal (MTP) joint and *varus* alignment of the hallux on the 1st MT
    i. Always associated with either congenital hallux varus or preaxial polydactyly
3. <u>Imaging</u>
  a. Simulated standing AP and lateral of the foot (Figure 6-3)
  b. Although it is *not* necessary if the plain x-rays are characteristically diagnostic, an MRI will show the pathoanatomy well (Figure 6-3).
4. <u>Natural history</u>
  a. Increasing or persistent varus deformity of the hallux, causing shoe-fitting difficulties
  b. Increasing length discrepancy between the 1st and 2nd MTs, resulting in stress overload and pain under the 2nd MT head (Figure 6-4)

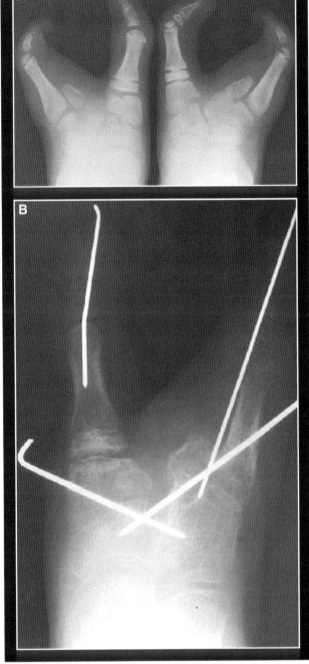

Figure 6-2. **A.** Preoperative AP x-ray of painful cleft feet. **B.** Postoperative AP x-ray of the right foot following medial and lateral column midfoot osteotomies and MTP joint capsulotomies. As anticipated, the toes returned to their original positions after the pins were removed, but the midfoot deformity correction persisted long term. (From Mosca VS. The foot. In: Weinstein SL, Flynn JM, eds. *Lovell and Winter's Pediatric Orthopaedics.* 7th ed. Philadelphia, PA: Lippincott Williams & Wilkins; 2013:1411, Figure 29-27.)

5. <u>Nonoperative treatment</u>
  a. None
6. <u>Operative indications</u>
  a. Presence of the malformation—it is best to operate when the child is over 6 months of age (due to technical

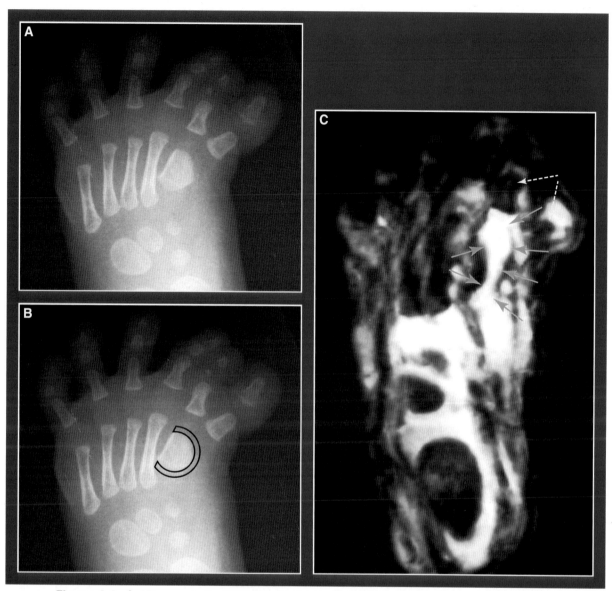

Figure 6-3. **A.** AP x-ray of a first MT LEB associated with preaxial polydactyly in an infant. The lateral cortex of the diaphysis is concave and has the normal density of cortical bone. The medial cortex is convex and does not have normal cortical bone density. It has the density more characteristic of metaphyseal bone adjacent to a normal physis. **B.** The LEB is outlined wrapping around the medial side of the 1st MT diaphysis connecting the normal proximal epiphysis with a distal pseudoepiphysis. **C.** An MRI of the same foot shows the LEB wrapping around the 1st MT shaft from proximal to distal (*green arrows outline it*). The two adjacent proximal phalanges (*dark rectangular shadows indicated by yellow dashed arrows*) can be seen distal and distal-medial to the LEB. **NOTE:** An MRI is not required if the plain x-rays are characteristically diagnostic.

considerations associated with the small size of the pathology) but under 1 year.

7. <u>Operative treatment</u> with reference to the surgical techniques section of the book for each individual procedure

   a. Resection of the LEB (**see Chapter 8**), with preservation of the normal proximal epiphysis and the distal pseudoepiphysis

     i. Concurrent soft tissue release of the congenital hallux varus, if present

     ii. Concurrent resection of a duplicate hallux, if present

Macrodactyly

1. <u>Definition</u>—**Malformation**, "Too large" (**see Table 1-1, Chapter 1**)

   a. Congenital enlargement of all tissue types in a ray (toe and MT) in a linear and circumferential array, starting distally at the tip of a toe and extending proximally to a variable extent along a ray (Figure 6-5)

   b. Occasionally, enlargement is present in adjacent rays to the same or a lesser extent, always starting distally at the tip of a toe and extending to a variable extent proximally along a ray (Figure 6-6).

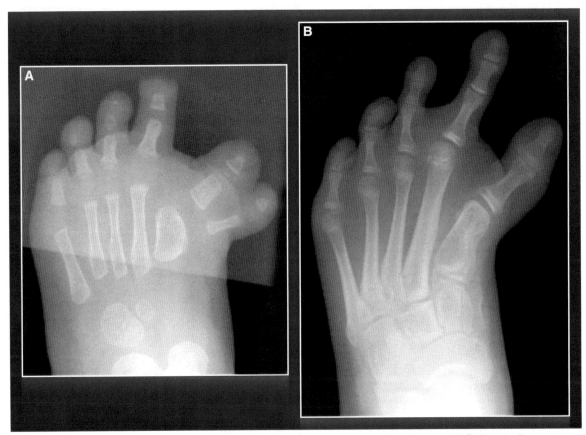

Figure 6-4. **A.** AP x-ray of preaxial polydactyly associated with a LEB of the 1st MT. **B.** The duplicate hallux was resected, but the LEB was not. Years later, there is a short 1st MT with varus deformity, hallux varus with toe pain when wearing shoes, and pain under the 2nd MT head due to stress transfer. Note the hypertrophy of the 2nd MT caused by the stress transfer.

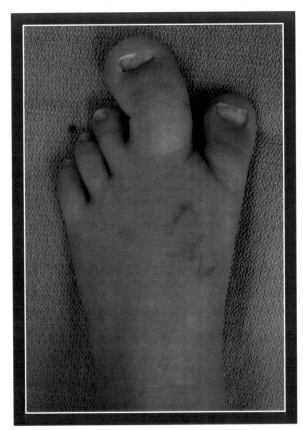

Figure 6-5. Typical macrodactyly of the 2nd ray in a foot.

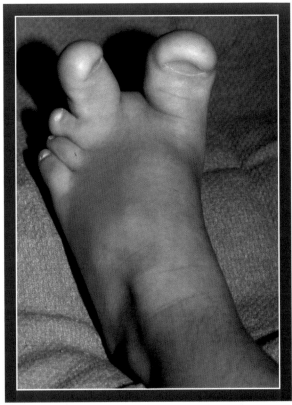

Figure 6-6. Macrodactyly of the 1st and 2nd rays in a foot.

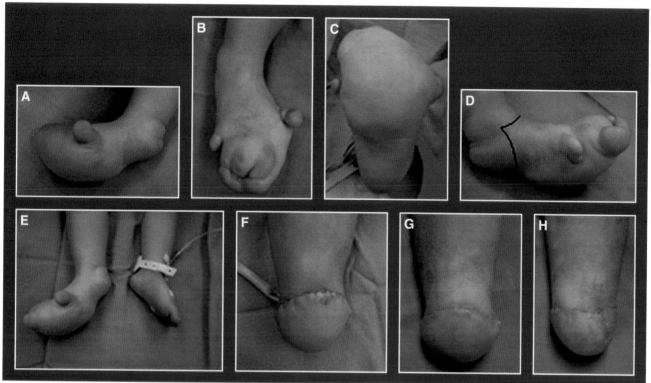

Figure 6-7. Macrodactyly or local gigantism (I have treated four of these). **A.** Medial view of the foot. **B.** Top view of the foot. **C.** Plantar view of the foot. Note the fairly sharp transverse demarcation between the enlarged forefoot soft tissues and the normal hindfoot soft tissues. **D.** Lateral view of the foot. Standard incision for a Syme amputation is indicated. It happens to cross the plantar surface of the foot immediately posterior to the pathologically enlarged soft tissues. **E.** Comparison view of feet confirms the need for ablation. **F.** Front view immediately after the Syme amputation. **G.** Front view of the residual limb 9 months later. Desirably bulbous, though not pathologic, heel pad is well centered under tibia. **H.** Side view of residual limb with heel pad well centered, i.e., slightly anterior to directly distal to the end of the tibia, anticipating slight posterior migration over time.

2. Elucidation of the segmental deformities
   a. Linear and circumferential enlargement of the bones and soft tissues along one or more adjacent rays of the foot, usually including or exclusive to the 2nd ray
   b. The enlargement of the bones and soft tissues is greatest distally, decreases in a gradual fashion proximally, and rarely extends proximal to the tarsometatarsal joint(s)
   c. Enlargement of the entire forefoot or the entire foot is perhaps best called localized gigantism (Figure 6-7)
   d. There is medial–lateral splaying and dorsal–plantar thickening of the forefoot due to a mass effect
3. Imaging
   a. Simulated standing or standing AP and lateral of the foot
4. Natural history
   a. Progressive enlargement of the affected bones and soft tissues, either proportionately or disproportionately faster than the normal adjacent tissues
   b. It is impossible to remove all of the abnormal soft tissues, as there is no distinct line of demarcation. Furthermore, it might be impractical to do so even if it were possible. Any remaining abnormal soft tissues will grow faster than the adjacent normal tissues, possibly

requiring subsequent and perhaps sequential soft tissue debulking operations (Figure 6-8).
5. Nonoperative treatment
   a. Accommodative shoe wear. This is rarely, if ever, an acceptable option.
6. Operative indications
   a. Anticipated and actual difficulty in fitting comfortably into normal shoes
   b. Objectionable appearance
      i. The appearance of the foot after surgery is never normal, but it is usually better than the original appearance. More importantly, more normal shoe wear is possible.
7. Operative treatment with reference to the surgical techniques section of the book for each individual procedure
   a. Individualized treatment
      i. Be creative
      ii. Be aggressive
         • It is impossible to remove all of the pathologic soft tissues with a segmental resection, even with a ray resection. There is no demarcation between the pathologic and normal soft tissues.

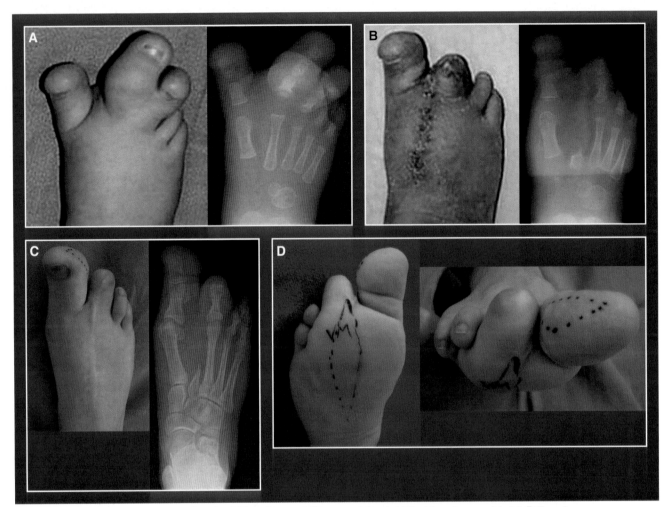

Figure 6-8. Macrodactyly. **A.** Top view and AP x-ray of the right foot in a 1-year-old girl. **B.** Top view and AP x-ray after 2nd ray resection and 3rd toe distal interphalangeal disarticulation. **C.** Top view and AP x-ray at age 17 years. There has been no change in the width of the foot. **D.** Remaining pathologic soft tissues at the margins of the resection site on the plantar surface of the forefoot grew faster than the adjacent normal soft tissues. This created a painful and callused "keel" that required resection. Painful enlarged soft tissues on the lateral side of the hallux were resected concurrently.

- The residual pathologic soft tissues will continue to grow disproportionately larger circumferentially than the adjacent normal soft tissues.
- It is almost guaranteed that a second operation will be required in the future to debulk the progressively enlarging/enlarged soft tissues (Figure 6-8).

b. Ray resection (**Figure 6-8; see Chapter 8**)—*perform this* for enlargement of an entire ray. This is the most important and successful of the proposed procedures used to treat macrodactyly.

c. Interphalangeal joint disarticulation (Figure 6-8)—*perform this* if there is no enlargement of the MT or the soft tissues around the MT.
   i. Disarticulate at the interphalangeal (IP) joint that will make the length of the residual toe equal to that of the adjacent lesser toe.
   ii. Do not perform an MTP joint disarticulation, because the adjacent toes will drift toward each other, creating joint incongruity.

d. MT epiphysiodesis
   i. It is challenging to calculate the timing for this procedure.
   ii. Does not address the main disability of macrodactyly, which is the circumferential enlargement of the soft tissues

e. MT shortening—*perform this* after skeletal maturity for a painful transfer stress lesion under the MT head of an elongated metatarsal.
   i. Does not address the circumferential enlargement of the soft tissues

f. Subsequent and sequential soft tissue debulking (Figure 6-8)—*perform this* for pain and progressive difficulty with shoe fitting due to circumferential enlargement of the soft tissues

g. Syme amputation (**see Chapter 7**)—*perform this* for enlargement of the entire forefoot (Figure 6-7)

h. Below-the-knee (transtibial and fibular) amputation—*perform this* for gigantism of the entire foot

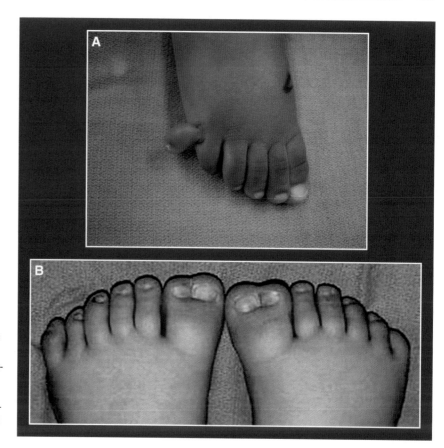

Figure 6-9. The extreme presentations of polydactyly. **A.** Postaxial polydactyly with only soft tissue and no bone or joint connection to the rest of the foot. **B.** Both feet have five well-formed lesser toes and MTs along with preaxial simple polysyndactyly consisting of complete duplication of the hallux and 1st MT bones.

Polydactyly

1. <u>Definition</u>—**Malformation, "Too many" (see Table 1-1, Chapter 1)**
   a. More than 5 complete toes per foot (Figure 6-9)
   b. Foot polydactyly is associated with hand polydactyly in 34% of cases
   c. Sporadic (most common) and hereditary types exist
   d. More than 1 extra digit per foot, especially if combined with syndactyly, is often the manifestation of a syndrome, such as Greig cephalopolysyndactyly (autosomal dominant) (Figure 6-10)
2. <u>Elucidation of the segmental deformities</u>
   a. Duplication of all or part of a toe, starting distally, and with or without segmentation/separation of the duplicate part(s)
   b. There may be widening and partial duplication without separation (double scoop) of the distal MT epiphysis, with one toe articulating with each half (Figure 6-10). This is frequently seen in the 5th MT with postaxial polydactyly.
   c. There may be complete duplication and separation of the distal end of the "normal" MT, creating a Y or T shape with each limb articulating with a toe.
   d. The duplicated toe may be associated with, and articulate with, a partially or completely duplicated MT (Figure 6-11).
   e. The duplicated toe may be separate or conjoined to an adjacent toe by soft tissue (simple syndactyly) or bone (complex syndactyly).

   f. There may be conjoined or separate duplicated toenails with syndactylized toes.
   g. Preaxial (great toe or medial border)—9% of the total (Figure 6-12)
      i. often associated with LEB of the 1st MT (**see this Chapter**)
   h. Central—6% of the total.
      i. These occur most commonly between the normal 4th and 5th rays. There is a partially formed MT with a synchondrosis to the 4th MT. And in many cases, there is osseous syndactyly/synostosis of the proximal phalanx to the 5th toe proximal phalanx (Figure 6-11)
   i. Postaxial (5th toe or lateral border)—85% of the total
      i. A commonly seen presentation is polysyndactyly. There is often duplication of the toenails (with or without segmentation), duplication of the distal and middle phalanges, but with a single proximal phalanx. All parts are contained within a single soft tissue envelope that has simple syndactyly to the normal 4th toe. Neither middle phalanx lines up axially with the proximal phalanx (Figure 6-13).
3. <u>Imaging</u>
   a. Simulated standing or standing AP and lateral of foot
4. <u>Natural history</u>
   a. Difficulty fitting comfortably in normal shoes due to excessive width of the toes in relation to the width of the shoe
5. <u>Nonoperative treatment</u>
   a. Wide shoes

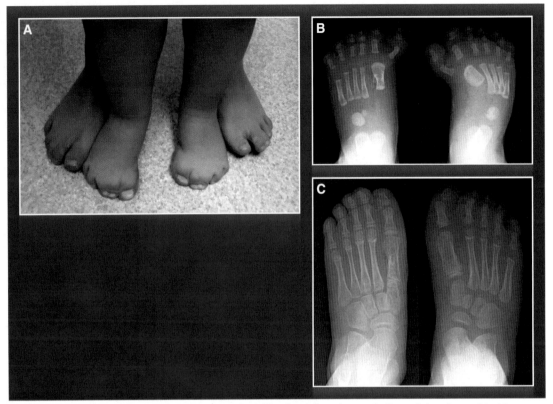

Figure 6-10. Greig cephalopolysyndactyly. **A.** The feet of mother and affected daughter with this autosomal dominant condition when the girl was 5 years old. **B.** AP x-rays of the girl's feet taken when she was an infant. At 10 months of age, she underwent resection of the left duplicate hallux and shaving of the enlarged 1st MT head, and resection of the right duplicate hallux and the 1st MT longitudinal epiphyseal bracket. **C.** AP x-rays of her feet taken at age 6 years, showing nearly normal appearances of both feet, including normal growth of the right 1st MT.

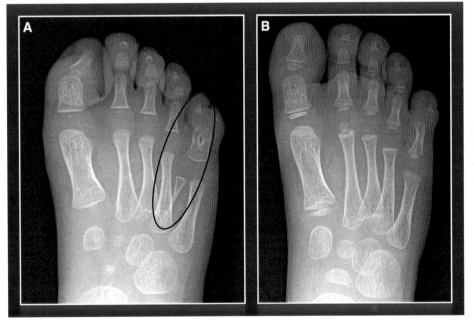

Figure 6-11. A. AP x-ray of a foot in a 3-year-old child with isolated central polysyndactyly between the 4th and 5th rays. There is a congenital synchondrosis of the partially formed duplicate MT to the normal 4th MT shaft, and a congenital synostosis of the duplicate proximal phalanx to the normal proximal phalanx of the 5th toe. This is one of the most common patterns of polydactyly that I have seen in recent years. **B.** Normal radiographic appearance of the foot 3 years after a ray resection. Separation of the proximal phalanges did not injure the physis of the 5th toe.

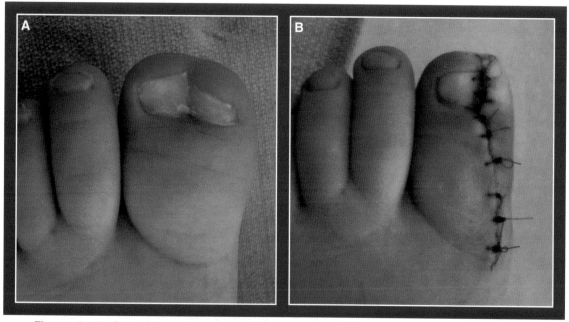

Figure 6-12. **A.** Preaxial polysyndactyly with a normal 1st MT. **B.** Appearance immediately after resection of the duplicate distal and proximal phalanges and toenail. A medial nail fold was carefully re-created with 4-0 chromic sutures.

Figure 6-13. Postaxial polysyndactyly. **A.** This is one of the most common patterns of polydactyly. The duplicate toenails are segmented (adjacent, but separate) in this case. The planned elliptical incision is marked. **B.** X-ray shows a single proximal phalanx and 2 middle phalanges, neither of which is aligned axially with the proximal phalanx. **C.** Intraoperative mini-fluoroscopy image shows the longitudinal osteotomy that was performed in the lateral duplicate middle phalanx. If the entire duplicate middle phalanx were removed, there would be instability at the proximal interphalangeal joint. **D.** Appearance of the toe after wound closure. 4-0 chromic sutures were used to enable the creation of a lateral nail fold that will prevent toenail ingrowth in the future. **E.** A soft tissue dressing is used following this short-duration day-surgery procedure. The child can bear weight immediately. The dressing is removed after 1 week.

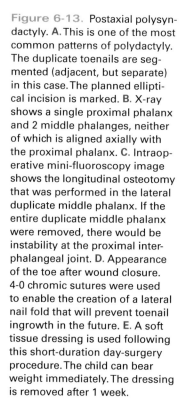

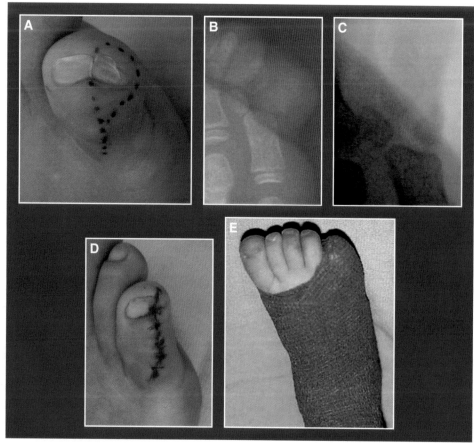

6. Operative indications
   a. Difficulty or anticipated difficulty fitting comfortably in normal shoes
   b. Objectionable appearance
7. Operative treatment with reference to the surgical techniques section of the book for each individual procedure
   a. Remove/disarticulate the abnormal (least well-aligned) toe through an elliptical skin incision
      i. It is both important and safe to create a Salter–Harris IV fracture-type resection of a partially duplicated and nonsegmented 5th MT head when removing an associated duplicated lateral toe (and certainly safe to resect the wide portion of a partially duplicated and nonsegmented 1st MT head (Figure 6-10) where no physis exists).
   b. Perform a ray resection (see Chapter 8) if an associated partially or completely duplicated MT is present (Figure 6-11)
   c. Remove the limb of a Y- or T-shaped MT along with the toe with which it articulates
      i. Perform a concurrent angular deformity corrective osteotomy of the residual MT for severe angular deformity
      ii. or delay/avoid the osteotomy if only a minor angular deformity exists, as it might correct spontaneously over time
   d. For polysyndactyly, remove the abnormal (least well-aligned) toe/toe parts/toenail through a dorsal elliptical incision; create a soft tissue lateral nail fold (Figures 6-12 and 6-13)
      i. When neither duplicated middle phalanx aligns with a single proximal phalanx, it is appropriate to longitudinally split the middle phalanx that is being removed, leaving the articular portion in the proximal interphalangeal joint rather than destabilizing the joint by removing the entire middle phalanx (Figure 6-13).
   e. Concurrently resect a LEB (see Chapter 8), if one exists
   f. Perform a percutaneous tenotomy of a contracted flexor digitorum longus tendon slip to the 4th and/or 5th toe if one exists (see Chapter 7); a common finding in postaxial polydactyly
   g. Do not separate 4th–5th toes syndactyly when associated with 5th toe polydactyly for the following reasons:
      i. It is dangerous to the vascularity of the remaining digit when both sides of the digit are operated on concurrently.
      ii. There are no functional or cosmetic advantages (the scar is less cosmetic than the syndactyly) achieved with separation of any toes, particularly the lateral toes (Figure 6-14).
      iii. Finally, there is a reasonably high risk of lateral drift of the lateral toe, which would cause pain and shoe-fitting difficulties—for which the treatment would be to re-create the syndactyly (Figure 6-14)!
   h. If a complete duplicate lateral 6th ray is resected, attach the peroneus brevis to the base of the 5th MT with sutures through drill holes.

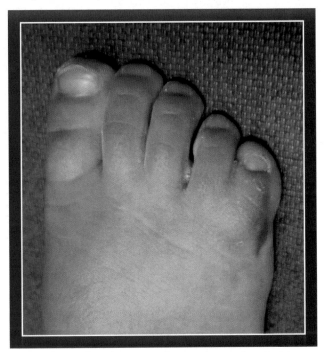

Figure 6-14. Excellent cosmetic appearance of postaxial polysyndactyly several years following resection of the duplicate lateral middle and distal phalanges and toenail, with maintenance of the simple syndactyly to the 4th toe. Also note the excellent cosmetic appearance of the surgically constructed lateral nail fold.

Syndactyly

1. Definition—Malformation, "Joined together (failed to separate)" (see Table 1-1, Chapter 1)
   a. Congenital failure of segmentation/separation of adjacent toes or of extra toes (polysyndactyly)
   b. Simple
      i. Congenital failure of segmentation/separation of the soft tissues of adjacent toes or of extra toes.
      ii. As an isolated malformation, it occurs most often between the 2nd and 3rd toes in normal children (Figure 6-15).

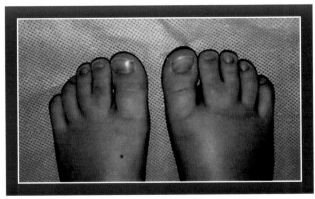

Figure 6-15. Simple syndactyly between the 2nd and 3rd toes of both feet. These are a cosmetic difference and rarely, if ever, a cause of pain or disability.

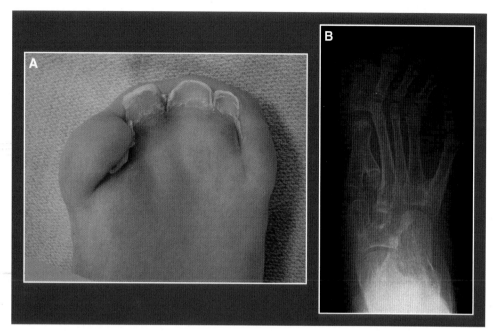

Figure 6-16. **A.** Typical appearance of the toes of a child with Apert syndrome. There is syndactyly of all toes. **B.** X-ray shows simple (soft tissue) and complex (osseous) polysyndactyly. Multiple synostoses and tarsal coalitions are seen in the forefoot, midfoot, and hindfoot.

- may be shallow (very close to the normal web position), intermediate, or complete (out to the tips of the toes)
- often bilateral
- often familial

iii. If more than 1 syndactyly per foot, the syndactylies are often manifestations of a syndrome, such as Greg cephalopolysyndactyly (autosomal dominant).

c. Complex
   i. Congenital failure of segmentation/separation of the soft tissues and bones of adjacent toes or of extra toes
   ii. Most often found in Apert syndrome or other syndromes (Figure 6-16)

d. Differentiate syndactyly from acrosyndactyly (*acro* means end or tip), a postseparation, acquired distal connection between toes that is due to an amniotic band (Streeter dysplasia) (Figure 6-17)

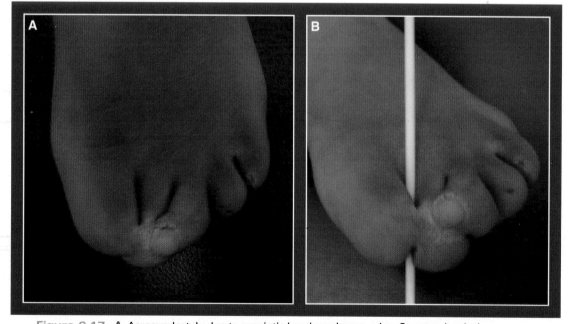

Figure 6-17. **A.** Acrosyndactyly due to amniotic band syndrome, a.k.a. Streeter dysplasia. **B.** Proximal separation is confirmed with a swizzle stick. Congenital syndactyly is a failure of separation. Acrosyndactyly, by way of contrast, is acquired and represents an injury to toes that have already separated in utero. The amniotic constriction band causes the developing fetal toes to unite or "spot weld" at the site of the band with amputation of the distal parts. Acrosyndactyly is neither a deformity nor a malformation, but instead an injury comparable to a burn.

2. Elucidation of the segmental deformities
   a. Simple
      i. Partial to complete (proximal to distal) failure of segmentation/separation of the soft tissue between 2 usually otherwise normal adjacent toes with normal bones, joints, tendons, neurovascular (NV) structures (though may be shared on the adjacent sides of the 2 toes), skin, nails.
   b. Complex
      i. Failure of segmentation/separation of the bones and soft tissues of 2 usually abnormal adjacent toes. The bones are frequently malformed as well as conjoined. Frequently, the joints are fused or ankylosed. The NV structures on adjacent sides of the toes are absent or malformed. Toenails are frequently unsegmented/conjoined.
3. Imaging
   a. None for simple syndactyly
   b. Simulated standing or standing AP and lateral of foot for complex syndactyly
4. Natural history
   a. Simple
      i. No pain or functional disability. The 2nd and 3rd toes typically grow at the same rate and achieve equal length. They perform identical tasks simultaneously that do not require independence.
      ii. Rarely, if ever, pain may develop if differential growth in length of the toes causes joint flexion of the longer toe, with painful callus formation over the dorsum of the flexed IP joint(s).
         • This can perhaps be anticipated in the unusual case of syndactyly between the hallux and 2nd toe.
   b. Complex
      i. Rarely a cause of pain or functional disability
5. Nonoperative treatment
   a. None needed or indicated for simple syndactyly
   b. Accommodative shoes for complex syndactyly and polysyndactyly which are often associated with other foot malformations, as in children with Apert syndrome
6. Operative indications
   a. Simple
      i. None
      ii. Except perhaps if differential growth in length of the toes causes joint flexion of the longer toe and painful callus formation over the dorsum of the flexed IP joint(s)
   b. Complex
      i. Pain that is directly related to the bony syndactyly. Occasionally, the joints spontaneously fuse in poor alignment (often plantar flexion of the 2nd MTP joint), creating poor plantar pressure distribution and soft tissue overload.
7. Operative treatment with reference to the surgical techniques section of the book for each individual procedure
   a. Syndactyly release (separation of the toes)—*perform this rarely*, and only if there is painful callus formation

over the dorsum of the flexed IP joint(s) of the longer toe in the clinical scenario in which the syndactylized toes have grown at different rates and to different lengths.
      i. The alternative, and perhaps preferred, treatment in this clinical scenario is to resect and fuse the painful, flexed IP joint(s).
   b. Anecdotally, I have seen a few children who had undergone syndactyly release between the hallux and 2nd toe with the goal of wearing thong-type sandals. The scars, in all cases, were too hypersensitive to enable the children to wear thong sandals comfortably. There was also web creep that re-created much of the syndactyly over time.

II. MIDFOOT

Accessory Navicular

1. Definition—**Malformation, "Too large" (see Table 1-1, Chapter 1)**
   a. Medial/plantar–medial enlargement of the tarsal navicular bone with a secondary ossification center that eventually coalesces with the main body of the navicular in most affected individuals (Figure 6-18).
   b. Prevalence is 10% to15% of the population. Most do not hurt.
   c. Accessory navicular may be coincident with a flexible flatfoot. Both conditions have high individual prevalence rates. A cause and effect relationship has not been established between the two conditions.
2. Elucidation of the segmental deformities
   a. Firm/bony prominence on the medial/plantar–medial aspect of the navicular/midfoot
   b. Forefoot—*neutral* or *supinated* (if associated with a *valgus/everted* hindfoot)
   c. Midfoot—*neutral*
   d. Hindfoot—*neutral* or *valgus/everted*
   e. Ankle—*neutral* or *plantar flexed (equinus)*
3. Imaging
   a. Standing AP, lateral, and *both* obliques of foot
      i. The *lateral (nonstandard) oblique* is the best view for revealing an accessory navicular (Figure 6-19).
      ii. Three types of accessory naviculars
         • Type I—small, separate ossicle in the posterior tibialis tendon adjacent to the main body of the navicular
         • Type II—bullet-shaped ossification center on the proximal medial/plantar–medial aspect of the navicular with a synchondrosis to the main body of the navicular
         • Type III—cornuate-shaped navicular—either a primary malformation or the result of metaplasia of a type II synchondrosis to a synostosis with the main body of the navicular

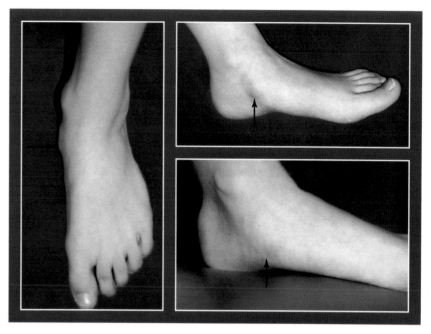

Figure 6-18. An accessory navicular (*black arrows*) creates a bony prominence on the medial/plantar–medial aspect of the midfoot. It moves with the navicular/acetabulum pedis during inversion and eversion of the subtalar joint. That is in contrast to the bony prominence on the medial/plantar–medial aspect of the midfoot in a flatfoot. The bony prominence in a flatfoot is the head of the talus. It does not move with inversion and eversion of the subtalar joint. In fact, the prominence of the head of the talus becomes obscured by the navicular when the subtalar joint in a flatfoot is inverted.

4. <u>Natural history</u>
   a. All three types create a bony prominence along the medial/plantar–medial midfoot that presses the overlying skin against the shoe or the ground, with the possible development of painful callus formation.
   b. The incidence of pain is not known, but is low.
   c. Pain can also be experienced in a type II accessory navicular if a crack develops in the synchondrosis. Such cracks typically result from repetitive stress rather than from an acute injury. Cartilage has poor vascularity. If a crack develops, it might not heal. The cyclic tension stress on the synchondrosis during weight-bearing leads to painful inflammation at the site. In these cases, maximum tenderness is elicited by plantar-to-dorsal (upward) pressure under the accessory navicular, rather than by direct medial-to-lateral pressure on the ossicle (Figure 6-20).

5. <u>Nonoperative treatment</u>
   a. Accommodative shoe wear
   b. Over-the-counter arch supports to move the navicular to a different position in relation to the shoe, and thereby decrease the pressure on the overlying skin, as well as to decrease tension stress on the posterior tibialis–accessory navicular complex

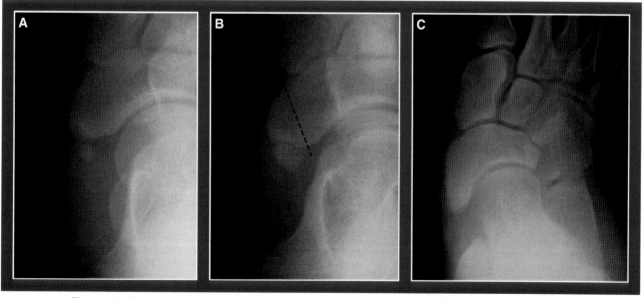

Figure 6-19. An accessory navicular is best seen on the lateral (nonstandard) oblique x-ray, as in A and B. **A.** Type I. **B.** Type II. Dashed black line is the site of resection of the accessory navicular and the enlarged medial body of the navicular. **C.** Type III.

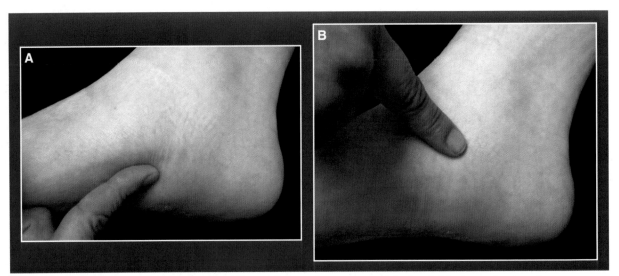

Figure 6-20. Adolescent male with a painful type II accessory navicular. **A.** Maximum tenderness to palpation is elicited by plantar-to-dorsal (upward) pressure under the accessory navicular. **B.** There is less tenderness to direct medial-to-lateral pressure over the ossicle.

c. If particularly inflamed and painful, temporary immobilization in a cast or CAM boot with or without nonsteroidal anti-inflammatory drugs

6. <u>Operative indications</u>
   a. Pain at the site of the accessory navicular that is not relieved by prolonged attempts at nonoperative treatment

7. <u>Operative treatment</u> with reference to the surgical techniques section of the book for each individual procedure
   a. Accessory navicular resection (**see Chapter 8**)—*perform this* for a painful accessory navicular in a well-aligned foot with normal ankle dorsiflexion.
   b. Accessory navicular resection (**see Chapter 8**) and gastrocnemius recession (**see Chapter 7**)—*perform this* combination of procedures for a painful accessory navicular in a well-aligned foot with a gastrocnemius contracture
   c. Accessory navicular resection (**see Chapter 8**) and calcaneal lengthening osteotomy (**see Chapter 8**) and gastrocnemius recession (**see Chapter 7**)—*perform this* combination of procedures for a painful accessory navicular in a severe flatfoot with a gastrocnemius contracture

III. HINDFOOT

Congenital Subtalar Synostosis

1. <u>Definition</u>—**Congenital mal-deformation,** "Joined together (failed to separate)" (**see Table 1-1, Chapter 1**)
   a. Congenital failure of segmentation/separation of the talus and calcaneus
      i. with translational valgus alignment of the calcaneus under the talus
      ii. usually associated with fibula hemimelia syndrome with

- Hypoplasia of the entire lower extremity in relation to the other lower extremity
- Genu valgum
- Often, cruciate ligament deficiency
- Valgus-oriented ball-and-socket ankle joint
- Often, lateral ray deficiency of the foot (Figure 6-21)

2. <u>Elucidation of the segmental deformities</u>
   a. Forefoot—*supinated* or *neutral* (if *neutral* in relation to the valgus hindfoot, the entire foot is pronated and the 5th MT head does not touch the ground in weight-bearing. **see Basic Principle #13, Figure 2-18B, Chapter 2)**
      i. There is usually complete absence of 1 to 3 lateral rays of the foot with associated absence of cuneiform bones.
   b. Midfoot—*neutral*
      i. Absence of cuneiform bones if lateral rays of the forefoot are absent
      ii. The cuboid is always present, though sometimes fused to the calcaneus.
   c. Hindfoot—*translational valgus* (without eversion)
      i. There is a synchondrosis (that eventually undergoes metaplasia to a synostosis) between the talus and calcaneus, with the calcaneus laterally positioned under the talus, thereby creating a congenital *translational valgus* deformity of the hindfoot. There is no rotational deformity of the foot. The talonavicular joint is usually well-aligned. The thigh–foot angle is neutral (**see similarities to translational valgus overcorrection of the subtalar joint in clubfoot, Chapter 5**).
      ii. The synchondrosis/synostosis sometimes extends to the calcaneocuboid joint ± the talonavicular joint.
   d. Ankle—*valgus*
      i. Ball-and-socket ankle joint in valgus alignment/orientation (Figure 6-22)

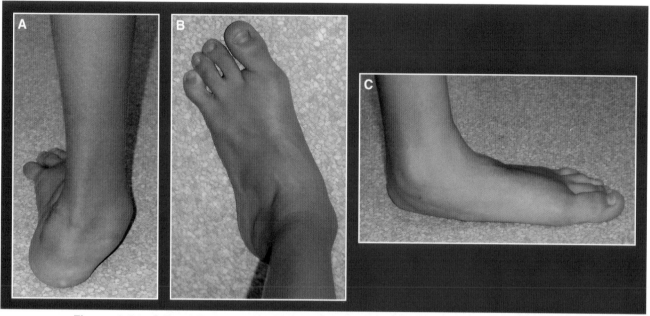

Figure 6-21. **A.** Type I fibula hemimelia syndrome with severe translational valgus alignment of a congenital subtalar synostosis and coincident severe valgus orientation of a ball-and-socket ankle joint. **B.** Absence of the lateral ray is apparent. **C.** Severe pes planus is seen.

3. Imaging
   a. Simulated standing or standing AP, lateral, and Harris axial views of the foot (Figure 6-23)
   b. AP, lateral, and mortis of the ankle (Figures 6-22 and 6-23)
4. Natural history
   a. Most often, there is no pain or functional disability. The associated congenital ball-and-socket ankle joint malformation is an excellent adaptation to congenital lack of subtalar motion, which is why a congenital subtalar synostosis does so much better than a surgically created subtalar arthrodesis. The ankle cannot convert

to a ball-and-socket joint later in life, or even later in childhood.
   b. In cases with exaggerated valgus alignment of the "talocalcaneal" bone, pain is related to the deformity. There may be lateral hindfoot impingement pain, medial collateral ligament stretch pain, and/or pain under the plantar–medial surface of the laterally displaced heel pad.
5. Nonoperative treatment
   a. Accommodative shoe wear, often with a shoe filler if there are absent rays

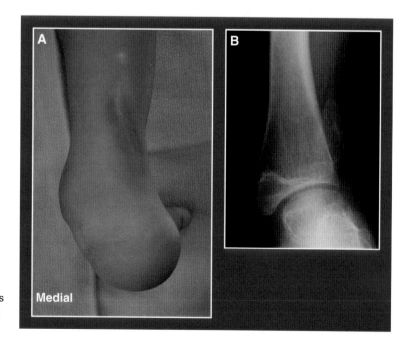

Figure 6-22. Incomplete fibula deficiency with congenital subtalar synostosis. **A.** Valgus deformity of the hindfoot. The scar was created by surgery to lengthen the peroneal tendons, obviously without benefit. **B.** AP x-ray of the ankle shows partial fibula hemimelia and a ball-and-socket ankle joint in valgus alignment. Congenital subtalar synostosis is always associated with a ball-and-socket ankle joint.

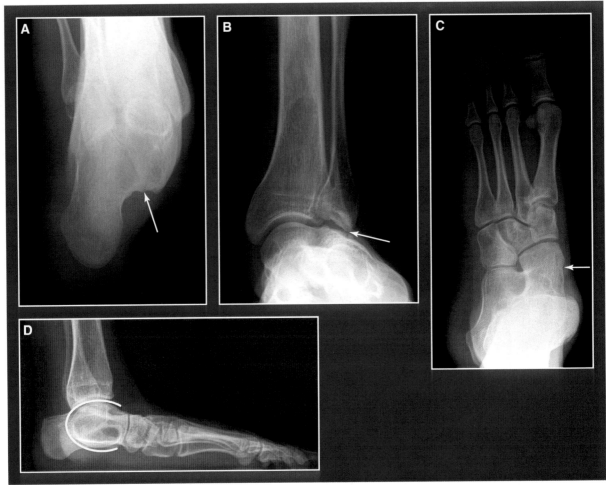

Figure 6-23. **A.** Harris axial x-ray showing a congenital synchondrosis of the subtalar joint (*white arrow*) undergoing metaplasia to a synostosis in a 16-year-old boy with hypoplasia of the lower extremity. The subtalar synchondrosis/synostosis is in valgus alignment. **B.** AP ankle x-ray shows a ball-and-socket joint with severe valgus orientation. The laterally translated calcaneus articulates with the lateral malleolus (*white arrow*). **C.** AP x-ray of the foot shows that the subtalar synostosis extends to the navicular (*white arrow indicates the site of the talonavicular synostosis*). There is normal axial alignment of the medial column of the foot. The lateral ray of the foot is absent, and there are only 2 cuneiform bones adjacent to the cuboid. **D.** Lateral x-ray shows a flatfoot and a dramatic C-sign of Lateur (*yellow C*) (**see Talocalcaneal Tarsal Coalition, Figure 5-48, Chapter 5**).

6. Operative indications
   a. Failure of nonoperative treatment to relieve
      i. lateral hindfoot impingement pain
      ii. medial collateral ligament stretch pain
      iii. pain under the plantar–medial surface of the laterally displaced heel pad
7. Operative treatment with reference to the surgical techniques section of the book for each individual procedure
   a. Posterior calcaneus displacement osteotomy (**see Chapter 8**)—*perform this* for lateral hindfoot impingement pain, medial collateral ligament stretch pain, and/or pain under the plantar–medial surface of the laterally displaced heel pad
   b. *Preliminary* correction of the ankle valgus deformity with medial distal tibia guided growth with a screw (**see Chapter 8**) or a distal tibial valgus corrective osteotomy (**see Chapter 8**)—*perform this* for lateral hindfoot

impingement pain, medial collateral ligament stretch pain, and/or pain under the plantar–medial surface of the laterally displaced heel pad if the ball-and-socket ankle joint is in severe valgus alignment.
   i. If the forefoot is pronated in relation to the hindfoot, the posterior calcaneus displacement osteotomy (**see Chapter 8**) is performed after the ankle deformity is improved and the plane of the forefoot is perpendicular to the tibia.
   ii. If the forefoot is supinated in relation to the hindfoot, the posterior calcaneus displacement osteotomy (**see Chapter 8**) is performed in conjunction with a medial cuneiform plantar flexion osteotomy (**see Chapter 8**) after the ankle deformity is improved.
   c. Possible Syme amputation (**see Chapter 7, and Figure 6-7 in this chapter**)—*perform this* as treatment for severe fibula hemimelia syndrome

CHAPTER 7

Soft Tissue Procedures

I. APONEUROTIC AND INTRAMUSCULAR RECESSIONS

PRINCIPLE: Aponeurotic and intramuscular recessions of contracted musculotendinous units can be carried out wherever there is an aponeurotic tendon that surrounds a muscle or a tendon that extends deep into a muscle. There is a limit to the amount of lengthening that can be achieved with an aponeurotic or an intramuscular recession, but overlengthening and permanent weakness are unlikely.

Gastrocnemius Recession (Strayer Procedure)

1. Indications
   a. Contracture of the gastrocnemius but not the soleus (**see Chapter 5**), as determined by the Silfverskiold test (**see Assessment Principle #12 and Figure 3-13, Chapter 3**), that is creating pain, functional disability, and/or gait disturbance
      i. The ankle joint can be dorsiflexed more than 10° with the subtalar joint locked in neutral alignment (**see Basic Principle #7, Chapter 2**) and the knee flexed, but less than 10° with the knee extended.
2. Technique (Figure 7-1)
   a. Make a 4- to 5-cm longitudinal incision approximately halfway between the knee and the ankle 2 finger-breadths posterior to the posterior edge of the medial face of the tibia
   b. Avoid and protect the long saphenous vein
   c. Open the facia longitudinally
   d. Identify the plantaris tendon along the medial edge of the gastrocnemius tendon and divide it
   e. Identify the musculotendinous junction of the gastrocnemius
   f. Clear all soft tissues off the posterior surface of the aponeurotic tendon of the gastrocnemius

   g. Identify the sural nerve in the fat on the posterior surface of the gastrocnemius, elevate it off the tendon, retract it, and protect it during the tenotomy
   h. Using finger-dissection or scissor spreading, elevate a *short segment* of the distal musculotendinous unit of the gastrocnemius off the soleus from medial to lateral until the muscle of the soleus can be visualized lateral to the aponeurotic tendon of the soleus
   i. Avoid extensive proximal-to-distal separation of the two aponeurotic tendons to prevent excessive retraction of the gastrocnemius muscle
   j. Cut the gastrocnemius aponeurosis as far distally as possible. Do not be concerned about cutting the distal-most fibers of the gastrocnemius. The gastrocnemius and soleus aponeurotic tendons are not always separate structures distal to all gastrocnemius muscle fibers. The last few fibers do not matter.
   k. Recheck the Silfverskiold test to ensure that the ankle can now be dorsiflexed at least 10° above neutral with the subtalar joint in neutral alignment and the knee extended (**see Assessment Principle #12 and Figure 3-13, Chapter 3**). There should be no difference in the degree of ankle dorsiflexion whether the knee is flexed or extended.
   l. There is no need to suture the gastrocnemius tendon to the soleus muscle as long as the blunt separation of the two aponeurotic tendons is limited to a few centimeters.
   m. There is no need to repair the compartment fascia.
   n. Close the deep fat with a few 2-0 absorbable sutures to prevent adherence of the skin to the muscle
   o. Approximate the skin edges with interrupted subcutaneous 3-0 absorbable sutures and a running subcuticular 4-0 absorbable suture
   p. Apply a short-leg walking cast with a neutral to 5° dorsiflexed ankle
   q. Maintain the cast for 5 to 6 weeks, or longer if needed for other concurrently performed procedures

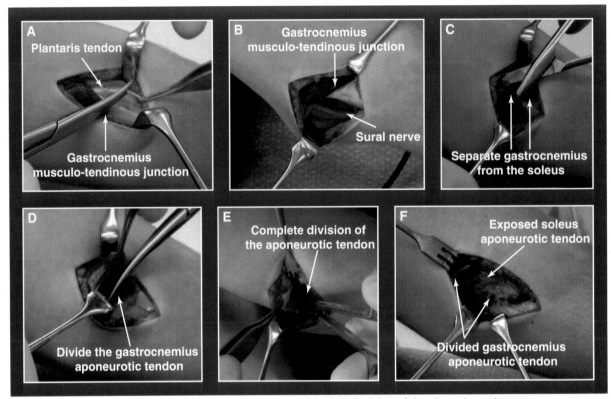

Figure 7-1. Strayer procedure (posteromedial left leg). **A.** Division of the plantaris tendon. **B.** Exposure and elevation of the sural nerve off the posterior surface of the gastrocnemius. **C.** Separation of the aponeurotic tendons of the gastrocnemius and the soleus. **D.** Initiation of the division of the gastrocnemius aponeurotic tendon. **E.** Completion of the division of the gastrocnemius aponeurotic tendon. **F.** Exposed soleus aponeurotic tendon.

3. Pitfalls
   a. Inadequate deformity correction due to incorrect determination of the appropriateness for a gastrocnemius recession when, in fact, the soleus is also contracted
   b. Release of both the gastrocnemius and the soleus aponeuroses, due to failure to separate them before release
4. Complications
   a. Injury to the sural nerve
      i. *Avoid by* isolating and protecting it before tenotomy
   b. Adherence of the skin to the muscle, creating an obvious tethering effect with muscle contraction
      i. *Avoid by* closing the deep fat with a few 2-0 absorbable sutures before closing the subcutaneous layer with interrupted 3-0 absorbable sutures
   c. Excessive migration of the gastrocnemius muscle with unusually prominent ball-like contours of the two heads of the muscle
      i. *Avoid by* limiting the extent of proximal-to-distal blunt separation of the two aponeurotic tendons

Distal Abductor Hallucis Recession

1. Indications
   a. Contracture of the abductor hallucis in:
      i. Congenital hallux varus (**see Chapter 5**)
         • Also see **Longitudinal Epiphyseal Bracket Resection, Chapter 8**
      ii. Dorsal bunion (**see Chapter 5**)

   • Also see **Reverse Jones Transfer of FHL to 1st MT Neck, this chapter**
      iii. Metatarsus adductus (**see Chapter 5**)
2. Technique (Figure 7-2)
   a. Make a 2-cm longitudinal incision medial to the distal end of the 1st metatarsal (MT)

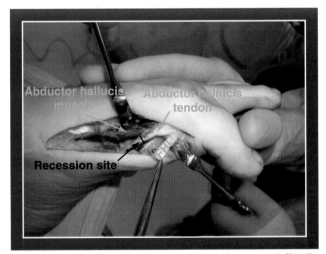

Figure 7-2. The abductor hallucis muscle is exposed distally through an incision that, in this photo, is longer than necessary for a simple recession, as it was being used for a concurrent reverse Jones transfer of the flexor hallucis longus (FHL) to the 1st metatarsal (MT) neck. The tendon is divided proximally within the substance of the muscle belly to avoid complete separation of the musculotendinous unit.

b. Identify the musculotendinous junction on the medial superficial surface of the abductor hallucis

c. Cut the tendon at its proximal end within the substance of the muscle, thereby creating a recession, and not a tenotomy

d. Approximate the skin edges with interrupted subcutaneous 3-0 absorbable sutures and a running subcuticular 4-0 absorbable suture

e. Apply a short-leg or long-leg weight-bearing or non–weight-bearing cast based on the requirements for the other concurrently performed procedures

3. Pitfalls

a. The use of this recession rather than proximal release of the three origins of the abductor hallucis for correction of cavovarus deformity (**see Superficial Medial Release, Deep Medial Release, Superficial Plantar-Medial Release, and Deep Plantar-Medial Release, this chapter**)

4. Complications

a. Complete tenotomy

i. *Avoid by* releasing the tendon at a level where there is adequate overlapping muscle, i.e., not too far distal

Abductor Digiti Minimi Recession

1. Indications

a. Performed in conjunction with a calcaneal lengthening osteotomy (CLO; **see Chapter 8**) for correction of symptomatic flatfoot deformity (**see Chapter 5**)

i. Necessary to release the lateral soft tissue tether that would otherwise impede distraction of the osteotomy fragments

2. Technique (Figure 7-3)

a. This procedure is rarely, if ever, performed in isolation, but always performed in conjunction with a CLO.

b. The incision is, therefore, a modified Ollier incision in a Langer's line over the sinus tarsi used for the CLO.

c. Clear the fat off the dorsal aponeurosis of the abductor digiti minimi with a Key elevator 1 to 3 cm proximal to the calcaneocuboid joint

d. Using a scalpel and/or scissors, divide the 1-mm-thick aponeurosis transversely starting medially at its attachment on the calcaneus and extending to its most lateral extent. Also release the aponeurosis from the lateral edge of the calcaneus 1 cm anterior and 1 cm posterior to the transverse aponeurotomy

e. Immobilization is based on the concurrently performed CLO—8 weeks in a non–weight-bearing short-leg cast, with a cast change at 6 weeks (**see Chapter 8**)

3. Pitfalls

a. There is no need to divide the muscle of the abductor digiti minimi. There are a few small veins immediately deep to the aponeurosis. By merely cutting the thin aponeurosis, the veins can often be avoided.

4. Complications

a. None

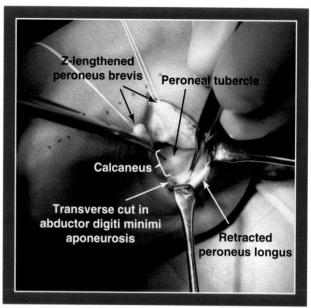

Figure 7-3. The abductor digiti minimi has been exposed through the plantar extent of a modified Ollier incision (used for a CLO) by retracting the peroneus longus (and sural nerve) laterally. The peroneus brevis has been Z-lengthened, and the soft tissue contents of the sinus tarsi have been elevated from the isthmus of the calcaneus in preparation for the osteotomy. The peroneal tubercle is seen on the lateral surface of the calcaneus. After scraping the fat (*held in the forceps*) off the dorsal surface of the aponeurosis of the abductor digiti minimi with a Key elevator, a transverse cut is made in this 1-mm-thick layer of collagen. It is only necessary to release the aponeurosis and not the muscle. Small veins immediately deep to the aponeurosis should be coagulated. The aponeurosis should also be released from the lateral edge of the calcaneus 1 cm anterior and 1 cm posterior to the aponeurotomy.

Posterior Tibialis Tendon Recession

1. Indications

a. Mild, *flexible* hindfoot varus and cavovarus deformities (**see Chapter 5**) with muscle imbalance; performed in conjunction with

i. a split anterior tibial tendon transfer (SPLATT) in CP (**see this chapter**)

ii. a superficial plantar-medial release (S-PMR) in mild forms of Charcot–Marie–Tooth (CMT) disease (**see this chapter**)

2. Technique

a. Make a 4-cm longitudinal incision along the posterior edge of the medial face of the tibia approximately 8 to 10 cm proximal to the tip of the medial malleolus

b. Release the fascia from the edge of the tibia

c. The first muscle encountered is the flexor digitorum longus. Confirm its identity by pulling proximally on its intramuscular tendon and observing flexion of the lesser toes. Retract it posteriorly.

d. The next muscle/tendon unit identified is the posterior tibialis. Confirm its identity by pulling proximally on its tendon and observing inversion of the foot. Divide the tendon within the substance of the muscle, cutting as few muscle fibers as possible.

e. Approximate the skin edges with interrupted subcutaneous 3-0 absorbable sutures and a running subcuticular 4-0 absorbable suture
f. Immobilization is based on the concurrently performed procedures, generally a short-leg non–weight-bearing cast for 6 weeks, followed by a short-leg walking cast for 2 weeks.

3. Pitfalls
   a. Recession of the flexor digitorum longus (FDL) rather than the posterior tibialis

4. Complications
   a. Complete tenotomy
      i. *Avoid by* releasing the tendon at a level where there is adequate overlapping muscle, i.e., not too far distal
   b. Division of tibial nerve
      i. *Avoid by* identifying the anatomy as described earlier and ensuring that the dense white cord-like structure has muscle fibers approaching it at oblique angles and firmly attached to it

II. TENDON LENGTHENINGS/RELEASES

PRINCIPLE: There is an almost unlimited amount of lengthening that can be achieved with a tendon lengthening, but overlengthening and permanent weakness are possible.

Lengthening the tendon of a contracted musculotendinous unit can be carried out when there is a long bare tendon distal to the muscle belly. These lengthenings are frequently employed in foot deformity corrections. It is important to set the proper tension on the musculotendinous unit when repairing the tendon. The proper tension is established by placing the foot and ankle (and knee, when indicated) at the extent of the desired range of motion and repairing the overlapping limbs of the tendon under slight tension in that position.

Percutaneous Tenotomies of the Flexor Hallucis Longus and Flexor Digitorum Longus to Toes 2 to 5

1. Indications
   a. Contracture of the flexor hallucis longus (FHL) and/or the FDL to one or more of the lesser toes
      i. in mallet, hammer, and curly toes (**see Chapter 5 and Figure 5-65, Chapter 5**)
      ii. in cavus, clubfoot, and equinus deformities (**see Chapter 5**)
      iii. applicable for infants through adolescents and young adults

2. Technique (Figures 7-4 and 7-5)
   a. Ask your assistant to dorsiflex the ankle to tension the long toe flexor tendons
   b. Maximally dorsiflex and release one toe at a time
   c. Using a #11 scalpel, cut the long flexor tendon to each toe using short-arc sweeping movements starting in the center of the toe at the proximal plantar flexion crease. The tip of the scalpel should be used both as a probe and a scalpel. The incision should be no more than about 3 to 4 mm. There will be a sudden release of tension and the interphalangeal (IP) joints will extend
   d. If the distal interphalangeal (DIP) joint extends but the proximal interphalangeal (PIP) does not, the flexor brevis is also contracted and should be released by probing with the tip of the scalpel and cutting deeper and wider as the bone is approached.
   e. If the IP joints of the toe extend fully in the relaxed position, there is no further treatment needed, except for immobilization.
   f. If the IP joints of the toe can be fully extended, but are flexed in the relaxed position due to skin or other soft

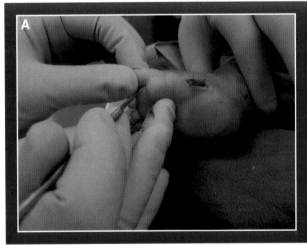
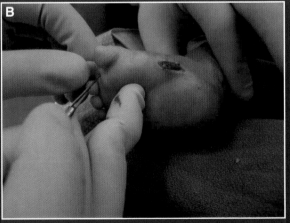

Figure 7-4. A. Percutaneous tenotomy of the FHL in an infant clubfoot. The ankle is dorsiflexed by the surgical assistant to tension the FHL. The surgeon further tensions the FHL by dorsiflexing the hallux while inserting the tip of a #11 scalpel in the medial-lateral center of the toe in the proximal plantar flexion crease. The scalpel is used as both a probe and a knife to first palpate and then divide the FHL using well-controlled short-arc sweeping movements (the NV bundles are very close by). There is a sudden and dramatic extension of the hallux when the FHL is completely released. Note the unrelated medial midfoot incision through which a plantar fasciotomy was performed. **B.** The same technique is used for each lesser toe with a contracted FDL tendon slip.

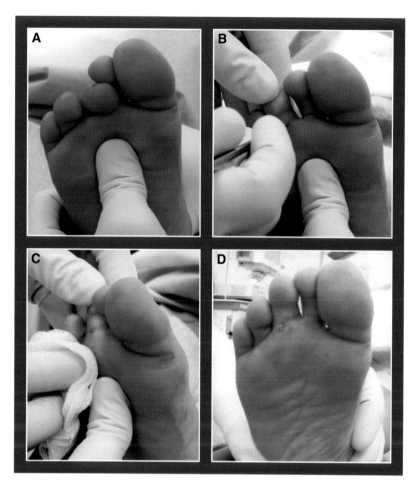

Figure 7-5. **A.** Four-year-old child with a severe, symptomatic curly 3rd toe. The assistant surgeon is dorsiflexing the ankle with a thumb under the MT heads to tension the FDL tendon. **B.** The surgeon dorsiflexes the toe. Using a #11 scalpel as both a probe and a cutting device, the FDL tendon is completely divided using short-arc sweeping motions after percutaneous insertion of the blade in the proximal plantar flexion crease of the toe. **C.** The release is dramatic as the toe suddenly extends. The tiny incision is seen. **D.** There is minimal (or no) bleeding if the scalpel is maintained in the midline of the toe. The associated varus and external rotation of the toe will gradually correct partially with time.

tissue contractures, insert a small gauge wire retrograde from the tip of the toe across the IP joints to the base of the proximal phalanx.

g. If the IP joints of the toe cannot be fully extended, a volar capsulotomy and pinning, or an arthrodesis, is indicated.

h. No wound closure is required (unless an open capsulotomy is performed).

i. Use a soft dressing with Coban extending above the ankle for a curly toe release. Remove the dressing in 1 week.

j. Use a soft dressing with an Ace bandage and an open-toed post-op shoe for mallet and hammer toes that do not require pinning.

  i. Return to clinic in 2 weeks for dressing removal and to initiate twice daily extension stretching exercises

k. Use a short-leg walking cast for mallet and hammer toes that require pinning

  i. Return to clinic in 4 to 6 weeks for cast and pin removal and to initiate twice daily extension stretching exercises

l. For toe flexor tenotomies performed as part of complex foot reconstruction surgery, immobilize based on the requirements of the other concurrently performed procedures

3. Pitfalls

a. Inserting the tip of the scalpel too rapidly and too deeply into the tendon so that it engages the tendon and cannot act as a probe to determine the position and limits of the tendon

4. Complications

a. Laceration of a digital nerve or artery

  i. *Avoid by* inserting the tip of the scalpel in the proximal plantar flexion crease centrally and carefully, using it both as a probe and a scalpel.

  ii. *Avoid* excessive medial and/or lateral excursion of the tip of the scalpel

Percutaneous Tendo-Achilles Tenotomy (TAT)

1. Indications

a. *Isolated* residual tendo-Achilles contracture in an infant with a clubfoot (**see Chapter 5**) treated by the Ponseti casting method

b. Applicable for a residual tendo-Achilles contracture in an infant with a congenital vertical talus (CVT; **see Chapter 5**) treated by the reverse Ponseti (Dobbs) casting method or the dorsal open reduction surgical technique (**see this chapter**)

  i. in combination with other procedures

c. A component of a limited, minimally invasive soft tissue release (**see this chapter**) for a severe, rigid, resistant arthrogrypotic clubfoot in an infant or young child (**see Chapter 5**)

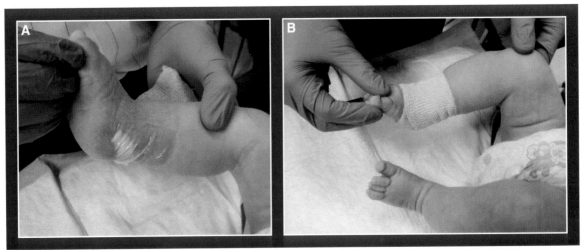

Figure 7-6. **A.** A small amount of lidocaine cream is placed over the intended site for the tenotomy and covered with a clear adhesive dressing. **B.** It is then covered with a loosely applied elastic bandage to prevent it from displacing during the 30 minutes it takes to penetrate the soft tissues.

  d. Upper age limit for tendo-Achilles tenotomy (TAT) is unknown, but it is at least age 2 years
2. <u>Technique</u> (Figures 7-6 to 7-10)
  a. In the *clinic*, for clubfoot
    i. Place a small amount of lidocaine cream over the hindfoot and ankle and cover with an occlusive dressing
    ii. Wipe off the cream after approximately 30 minutes.
    iii. Ask your assistant to hold the forefoot with one hand and the thigh with the other hand while positioning the foot and leg parallel with the procedure table
    iv. Prep the hindfoot and ankle with iodine prep solution
    v. Using a narrow Beaver scalpel, completely divide the tendo-Achilles 1 cm proximal to its insertion

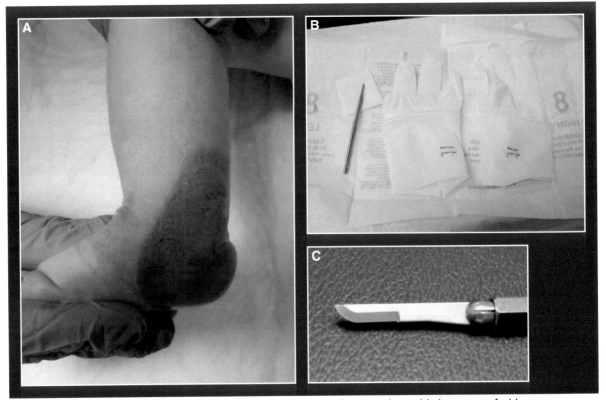

Figure 7-7. **A.** The foot and leg are all held parallel with the procedure table in a secure fashion by the surgical assistant. The hindfoot is prepped with iodine solution. **B.** Sterile gloves and scalpel are opened on a Mayo stand. **C.** A narrow scalpel is used. I prefer the shape shown in this image, rather than a pointed tip, because the former can be used as a probe to palpate the tendon and move around it without impaling it prematurely.

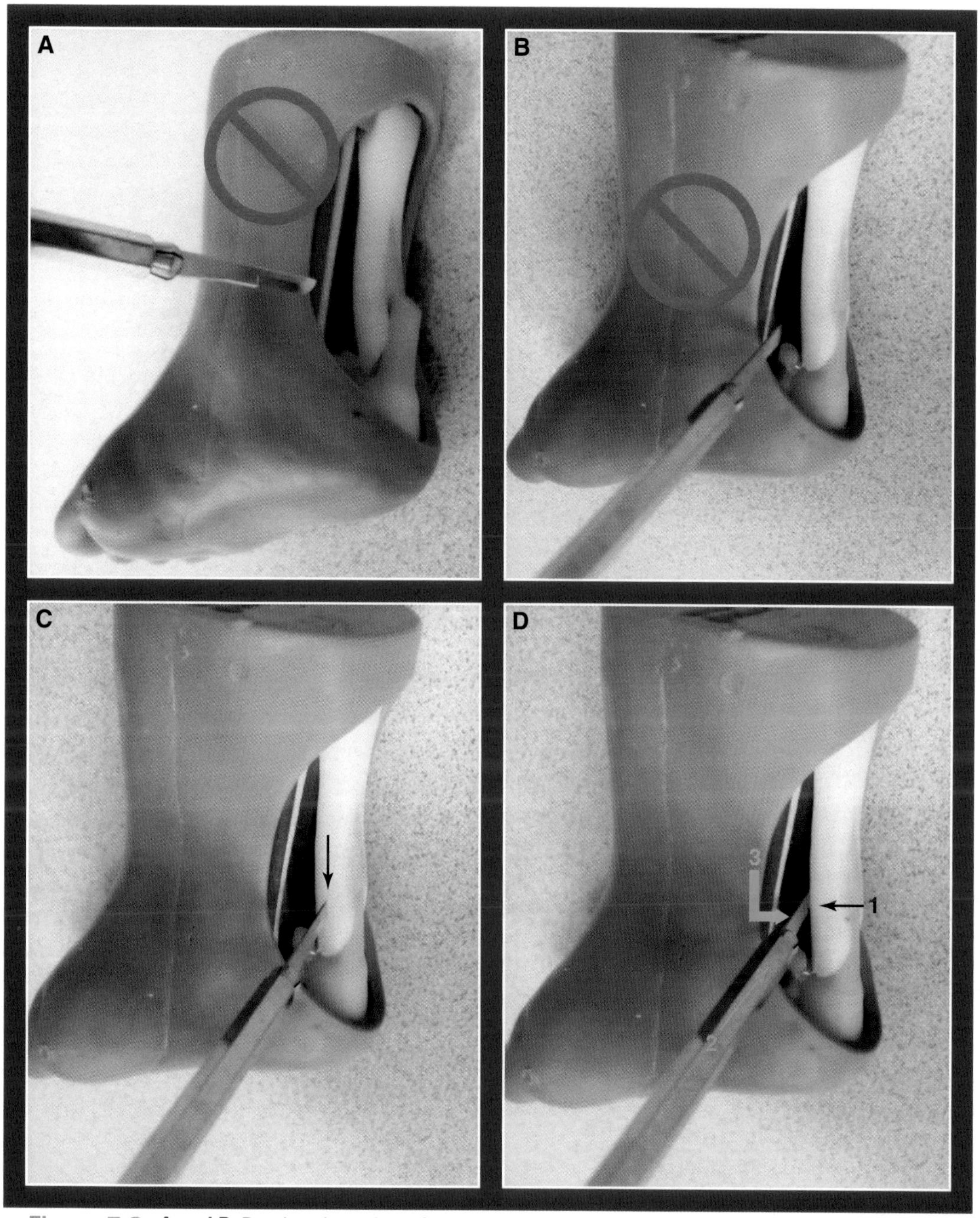

Figure 7-8. **A and B.** Random insertion of the scalpel on the medial side of the ankle can result in injury to the posterior tibial NV bundle. There are only a few millimeters of space between the NV bundle and the tendo-Achilles in infants and young children. **C.** To avoid injury to the NV bundle, insert the scalpel aimed directly at the medial side of the tendo-Achilles with the face of the blade parallel with the axis of the tendon and perpendicular to the long axis of the foot, i.e., in the coronal plane (*black arrow*). There can then only be skin and a little fat before the tip of the scalpel encounters the tendon. **D.** Once through the skin, use the scalpel as a probe to slowly translate anteriorly on the tendon (*black arrow 1*). When it reaches the anterior margin of the tendo-Achilles, slide it into the fat that is immediately anterior to the tendon (*green arrow 2*). Turn the scalpel 90° posteriorly and translate it in that direction (*blue angled arrow 3*) to cut the tendo-Achilles that is being held under dorsiflexion tension by the surgical assistant. Maintain control of the scalpel to avoid enlarging the skin incision (which should be no longer than the height of the blade).

on the calcaneus (and the deep posterior heel crease) from an anteromedial approach

vi. In order to avoid injury to the posterior tibial neurovascular (NV) structures, insert the scalpel through the skin directly medial to the tendo-Achilles and perpendicular to the foot in the coronal plane with the face of the blade parallel with the fibers of the tendo-Achilles

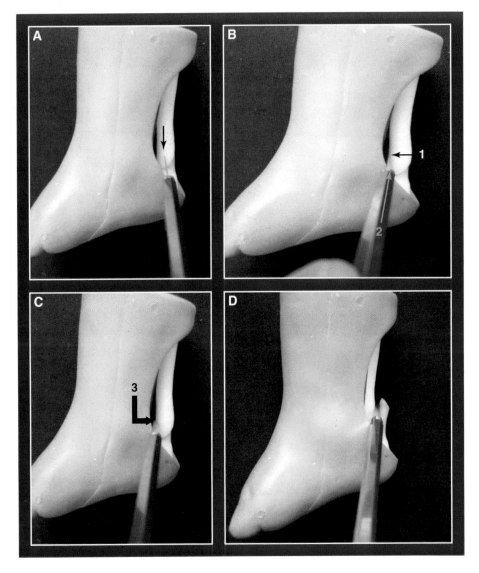

Figure 7-9. Different views of the technique shown in Figure 7-8. **See legend**.

vii. Using the tip of the scalpel as a probe, slowly advance it anteriorly until it falls into the fat immediately anterior to the tendon

viii. Rotate the scalpel blade 90° and translate it posteriorly to divide the tensioned tendo-Achilles

ix. The release will be experienced by the surgeon and the assistant (and often by observers).

x. Acceptable dorsiflexion is 15° to 20°.

xi. Inject a small volume of 1% lidocaine locally

xii. Apply a pressure dressing for several minutes before applying a long-leg clubfoot cast with the ankle dorsiflexed at least 10° and a 70° external thigh–foot angle

xiii. The children rarely require more than acetaminophen for pain control, though one to two doses of a liquid narcotic medication can be prescribed safely.

xiv. Have the child return to clinic in 3 weeks for cast removal and application of a foot abduction brace (FAB)

b. In the *OR* for clubfoot, merely eliminate the initial lidocaine cream step

c. In the *OR* for congenital vertical and oblique talus treated by the reverse Ponseti (Dobbs) casting method,

i. Eliminate the initial lidocaine cream step

ii. Perform a full sterile prep and draping of the lower extremity

iii. Perform a TAT as described

iv. Then make a 3-cm longitudinal incision medial to the talonavicular (TN) joint

v. Release the TN joint capsule medially for visual inspection and confirmation that the joint reduces anatomically with inversion of the subtalar joint

vi. Under direct vision and with mini-fluoroscopic guidance, insert a 0.062″ smooth Steinmann pin retrograde across the TN joint starting dorsal to the 1st MT

vii. Insert a second 0.062″ smooth Steinmann pin retrograde across the TN joint starting medially

viii. Cut the pins and bury the ends under the skin

ix. Use a 3-0 absorbable suture in the subcutaneous tissues and a running 4-0 subcuticular suture in the skin

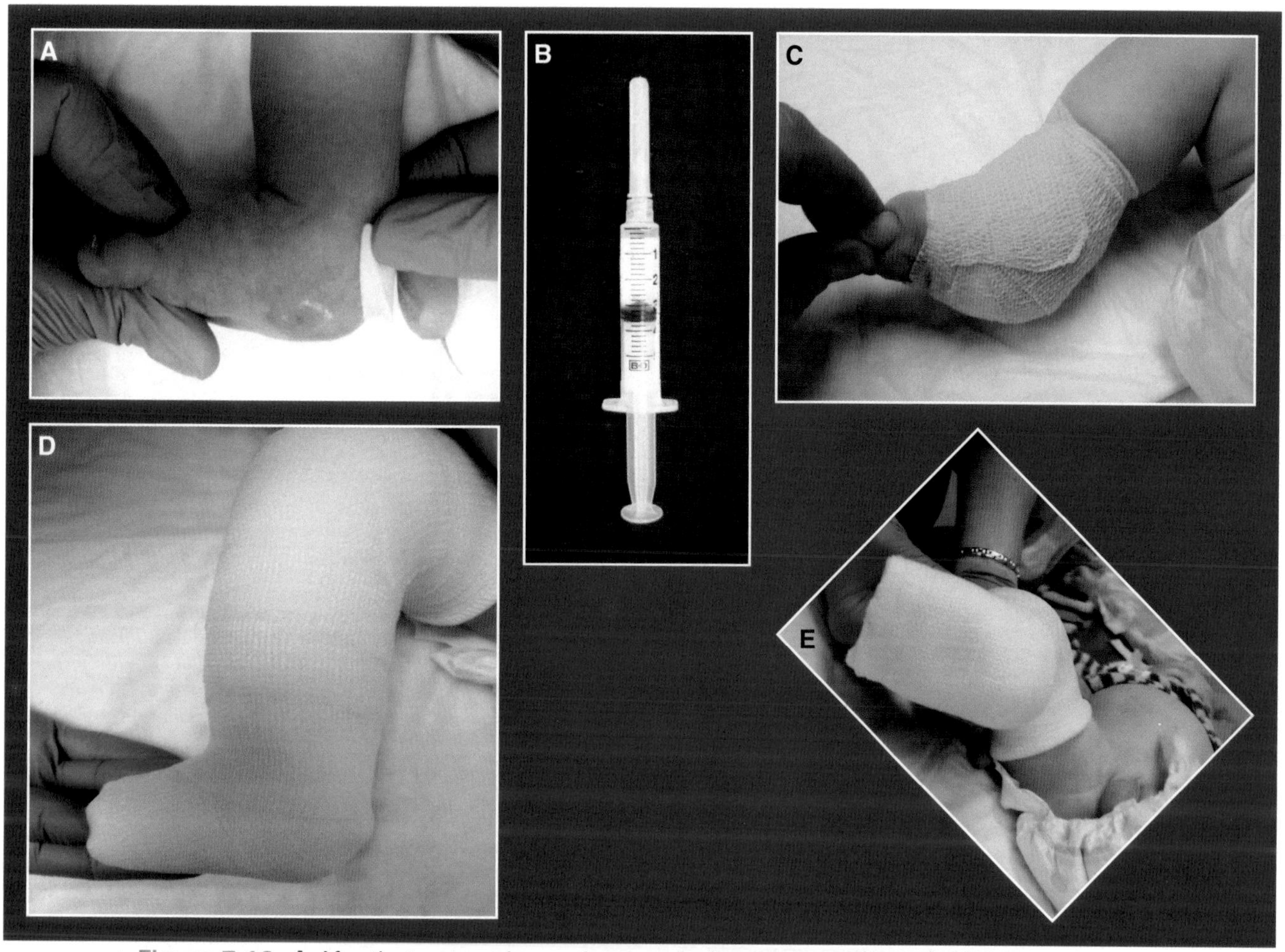

Figure 7-10. **A.** After the tenotomy is completed, apply direct pressure. There should be no more than a few drops of capillary bleeding, and there should be excellent perfusion of the foot and toes. **B.** Inject a small amount of lidocaine at the site. I prefer not to inject before the tenotomy, because the infusion will dilate the soft tissues, making it difficult to palpate the tendo-Achilles. **C.** Loosely wrap the ankle with a sterile gauze pad, cast padding, and an elastic wrap. Maintain the wrap for several minutes while the lidocaine takes effect. **D** and **E.** Apply a long-leg clubfoot cast with the ankle dorsi-flexed 10° and a thigh–foot angle of 70° external.

    x. Apply adhesive strips, a gauze dressing, and a long-leg cast with inversion molding of the subtalar joint, neutral to 5° of dorsiflexion at the ankle, and a 0° thigh–foot angle

    xi. Return to clinic in 2 weeks for a long-leg cast change, this time with inversion molding of the subtalar joint, 10° to 15° of ankle dorsiflexion, and a 0° thigh–foot angle

    xii. Return to clinic in 3 weeks for another long-leg cast change—same foot and ankle position as the last cast change

    xiii. Return to clinic in 3 weeks for the final long-leg cast change—same foot and ankle position as the last two cast changes

    xiv. Return to the OR in 1 to 2 weeks for pin removal and to initiate FAB wear with *parallel* shoes

3. Pitfalls

    a. Incomplete tenotomy

      i. This occurs infrequently with the described technique, but should be addressed by reinserting the scalpel to

release residual uncut tendon fibers using the same steps used initially. Incomplete tenotomy occurs perhaps more frequently if the scalpel is inserted directly from posterior to anterior in the sagittal plane in line with the axis of the foot. The tendo-Achilles is quite wide as it approaches its calcaneal insertion, making complete tenotomy difficult with this approach. The tendon is much thinner from anterior to posterior at that level, so it is easier to release it completely using the technique described earlier. Additionally, it is challenging to know how deep to insert the scalpel when using a direct posterior-to-anterior technique. This uncertainty puts the posterior tibial NV bundle at risk, particularly when the tendon is closer than average to the NV bundle and when there is more than normal subcutaneous fat in the area (Figures 7-11 and 7-12).

    b. Unanticipated posterior ankle joint contracture

      i. In an older child, the posterior ankle joint capsule may have become contracted, thereby limiting dorsiflexion following a TAT. If inadequate dorsiflexion is

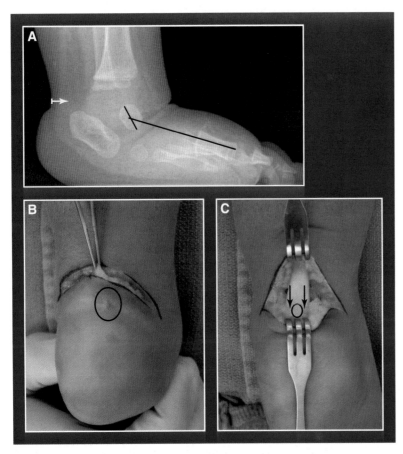

Figure 7-11. **A.** Lateral x-ray of a left clubfoot in a 7-month-old boy who underwent attempted percutaneous Achilles tenotomy from a direct posterior to anterior sagittal approach at age 3 months (*yellow arrow*). The incomplete tenotomy was unrecognized, and he was placed in an FAB, which he wore 23 hours per day for several months. A severe and rigid rocker-bottom deformity resulted from the abnormally applied pressures. A series of plantar flexion (CVT-type) casts were applied. The forefoot became aligned with the hindfoot, but the ankle could not be dorsiflexed. **B.** Photo of the scar from the previous percutaneous midline TAT incision (*black circle*) obtained at the time of an open TAL and posterior capsulotomy. **C.** There was scar tissue in the center of the tendo-Achilles (*small black circle*), but the medial and lateral margins of the tendon had never been cut (*black arrows*). Another potential pitfall/complication that could have occurred in this case was division of the calcaneal apophysis, due to the distal position of the tenotomy in the posterior heel crease. The tendon should be cut at least 1 cm proximal to the posterior heel crease.

achieved after the TAT, consider further serial casting. It is not reasonable to proceed with an open posterior ankle capsulotomy immediately after a TAT. The local environment is favorable for scar tissue to create a new, "normal" tendo-Achilles segment to fill the gap following a *percutaneous* TAT in an infant or very

young child. But the local environment is disrupted by an open exposure and release of the posterior ankle capsule. The tendo-Achilles cannot repair itself in the same way. If the possibility of a capsular contracture is anticipated in an older child, perform an open tendo-Achilles Z-lengthening (**see this chapter**) through a

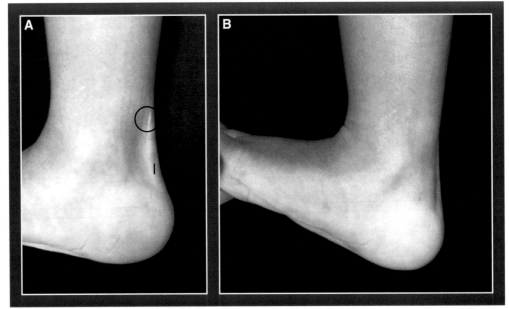

Figure 7-12. **A.** Two-and-a-half-year follow-up of a well-executed coronal plane percutaneous TAT that was performed at age 3 months. The black line represents the original size and location of the tenotomy incision. It is normal for the scar to migrate proximally. Note its present location (*within the black circle*). **B.** Excellent dorsiflexion is appreciated.

short segment Cincinnati incision. Proceed with the capsulotomy, if necessary, followed by repair of the tendon at the appropriate tension. If a capsulotomy is not deemed necessary, merely repair the Z-lengthened tendo-Achilles at the appropriate tension.

4. Complications
   a. Nerve injury
      i. *Avoid by* following the technique exactly as described earlier
   b. Vascular injury
      i. *Avoid by* following the technique exactly as described earlier
   c. Laceration of cartilaginous calcaneal apophysis
      i. *Avoid by* following the technique exactly as described earlier, inserting the scalpel at least 1 cm above the posterior heel crease

Tendo-Achilles Lengthening (TAL)

1. Indications
   a. Contracture of the entire triceps surae/tendo-Achilles (**see Chapter 5**), as determined by the Silfverskiold test (**see Assessment Principle #12 and Figure 3-13, Chapter 3**), that is creating pain, functional disability, and/or gait disturbance
      i. The ankle joint cannot be dorsiflexed at least 10° with the subtalar joint locked in neutral alignment (**see**

Basic Principle #7, Chapter 2) and the knee flexed 90° (with an even greater lack of ankle dorsiflexion with the knee extended) (**see Assessment Principle #12 and Figure 3-13, Chapter 3**)

2. Technique
   a. There are several ways to lengthen the tendo-Achilles and each has its advantages and disadvantages. Some are performed open or semi-open (for more control) and others percutaneously. Some consider and take advantage of the 90° of internal rotation of the tendo-Achilles fibers that takes place in the distal 6 to 8 cm of the tendon, whereas others disregard the rotation of the tendon fibers.

   b. **Percutaneous Triple-Cut Tendo-Achilles Lengthening (TAL), a.k.a. Hoke Procedure** (Figure 7-13)
      i. The advantages of this technique are speed and cosmesis.
      ii. The disadvantage/risk with this technique is that a complete tenotomy can be inadvertently created; therefore, use it:
         • with a thick tendo-Achilles (easier to feel the edges), and
         • when the ankle can be dorsiflexed to approximately neutral (90°) with the knee flexed. Using this technique to correct greater degrees of

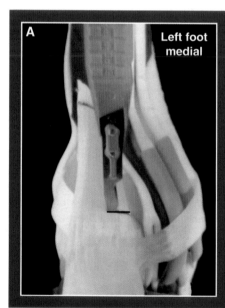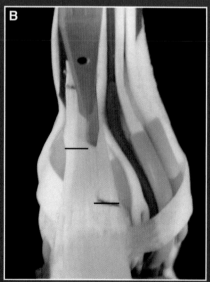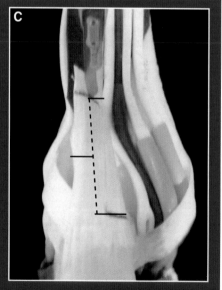

Figure 7-13. Triple cut TAL. **A.** Insert a #15 scalpel through the skin from posterior to anterior (*in the sagittal plane*) just proximal to the calcaneus with the face of the blade parallel with the direction of the tendon fibers. Then use it as a probe to identify the sagittal midline of the tendon. Rotate it 90° and translate it medially (for a varus hindfoot deformity) or laterally (for a valgus hindfoot deformity) to cut the desired half of the tendon's fibers. Avoid making the percutaneous incision any larger than is required for the scalpel to pass through the skin. **B.** Reinsert the scalpel in the same manner approximately 10 to 15 mm more proximally (depending on the length of the tendon), rotate it 90° in the opposite direction, and translate it until the opposite half of the tendon is released (ignoring the anatomic rotation of the fibers). **C.** Reinsert the scalpel in the same manner approximately 10 to 15 mm more proximally (depending on the length of the tendon), rotate it 90° in the direction of the first cut, and translate it until the same half of the tendon is released as was released with the first cut. Dorsiflex the ankle with the knee extended until a noticeable, and often dramatic, release is appreciated. Check the Thompson test to ensure that continuity of the musculotendinous unit persists.

contracture risks the loss of contact between the tendon segments, i.e., a complete tenotomy.

iii. This technique *disregards* the 90° rotation of the tendon fibers that takes place as they approach their insertion on the calcaneus.

iv. Use a standard lower limb prep and drape

v. Ask your assistant to hold the forefoot with one hand and the leg with the other hand while positioning the foot and leg parallel with the OR table

vi. Place your nondominant thumb and index finger on either side of the tendo-Achilles immediately proximal to its insertion on the calcaneus

vii. Insert a #15 scalpel through the skin from posterior to anterior in the midsagittal plane with the face of the blade in line with the direction of the tendon fibers just proximal to the calcaneus

viii. Use the scalpel as a probe to find the sagittal midline of the tendon by dragging the skin medial and lateral until the midpoint is determined

ix. Insert the scalpel through the tendon in the sagittal midline to the presumed thickness of the tendon (at least 1 cm), turn it 90° (medially for a varus hindfoot and laterally for a valgus hindfoot), and cut the fibers by translating the blade in the desired direction. The skin incision should not enlarge

x. Remove the scalpel and reinsert it 10 to 15 mm more proximally finding the sagittal midline in the same way

xi. This time, cut the opposite half of the tendon

xii. Remove the scalpel and reinsert it 10 to 15 mm more proximally finding the sagittal midline in the same way

xiii. This time, cut the same half of the tendon that was cut distally

xiv. With the knee extended and the subtalar joint in neutral alignment, dorsiflex the ankle to approximately 10°. There should be a sudden release of tension to allow the ankle to dorsiflex, but also a sense of resistance to excessive dorsiflexion
  • Perform the Thompson test, by squeezing the calf musculature and watching the ankle plantar flex, to confirm maintenance of musculotendinous continuity

xv. If the ankle does not dorsiflex, palpate each incisional site to determine which one(s) requires reinsertion of the scalpel to release additional fibers
  • Perform the Thompson test again

xvi. Apply adhesive strips, a gauze dressing, and a short-leg walking cast with the ankle dorsiflexed no more than 10°

xvii. Remove the cast at 6 weeks and prescribe daily strengthening and stretching exercises to be performed indefinitely

xviii. If both tendo-Achilless are lengthened, consider providing CAM boots to help with mobility during the time it takes to get strong and stable on both legs

c. ***Open Double Cut Slide TAL*** (Figure 7-14)

i. The advantage of this technique is that there is little risk for overlengthening or complete tenotomy

ii. The disadvantages/risks with this technique are:
  • With extensive lengthenings, it may be hard to identify the opposite fibers. Release of additional fibers, even under direct vision, could inadvertently result in complete tenotomy.
  • This technique requires an incision that is larger and, therefore, less cosmetic than the incisions used for the mini-open double cut slide TAL and the percutaneous triple-cut technique.

iii. This technique *considers* and takes advantage of the 90° of internal rotation of the tendon fibers that takes place as they approach their insertion on the calcaneus (Figures 7-15 and 7-16).

iv. Use a standard lower limb prep and drape with the patient in the supine position

v. Make a 5- to 7-cm longitudinal incision anteromedial to the tendo-Achilles in the concavity between the tendo-Achilles and the posterior edge of the tibia. *Never* make the incision directly posterior where the shoe counter will later rub and cause irritation. Directly posterior incisions also tend to be uncosmetic, as they often heal thick and wide (Figure 7-17).

vi. Incise the anteromedial aspect of the tendon sheath from proximal to distal

vii. Avoid disruption of the posterior tendon sheath and subcutaneous fat. By so doing, there will be less adherence of the tendon to the skin.

viii. Divide the plantaris tendon distally—if an inadvertent tenotomy occurs, the plantaris can be used as an intercalary graft

ix. Insert a #15 scalpel into the tendon from posterior to anterior with the face of the blade in line with the direction of the tendon fibers and in the sagittal midline of the tendon immediately proximal to the insertion on the calcaneus

x. Insert the scalpel through the tendon to the presumed thickness of the tendon (at least 1 cm), turn it 90° medially, and cut the *medial* half of the fibers by translating the blade in that direction

xi. Insert a #15 scalpel into the tendon from medial to lateral with the face of the blade in line with the direction of the tendon fibers and in the midcoronal plane of the tendon approximately 4 to 6 cm more proximal than the first cut

xii. Insert the scalpel through the tendon, turn it 90° posteriorly, and cut the *posterior* half of the fibers by translating the blade in that direction

xiii. With the knee extended and the subtalar joint in neutral alignment, dorsiflex the ankle to approximately 10°. There should be a sudden release of tension to allow the ankle to dorsiflex, and also a sense of resistance to excessive dorsiflexion. The overlapping

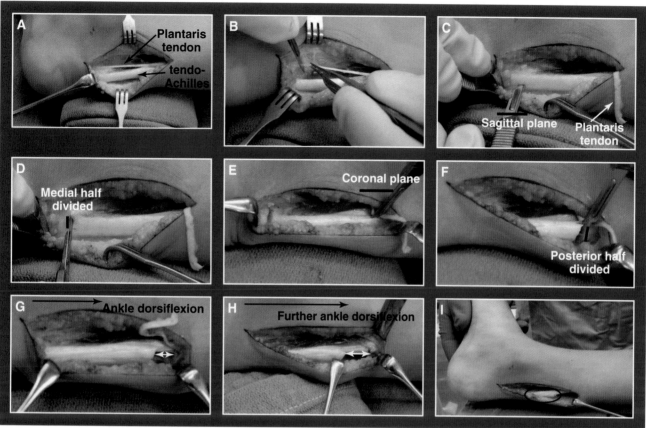

Figure 7-14. Open double cut slide TAL. **A.** Wide exposure of Achilles and plantaris tendons through a posteromedial incision. **B.** Distal release of plantaris tendon. **C.** Scalpel is inserted distally in the midsagittal plane of the tendo-Achilles. **D.** The scalpel is rotated 90° medially and translated until the hemitendon is released. **E.** Scalpel inserted proximally in the midcoronal plane of the tendon. **F.** The scalpel is rotated 90° posteriorly and translated until the hemitendon is released. **G.** As the ankle is dorsiflexed, the tendon halves begin to slide past each other. **H.** Even further dorsiflexion of the ankle results in further longitudinal translation of the tendon halves relative to each other. **I.** Ten degrees of ankle dorsiflexion with the knee extended should be sought—not less and not much more. Ensure that there is enough distance between the proximal and distal cuts that the tendon halves will maintain some side-to-side contact at the final lengthened position. Though not intuitive, translation/ lengthening of even 3 to 4 cm can take place without loss of "stable" side-to-side contact between the tendon halves (*black oval*). Reinforcing sutures can be used, but are often unnecessary.

halves of the tendon should maintain side-to-side contact even with lengthenings of 3 to 4 cm or more. Reinforcing sutures are rarely required.
- Perform the Thompson test, by squeezing the calf musculature and watching the ankle plantar flex, to confirm maintenance of musculotendinous continuity

xiv. If the ankle does not dorsiflex, carefully release only the fibers that appear to be resisting deformity correction
- Perform the Thompson test again

xv. Use a 3-0 absorbable suture in the subcutaneous tissues and a running 4-0 subcuticular suture in the skin of the proximal incision. Apply adhesive strips, a gauze dressing, and a short-leg walking cast with the ankle dorsiflexed no more than 10°

xvi. Remove the cast at 6 weeks and prescribe daily strengthening and stretching exercises to be performed indefinitely

xvii. If both tendo-Achilless are lengthened, consider providing CAM boots to help with mobility during the time it takes to get strong and stable on both legs

d. **Mini-Open Double Cut Slide TAL** (Figure 7-18)

i. The advantages of this technique are:
- There is little risk for overlengthening or complete tenotomy.
- The incisions are smaller and, therefore, more cosmetic than the incision used for the open double cut slide TAL.

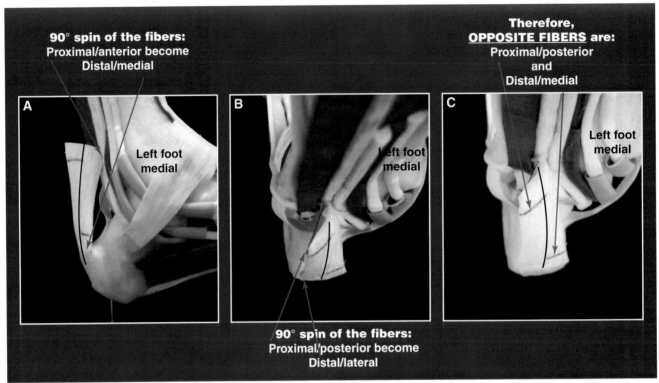

Figure 7-15. **A.** The tendo-Achilles fibers internally rotate 90° in their terminal few inches as they approach their insertion on the calcaneus. In this lateral view of a left foot model, it can be appreciated that the proximal/anterior tendon fibers become distal/medial at the calcaneus. **B.** The proximal/posterior fibers become distal/lateral at their insertion. **C.** Therefore, the opposite fibers are the posterior ones proximally and the medial fibers distally.

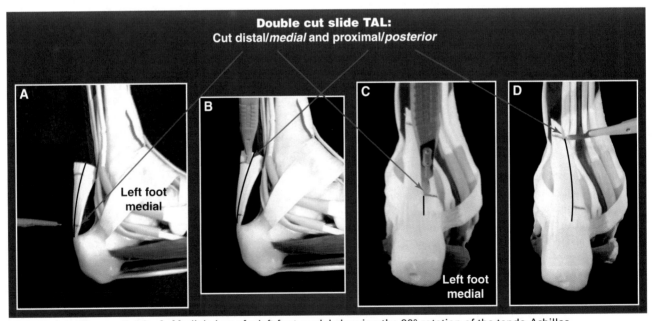

Figure 7-16. **A.** Medial view of a left foot model showing the 90° rotation of the tendo-Achilles. The medial half of the tendon is cut distally. **B.** The posterior half of tendon, which contains the opposite half of the fibers, is cut proximally. **C.** Posterior view of the foot model showing the medial half of the tendo-Achilles being cut distally. **D.** The posterior half of the tendon is cut proximally.

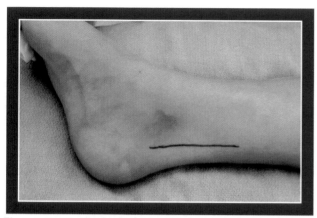

Figure 7-17. The incision for an open tendo-Achilles lengthening should be along the posteromedial aspect of the ankle. Avoid directly posterior incisions.

ii. The disadvantages/risks with this technique are:
- With extensive lengthenings, it may be hard to identify the opposite fibers. Release of additional fibers, even under direct vision, could inadvertently result in complete tenotomy.
- The incisions are larger than those used for the percutaneous triple-cut technique.

iii. This technique *considers* and takes advantage of the 90° of internal rotation of the tendon fibers that takes place as they approach their insertion on the calcaneus (Figures 7-15 and 7-16).

iv. Use a standard lower limb prep and drape with the patient in the supine position

v. This procedure is *identical* to the open double cut slide, *except* that it is performed through a percutaneous distal incision and a short proximal incision (that is the upper portion of the incision used for the open technique).

vi. Place your nondominant thumb and index finger on either side of the tendo-Achilles immediately proximal to its insertion on the calcaneus

vii. Insert a #15 scalpel through the skin from posterior to anterior in the midsagittal plane with the face of the blade in line with the direction of the tendon fibers just proximal to the calcaneus

viii. Use the scalpel as a probe to find the sagittal midline of the tendon by dragging the skin medial and lateral until the midpoint is determined

ix. Insert the scalpel through the tendon to the presumed thickness of the tendon (at least 1 cm), turn it 90° medially, and cut the *medial* half of the fibers by translating the blade in that direction

x. Make a 1.5- to 2.0-cm longitudinal incision slightly anteromedial to the tendo-Achilles starting at least 5 cm proximal to the distal cut

xi. Under direct vision, release the plantaris tendon and open the tendo-Achilles sheath

xii. Insert a #15 scalpel into the tendon from medial to lateral with the face of the blade in line with the direction of the tendon fibers and in the midcoronal plane of the tendon approximately 4 to 6 cm more proximal than the first cut

xiii. Insert the scalpel through the tendon, turn it 90° posteriorly, and cut the *posterior* half of the fibers by translating the blade in that direction

xiv. With the knee extended and the subtalar joint in neutral alignment, dorsiflex the ankle to approximately 10°. There should be a sudden release of tension to allow the ankle to dorsiflex, and also a sense of resistance to excessive dorsiflexion. The overlapping halves of the tendon should maintain side-to-side contact even with lengthenings of 3 to 4 cm or more. Reinforcing sutures are rarely required.
- Perform the Thompson test, by squeezing the calf musculature and watching the ankle plantar flex, to confirm maintenance of musculotendinous continuity

xv. If the ankle does not dorsiflex, carefully release only the fibers that appear to be resisting deformity correction
- Perform the Thomson test again

xvi. Use a 3-0 absorbable suture in the subcutaneous tissues and a running 4-0 subcuticular suture in the skin of the proximal incision. Apply adhesive strips, a gauze dressing, and a short-leg walking cast with the ankle dorsiflexed no more than 10°

xvii. Remove the cast at 6 weeks and prescribe daily strengthening and stretching exercises to be performed indefinitely

xviii. If both the tendo-Achilless are lengthened, consider providing CAM boots to help with mobility during the time it takes to get strong and stable on both legs.

e. **Open Z-lengthening TAL** (Figure 7-19)

i. The advantage of this technique is its ability to correct the most severe contractures that require the greatest amount of lengthening without risk of running out of tendon ends to overlap, as long as adequate length is considered at the time of release.

ii. The disadvantages/risks with this technique are:
- Overlengthening
- This technique requires an incision that is larger and, therefore, less cosmetic than the incisions used for the mini-open double cut slide TAL and the percutaneous triple-cut technique.

iii. This technique *disregards* the 90° rotation of the tendon fibers that takes place as they approach their insertion on the calcaneus.

iv. Make a 5- to 7-cm longitudinal incision anteromedial to the tendo-Achilles in the concavity between

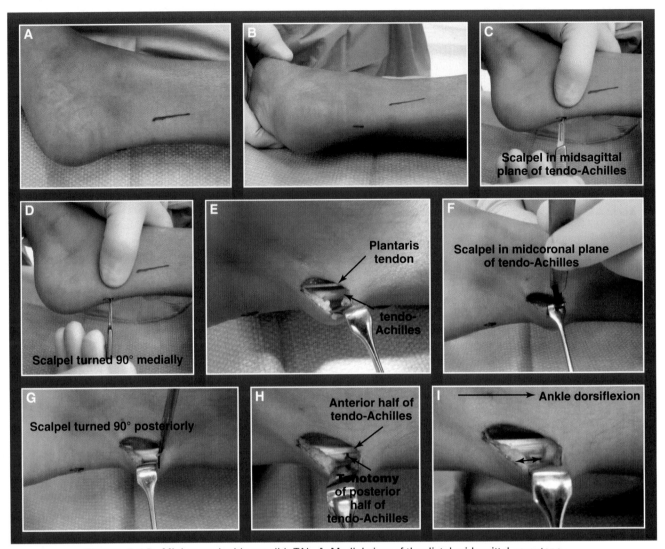

Figure 7-18. Mini-open double cut slide TAL. **A.** Medial view of the distal midsagittal percutaneous incision and the proximal mini-posteromedial incision marked on the skin. **B.** Posterior view. **C.** Scalpel is inserted percutaneously distally in the midsagittal plane of the tendo-Achilles. **D.** The scalpel is rotated 90° medially and translated until the hemitendon is released. **E.** The plantaris and tendo-Achilless are exposed through a short posteromedial incision, which is the upper portion of the long incision used for an open tendo-Achilles lengthening (Figure 7-17). The plantaris is divided (not shown). **F.** The scalpel is inserted in the midcoronal plane of the tendon with the blade parallel with the tendon fibers (*black line*). **G.** The scalpel is rotated 90° posteriorly and translated until the hemitendon is released. **H.** Tenotomy of the posterior half of the tendon fibers is evident. **I.** As the ankle is dorsiflexed, the ends of the divided posterior half of the tendon begin to separate from each other (*double-ended arrow*). Ten degrees of ankle dorsiflexion with the knee extended should be sought— not less and not much more. Ensure that there is enough distance between the proximal and distal cuts that the tendon halves will maintain some side-to-side contact at the final lengthened position. Though not intuitive, translation/lengthening of even 3 to 4 cm can take place without loss of "stable" side-to-side contact between the tendon halves. If reinforcing sutures are deemed necessary, the posteromedial incision should be extended distally for visualization.

tendo-Achilles and the posterior edge of the tibia. *Never* make the incision directly posterior where the shoe counter will later rub and cause irritation. Directly posterior incisions also tend to be uncosmetic, as they often heal thick and wide (Figure 7-17).

v. Incise the anteromedial aspect of the tendon sheath from proximal to distal (Figure 7-16)

vi. Avoid disruption of the posterior tendon sheath and subcutaneous fat. By so doing, there will be less adherence of the tendon to the skin.

vii. Divide the plantaris tendon distally—if an inadvertent tenotomy occurs, the plantaris can be used as an intercalary graft

viii. Split the tendo-Achilles longitudinally in the sagittal plane

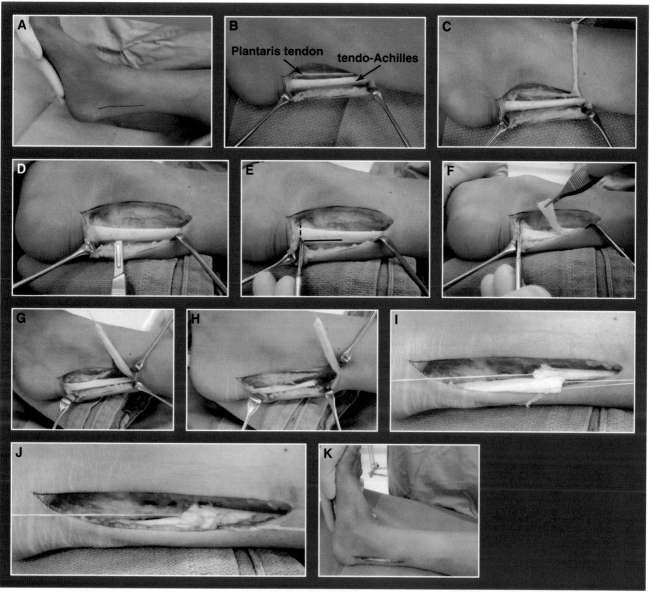

Figure 7-19. Open Z-lengthening TAL. **A.** Severe tendo-Achilles contracture with inability to dorsiflex the ankle. The planned posteromedial incision site is marked. **B.** The Achilles and plantaris tendons are exposed. **C.** The plantaris tendon is released distally and reflected away. **D.** The scalpel is inserted into the tendo-Achilles in the midsagittal plane proximal to its insertion on the calcaneus. Midcoronal plane lengthening is also possible. **E.** The scalpel is advanced distally to the insertion site on the calcaneus and turned 90° medially. **F.** The medial half of the tendon fibers are released from the calcaneus and the free end is elevated. **G.** The tendon division is continued proximally. **H.** The lateral half of the tendon is divided approximately 5 to 6 cm. proximal to the distal cut. **I.** With the ankle dorsiflexed 10° and the knee extended, the lead sutures are pulled in opposite directions to create moderate tension on the overlapping halves of the tendon. **J.** Figure-of-8 2-0 absorbable sutures are used for the repair. **K.** Final position of 5° to 10° of dorsiflexion.

ix. For a varus hindfoot, release the medial half of the fibers distally and the lateral half proximally—this will shift the vector of pull on the calcaneus laterally

x. For a valgus hindfoot, release the lateral half of the fibers distally and the medial half proximally—this will shift the vector of pull on the calcaneus medially

xi. Place tagging sutures in both tendon ends

xii. Extend the knee, dorsiflex the ankle to 10°, and repair the overlapping ends of the tendon under moderate tension with 2-0 absorbable sutures

xiii. Use a 3-0 absorbable suture in the subcutaneous tissues and a running 4-0 subcuticular suture in the skin of the proximal incision. Apply adhesive strips, a gauze dressing, and a short-leg walking cast with the ankle dorsiflexed no more than 10°

   xiv. Remove the cast at 6 weeks and prescribe daily strengthening and stretching exercises to be performed indefinitely

   xv. If both the tendo-Achilless are lengthened, consider providing CAM boots to help with mobility during the time it takes to get strong and stable on both legs

3. Pitfalls for *all* Achilles lengthening techniques
   a. Underlengthening
   b. Overlengthening
   c. Failure to appreciate the rotation of tendon fibers in the double cut techniques, resulting in complete tenotomy after additional fibers are cut

4. Complications for *all* Achilles lengthening techniques
   a. Complete tenotomy, rather than a lengthening, due to:
     i. Inadequate distance between cuts in both the open and percutaneous techniques
      • *Avoid by* becoming expert at the open Z-lengthening technique and then the open double cut slide technique before attempting the other techniques
     ii. Excessive release of fibers in the percutaneous technique
      • *Avoid by* practicing the technique open, and then by using it only with thick tendo-Achilless in older children and adolescents

III. TENDON TRANSFERS

PRINCIPLE: Transfer the right tendon to the right location at the right tension (**see Management Principle #22-1, Chapter 4**).

Anchoring techniques—it is not known if a tendon can reliably anchor/heal into a cartilage anlage of a bone. The reliable anchoring techniques are:
1. Pulvertaft weave into another tendon
2. Drill hole in a bone with lead sutures tied over a button and felt pad on the plantar aspect of the foot
   a. Commercial tendon anchor (rarely indicated in children)

Jones Transfer of Extensor Hallucis Longus to 1st MT Neck

1. Indications
   a. Claw deformity of the hallux (**see Chapter 5**) that causes pain and skin irritation over the dorsum of the IP joint and/or under the 1st MT head
     i. usually associated with a cavovarus foot deformity, as in CMT or other neuromuscular disorder (**see Cavovarus Foot, Chapter 5**)
   b. Can be performed as an isolated procedure, but is most often performed during the second stage of a two-stage reconstruction for cavovarus deformity with clawing of the hallux
   c. Combine with percutaneous tenotomy of the FHL (**see this chapter**)

2. Technique (Figure 7-20)
   a. If this is an isolated procedure, perform a percutaneous tenotomy of the FHL (**see this chapter**)
   b. If this procedure is being performed in conjunction with other procedures during the second-stage reconstruction of a cavovarus foot, the FHL was already released in stage 1.

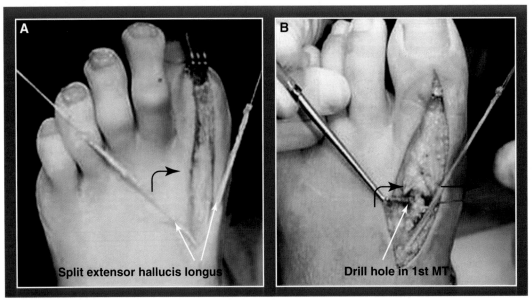

Figure 7-20. Jones transfer. **A.** Extensor hallucis longus is released from the hallux asymmetrically. **B.** The long lateral slip is passed transversely through a drill hole in the distal metaphysis of the 1st MT. **C.** The transferred EHL slip is brought back firmly into the split in the tendon and sutured securely. Ensure that the FHL has been released.

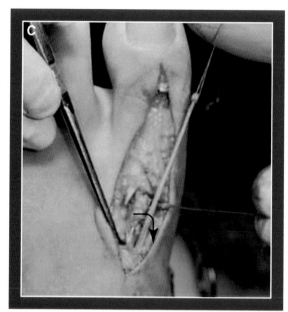

Figure 7-20. *(Continued)*

c. Make a longitudinal incision dorsal to the extensor halluces longus (EHL) starting just distal to the hallux IP joint and extending proximally to the base of the 1st MT

d. Release the EHL from its tendon sheath and release all soft tissue attachments to it

e. Split the EHL longitudinally

f. Release the lateral half of the tendon from its insertion on the distal phalanx and insert a Bunnell-type 2-0 absorbable suture in its end

g. Divide the medial half of the tendon immediately proximal to the metatarsophalangeal (MTP) joint and insert a tagging 2-0 absorbable suture in both ends

h. Make a transverse tunnel in the 1st MT neck with a small-diameter power drill

i. Pass the long lateral half of the EHL through the tunnel from lateral to medial

j. Complete all other bone and soft tissue procedures. Importantly, complete the medial cuneiform plantar-based opening wedge osteotomy. Setting the tension on this transfer should be the *last* procedure performed (or second to last if a SPLATT [**see this chapter**] is being performed concurrently) before final wound closure and cast application (**see Management Principle #24, Chapter 4**).

k. With the foot and ankle in anatomic alignment, pull the lateral half of the EHL through the tunnel in the 1st MT and *firmly* back upon itself

l. Position the transferred half of the EHL in the proximal extent of the split in the EHL and suture the 3 half tendons together with 2-0 absorbable sutures. This effectively simulates a Pulvertaft weave.

m. Pass the long medial distally-based slip of the EHL through a transverse slit in the extensor hallucis brevis/dorsal capsule of the MTP joint. Pull the tendon firmly back upon itself, thereby extending the IP and MTP joints, and suture the afferent and efferent limbs to each other with 2-0 absorbable sutures. This creates an extension tenodesis (Figure 7-21).

n. The alternative is a hallux IP joint arthrodesis (**see Chapter 8**), which is not indicated in children with open growth plates. The described tenodesis works very well in most cases.

o. Approximate the skin edges with interrupted subcutaneous 3-0 absorbable sutures and a running subcuticular 4-0 absorbable suture

p. Apply a short-leg non–weight-bearing cast

q. Change to a short-leg walking cast after 6 weeks and maintain it until 8 weeks postoperatively

3. Pitfalls

a. Insufficient tension on the distal tenodesis of the EHL to the extensor hallucis brevis to create an extension tenodesis

b. Insufficient tension on the transfer of the EHL to the 1st MT

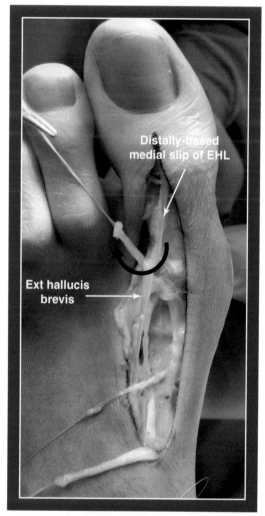

Figure 7-21. EHL tenodesis. The long medial distally-based slip of the asymmetrically cut split EHL is passed transversely through a slit in the extensor hallucis brevis/dorsal capsule of the MTP joint. It is pulled back firmly to extend the IP joint and then sutured securely to itself to create a tenodesis.

c. Failure to release the FHL

d. Failure to release the volar capsule of the IP joint and longitudinally pin across the joint if it does not fully extend following FHL tenotomy

e. Assuming that the EHL transfer will correct forefoot pronation deformity. It will not. A medial cuneiform osteotomy is needed to correct the deformity, whereas the EHL transfer will help prevent recurrent deformity by supplementing the weak anterior tibialis (**see Management Principles #5, 6, 15, 22-2, Chapter 4**).

4. Complications

a. Drop toe due to insufficient tension, rupture, or stretching out of the tenodesis

i. *Avoid by*
   - setting exaggerated tension initially
   - cautioning against barefoot walking

Reverse Jones Transfer of FHL to 1st MT Neck

1. Indications

a. Dorsal bunion (**see Chapter 5**)

i. Often combined with transfer of the anterior tibialis to the middle (2nd) cuneiform (**see this chapter**) and a medial cuneiform plantar flexion osteotomy (**see Chapter 8**)

2. Technique (Figure 7-22)

a. Make a longitudinal incision along the medial border of the forefoot from the 1st MTP joint to the base of the 1st MT

b. Perform an intramuscular recession of the tendon of the abductor hallucis

c. Retract the abductor hallucis plantarward

d. Isolate and release the FHL tendon sheath under the 1st MT from the distal phalanx to the base of the 1st MT. Hyperflex the IP and MTP joints to aid with exposure of the FHL insertion on the distal phalanx

e. Release the FHL from the distal phalanx and split it longitudinally

f. Insert a Bunnell-type 2-0 absorbable suture in the end of one slip of the FHL, leaving long tails on both limbs of the suture; and insert a tagging 2-0 absorbable suture in the other slip

g. If it is not possible to easily dorsiflex the MTP joint past neutral, release the plantar capsule sharply from medial to lateral

h. Make a vertical tunnel in the 1st MT neck with a drill bit a little larger than the thickness of the split half of the FHL

i. Pass the FHL slip with the Bunnell suture through the tunnel from plantar to dorsal

j. Importantly, complete the medial cuneiform plantar flexion osteotomy before setting the tension on the transfer. Setting the tension on this transfer should be the *second* to last procedure performed before final wound closure and cast application. The last procedure should be setting the tension on the anterior tibialis tendon transfer to the middle (2nd) cuneiform (**see Management Principle #24, Chapter 4**).

k. With the foot and ankle in anatomic alignment, pull the transferred slip of the FHL (that was passed through the tunnel in the 1st MT) *firmly* back upon itself

l. Position the transferred slip in the proximal extent of the split in the FHL and suture the 3 half tendons together with 2-0 absorbable sutures. This effectively simulates a Pulvertaft weave.

m. Tension the anterior tibialis tendon transfer to the middle (2nd) cuneiform, if applicable

n. Approximate the skin edges with interrupted subcutaneous 3-0 absorbable sutures and a running subcuticular 4-0 absorbable suture

o. Apply a short-leg non–weight-bearing cast

p. Change to a short-leg walking cast after 6 weeks and maintain it until 8 weeks postoperatively

3. Pitfalls

a. Failure to release a contracted volar capsule of the 1st MTP joint

b. Insufficient tension placed on the transfer

c. Assuming that the transfer will correct forefoot supination deformity. It will not. A medial cuneiform osteotomy is needed to correct the deformity, whereas the FHL transfer will help prevent recurrent deformity by substituting for the weak peroneus longus (**see Management Principles #5, 6, 15, 22-2, Chapter 4**).

4. Complications

a. None

Hibbs Transfer of Extensor Digitorum Communis to Cuboid or Peroneus Tertius

1. Indications

a. Claw deformity of the lesser toes (**see Chapter 5**) that causes pain and skin irritation over the dorsum of the IP joints and/or under the MT heads

i. usually associated with a cavovarus foot deformity, as in CMT or other neuromuscular disorder (**see Cavovarus Foot, Chapter 5**)

b. Can be performed as an isolated procedure, but is most often performed during the second stage of a two-stage reconstruction for cavovarus deformity with clawing of the lesser toes

c. Combine with percutaneous tenotomy of the FDL to all affected toes (**see this chapter**)

2. Technique (Figure 7-23)

a. If this is an isolated procedure, perform a percutaneous tenotomy of the FDL to toes 2 to 5 (**see this chapter**)

b. If this procedure is being performed in conjunction with other procedures during the second-stage reconstruction of a cavovarus foot, the FDL to toes 2 to 5 was already released in stage 1.

c. Make a longitudinal incision over the dorsolateral midfoot following the course of the extensor digitorum communis (EDC) and peroneus tertius. Avoid/retract the superficial peroneal nerve.

d. Isolate the peroneus tertius if one exists (approximately 15% of people do not have a peroneus tertius)

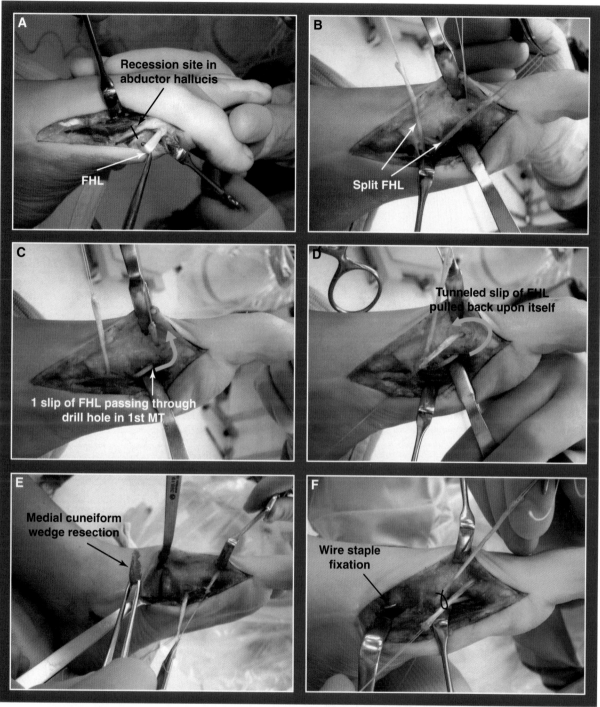

Figure 7-22. Reverse Jones transfer. **A.** The site of the abductor hallucis intramuscular recession is marked. The FHL is exposed, retracted, and released from its insertion on the distal phalanx of the hallux. **B.** The FHL is split longitudinally and a tagging suture is inserting in both ends. **C.** One slip of the FHL is passed through a vertical drill hole in the 1st MT from plantar to dorsal. **D.** The slip is pulled back on itself. **E.** A plantar-based wedge of bone has been removed from the medial cuneiform. Plantar flexion of the 1st ray brings the osteotomy surfaces into apposition. **F.** A wire staple has been inserted from plantar to dorsal to internally fixate the osteotomy. The tendon slip of the FHL that was passed through the drill hole is firmly pulled back upon itself and sutured to itself as well as the other slip of the tendon.

e. Release the EDC slip to the 5th toe as far distal as possible and insert a Bunnell-type #0 absorbable suture in its end, leaving long tails on both limbs of the suture

f. Resect a 2-cm section from the EDC slips to toes 2 to 4

g. If there is a peroneus tertius:

  i. pass the EDC slip #5 through a slit in the tertius

  ii. complete all other bone and soft tissue procedures. Setting the tension on this transfer should be the last, or second to last (before the Jones transfer), procedure performed before final wound closure and cast application (**see Management Principle #24, Chapter 4**).

  iii. with the foot and ankle in anatomic alignment, pull the EDC slip #5 firmly through the slit in the peroneus tertius while the latter tendon is pulled proximally with a button hook

  iv. repair this Pulvertaft weave with figure-of-8 2-0 absorbable sutures

h. If there is no peroneus tertius:

  i. drill a hole in the cuboid from dorsal to plantar that is slightly larger in diameter than the EDC slip #5

  ii. thread one of the long suture tails into each of two large Keith needles. Pass one of the needles through the hole until the tip pierces the plantar skin, but *do not* pull it through yet. Leave the needle shaft in the hole. Pass the other needle, exiting 5 to 7 mm away from the first on the plantar surface of the midfoot. If the first suture were left bare in the hole, the second Keith needle would almost certainly pierce and weaken it. Pull both needles and sutures through the hole and out the plantar surface of the foot.

  iii. pass the needles through a thick felt pad and through different holes in a large button

  iv. complete all other bone and soft tissue procedures. Setting the tension on this transfer should be the last, or second to last (before the Jones transfer), procedure performed before final wound closure and cast application (**see Management Principle #24, Chapter 4**).

  v. with the foot and ankle in anatomic alignment, pull the EDC slip #5 firmly into the hole in the cuboid and tie the sutures over a button and thick felt pad on the plantar aspect of the midfoot

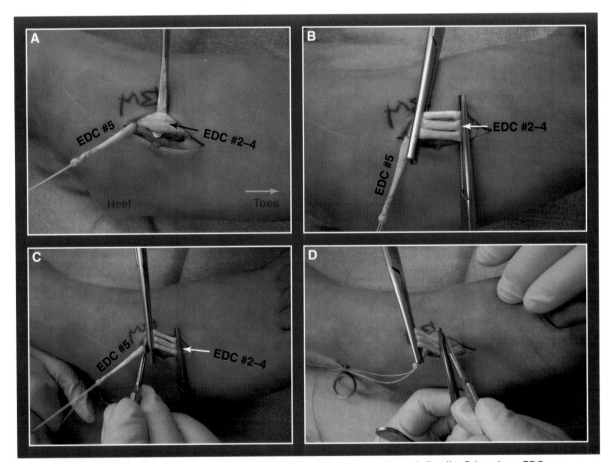

Figure 7-23. Hibbs transfer. **A.** The EDC slip to the 5th toe was released distally. Other three EDC slips are exposed. **B.** Kocher clamps are placed on the EDC slips to toes 2 to 4 approximately 2 cm apart. **C.** Those three slips are divided immediately proximal to the proximal clamp. **D.** The three slips are divided immediately distal to the distal clamp to complete the segmental resections. **E.** For feet in which there is no peroneus tertius (~15%), the lead sutures on EDC slip #5 are passed through a drill hole in the cuboid on Keith needles. **F.** They exit 5 to 7 mm apart on the plantar surface of the midfoot. **G.** The tendon is pulled into the hole and the sutures are tied under tension over a thick felt pad and button. **H.** For feet with a peroneus tertius (~85%), EDC slip #5 is passed through a slit in that tendon for repair as a Pulvertaft weave.

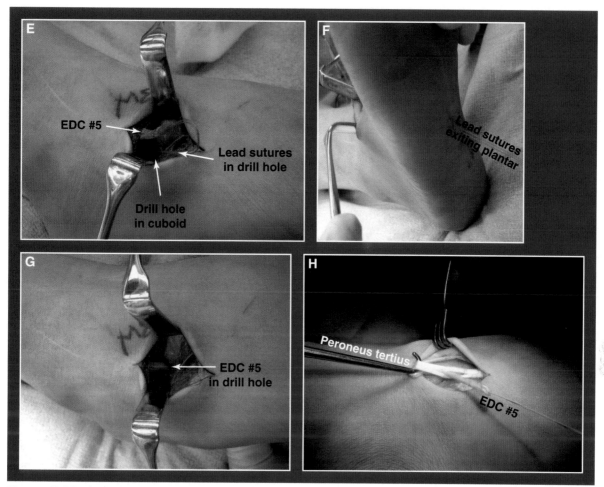

Figure 7-23. *(continued)*

vi. supplement the button fixation by suturing the tendon to the dorsal periosteum of the cuboid with a 2-0 absorbable suture

i. Approximate the skin edges with interrupted subcutaneous 3-0 absorbable sutures and a running subcuticular 4-0 absorbable suture

j. Apply a short-leg non–weight-bearing cast

k. Change to a short-leg walking cast after 6 weeks and maintain it until 8 weeks postoperatively

3. Pitfalls

a. Insufficient tension on the transfer of the EDC to the peroneus tertius or the cuboid

b. Failure to release the FDL to toes 2 to 5

c. Failure to longitudinally pin the toes temporarily if they do not fully passively extend following release of the FDL

d. Assuming that the EDC transfer will correct foot deformity. It will not (**see Management Principles #5, 6, 15, 22-2, Chapter 4**).

4. Complications

a. Injury to the superficial peroneal nerve

i. *Avoid by* careful dissection, identification, and retraction

b. Pull-out of the tendon from the bone

i. *Avoid by:*

• anchoring the tendon securely with the #0 lead suture tied over a plantar button and adding a

supplemental suture between the tendon and the dorsal periosteum of the cuboid

• immobilizing in a cast for at least 6 weeks

Anterior Tibialis Tendon Transfer to the Lateral (3rd) Cuneiform (ATTTx)

1. Indications

a. Clubfoot (**see Chapter 5**) with full correction of all deformities and with good flexibility, but with muscle imbalance that is characterized by overpull of the anterior tibialis in relation to the peroneus longus and peroneus tertius

i. If residual or recurrent deformities coexist, preoperative serial casting should be performed to correct them.

ii. If any of the segmental deformities cannot be corrected by a series of preoperative casts, they can be surgically corrected concurrent with the tendon transfer (**see Management Principles #5, 6, 15, 22-2, Chapter 4**).

2. Technique (Figure 7-24)

a. If any residual deformities exist despite preoperative serial casting, they should be corrected before performing the tendon transfer. For example, a TAT (**see this chapter**) or plantar fasciotomy (PF) (**see this chapter**) should be performed first.

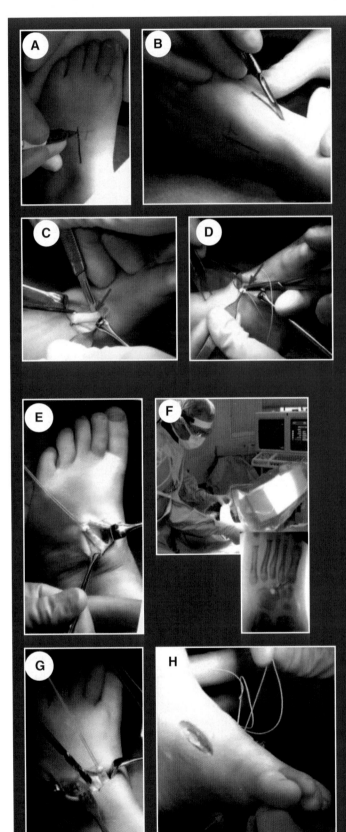

Anterior Tibialis Transfer

Indication

Transfer is indicated if the child has persistent varus and supination during walking. The sole shows thickening of the lateral plantar skin. Make certain that any fixed deformity is corrected by two or three casts before performing the transfer. Transfers are best performed when the child is between 3 and 5 years of age.

Often, the need for transfer is an indication of poor compliance with brace management.

Mark the sites for incisions

The dorsolateral incision is marked on the mid-dorsum of the foot [A].

Make medial incision

The dorsomedial incision is made over the insertion of the anterior tibialis tendon [B].

Expose anterior tibialis tendon

The tendon is exposed and detached at its insertion [C]. Avoid extending the dissection too far distally to avoid injury to the growth plate of the first metatarsal.

Place anchoring sutures

Place a #0 dissolving anchoring suture [D]. Make multiple passes through the tendon to obtain secure fixation.

Transfer the tendon

Transfer the tendon to the dorsolateral incision [E]. The tendon remains under the extensor retinaculum and the extensor tendons. Free the subcutaneous tissue to allow the tendon a direct course laterally.

Option: localize site for insertion

Using a needle as a marker, radiography may be useful in exactly localizing the site of transfer in the third cuneiform [F]. Note the position of the hole in the radiograph (arrow).

Identify site for transfer

This should be in the mid-dorsum of the foot and ideally into the body of the third cuneiform. Make a drill hole large enough to accommodate the tendon [G].

Thread sutures

Thread a straight needle on each of the securing sutures. Leave the first needle in the hole while passing the second needle to avoid piercing the first suture [H]. Note that the needle penetrates the sole of the foot (arrow).

Figure 7-24. Anterior tibialis tendon transfer to the lateral (3rd) cuneiform. See text within figures. (From Mosca VS. In: Lynn Staheli, ed. *Clubfoot: Ponseti Management*, 3rd ed., www.Global-HELP.org, 2009.)

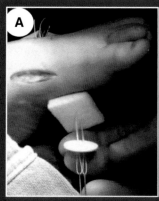

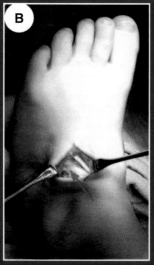

Pass two needles
Place the needles through a felt pad and then through different holes in the button to secure the tendon [A].

Secure tendon
With the foot held in dorsiflexion, pull the tendon into the drill hole by traction on the fixation sutures and tie the fixation sutures with multiple knots [B].

Supplemental fixation
Supplement the button fixation by suturing the tendon to the periosteum at the site where the tendon enters the cuneiform [C], using a heavy absorbable suture.

Neutral position without support
Without support, the foot should rest in approximately 5–10 degrees of plantar flexion [D] and neutral valgus-varus.

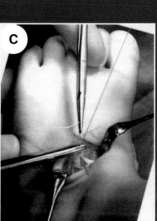

Local anesthetic
A long-acting local anesthetic is injected into the wound [E] to reduce immediate postoperative pain.

Skin closure
Close the incisions with absorbable subcutaneous sutures [F]. Tape strips reinforce the closure.

Cast immobilization
A sterile dressing is placed [G], and a long leg cast is applied [H].

Postoperative care
This patient was discharged on the same day of the procedure. Usually, the patients remain hospitalized overnight. The sutures absorb. Remove the cast at 6 weeks. No bracing is necessary after the procedure. See the child again in 6 months to assess the effect of the transfer.

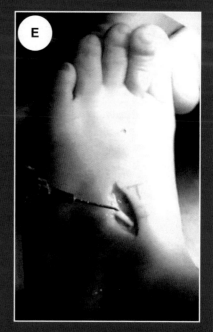

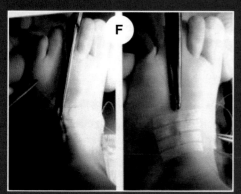

Figure 7-24. (continued)

b. Make a 4-cm longitudinal incision over the dorsome-dial midfoot in line with the anterior tibialis tendon

c. Expose and isolate the anterior tibialis tendon from the distal edge of the extensor retinaculum to the base of the 1st MT. Carefully expose the distal end of the tendon without injuring the 1st MT physis

d. Taper the flared end of the tendon to the thickness of the more proximal visible portion and release it from the 1st MT far distally.

e. Insert a Bunnell-type #0 absorbable suture in its end, leaving long tails on both limbs of the suture

f. Make a 4-cm longitudinal incision over the central midfoot in line with the 3rd MT/lateral (3rd) cuneiform. Avoid/retract the superficial peroneal nerve.

g. Bluntly expose the lateral cuneiform between the EDC and the peroneus tertius

h. Using a 25G needle and mini-fluoroscopy, identify the lateral cuneiform

i. Make a cruciate incision in the periosteum and elevate the four triangular corners with a Freer elevator

j. Make a drill hole through the lateral cuneiform, including the plantar cortex, aimed somewhat lateral to the mid-arch. The diameter of the hole should be slightly greater than the diameter of the tendon.

k. Transfer the tendon laterally from the dorsomedial incision to the central incision remaining deep to the extensor tendons, and certainly deep to the extensor retinaculum. Release fatty or fibrous bands that prevent the tendon from assuming a reasonably straight vector from proximal to distal in its new location.

l. Thread one of the long suture tails into each of two large Keith needles. Pass one of the needles through the hole until the tip pierces the plantar skin, but *do not* pull it through yet. Leave the needle shaft in the hole. Pass the other needle, exiting 5 to 7 mm away from the first on the plantar surface of the midfoot. If the first suture were left bare in the hole, the second Keith needle would almost certainly pierce and weaken it. Pull both needles and sutures through the hole and out the plantar surface of the foot.

m. Pass the needles through a thick felt pad and through different holes in a large button

n. With the foot held in at least 10° of dorsiflexion, pull the tendon firmly into the drill hole and tie the sutures over the felt pad and button on the plantar surface of the midfoot

o. Supplement the button fixation by suturing the tendon to the dorsal periosteum of the lateral cuneiform with a 2-0 absorbable suture

p. Approximate the skin edges with interrupted subcutaneous 3-0 absorbable sutures and a running subcuticular 4-0 absorbable suture

q. Apply a long-leg, bent knee clubfoot cast with maximum dorsiflexion and abduction/eversion molding

r. Remove the cast 6 weeks later

s. A CAM boot can be used for an additional 2 weeks in children over 4 years of age

3. Pitfalls

a. Failure to correct residual or recurrent deformities either before surgery with serial casting or during the operation with the appropriate surgical procedure(s) (**see Management Principles #5, 6, 15, 22-2, Chapter 4**)

b. Incorrect destination for transfer, because of failure to confirm the site with mini-fluoroscopy

c. Insufficient tension placed on the transfer

4. Complications

a. Injury to the superficial peroneal nerve
   i. *Avoid by* careful dissection, identification, and retraction

b. Pull-out of the tendon from the bone
   i. *Avoid by:*
   • waiting to operate until there is a large ossification center in the lateral cuneiform. Tendon likely heals better to bone than to cartilage, though this has not been proven
   • anchoring the tendon securely with the #0 lead suture tied over a plantar button and adding a supplemental suture between the tendon and the dorsal periosteum of the lateral cuneiform
   • immobilizing in a cast for at least 6 weeks

Anterior Tibialis Tendon Transfer to the Middle (2nd) Cuneiform

1. Indications
a. Dorsal bunion (**see Chapter 5**)
   i. Often combined with a reverse Jones transfer of the FHL to the 1st MT (**see this chapter**) and a medial cuneiform plantar flexion osteotomy (**see Chapter 8**)

2. Technique (**see Figure 7-24, above**)
a. Make a 4-cm longitudinal incision over the dorsomedial midfoot in line with the 2nd MT/middle (2nd) cuneiform

b. Expose and isolate the anterior tibialis tendon from the distal edge of the extensor retinaculum to the base of the 1st MT. Carefully expose the distal end of the tendon without injuring the 1st MT physis

c. Taper the flared end of the tendon to the thickness of the more proximal visible portion and release it from the 1st MT far distally.

d. Insert a Bunnell-type #0 absorbable suture in its end, leaving long tails on both limbs of the suture

e. Bluntly expose the dorsum of the middle (2nd) cuneiform and confirm its location using a 25G needle and mini-fluoroscopy

f. Make a cruciate incision in the periosteum and elevate the four triangular corners with a Freer elevator

g. Make a drill hole through the middle cuneiform, including the plantar cortex. The diameter of the hole should be slightly greater than the diameter of the tendon

h. Shift the tendon laterally releasing any fatty or fibrous bands that prevent the tendon from assuming a straight vector from proximal to distal in its new location

i. Thread one of the long suture tails into each of two large Keith needles. Pass one of the needles through the hole until the tip pierces the plantar skin, but *do not* pull it through yet. Leave the needle shaft in the hole. Pass the other needle, exiting 5 to 7 mm away from the first on the plantar surface of the midfoot. If the first suture were left bare in the hole, the second Keith needle would almost certainly pierce and weaken it. Pull both needles and sutures through the hole and out the plantar surface of the foot.

j. Pass the needles through a thick felt pad and through different holes in a large button

k. Complete all other bone and soft tissue procedures, including the medial cuneiform osteotomy and the reverse Jones transfer of the FHL to the first MT, and close all other incisions (**see Management Principle #24, Chapter 4**)

l. With the foot held in at least 10° of dorsiflexion, pull the tendon firmly into the drill hole and tie the sutures over the felt pad and button on the plantar aspect of the midfoot

m. Supplement the button fixation by suturing the tendon to the dorsal periosteum of the middle cuneiform with a 2-0 absorbable suture

n. Approximate the skin edges with interrupted subcutaneous 3-0 absorbable sutures and a running subcuticular 4-0 absorbable suture

o. Apply a short-leg non–weight-bearing cast with neutral positioning of the ankle and subtalar joints and with forefoot pronation

p. Change the cast to a short-leg walking cast after 6 weeks and remove that 1 to 2 weeks later

3. Pitfalls
a. Incorrect destination for transfer, because of failure to confirm the site with mini-fluoroscopy
b. Insufficient tension placed on the transfer

4. Complications
a. Pull-out of the tendon from the bone
   i. *Avoid by:*
   • anchoring the tendon securely with the #0 lead suture tied over a plantar button and adding a supplemental suture between the tendon and the dorsal periosteum of the middle cuneiform
   • immobilizing in a cast for at least 6 weeks

Split Anterior Tibial Tendon Transfer (SPLATT)

1. Indications
a. Varus or cavovarus foot deformity in a child with cerebral palsy (**see Chapter 5**)
b. Cavovarus foot deformity in a child with other neuromuscular disorder, such as CMT (**see Chapter 5**)
c. Often combined with a posterior tibialis tendon recession or lengthening with or without a medial or plantar-medial release (**see this chapter**)

2. Technique (Figure 7-25)
a. Make a 4-cm longitudinal incision over the dorsomedial midfoot in line with the anterior tibialis tendon

b. Expose and isolate the anterior tibialis tendon from the distal edge of the extensor retinaculum to the base of the 1st MT. Carefully expose the distal end of the tendon without injuring the 1st MT physis

c. Split the anterior tibialis tendon longitudinally (there is often a natural longitudinal cleft/split in the tendon, as if there are two adjacent adherent tendons, that can be used to easily create the split)

d. Release one of the slips from the 1st MT

e. Insert a Bunnell-type #0 absorbable suture in its end, leaving long tails on both limbs of the suture

f. Without releasing the extensor retinaculum, split the anterior tibialis as far proximal as possible while removing all soft tissue connections, including vinculae. Dorsiflexion of the ankle and distal traction on the 2 limbs of the tendon will help with proximal exposure of the tendon

g. Make a 5- to 6-cm longitudinal incision anterior to the crest of the distal tibial metaphysis

h. Release the anterior compartment fascia longitudinally

i. The anterior tibialis is the thick tendon immediately lateral to the tibial crest. Release all soft tissue attachments to the tendon.

j. Dorsiflex the ankle while pulling the anterior tibialis tendon proximally into the anterior ankle incision using a button hook. The split in the tendon should become visible just proximal to the extensor retinaculum. Retrieve the split half and pull it retrograde into the anterior ankle wound

k. Continue splitting the tendon proximally to the level of the musculoskeletal junction

l. At that level, place a simple 2-0 absorbable suture on both corners of the limit of the split. This will prevent the tendon from splitting any further, thereby ensuring that the tension that is set will persist

m. Make a longitudinal incision over the dorsolateral midfoot following the course of the peroneus tertius. Avoid/retract the superficial peroneal nerve

n. Isolate the peroneus tertius, if one exists (approximately 15% of people do not have a peroneus tertius)

o. Using a retrograde tonsil clamp, pull the lead sutures on the split half of the anterior tibialis antegrade *deep* to the extensor retinaculum and adjacent to the peroneus tertius from the anterior ankle incision to the dorsolateral incision

p. If there is a peroneus tertius:
   i. pass the split half of the anterior tibialis through a slit in the tertius
   ii. complete all other procedures and close all other incisions. Setting the tension on this transfer should be the last procedure performed before final wound closure and cast application (**see Management Principle #24, Chapter 4**)
   iii. with the ankle in slight dorsiflexion and the subtalar joint everted, pull the split half of the anterior tibialis firmly through the slit in the peroneus tertius while the latter tendon is pulled proximally with a button hook. Repair this Pulvertaft weave with figure-of-8 2-0 absorbable sutures

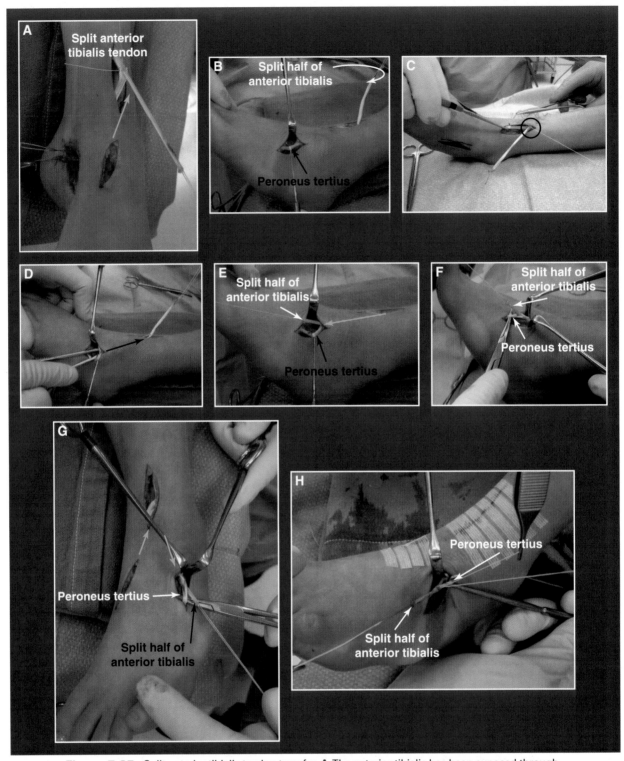

Figure 7-25. Split anterior tibialis tendon transfer. **A.** The anterior tibialis has been exposed through a dorsomedial incision, split longitudinally, and one of the slips has been released from the 1st MT. That slip has been retracted retrograde (*blue arrow*) to an incision anterior to the distal tibial metaphysis. **B.** The peroneus tertius is exposed through a dorsolateral incision. For the approximately 15% of individuals without a peroneus tertius, the cuboid can be exposed through this incision for transfer of the tendon into a drill hole in that bone. **C.** Absorbable 2-0 sutures are placed at the proximal extent of the split in the tendon (*at the musculoskeletal junction—black circle*) to prevent further inadvertent splitting of the tendon. **D.** A tonsil clamp is passed retrograde deep to the peroneus tertius and extensor retinaculum to the anterior ankle incision (*black arrow*). **E.** There, it captures the sutures on the split half of the anterior tibialis for antegrade delivery (*blue arrow*) of the tendon to the dorsolateral incision. **F.** The anterior tibialis tendon is passed through a slit in the peroneus tertius for later tensioning. **G.** The pathway for the split transfer is indicated by the blue arrows. **H.** With the subtalar joint everted and the ankle dorsiflexed, the Pulvertaft weave is being tensioned and secured with 2-0 absorbable sutures. Note that the other incisions have already been sutured closed. Securing the tendon transfer and closing that incision are the last procedures performed before cast application (**see Management Principle #24, Chapter 4**).

162

q. If there is no peroneus tertius:
  i. drill a hole in the cuboid from dorsal to plantar
  ii. thread one of the long suture tails into each of two large Keith needles. Pass one of the needles through the hole until the tip pierces the plantar skin, but *do not* pull it through yet. Leave the needle shaft in the hole. Pass the other needle, exiting 5 to 7 mm away from the first on the plantar surface of the midfoot. If the 1st suture were left bare in the hole, the second Keith needle would almost certainly pierce and weaken it. Pull both needles and sutures through the hole and out the plantar surface of the foot
  iii. complete all other procedures and close all other incisions. Setting the tension on this transfer should be the last procedure performed before final wound closure and cast application (**see Management Principle #24, Chapter 4**)
  iv. with the ankle in slight dorsiflexion and the subtalar joint everted, pull the split half of the anterior tibialis firmly into the hole in the cuboid and tie the sutures over a button and thick felt pad on the plantar aspect of the midfoot
  v. supplement the button fixation by suturing the tendon to the dorsal periosteum of the cuboid with a 2-0 absorbable suture
r. Approximate the skin edges with interrupted subcutaneous 3-0 absorbable sutures and a running subcuticular 4-0 absorbable suture
s. Apply a short-leg non–weight-bearing cast with neutral rotation of the forefoot, eversion of the subtalar joint, and slight dorsiflexion of the ankle
t. Change the cast to a short-leg walking cast after 6 weeks and remove that one 2 weeks later

3. Pitfalls
  a. Insufficient tension placed on the transfer
  b. Failure to recognize and concurrently correct structural deformities of the foot, such as fixed inversion of the subtalar joint, severe cavus, and rigid pronation of the forefoot (**see Management Principles #5, 6, 15, 22-2, Chapter 4**)
  c. If there is severe pronation of the forefoot (plantar flexion of the 1st ray), a SPLATT will further weaken dorsiflexion of the 1st ray and potentiate the power of the peroneus longus (the plantar flexor of the 1st ray), resulting in further pronation of the forefoot. In this scenario, one should consider a PF (**see this chapter**), a medial cuneiform dorsiflexion osteotomy (**see Chapter 8**), and/or a peroneus longus to peroneus brevis transfer (**see this chapter**).

4. Complications
  a. Injury to the superficial peroneal nerve
    i. *Avoid by* careful dissection, identification, and retraction
  b. Pull-out of the tendon from the bone
    i. *Avoid by:*
      • anchoring the tendon securely with the #0 lead suture tied over a plantar button and adding a supplemental suture between the tendon and the dorsal periosteum of the cuboid
      • immobilizing in a cast for at least 6 weeks

Peroneus Longus to Peroneus Brevis Transfer (PL to PB tx)

1. Indications
  a. Cavovarus foot deformity with pronation of the forefoot in a child with CMT or other neuromuscular disorder, including some with CP (**see Chapter 5**)
    i. This is the most important tendon transfer for most cavovarus foot deformities. The primary deformity in a cavovarus foot is plantar flexion of the 1st ray (pronation of the forefoot). The peroneus longus plantar flexes the 1st ray. The second deformity in a cavovarus foot is inversion of the hindfoot because of relative weakness of the evertor (peroneus brevis) compared with the invertor (posterior tibialis). Transfer of the peroneus longus to the peroneus brevis removes the primary deforming forces and enhances the power of hindfoot eversion (**see Management Principle #22, Chapter 4**).
  b. Often performed as one of several concurrent or staged procedures to correct cavovarus deformity, including plantar-medial release (**see this chapter**), medial cuneiform dorsiflexion osteotomy (**see Chapter 8**), SPLATT (**see this chapter**), Jones transfer (**see this chapter**), Hibbs transfer (**see this chapter**), and posterior calcaneus displacement osteotomy (**see Chapter 8**)

2. Technique (Figure 7-26)
  a. This transfer is usually performed along with one or more other procedures during the second stage of a two-stage cavovarus foot reconstruction.
  b. Make a slightly curved incision on the lateral aspect of the calcaneus following the course of the peroneal tendons starting posterior to the lateral malleolus and ending at the glabrous skin plantarward. This is the same incision used for a posterior calcaneus displacement osteotomy (**see Chapter 8**).
  c. Isolate and protect the sural nerve
  d. Release the peroneus longus and brevis from their tendon sheaths
  e. Resect the septum (the conjoined tendon sheaths) that separates them. Resect the peroneal tubercle if it is large
  f. Make a long Z-cut in the peroneus longus and place a tagging 2-0 absorbable suture in the free end of the proximal slip. Pass this slip through a slit in the peroneus brevis for later tensioning
  g. The exposed portion of the distal slip of the peroneus longus can be resected. If there is concern that the forefoot might overcorrect to supination, this slip can be sutured to the periosteum on the lateral surface of the calcaneus, thereby changing the tendon into a ligament and creating a tenodesis.
  h. Complete all other procedures and close all other incisions. If a posterior calcaneus displacement osteotomy (**see Chapter 8**) is being performed concurrently, displace and internally fixate the posterior bone fragment before setting the tension on the tendon transfer. Setting

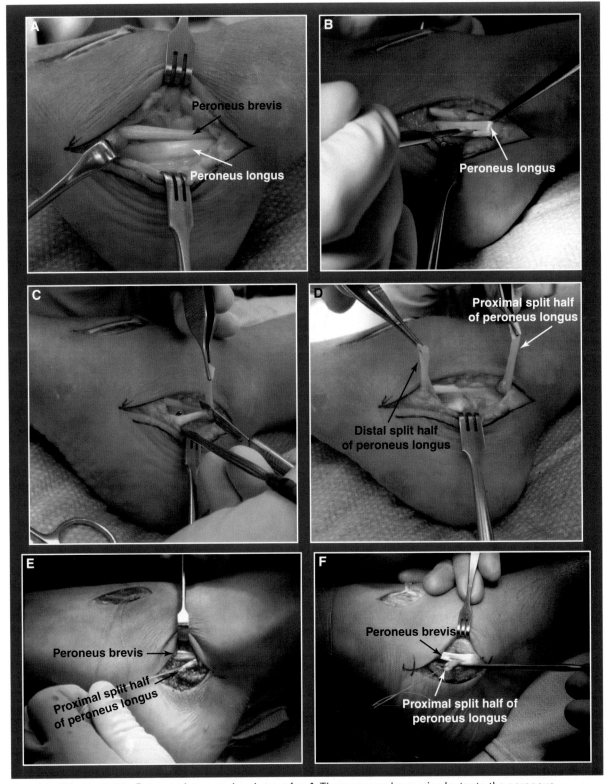

Figure 7-26. Peroneus longus to brevis transfer. **A.** The peroneus longus is plantar to the peroneus brevis tendon along the lateral surface of the calcaneus. Both are released from their tendon sheaths. Ensure that they are appropriately identified by observing the effect of traction on each one using a button/tendon hook. **B–D.** The peroneus longus is cut in a Z-fashion. **E.** A lead suture is placed in the end of the proximal slip as a handle. **F.** The proximal slip of the peroneus longus is passed through a slit in the peroneus brevis. **E.** A lead suture is placed in the end of the proximal slip as a handle. **F.** The proximal slip of the peroneus longus is passed through a slit in the peroneus brevis. **G.** This Pulvertaft weave is secured under firm tension with figure-of-8 sutures of 2-0 absorbable sutures.

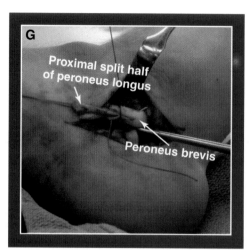

Figure 7-26. *(continued)*

the tension on this transfer should be the last (or one of the last) procedure performed before final wound closure and cast application (**see Management Principle #24, Chapter 4**)

i. Dorsiflex the ankle to neutral and fully evert the subtalar joint. Firmly pull the proximal slip of the peroneus longus tendon distally through the slit in the peroneus brevis while the latter tendon is pulled proximally with a button hook. Repair this Pulvertaft weave with multiple figure-of-8 2-0 absorbable sutures

j. Approximate the skin edges with interrupted subcutaneous 3-0 absorbable sutures and a running subcuticular 4-0 absorbable suture

k. Apply a short-leg cast with weight-bearing status and duration of casting dependent the other procedures that were performed concurrently. Generally, a short-leg non–weight-bearing cast is used for 6 weeks followed by 2 weeks in a short-leg weight-bearing cast

3. <u>Pitfalls</u>

a. Failure to recognize and concurrently correct structural deformities of the foot, such as fixed inversion of the subtalar joint, severe cavus, and rigid pronation of the forefoot (**see Management Principles #5, 6, 15, 22-2, Chapter 4**)

b. Insufficient tension placed on the transfer

4. <u>Complications</u>

a. Injury to the sural nerve

   i. *Avoid by* careful dissection, identification, and retraction

Anterior Tibialis Tendon Transfer to the Tendo-Achilles (AT to TA tx)

1. <u>Indications</u>

a. Acquired calcaneus foot deformity (**see Chapter 5**) due to a strong anterior tibialis and a weak triceps surae, typically in a child with myelomeningocele

2. <u>Technique</u> (Figure 7-27)

a. Make a 4-cm longitudinal incision over the dorsomedial midfoot in line with the anterior tibialis tendon

b. Expose and isolate the anterior tibialis tendon from the distal edge of the extensor retinaculum to the base of the 1st MT. Carefully expose the distal end of the tendon without injuring the 1st MT physis

c. Taper the flared end of the tendon to the thickness of the more proximal visible portion and release it from the 1st MT far distally.

d. Insert a Bunnell-type #0 absorbable suture in its end, leaving long tails on both limbs of the suture

e. Make a 5- to 6-cm longitudinal incision anterior to the crest of the distal tibial metaphysis

f. Release the anterior compartment fascia longitudinally. The anterior tibialis is the thick tendon immediately lateral to the tibial crest.

g. Release all soft tissue attachments from the tendon and pull the entire tendon retrograde from the foot to this incision on the lower leg.

h. Expose the interosseous membrane by retracting the soft tissues laterally away from the tibia. Gently retract the NV bundle.

i. Approximately 5 to 7 cm proximal to the ankle joint, make a window in the interosseous membrane that is the full width of the membrane and at least 1.5 cm long

j. Make a longitudinal incision along the posteromedial aspect of the ankle half way between the tendo-Achilles and the tibia. Expose and isolate the tendo-Achilles

k. Pass a tonsil clamp through the window in the interosseous membrane from anterior/proximal (in the anterior ankle incision) to posteromedial/distal (in the posteromedial incision). Keep the tonsil clamp adjacent to the tibia while spreading the soft tissues without closing the clamp in the depths of the wound.

l. The tonsil clamp should emerge in the distal aspect of the posteromedial incision *lateral* to the posterior tibial NV bundle and anteromedial to the tendo-Achilles.

m. Perform a reverse passage of a second tonsil clamp (clamped to the first clamp). Use it to clamp the lead suture on the anterior tibialis tendon and pull the tendon distally into the posteromedial wound

n. Confirm that the path of the tendon is fairly straight and not bound or deviated by the window in the interosseous membrane

o. Pass the anterior tibialis tendon through a slit in the tendo-Achilles

p. Ensure that the ankle can be plantar flexed beyond neutral. If not, release any tethering anterior and dorsal soft tissues.

q. Plantar flex the ankle 10° by pulling the tendo-Achilles proximally with a button hook, while pulling the anterior tibialis firmly through the slit in the tendo-Achilles and back upon itself. Repair this Pulvertaft weave with multiple figure-of-8 #0 absorbable sutures

r. Approximate the skin edges with interrupted subcutaneous 3-0 absorbable sutures and a running subcuticular 4-0 absorbable suture

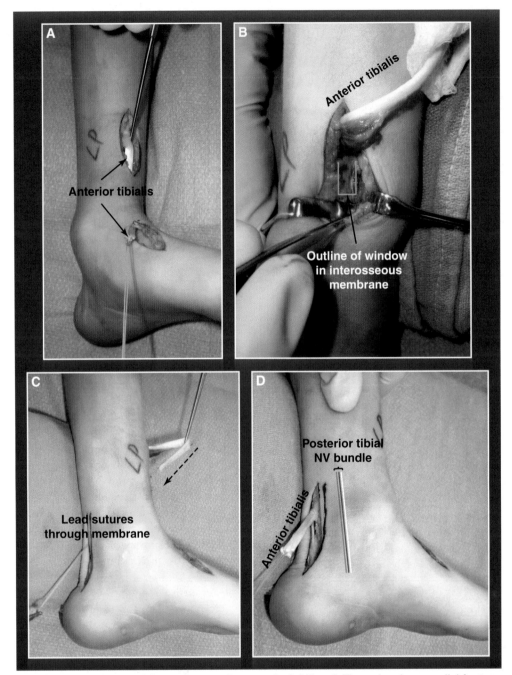

Figure 7-27. Anterior tibialis tendon transfer to tendo-Achilles. **A.** Through a dorsomedial foot incision, the anterior tibialis is released from the 1st MT and a tagging suture is placed in its distal end. Through an incision anterior to the distal tibial metaphysis, the tendon is again identified. **B.** The anterior tibialis anterior tendon is retracted proximally. While protecting the anterior tibial NV bundle, the interosseous membrane is exposed. An adequate size window is made in the membrane at least 5 to 7 cm proximal to the ankle joint (*green U*). **C.** The lead sutures are passed from anterior/proximal to posteromedial/distal through the window in the membrane, exiting through a longitudinal incision anteromedial to the tendo-Achilles. **D.** The anterior tibialis is pulled through the window. The sutures/tendon pass *lateral* to the posterior tibial NV bundle. **E.** The anterior tibialis is passed through a slit in the tendo-Achilles. The tendo-Achilles is pulled proximally to place the ankle in slight plantar flexion while the anterior tibialis is pulled distally. This Pulvertaft weave is sutured under tension with 2-0 absorbable sutures. **F.** The anterior tibialis is pulled back upon itself where additional sutures are placed.

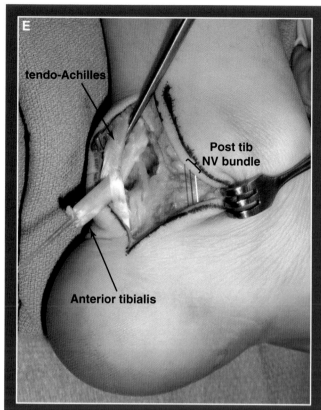
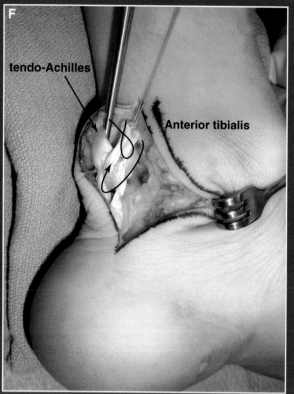

Figure 7-27. *(continued)*

s. Apply a short-leg non–weight-bearing cast with the ankle in 10° of plantar flexion
t. Remove the cast after 6 weeks and take a mold for an ankle-foot-orthotic (AFO)
u. Apply a short-leg walking cast that will be worn for the 1 to 2 weeks needed to fabricate the AFO

3. Pitfalls
   a. Failure to release a dorsiflexion contracture at the ankle that is due to structures other than the anterior tibialis
   b. Insufficient tension placed on the transfer

4. Complications
   a. Injury to the anterior tibial NV bundle
      i. *Avoid by* careful dissection, identification, and retraction
   b. Injury to the posterior tibial NV bundle
      i. *Avoid by* careful dissection, identification, and passage of the tendon posterior to the bundle

Posterior Tibialis Tendon Transfer to the Dorsum of the Foot (PT tx dorsum)

1. Indications
   a. Cavovarus foot (**see Chapter 5**) in which the posterior tibialis is the only functioning muscle, i.e., *not* cavovarus due to CMT
      i. This is an out of phase transfer, so it should not be a transfer of first choice in most cavovarus foot

deformities. In most cases, this transfer acts as a tenodesis (**see Management Principle #22-1, Chapter 4**).

2. Technique (Figure 7-28)
   a. Make a longitudinal incision along the medial border of the midfoot/hindfoot over the posterior tibialis tendon extending posteriorly to the posterior tibial NV bundle
   b. Release the posterior tibialis tendon sheath from the tip of the medial malleolus distally
   c. Release the tendon from the navicular as far plantar-distally as possible, so as to have enough tendon length for transfer
   d. Insert a Bunnell-type #0 absorbable suture in its end, leaving long tails on both limbs of the suture
   e. Make a 5- to 6-cm longitudinal incision anterior to the crest of the distal tibial metaphysis
   f. Release the anterior compartment fascia longitudinally
   g. Expose the interosseous membrane by retracting the soft tissues laterally away from the tibia. Gently retract the anterior tibial NV bundle.
   h. Approximately 5 to 7 cm proximal to the ankle joint, make a window in the interosseous membrane that is the full width of the membrane and at least 1.5 cm long
   i. Make a 5-cm longitudinal incision along the posterior edge of the medial face of the tibia approximately 8 to 10 cm proximal to the tip of the medial malleolus
   j. Release the fascia from the edge of the tibia

k. The first muscle encountered is the FDL. Confirm its identity by pulling proximally on its intramuscular tendon and observing flexion of the lesser toes. Retract it posteriorly.

l. The next muscle/tendon unit identified is the posterior tibialis. Confirm its identity by pulling distally on the released tendon in the foot

m. Pull the tendon retrograde to the proximal wound

n. Pass a tonsil clamp or tendon passer through the window in the interosseous membrane from anterolateral to posteromedial. Remain *strictly adjacent* to the posterior surface of the tibia while spreading the soft tissues, without closing the clamp in the depths of the wound. Also, keep the clamp *anterior* to the posterior tibial NV bundle

o. Clamp the lead sutures on the posterior tibialis tendon and pull them through the interosseous membrane from posteromedial to anterolateral. By staying anterior to the posterior tibial NV bundle, the tendon will not wrap around and compress the NV bundle.

p. Make a longitudinal incision on the dorsolateral midfoot. Avoid/retract the superficial peroneal nerve.

q. Expose the dorsum of the cuboid or the lateral cuneiform depending on your assessment of the degree of lateral positioning required

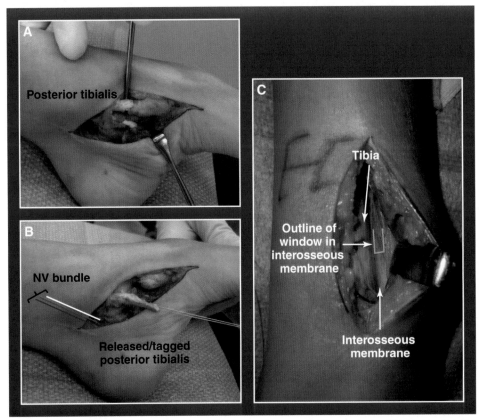

Figure 7-28. Posterior tibialis tendon transfer to the dorsum. **A.** The posterior tibialis tendon is exposed through a longitudinal midfoot/hindfoot incision. **B.** It is released from its distal/plantar-most insertion on the navicular. A tagging Bunnell-type #0 absorbable lead suture is inserted. The tendon remains anterior to the posterior tibial NV bundle at *all* times. **C.** Through a longitudinal incision anterior to the distal tibial metaphysis, the anterior compartment fascia is released. The interosseous membrane is exposed by retracting the soft tissues laterally and protecting the anterior tibial NV bundle. An adequate size window is made in the membrane at least 5 to 7 cm proximal to the ankle joint (*green U*). **D.** A longitudinal incision is made along the posteromedial edge of the tibia approximately 8 to 10 cm proximal to the tip of the medial malleolus. The posterior tibialis is pulled retrograde to that incision. A tonsil clamp is passed from anterior to posteromedial through the window in the interosseous membrane staying *strictly adjacent* to the posterior surface of the tibia and *anterior* to the posterior tibial NV bundle. The lead sutures on the tendon are grasped. **E.** The sutures are pulled through the window from posteromedial to anterior. **F.** The posterior tibialis follows. **G.** The tendon should have free excursion and a straight line vector through the window in the interosseous membrane. **H.** A tonsil clamp is passed retrograde (*dashed black arrow*) from an incision on the dorsolateral midfoot staying deep to the extensor retinaculum and ending in the anterior compartment that was previously exposed. The lead sutures are grasped. **I–K.** The sutures are pulled antegrade (*dashed black arrow*) until the tip of the tendon is exposed in the dorsolateral midfoot incision. **L.** A drill hole is made in the bone that is to accept the transfer (typically the lateral cuneiform). In adolescents, it is appropriate to supplement fixation with a suture anchor. **M and N.** The tendon has been pulled into the hole in the bone by the lead sutures that are tied under tension over a thick felt pad and button. **O.** The supplemental suture anchor has been used.

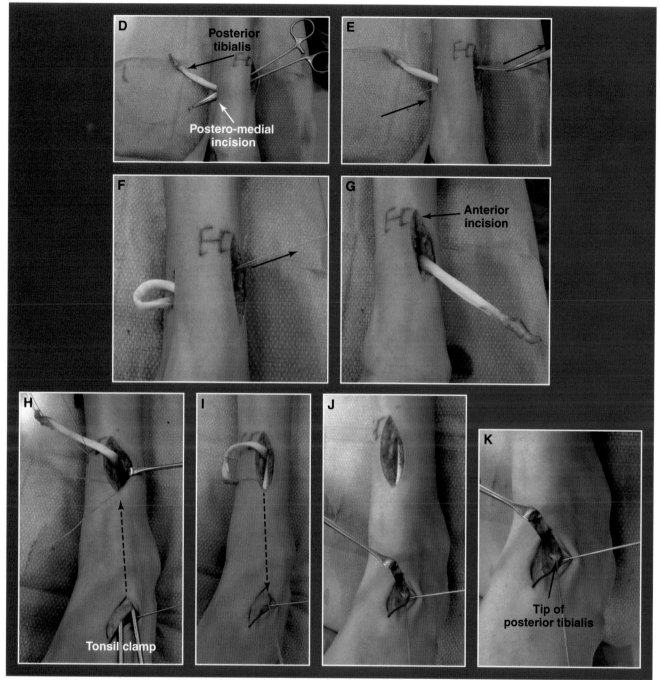

Figure 7-28. *(continued)*

r. Drill a hole through the entire bone that is chosen
s. Pass a tonsil clamp or a tendon passer retrograde from the dorsal foot wound to the anterior leg wound staying deep to the extensor retinaculum
t. Pull the lead sutures on the posterior tibialis and, thereby, the end of the posterior tibialis tendon into the dorsal foot wound
u. Thread one of the long suture tails into each of two large Keith needles. Pass one of the needles through the hole in the bone until the tip pierces the plantar skin, but *do not* pull it through yet. Leave the needle shaft in the hole. Pass the other needle, exiting 5 to 7 mm away from

the first on the plantar surface of the midfoot. If the first suture were left bare in the hole, the second Keith needle would almost certainly pierce and weaken it. Pull both needles and sutures through the hole and out the plantar surface of the foot.
v. Pass the needles through a thick felt pad and through different holes in a large button
w. Complete all other procedures and close all other incisions. Setting the tension on this transfer should be the last procedure performed before final wound closure and cast application (**see Management Principle #24, Chapter 4**)

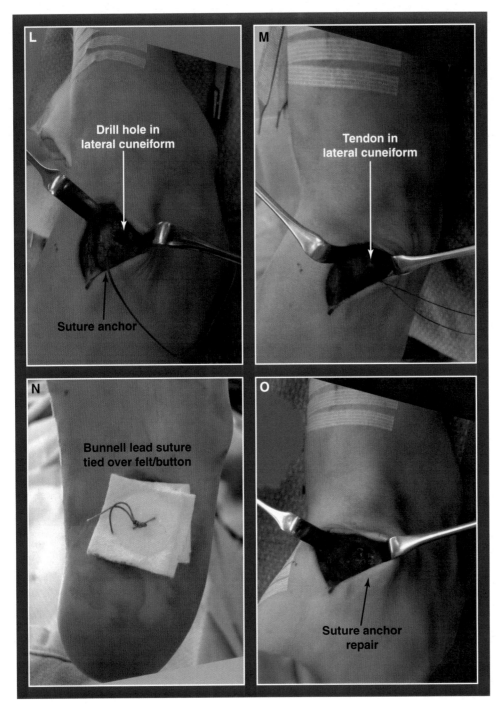

Figure 7-28. *(continued)*

x. With the foot held in at least 10° of dorsiflexion and full eversion, pull the tendon firmly into the drill hole and tie the sutures over the felt pad and button on the plantar surface of the midfoot

y. Supplement the button fixation by suturing the tendon to the dorsal periosteum of the bone with a 2-0 absorbable suture

   i. A suture anchor can also be used in older children and adolescents

z. Apply a short-leg non–weight-bearing cast

aa. Convert to a short-leg walking cast 6 weeks later after taking a mold for an AFO

ab. Remove the final cast 2 weeks later and transition to the AFO

3. Pitfalls

a. Failure to recognize and concurrently correct structural deformities of the foot, such as fixed inversion of the subtalar joint, severe cavus, and rigid pronation of the forefoot (**see Management Principles #5, 6, 15, 22-2, Chapter 4**)

b. Insufficient tension placed on the transfer

4. Complications

a. Injury to the anterior tibial NV bundle

   i. *Avoid by* careful dissection, identification, and retraction

b. Injury to the posterior tibial NV bundle

   i. *Avoid by* careful dissection, identification, and passage of the tendon anterior to the bundle

c. Pull-out of the tendon from the bone
   i. *Avoid by:*
      • anchoring the tendon securely with the #0 lead suture tied over a plantar button and adding a supplemental suture between the tendon and the dorsal periosteum of the bone
      • supplementing the tendon fixation to the bone with a suture anchor in older children and adolescents
      • immobilizing in a cast for at least 6 weeks

IV. RELEASES—COMBINATIONS OF APONEUROTIC AND/OR INTRAMUSCULAR RECESSIONS, TENDON LENGTHENINGS, MUSCLE DIVISIONS/RELEASES, AND CAPSULOTOMIES

PRINCIPLE: A combination of two or more soft tissue procedures is often needed to correct specific deformities.

Plantar Fasciotomy/Release (PF/PR)

1. Indications
   a. Isolated cavus foot deformity (**see Chapter 5**) without significant hindfoot varus or forefoot pronation

b. Combined with superficial and/or deep medial releases (S-PMR, D-PMR) (**see this chapter**) as well as osteotomies and tendon transfers for cavovarus deformities (**see Chapter 5**)

2. Technique
   a. Plantar fasciotomy (PF) for mild transtarsal cavus (Figure 7-29):
      i. Make a 4-cm longitudinal incision along the medial border of the midfoot/hindfoot just dorsal to the edge of the glabrous skin
      ii. Retract the lowest origin of the abductor hallucis muscle dorsally
      iii. Isolate the plantar fascia on its plantar and dorsal surfaces from medial to lateral using Metzenbaum scissors
      iv. Divide the plantar fascia transversely directly plantar to the head/neck of the talus
      v. The muscles of the short toe flexors create a layer of protection to prevent inadvertent injury to the posterior tibial plantar NV structures.
      vi. Release the tourniquet and achieve good hemostasis
      vii. Approximate the skin edges with interrupted subcutaneous 3-0 absorbable sutures and a running subcuticular 4-0 absorbable suture
      viii. Apply a short-leg non–weight-bearing cast with the neutrally rotated forefoot dorsiflexed against

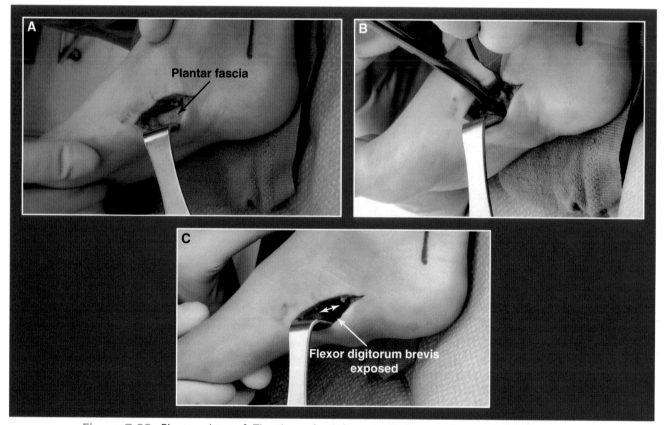

Figure 7-29. Plantar release. **A.** The plantar fascia is exposed plantar and lateral to the abductor hallucis muscle. **B.** The plantar fascia is isolated on its dorsal and plantar surfaces from medial to lateral using Metzenbaum scissors. **C.** Following release of the plantar fascia (*double-headed white arrow*), the short toe flexor muscles are visible as a layer of safety between the released plantar fascia and the NV bundles. **D & E.** Artist's sketches of plantar fasciotomy.

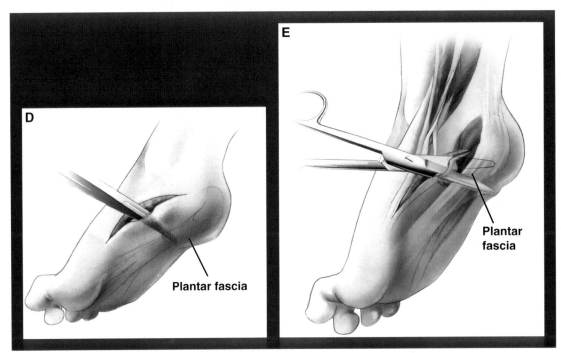

Figure 7-29. *(continued)*

the resistance of the ankle/heel cord. There is no need to bivalve the cast.

  ix. Remove the cast after 6 weeks

b. Plantar release for moderate-to-severe transtarsal cavus and cavovarus deformities (**see Superficial Plantar-Medial Release, Figure 7-31, below**)

  i. Make a longitudinal incision along the medial border of the midfoot/hindfoot more dorsal than for an isolated PF (almost to the distal tip of the medial malleolus) and extending posteriorly to the posterior tibial NV bundle

  ii. Isolate the posterior tibial NV bundle posterior to the medial malleolus and proximal to the posterosuperior border of the flexor retinaculum

  iii. Release the flexor retinaculum (laciniate ligament) vertically in line with the NV bundle for full exposure of these important structures

  iv. Release the lowest and largest origin of the abductor hallucis muscle from its origin on the calcaneus while protecting the lateral plantar NV bundle. In moderate-to-severe cavus deformity, the lowest origin of the abductor hallucis muscle is so far plantar that its contracture is similar to that of the plantar fascia, so it must be released.

  v. Expose the tunnel through which the lateral plantar NV bundle travels across the foot deep to the flexor digitorum brevis

  vi. Bluntly and carefully develop some space between the lateral plantar NV bundle and the plantar roof of this tunnel, which is made up of the flexor digitorum brevis and the plantar fascia

  vii. Release the plantar fascia and flexor digitorum brevis from medial to lateral while visualizing and protecting the lateral plantar NV bundle

  viii. Release the tourniquet and achieve good hemostasis

  ix. Approximate the skin edges with interrupted subcutaneous 3-0 absorbable sutures and a running subcuticular 4-0 absorbable suture

  x. Apply a short-leg non–weight-bearing cast with the neutrally rotated forefoot dorsiflexed against the resistance of the ankle/heel cord. There is no need to bivalve the cast.

  xi. Remove the cast after 6 weeks

3. Pitfalls

a. Uncertainty regarding the location of the posterior tibial NV bundles, thereby creating unnecessary caution, concern, and slow progress. Find the NV structures first to improve confidence, accuracy, and speed.

4. Complications

a. Injury to the posterior tibial NV structures

  i. *Avoid by* isolating them proximally and trace them through the plantar tunnel

Limited, Minimally Invasive Soft Tissue Releases for Clubfoot

1. Indications

a. Little (or no) improvement after a long series of clubfoot casts in *an infant* or *young child* (and perhaps an older child) with a severe, rigid, resistant, non-surgically treated arthrogrypotic (or idiopathic) clubfoot (**see Chapter 5**)

  i. The *presumption* is that it would be challenging to stretch the posterior ankle skin and align the foot in the ankle mortis even if a talectomy were performed

  ii. The operative *expectation* is that, following surgery, the deformities will be improved and serial casting will be reinitiated. The deformities might then be corrected with further serial casting or improved enough with further serial casting that subsequent conventional á la carte partial-to-complete circumferential release will be successful.

2. Technique (Figure 7-30)
   a. Percutaneous tendo-Achilles tenotomy (TAT) (**see this chapter**)
   b. Limited open plantar fasciotomy (PF) (**see this chapter**)
   c. Limited open posterior tibialis tenotomy
      i. Dissect dorsally between the abductor hallucis and the subcutaneous fat to expose the posterior tibialis tendon sheath
      ii. Open the sheath and release the posterior tibialis from the navicular
   d. Percutaneous tenotomies of FHL and FDL to toes 2 to 5 (**see this chapter**)
   e. Release the tourniquet and achieve good hemostasis
   f. Approximate the skin edges of the plantar–medial incision with interrupted subcutaneous 3-0 absorbable sutures and a running subcuticular 4-0 absorbable suture
   g. Apply a long-leg clubfoot cast without excessive corrective forces on the foot. Allow the tissues to relax
   h. Reinitiate serial long-leg clubfoot casting in clinic in 1 to 2 weeks
3. Pitfalls
   a. Incomplete TAT (**see this chapter**)

b. Inserting the tip of the scalpel too rapidly and too deeply into the toe flexor tendon so that it cannot act as a probe to determine the position and limits of the tendon
4. Complications
   a. Posterior tibial NV injury
      i. *Avoid by* following the TAT technique exactly as described (**see this chapter**)
      ii. *Avoid by* releasing the plantar fascia but not the short toe flexor muscles
   b. Laceration of a digital nerve or artery
      i. *Avoid by* inserting the tip of the scalpel centrally and carefully into the plantar base of the toe, using it both as a probe and a scalpel (**see this chapter**).
      ii. *Avoid* excessive medial and/or lateral excursion of the tip of the scalpel
   c. Laceration of cartilaginous calcaneal apophysis
      i. *Avoid by* following the TAT technique exactly as described, inserting the scalpel at least 1 cm above the posterior heel crease (**see this chapter**)

Superficial Medial Release (S-MR)

1. Indications
   a. Pain and/or gait instability due to flexible hindfoot varus, i.e., *corrects* with the Coleman block test

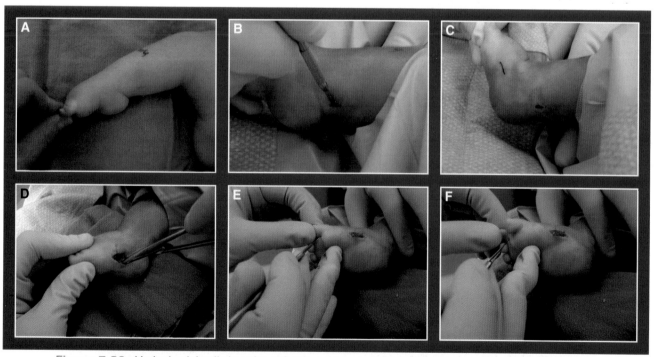

Figure 7-30. Limited, minimally invasive soft tissue releases. **A.** Medial image of maximum dorsiflexion of a severe, rigid, resistant clubfoot in an infant with arthrogryposis that had undergone eight serial Ponseti-type long-leg casts. The concern was that either (1) a Cincinnati incision might be under too much tension to close at the completion of a circumferential clubfoot release, or (2) a talectomy would be used unnecessarily (and it still might not be possible to bring the foot to a neutral position). **B.** Limited, minimally invasive soft tissue releases were carried out starting with a percutaneous TAT. **C.** Improvement following the TAT, but equinus persisted. **D.** Mini-open PF and posterior tibialis tenotomy. **E.** Percutaneous tenotomy of FHL. **F.** Percutaneous tenotomy of FDL to toe 2 (FDL to toes 3 to 5 were subsequently released). Serial casting was reinitiated for this child's foot. Two months later, a simple posterior release was performed and there was full and lasting deformity correction.

(see Assessment Principles #9 and 19, Chapter 3), and *without* forefoot pronation or cavus

   i. Seen in some clubfeet and in some spastic varus feet
      • Often used as an adjunct procedure with tendon transfers in these feet

2. Technique (see **Superficial Plantar-Medial Release [Figure 7-31], but do *not* perform the plantar release**)

   a. Make a longitudinal incision along the medial border of the midfoot/hindfoot just dorsal to the edge of the glabrous skin and extending posterior to the posterior tibial NV bundle
   b. Isolate the posterior tibial NV bundle posterior to the medial malleolus and proximal to the posterosuperior border of the flexor retinaculum
   c. Release the flexor retinaculum (laciniate ligament) vertically in line with the NV bundle for full exposure of these important structures
   d. Release the lowest and largest origin of the abductor hallucis muscle from its origin on the calcaneus while protecting the lateral plantar NV bundle.
   e. Expose and release the very thin interfascicular septum (the middle origin of the abductor hallucis on the calcaneus) that separates the medial and lateral plantar NV bundles. It is only 1 to 2 mm long and 1 to 2 mm wide

   f. Release from the calcaneus the most dorsal origin of the abductor hallucis, which is the dorsal edge of the tunnel through which the medial plantar NV bundle travels within the abductor hallucis muscle
   g. This completes the release of the three origins of the abductor hallucis muscle.
   h. Release the tourniquet and achieve good hemostasis
   i. Approximate the skin edges with interrupted subcutaneous 3-0 absorbable sutures and a running subcuticular 4-0 absorbable suture
   j. Apply a short-leg non–weight-bearing cast with the ankle joint at neutral and the subtalar joint everted
   k. Remove the cast after 6 weeks

3. Pitfalls
   a. Uncertainty regarding the location of the posterior tibial NV bundles, thereby creating unnecessary caution, concern, and slow progress. Find the NV structures first to improve confidence, accuracy, and speed.
   b. Failure to recognize the need for a D-MR, i.e., the subtalar joint does not fully evert

4. Complications
   a. Injury to the posterior tibial NV structures
      i. *Avoid by* isolating them proximally and tracing them between the three origins of the abductor hallucis

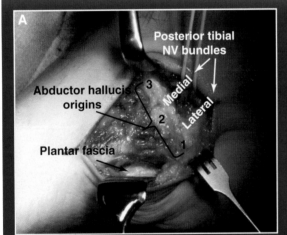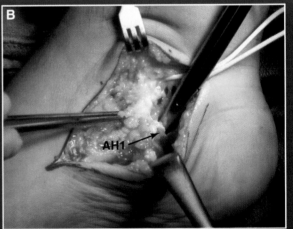

Figure 7-31. Superficial plantar-medial release. **A.** The abductor hallucis muscle has three origins on the medial surface of the calcaneus (labeled *1, 2,* and *3* from plantar to dorsal). The posterior tibial NV bundle (*with white vessel loop around it*) divides into medial and lateral plantar NV bundles immediately before passing into the muscle. The laciniate ligament (flexor retinaculum) has been incised vertically in line with the NV bundles to expose the bundles. The plantar fascia is seen as a white band of dense collagen plantar-lateral to the abductor hallucis. It is sharply separated from the thick layer of plantar fat. **B.** Metzenbaum scissors are used to enter the tunnel through which the lateral plantar NV bundle passes obliquely across the plantar aspect of the foot. The NV bundle is gently swept away from the muscles on the plantar–medial surfaces of the tunnel. **C.** The lowest/largest origin of the abductor hallucis muscle (AH 1) and the plantar fascia and short toe flexors are divided. Release of those soft tissues using the tunnel of the NV bundle for guidance obviates injury to those important structures. **D.** The lateral plantar NV bundle can be seen traversing the foot in a distal–lateral direction. **E.** The thin septum, and 2nd origin, of the abductor hallucis (AH 2) that separates the medial and lateral plantar NV bundles is exposed. **F.** It is divided under direct vision. **G.** The most dorsal origin of the abductor hallucis (AH 3), which is dorsal to the medial plantar NV bundle, is released. **H.** The three origins of the abductor hallucis muscle have been released from the calcaneus while carefully protecting the medial and lateral plantar posterior tibial NV bundles. The plantar fascia and the flexor digitorum brevis have been released. This completes the S-PMR for a cavovarus foot deformity with flexible hindfoot varus.

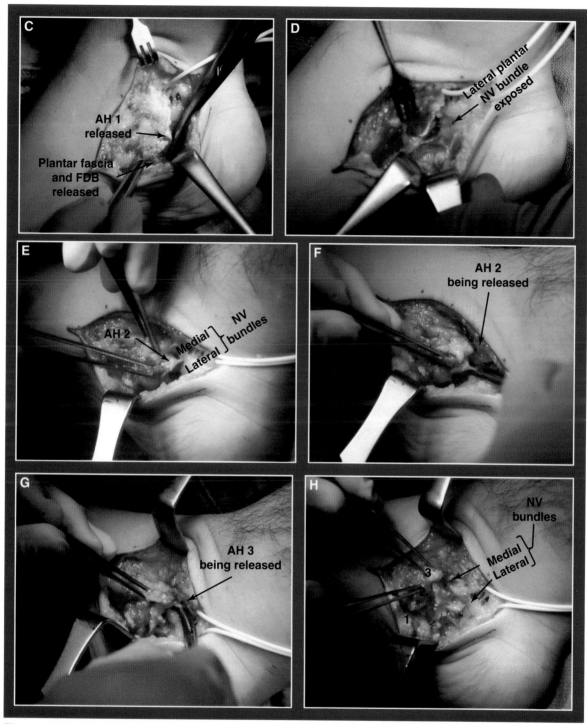

Figure 7-31. *(continued)*

Deep Medial Release (D-MR)

1. Indications
   a. Pain and/or gait instability due to stiff/rigid hindfoot varus, i.e., *does not correct* with the Coleman block test (**see Assessment Principles #9 and 19, Chapter 3**), and *without* forefoot pronation or cavus
      i. Seen in some clubfeet and in some spastic varus feet
         • Often used as an adjunct procedure with tendon transfers in these feet

2. Technique (**see Superficial Plantar-Medial Release [Figure 7-31] and Deep Plantar-Medial Release [Figure 7-32], but do *not* perform the plantar release**)
   a. Make a longitudinal incision along the medial border of the midfoot/hindfoot just dorsal to the edge of the glabrous skin and extending posterior to the posterior tibial NV bundle
   b. Perform a superficial medial release exactly as described previously

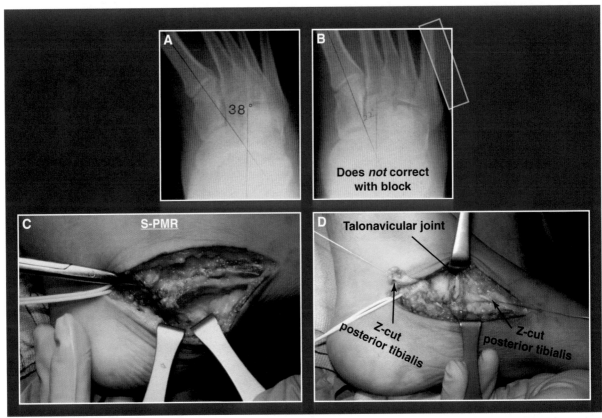

Figure 7-32. Deep plantar-medial release. **A.** Standing AP x-ray of a cavovarus foot. The foot-CORA is in the TN joint, confirming that the deformity is hindfoot varus and not midfoot adductus (**see Assessment Principle #18, Figure 3-20, Chapter 3**). **B.** The varus deformity does not correct fully, as confirmed by a standing Coleman-type block test x-ray. The foot-CORA is still in the TN joint, but the forefoot axis (and acetabulum pedis) is still medially deviated. This is the indication for a D-PMR. The subtalar joint inversion requires release, just as it would if this were a clubfoot. **C.** The S-PMR is performed first (**see above**). Besides providing the necessary release of the contracted more superficial structures, it provides access to the deep structures. **D.** The posterior tibialis tendon is Z-lengthened and the TN joint is released dorsal to plantar, including release of the spring (calcaneonavicular) ligament. Again consider the analogy to a clubfoot release.

c. Release the posterior tibialis tendon sheath from the tip of the medial malleolus distally

d. Z-lengthen the posterior tibialis, releasing the plantar limb from the navicular

e. Release the TN joint capsule medially and plantar-medially, including release of the spring (calcaneonavicular) ligament, to enable passive eversion of the subtalar joint beyond neutral—confirmed with mini-fluoroscopy

f. Repair the overlapping limbs of the posterior tibialis under minimal tension using 2-0 absorbable sutures with the ankle in maximum dorsiflexion and the subtalar joint fully everted

g. Release the tourniquet and achieve good hemostasis

h. Approximate the skin edges with interrupted subcutaneous 3-0 absorbable sutures and a running subcuticular 4-0 absorbable suture.

i. Apply a short-leg non–weight-bearing cast with the ankle in unforced dorsiflexion, the subtalar joint in unforced eversion, and the forefoot in neutral rotation and angulation. Excessive corrective forces could lead to wound edge necrosis, especially in feet that were severely deformed. There is no need to bivalve the cast.

j. Remove the cast after 6 weeks

3. Pitfalls

a. Uncertainty regarding the location of the posterior tibial NV bundles, thereby creating unnecessary caution, concern, and slow progress. Find the NV structures first to improve confidence, accuracy, and speed.

4. Complications

a. Injury to the posterior tibial NV bundles

i. *Avoid by* isolating them proximally and tracing them between the three origins of the abductor hallucis

Superficial Plantar-Medial Release (S-PMR)

1. Indications

a. Pain and/or gait instability due to cavovarus foot deformity (**see Chapter 5**) with flexible hindfoot varus, i.e., *corrects* with the Coleman block test (**see Assessment**

Principles #9 and 19, Chapter 3), and *with* stiff/rigid forefoot pronation and cavus

2. Technique (Figure 7-31)
   a. Make a longitudinal incision along the medial border of the midfoot/hindfoot just dorsal to the edge of the glabrous skin and extending posterior to the posterior tibial NV bundle
   b. Isolate the posterior tibial NV bundle posterior to the medial malleolus and proximal to the superior edge of the flexor retinaculum. Tag it with a vessel loop.
   c. Release the flexor retinaculum (laciniate ligament) vertically in line with the NV bundle for full exposure of these important structures
   d. Release the lowest and largest origin of the abductor hallucis muscle from its origin on the calcaneus while protecting the lateral plantar NV bundle.
   e. Expose the tunnel through which the lateral plantar NV bundle travels across the foot deep to the flexor digitorum brevis
   f. Bluntly and carefully develop some space between the lateral plantar NV bundle and the plantar roof of this tunnel, which is made up of the flexor digitorum brevis and the plantar fascia
   g. Elevate the plantar fat off the plantar fascia
   h. Release the plantar fascia and flexor digitorum brevis from medial to lateral while visualizing and protecting the lateral plantar NV bundle (**see Plantar release, this Chapter**)
   i. Expose and release the very thin interfascicular septum (the middle origin of the abductor hallucis on the calcaneus) that separates the medial and lateral plantar NV bundles. It is only 1 to 2 mm long and 1 to 2 mm wide
   j. Release from the calcaneus the most dorsal origin of the abductor hallucis, which is the dorsal edge of the tunnel through which the medial plantar NV bundle travels within the abductor hallucis muscle
   k. This completes the release of the three origins of the abductor hallucis muscle, the plantar fascia, and flexor digitorum brevis from the calcaneus.
   l. Release the tourniquet and achieve good hemostasis
   m. Approximate the skin edges with interrupted subcutaneous 3-0 absorbable sutures and a running subcuticular 4-0 absorbable suture
   n. If this is the first of a two-stage reconstruction for a cavovarus foot deformity, use a running subcuticular pull-out 3-0 Proline suture. This will decrease the soft tissue reaction that might otherwise complicate wound closure at the completion of the second stage procedure 2 weeks later
   o. Apply a short-leg cast with the ankle in unforced dorsiflexion, the subtalar joint in unforced eversion, and the forefoot in unforced supination and abduction. Excessive corrective forces could lead to wound edge necrosis, especially in feet that were severely deformed. There is no need to bivalve the cast.
   p. The cast will be removed (in most cases) 2 weeks later at the start of the second-stage reconstruction of the cavovarus foot deformity.
   q. If this is the only procedure to be performed, remove the cast after 6 weeks.

3. Pitfalls
   a. Uncertainty regarding the location of the posterior tibial NV bundles, thereby creating unnecessary caution, concern, and slow progress. Find the NV structures first to improve confidence, accuracy, and speed.
   b. Failure to recognize the need for a D-MR, i.e., the subtalar joint does not fully evert

4. Complications
   a. Wound edge necrosis
      i. *Avoid by* using good tissue handling techniques and/or by limiting exaggerated corrective forces in the cast
   b. Injury to the posterior tibial NV bundles
      i. *Avoid by* isolating them proximally and tracing them between the three origins of the abductor hallucis and through the plantar tunnel under direct vision

Deep Plantar-Medial Release (D-PMR)

1. Indications
   a. Pain and/or gait instability due to cavovarus foot deformity (**see Chapter 5**) with stiff/rigid hindfoot varus, i.e., *does not correct* with the Coleman block test (**see Assessment Principles #9 and 19, Chapter 3**), and *with* stiff/rigid forefoot pronation and cavus

2. Technique (Figure 7-32)
   a. Make a longitudinal incision along the medial border of the midfoot/hindfoot just dorsal to the edge of the glabrous skin and extending posterior to the posterior tibial NV bundle
   b. Perform a S-PMR exactly as described previously
   c. Release the FDL tendon sheath plantar-medial to the talus and navicular starting from the medial malleolus and progressing anteriorly
   d. Retract the FDL plantarward
   e. Release the posterior tibialis tendon sheath plantar-medial to the talus between the tip of the medial malleolus and the navicular
   f. Z-lengthen the posterior tibialis, releasing the *plantar* limb from the navicular
   g. Release the TN joint capsule medially and plantar-medially, including release of the spring (calcaneonavicular) ligament, to enable passive eversion of the subtalar joint slightly beyond neutral—confirmed with mini-fluoroscopy. Avoid circumferential release of the TN capsule as excessive instability of the joint could result
   h. Repair the overlapping limbs of the posterior tibialis under minimal tension using 2-0 absorbable sutures with the ankle in maximum dorsiflexion and the subtalar joint fully everted
   i. Release the tourniquet and achieve good hemostasis

j. Approximate the skin edges with interrupted subcutaneous 3-0 absorbable sutures and a running subcuticular pull-out 3-0 Proline suture. A deep plantar-medial release (D-PMR) is almost always the first of a two-stage reconstruction. Using the Proline will decrease the soft tissue reaction that might otherwise complicate wound closure at the completion of the second stage procedure 2 weeks later

k. Apply a short-leg cast with the ankle in unforced dorsiflexion, the subtalar joint in unforced eversion, and the forefoot in unforced supination and abduction. Excessive corrective forces could lead to wound edge necrosis, especially in feet that were severely deformed. There is no need to bivalve the cast.

l. The cast will be removed (in most cases) 2 weeks later at the start of the second-stage reconstruction of the cavovarus foot deformity

3. Pitfalls

a. Uncertainty regarding the location of the posterior tibial NV bundles, thereby creating unnecessary caution, concern, and slow progress. Find the NV structures first to improve confidence, accuracy, and speed.

4. Complications

a. Wound edge necrosis

   i. *Avoid by* using good tissue handling techniques and/or by limiting exaggerated corrective forces in the cast

b. Injury to the posterior tibial NV bundles

   i. *Avoid by* isolating them proximally and tracing them between the three origins of the abductor hallucis and through the plantar tunnel under direct vision

Dorsal Approach Release for Congenital Vertical Talus and Congenital Oblique Talus (DR)

1. Indications

a. Failure of the reverse Ponseti (Dobbs) nonoperative method to align the TN joint and, thereby, correct a CVT or congenital oblique talus deformity (**see Chapter 5**)

2. Technique (Figure 7-33)

a. Make a transverse incision in the anterior ankle crease from the tip of the medial malleolus to the tip of the lateral malleolus

b. Isolate and protect the superficial peroneal nerve and the anterior tibialis NV bundle

c. Z-lengthen the anterior tibialis and the EHL tendons in idiopathic cases. Perform tenotomies of those tendons in children with arthrogryposis and myelomeningocele

d. Retract the EDC tendons unless they are too contracted to retract—in which case they can be released

e. Release the peroneus tertius

f. Bluntly elevate the fat from the dorsal and medial surfaces of the tibio-navicular joint capsule, extending plantar-medially

g. The posterior tibial NV bundle is quite plantar and should be considered and avoided when dissecting far plantarward.

h. Release the posterior tibialis tendon from its sheath. The tendon can be used to help identify the location of the dorsally dislocated navicular

i. Release the peroneus brevis and longus from their tendon sheaths laterally and transect them.

j. The very contracted dorsal "tibio-talo-navicular" joint capsule can now be appreciated by dorsiflexing and plantar flexing the foot and observing as it slightly relaxes and tightens

k. Release the capsule between the navicular and tibia transversely, starting medial to the TN joint and extending laterally into the sinus tarsi. The dome and neck of the talus will be exposed. The head of the talus is not readily visible initially because the talus is so plantar flexed.

l. Release the dorsal capsule of the calcaneocuboid joint if the cuboid is dorsally subluxated (check preoperative lateral x-ray and intraoperative lateral mini-fluoroscopy image)

m. Perform a percutaneous TAT (**see this chapter**). Consider releasing this initially.

n. Using a Freer or Joker elevator with a dorsal-to-plantar trajectory between the navicular and talus, lever and elevate the head of the talus while depressing the navicular

o. While maintaining this position, insert a 0.062″ smooth Steinmann pin retrograde from the anatomic center of the talar head, along the central axis of the talus, exiting through the skin of the posterior ankle. Use mini-fluoroscopy to ensure that this pin is in the proper position three-dimensionally, repositioning it if necessary

p. With the drill transferred to the exposed wire posteriorly, pull it back until the anterior sharpened tip is flush with the articular surface of the talar head

q. Align the TN joint/subtalar joint anatomically

r. If the dorsal capsule is adequately released and the subtalar joint will not invert, the problem could be contracted soft tissues in the sinus tarsi.

s. Use the wire to dorsiflex the talus while inserting it antegrade across the TN joint. Advance it until it exits the skin on the dorsal forefoot. Confirm anatomic alignment of the foot with mini-fluoroscopy. Realign the foot and reinsert the wire if necessary.

t. Add a second wire across the TN joint from anterior-medial to posterior-lateral. In my experience, a single wire has been known to migrate out of the foot prematurely, so having a backup wire is wise

u. Cut the wires flush with the skin and allow them to retract subcutaneously (for anticipated removal under anesthesia) or bend them at the insertion sites and cut them long (for easy removal in clinic).

v. Repair the anterior tibialis and the EHL tendons with 2-0 absorbable sutures in idiopathic cases. Do not repair them in children with arthrogryposis and myelomeningocele

w. Approximate the skin edges with interrupted subcutaneous 3-0 absorbable sutures and a running subcuticular 4-0 absorbable suture

x. Apply a long-leg cast with slight inversion molding of the subtalar joint, pronation molding of the forefoot, a well-molded longitudinal arch, and with the ankle at neutral-to-slight dorsiflexion. Flex the knee 90° and set the thigh–foot angle at neutral (0°)

y. Change to a new long-leg cast in clinic in 3 weeks

z. Remove the cast and the two buried pins in the OR, or the exposed pins in the clinic, 6 weeks postoperatively

  i. Idiopathic cases: apply a short-leg cast. Three weeks later, remove the cast in clinic and initiate a Ponseti-type FAB with the shoes parallel to each other on the

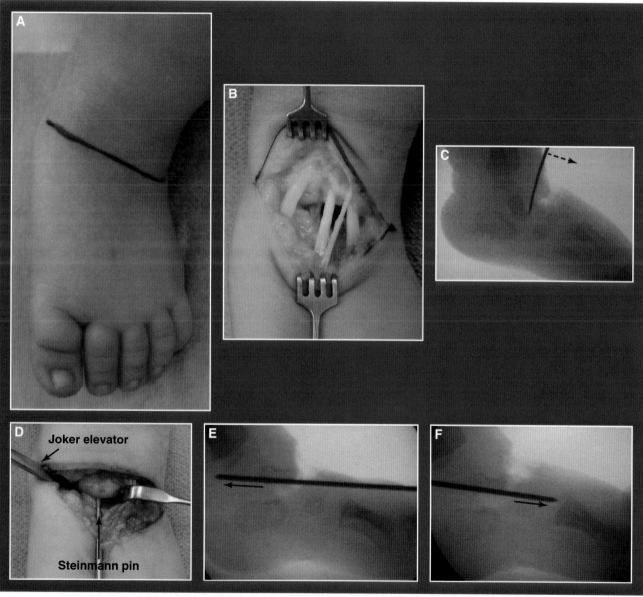

Figure 7-33. Dorsal release for CVT. **A.** Transverse anterior ankle incision. **B.** Exposed extensor tendons and superficial peroneal nerve. **C.** Following release of the dorsal tibio-navicular joint capsule, a Freer elevator (*thin black line*) is inserted and used as a lever to elevate/dorsiflex the talus. **D.** A 0.062″ smooth Steinmann pin is inserted retrograde into the center of the articular surface of the talar head. A Joker elevator can be used to maintain elevation of the talar head during insertion of the pin. **E.** The pin is advanced retrograde through the center of the body of the talus and out the back of the ankle. **F.** The pin is then inserted antegrade across the anatomically aligned TN joint and out the dorsum of the forefoot. **G.** Dorsal appearance of the anatomically aligned foot. **H.** Medial side appearance of the anatomically aligned foot. **I.** AP fluoroscopic image. The pin does not have to be in the exact axis of the medial column of the foot, but the talus and the first MT should be aligned, as they are in this foot. **J.** Lateral fluoroscopic image of the foot showing anatomic alignment.

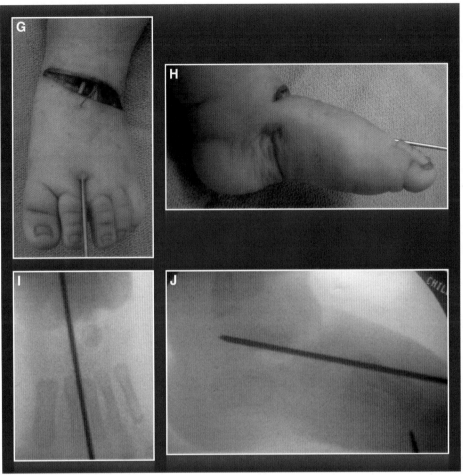

Figure 7-33. *(continued)*

bar. Request that the child wear the FAB 23 hours per day for 3 months and at night/naps till age 2 years

aa. Arthrogryposis and myelomeningocele cases: mold for an AFO with neutral ankle, varus hindfoot, pronated forefoot, and well-molded arch in clinic at 6 weeks. Apply a short-leg cast. Three weeks later, remove the cast and buried pins in the OR and fit the AFO, to be worn 23 hours per day

3. Pitfalls

a. Inadequate release of the anterior capsule and/or peroneus brevis and/or tendo-Achilles, thereby preventing full deformity correction

b. Nonanatomic alignment of the TN and subtalar joints before pinning

4. Complications

a. Injury to the posterior tibial NV bundle

i. *Avoid by* careful medial dissection and soft tissue retraction before capsulotomy

b. Migration of a single pin out from across the TN joint, resulting in subluxation of the joint with recurrent deformity

i. *Avoid by*

• having a backup second pin

• cutting the pins immediately subcutaneously, rather than leaving them exposed is very small feet.

3rd Street Procedure (Barnett Procedure)

1. Indications

a. Iatrogenically acquired dorsal subluxation or dislocation of the navicular on the head of the talus in an operatively treated clubfoot (**see Chapter 5**) in a child under the age of 6 to 7 years

i. In children with this iatrogenic deformity, simple TN joint release and realignment are rarely successful

2. Technique (Figures 7-34 and 7-35)

a. Make a longitudinal incision along the medial border of the midfoot. Incision through the scar from the original clubfoot release is ideal.

b. Release the posterior tibialis tendon from the dense scar tissue surrounding it and cut it in a Z-fashion

c. Release the TN joint capsule circumferentially as completely as possible from this approach. Release intra-articular adhesions with a Freer elevator.

d. Attempt to align the joint anatomically. If it does not easily realign, proceed with the 3rd street procedure.

e. Make a longitudinal incision on the dorsum of the midfoot starting proximally over the navicular–cuboid joint and extending distally over the interval between the base of the 3rd and 4th MTs (the "3rd street")

f. Identify and protect the superficial peroneal nerve

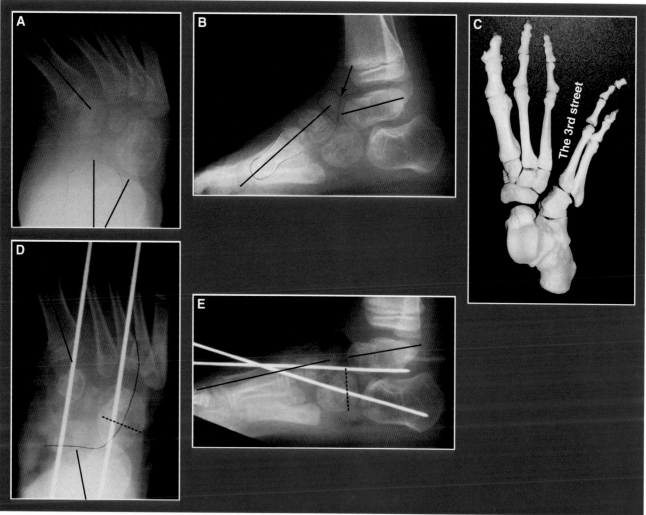

Figure 7-34. 3rd Street procedure. A. Standing AP x-ray shows severe forefoot adductus in this 5-year-old boy who underwent a circumferential clubfoot release at age 6 months. The relationship of the talus to the calcaneus is normal. B. Standing lateral x-ray shows dorsal subluxation of the navicular on the head of the talus (*arrow*). The cartilaginous anlage of the navicular is outlined. The relationships of the tibia, talus, and calcaneus are normal. The 1st ray of the foot (including the 1st MT, medial cuneiform, and navicular) is dorsally translated and plantar flexed. C. The "3rd street," according to Barnett, is the interval between the 3rd MT–3rd cuneiform–navicular bones and the 4th MT–cuboid bones. D. Barnett suggested correcting iatrogenic dorsal subluxation of the navicular on the head of the talus by performing a circumferential release of the TN joint and extending the cap-sulotomies distally along the dorsal surface of the 3rd street (indicated by the *black curved line*). The dotted line represents the closing wedge osteotomy of the cuboid that was indicated in this foot to correct the additional rigid adductus deformity of the midfoot that existed. The medial white line is the Steinmann pin that was used for temporary internal fixation of the TN joint. The lateral white line is the Steinmann pin that was used for temporary internal fixation of the lateral column, including the cuboid osteotomy. Correction of the talus–1st MT alignment is shown with the axis lines. E. Lateral intraoperative radiograph shows the reestablished anatomic alignment of the talus and 1st MT (*black lines*) held in place by the Steinmann pins (*white lines*). The location of the cuboid closing wedge osteotomy (*dotted line*) is indicated. F. Standing lateral x-ray obtained 3.9 years later shows main-tenance of anatomic alignment. Note the straight alignment of the axes of the 1st MT and the talus. The dorsal surface of the navicular is slightly dorsal to the dorsal surfaces of the medial cuneiform and talus, suggesting dorsal overgrowth of the navicular but with good alignment at the TN joint. The wire staple was inserted during the operation for additional internal fixation of the cuboid after the Steinmann pins were inserted, but before the previous intraoperative x-rays were obtained. G. Stand-ing lateral x-ray taken 13 years after the operation showing good maintenance of alignment in this asymptomatic 18-year-old young man. H. Standing AP x-ray taken at the same time.

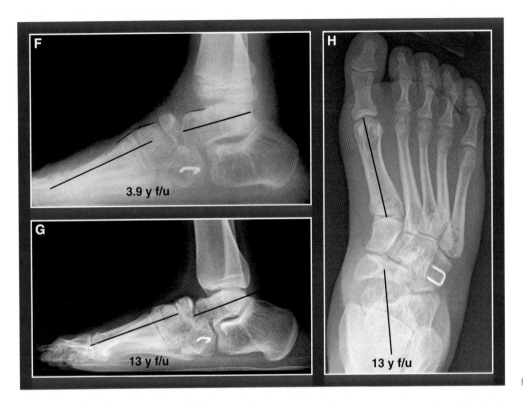

F 3.9 y f/u

G 13 y f/u

H 13 y f/u

Figure 7-34. *(continued)*

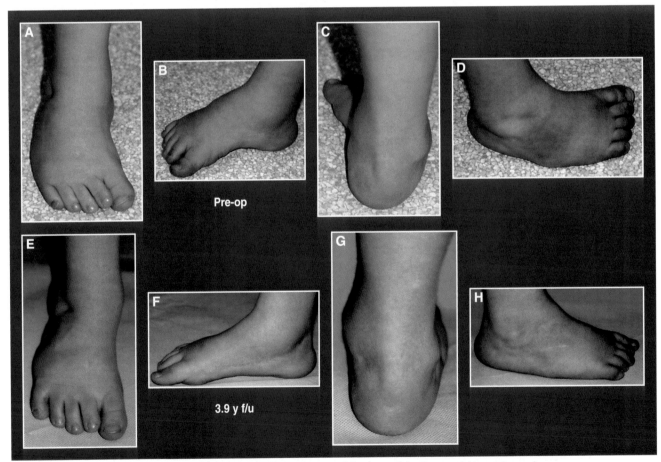

Pre-op

3.9 y f/u

Figure 7-35. **A–D.** Preoperative standing images of the foot of the 5-year-old boy, shown in Figure 7-34, with iatrogenic acquired dorsal subluxation of the navicular on the head of the talus following clubfoot surgery in infancy. **E–H.** Standing images of his foot 3.9 years after he underwent a 3rd street procedure and concurrent closing wedge osteotomy of the cuboid. **I–L.** Standing images of his foot 13 years later at age 18 years. He was asymptomatic at the time, despite marked restriction of subtalar motion.

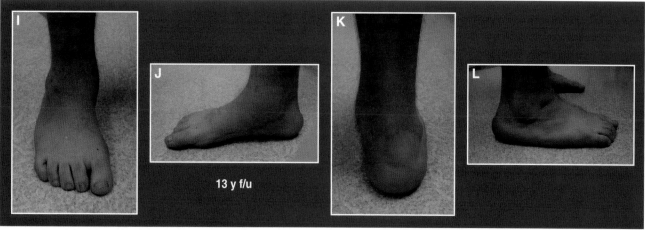

13 y f/u

Figure 7-35. *(continued)*

g. Release the lateral TN joint capsule to complete the circumferential release of that joint

h. Release the dorsal capsule of the navicular–cuboid joint

i. Release the dorsal capsule of the lateral cuneiform–cuboid joint

j. Release the dorsal capsule and ligaments between the base of the 3rd and 4th MTs

k. There is now a continuous capsular release from the medial TN joint to the interval between the base of the 3rd and 4th MTs.

l. The navicular will easily align anatomically with the head of the talus by pronating the medial forefoot on the hindfoot

m. Insert 1 to 2 smooth 0.062″ Steinmann pins retrograde across the TN joint. Use mini-fluoroscopy to confirm TN joint alignment and appropriate position of the pins.

n. Bend the pins at their insertion sites on the dorsum of the foot and cut them long for easy retrieval in clinic

o. Perform a deep plantar–medial plication (**see this chapter**)

p. Apply a long-leg non–weight-bearing cast

q. Change to a short-leg walking cast with exaggerated cavovarus molding after removal of the pins in clinic 6 weeks later. The second cast is worn for 3 weeks

3. Pitfalls

a. Incomplete deformity correction because of inadequate capsular releases.

4. Complications

a. Injury to the superficial peroneal nerve

i. *Avoid by* careful dissection, identification, and retraction

b. Recurrent deformity

i. *Avoid by* casting no less than 9 weeks as prescribed above

Butler Procedure for Congenital Overriding 5th Toe

1. Indications

a. Congenital overriding 5th toe (**see Chapter 5**)

2. Technique (Figure 7-36)

a. Make an elliptical V-shaped dorsomedial and Y-shaped plantar–lateral incision around the base of the 5th toe passing through the 4th and 5 web space medially.

b. After incising the skin, carefully spread the soft tissues with iris or tenotomy scissors to free the skin from the fat that contains the NV bundles, thereby keeping the NV bundles with the toe

c. Expose and Z-lengthen the EDC tendon to the toe

d. Release the dorsal and dorsomedial portions of the MTP joint capsule

e. Release the tourniquet, assess vascularity of the toe, and achieve hemostasis.

f. Gently pronate the toe and reposition it plantar-laterally in line with the 5th MT head/shaft, advancing it into the longitudinal portion of the Y-shaped plantar–lateral skin incision

g. Reposition the toe slowly and gently so as not to over-stretch the NV bundles. If the toe loses vascularity, return it to the deformed position and try again more slowly

h. Using 4-0 chromic simple sutures, convert the plantar–lateral incision from a Y-shape to a V-shape to hold the toe in the proper position

i. Using 4-0 chromic simple sutures, convert the dorso-medial incision from a V-shape to a Y-shape to hold the toe in the proper position

j. Wire fixation should not be necessary

k. Apply a short-leg cast over dressings and cast padding that are applied in a way so as to maintain the proper position of the toe. Check the vascularity of the toe by viewing it through the end of the cast

l. Remove the cast after 4 to 6 weeks, based on the age of the patient

3. Pitfalls

a. Inaccurate positioning of the handles of the longitudinal incisions, thereby resulting in less than ideal final position of the toe

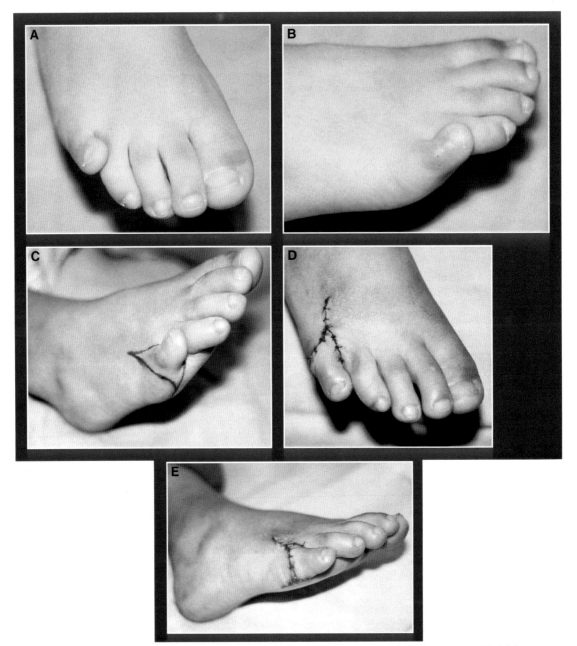

Figure 7-36. Butler procedure. **A.** Top view of a congenital overriding 5th toe in a 7-year-old child with pain and callus formation over the dorsum of the toe from shoe pressure. **B.** Side view. **C.** Double racket handle (V-Y, Y-V) incision is marked with plantar–lateral position of the Y-V racket handle. This will ensure plantar–lateral translation and pronation of the toe to correct the dorsomedial malposition and supination. **D.** Top view after correction. The translational and rotational deformities have been corrected. 4-0 absorbable simple sutures were used. **E.** Side view shows excellent correction of the deformities and no need for fixation. Comparison with image C reveals the conversion of the dorsal V-shaped incision into a Y-shaped scar. (From Mosca VS. The foot. In: Weinstein S, Flynn J, eds. *Lovell and Winter's Pediatric Orthopaedics*, 7th ed. Philadelphia, PA: Lippincott Williams & Wilkins, 2013:1493, Figure 29-71.)

4. Complications
   a. Vascular compromise to the toe
      i. *Avoid by:*
         • careful dissection around the base of the toe
         • releasing the tourniquet before repositioning the toe
         • assuring good blood supply to the toe after it is repositioned and before/after the incisions are closed and the dressing is applied

Posterior Release (Post-R)

1. Indications
   a. Clubfoot (**see Chapter 5**) with full correction of cavus, adductus, and varus, but with residual or recurrent equinus due to contractures of the tendo-Achilles and the posterior ankle joint capsule
   b. Long-standing acquired equinus deformity

2. Technique (Figure 7-37)
   a. Make a Cincinnati incision 1 cm proximal to, and parallel with, the posterior heel crease
   b. Isolate the posterior tibial NV bundle posterior to the medial malleolus and proximal to the superior edge of the flexor retinaculum. Tag it with a vessel loop.
   c. Z-lengthen the tendo-Achilles, releasing its medial fibers from the calcaneus and its lateral fibers proximally
      i. In the rare situation in which a posterior release is performed for an equinovalgus deformity, release the lateral fibers from the calcaneus and the medial fibers proximally
   d. Identify the FHL posteromedially as the tendon with the most distal musculotendinous junction in the field. It is immediately lateral to the PT NV bundle
   e. Release the tendon sheath of the FHL from proximal to distal, following the tendon until it disappears under the sustentaculum tali
   f. The sustentaculum tali is directly medial to the posterior facet of the subtalar joint and is, therefore, a good reference point for identifying that joint
   g. The posterior facet of the subtalar joint can be partially or completely released posteriorly, based on the severity of deformity at that level
   h. Release the calcaneofibular ligament and the adjacent short section of the peroneal tendon sheath from the calcaneus. Do not release the peroneal tendon sheath from the fibula as that could result in anterolateral subluxation of the tendons
   i. Identify the ankle joint proximal/cephalad to the subtalar joint taking care not to injure the perichondrial ring of the distal tibial physis, a particular risk in very young children with severe equinus deformity in which the ankle and subtalar joints are essentially unified by a single posterior joint capsule
   j. Release the tibiotalar (ankle) joint capsule posteriorly and around both corners of the dome of the talus down

to, but not including, the distal-most fibers of the deep deltoid ligament and the distal talofibular ligament
   k. Do *not* release the talocalcaneal interosseous ligament located anterior to the posterior facet
   l. Confirm full dorsiflexion of the hindfoot clinically and radiographically
      i. on mini-fluoroscopy, the talus should dorsiflex to within 10° of perpendicular to the tibia and the calcaneus to at least 15° above perpendicular to the tibia
   m. Repair the overlapping limbs of the tendo-Achilles with 2-0 absorbable sutures under moderate tension with the knee extended and the ankle dorsiflexed 10°
   n. Approximate the skin edges with interrupted subcutaneous 3-0 absorbable sutures and a running subcuticular 4-0 absorbable suture
   o. Apply a short-leg cast with 10° dorsiflexion. Use a long-leg cast in infants and young children in whom the cast might otherwise slip off. There is no need to bivalve the cast.

3. Pitfalls
   a. Inappropriate release of the subtalar joint rather than the ankle joint, because of inaccurate identification. Tracing the FHL to the subtalar joint for orientation will prevent this error.
   b. Incomplete release of the ankle joint, because of failure to release around both corners of the dome of the talus

4. Complications
   a. Heel pad slough due to dysvascularity
      i. *Avoid by* ensuring that the Cincinnati incision is at least 1 cm proximal to, and parallel with, the deep posterior heel crease (the crease is usually at the insertion of the tendo-Achilles on the calcaneus)
   b. Posterior distal tibial physeal injury with progressive procurvatum deformity, due to imprecise identification of the ankle joint and resultant direct trauma to the physis (**see Figure 5-21, Chapter 5**)
      i. *Avoid by* tracing the FHL to the subtalar joint and then carefully probing more proximally for the ankle joint. If the ankle joint is incorrectly thought to be the subtalar joint, the more proximal probing for the "ankle joint" could result in damage to the perichondrial ring of the distal tibial physis

Circumferential Clubfoot Release (Postero-Plantar-Medial Release)—Á la Carte (Post-PMR)

1. Indications
   a. Failure to achieve full correction of some or all of the clubfoot deformities with serial casting (**see Chapter 5**)
   b. An á la carte approach is used starting posterolaterally and progressing posteromedially and then plantar-medially, releasing only those soft tissue structures that have not fully corrected with the preoperative serial casting

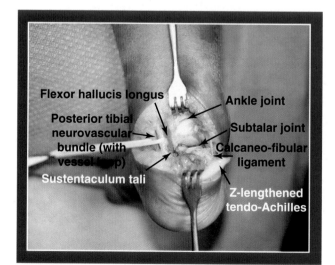

Figure 7-37. Posterior release. The anatomic structures are labeled.

2. <u>Technique</u>

  a. Make a Cincinnati incision 1 cm proximal to, and parallel with, the posterior heel crease. Start at the distal tip of the lateral malleolus and pass distal to the tip of the medial malleolus before progressing anteriorly along the medial border of the hindfoot and midfoot ending adjacent to the medial cuneiform.

  Posterior release (**see Post-R Technique b–k [repeated here for convenience and continuity], Figure 7-37**)

  b. Isolate the posterior tibial NV bundle posterior to the medial malleolus and proximal to the superior edge of the flexor retinaculum. Tag it with a vessel loop.

  c. Z-lengthen the tendo-Achilles, releasing its medial fibers from the calcaneus and its lateral fibers proximally

  d. Identify the FHL posteromedially as the tendon with the most distal musculotendinous junction in the field. It is immediately lateral to the posterior tibial NV bundle

  e. Release the tendon sheath of the FHL from proximal to distal, following the tendon until it disappears under the sustentaculum tali

  f. The sustentaculum tali is directly medial to the posterior facet of the subtalar joint and is, therefore, a good reference point for identifying that joint.

  g. The posterior facet of the subtalar joint can be partially or completely released posteriorly, based on the severity of deformity at that level.

  h. Release the calcaneofibular ligament and the adjacent short section of the peroneal tendon sheath from the calcaneus. Do not release the peroneal tendon sheath from the fibula as that could result in anterolateral subluxation of the tendons

  i. Identify the ankle joint proximal/cephalad to the subtalar joint taking care not to injure the perichondrial ring of the distal tibial physis, a particular risk in very young children with severe equinus deformity in which the ankle and subtalar joints are essentially unified by a single posterior joint capsule

  j. Release the tibiotalar (ankle) joint capsule posteriorly and around both corners of the dome of the talus down to, but not including, the distal-most fibers of the deep deltoid ligament and the distal talofibular ligament

  k. Do *not* release the talocalcaneal interosseous ligament located anterior to the posterior facet

  Plantar-medial clubfoot release (**also see S-PMR Technique c–j and D-PMR Technique c-g [repeated here for convenience and continuity], Figure 7-38**)

  l. Release the flexor retinaculum (laciniate ligament) vertically in line with the NV bundle for full exposure of these important structures

  m. Release the lowest and largest origin of the abductor hallucis muscle from its origin on the calcaneus while protecting the lateral plantar NV bundle.

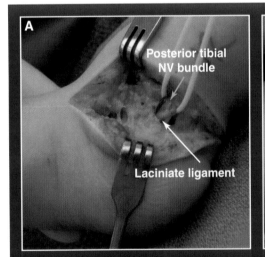 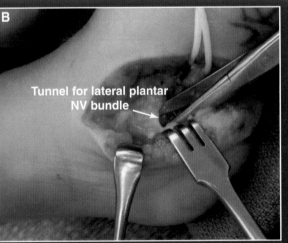

Figure 7-38. Plantar-medial release for clubfoot. Following a posterolateral release, a plantar-medial release is performed through the medial extent of the Cincinnati incision. **A.** The posterior tibial NV bundle is isolated behind the medial malleolus and tagged with a vessel loop. The laciniate ligament (flexor retinaculum) is released. **B.** The tunnel through which the lateral plantar NV bundle travels under the hindfoot/midfoot is carefully and bluntly exposed. **C.** The lowest and largest origin of the abductor hallucis muscle, which makes up the plantar–medial roof of the tunnel, is released from the calcaneus. **D.** The plantar fascia and the short toe flexors, which make up the plantar roof of the tunnel, are released from the calcaneus. The lateral plantar NV bundle is now completely exposed. **E.** The middle and thinnest origin of the abductor hallucis muscle, that separates the medial and lateral plantar NV bundles, is released from the calcaneus. **F.** The highest (most dorsal) origin of the abductor hallucis, that is dorsal to the medial and lateral plantar NV bundles, is released from the calcaneus. **G.** An S-PMR has been completed (**also see Superficial Plantar-Medial Release, this chapter**). The posterior tibialis and FDL tendons have been released from their respective tendon sheaths. **H.** A D-PMR is completed by Z-lengthening the posterior tibialis tendon and performing a TN joint capsulotomy (**also see Deep Plantar-Medial Release, this chapter**).

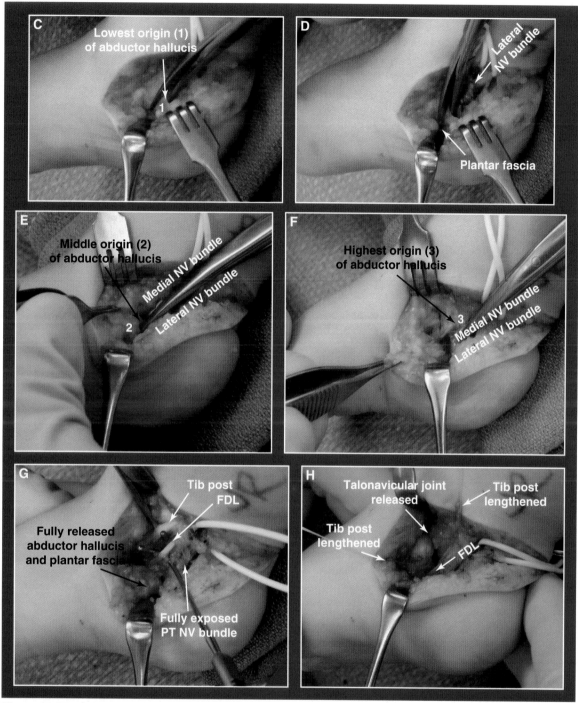

Figure 7-38. *(continued)*

n. Expose the tunnel through which the lateral plantar NV bundle travels across the foot deep to the flexor digitorum brevis

o. Bluntly and carefully develop some space between the lateral plantar NV bundle and the plantar roof of this tunnel, which is made up of the flexor digitorum brevis and the plantar fascia

p. Elevate the plantar fat off the plantar fascia

q. Release the plantar fascia and flexor digitorum brevis from medial to lateral while visualizing and protecting the lateral plantar NV bundle (**see Plantar release, this chapter**)

r. Expose and release the very thin interfascicular septum (the middle origin of the abductor hallucis on the calcaneus) that separates the medial and lateral plantar NV bundles. It is only 1 to 2 mm long and 1 to 2 mm wide.

s. Release from the calcaneus the most dorsal origin of the abductor hallucis, which is the dorsal edge of the tunnel through which the medial plantar NV bundle travels within the abductor hallucis muscle

t. Release the FDL tendon sheath plantar-medial to the talus and navicular starting from the medial malleolus and progressing anteriorly.

u. Retract the FDL plantarward

v. Release the posterior posterior tibialis tendon sheath plantar-medial to the talus between the tip of the medial malleolus and the navicular

w. Z-lengthen the posterior tibialis, releasing the *plantar* limb from the navicular

x. Release the TN joint capsule medially and plantar-medially, including release of the spring (calcaneo-navicular) ligament, to enable passive eversion of the subtalar joint slightly beyond neutral—confirmed with mini-fluoroscopy. Avoid circumferential release of the TN capsule as excessive instability of the joint could result.

Percutaneous tenotomies of FHL and FDL to toes 2 to 5 (**see Perc. FHL/FDL Technique a–d [repeated here for convenience and continuity], Figure 7-4, this chapter**)

y. Dorsiflex the ankle to tension the long toe flexor tendons

z. Maximally dorsiflex one toe at a time

aa. Using a #11 scalpel, cut the long flexor tendon to each toe using short-arc sweeping movements starting in the center of the toe at the proximal plantar flexion crease. The tip of the scalpel should be used both as a probe and a scalpel. The incision should be no more than about 3 to 4 mm. There will be a sudden release of tension and the IP joints will extend.

bb. If the DIP joint extends but the PIP does not, the flexor brevis is also contracted and should be released using the same technique.

Final assessment and closure

cc. Confirm full dorsiflexion of the hindfoot clinically and radiographically

  i. on mini-fluoroscopy, the talus should dorsiflex to within 10° of perpendicular to the tibia and the calcaneus to at least 15° above perpendicular to the tibia

dd. Confirm full eversion of the subtalar joint clinically and radiographically

  i. on mini-fluoroscopy, there should be straight axial alignment of the axis of the 1st MT with the axis of the talus on the lateral image, and straight axial alignment to slight abduction of the axis of the 1st MT with the axis of the talus on the anteroposterior (AP) image

ee. Repair the overlapping limbs of the posterior tibialis under minimal tension using 2-0 absorbable sutures with the subtalar joint fully everted and the ankle dorsiflexed 10°

ff. Repair the overlapping limbs of the tendo-Achilles with 2-0 absorbable sutures under moderate tension with the knee extended and the ankle dorsiflexed 10°

gg. There is no need for pins across the joints unless the joint capsules have been released excessively, rather than sufficiently. Try to avoid that.

hh. Release the tourniquet and achieve good hemostasis

  ii. Approximate the skin edges with interrupted subcutaneous 3-0 absorbable sutures and a running subcuticular 4-0 absorbable suture

jj. First, apply a short-leg cast with 10° of ankle dorsiflexion, full eversion of the subtalar joint, midfoot abduction, and slight forefoot supination—only if the skin edges remained pink following wound closure and assumption of this position (**see Complication "e" below**). Then extend it to a long-leg cast with the knee flexed 90° and a thigh–foot angle of approximately 45° external. There is no need to bivalve the cast.

3. Pitfalls

a. Uncertainty regarding the location of the posterior tibial NV bundles, thereby creating unnecessary caution, concern, and slow progress. Find the NV structures first to improve confidence, accuracy, and speed.

b. Inappropriate posterior release of the subtalar joint rather than the ankle joint, because of inaccurate identification. Tracing the FHL to the subtalar joint will prevent this error.

c. Incomplete release of the ankle joint, because of failure to release around both corners of the dome of the talus

d. Inserting the tip of the scalpel too rapidly and too deeply into the FHL or FDL tendon so that it cannot act as a probe to determine the position and limits of the tendon during percutaneous tenotomy

e. Excessive release of joint capsules and/or the interosseous talocalcaneal ligament, which will often result in overcorrection of deformities

4. Complications

a. Heel pad slough due to dysvascularity

  i. *Avoid by* ensuring that the Cincinnati incision is at least 1 cm proximal to, and parallel with, the deep posterior heel crease (the crease is usually at the insertion of the tendo-Achilles on the calcaneus)

b. Injury to the posterior tibial NV bundles

  i. *Avoid by* isolating them proximally and tracing them between the three origins of the abductor hallucis and through the plantar tunnel under direct vision

c. Posterior distal tibial physeal injury with progressive procurvatum deformity, due to imprecise identification of the ankle joint and resultant direct trauma to the physis (**see Figure 5-21, Chapter 5**)

  i. *Avoid by* tracing the FHL to the subtalar joint and then carefully probing more proximally for the ankle joint. If the ankle joint is incorrectly thought to be the subtalar joint, the more proximal probing for the "ankle joint" could result in damage to the perichondrial ring of the distal tibial physis

d. Laceration of a digital nerve or artery during percutaneous tenotomy of the FHL or FDL

  i. *Avoid by*
    • inserting the tip of the scalpel centrally and carefully, using it both as a probe and a scalpel
    • limiting medial and/or lateral excursion of the tip of the scalpel

e. Wound edge necrosis
  i. *Avoid by*
    • using good tissue handling techniques
    • limiting exaggerated corrective forces in the cast
      • Achieve full correction of all deformities
      • Close the incision
      • Dorsiflex the ankle and evert the subtalar joint to the point at which the wound edges blanch
      • The position for cast molding is slightly less than that.
      • If that position is less than the full deformity correction position achieved with the incision open, serial postoperative casting is required.
      • The skin will stretch by creep and stress relaxation.
      • For slight limitation from the fully corrected position, serial casting can be performed in clinic starting in 2 to 3 weeks.
      • For severe limitation from the fully corrected position, serial casting should be performed in the OR starting in 1 to 2 weeks.

V. PLICATIONS—TENDON SHORTENINGS AND CAPSULAR TIGHTENINGS

PRINCIPLE: A combination of two or more soft tissue procedures is often needed to correct specific deformities.

Plantar–Medial Plication (PMP)

1. Indications
   a. In combination with a calcaneal lengthening osteotomy (CLO) (**see Chapter 8**) in a flatfoot (**see Chapter 5**)
   b. In combination with a CLO (**see Chapter 8**) in a skewfoot (**see Chapter 5**)
   c. In combination with a CLO (**see Chapter 8**) for deformity correction in certain tarsal coalitions (**see Chapter 5**)
   d. In combination with a circumference release for resistant congenital vertical talus (**see Chapter 5**)
   e. In combination with a circumference release for resistant congenital oblique talus (**see Chapter 5**)
   f. In combination with the 3rd street procedure (**see this chapter**)
2. Technique (Figure 7-39)
   a. Make a longitudinal incision along the medial border of the foot dorsal to the edge of the glabrous skin starting at a point just distal to the medial malleolus and continuing to the base of the first MT. Release the posterior tibialis from its tendon sheath.
   b. Cut the posterior tibialis tendon in a Z-fashion, releasing its *dorsal* one-third to half from the navicular. The stump of the tendon remaining attached to the navicular contains the *plantar* one-half to two-thirds of the fibers.
   c. Incise the TN joint capsule from dorsal-lateral to plantar-lateral around the medial side, including the

spring ligament. Resect a 5- to 7-mm-wide strip of capsule from the medial and plantar aspects of this redundant tissue.
   d. Perform other concurrent procedures, such as a CLO (**see Chapter 8**), TAL (**see this chapter**), TAT (**see this chapter**), 3rd street procedure (**see this chapter**)
   e. Plicate the TN joint capsule plantar-medially, but not dorsally, with multiple figure-of-8 2-0 absorbable sutures
   f. Advance the proximal slip of the posterior tibialis tendon approximately 5 to 7 mm through a slit in the distal stump of the tendon. Secure this Pulvertaft weave with multiple figure-of-8 2-0 absorbable sutures.
   g. Approximate the skin edges with interrupted subcutaneous 3-0 absorbable sutures and a running subcuticular 4-0 absorbable sutures
3. Pitfalls
   a. Plication without complete deformity correction
   b. Substitution of plantar–medial plication for osseous deformity correction in a valgus hindfoot. The default position of the hindfoot is valgus (**see Basic Principle #9, Chapter 2**). Therefore, except in babies with CVT and congenital oblique talus, a PMP is supplemental to a CLO in valgus hindfoot deformity correction, but not an alternative to a CLO (**see Management Principle #17, Chapter 4**).
4. Complications
   a. None

VI. DISARTICULATIONS

PRINCIPLE: A good disarticulation/amputation can provide better comfort and function than some deformity and malformation reconstructions. (**see Management Principle #29, Chapter 4**).

Syme Ankle Disarticulation

1. Indications
   a. Severe malformations, deformities, and injuries of the foot and/or leg, in which a good heel pad exists (**see Management Principle #29, Chapter 4**).
   b. Forefoot gigantism (transverse macrodactyly) with a normal heel pad (**see Macrodactyly, Chapter 6**)
2. Technique (**see Figure 6-7, Chapter 6**) (Figure 7-40)
   a. Make a fishmouth incision at the ankle/hindfoot
     i. Incise across the anterior ankle from the tip of the medial malleolus to the tip of the lateral malleolus (or the lateral hindfoot if there is no lateral malleolus, as in the case of fibula hemimelia)
     ii. Create a U-shaped flap extending across the plantar midfoot starting at the medial extent of the anterior ankle incision and ending at the lateral extent of the anterior ankle incision
   b. Dorsally, isolate the superficial peroneal nerve branches, pull them distally, sharply transect them, and allow them to retract proximally

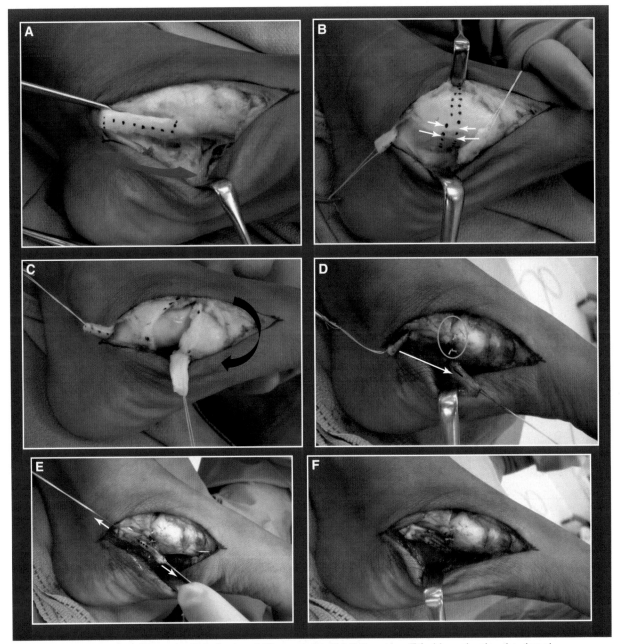

Figure 7-39. Plantar-medial plication. **A.** The posterior tibialis is cut in a Z-fashion releasing the *dorsal* slip from the navicular. **B.** The TN joint capsule is released from dorsolateral to plantar-lateral around the medial side, including release of the spring ligament. A 5- to 7-mm-wide strip of redundant capsule is resected from its plantar–medial aspect. **C.** The strip of redundant capsule has been resected. **D.** The plantar and medial aspects of the TN joint capsule are repaired anterior to posterior with large-gauge dissolving suture material (*outlined by purple oval*), having already resected the redundant capsule. The proximal slip of the posterior tibialis is advanced distally through a slit in the distal stump of the tendon. **E.** This Pulvertaft weave is repaired under firm tension with large-gauge dissolving sutures. **F.** A very cosmetic and sound repair is achieved. By performing the plications in this way, one can avoid creating excessive soft tissue bulk that might otherwise be as prominent as the head of the talus was initially. (From Mosca VS. Calcaneal lengthening osteotomy for valgus deformity of the hindfoot. In: Skaggs DL and Tolo VT, editors. *Master Techniques in Orthopaedic Surgery: Pediatrics.* Philadelphia: Lippincott Williams & Wilkins, 2008; 263–276.)

c. Isolate the anterior tibialis, extensor hallucis longus, extensor digitorum communis, and peroneus tertius, pull them distally, sharply transect them, and allow them to retract proximally

d. Isolate the anterior tibial NV bundle. Isolate the deep peroneal nerve, pull it distally, sharply transect it, and allow it to retract proximally. Ligate the artery and vein.

e. Release the anterior ankle capsule from the medial malleolus to the lateral malleolus

f. Release the medial and lateral collateral ligaments

g. Release the anterior edge of the flexor retinaculum (laciniate ligament) on the medial side of the hindfoot

h. Bluntly elevate the soft issues, including the posterior tibial NV bundle, from the flexor tendons and the

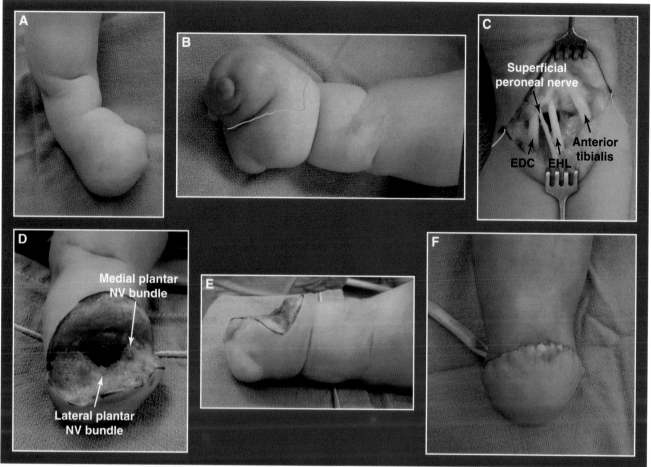

Figure 7-40. Syme amputation. **A.** Foot malformation in an infant with Streeter dysplasia (amniotic band syndrome). The deep band on the lower leg was previously reconstructed by Z-plasty and time has passed to ensure establishment of good vascularity and lymphatic flow to and from the distal part. **B.** The planned fishmouth incision is marked. **C.** All dorsal tendons and nerves are pulled distally, cut proximally, and allowed to retract. Vascular structures are ligated. **D.** The posterior tibial NV bundle is carefully protected and retracted with the heel pad away from the hindfoot bones. After the foot is disarticulated from the ankle, the plantar soft tissues are transected transversely at the midfoot. The medial and lateral plantar nerves are pulled distally, cut proximally, and allowed to retract. The arteries and veins are ligated/coagulated. **E.** Medial view of the limb after disarticulation of the foot. **F.** Appearance of the residual limb after repair of the midfoot soft tissues to the anterior ankle soft tissues. A Penrose drain is visible laterally.

talus and calcaneus. The NV bundle remains with the heel pad.

i. Release the posterior tibialis (PT) tendon sheath, pull the PT distally, sharply transect it, and allow it to retract proximally

j. Release the flexor digitorum longus (FDL) tendon sheath, pull the FDL distally, sharply transect it, and allow it to retract proximally

k. Release the flexor hallucis longus (FHL) tendon from the sustentaculum tali, pull the FHL distally, sharply transect it, and allow it to retract proximally

l. Release the peroneus longus and brevis tendon sheaths, pull the peroneal tendons distally, sharply transect them, and allow them to retract proximally

m. Release the posterior ankle capsule

n. Pull the foot anteriorly out of the ankle joint with a towel clip

o. Sharply resect all soft tissues off the calcaneus

p. At the plantar midfoot, in line with the previously created transverse skin incision, sharply transect the plantar soft tissues. Identify and coagulate/ligate the medial and lateral plantar posterior tibial vascular structures. Pull the medial and lateral plantar posterior tibial nerves distally, cut them proximally, and allow them to retract.

q. Finally, pull the foot distally, isolate the tendo-Achilles far proximally, and transect the tendo-Achilles as far proximally as possible. Remove the foot from the surgical site.

r. The cartilaginous malleoli can be shaved off with a scalpel

s. Release the tourniquet and achieve complete hemostasis, while also confirming excellent vascularity to the entire heel pad

t. Place a small Penrose drain transversely in the posterior aspect of the resection cavity exiting through a stab wound through the skin on the lateral side

u. Adjust the length of the plantar flap to ensure that the heel pad can be pulled slightly anteriorly, thereby positioning the posteroplantar corner of the heel pad directly distal to the tibial shaft. In case of posterior heel pad migration, there will still be heel pad distal to the tibia (Figure 7-41).
v. Suture the plantar fascia to the anterior ankle capsule with #0 absorbable sutures
w. Approximate the skin edges with interrupted subcutaneous 3-0 absorbable sutures and a running subcuticular 4-0 absorbable suture

x. Apply a single hip spica cast in an infant (to prevent the cast from falling off), and a long-leg, bent knee cast in an older child (Figure 7-42)
y. Maintain the cast for 6 weeks, then use a stump shrinker for at least one week before molding for the Syme prosthesis
3. Pitfalls
a. Shaving unossified cartilage off the calcaneus that will eventually ossify
b. Poor design of the fishmouth incision resulting in excessive tension on the wound closure

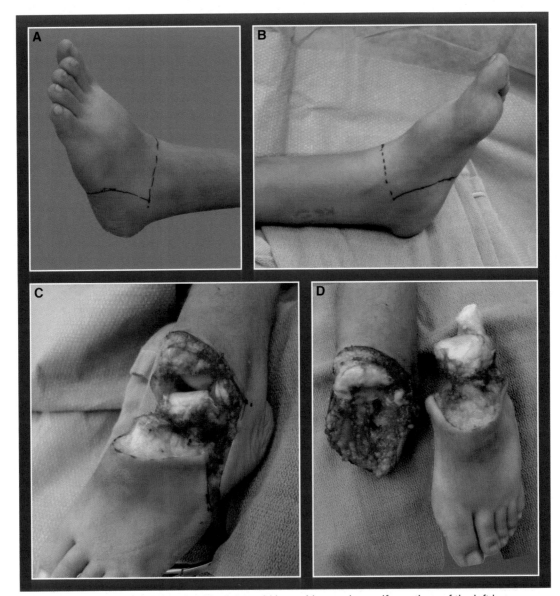

Figure 7-41. Syme amputation in a 4-year-old boy with complex malformations of the left lower extremity. A. Lateral view of the fishmouth incision marked on the skin. B. Medial view of the fishmouth incision marked on the skin. C. Disarticulation of the foot at the ankle is near completion. D. The foot has been disarticulated. The large cartilaginous medial and lateral malleoli have been shaved off with a scalpel to provide a flat weight-bearing surface. E. Lateral view of the residual limb after removal of the foot. F. The plantar flap is pulled proximally to determine whether the appropriate amount of soft tissue has been resected to place the posteroplantar corner of the heel pad in line with the axis of the tibial shaft. If not, more needs to be resected. G. The closure has been completed with layers of absorbable sutures. H. Lateral view of the repair with the heel pad appropriating aligned and with the Penrose drain exposed.

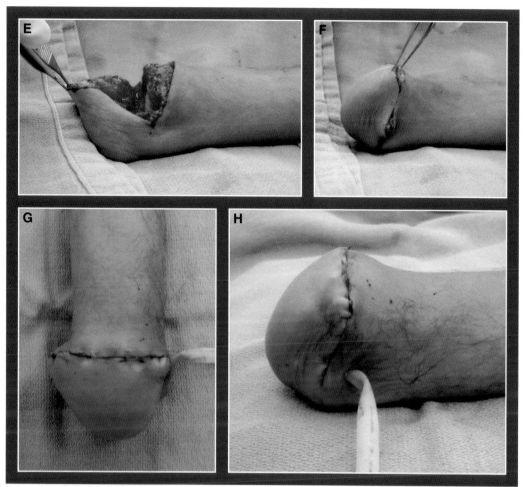

Figure 7-41. *(continued)*

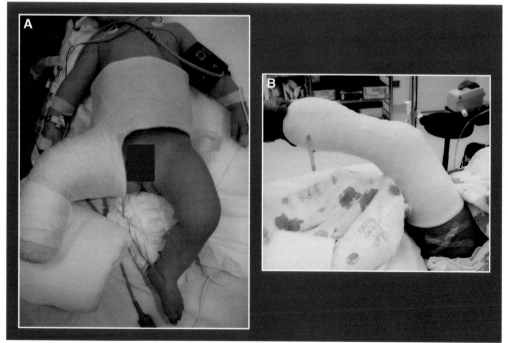

Figure 7-42. **A.** Single hip spica cast applied following Syme amputation in an infant.
B. Long-leg bent knee cast applied following Syme amputation in a 4-year-old child.

  c. Excessive posterior positioning of the heel pad under the tibia that may contribute to posterior migration of the heel pad
4. <u>Complications</u>
  a. Damage to the posterior tibial NV structures resulting in necrosis and/or loss of sensation of the heel pad
    i. *Avoid by* careful isolation and retraction of the NV bundle with the heel pad before releasing the flexor tendons and resecting the soft tissues off the calcaneus. Transect the NV bundles at the edge of the plantar incision.
  b. Posterior migration of the heel pad
    i. *Avoid by*
      • transecting the tendo-Achilles as far proximally as possible
      • positioning the posteroplantar corner of the heel pad directly distal to the tibial shaft, anticipating slight posterior migration over time

Bone Procedures

I. GUIDED GROWTH

Medial Distal Tibia Guided Growth with Retrograde Medial Malleolus Screw

1. Indications
   a. Pain due to lateral hindfoot impingement and/or medial hindfoot soft tissue strain caused by exaggerated congenital or acquired valgus deformity of the ankle joint (**see Assessment Principles #11 and 21, Chapter 3; Valgus Deformity of the Ankle Joint, Chapter 5**)
   b. If there is coincident valgus deformity of the ankle joint and the subtalar joint, the ankle deformity should be corrected first (**see Management Principle #23-6, Chapter 4; Valgus Deformity of the Ankle Joint and the Hindfoot, Chapter 5**).

2. Technique (Figure 8-1)
   a. Make a 7-mm longitudinal incision immediately distal to the medial malleolus in the midcoronal plane of the tibia
   b. Insert a guide pin for the 4.5-mm cannulated screws retrograde from the intersection of the medial-to-lateral center of the medial malleolus with the midcoronal plane of the tibia, using mini-fluoroscopy for guidance. Anterior placement could result in recurvatum and posterior placement in procurvatum.
      i. Ensure placement in the midcoronal plane of the tibia by visualizing a true lateral image of the ankle on mini-fluoroscopy, i.e., the posterior cortex of the fibula and the posterior cortex of the tibia are colinear. Using the "dome of the talus" as the alignment guide for a true lateral image of the ankle is unreliable in children because of immature ossification of the talus and/or malformations/deformities of the talus. The midcoronal plane of the tibia is typically in line with the anterior cortex of the fibula.

   c. Insert the guide pin parallel with, and immediately adjacent to, the medial cortex of the tibial metaphysis. The more medial the screw, the more medial the mechanical center of rotation of angulation (CORA), and the more rapid will be the deformity correction.
   d. Use the cannulated reamer up to, but not across, the physis
   e. Insert a fully threaded cannulated 4.5-mm screw. Generally, a 52-mm-long screw is a good length.
   f. Countersink the head of the screw into the medial malleolus. Be aware that the tip of the medial malleolus might be cartilaginous and, therefore, not visible on fluoroscopy.
   g. Use a 4-0 absorbable subcuticular suture
   h. No immobilization is required.

3. Pitfalls
   a. Correction of subtalar/hindfoot valgus deformity *before* correction of ankle valgus
   b. Failure to countersink the head of the screw, thereby leaving a metallic prominence under the medial malleolus
   c. Anterior screw placement resulting in the development of recurvatum while correcting the valgus deformity
   d. Posterior screw placement resulting in the development of procurvatum while correcting the valgus deformity
   e. Lateral screw placement across the physis. The more lateral the screw crosses the physis, the more lateral the CORA and the longer the time to deformity correction. If the screw crosses the center of the physis, it could result in epiphysiodesis. Crossing the physis lateral to the midline will result in *increasing* the valgus deformity.
   f. Failure to account for rebound valgus deformity. Several degrees of recurrent valgus deformity develop after screw removal in most cases. Therefore, overcorrect a few degrees before removing the screw.

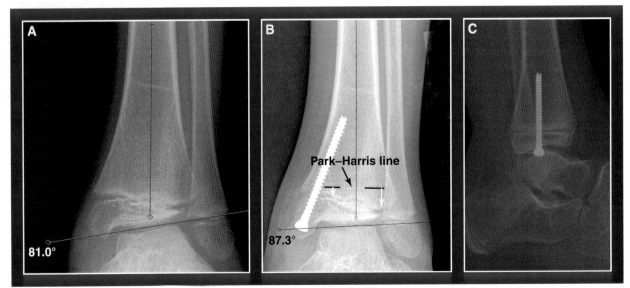

Figure 8-1. Medial malleolus screw hemiepiphysiodesis for guided growth correction of ankle valgus deformity. **A.** Preoperative AP ankle x-ray showing 9° of valgus deformity. **B.** 3° of valgus deformity persist 6 months after retrograde insertion of a screw across the medial side of distal tibial physis with a starting point in the center of the medial malleolus. The Park–Harris line (*dashed black lines* with white P–H line visible between them) confirms deformity correction. The yellow arrows indicate the differential growth of the physis from the P–H line following screw insertion months earlier. **C.** Lateral radiograph shows that the screw is in the midcoronal plane. This is a true lateral projection of the ankle joint, confirmed by colinear alignment of the posterior cortices of the tibia and fibula at the level of the tibial meta-epiphysis. **(see Assessment Principle #20, Chapter 3)**.

4. Complications
   a. Broken screw
      i. *Avoid by* using a large enough screw, which is 4.5 mm in diameter in all but the youngest children. The screw must bend as the angular deformity is corrected. Larger screws resist fracture.
   b. Continued physeal growth
      i. *Avoid by* using a fully threaded screw. The threads of a fully threaded and a partially threaded screw are stable in the metaphysis. The head of the screw and the smooth shank of a partially threaded screw are not sufficient to keep the distal portion of the screw stable in the epiphysis of the medial malleolus. The physis will continue to grow, effectively dragging the head of the screw into the medial malleolus. The threads of a fully threaded screw maintain stable fixation in the medial malleolus.
   c. Exaggerated overcorrection
      i. *Avoid by* ensuring timely patient follow-up with radiographs. Anticipate deformity correction at approximately 1° per month.

Anterior Distal Tibia Guided Growth with Anterior Plate–Screw Construct

1. Indications
   a. Failure of non-operative management to relieve the anterior ankle impingement pain that is most often due to a flat-top talus in a treated clubfoot (**see Chapter 5**)

2. Technique (Figure 8-2)
   a. Make a 4- to 5-cm longitudinal incision over the anterior aspect of the ankle joint lateral to the anterior tibialis tendon
   b. Avoid or retract the superficial peroneal nerve
   c. Release the proximal portion of the extensor retinaculum longitudinally
   d. Incise the anterior ankle joint capsule longitudinally and retract the edges medially and laterally to expose the distal tibial metaphysis and epiphysis
   e. Apply a guided growth plate–screw construct across the physis in the midsagittal plane of the tibia using mini-fluoroscopy for assistance.
      i. Insert the epiphyseal screw half way between the physis and the articular cartilage
      ii. Insert the metaphyseal screw perpendicular to the shaft of the tibia
   f. Repair the capsule over the plate with 2-0 absorbable sutures, if possible
   g. Repair the extensor retinaculum with 2-0 absorbable sutures
   h. Approximate the skin edges with interrupted subcutaneous 3-0 absorbable sutures and a running subcuticular 4-0 absorbable suture
   i. *Do not* lengthen the tendo-Achilles. That would increase the anterior ankle impingement. Reorientation of the ankle joint into recurvatum will improve painless ankle dorsiflexion.
   j. Immobilize the ankle in a CAM boot for 1 week to allow the soft tissues to heal

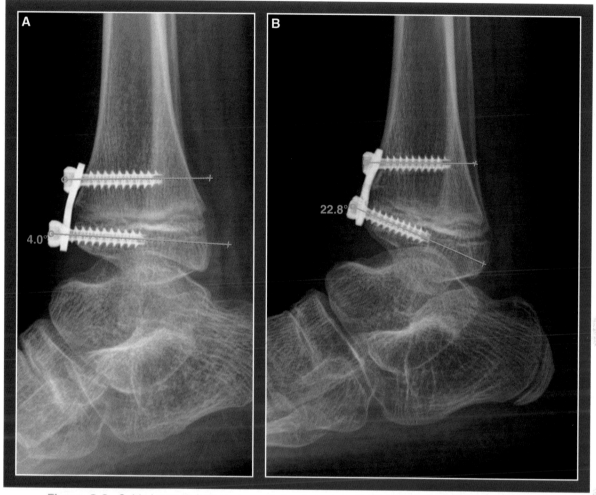

Figure 8-2. Guided growth for anterior ankle impingement. **A.** Plate/screw construct is seen bridging the anterior distal tibial physis. **B.** Several months later, the joint has reoriented and grown into recurvatum, thereby increasing dorsiflexion and decreasing the painful anterior ankle impingement.

k. Remove the plate and screws after the joint has reoriented and the pain has been resolved for a few months
3. Pitfalls
   a. Using a plate so large or poorly positioned that it impinges on the dorsal talar neck more than the offending anterior distal tibial epiphysis already was
   b. Concurrent lengthening of the tendo-Achilles. The goal is to move the anterior distal tibial epiphysis away from the dorsal talar neck. Therefore, first reorient the joint into recurvatum/dorsiflexion with guided growth. Then determine if a heel cord lengthening is necessary.
4. Complications
   a. Overcorrection
      i. *Avoid by* ensuring patient follow-up
   b. Screw insertion into the physis or the joint
      i. *Avoid by* inserting the epiphyseal screw first and using mini-fluoroscopy for guidance
   c. Injury to the superficial peroneal nerve
      i. *Avoid by* isolating and retracting/protecting it

II. RESECTIONS

Accessory Navicular Resection

1. Indications
   a. Pain at the site of the accessory navicular that is not relieved by prolonged attempts at nonoperative treatment (**see Chapter 6**)
2. Technique (Figure 8-3)
   a. Make a 4-cm longitudinal incision along the medial border of the midfoot from the medial cuneiform to the talar neck along the course of the posterior tibialis tendon
   b. Incise the soft tissues on the medial surface of the navicular/accessory navicular longitudinally in line with the fibers of the distal extension of the posterior tibialis tendon
   c. Continue the incision into the posterior tibialis tendon in the transverse plane for 1 cm
   d. Sharply elevate the periosteum/posterior tibialis tendon fibers dorsally and plantarward from the navicular/accessory navicular, exposing the entire accessory

198   Principles and Management of Pediatric Foot and Ankle Deformities and Malformations

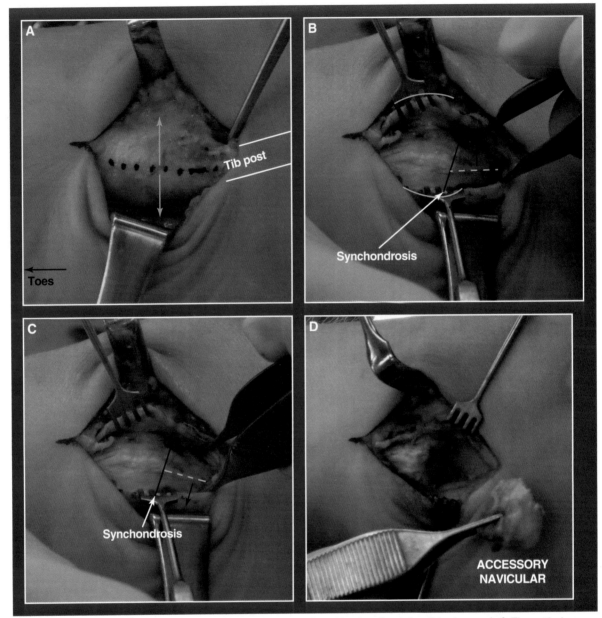

Figure 8-3. Accessory navicular resection (toes to the left and heel to the right of the images). **A.** The pathology is exposed through a 4-cm longitudinal skin incision directly medial to the bony prominence. An incision is made in the soft tissues on the medial surface of the navicular and accessory navicular in line with the posterior tibialis tendon fibers (*dotted blue line*). The division of the tendon fibers extends 1 to 2 cm proximally into the posterior tibialis tendon. The button hook is around the tendon as it approaches the navicular from the right side of the image. The green arrows indicate the directions that the dorsal and plantar soft tissue flaps will be elevated. **B.** The periosteum/tendon fiber flaps (*curved green lines*) have been sharply elevated both dorsally and plantarward off the navicular and the accessory navicular *without* detaching them transversely from the navicular. The small four-pronged hooks are shown retracting these soft tissue flaps. The black line indicates the location of the synchondrosis of the accessory navicular with the main body of the navicular. The dotted green line indicates the longitudinal axis of the accessory navicular. The forceps are shown rotating the accessory navicular dorsally at the synchondrosis. **C.** The forceps are shown rotating the accessory navicular plantarward, thereby demonstrating hypermobility of the accessory navicular at the synchondrosis. **D.** The accessory navicular has been resected at the synchondrosis. **E.** The enlarged medial extension of the main body of the navicular is resected flush with the medial surface of the medial cuneiform using an osteotome. **F.** Forceps are holding the resected bone. **G.** Multiple vest-over-pants imbrication-type 2-0 absorbable sutures are placed in the flaps in preparation for plantar-to-dorsal plication and tubularization of the tendon. **H.** Sutures are pulled dorsally to close the dead space that was created by the bone resection. **I.** The vest-over-pants sutures have been tied. **J.** A running 2-0 absorbable suture is initiated between the free edge of the plantar flap and the adjacent fibers of the dorsal flap of the posterior tibialis tendon at the proximal (heel) end of the plicated tissues. **K.** The suture is run along the free edge to smooth the repair. **L.** Final, smooth imbricated repair.

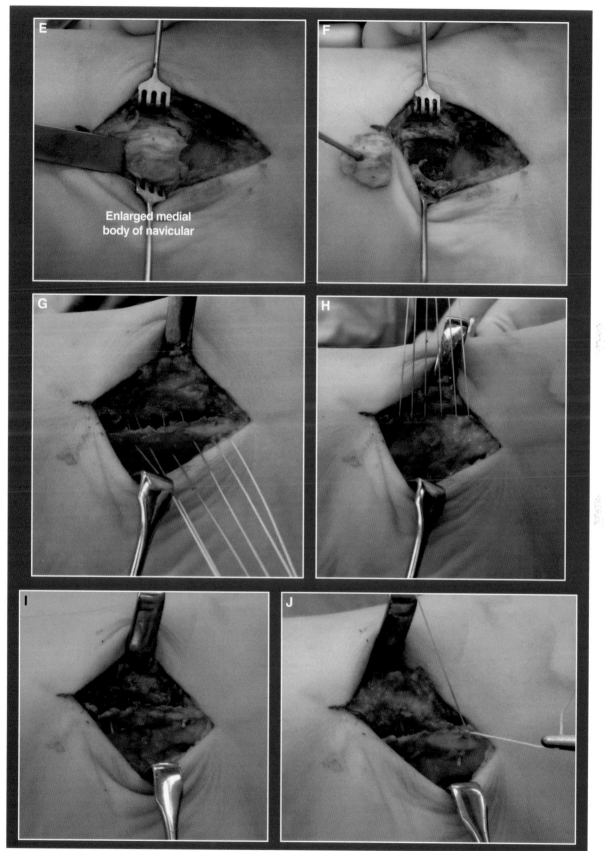

Figure 8-3. *(continued)*

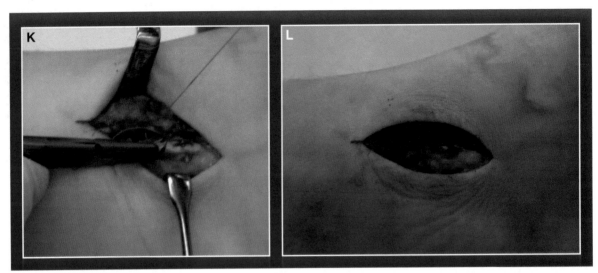

Figure 8-3. *(continued)*

navicular and the enlarged medial extension of the main body of the navicular. Preserve these flaps for later repair. Do not release them transversely.
e. Identify the synchondrosis, incise it, and remove the accessory navicular
f. Using an osteotome, resect the enlarged medial extension of the navicular flush with the medial surface of the medial cuneiform. Confirm adequate resection with mini-fluoroscopy
g. Plicate the soft tissue flaps over the resection site using a dorsal–plantar vest-over-pants technique with 2-0 absorbable sutures
h. Finish the free edge of the superficial flap with a running 2-0 absorbable suture
i. Approximate the skin edges with interrupted subcutaneous 3-0 absorbable sutures and a running subcuticular 4-0 absorbable suture
j. Apply a short-leg non–weight-bearing cast
k. Remove the cast after 6 weeks and initiate weight-bearing
3. Pitfalls
a. Failure to resect the enlarged medial/plantar–medial extension of the main body of the navicular
4. Complications
a. Weakening, stretching, or rupture of the posterior tibialis tendon attachment on the navicular
   i. *Avoid by* preserving the dorsal and plantar soft tissue flaps as described earlier

Calcaneonavicular Tarsal Coalition Resection

1. Indications
a. Activity-related pain in the sinus tarsi region, and occasionally under the medial midfoot, caused by a calcaneonavicular tarsal coalition (**see Chapter 5**) that is not relieved despite prolonged attempts at nonoperative treatment
2. Technique (Figure 8-4)
a. Use a sterile tourniquet and hindquarter prep if the fat graft will be taken from the posterior buttock crease.

A nonsterile tourniquet can be used if the fat graft will be taken from the posteromedial distal thigh
b. Make an oblique incision over the midfoot from the dorsal midline of the navicular to the midlateral point of the anterior calcaneus in a Langer's line
c. Isolate, retract, and protect the superficial peroneal nerve
d. Elevate the extensor muscles from the sinus tarsi and the coalition from posterior to anterior, tagging the proximal margin for ease of reattachment
e. Place Joker elevators posterior and anterior to the coalition with the tips meeting under the coalition, which is usually around 2.5 cm in depth
f. Using a 10-mm osteotome, cut the navicular from dorsolateral to plantar-medial in line with the head and neck of the talus
g. Using a 10-mm osteotome, cut the calcaneus from dorsolateral to plantar-medial in line with the cuboid/lateral cuneiform joint, trying to preserve as much normal calcaneocuboid joint articulation as possible
h. The two cuts should be approximately 10 to 12 mm apart and parallel to nearly parallel
i. The coalition will be in the resected specimen.
j. If necessary, use a Kerrison rongeur to remove bone and bone fragments from the depths of the resection cavity
k. The spring (calcaneonavicular) ligament should be visible at the base of the resection cavity.
l. Cover the exposed bone surfaces with bone wax
m. Obtain a large fat graft from the posterior–medial aspect of the distal thigh or from the posterior buttock crease and overfill the resection cavity
n. Replace the short toe extensors to their origin with 2-0 absorbable sutures, covering the fat graft
o. Approximate the skin edges with interrupted subcutaneous 3-0 absorbable sutures and a running subcuticular 4-0 absorbable suture
p. Apply a short-leg non–weight-bearing cast. The cast is worn for 2 weeks to allow the soft tissues to heal before initiating range-of-motion exercises

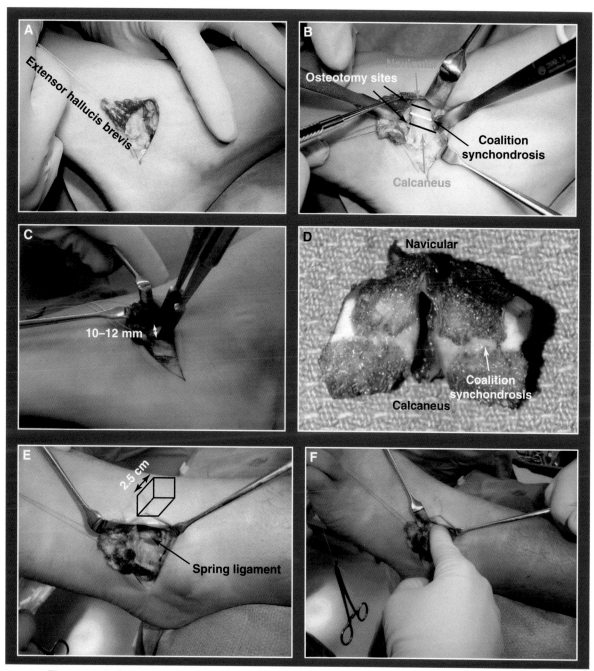

Figure 8-4. Resection of a calcaneonavicular tarsal coalition. **A.** The EHB is elevated from the sinus tarsi and reflected anteriorly. **B.** The synchondrosis and adjacent portions of the calcaneus and the navicular are exposed. **C.** Ten-millimeter osteotomes are positioned 10 to 12 mm apart and parallel to each other for the osteotomies. **D.** A resected coalition has been bisected to reveal the pathoanatomy. **E.** The 3D rectangle-shaped resection cavity is visualized with the spring ligament exposed at its base. **F.** The resection cavity is large enough to accept the surgeon's index finger. **G.** The cavity is 2.5 cm deep. **H.** After the osteotomy surfaces are coated with bone wax, a large free fat graft is inserted to completely fill the cavity. The EHB is pulled over the fat graft and reattached to its origin in the sinus tarsi. **I.** Preresection oblique intraoperative fluoroscopy image with osteotome in place. **J.** Postresection oblique image. The navicular osteotomy is made in line with the head/neck of the talus. The calcaneus osteotomy is made in line with cuboid/lateral cuneiform joint.

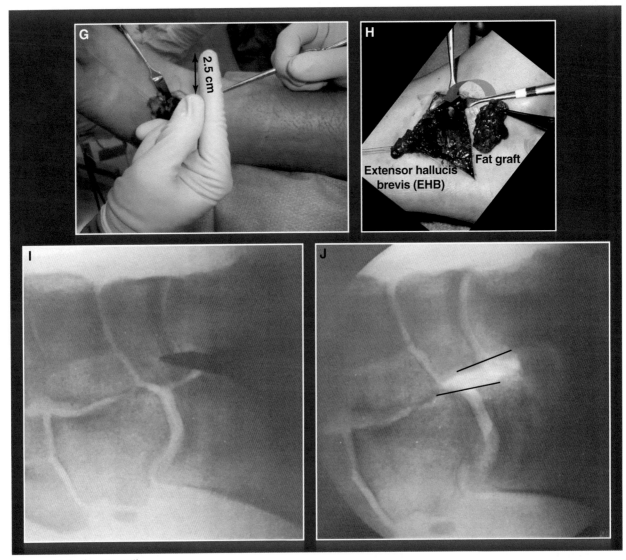

Figure 8-4. *(continued)*

q. Prescribe a dosage of a nonsteroidal anti-inflammatory drug (NSAID) for 4 weeks
r. Remove the cast after 2 weeks, but continue non–weight-bearing for an additional 4 weeks while the patient regains comfortable range of motion
s. Initiate gradual return to weight-bearing after 6 weeks, using crutches at first to ensure comfort

3. Pitfalls
    a. Excessive resection of the articular surface of the calcaneus, resulting in instability at the calcaneocuboid joint
    b. Excessive resection of the articular surface of the navicular resulting in instability at the talonavicular (TN) joint

4. Complications
    a. Injury to the superficial peroneal nerve
        i. *Avoid by:*
            • isolating, retracting, and protecting it
    b. Persistence of the coalition

        i. *Avoid by:*
            • ensuring that the coalition is completely resected, including at its plantar extent
                • Visualize the spring (calcaneonavicular) ligament.
                • Probe the depths of the resection cavity with a Freer elevator.
                • Obtain an intraoperative oblique fluoroscopic or radiographic image.
    c. Recurrence of the coalition
        i. *Avoid by:*
            • applying bone wax to the resection surfaces
            • inserting a large free fat graft to completely fill the resection cavity and covering it with the EHB

Talocalcaneal Tarsal Coalition Resection

1. Indications
    a. Activity-related pain in the medial hindfoot, the sinus tarsi region, and occasionally under the medial

midfoot, caused by a talocalcaneal tarsal coalition (**see Chapter 5**) that is not relieved despite prolonged attempts at nonoperative treatment

b. A coalition of the middle facet in which the size of the coalition is less than 50% the surface area of the posterior facet

c. *And* with a normal posterior facet, defined as "normal" thickness on coronal CT scan images

2. Technique (Figure 8-5)

a. Use a sterile tourniquet and hindquarter prep if the fat graft will be taken from the posterior buttock crease. A nonsterile tourniquet can be used if the fat graft will be taken from the posteromedial distal thigh

b. Make a longitudinal incision medial to the subtalar joint from the posterior tibial (PT) neurovascular bundle to the TN joint

c. Incise the laciniate ligament (flexor retinaculum) longitudinally directly over the middle facet. Tag the edges with 2-0 absorbable sutures for later identification and repair

d. Retract the flexor digitorum longus (FDL) dorsally or plantarward, depending on the dorsal–plantar location of the coalition and the ease of exposure

e. Retract the flexor hallucis longus (FHL) plantarward from the sustentaculum tali

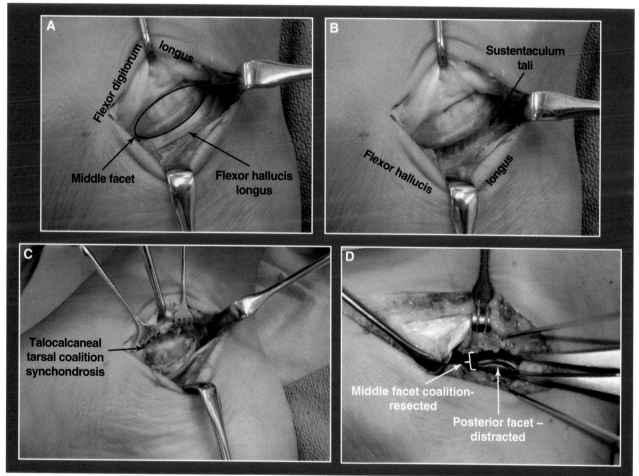

Figure 8-5. Resection of a talocalcaneal tarsal coalition. **A.** The FDL is retracted dorsally to expose the middle facet, though it might be easier to retract it plantarward in some feet. **B.** The FHL is retracted plantarward from the sustentaculum tali. **C.** The periosteum is sharply elevated from the medial surfaces of the talus and calcaneus at the middle facet. The synchondrosis is exposed. **D.** The middle facet coalition has been resected. The posterior facet is visualized at the base of the resection cavity. A smooth-toothed laminar spreader in the resected middle facet cavity has been used to distract the posterior facet to ensure that there are no remaining bony or cartilaginous connections between the talus and calcaneus. **E.** Steinmann pins are inserted in the talus and calcaneus from medial to lateral before resection of the coalition. There is no motion between them with attempted inversion and eversion of the subtalar joint. **F.** Following resection, convergence and divergence of the pins confirms restoration of subtalar motion. **G** and **H.** Direct visualization of the resection cavity during eversion and inversion of the subtalar joint, with widening and narrowing of the resection cavity, further confirms complete resection of the coalition. **I.** Bone wax is applied to the resected bone surfaces. **J.** A large free fat graft is inserted. **K.** The fat graft completely fills the cavity. **L.** The periosteum is repaired over the fat. The flexor retinaculum is subsequently repaired over the graft and the flexor tendons.

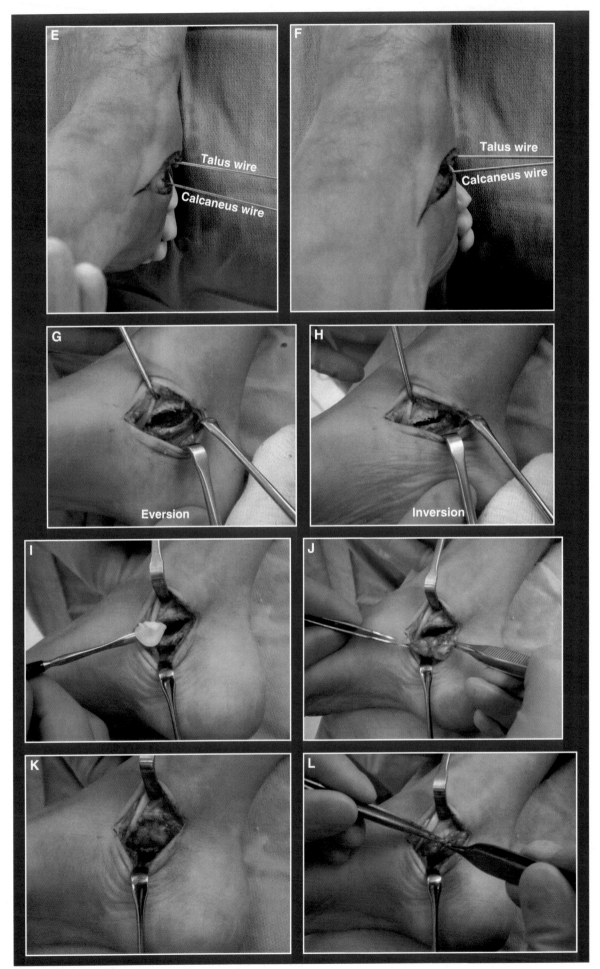

Figure 8-5. *(continued)*

f. Bluntly identify the posterior edge of the middle facet. Place a baby Hohman retractor there to both identify the posterior extent of the pathologic facet and retract and protect the FHL and PT neurovascular bundle

g. Bluntly identify the anterior edge of the middle facet. Place a baby Hohman retractor there

h. Longitudinally (from anterior to posterior) incise the periosteum in the center of the medial face of the middle facet

i. Sharply elevate the periosteum from the middle facet dorsally and plantarward. Try to preserve it for later repair, if possible

j. Identify the synchondrosis

k. Using a high-speed 3- to 4-mm burr, remove the synchondrosis from anterior to posterior and medial to lateral. The height of the resection cavity should be 6 to 8 mm

l. The resection is complete when:
    i. the healthy posterior facet is visualized.
    ii. the talocalcaneal interosseous ligament and surrounding fat are visualized.
    iii. the healthy anterior facet is visualized.
    iv. the posterior and anterior facets can be distracted easily with a smooth-toothed laminar spreader in the resection cavity of the middle facet.
    v. the subtalar joint can be inverted and everted. Do not expect dramatic improvement in range of motion in long-standing cases, but ensure that there are no pathologic bony or cartilaginous connections remaining between the talus and calcaneus
        • Insert parallel 0.062″ smooth Steinmann pins from medial to lateral in the talus and calcaneus adjacent to the resection cavity. Invert and evert the subtalar joint to confirm that there is restoration of motion by observing the movement between the pins. If there is limited or no subtalar motion despite confirmed distraction of the posterior facet with the laminar spreader, release the dorsolateral TN joint capsule through a dorsolateral incision. In long-standing coalitions, a contracture/synchondrosis sometimes develops at that location between a dorsal talar beak and a dorsal navicular osteophyte.

m. Cover the exposed bone surfaces with bone wax

n. Obtain a large fat graft from the posterior–medial aspect of the distal thigh or from the posterior buttock crease and use it to overfill the resection cavity

o. Replace the FHL under the sustentaculum tali

p. Repair the periosteum over the fat graft, if possible

q. Replace the FDL to its normal position medial to the middle facet, and repair the laciniate ligament (flexor retinaculum) with 2-0 absorbable sutures over the fat graft

r. Approximate the skin edges with interrupted subcutaneous 3-0 absorbable sutures and a running subcuticular 4-0 absorbable suture

s. Apply a short-leg non–weight-bearing cast. The cast is worn for 2 weeks to allow the soft tissues to heal before initiating range-of-motion exercises

t. Prescribe a dosage of an NSAID for 4 weeks

u. Remove the cast after 2 weeks, but continue non–weight-bearing for an additional 4 weeks while the patient regains comfortable range of motion

v. Initiate gradual return to weight-bearing after 6 weeks, using crutches at first to ensure comfort

3. Pitfalls
    a. Inappropriate resection in a foot with an unresectable coalition characterized by an ankylosed and narrow posterior facet and/or an extremely large middle facet coalition
    b. Failure to correct severe associated valgus hindfoot deformity either concurrently or staged

4. Complications
    a. Persistence of the coalition
        i. *Avoid by:*
            • ensuring complete resection. See "l" above in the Technique section.
    b. Recurrence of the coalition
        i. *Avoid by:*
            • making a large resection cavity
            • applying bone wax to the resection surfaces
            • inserting a large free fat graft to completely fill the resection cavity and covering it with the periosteum and flexor retinaculum
    c. Injury to the PT neurovascular bundle
        i. *Avoid by* retracting and protecting it from the burr

Lichtblau Distal Calcaneus Resection

See under Lateral Column Shortening Procedures later.

Longitudinal Epiphyseal Bracket Resection

1. Indications
    a. The presence of a longitudinal epiphyseal bracket (LEB; **see Chapter 6**)
        i. LEB is always associated either with congenital hallux varus (**see Chapter 5**) or with preaxial polydactyly (**see Chapter 6**)

2. Technique (Figures 8-6 and 8-7)
    a. Make a longitudinal incision along the medial border of the forefoot extending from the hallux to the medial cuneiform
    b. If preaxial polydactyly exists, continue the incision distally as an ellipse around the duplicate hallux on the medial side. Resect the duplicate hallux
    c. The abductor hallucis is contracted and often exists as a fibrous cord/band in a foot with either congenital hallux varus or preaxial polydactyly. Release it distally (or excise it) (**see Chapter 7**).
    d. Expose the 1st metatarsal (MT) shaft extraperiosteally on its dorsal, medial, and plantar surfaces

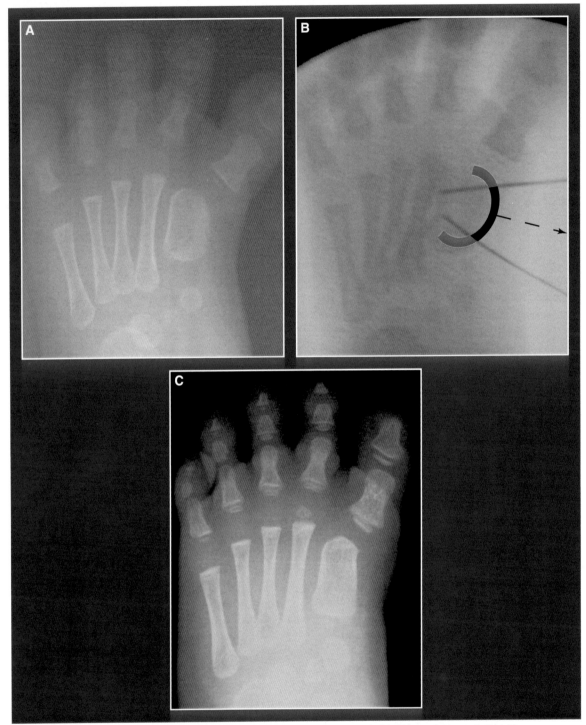

Figure 8-6. **A.** AP x-ray of a 1st MT LEB associated with congenital hallux varus in an infant. The lateral cortex of the diaphysis is concave, whereas the medial cortex is convex and poorly ossified. The hallux is in varus alignment. **B.** The purple and black arc represents the LEB. The black central section represents the abnormal portion of the LEB along the medial side of the 1st MT shaft. The convergent black lines are the 25G needles that were inserted to mark the planned extent of resection. **C.** One year later, the medial cortex of the 1st MT diaphysis is concave and has the normal density of cortical bone. Longitudinal growth of the MT has been established. It is unknown at this time if catch up longitudinal growth will take place.

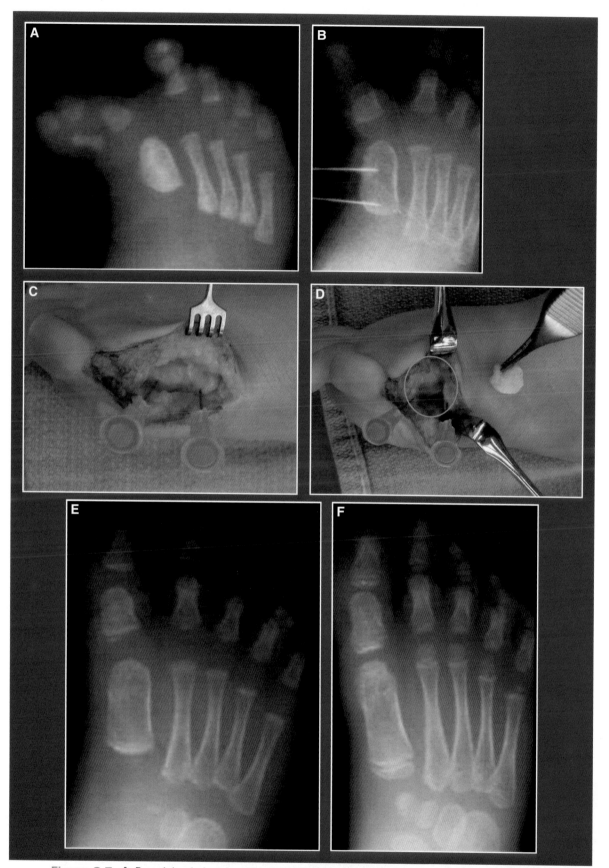

Figure 8-7. **A.** Preaxial polydactyly with a 1st MT LEB in a newborn infant. **B.** Intraoperative x-ray obtained when the child was 9 months old. The two 25G needles mark the proximal and distal limits of the planned LEB resection (the distal needle was moved further distally before resection). **C.** The shiny cartilage of the LEB along the medial surface of the MT shaft can be seen between the needles. **D.** The 1-cm-thick (medial to lateral) abnormally positioned epiphyseal cartilage (held in the forceps) was resected, sharply exposing metaphyseal-type bone where cortical bone should be (*purple oval*). **E.** Normal-appearing medial cortex on the 1st MT shaft 2 years later. **F.** At 4 years postoperatively, the 1st MT appears normal in length and shape, and the mild residual varus alignment of the 1st MTP joint has corrected to physiologic alignment.

e. Using mini-fluoroscopy for guidance, insert a 25G needle from medial to lateral at the transverse level of the normal physis proximally and another at the level of the normal articular cartilage distally

f. Use a scalpel to incise the thick, abnormally placed epiphyseal cartilage on the medial side of the shaft, cutting from dorsal to plantar immediately distal to the proximal needle and immediately proximal to the distal needle. The epiphyseal cartilage extends dorsomedially and plantar-medially approximately to the midsagittal plane of the MT.

g. Identify the junction between the abnormal epiphyseal cartilage and the normal periosteum on the dorsal and plantar surfaces

h. Incise the periosteum longitudinally on the dorsal and plantar surfaces immediately adjacent to the LEB

i. Use a Freer elevator to separate, or "pop off," the abnormal epiphyseal cartilage from the shaft of the MT. The technique is similar to separating the iliac apophysis from the iliac crest during hip surgery in children. The exposed bone on the MT shaft is not cortex, but instead juxtaphyseal metaphyseal bone as seen at the iliac crest or during operative treatment of a physeal injury. Make sure all abnormal cartilage is removed, leaving only normal periosteum on the dorsal and plantar surfaces of the MT shaft.

j. The subcutaneous fat and abductor hallucis muscle fall into the gap upon closure of the wound, though a deep fat stitch of a 3-0 absorbable material can be used to ensure that soft tissues fill the gap.

k. Approximate the skin edges with interrupted subcutaneous 3-0 absorbable sutures and a running subcuticular 4-0 absorbable suture

l. If the skin is particularly contracted, the incision can be converted to a Z-plasty (Figure 8-8).

m. It is uncommon to require pin fixation of the metatarsophalangeal (MTP) joint. The articular cartilage of the 1st MT is medially deviated (essentially a reverse, or negative, distal metatarsal articular angle [DMAA]— **see Juvenile Hallux Valgus, Chapter 5**) and the MTP

joint is generally congruous. After establishing longitudinal growth of the MT, the joint tends to reorient itself.

n. Use a long-leg cast (to prevent it from slipping off the infant) for 4 weeks

3. Pitfalls

a. Failure to release the abductor hallucis contracture

b. Failure to resect the proximal-to-distal and dorsal-to-plantar full extent of the abnormal epiphysis. Whereas taking too much of the epiphysis is not good for the remaining bone ends, resecting too little might result in incomplete establishment of normal growth of the MT.

c. Performing a concurrent angular deformity correction osteotomy in infants. In most cases, the varus deformity of the 1st MT and the varus orientation of the 1st MTP joint correct spontaneously. If they do not, an osteotomy can be performed later in childhood.

4. Complications

a. Incomplete resection of the abnormal epiphysis with persistent deformity

  i. *Avoid by* ensuring that the dorsomedial and plantar–medial extensions of the abnormal epiphysis are resected along with the medial portion. Periosteum must be seen on the dorsal and plantar surfaces of the MT shaft.

b. Incision wound edge necrosis

  i. *Avoid by* performing a Z-plasty if the skin appears to be excessively tight upon wound closure and passive abduction of the hallux to approximately neutral alignment on the 1st MT

Resection of Impinging Portion of Dorsally Subluxated Navicular

1. Indications

a. Painful anterior ankle impingement (**see Chapter 5**) from dorsal subluxation of the navicular on the head of the talus in an adolescent/young adult who underwent surgical treatment for a clubfoot early in life and does *not* have evidence for arthritis in the TN joint

2. Technique (Figure 8-9)

a. Make a 4- to 5-cm longitudinal incision over the anterior aspect of the ankle joint lateral to the anterior tibialis tendon

b. Avoid or retract the superficial peroneal nerve

c. Release the extensor retinaculum longitudinally

d. Incise the anterior ankle joint capsule longitudinally and retract the edges medially and laterally

e. Reshape the prominent dorsal portion of the navicular with an osteotome

f. Debride surrounding thick abnormal callus tissue, if present

g. Maximally dorsiflex the ankle to confirm, under direct visualization, that there is no residual contact between the navicular and the tibia

h. Repair the ankle joint capsule with 2-0 absorbable sutures

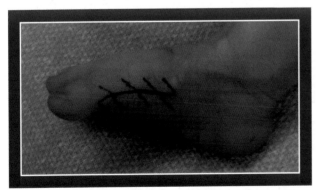

Figure 8-8. Z-plasty of the skin on the medial side of the forefoot may be necessary when correcting congenital hallux varus or preaxial polydactyly with or without resection of a 1st MT LEB.

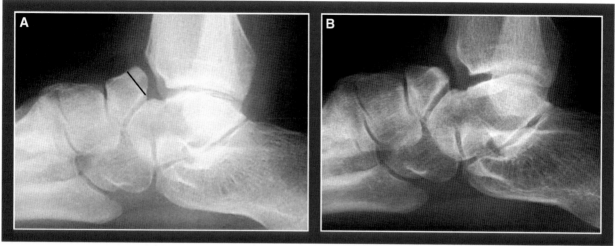

Figure 8-9. **A.** Standing lateral x-ray of the ankle and hindfoot in a skeletally mature adolescent who underwent clubfoot surgery as an infant and presented at age 16 with intractable impingement-type anterior ankle pain. Her symptoms were not consistent with TN joint arthritis; therefore, TN joint arthrodesis was not indicated. Her overall foot shape was acceptable and, although her foot was very stiff, she had no other symptoms. Black line indicates the level of resection of the dorsally subluxated navicular. **B.** This x-ray image was taken several months later at which time she was asymptomatic and had improved dorsiflexion.

i. Repair the extensor retinaculum with 2-0 absorbable sutures

j. Approximate the skin edges with interrupted subcutaneous 3-0 absorbable sutures and a running subcuticular 4-0 absorbable suture

k. Apply a non–weight-bearing CAM boot for 2 to 3 weeks to provide comfort during the early healing phase

l. Then initiate active range-of-motion exercises and continue non–weight-bearing for an additional 4 weeks; use of the CAM boot is optional for comfort during this time.

3. Pitfalls

a. Inadequate resection of bone

b. Failure to repair the extensor retinaculum with resultant bow-stringing of the extensor tendons

4. Complications

a. Injury to the superficial peroneal nerve
   i. *Avoid by* isolating and retracting/protecting it

Debridement of Dorsal Talar Neck

1. Indications

a. Painful anterior ankle impingement (**see Chapter 5**) from a flat-top talar dome with a shallow or flat dorsal talar neck, typically found in a previously treated clubfoot

2. Technique (Figure 8-10)

a. Make a 4- to 5-cm longitudinal incision over the anterior aspect of the ankle joint lateral to the anterior tibialis tendon

b. Avoid or retract the superficial peroneal nerve

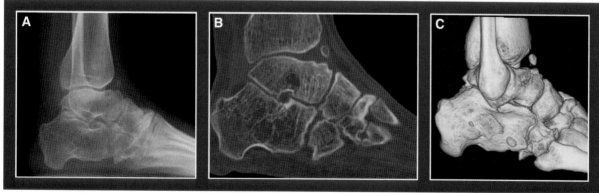

Figure 8-10. Multiply operated, stiff clubfoot in a 15-year-old girl with pain from anterior ankle impingement. **A.** Flat-top talus with shallow/absent dorsal talar neck concavity (and small heterotopic ossicle) causing anterior ankle impingement and pain. **B.** Sagittal CT scan image confirming the deformity. **C.** Three-dimensional CT scan image confirming the deformity. **D.** Lateral x-ray with purple markings indicating the resections to be performed. **E.** Lateral x-ray of the ankle in plantar flexion following resection of heterotopic ossicle and reshaping of the dorsal talar neck. **F.** Lateral x-ray of the ankle in dorsiflexion following resection of heterotopic ossicle and reshaping of dorsal talar neck.

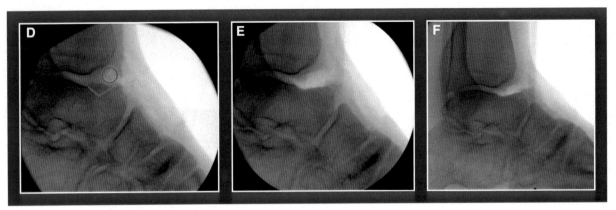

Figure 8-10. *(continued)*

c. Release the extensor retinaculum longitudinally
d. Incise the anterior ankle joint capsule longitudinally and retract the edges medially and laterally
e. Reshape the dorsal talar neck with an osteotome and high-speed burr
f. Resect osteophytes from the anterior distal tibial epiphysis, if present
g. Debride surrounding thick abnormal callus tissue, if present
h. Maximally dorsiflex the ankle to confirm, under direct visualization, that there is no residual contact between the talus and the tibia
i. Repair the ankle joint capsule with 2-0 absorbable sutures
j. Repair the extensor retinaculum with 2-0 absorbable sutures
k. Approximate the skin edges with interrupted subcutaneous 3-0 absorbable sutures and a running subcuticular 4-0 absorbable suture
l. Apply a non–weight-bearing CAM boot for 2 to 3 weeks to provide comfort during the early healing phase

m. Then initiate active range-of-motion exercises and continue non–weight-bearing for an additional 4 weeks; use of the CAM boot is optional for comfort during this time.
3. Pitfalls
   a. Inadequate resection of bone
   b. Failure to repair the extensor retinaculum with resultant bow-stringing of the extensor tendons
4. Complications
   a. Injury to the superficial peroneal nerve
      i. *Avoid by* isolating and retracting/protecting it

Ray Resection

1. Indications
   a. Macrodactyly (**see Chapter 6**)
   b. Polydactyly (**see Chapter 6**)
2. Technique (Figure 8-11)
   a. Make a V-shaped incision on both the dorsal and plantar surfaces of the foot with the apices at the tarsometatarsal

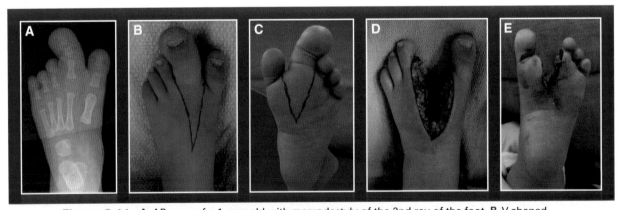

Figure 8-11. **A.** AP x-ray of a 1-year-old with macrodactyly of the 2nd ray of the foot. **B.** V-shaped incision is marked on the dorsum. **C.** V-shaped incision is marked on the plantar aspect. **D.** Dorsal view after the ray has been resected. **E.** Plantar view after the ray has been resected. **F.** AP x-ray after the resection. **G.** Intraoperative appearance of the dorsum of the foot immediately after the resection. Note the markedly improved appearance of the foot and the cosmetic appearance of the subcuticular suture wound closure. **H.** Intraoperative appearance of the plantar surface of the foot immediately after the resection. **I.** Dorsal appearance of the foot 18 months later. Note the cosmetic appearance of the scar (disregard the small recent abrasion at the proximal end). **J.** Plantar appearance of the foot 18 months later. The scar is barely noticeable.

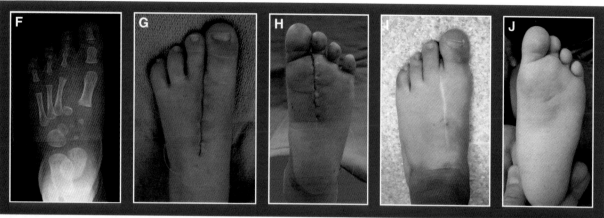

Figure 8-11. *(continued)*

joint level and connecting distally in the web spaces on both sides of the ray to be removed
b. From the dorsal approach, incise sharply and directly to the intermetatarsal spaces on both sides of the MT to be removed
c. Expose the common digital neurovascular bundles in the web spaces and transect the branches to the toe being removed
d. Expose the MT shaft extraperiosteally on its dorsal, medial, and lateral surfaces
e. Transect the MT at the proximal meta-diaphysis, rather than disarticulating the MT Removing the entire MT risks upsetting the congruity of the remaining MTs and tarsometatarsal joints
f. Divide the plantar soft tissues in line with the V-shaped skin incision
g. Release the tourniquet and achieve hemostasis
h. Approximate the distal intermetatarsal ligaments of the adjacent MTs with 2-0 absorbable sutures
i. Resect any excess skin and fat
j. Approximate the skin edges with interrupted subcutaneous 3-0 absorbable sutures and a running subcuticular 4-0 absorbable suture
k. Use a long-leg cast (to prevent it from slipping off the infant) for 4 to 6 weeks
3. Pitfalls
a. Inadequate soft tissue resection, particularly on the plantar surface
4. Complications
a. Necrosis of the lateral toes
i. *Avoid by* limiting the plantar muscle resection to that under the distal two-third of the MT being resected (the lateral plantar neurovascular bundle travels lateral to the 2nd ray). Resecting plantar subcutaneous fat is generally safe.
b. Progressive overgrowth of residual macrodactyly soft tissues at the resection site
i. *Avoid by*—it is *almost impossible* to remove all of the pathological soft tissues because there is no clear

demarcation between normal and abnormal. That said, be aggressive and remove all of the soft tissues that appear safe to remove. Prepare the family for the possible need for a debulking procedure (or two) in the future (**see Management Principle #10, Chapter 4**).

Naviculectomy

1. Indications
a. Neglected/recurrent/residual congenital vertical talus (**see Chapter 5**) in which:
i. the TN joint is well-aligned or becomes well-aligned in the frontal plane yet the deformity persists (**see Figure 5-29, Chapter 5**)
ii. or, the TN joint cannot be aligned with a posterolateral soft tissue release because of resistance of the lateral soft tissues or too short a lateral column of the foot
2. Technique (Figures 8-12 and 8-13)
a. Perform a posterior/posterolateral release (**see Chapter 7**) if indicated
b. Make a longitudinal incision along the medial border of the midfoot from the base of the 1st MT to a point just distal to the medial malleolus
c. Retract the abductor hallucis plantarward
d. Release the posterior tibialis tendon sheath and expose the tendon from the medial malleolus to its insertion on the navicular
e. Z-lengthen the posterior tibialis tendon to expose the TN joint capsule
f. Release the TN joint circumferentially
g. If the navicular is dorsolaterally displaced, try to reduce it onto the head of the talus. If it cannot be reduced, or if the TN joint is already reduced but severe deformity persists, elevate the distally based Z-lengthened slip of the posterior tibialis off the navicular while maintaining its connections with the cuneiform bones.
h. Release the joint capsules between the navicular and the medial, middle, and lateral cuneiforms
i. Remove the navicular from the foot

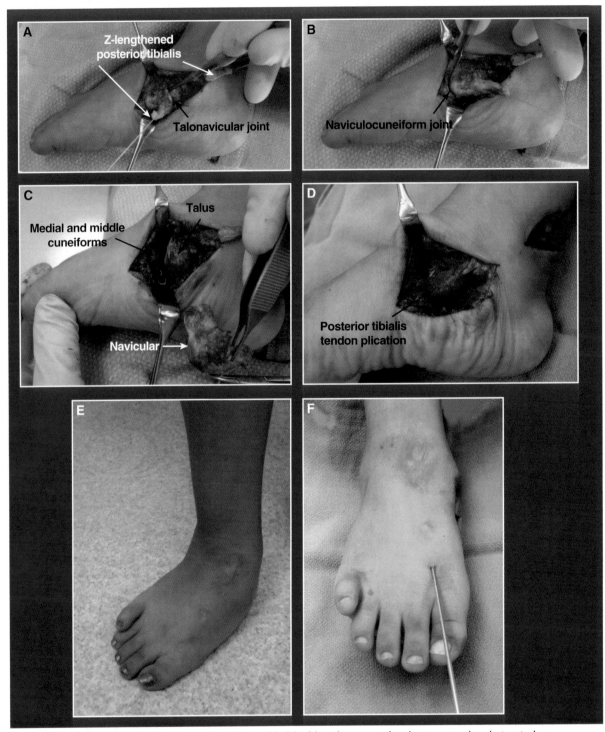

Figure 8-12. Naviculectomy in a 6-year-old girl with arthrogryposis who was previously treated unsuccessfully with a circumferential release. A. The posterior tibialis is Z-lengthened and the TN joint capsule is released circumferentially. B. The naviculocuneiform joints are released. C. The navicular has been removed from the foot. The articular surfaces of the cuneiform bones are exposed. D. The posterior tibialis tendon is plicated. E. Preoperative standing top image of the foot. F. Intraoperative top image of the foot following naviculectomy. The first of two Steinmann pins is in place across the talocuneiform joint. G. Preoperative standing medial image of the foot. H. Intraoperative medial image of the foot following naviculectomy, plantar–medial soft tissue plication, and Steinmann pin fixation. The incision for the posterior release is visualized.

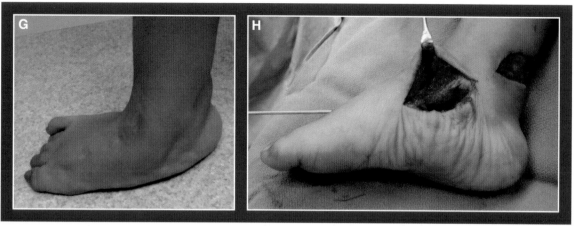

Figure 8-12. *(continued)*

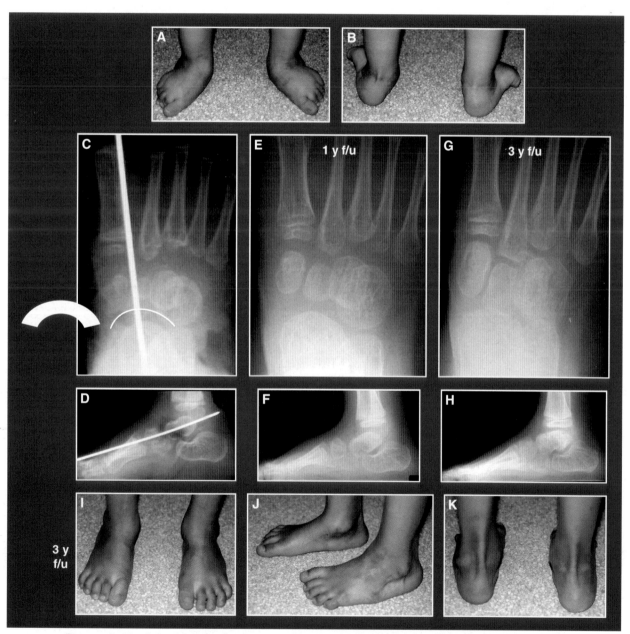

Figure 8-13. **A.** Preoperative standing top images of recurrent/residual congenital vertical talus deformities in a 3-year-old with arthrogryposis. **B.** Preoperative standing posterior images. **C.** AP x-ray of the right foot immediately following naviculectomy, with Steinmann pin fixation in place. The thick arc represents the navicular. The thin arc represents the talocuneiforms joint that resulted from the naviculectomy. **D.** Lateral x-ray with Steinmann pin in place. **E** and **F.** AP and lateral x-rays 1 year post-op. **G** and **H.** AP and lateral x-rays 3 years following naviculectomy. **I–K.** Top, side, and back views of the feet 3 years post-op.

j. Align the proximal articular surfaces of the 3 cuneiform bones with the articular surface of the talar head. They should be fairly congruous and match fairly well.

k. With the foot deformity corrected, insert two crossed 0.062″ smooth Steinmann pins retrograde across the resection site, using mini-fluoroscopic guidance

l. Bend the pins at the insertion sites and cut them long for easy retrieval in clinic in larger feet, or cut the pins short and bury them under the skin in smaller feet (to prevent spontaneous dislodgement)

m. If there is adequate capsular tissue remaining on the medial cuneiform and the talus, repair this tissue plantar-medially with 2-0 absorbable sutures

n. Advance and plicate the two slips of the posterior tibialis tendon with figure-of-8 2-0 absorbable sutures. The tendon can also be sutured to the capsule, thereby creating additional scar at the talocuneiform joint

o. Approximate the skin edges with interrupted subcutaneous 3 0 absorbable sutures and a running subcuticular 4-0 absorbable suture

p. Apply a long-leg, bent knee, non–weight-bearing cast if the child will not be compliant with non–weight-bearing in a short-leg cast

q. At 6 weeks, remove the exposed pins in clinic or the buried pins in the OR and apply another non–weight-bearing cast that will be worn for an additional 3 weeks

r. If the child has arthrogryposis or myelomeningocele, an ankle-foot-orthotic (AFO) can be molded at the 6-week cast change and fitted at the 9-week post-op visit

3. Pitfalls
    a. Incomplete removal of the navicular
    b. Incomplete posterolateral release
    c. Inaccurate alignment of the talocuneiform joints

4. Complications
    a. Recurrence of deformity
        i. *Avoid by* plicating the plantar–medial soft tissues (**see Plantar–Medial Plication, Chapter 7**) at the resection site and maintaining cast immobilization for at least 9 weeks
    b. Overcorrection of deformity
        i. *Avoid by* ensuring that the navicular cannot be anatomically positioned on the head of the talus before resecting it
    c. Incomplete removal of the navicular
        i. *Avoid by* careful dissection using fluoroscopic guidance if necessary

Talectomy

1. Indications
    a. Severe, rigid clubfoot in an infant or young child with arthrogryposis that has not responded adequately to serial casting and limited, minimally invasive soft tissue releases, followed by ongoing serial casting (**see Severe, Rigid, Resistant Arthrogrypotic Clubfoot in an Infant or Young Child, Chapter 5**)

2. Technique (Figures 8-14 and 8-15)
    a. First perform a percutaneous tendo-Achilles tenotomy (**see Chapter 7**)
    b. There are several possible incisions to choose from. My recent personal favorite is a curved incision over the dorsum of the midfoot from posterolateral to anteromedial coursing over the prominent talar head.
    c. Isolate and retract the superficial peroneal nerve
    d. Transect all extensor tendons to the foot and toes

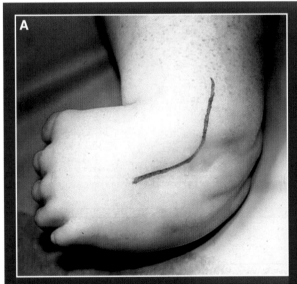 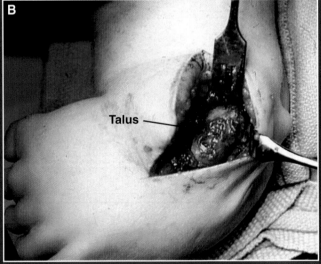

Figure 8-14. A. A curved dorsal incision is centered over the prominent head of the talus. **B.** The talus is exposed by transection of the extensor tendons and retraction of the superficial peroneal nerve. **C.** The TN joint is released circumferentially. **D.** The ankle and subtalar joints are released circumferentially and the talus is extracted from the foot.

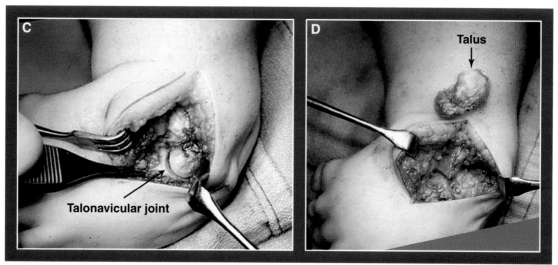

Figure 8-14. *(continued)*

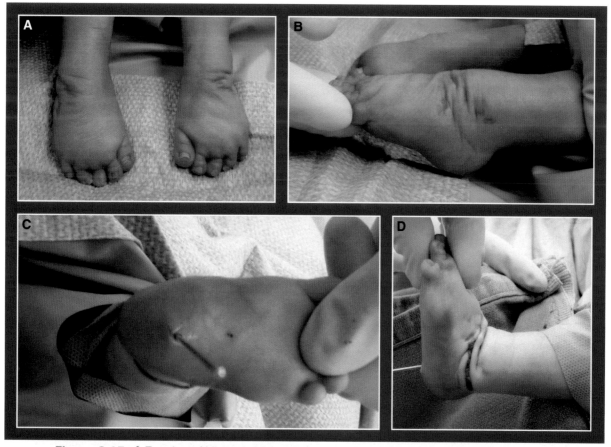

Figure 8-15. **A.** Top view of bilateral clubfoot deformities in a 1-year-old boy with Freeman–Sheldon syndrome. The cavus, adductus, and varus deformities have been corrected after 20 casts. **B.** But the navicular is plantar to the head of the talus in both feet and the talus is in extreme and rigid plantar flexion, despite two percutaneous Achilles tenotomies in both feet. **C.** Following talectomy, the calcaneus is positioned in the ankle mortis and a Steinmann pin is inserted retrograde for temporary fixation. **D.** The foot is dorsiflexed to 90° or higher.

e. Bluntly elevate the soft tissues from the medial side of the hindfoot bones (talus and calcaneus)

f. Isolate and retract the PT neurovascular bundle posteriorly

g. Incise the posterior tibialis tendon sheath distal and anterior to the medial malleolus and follow the tendon to the TN joint

h. Transect the posterior tibialis tendon

i. Transect the FHL and FDL tendons immediately plantar to the posterior tibialis tendon

j. Release the TN joint circumferentially

k. Release the ankle joint anteriorly and medially with release of the deep deltoid ligament

l. Release the lateral collateral ligaments of the ankle joint

m. Release the subtalar joint medially, laterally, and centrally (release the talocalcaneal interosseous ligament)

n. Finally, release the posterior ankle joint and subtalar joint capsules

o. Remove the talus from the operative field

p. Inset the calcaneus into the ankle joint mortis, moving it posteriorly until the navicular abuts the anteromedial aspect of the distal tibial epiphysis

q. Dorsiflex the calcaneus 5° to 10° from perpendicular to the tibia and insert a 0.062″ smooth Steinmann pin retrograde from the center of the heel pad up into the central canal of the tibial shaft

r. Bend the pin at the insertion site for easy retrieval in clinic

s. Resect a strip of excessively redundant skin from the wound edges if necessary

t. Approximate the skin edges with interrupted subcutaneous 3-0 absorbable sutures and a running subcuticular 4-0 absorbable suture

u. Apply a long-leg bent knee cast with 5° to 10° of ankle dorsiflexion and a neutral thigh–foot angle

v. Change to a fresh long-leg cast at 3 weeks

w. Change the cast again at 6 weeks, at which time the pin can be removed from the heel and a mold can be taken for a 5° to 10° dorsiflexed solid AFO

x. Apply a short-leg cast with 5° to 10° of ankle dorsiflexion and maintain it for 2 to 3 more weeks

y. Remove the cast at that time and replace it with the AFO

3. Pitfalls

a. Incomplete removal of the talus

4. Complications

a. Recurrence of equinus deformity

    i. *Avoid by:*

    • first, achieving full deformity correction with 5° to 10° of dorsiflexion held with a retrograde-inserted Steinmann pin

    • maintaining deformity correction with full-time use (23 hours per day) of a dorsiflexed AFO

b. Incomplete removal of the talus

    i. *Avoid by* carefully identifying the ankle and subtalar joints with the aid of a Freer elevator and mini-fluoroscopy

III. OSTEOTOMIES

Calcaneal Lengthening Osteotomy (CLO)

1. Indications

a. A flexible or rigid valgus/eversion deformity of the hindfoot that

    i. is almost always associated with an tendo-Achilles or gastrocnemius tendon contracture, and that

    ii. has resulted in intractable pain under the medial midfoot and/or in the sinus tarsi area that

    • has not been relieved despite prolonged attempts at nonoperative management

b. Perform a calcaneal lengthening osteotomy (CLO) for the signs and symptoms presented in "a" in

    i. flexible flatfoot with a short (tight) Achilles or gastrocnemius tendon (**see Chapter 5**)

    ii. skewfoot (**see Chapter 5**)

    iii. tarsal coalition (**see Chapter 5**)

    iv. rotational valgus overcorrection of the subtalar joint in a surgically treated clubfoot (**see Chapter 5**)

c. The CLO, in isolation, does *not* correct flatfoot deformity (or the other named complex multisegment foot deformities, such as skewfoot, that include valgus/eversion deformity of the hindfoot as one of the segmental deformities). It corrects all components of valgus/eversion deformity of the hindfoot (**see Basic Principle #6, Chapter 2**) at the site of the deformity in the named complex multisegment foot deformities. The success of the osteotomy for hindfoot deformity correction is significantly increased by appropriate management of the soft tissues and concurrent correction of the other segmental deformities of the foot (**see Basic Principle #5, Chapter 2; Assessment Principle #8, Table 3-1, Chapter 3**). Therefore, the CLO is usually combined with other concurrently performed procedures, including:

    i. plantar–medial plication (**see Chapter 7**)

    ii. medial cuneiform osteotomy (**see this Chapter**)

    iii. tendo-Achilles lengthening (**see Chapter 7**)

    iv. gastrocnemius recession (**see Chapter 7**)

    v. resection of tarsal coalition (**see this chapter**)

2. Technique

Background: In 1961, Dillwyn Evans proposed shortening the lateral column of the foot by means of a calcaneocuboid joint arthrodesis to correct cavovarus deformity in the older child with a residual or recurrent clubfoot. It was his concept that one element of clubfoot deformity was relative overgrowth of the lateral column of the foot. This is the original Evans procedure. He apparently removed too much bone from the lateral column in some feet and created valgus deformities. He proposed that varus and valgus of the hindfoot are opposite deformities based on the relative length of the medial and lateral columns of the foot. In 1975, he proposed lengthening the lateral column of the foot by means of a CLO to correct so-called calcaneovalgus (flatfoot) deformity. This would then best be labeled the reverse Evans procedure. The surgical description in his article was terse, stating only:

"An incision is made over the lateral surface of the calcaneus parallel with, and just above, the peroneal tendons, avoiding the sural nerve lest it be involved in the scar. The anterior half of the bone is exposed and the calcaneocuboid joint is identified. The anterior end of the calcaneus is then divided through its narrow part in front of the peroneal tubercle by an osteotome, the line of division being parallel with and about 1.5 cm behind the calcaneocuboid joint. The cut surfaces of the calcaneus are then prised apart by means of a spreader and a graft of cortical bone taken from the tibia is inserted between the blades of the spreader to maintain separation of the two pieces of the calcaneus."

Evans D. Calcaneo-valgus deformity. *J Bone Joint Surg Br.* 1975;57:270–278

The intermediate-term surgical results in his patients, as reported by Phillips in 1983, indicate that Evans was consistently successful in achieving his goals. I have come to learn that many orthopedic surgeons in the United States attempted to perform the procedure after reading Evans's article and had variable, but generally poor, results. They, therefore, abandoned it. Recall **Management Principle #2 in Chapter 4**: A less-than-ideal surgical outcome can be due to a poor technique, a poor technician, or both. A corollary might be: A less-than-ideal surgical outcome can be due to a poor description of a good concept.

Encouraged by Phillips's report, dissatisfied with other proposed surgical treatments for painful flatfoot deformities, and using my "developing" principles of assessment and management of foot deformities in children, I attempted to interpret what Evans meant and probably did, but did not elaborate upon. The result, published in 1995, was a treatment method for complex multisegment foot deformities that include valgus/eversion deformity of the hindfoot as one of the segmental deformities.

My contributions to Evans's concept include:

1. *Strict indications for surgery*—A flexible *or* rigid valgus/eversion deformity of the hindfoot that is almost always associated with an tendo-Achilles or gastrocnemius tendon contracture, and that has resulted in intractable pain under the medial midfoot and/or in the sinus tarsi area that has not been relieved despite prolonged attempts at nonoperative management.
2. *Use of an Ollier incision*—It is more cosmetic and extensile than the longitudinal incision proposed by Evans.
3. *Location of the osteotomy*—It starts laterally at the "isthmus" of the calcaneus. For lack of a better term, I have defined the isthmus as the narrowest dorsal–plantar site of this bone. It is the anatomic manifestation of the radiographic "critical angle of Gissane" that is located where the downward slope of the beak of the calcaneus meets the reverse downward slope of the posterior facet/lateral process of the talus. It is approximately 2 cm posterior to the calcaneocuboid joint. That starting point ensures that the beak of the calcaneus is moved away from the lateral process of the

talus, thereby eliminating impingement and its associated pain at that site. The osteotomy ends medially between the anterior and middle facets of the calcaneus/subtalar joint.

In 2003, Ragab et al. published a study of cadaver feet in which they found that 54% of the feet (67% of whites and 40% of blacks) had separate anterior and middle facets or no anterior facet. Forty-six percent of the feet (33% of whites and 60% of blacks) had conjoined anterior and middle facets. Bunning and Barnett, in 1963, first reported on the anatomy of the subtalar joint. They reported separate facets in 67% of whites and 36% of blacks, remarkably similar findings. The authors of the recent study raised a theoretic concern that the CLO could lead to early degenerative arthritis in the subtalar joint if performed in feet with conjoined facets, because the osteotomy in those feet would be intra-articular. Arguments in favor of the CLO for valgus deformity of the hindfoot, despite the apparent anatomy of the subtalar joint, are many:

a. There are no published clinical studies of the CLO in which subtalar joint arthritis was identified. Phillips did not identify subtalar joint arthritis in his average 13-year follow-up study of Evans's patients. That is significant because Evans very likely cut into the middle facet in most of his patients by cutting "parallel with and about 1.5 cm behind the calcaneocuboid joint." Phillips reported arthritis in some calcaneocuboid joints, but those joints were not protected from subluxation by pinning, as I have recommended.

b. There is no evidence that the same ratio of separate to conjoined anterior and middle calcaneal facets exists in flatfeet as in other foot shapes. In the referenced studies, there were significant racial differences found in the facet anatomy. Variation in anatomy based on foot shape with either a higher or lower percentage of separate facets is certainly conceivable.

c. The subtalar joint complex is unlike any other joint in the body, except the hip joint, and it is more open and unconstrained than the hip. The anterior facet acts as a small platform that partially supports the plantar–lateral aspect of the head of the talus in a foot with neutral hindfoot alignment, though its primary function might, in fact, be as the lateral attachment point for the spring ligament which actually supports the talar head (**see Basic Principle #6, Chapter 2**). In a flatfoot, the anterior facet is rotated dorsolaterally around the talar head and the support is lost. The CLO rotates the so-called acetabulum pedis (including the anterior facet) plantar-medially around the head of the talus in the axis of the subtalar joint. This replaces it to its anatomic alignment where it can again provide the needed support for the head of the talus.

d. The actual separation of the calcaneal fragments along the medial column of the calcaneus is small, perhaps 1 to 3 mm. As long as the fragments do not translate vertically, the linear separation should be well tolerated as a simple, small enlargement of the platform that follows the shape and contour of the talar head and subtalar joint.

e. The alternatives of arthroereisis, arthrodesis, and soft tissue plications have higher reported complication rates than calcaneal lengthening in clinical studies. The posterior calcaneal displacement osteotomy creates a compensating deformity rather than correcting the primary deformity. It does not have the power to correct severe deformities and to realign the TN joint.

4. *Shape of the bone graft*—It should be trapezoidal, rather than triangular, because the foot-CORA (**see Assessment Principle #18, Chapter 3**) is in the center of the head of the talus (Dumontier et al. 2005), not at the medial cortex of the calcaneus. Therefore, it is a distraction wedge osteotomy rather than an opening wedge osteotomy.

5. *Management of the lateral soft tissue restraints*—The peroneus brevis (PB) tendon should be lengthened and the abductor digiti minimi aponeurosis should be released, because they are lateral soft tissue restraints that will otherwise impede distraction of the calcaneal bone fragments. The peroneus longus (PL) should be retracted and *not* lengthened. It is the pronator of the forefoot. As the lateral column of the foot is lengthened, the PL is effectively shortened, thereby pronating the supinated forefoot. And because its insertion is on the medial column of the foot, it does not impede calcaneal lengthening.

6. *Management of the medial soft tissue redundancy*—The posterior tibialis tendon and the talonavicular joint capsule should be plicated plantar-medially to eliminate the redundancy of those tissues that develops following hindfoot deformity correction with the CLO. This soft tissue plication reinforces and further stabilizes the primary bony structural deformity correction.

7. *Stabilization of the calcaneocuboid joint*—One or two Steinmann pins should be inserted retrograde across that joint before distraction of the osteotomy to prevent subluxation that would otherwise compromise the outcome.

8. *Lengthening of the Achilles or gastrocnemius tendon*—Contracture of the heel cord is usually the deformity that converts a painless flexible valgus/eversion hindfoot deformity into a painful deformity. Therefore, it must be eliminated at the time of hindfoot deformity correction with the CLO. The CLO eliminates the pathologic dorsiflexion of the subtalar joint by converting "up (dorsiflexion) and out" to "down (plantar flexion) and in" (**see Basic Principle #6, Chapter 2**). It does not create ankle joint equinus, it uncovers it. The Silfverskiold test (**see Assessment Principle #12, Chapter 3**) is used to determine whether the tendo-Achilles or the gastrocnemius tendon alone is contracted so the appropriate site of lengthening can be chosen.

9. *Identification and correction of forefoot deformity*—Forefoot supination deformity exists in all flatfoot deformities. It is initially flexible and corrects spontaneously immediately following insertion of the graft into the calcaneal osteotomy. In long-standing deformities, the forefoot supination deformity is rigid and does not correct spontaneously. A medial cuneiform osteotomy (MCO) is required to correct this independent segmental deformity or else the hindfoot deformity will likely recur. The CLO does not create forefoot supination deformity, it uncovers it (**see Basic Principle #5, Chapter 2; Assessment Principle #8, Figure 3-2, Chapter 3**).

a. Attention to *all* of the details of the technique is *critical* for consistently good results. There are only two intraoperative decisions that need to be made: (1) whether rigid forefoot supination deformity exists and requires a MCO for correction, and (2) whether the heel cord contracture is in the gastrocnemius alone or in the entire triceps surae.

b. Special equipment: sagittal saw, smooth Steinmann pins, straight osteotomes, laminar spreader with smooth teeth, Joker elevators and narrow Crego retractors (Figure 8-16), and a mini-fluoroscope

c. Place the patient supine with a folded towel under the ipsilateral buttock and put a cushioned ramp under the extremity

d. Prep and drape from the iliac crest to the toes and use a sterile tourniquet if using autograft. If using allograft, prep the lower extremity only and use a nonsterile tourniquet.

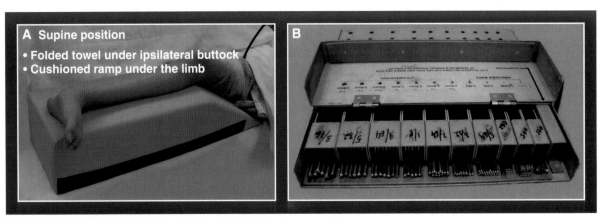

Figure 8-16. **A.** The patient is placed supine on the operating table with the deformed lower extremity on a cushioned ramp. A folded towel is placed under the ipsilateral buttock. **B.** Steinmann pins are used for internal fixation. **C.** Narrow Crego retractors (*left*), Joker elevators (*center*), and laminar spreader with smooth teeth (*right*). **D.** Sagittal saw.

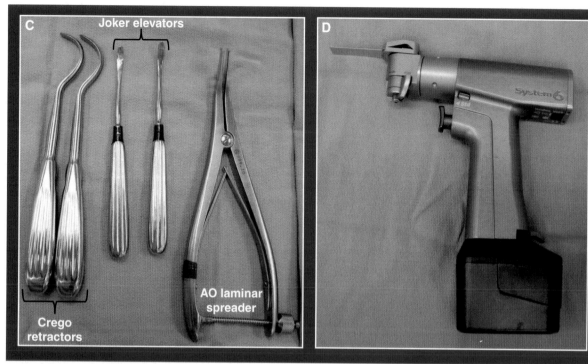

Figure 8-16. *(continued)*

e. Make a modified Ollier incision in a Langer's skin line from the superficial peroneal nerve to the sural nerve half way between the beak of the calcaneus and the tip of the lateral malleolus (Figure 8-17)

f. Release the PL and the PB from their tendon sheaths on the lateral surface of the calcaneus. Resect the intervening septum. Resect the peroneal tubercle if it is large

g. Z-lengthen the PB tendon

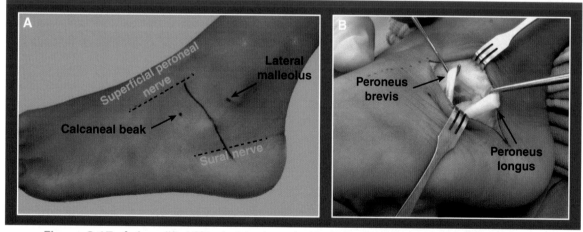

Figure 8-17. **A.** A modified Ollier incision is marked in a Langer's line half way between the tip of the lateral malleolus and the beak of the calcaneus. It extends from the superficial peroneal nerve to the sural nerve. **B.** The PB and PL tendons are released from their sheaths. The septum between them is resected. A very large peroneal tubercle should be resected. **C.** The PB is Z-lengthened. The PL is retracted. The aponeurosis of the abductor digiti minimi is divided transversely 2 cm posterior to the calcaneocuboid joint (*yellow line*). **D.** The soft tissue contents of the sinus tarsi are elevated from the dorsum of the calcaneus. A Freer elevator is inserted perpendicular to the lateral surface of the calcaneus at the isthmus of the calcaneus (**see Technique Background, Location of the osteotomy—earlier**), which is approximately 2 cm posterior to the calcaneocuboid (CC) joint. The Freer is inserted until it makes contact with the middle facet. **E.** The Freer is then externally rotated (*purple curved arrow*) and advanced (*yellow arrow*) until the tip falls into the interval between the anterior and middle facets. **F.** The position of the Freer is confirmed with mini-fluoroscopy. (From Mosca VS. Calcaneal lengthening osteotomy for valgus deformity of the hindfoot. In: Skaggs DL and Tolo VT, editors. *Master Techniques in Orthopaedic Surgery: Pediatrics.* Philadelphia: Lippincott Williams & Wilkins. 2008; 263–276.)

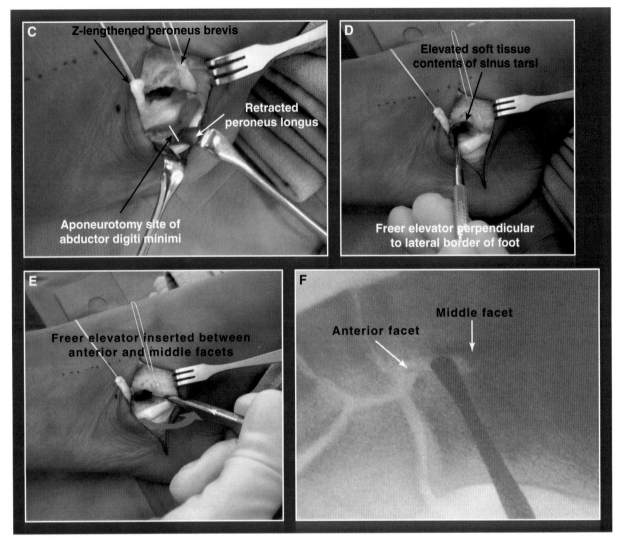

Figure 8-17. *(continued)*

h. Do *not* lengthen the PL

i. Divide the aponeurosis of the abductor digiti minimi transversely at a point approximately 2 cm proximal to the calcaneocuboid (CC) joint (**see Chapter 7**)

j. Elevate the soft tissues from the dorsal surface of the anterior calcaneus in the sinus tarsi. Avoid exposure of, or injury to, the capsule of the calcaneocuboid joint

k. Insert a Freer elevator in the sinus tarsi perpendicular to the lateral surface of the calcaneus at the lowest (most plantar) point of the dorsal surface of the calcaneus, the so-called "isthmus" of the calcaneus (**see Technique Background, Location of the osteotomy—earlier**). The Freer is inserted until it makes contact with the middle facet.

l. Externally rotate and advanced the Freer until the tip falls into the interval between the anterior and middle facets

m. Although there are not separate anterior and middle facets in a large percentage of calcaneus bones (**see above**), this interval is very easy to identify in all feet, in my experience. The interval and the position of the Freer can be readily confirmed with an oblique image obtained on mini-fluoroscopy.

n. Replace the Freer with a curved Joker elevator. Place a narrow curved Crego retractor around the plantar

aspect of the calcaneus in an extraperiosteal plane in line with the dorsally placed Joker. Remove the retractors and prepare the other surgical sites before performing the calcaneal osteotomy

o. Make a longitudinal incision along the medial border of the midfoot and hindfoot to perform the plantar–medial plication (**see Chapter 7**). Start at a point just plantar to the medial malleolus and continue anteriorly to the medial cuneiform. This incision can be extended to the base of the 1st MT if an MCO is determined to be necessary.

p. Release the posterior tibialis from its tendon sheath from the medial malleolus to the navicular

q. Cut the posterior tibialis tendon in a Z-fashion, releasing its *dorsal* one-third to one-half from the navicular. The stump of tendon that remains attached to the navicular contains the *plantar* one-half to two-third of the fibers (**see Plantar–Medial Plication, Figure 7-39, Chapter 7**)

r. Incise the TN joint capsule from dorsal-lateral around medially to plantar-lateral, including release of the spring ligament. Resect a 5- to 7-mm-wide strip of redundant capsule from the medial and plantar aspects of the joint (**see Plantar–Medial Plication, Figure 7-39, Chapter 7**)

s. In a foot with a *long-standing talocalcaneal tarsal coalition*, the dorsolateral TN joint capsule may become tightly contracted. In some cases, adjacent dorsolateral osteophytes on the talus and navicular may become partially fused together. Release and/or resect this connection with Mayo scissors or an osteotome.

t. Assess the equinus contracture by the Silverskiold test (**see Assessment Principle #12, Figure 3-13, Chapter 3**) with the subtalar joint inverted to neutral and the knee both flexed and extended. Perform

a gastrocnemius recession (**see Chapter 7**) if 10° of dorsiflexion can be achieved with the knee flexed, but not with the knee extended. Perform an open or percutaneous tendo-Achilles lengthening (**see Chapter 7**) if 10° of dorsiflexion cannot be obtained even with the knee flexed

u. Replace the Joker elevator and Crego retractor respectively dorsal and plantar to the isthmus of the calcaneus meeting in the interval between the anterior and middle facets of the subtalar joint (Figure 8-18)

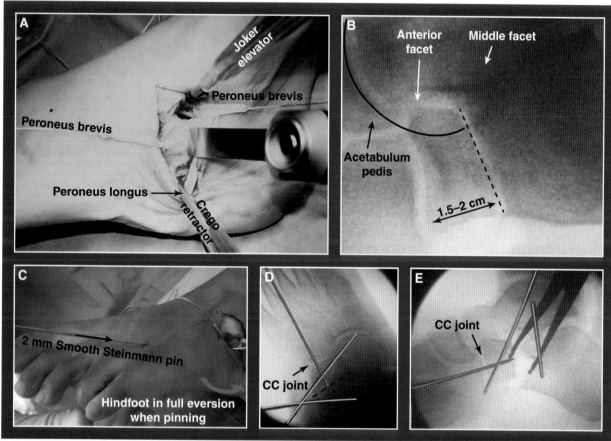

Figure 8-18. **A.** A Joker elevator is inserted above the isthmus of the calcaneus and a narrow Crego retractor is inserted extraperiosteally from below. They meet in the interval between the anterior and middle facets. A sagittal saw is used to create the osteotomy in line with the retractors. **B.** The osteotomy (*black dashed line*) begins laterally at the isthmus of the calcaneus (at or near the "critical angle of Gissane"), which is approximately 2 cm posterior to the calcaneo-cuboid (CC) joint, and ends between the anterior and middle facets medially (**see Technique Background, Location of the osteotomy—earlier**). The acetabulum pedis is indicated here (**see Basic Principle #6, Chapter 2**). **C.** A 2-mm smooth Steinmann pin is inserted retrograde from the dorsolateral forefoot across the anatomic center of the CC joint while holding the foot in the fully everted/flat position. **D and E.** Mini-fluoroscopy is used to ensure that the pin (*purple line*) crosses the anatomic center of the CC joint and is advanced to the osteotomy. 0.062″ smooth Steinmann pin joy sticks are inserted from lateral to medial in the anterior and posterior calcaneal fragments (*blue lines*). They are inserted in a divergent pattern, so they will become more parallel after the fragments are distracted. **F.** Smooth-toothed laminar spreader is inserted in the osteotomy to determine the size of graft that is required to correct the deformity three-dimensionally, as confirmed by mini-fluoroscopy. **G.** An iliac crest corticocancellous bone graft is fashioned into a trapezoid shape with its lateral length based on direct measurement of the distracted bone fragments and the medial length approximately 2 to 4 mm. **H.** The trapezoid-shaped allograft is being inserted while using the joy sticks to open the space. **I.** The cortical surfaces are axially aligned with the dorsal, lateral, and plantar cortical surfaces of the calcaneus. The graft is firmly impacted (*black arrow over the tamp*), making it inherently stable. **J.** Artist's sketch of a foot with the graft inserted. **K.** Same intraoperative image as in D, but with the foot-CORA (**see Assessment Principle #18, Chapter 3**) indicated. **L.** The laminar spreader has distracted the osteotomy, thereby rotating the acetabulum pedis into anatomic alignment (*purple curved arrow*). **M.** With the graft partially inserted, the deformity is almost completely corrected, as confirmed by the correction of deformity at the foot-CORA. Following full insertion of the graft, the 2-mm Steinmann pin (*purple line*) is inserted retrograde through the graft and into the posterior calcaneus. **N.** The foot is in the fully everted (up and out/flat) baseline position with the Steinmann pin joy sticks in place and the osteotomy completed. **O.** The laminar spreader has been opened in the osteotomy thereby creating full inversion (down and in/arched) of the acetabulum pedis/subtalar joint. (From Mosca VS. Calcaneal lengthening osteotomy for valgus deformity of the hindfoot. In: Skaggs DL and Tolo VT, editors. *Master Techniques in Orthopaedic Surgery: Pediatrics.* Philadelphia: Lippincott Williams & Wilkins. 2008; 263–276.)

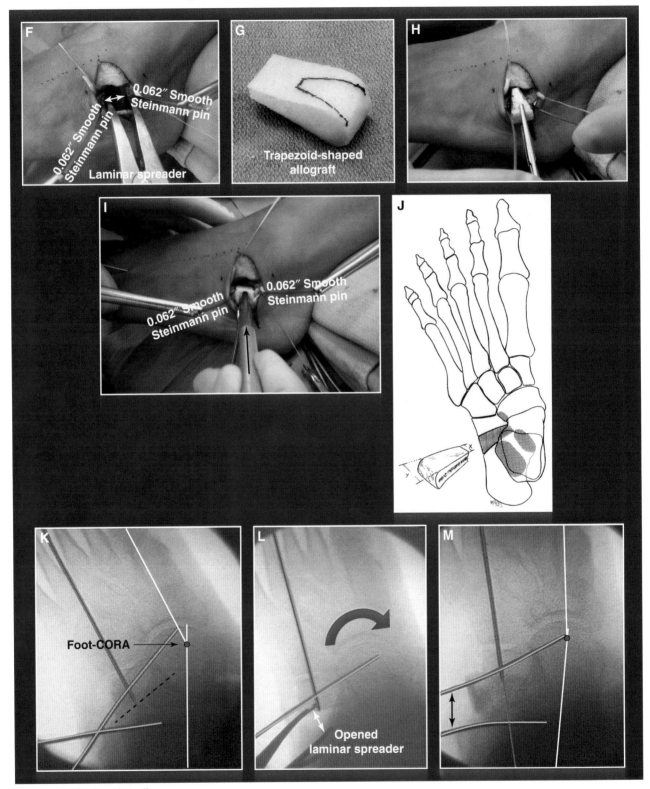

Figure 8-18. *(continued)*

v. Perform an osteotomy of the calcaneus using a sagittal saw
w. It is an oblique osteotomy from posterolateral to anteromedial that starts at the "isthmus" of the calcaneus, defined as the narrowest dorsal–plantar site of this bone. It is the anatomic manifestation of the radiographic "critical angle of Gissane" that is located where

the downward slope of the beak of the calcaneus meets the reverse downward slope of the posterior facet/lateral process of the talus. It is approximately 2 cm posterior to the calcaneocuboid joint. The osteotomy exits medially between the anterior and middle facets (**see Technique Background, Location of the osteotomy—earlier**).

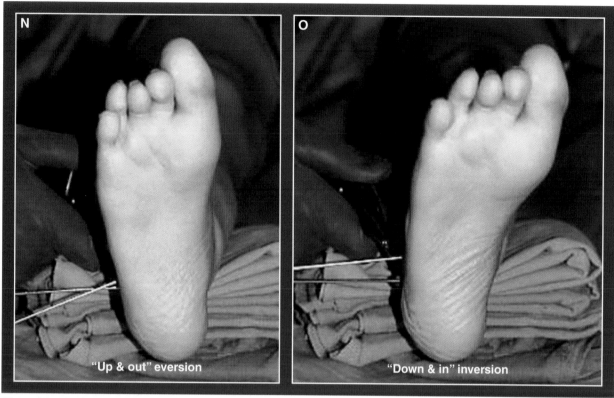

Figure 8-18. *(continued)*

x. It is a complete osteotomy through the medial cortex of the calcaneus. Cut the plantar periosteum and long plantar ligament, a.k.a. lateral plantar fascia (*not* the plantar fascia) under direct vision if necessary, i.e., if these soft tissues resist distraction of the bone fragments.

y. Insert a 2-mm smooth Steinmann pin retrograde from the dorsum of the foot passing through the cuboid, *across the anatomic center* of the calcaneocuboid joint, stopping at the osteotomy. This is performed with the foot in the *original fully everted, deformed position before* the osteotomy is distracted. By so doing, the pes acetabulum (navicular, spring ligament, anterior facet of calcaneus) will remain intact and the distal fragment of the calcaneus will not subluxate dorsally on the cuboid during distraction of the osteotomy. <u>Take time on this step</u> and <u>use mini-fluoroscopy </u>to ensure that the calcaneo-cuboid joint is perfectly aligned and that the pin crosses the anatomic center of the joint to prevent subluxation

z. Insert a 0.062″ smooth Steinmann pin from lateral to medial in both of the calcaneal fragments immediately adjacent to the osteotomy. These will be used as joy sticks to distract the osteotomy at the time of graft insertion.

aa. Place a smooth-toothed laminar spreader in the osteotomy and distract maximally, trying to avoid crushing the bone

bb. Assess deformity correction of the hindfoot clinically and using mini-fluoroscopy. The deformity is corrected when the axes of the talus and 1st MT are collinear in both the anteroposterior (AP) and lateral planes

cc. The CLO is a distraction wedge rather than a simple opening wedge, as the center of rotation for angular deformity correction is within the talar head, rather than the medial cortex of the calcaneus.

dd. Measure the distance between the lateral cortical margins of the calcaneal fragments. This is the lateral length dimension of the trapezoid-shaped iliac crest graft that will be obtained either from the child's iliac crest or from the bone bank. There is no difference in healing rate or complication rate between tricortical iliac crest allograft and bicortical (in a young child) or tricortical (in the adolescent) iliac crest autograft, though there is unnecessary added pain morbidity when autograft is used.

ee. The length of the medial edge of the trapezoid should be 20% to 30% of the length of the lateral edge.

ff. Remove the laminar spreader and use the Steinmann pin joysticks free-hand to distract the calcaneal fragments. *Do not* use a fixed angle distractor, such as a mini-lengthening rail. This is *not* a pure linear lengthening osteotomy. It is a three-dimensional distraction wedge. The acetabulum pedis must be allowed to follow the axis of the subtalar joint "down and in" (**see Basic Principles #6 and 7, Chapter 2**) as it rotates around the head of the talus. A fixed distractor can/will subluxate the TN joint, whereas manual distraction of the osteotomy with Steinmann pins will maintain articular contact as the acetabulum pedis naturally inverts around the head of the talus.

gg. Insert and impact the graft with the cortical surfaces aligned with those of the calcaneal fragments from anterior to posterior in the long axis of the foot. This will place the cancellous bone of the graft in direct contact with the cancellous bone of the calcaneal fragments.

hh. Use mini-fluoroscopy to confirm that there is full three-dimensional correction of all components of hindfoot eversion and that there is no subluxation at the CC joint. If CC joint subluxation is identified, the joint has not been adequately stabilized. Remove the bone graft, reposition the pin more centrally across the joint, and/or add another pin! It is *impossible* for the CC joint to subluxate if the pin is properly positioned. That is a basic orthopedic principle of bone/joint internal fixation.

ii. Advance the previously inserted 2-mm Steinmann pin retrograde through the graft and into the posterior calcaneal fragment. Bend the pin at its insertion site on the dorsum of the foot for ease of retrieval in clinic. No additional fixation is required. In fact, were the pin not needed to prevent subluxation at the calcaneocuboid joint, no graft fixation would be needed.

jj. Repair the PB tendon with a 2-0 absorbable suture after a 5- to 7-mm lengthening

kk. Plicate the TN joint capsule plantar-medially, but not dorsally, with multiple figure-of-8 2-0 absorbable sutures (**see Figure 7-39, Chapter 7**)

ll. Advance the proximal slip of the posterior tibialis tendon approximately 5 to 7 mm through a slit in the distal stump of the tendon. Secure this tensioned Pulvertaft weave with a 2-0 absorbable suture (**see Figure 7-39, Chapter 7**)

mm. Assess the forefoot for structural supination deformity by cupping the heel in one hand, while maintaining neutral ankle dorsiflexion, and visually sighting down the long axis of the foot from toes to heel. If the plane of the MT heads is supinated in relation to the long axis of the tibia or there is dorsal–plantar hypermobility of the 1st MT–medial cuneiform joint, a plantar flexion plantar-based closing wedge osteotomy of the medial cuneiform is needed (**see this chapter, and Figure 8-19**).

nn. Approximate the skin edges of all incisions with interrupted subcutaneous 3-0 absorbable sutures and a running subcuticular 4-0 absorbable suture

oo. Apply a well-padded short-leg fiberglass non–weight-bearing cast and immediately bivalve it to allow for swelling overnight. Obtain final radiographs of the foot in the cast in the recovery room (Figure 8-20)

pp. Discharge the patient from the hospital the following day after the bivalved cast is overwrapped with fiberglass (**see Management Principle #26, Figure 4-20, Chapter 4**)

qq. Postoperative management:
i. The patient is immobilized in a below-the-knee cast and is not permitted to bear weight on the operated extremity for 8 weeks. At 6 weeks, the cast is removed to obtain simulated standing AP and lateral radiographs of the foot and to remove the Steinmann pin. Another below-the-knee non–weight-bearing cast is applied. Upon removal of this cast 2 weeks later, final

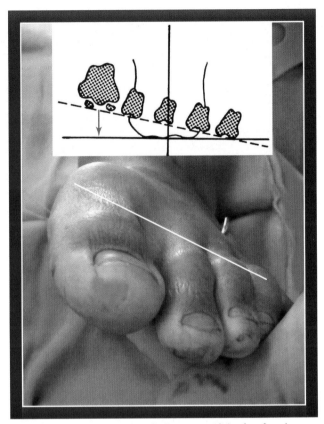

Figure 8-19. The rotational alignment of the forefoot is assessed following correction of the hindfoot deformity and the heel cord contracture. If, as in this case, the forefoot is rigidly supinated, an osteotomy of the medial cuneiform is required (**see Medial Cuneiform Plantar Flexion Plantar-Based Closing Wedge Osteotomy [MC-PF-CWO], this chapter**). (From Mosca VS. Calcaneal lengthening osteotomy for valgus deformity of the hindfoot. In: Skaggs DL and Tolo VT, editors. *Master Techniques in Orthopaedic Surgery: Pediatrics.* Philadelphia: Lippincott Williams & Wilkins. 2008; 263–276.)

simulated standing AP and lateral radiographs of the foot are obtained. Over-the-counter arch supports are used initially and indefinitely to provide added cushioning and comfort for the "new" weight-bearing surfaces of the foot. Physical therapy is rarely needed.

3. Pitfalls
a. Failure to pay attention to *all* of the details of the technique as described.
b. Failure to create the osteotomy between the anterior and middle facets of the calcaneus. Try to find the interval between the anterior and middle facets of the subtalar joint to create an extra-articular osteotomy, acknowledging that perhaps only approximately 54% of individuals have separate facets.
c. Failure to lengthen the PB and the aponeurosis of the abductor digiti minimi, while preserving the PL
d. Failure to prevent subluxation of the CC joint by predistraction retrograde pinning
e. Failure to appreciate and correct rigid supination deformity of the forefoot
f. Failure to lengthen a contracted gastrocnemius or tendo-Achilles

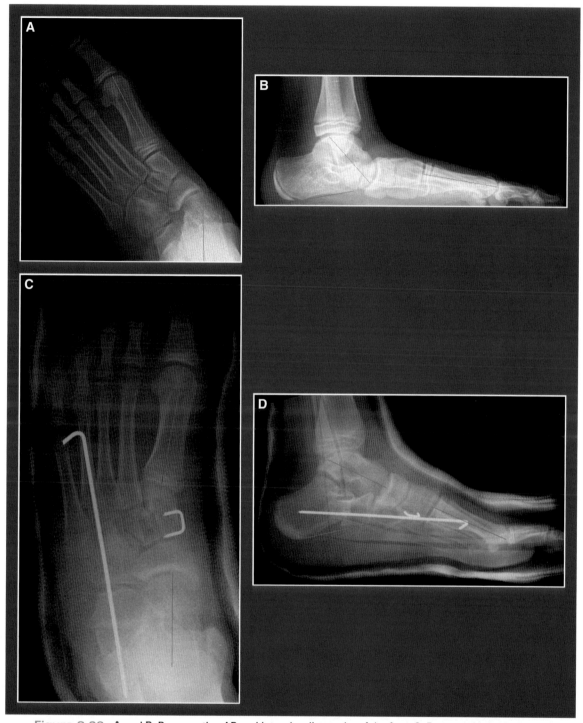

Figure 8-20. **A** and **B**. Preoperative AP and lateral radiographs of the foot. **C**. Postoperative AP view in the bivalved cast. Note the correction of the external rotation component of eversion deformity of the subtalar joint with alignment of the TN joint and correction of the talo–1st MT angle. **D**. Postoperative lateral view demonstrates dorsiflexion of the talus, alignment of the TN joint, correction of the talo–1st MT angle, and normalization of the calcaneal pitch. (From Mosca VS. Calcaneal lengthening osteotomy for valgus deformity of the hindfoot. In: Skaggs DL and Tolo VT, editors. *Master Techniques in Orthopaedic Surgery: Pediatrics*. Philadelphia: Lippincott Williams & Wilkins. 2008; 263–276.)

4. Complications
   a. Subluxation of the CC joint, with resultant incomplete deformity correction and the eventual development of premature arthritis
      i. *Avoid by* retrograde insertion of a pin across the anatomic center of the CC joint, with the foot held in the fully everted position, after the osteotomy is created but before the osteotomy is distracted
   b. Incomplete deformity correction
      i. *Avoid by:*
         • releasing the lateral soft tissues (PB and abductor digiti minimi aponeurosis)

- releasing the dorsolateral aspect of the TN joint capsule in long-standing cases and in feet with talocalcaneal tarsal coalitions
- pinning the CC joint before distraction of the osteotomy
- inserting the proper size graft
- confirming adequate correction intraoperatively with mini-fluoroscopy

c. Persistent equinus

  i. *Avoid by* lengthening the Achilles or gastrocnemius tendon, based on the Silfverskiold test, and confirming adequacy of ankle dorsiflexion with the knee extended after deformity correction

d. Persistent forefoot supination

  i. *Avoid by* assessing forefoot supination intraoperatively after the calcaneus and the heel cord have been lengthened. Correct it with an MCO if identified

e. Recurrence of deformity

  i. *Avoid by* paying attention to all of the details of the procedure as outlined.

Posterior Calcaneus Displacement Osteotomy (PCDO)

1. Indications

   a. Lateral hindfoot impingement pain and/or medial hindfoot soft tissue strain due to exaggerated *valgus* deformity of the hindfoot *without* eversion of the subtalar joint

      i. This deformity is most often due to lateral translational overcorrection of the subtalar joint in a surgically treated clubfoot (**see Chapter 5**).

      ii. Also indicated for symptomatic hindfoot valgus malformation in congenital synostosis of the subtalar joint (**see Chapter 6**)

   b. Residual *varus* deformity of the subtalar joint in a cavovarus foot (**see Chapter 5**) that does not correct fully with a deep plantar-medial release (D-PMR; **see Chapter 7**)

      i. The usual reason for incomplete deformity correction after a D-PMR is that the deformity has been present for too long and the tissues are unyielding.

   c. Because the foot-CORA (**see Assessment Principle #18, Chapter 3**) is the nearby subtalar joint, translation of the posterior fragment is more powerful and effective than angulation in deformity "correction".

2. Technique (Figure 8-21)

   a. The posterior calcaneus displacement osteotomy can be used to correct valgus, varus, planus, cavus, and combinations of these deformities, depending on the direction of displacement.

   b. If the only procedure being performed under the anesthetic is the posterior calcaneus displacement osteotomy, place the patient prone to improve visual confirmation of the deformity correction. If other procedures are to be performed concurrently, it is generally easier to carry out all procedures with the patient supine.

   c. Make a slightly curved incision on the lateral aspect of the calcaneus following the course of the peroneal tendons starting posterior to the lateral malleolus and ending at the glabrous skin plantarward. This is the same incision used for a PL to PB transfer (**see Chapter 7**).

d. Isolate and protect the sural nerve

e. Expose the tuber of the calcaneus extraperiosteally on its dorsal, lateral, and plantar surfaces using blunt dissection

f. Use a Joker elevator to elevate the soft tissues extraperiosteally off the dorsal aspect of the tuber calcanei immediately posterior to the posterior facet of the subtalar joint, continuing around the medial side of the calcaneus deep to the PT neurovascular bundles

g. Use a Joker elevator to elevate the soft tissues extraperiosteally off the plantar aspect of the tuber calcanei approximately 1.5 to 2 cm anterior to the dorsally placed Joker, continuing around the medial side of the calcaneus deep to the PT neurovascular bundles

h. Replace the Jokers with narrow Crego retractors. They will overlap on the medial side of the calcaneus deep to the neurovascular bundles. The Crego retractors define the plane of the planned osteotomy in relation to the plantar aspect of the foot. Prepare for a more vertical osteotomy if planning some dorsal displacement (to correct cavus) or plantar displacement (to correct planus/flatfoot) in addition to the lateral or medial displacement.

i. Insert a 2-mm threaded Steinmann pin from medial to lateral through the posteroplantar corner of the calcaneus *in the plane of the MT heads*. This pin will be used as a joy stick. More importantly, it defines the translational plane of the osteotomy, which is *not* perpendicular to the lateral cortex of the calcaneus.

   i. An osteotomy perpendicular to a varus calcaneus will result in plantar displacement of the posterior fragment during lateralization and may prevent full lateral displacement

   ii. An osteotomy perpendicular to a valgus calcaneus will result in plantar displacement of the posterior fragment during medialization and may prevent full medial displacement

j. Cut the calcaneus with a sagittal saw in line with the Crego retractors (more or less vertically—**see "h" above**) and parallel with the threaded Steinmann pin. With the Crego's in place, there should be little concern for injury to the medial soft tissues (Figure 8-22)

k. Use a wide, straight osteotome to lever the posterior calcaneal fragment away from the body of the calcaneus and, thereby, elevate the periosteum on the medial side of the bone fragments

l. Translate the posterior fragment in the desired direction(s). Plantar flex the ankle to relax the tension on the tendo-Achilles and to facilitate movement of the fragment

m. *If,* despite adequate elevation of the periosteum on the medial side and maximum displacement of the posterior fragment, the deformity does *not* fully correct, a wedge of bone can be removed from the medial side of the posterior fragment in a valgus deformity or the lateral side of the posterior fragment in a varus deformity

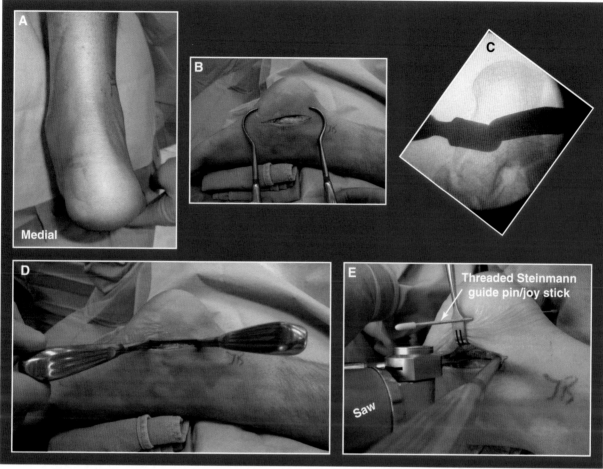

Figure 8-21. Posterior calcaneus displacement osteotomy. A. Posterior view of a symptomatic lateral translational valgus hindfoot deformity. B. Curved lateral incision over the peroneal tendons and sural nerve. Protect all three structures. C. Radiographic appearance of Crego retractors passed extraperiosteally around the tuber of the calcaneus deep to the PT neurovascular bundles on the medial side. D. Clinical appearance of the Crego retractors in place. E. A 2-mm threaded Steinmann pin has been inserted transversely in the calcaneus in the plane of the MT heads to act as a guide pin defining the true transverse plane. A sagittal saw is used to create the osteotomy in the plane defined by the Steinmann pin and angled approximately 45° from the plantar surface of the foot. The Crego retractors protect the medial soft tissues.

i. When correcting a varus deformity, a plantar fasciotomy is frequently necessary. This can be performed in the standard manner as described in **Chapter 7**.

n. Internally stabilize the osteotomy (Figure 8-23)
   i. In a skeletally immature child, use a 2.4- to 2.8-mm smooth Steinmann pin that aligns with the posterior surface of the os calcis apophysis and exits on the dorsolateral midfoot/forefoot. Bend the pin at the skin penetration site on the dorsum of the foot for ease of removal in clinic.
   ii. In a skeletally mature adolescent, use a cannulated 6.5-mm or larger partially threaded screw inserted antegrade into the anterior calcaneus and with the screw head countersunk into the posterior calcaneus.

o. Approximate the skin edges with interrupted subcutaneous 3-0 absorbable sutures and a running subcuticular 4-0 absorbable suture

p. A short-leg non–weight-bearing fiberglass cast is applied and bivalved. It is overwrapped with fiberglass before discharge from the hospital the following day

q. The cast is changed to a walking cast at 6 weeks postoperatively after obtaining simulated standing lateral and Harris x-rays
   i. and removing the Steinmann pin in the young children

3. Pitfalls
   a. Inability to adequately displace the posterior calcaneus fragment due to
      i. insufficient elevation of the periosteum on the medial side of the bone fragments
      ii. obliquity of the plane of the osteotomy
      iii. contracture of the plantar fascia in a cavovarus foot deformity
   b. Incomplete deformity correction because of poor visualization of the hindfoot. Prone positioning obviates this problem, but is not possible if other procedures are being performed concurrently

4. Complications
   a. Injury to the PT neurovascular bundles
      i. *Avoid by:*
         • careful extraperiosteal dissection on the medial side of the tuber calcanei with a Joker elevator

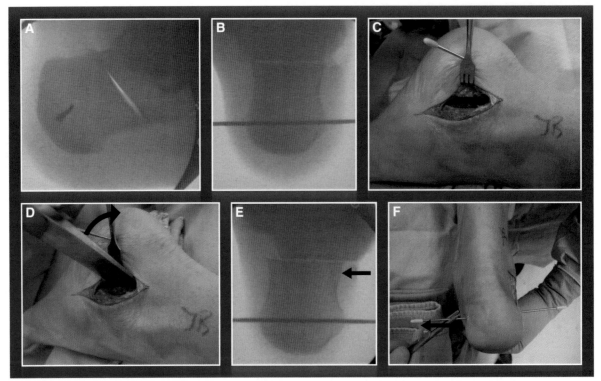

Figure 8-22. **A.** Lateral x-ray shows completed osteotomy. Threaded Steinmann guide pin/joy stick is seen. **B.** Harris axial x-ray shows completed osteotomy and threaded Steinmann guide pin/joy stick. **C.** The osteotomy is visualized with the posterior calcaneal fragment displaced slightly medially. **D.** A broad, straight osteotome is used as a lever (*black curved arrow*) to elevate the periosteum on the medial side of the fragments and to displace the posterior calcaneal fragment further medially. **E.** Initial medial displacement of the posterior fragment can be seen. **F.** The posterior fragment is displaced using pressure on the lateral side of the fragment and with assistance of the Steinmann pin joy stick. Plantar flexion of the ankle will facilitate movement of the fragment medially by relaxing the tendo-Achilles.

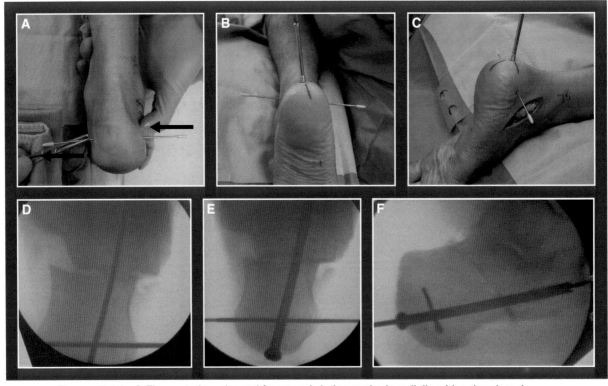

Figure 8-23. **A.** The posterior calcaneal fragment is being pushed medially with a thumb and pulled medially with a Kocher clamp on the Steinmann pin joy stick. **B** and **C.** A 6.5-mm partially threaded, cannulated screw is being inserted. **D.** Harris axial mini-fluoroscopy image with cannulated screw guide pin in place. **E** and **F.** Harris and lateral mini-fluoroscopy images with cannulated screw in place (before removal of guide pins).

- placement of narrow Crego retractors around the tuber calcanei in the line of the osteotomy that act as targets for the saw blade
  b. Injury to the sural nerve
    i. *Avoid by* careful identification, dissection, and retraction

Medial Cuneiform Osteotomy— "Generic" (MCO)

1. Indications
   a. The medial cuneiform contains the foot-CORA for forefoot pronation, forefoot supination, midfoot adduction, and midfoot abduction (**see Assessment Principle #18, Figures 3-21** and **3-22, Chapter 3**). Osteotomies in this bone can be used to correct all of these individual deformities as well as combinations of them. The medial cuneiform is, therefore, the workhorse of the medial column of the foot (**see Management Principle #19, Chapter 4**).
2. Technique—*This technique section is the basis for all types of medial cuneiform osteotomies and will be so-referenced in the subsequent operative procedure outlines.* (Figure 8-24)
   a. Make a longitudinal incision along the medial midfoot centered on the medial cuneiform

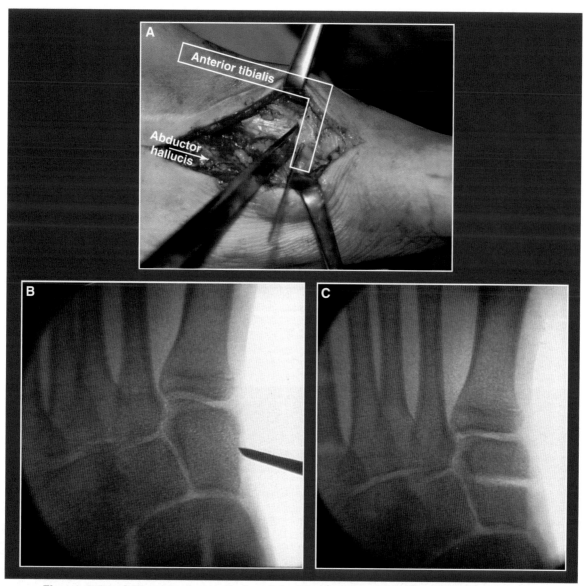

Figure 8-24. **A.** Through a longitudinal medial midfoot incision, the abductor hallucis is retracted plantarward. The anterior tibialis is released from its tendon sheath and elevated from the dorsal and medial surfaces of the proximal half of the medial cuneiform without detaching it from the distal half of the bone. Baby Hohmann or Langenbeck (*shown*) retractors can be used for exposure. An osteotome is used to identify the proper starting point for the osteotomy. A Steinmann pin can be inserted under mini-fluoroscopy as a guide pin for the direction of the osteotomy, but is not necessary. **B.** The starting point for the osteotomy is confirmed by mini-fluoroscopy to be half way between the distal and proximal ends of the bone. It is directed slightly distal-lateral to end adjacent to the 2nd MT–middle cuneiform joint. **C.** The completed osteotomy is in line with the 2nd MT–middle cuneiform joint, thereby creating a "joint" next to a joint (**see Assessment Principle #18, Figure 3-21, Chapter 3**).

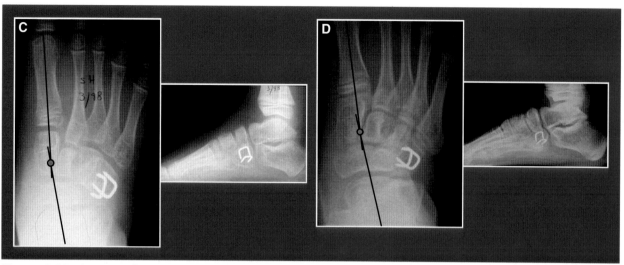

Figure 8-25. *(continued)*

ii. perform the cuboid closing wedge osteotomy (**see this chapter**)

iii. abduct the 1st ray and open the osteotomy with the joy sticks

iv. insert the bone wedge from the cuboid (Figure 8-26)

i. In metatarsus primus varus:

  i. initiate all other procedures that are being performed concurrently

  ii. abduct the 1st ray and open the osteotomy with the joy sticks

iii. fashion a tricortical iliac crest allograft or autograft into a triangle of the appropriate size and shape. Often, the length of the medially-based wedge is 5 to 8 mm

iv. insert and impact the wedge—base medial and apex lateral

j. The graft will, in most cases, be inherently stable and not require fixation.

k. If the graft is not inherently stable, insert a 0.062″ smooth Steinmann pin retrograde across the site from

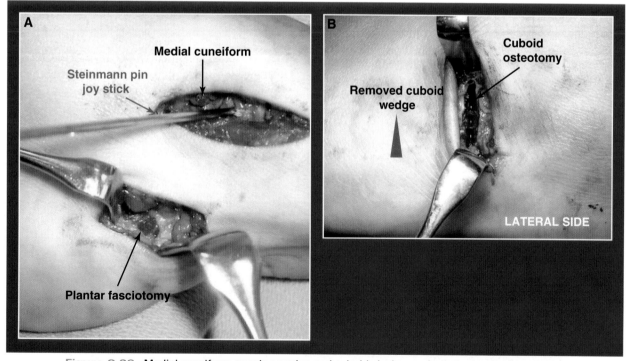

Figure 8-26. Medial cuneiform opening wedge and cuboid closing wedge osteotomies for metatarsus adductus. **A.** The plantar fasciotomy can be seen (**see Chapter 7**). A Steinmann pin has been inserted as a joy stick from medial to lateral into the distal fragment of the medial cuneiform after the osteotomy has been performed. A proximal pin was not used in this case. **B.** A laterally-based wedge of bone has been resected with a sagittal saw from the middle of the cuboid (**see this chapter**). **C.** The wedge of bone is inserted into the MCO. **D.** The osteotomy surfaces of the cuboid are brought into apposition by abducting the forefoot on the hindfoot. A wire staple is used for internal fixation.

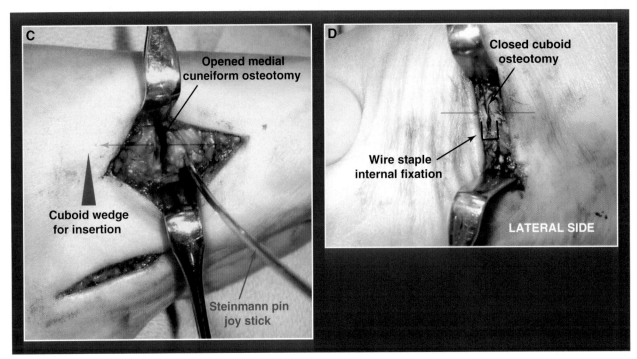

Figure 8-26. *(continued)*

the dorsal forefoot. Add a supplemental wire or a staple if necessary. Bend the wire(s) at the insert site(s) and leave long for easy retrieval in clinic.

l. Approximate the skin edges with interrupted subcutaneous 3-0 absorbable sutures and a running subcuticular 4-0 absorbable suture

m. Apply a short-leg non–weight-bearing cast

n. Six weeks later, obtain simulated standing AP and lateral x-rays of the foot out of the cast, remove the wire(s) if present, and replace the cast with a short-leg walking cast that will be worn for 2 weeks

3. Pitfalls

a. Failure to identify the ideal medial starting point for the osteotomy. Mini-fluoroscopy will provide the desired assistance.

b. Failure to cut the lateral cortex adjacent to the 2nd MT–middle cuneiform joint. Though not a disaster if the cut is not located there, the recommended position for the osteotomy will improve the mobility of the fragments and the ability to achieve the desired outcome.

c. Failure to cut the dorsal cortex. It is hidden under the anterior tibialis and much more dorsal than expected. It must be cut or the fragments will resist repositioning.

4. Complications

a. Creating the osteotomy too far distal or proximal, resulting in the smaller fragment being unstable and/or subject to dysvascularity

   i. *Avoid by* using mini-fluoroscopy for guidance

b. Extrusion of the graft

   i. *Avoid by* using internal fixation if there is any concern about the stability of the graft in the osteotomy

Medial Cuneiform (Dorsiflexion) Plantar-Based Opening Wedge Osteotomy (MC-DF-OWO)

(see Assessment Principle #18, Figure 3-22, Chapter 3; and Management Principle #19, Figure 4-9A, Chapter 4)

1. Indications

a. Rigid pronation deformity (plantar flexion of the 1st ray) of the forefoot in a *cavovarus* foot (**see Chapter 5**)

b. Adduction/pronation (plantar flexion of the 1st ray) deformities of the forefoot in a *skewfoot* (**see Chapter 5**)

2. Technique (Figures 8-27 and 8-28)

a. **See Medial cuneiform osteotomy "generic," Technique a–f**

g. Complete other structural deformity corrections of the foot and, in the case of a cavovarus foot, prepare the tendons for transfer (without setting the tension on them until after the MCO)

h. Insert 0.062″ smooth Steinmann pin joy sticks from plantar to dorsal in the proximal and distal bone fragments

i. Dorsiflex the 1st ray with the distal joy stick and open the osteotomy to determine the size of bone graft required. A laminar spreader may be helpful.

j. Fashion a tricortical iliac crest allograft or autograft into a triangle of the appropriate size and shape. The length of the base of the wedge is 7 to 10 mm in severe deformities.

k. For cavovarus (**see Chapter 5**)

   i. insert and impact the wedge of bone into the medial cuneiform with the base plantar and apex dorsal.

The dorsal cortices of the 2 medial cuneiform fragments will automatically remain in contact.

l. For skewfoot (see Chapter 5)
    i. in the young child without severe hindfoot equinovalgus

• insert and impact the wedge of bone into the medial cuneiform with the base plantar-medial.

    ii. in the older child and adolescent with severe, symptomatic hindfoot equinovalgus

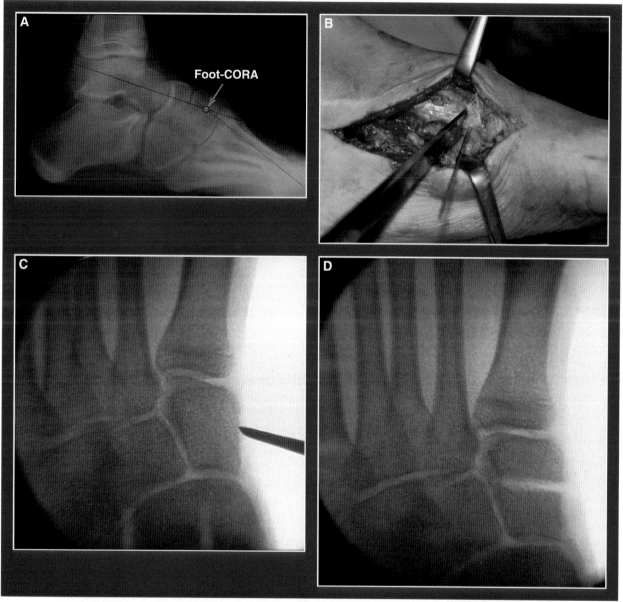

Figure 8-27. A. Standing lateral x-ray of a cavovarus foot deformity. The foot-CORA for the cavus deformity is in the medial cuneiform (see Assessment Principle #18, Figure 3-22, Chapter 3). B. An osteotome is used to site the osteotomy, using mini-fluoroscopic guidance. C. Fluoroscopic image shows the starting point for the osteotomy half way between the distal and proximal ends of the bone, which is usually at the proximal edge of the anterior tibialis tendon as it crosses the medial surface of the medial cuneiform. The osteotomy is angled slightly distal-lateral to end adjacent to the 2nd MT–middle cuneiform joint. D. Fluoroscopic image shows the completed osteotomy in the ideal position. It was performed with a sagittal saw. E. Steinmann pin joy sticks, that were inserted from plantar to dorsal, are used to open the osteotomy on the plantar surface. A freeze-dried tricortical iliac crest allograft is fashioned into a triangle. F. The graft is inserted and impacted into the osteotomy with the base plantar and the apex dorsal. G. The graft is usually inherently stable and, therefore, does not require internal fixation. There will be slight abduction through the osteotomy despite attempts to place the base of the graft directly plantar, which is actually a desirable effect in a cavovarus foot deformity (see Management Principle #19, Figure 4-9A, Chapter 4).

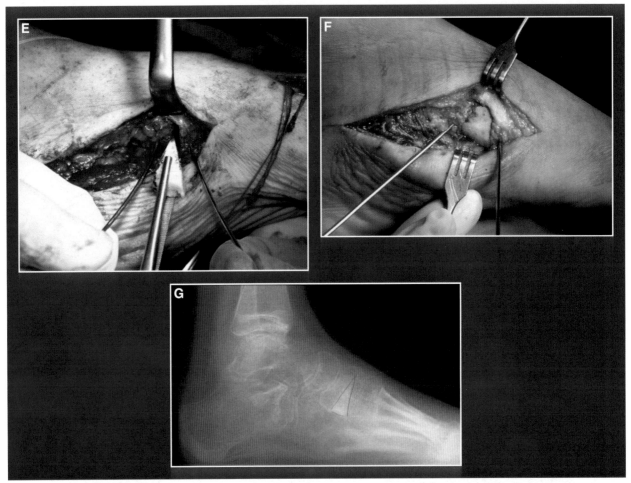

Figure 8-27. *(continued)*

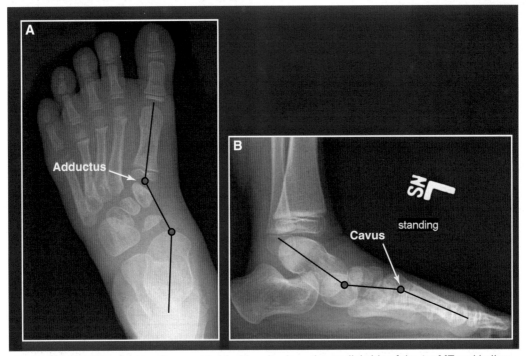

Figure 8-28. Skewfoot in a 7-year-old girl with pain along the medial side of the 1st MT and hallux when wearing shoes. **A** and **B**. Standing AP and lateral x-rays show skew deformities in both planes, but without severe hindfoot equinus (this is typical for a skewfoot in a young child [**see Skewfoot, Chapter 5**]). There are adductus and cavus deformities at the midfoot-forefoot-CORAs based on the tarsal–1st MT angles (**see Assessment Principle #18, Figure 3-23, Chapter 3**). **C** and **D**. Following an MC-DF/abduction-OWO (the base of the wedge was aligned plantar-medially [*yellow dashed triangles*] to correct both deformities concurrently (**see Management principle #19, Figure 4-9A' Chapter 4**), both deformities were improved and her symptoms were relieved. By stretching the plantar–medial soft tissues, there was incidental improvement in eversion of the subtalar joint. This is manifest by improved alignment of the navicular on the head of the talus (note talotarsal angles) in both planes.

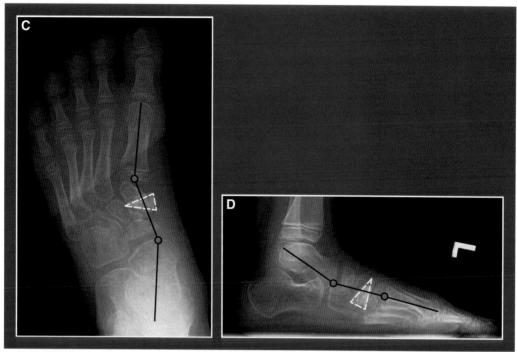

Figure 8-28. *(continued)*

- first perform a CLO (**see this chapter**) and a gastrocnemius recession (**see Chapter 7**) or tendo-Achilles lengthening (**see Chapter 7**), based on the results of the Silfverskiold test (**see Assessment Principle #12, Chapter 3**)
  - insert and impact the wedge of bone into the medial cuneiform with the base plantar-medial.
m. The graft will, in most cases, be inherently stable and not require fixation.
n. If the graft is not inherently stable, insert a 0.062" smooth Steinmann pin retrograde across the site from the dorsal forefoot. Add supplemental wire fixation if necessary. Bend the wire(s) at the insert site(s) and leave them long for easy retrieval in clinic.
o. Approximate the skin edges with interrupted subcutaneous 3-0 absorbable sutures and a running subcuticular 4-0 absorbable suture
p. Apply a short-leg non–weight-bearing cast
q. Six weeks later, obtain simulated standing AP and lateral x-rays of the foot out of the cast, remove the wire(s) if present, and replace the cast with a short-leg walking cast that will be worn for 2 weeks. If a CLO is performed concurrently for a skewfoot in an older child, maintain non–weight-bearing in the final cast.
3. Pitfalls
a. Failure to identify the ideal medial starting point for the osteotomy. Mini-fluoroscopy will provide the desired assistance.
b. Failure to cut the lateral cortex adjacent to the 2nd MT–middle cuneiform joint. Though not a disaster if the cut is not located there, the recommended position for the osteotomy will improve the mobility of the fragments and the ability to achieve the desired outcome.

c. Failure to cut the dorsal cortex. It is hidden under the anterior tibialis and much more dorsal than expected. It must be cut or the fragments will resist repositioning.
4. Complications
a. Creating the osteotomy too far distal or proximal, resulting in the smaller fragment being unstable and/or subject to dysvascularity
   i. *Avoid by* using mini-fluoroscopy for guidance
b. Extrusion of the graft
   i. *Avoid by* using internal fixation if there is any concern about the stability of the graft in the osteotomy

Medial Cuneiform (Plantar Flexion) Plantar-Based Closing Wedge Osteotomy (MC-PF-CWO)

(see Management Principle #19, Figure 4-9B, Chapter 4)
1. Indications
a. Structural supination deformity of the forefoot with a normal rectangle-shaped medial cuneiform and *no* adduction deformity of the midfoot (including absence of metatarsus primus varus) as seen in most
   i. flatfoot deformities (**see Chapter 5**) and
   ii. dorsal bunion deformities (**see Chapter 5**)
2. Technique (Figure 8-29)
a. **See Medial cuneiform osteotomy "generic," Technique a–f**
g. Complete the structural correction of the hindfoot deformity in a *flatfoot* using a CLO (**see this chapter**) and lengthen the gastrocnemius (**see Chapter 7**) or the tendo-Achilles (**see Chapter 7**), based on the results of the Silfverskiold test (**see Assessment Principle #12, Chapter 3**)

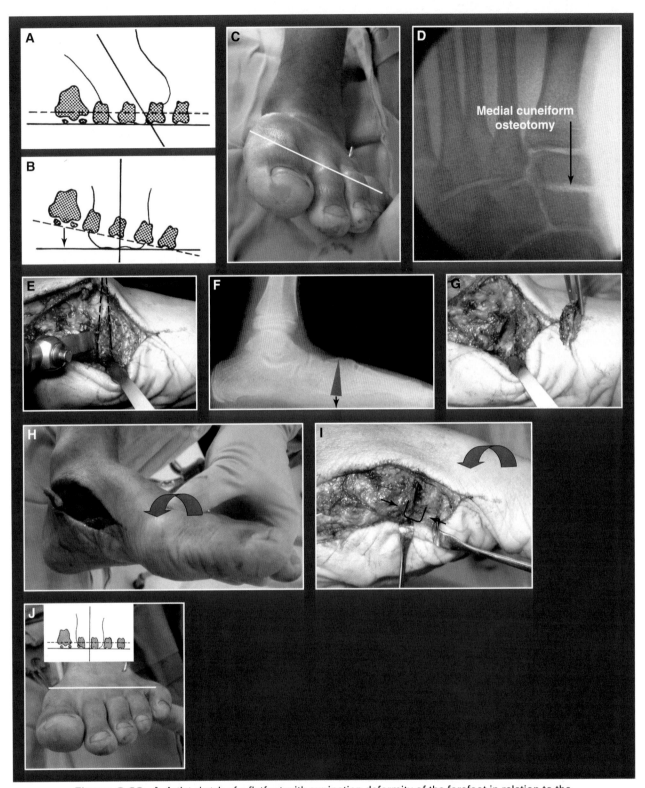

Figure 8-29. **A.** Artist sketch of a flatfoot with supination deformity of the forefoot in relation to the valgus deformity of the hindfoot (**see Basic Principle #5, Chapter 2**). **B.** This is better appreciated after the hindfoot valgus has been corrected to neutral, as after a CLO. The black arrow indicates the need to pronate the forefoot (plantar flex the 1st ray) to establish a balanced tripod (**see Basic Principle #5, Chapter 2; Assessment Principle #8, Figure 3-2, Chapter 3; and Management Principle #23-3, Chapter 4**). **C.** A clinical photo of a flatfoot taken intraoperatively after a CLO reveals rigid, structural supination deformity of the forefoot. The white line indicates the plane of the MT heads. The CLO did *not create* the forefoot supination, it *exposed* it. **D.** The MCO in its ideal position is identified on the mini-fluoroscopic image. **E.** A plantar-based closing wedge osteotomy of the medial cuneiform is indicated by the dashed lines. **F.** X-ray representation of the osteotomy. **G.** The wedge has been removed from the medial cuneiform. **H.** The forefoot is pronated, which plantar flexes the 1st ray and brings the osteotomy surfaces into apposition. **I.** A wire staple fabricated from a 0.062″ smooth Steinmann pin is inserted from plantar to dorsal across the osteotomy while the forefoot is held in forced pronation. **J.** The forefoot and hindfoot deformities are now corrected. (From Mosca VS. Calcaneal lengthening osteotomy for valgus deformity of the hindfoot. In: Skaggs DL and Tolo VT, editors. *Master Techniques in Orthopaedic Surgery: Pediatrics.* Philadelphia: Lippincott Williams & Wilkins, 2008; 263–276.)

h. Prepare the tendon transfers for a *dorsal bunion* reconstruction, but do not set their tensions until the MCO is completed

i. Remove a plantar-based wedge of bone from the cut surfaces of both fragments of the previously osteotomized medial cuneiform, or simply remove a plantar-based wedge of bone initially

j. Plantar flex the 1st ray to bring the cut surfaces into apposition

k. Keep taking small wedges of bone until the supination deformity (dorsiflexion of the 1st ray) is fully corrected. Often, the total length of resected bone from the plantar cortex is 5 to 8 mm

l. The osteotomy is closed and internally fixed with a 0.062″ smooth wire staple (fabricated from a Steinmann pin intraoperatively) that is inserted from plantar to dorsal.

m. Approximate the skin edges with interrupted subcutaneous 3-0 absorbable sutures and a running subcuticular 4-0 absorbable suture

n. Apply a short-leg non–weight-bearing cast

o. Six weeks later, obtain simulated standing AP and lateral x-rays of the foot out of the cast, and replace the cast with a short-leg walking cast that will be worn for 2 weeks. If a CLO is performed concurrently, maintain non–weight-bearing in the final cast.

3. Pitfalls
   a. Failure to identify the ideal medial starting point for the osteotomy. Mini-fluoroscopy will provide the desired assistance.
   b. Failure to cut the lateral cortex adjacent to the 2nd MT–middle cuneiform joint. Though not a disaster if the cut is not located there, the recommended position for the osteotomy will improve the mobility of the fragments and the ability to achieve the desired outcome.
   c. Failure to cut the dorsal cortex. It is hidden under the anterior tibialis and much more dorsal than expected. It must be cut or the fragments will resist repositioning.

4. Complications
   a. Creating the osteotomy too far distal or proximal, resulting in the smaller fragment being unstable and/or subject to dysvascularity
      i. *Avoid by* using mini-fluoroscopy for guidance.
   b. Loss of fixation
      i. *Avoid by* using two staples if the first one has tenuous purchase.

Medial Cuneiform (Plantar Flexion) Dorsal-Based Opening Wedge Osteotomy (MC-PF-OWO)

(see Management Principle #19, Figure 4-9C, Chapter 4)
1. Indications
   a. Structural supination deformity of the forefoot with a trapezoid-shaped medial cuneiform and mild-to-severe adduction deformity of the midfoot as seen in
      i. some flatfoot deformities
      ii. some skewfoot deformities
      iii. some dorsal bunion deformities

2. Technique
   a. **See Medial cuneiform osteotomy "generic," Technique a–f**
   g. Complete the structural correction of the hindfoot deformity in a *flatfoot* or *skewfoot* using a CLO (**see this chapter**) and lengthen the gastrocnemius (**see Chapter 7**) or the tendo-Achilles (**see Chapter 7**), based on the results of the Silverskiold test (**see Assessment Principle #12, Chapter 3**)
   h. Prepare the tendon transfers for a *dorsal bunion* reconstruction, but do not set their tensions until the MCO is completed
   i. Insert 0.062″ smooth Steinmann pin joy sticks from dorsal to plantar in the distal and proximal bone fragments of the medial cuneiform
   j. Plantar flex the 1st ray with the joy stick in the distal fragment and open the osteotomy to determine the size of the required bone graft
   k. Fashion a tricortical iliac crest allograft or autograft into a triangle of the appropriate size and shape. Often, the length of the base of the wedge is 5 to 8 mm
   l. Insert and impact the wedge of bone into the osteotomy with its base dorsal and apex plantar. Adjust the position of the base of the wedge more or less medially depending on the amount of adductus deformity to be corrected concurrently.
   m. This is a challenging osteotomy because the anterior tibialis acts like a dorsal tension band that resists dorsal distraction of the bone fragments. Maintenance of contact between the plantar cortices of the bone fragments is also difficult, but very important.
   n. Plantar flex the 1st ray to keep the plantar cortices of the 2 medial cuneiform fragments in contact while inserting a 0.062″ smooth Steinmann pin retrograde across the site from the dorsal forefoot. Add supplemental wire fixation if necessary. Bend the wire(s) at the insert site(s) and leave long for easy retrieval in clinic.
   o. Approximate the skin edges with interrupted subcutaneous 3-0 absorbable sutures and a running subcuticular 4-0 absorbable suture
   p. Apply a short-leg non–weight-bearing cast
   q. Six weeks later, obtain simulated standing AP and lateral x-rays of the foot out of the cast, remove the wire(s), and replace the cast with another short-leg non–weight-bearing cast that will be worn for 2 weeks

3. Pitfalls
   a. Failure to identify the ideal medial starting point for the osteotomy. Mini-fluoroscopy will provide the desired assistance.
   b. Failure to cut the lateral cortex adjacent to the 2nd MT–middle cuneiform joint. Though not a disaster if the cut is not located there, the recommended position for the osteotomy will improve the mobility of the fragments and the ability to achieve the desired outcome.
   c. Failure to cut the entire dorsal cortex. It is hidden under the anterior tibialis and much more dorsal than

expected. It must be cut or the fragments will resist repositioning.

    d. Incomplete deformity correction, because of failure to maintain contact between the plantar cortices of the 2 medial cuneiform fragments at the time of wire fixation

4. Complications
    a. Creating the osteotomy too far distal or proximal, resulting in the smaller fragment being unstable and/or subject to dysvascularity
        i. *Avoid by* using mini-fluoroscopy for guidance
    b. Loss of fixation.
        i. *Avoid by* using one or two well-positioned and stable smooth Steinmann pins

Medial Cuneiform (Dorsiflexion) Dorsal-Based Closing Wedge Osteotomy (MC-DF-CWO)

(see Management Principle #19, Figure 4-9D, Chapter 4)

1. Indications
    a. Pronation/abduction deformity of the forefoot (extremely rare, and probably only seen as an iatrogenic deformity)

2. Technique
    a. **See Medial cuneiform osteotomy "generic," Technique a–f**
    g. Complete other structural deformity corrections
    h. Remove a dorsally-based wedge of bone from the cut surfaces of both fragments
    i. Dorsiflex the 1st ray to bring the cut surfaces into apposition
    j. Keep taking small wedges of bone until the pronation deformity (plantar flexion of the 1st ray) is fully corrected. The total length of resected bone from the dorsal cortex may be 5 to 8 mm
    k. The osteotomy is closed and internally fixed with a 0.062″ smooth wire staple (fabricated from a Steinmann pin intraoperatively) that is inserted from dorsal to plantar
    l. Approximate the skin edges with interrupted subcutaneous 3-0 absorbable sutures and a running subcuticular 4-0 absorbable suture
    m. Apply a short-leg non–weight-bearing cast
    n. Six weeks later, obtain simulated standing AP and lateral x-rays of the foot out of the cast, and replace the cast with a short-leg walking cast that will be worn for 2 weeks

3. Pitfalls
    a. Failure to identify the ideal medial starting point for the osteotomy. Mini-fluoroscopy will provide the desired assistance.
    b. Failure to cut the lateral cortex adjacent to the 2nd MT–middle cuneiform joint. Though not a disaster if the cut is not located there, the recommended position for the osteotomy will improve the mobility of the fragments and the ability to achieve the desired outcome.

4. Complications
    a. Creating the osteotomy too far distal or proximal, resulting in the smaller fragment being unstable and/or subject to dysvascularity
        i. *Avoid by* using mini-fluoroscopy for guidance
    b. Loss of fixation
        i. *Avoid by* using two staples if the first one has tenuous purchase

Cuboid Closing Wedge Osteotomy (CCWO)

1. Indications
    a. Lateral column shortening for midfoot adduction deformity
        i. often performed in combination with a MC-Medial-OWO (see **Figure 8-25 in this chapter, and Assessment Principle #18, Figure 3-21 in Chapter 3**) to treat
            • metatarsus adductus—as an isolated idiopathic deformity (**see Chapter 5**) or as a component of recurrent or persistent clubfoot deformity (**see Chapter 5**)
            • skewfoot (**see Chapter 5**)
        ii. This osteotomy is *too far distal* to have an effect on TN joint alignment (**see Management Principle #18, Figure 4-7, Chapter 4**)

2. Technique (Figure 8-30)
    a. Make a longitudinal incision along the lateral border of the midfoot centered on the cuboid
    b. Isolate and retract, or avoid, the sural nerve
    c. Release the PB from its tendon sheath and retract it plantarward
    d. Expose the cuboid extraperiosteally on its dorsal, lateral, and plantar surfaces
    e. Insert two 25G hypodermic needles in the cuboid in the desired locations of the osteotomy cuts that will result in removal of a wedge of bone large enough to correct the adduction deformity of the lateral border of the foot. The proximal needle should be perpendicular to the axis of the calcaneus and the distal needle should be perpendicular to the axis is of the 5th MT. Use mini-fluoroscopy for guidance.
    f. Resect the wedge of bone with a small sagittal saw by cutting between and immediately adjacent to the needles
    g. Preserve the bone for insertion in the medial cuneiform
    h. Perform a **medial cuneiform osteotomy "generic" technique a–f and MC-medial-OWO technique g, h, j, and k (this chapter)**
    i. Abduct the forefoot on the hindfoot to approximate the cut surfaces of the cuboid. Remove more bone, if necessary, to align the axis of the forefoot on the hindfoot. Use mini-fluoroscopy for guidance.
    j. Insert a staple made from a 0.062″ smooth Steinmann pin across the osteotomy while holding the forefoot firmly abducted on the hindfoot. Alternatively, insert a 0.062″ smooth Steinmann pin retrograde across the

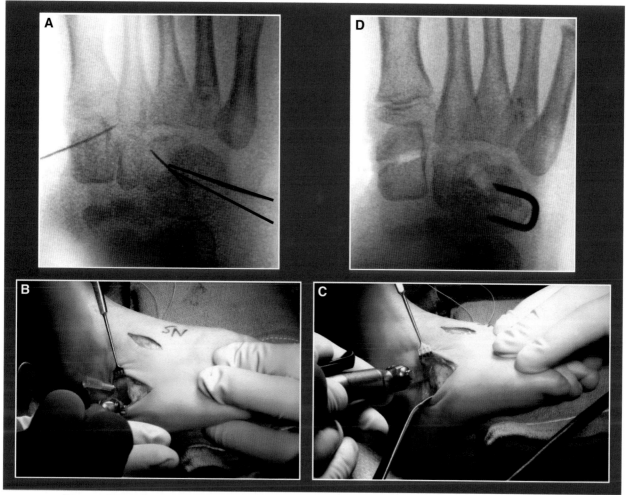

Figure 8-30. **A.** AP intraoperative mini-fluoroscopy image showing a 25G needle marking the site of the MCO (*left*) and another marking the lateral cuneiform (*central*) through which a drill hole will be made for a anterior tibialis tendon transfer. The two thick black lines (*right*) represent the locations for the 25G needles that are inserted in the cuboid to mark the location of the closing wedge osteotomy. **B.** The distal osteotomy is created with a microsagittal saw. **C.** The proximal osteotomy is created with the microsagittal saw. The lateral base length of the wedge is at least 4 to 5 mm. **D.** With the forefoot abducted on the hindfoot, the wedge of bone removed from the cuboid was inserted into the MCO. A wire staple (made from a 0.062″ smooth Steinmann pin) was inserted across the osteotomy site in the cuboid for internal fixation.

resection site of the cuboid from the dorsolateral aspect of the foot. Bend the wire at the insertion site and cut it long for ease of removal in clinic.

   k. Approximate the skin edges with interrupted subcutaneous 3-0 absorbable sutures and a running subcuticular 4-0 absorbable suture

   l. Apply a short-leg non–weight-bearing cast

   m. Six weeks later, obtain simulated standing AP and lateral x-rays of the foot out of the cast, remove the wire(s), and replace the cast with a short-leg walking cast that will be worn for 2 weeks

3. Pitfalls

   a. Inadequate resection of bone resulting in

     i. persistence of deformity

     ii. inadequate graft size/strength for correction of the medial cuneiform deformity

4. Complications

   a. Injury to the sural nerve

     i. *Avoid by* isolating and protecting it

Calcaneocuboid Joint Resection/Arthrodesis

(the "original" Evans procedure; see Calcaneal Lengthening Osteotomy Technique Background, this chapter)

1. Indications

   a. Lateral column shortening for resistant subtalar joint inversion in a recurrent, persistent, or neglected clubfoot (**see Chapter 5**), typically in a child with *arthrogryposis* who is *at least 8 years old*

2. Technique (Figure 8-31)

   a. Perform a D-PMR (**see Chapter 7**). The soft tissues along the plantar–medial midfoot/hindfoot, including

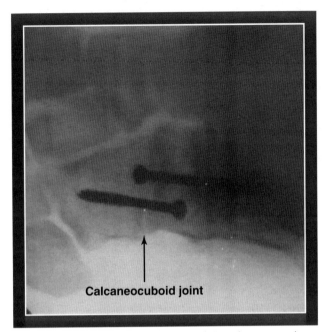

Figure 8-31. The articular surfaces of the calcaneus and cuboid were resected at the CC joint. Crossed screws were used for internal fixation in this teenager.

the TN joint capsule, must be released in an effort to align the navicular with the head of the talus.

b. If the subtalar joint does not evert completely and the navicular remains medially positioned on the head of the talus in a child who is at least 8 years old, a calcaneocuboid joint resection/arthrodesis is indicated to pull the navicular laterally (**see Management Principle #18, Figure 4-7, Chapter 4**).

c. Make a longitudinal incision along the lateral border of the midfoot centered on the calcaneocuboid joint

d. Isolate and retract, or avoid, the sural nerve

e. Release the PB from its tendon sheath and retract it plantarward

f. Release/resect the calcaneocuboid joint capsule

g. Place a Freer or Joker elevator over the dorsum of the calcaneocuboid joint

h. Place a Joker elevator or narrow Crego retractor plantar to the calcaneocuboid joint

i. Using a sagittal saw, cut the calcaneus perpendicular to the longitudinal axis of the bone starting 3 to 5 mm proximal to the distal articular surface of the bone

j. Using a sagittal saw, cut the cuboid perpendicular to the longitudinal axis of the 5th MT starting 3 to 5 mm distal to the proximal articular surface of the bone

k. Abduct the forefoot/midfoot on the hindfoot to approximate the cut surfaces of the bones and to pull the navicular laterally to align it with the talar head. Remove more bone from either or both of the bones, if necessary, to align the axis of the forefoot with that of the hindfoot. Use mini-fluoroscopy for guidance.

l. Internally fixate the arthrodesis using one of several methods:

i. Insert one or two 0.062″ smooth Steinmann pin(s) retrograde across the fusion site from the dorsolateral aspect of the forefoot. Bend the wire(s) at the insertion site(s) and cut them long for ease of removal in clinic.

ii. Insert one or two wire staples made from a 0.062″ smooth Steinmann pin across the fusion site from lateral to medial

iii. Insert crossed screws

m. Approximate the skin edges with interrupted subcutaneous 3-0 absorbable sutures and a running subcuticular 4-0 absorbable suture

n. Apply a well-padded short-leg non–weight-bearing cast with the ankle at neutral, the subtalar joint everted, and the midfoot abducted

o. At 6 weeks, remove the cast (and exposed pin(s) if used for fixation) in the clinic and apply a short-leg walking cast that will be worn for an additional 3 to 6 weeks

3. Pitfalls

a. Inadequate resection of the bones, resulting in persistence of the deformity

b. Inadequate D-PMR

4. Complications

a. Injury to the sural nerve

i. *Avoid by* isolating and protecting it

b. Excessive resection of the bones, thereby creating a flatfoot or creating a large gap that leads to nonunion

i. *Avoid by* removing a little bone at a time

Lichtblau Anterior Calcaneus Resection

1. Indications

a. Lateral column shortening for resistant subtalar joint inversion in a recurrent, persistent, or neglected clubfoot (**see Chapter 5**), typically in a child with *arthrogryposis* who is *between 3 and 8 years of age*

2. Technique (Figure 8-32)

a. Perform a D-PMR (**see Chapter 7**). The soft tissues along the plantar–medial midfoot/hindfoot, including the TN joint capsule, must be released in an effort to align the navicular with the head of the talus.

b. If the subtalar joint does not evert completely and the navicular remains medially positioned on the head of the talus in a child between the ages of 3 and 8 years, a Lichtblau procedure is indicated to pull the navicular laterally (**see Management Principle #18, Figure 4-7, Chapter 4**).

c. Make a longitudinal incision along the lateral border of the midfoot centered on the anterior calcaneus

d. Isolate and retract, or avoid, the sural nerve

e. Release the PB from its tendon sheath and retract it plantarward

f. Release the calcaneocuboid joint capsule

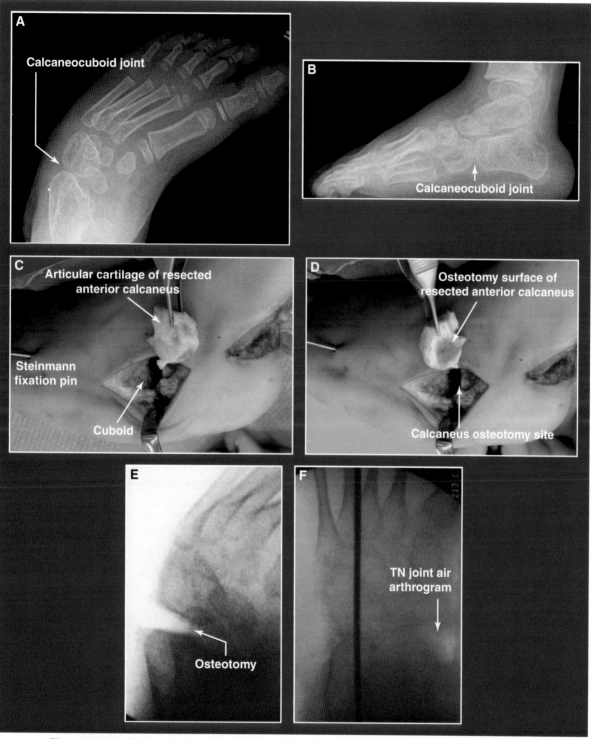

Figure 8-32. **A.** Simulated standing AP x-ray of a severe, recurrent clubfoot deformity in a 6-year-old child with distal arthrogryposis. Varus malorientation/subluxation of the calcaneocuboid joint can be seen. **B.** Simulated standing lateral x-ray of the same foot. **C.** The anterior calcaneus has been resected. The articular cartilage surface of the fragment is shown. The longitudinal internal fixation wire has been inserted up to, but not yet across, the resection site. **D.** The osteotomy surface of the fragment is shown. **E.** An intraoperative mini-fluoroscopy image shows the osteotomy site after the fragment was removed. **F.** The Steinmann pin has been advanced across the resection site. An air arthrogram was created at the TN joint following the capsular release. **G.** AP x-ray of the foot 1 year later shows improved alignment and a pseudo-calcaneo-cuboid joint. **H.** The lateral x-ray from that clinic visit shows the pseudo-joint even better than the AP image does.

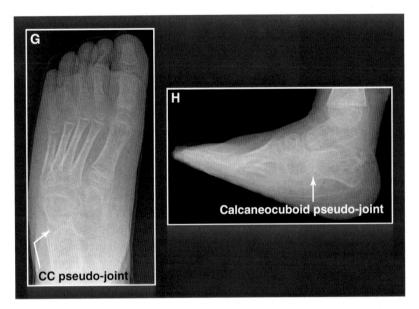

Figure 8-32. *(continued)*

g. Place a Freer or Joker elevator over the dorsum of the anterior calcaneus proximal to the anterior facet
h. Place a Joker elevator or narrow Crego retractor plantar to the anterior calcaneus
i. Using a sagittal saw, cut the calcaneus perpendicular to the longitudinal axis of the bone starting 5 to 8 mm proximal to the distal articular surface of the bone
j. Abduct the forefoot/midfoot on the hindfoot to approximate the articular cartilage surface of the cuboid with the cut surface of the calcaneus and to pull the navicular laterally to align it with the talar head. Remove more bone from the calcaneus, if necessary, to align the axis of the forefoot with that of the hindfoot. Use mini-fluoroscopy for guidance
k. Insert one or two 0.062″ smooth Steinmann pin(s) retrograde across the resection site from the dorsolateral aspect of the forefoot. Bend the wire(s) at the insertion site(s) and cut them long for ease of removal in clinic
l. Approximate the skin edges with interrupted subcutaneous 3-0 absorbable sutures and a running subcuticular 4-0 absorbable suture
m. Apply a well-padded long-leg cast (to ensure non–weight-bearing in these young children) with the ankle at neutral, the subtalar joint everted, and the midfoot abducted
n. At 6 weeks, remove the cast and pin(s) in the clinic and apply a short-leg walking cast that will be worn for an additional 2 weeks

3. Pitfalls
   a. Inadequate resection of the distal calcaneus resulting in persistence of the deformity
   b. Inadequate D-PMR

4. Complications
   a. Injury to the sural nerve
      i. *Avoid by* isolating and protecting it
   b. Excessive resection of the distal calcaneus, thereby creating a flatfoot or creating a large gap
      i. *Avoid by* removing a little bone at a time

Anterior Calcaneus Closing Wedge Osteotomy

(Reverse Calcaneal Lengthening Osteotomy)

1. Indications
   a. Lateral column shortening for resistant subtalar joint inversion in a recurrent, persistent, or neglected *idiopathic* clubfoot (**see Chapter 5**), typically in a *3- to 8-year-old child*

2. Technique (Figure 8-33)
   a. Perform a D-PMR (**see Chapter 7**). The soft tissues along the plantar–medial midfoot/hindfoot, including the TN joint capsule, must be released in an effort to align the navicular with the head of the talus.
   b. If the subtalar joint does not evert completely and the navicular remains medially positioned on the head of the talus in a child between the ages of 3 and 8 years, an anterior calcaneus closing wedge osteotomy is indicated to pull the navicular laterally (**see Management Principle #18, Figure 4-7, Chapter 4**).
   c. Make a longitudinal incision along the lateral border of the hindfoot centered on the anterior calcaneus
   d. Isolate and retract, or avoid, the sural nerve
   e. Release the PL and the PB from their tendon sheaths and retract them plantarward
   f. Avoid exposure of, or injury to, the capsule of the calcaneocuboid joint.
   g. Elevate the soft tissues from the sinus tarsi
   h. Insert a Freer elevator into the sinus tarsi perpendicular to the lateral cortex of the calcaneus at the level of the "isthmus," the narrowest dorsal–plantar site of this bone that is located immediately anterior to the posterior facet and posterior to the calcaneal beak (**see Calcaneal Lengthening Osteotomy, this chapter**). Rotate the Freer anteriorly until it falls into the interval between the anterior and middle facets of the subtalar joint
   i. Place a Joker elevator plantar to the dorsally placed Freer elevator

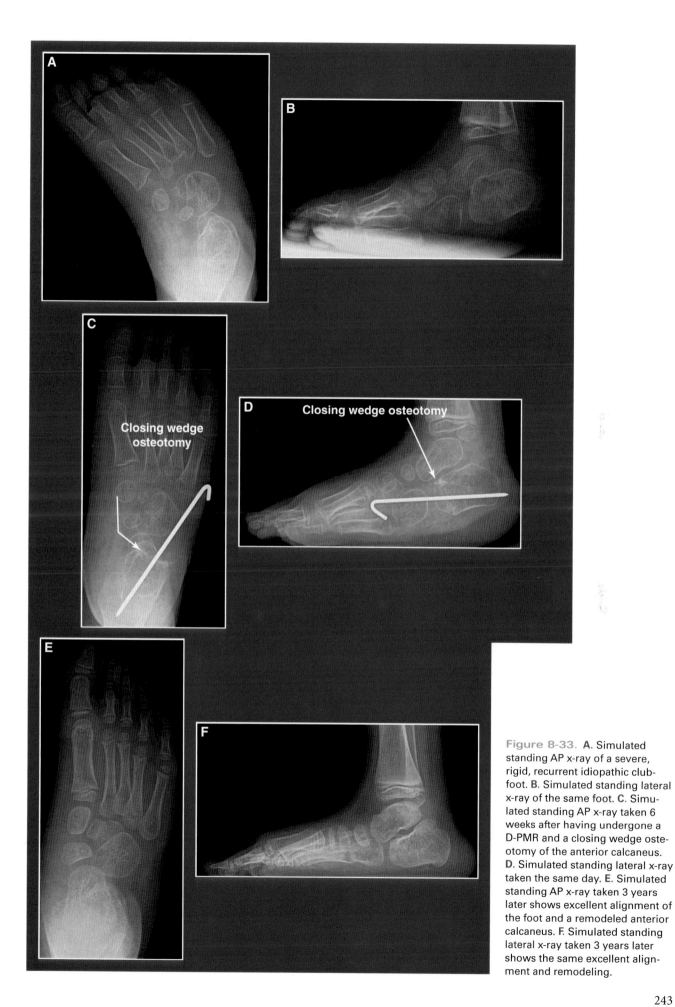

Figure 8-33. **A.** Simulated standing AP x-ray of a severe, rigid, recurrent idiopathic clubfoot. **B.** Simulated standing lateral x-ray of the same foot. **C.** Simulated standing AP x-ray taken 6 weeks after having undergone a D-PMR and a closing wedge osteotomy of the anterior calcaneus. **D.** Simulated standing lateral x-ray taken the same day. **E.** Simulated standing AP x-ray taken 3 years later shows excellent alignment of the foot and a remodeled anterior calcaneus. **F.** Simulated standing lateral x-ray taken 3 years later shows the same excellent alignment and remodeling.

243

j. Using a microsagittal saw and starting at the isthmus, cut the calcaneus in line with the retractors, exiting medially between the anterior and middle facets

k. Remove a laterally-based wedge of bone from one or the other of the calcaneal fragments. Keep removing small wedges of bone until the lateral border of the foot is straight (and the TN joint is confirmed to be aligned using mini-fluoroscopy)

l. Insert one or two 0.062″ smooth Steinmann pin(s) retrograde across the resection site from the dorsolateral aspect of the forefoot. Bend the wire(s) at the insertion site(s) and cut them long for ease of removal in clinic

m. Approximate the skin edges with interrupted subcutaneous 3-0 absorbable sutures and a running subcuticular 4-0 absorbable suture

n. Apply a well-padded long-leg cast (to ensure non–weight-bearing in these young children) with the ankle at neutral, the subtalar joint everted, and the midfoot abducted

o. At 6 weeks, remove the cast and pin(s) in the clinic and apply a short-leg walking cast that will be worn for an additional 2 weeks

3. Pitfalls
   a. Inadequate wedge resection of the anterior calcaneus resulting in persistence of the deformity
   b. Inadequate D-PMR

4. Complications
   a. Injury to the sural nerve
      i. *Avoid by* isolating and protecting it

1st Metatarsal Base Osteotomy

1. Indications
   a. Metatarsus primus varus in a skeletally *mature* adolescent with juvenile hallux valgus (see Chapter 5)
   b. NOTE:
      i. The base of the 1st MT is NOT the foot-CORA (see Assessment Principle #18, Chapter 3) for *any* forefoot or midfoot deformity. The *medial cuneiform* is the foot-CORA for cavus (plantar flexion of the 1st ray, pronation of the forefoot), supination of the forefoot (dorsiflexion of the 1st ray), metatarsus adductus (midfoot adductus), and metatarsus primus varus.
      ii. Therefore, a *medial cuneiform osteotomy* (see this Chapter) is *preferred* over a 1st MT base osteotomy to correct
         • pronation of the forefoot (plantar flexion of the 1st ray) in a cavovarus foot
         • supination of the forefoot (dorsiflexion of the 1st ray) in a flatfoot
         • adduction of the midfoot in metatarsus adductus and skewfoot
         • adduction of the 1st ray in some cases of metatarsus primus varus.
      iii. If a 1st MT base osteotomy is used to correct cavus deformity, the shaft fragment must be dorsally translated as well as dorsally angulated, because the

deformity correction is occurring away from the foot-CORA.
      iv. 1st MT base osteotomies for cavus deformity correction have a greater likelihood of creating stress transfer to the 2nd MT head than medial cuneiform osteotomies.

2. Technique (see Figure 5-61, Chapter 5)
   a. There are many techniques for creating a 1st MT base osteotomy, but I prefer the oblique rotational osteotomy
   b. Make a longitudinal incision along the medial border of the midfoot centered on the base of the 1st MT
   c. Expose the proximal half of the 1st MT extraperiosteally
   d. Insert a 0.045″ smooth Steinmann pin from medial to lateral through the MT heads and in the transverse plane of the MT heads. This is a guide pin that will be referenced to ensure that the osteotomy is performed in the proper plane. If the osteotomy is rotated from the plane of the MT heads, it will create either dorsiflexion or plantar flexion of the 1st MT when the shaft fragment is rotated on the base fragment.
   e. Begin the osteotomy as far proximal as possible in the 1st MT using a small sagittal saw cutting from medial to lateral. It should be rotated at least 45° from perpendicular to the MT shaft and inclined from dorsal/proximal to plantar/distal. Importantly, it should be in the transverse plane defined by the guide pin in the MT heads.
   f. Before completing the osteotomy, create a lag screw hole for a 2.8- to 3.5-mm-diameter cortical screw that crosses the osteotomy at a right angle. Create a countersink recess in the dorsal cortex to prevent prominence of the screw head.
   g. Complete the osteotomy, remove the guide pin from the MT heads, rotate the shaft fragment laterally, and insert the proper length screw in the prepared hole. Fixation should be excellent with the single screw.
   h. Complete the other procedures that are being performed concurrently
   i. Approximate the skin edges with interrupted subcutaneous 3-0 absorbable sutures and a running subcuticular 4-0 absorbable suture
   j. Apply a short-leg non–weight-bearing cast. It will take approximately 6 weeks to heal.

3. Pitfalls
   a. Failure to ensure proper alignment of the 1st MTP joint by failing to perform the appropriate associated procedures for correction of hallux valgus

4. Complications
   a. Performing a 1st MT base osteotomy before skeletal maturity and, thereby, either damaging the growth plate or performing the osteotomy far from the foot-CORA for metatarsus primus varus which, as in metatarsus adductus (see Assessment Principle #18, Chapter 3), is in the medial cuneiform.
      i. *Avoid by* delaying surgery for JHV until skeletal maturity. Then one can perform a 1st MT base osteotomy or a medial cuneiform medial opening wedge osteotomy (see this chapter)

b. Rotational malinclination of the osteotomy, thereby creating plantar flexion or dorsiflexion of the 1st MT
   i. *Avoid by* inserting a Steinmann pin from medial to lateral through the MT heads in the transverse plane of the MT heads to act as a guide pin that defines the true transverse plane of the forefoot
c. Prominence of the screw head requiring a second operation to remove it
   i. *Avoid by* countersinking the screw head

5th Metatarsal Osteotomy

1. Indications
   a. Bunionette (Tailor's bunion) (**see Chapter 5**)
2. Technique (Figure 8-34)
   a. Make a longitudinal incision lateral to the 5th MT extending distal to the MTP joint
   b. Expose the 5th MT shaft extraperiosteally
   c. Insert a 0.045″ smooth Steinmann pin from lateral to medial within the MT heads and in the transverse

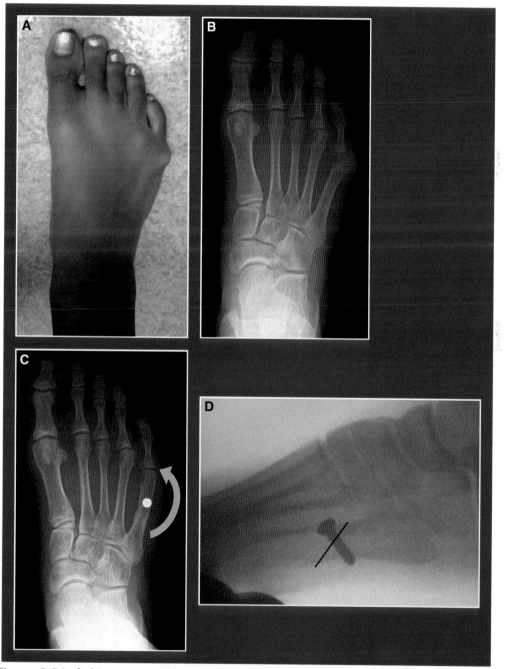

Figure 8-34. A. Clinical photo of a bunionette deformity in a teenage girl. **B.** Standing AP x-ray of her foot. **C.** Standing AP x-ray taken 1 year after an oblique, rotational osteotomy of the 5th MT. The blue curved arrow shows the effect of the rotation around the screw. The lateral exostosis of the MT head was resected and the lateral capsule was plicated. **D.** An intraoperative mini-fluoroscopic image shows the position of the oblique transverse plane osteotomy (*black line*).

plane of the MT heads. This is the guide pin that will be referenced to ensure that the osteotomy is in the proper plane. If the osteotomy is rotated from the plane of the MT heads, it will create either dorsiflexion or plantar flexion of the 5th MT when the shaft is rotated on the base.

   d. Begin the osteotomy at the CORA of the bone deformity or as far proximal as possible in the 5th MT using a small sagittal saw cutting from lateral to medial. The blade should be rotated at least 45° from perpendicular to the MT shaft and inclined from dorsal/posterior to plantar/anterior. It is, therefore, an oblique transverse plane osteotomy in which the transverse plane is defined by the guide pin in the MT heads.

   e. Before completing the osteotomy, create a lag screw hole for a 2.0- to 3.5-mm-diameter cortical screw that crosses the osteotomy at a right angle. Create a countersink in the dorsal cortex to avoid prominence of the screw head

   f. Complete the osteotomy, remove the MT heads guide pin, rotate the shaft medially, and insert the proper length screw. Fixation should be excellent with the single screw.

   g. Complete the other procedures that are being performed concurrently, such as medial 5th MTP capsulotomy, lateral 5th MT head shaving, and lateral 5th MTP joint capsular plication

   h. Approximate the skin edges with interrupted subcutaneous 3-0 absorbable sutures and a running subcuticular 4-0 absorbable suture

   i. Apply a short-leg non–weight-bearing cast. It will take approximately 6 weeks to heal.

3. Pitfalls
   a. Failure to ensure proper alignment of the 5th MTP joint by failing to perform the appropriate associated procedures for correction of a tailor's bunion

4. Complications
   a. Rotational malinclination of the osteotomy, thereby creating plantar flexion or dorsiflexion of the 5th MT
      i. *Avoid by* inserting a Steinmann pin in the MT heads to act as a guide pin that defines the true transverse plane of the forefoot
   b. Prominence of the screw head requiring a second operation to remove it
      i. *Avoid by* countersinking the screw head

1st Metatarsal Distal Osteotomy

1. Indications
   a. High DMAA of the 1st MT, usually with a congruent 1st MTP joint, in JHV (**see Figures 5-55 and 5-56, Chapter 5**)

2. Technique (**see Figure 5-60, Chapter 5**)
   a. There are many techniques for creating a distal 1st MT osteotomy, but I prefer a simple medially-based closing wedge osteotomy.
   b. Make a longitudinal incision along the medial border of the proximal phalanx and distal half of the 1st MT.

Gently curve the incision dorsally over the bunion (1st MT head). The incision can be continued proximally to concurrently perform a 1st MT base osteotomy (**see this chapter**) or a MCO (**see this chapter**).

   c. Create a U-shaped capsular flap, sharply elevating the thick capsule off the medial side of the 1st MT head and reflecting it distally on its proximal phalanx attachment

   d. Using an osteotome or small sagittal saw, resect the medial exostosis of the 1st MT head retrograde from the sulcus on the medial edge of the articular surface in line with the medial cortex of the MT shaft

   e. Do *not* release the adductor hallucis or the lateral capsule of the 1st MTP joint. The joint is congruous but maloriented in most cases, so lateral capsular release is not indicated. There is a risk of devascularizing the MT head when lateral soft tissue release is combined with a distal 1st MT osteotomy.

   f. Start to create an osteotomy with a small sagittal saw that is parallel with and 1 to 1.5 cm proximal to the articular surface of the 1st MT head

   g. Before completing the first cut, start a second osteotomy that is perpendicular to the 1st MT shaft and designed to intersect with the more distal cut at the lateral cortex

   h. Insert a 0.045″ or 0.062″ smooth Steinmann pin from distal/medial to proximal/lateral in the head fragment stopping at the distal osteotomy

   i. Insert a 0.045″ or 0.062″ smooth Steinmann pin from proximal/medial to distal/lateral in the shaft fragment stopping at the proximal osteotomy

   j. Complete both osteotomies

   k. Adduct and laterally displace the MT head fragment (the CORA is distal to the osteotomy) to bring the osteotomy surfaces into apposition with the proper axial alignment of the head on the shaft

   l. Advance the pins across the osteotomy capturing the far cortices for stable fixation

   m. Advance the capsular flap proximally on the medial surface of the MT shaft and repair it with multiple figure-of-8 2-0 absorbable sutures

   n. Confirm correction of all deformities with mini-fluoroscopy

   o. Approximate the skin edges with interrupted subcutaneous 3-0 absorbable sutures and a running subcuticular 4-0 absorbable suture

   p. Apply a short-leg non–weight-bearing cast. It will take approximately 6 weeks to heal.

3. Pitfalls
   a. Failure to ensure proper alignment of the 1st MTP joint by failing to perform the appropriate associated procedures for correction of hallux valgus. There are many. Treatment must be individualized.

4. Complications
   a. Avascular necrosis of the 1st MT head
      i. *Avoid by* performing either a distal 1st MT osteotomy *or* a lateral 1st MTP joint capsular release. The former is indicated if there is a congruent joint

and a high DMAA. The lateral is indicated if there is an incongruent joint and a normal DMAA.

   b. The list of complications following surgery for hallux valgus is exceedingly high

     i. *Avoid by*:

- avoiding hallux valgus surgery, except when prolonged attempts at nonoperative treatment fail to relieve the pain
- studying the unique anatomic variations and deformities in the patient's foot and lower extremity and having a surgical plan for each one. Individualize treatment.

Distal Tibia and Fibula Varus, Valgus, Flexion, Extension, Rotational Osteotomies

1. Indications

   a. Distal tibia and fibula varus, valgus, extension, flexion, and/or rotational deformities

2. Technique (**see Management Principle #20, Figures 4-10 to 4-16, Chapter 4**)

   a. Prep the entire lower extremity and use a sterile tourniquet. This will enable accurate assessment of the thigh–foot angle, which is particularly important when correcting rotational deformities

   b. Make a 3- to 4-cm longitudinal incision along the posterolateral edge of the distal *fibula* meta-diaphysis, i.e., adjacent to the intended site of the tibial osteotomy

   c. Incise the periosteum and expose the fibula subperiosteally

   d. Place Joker elevators around the fibula as tissue protectors

   e. Using a small sagittal saw, create an oblique osteotomy in the predetermine proper plane (**see Management Principle #20-2, Chapter 4**)

   f. Irrigate and then close this incision with interrupted subcutaneous 3-0 absorbable sutures and a running subcuticular 4-0 absorbable suture

   g. Make a 5- to 7-cm longitudinal incision 1 cm lateral to the anterior crest of the distal *tibial* metaphysis

   h. Incise the periosteum along the crest and expose the tibial metaphysis subperiosteally to no closer than 1 cm from the growth plate

   i. *For a pure rotational tibial osteotomy:*

     i. Make sure the fibula osteotomy is in the *oblique sagittal* plane (**see Figures 4-11 and 4-13, Chapter 4**)

     ii. Precontour a five-hole dynamic compression plate or locking plate to the flair of the tibial metaphysis

     iii. With the distal end of the plate approximately 1 cm from the physis and the plate axially aligned with the shaft of the tibia, insert fully threaded cortical screws in the two distal holes (**see Management Principle #20-3, Figure 4-14, Chapter 4**)

     iv. Make a notch in the tibia with an osteotome half way between screw holes 2 and 3, the planned site for the osteotomy

     v. Also make a longitudinal score with the osteotome along the cortex adjacent to the plate. This will be a reminder of the rotational alignment of the bone before the osteotomy was performed

     vi. Remove the plate and two screws

     vii. With narrow Crego retractors surrounding the tibia subperiosteally at the level of the notch, perform an osteotomy with a sagittal saw that is perpendicular to the shaft of the tibia (**see Management Principle #20-4, Figure 4-15, Chapter 4**)

     viii. Reattach the plate and two screws to the distal fragment

     ix. Rotate the foot/distal fragment until the thigh–foot angle is neutral (0°). Hold that position with a Verbrugge clamp

     x. Fasten the plate to the tibial shaft with three fully threaded cortical screws, dynamizing at least one of them

   j. *For a valgus-correcting, or a valgus-correcting* and *rotational osteotomy:*

     i. Make sure the fibula osteotomy is in the *oblique coronal* plane (**see Figures 4-10 and 4-12, Chapter 4**)

     ii. A plate and screws can be used on the tibia, but the angular deformity can make it difficult to properly align and fix the plate distally before the osteotomy is performed.

     iii. Measure and mark the approximate distance needed on the tibia for the osteotomy to be performed between what would/will be the second and third holes on the plate.

     iv. Insert a 0.062″ smooth Steinmann pin retrograde from the medial malleolus stopping short of the intended distal osteotomy site

     v. Insert a second 0.062″ smooth Steinmann pin retrograde from the anterolateral corner of the epiphysis stopping short of the intended distal osteotomy site

     vi. Make sure both pins are parallel with the longitudinal axis of the tibia in the coronal plane. They provide assessment of alignment and control of the distal tibial fragment (**see Management Principle #20-3, Figure 4-14, Chapter 4**).

     vii. With narrow Crego retractors surrounding the tibia subperiosteally at the level of the notch, perform an osteotomy with a sagittal saw that is *parallel* with the ankle joint

     viii. Then perform the second and more proximal osteotomy on the shaft fragment. It is *perpendicular* to the shaft and designed to meet the first osteotomy at the lateral cortex (**see Management Principle #20-5, Figure 4-16, Chapter 4**).

     ix. Bring the osteotomy surfaces into apposition and translate the distal fragment *laterally* until the medial cortices of the two fragments align. That is usually sufficient to centralize the ankle under the tibia (**see Management Principle #20-1, Figure 4-10, Chapter 4**).

     x. Rotate the distal fragment to correct rotational deformity, if indicated

xi. Advance the Steinmann pins retrograde across the osteotomy and into the opposite tibial cortices of the shaft. Check the thigh–foot angle and adjust rotation, if indicated

xii. Either use these pins as definitive fixation or apply a plate and screws on the smoothest surface

k. *For a varus-correcting osteotomy in a skeletally mature (or nearly mature) adolescent, as following a medial malleolus fracture with medial growth arrest (Figure 8-35):*

i. Make sure the fibula osteotomy is in the *oblique coronal* plane (**see Figures 4-10 and 4-12, Chapter 4**)

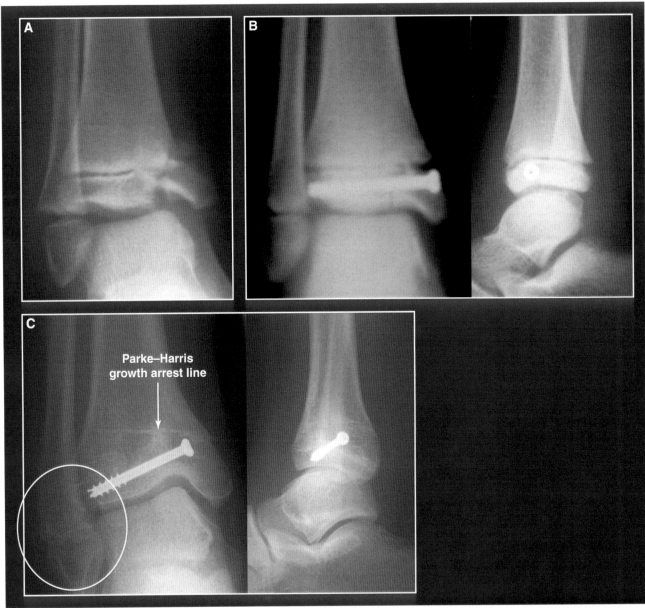

Figure 8-35. **A.** AP x-ray of a Salter–Harris IV medial malleolus fracture in an 8-year-old girl. **B.** AP and lateral x-rays after open reduction internal fixation. **C.** AP and lateral x-rays after failing to follow-up for 4 years and 4 months. Medial distal tibial growth arrest is apparent. The Park–Harris growth arrest line and the physis converge medially. The distal fibula and lateral distal tibial growth plates are still open (inside the *yellow circle*). **D.** Distal fibula and lateral distal tibia epiphysiodeses (*purple ovals*) were performed at the same time as the deformity correction osteotomies. An *oblique coronal plane* fibula osteotomy was performed. The lateral extent of the oblique distal tibial osteotomy was located at the CORA (the lateral margin of the physis), so translation was not required. Fairly minimal fixation was required because of the significant compression forces across the medial aspect of the opening wedge osteotomy and the inherent stability of the structural bone grafts. **E.** Early postoperative lateral x-ray. **F.** AP x-ray taken 6 months later shows excellent healing and deformity correction. The center of the talus is directly in line with the mid-axis of the tibia. **G.** Lateral x-ray obtained the same day shows excellent sagittal plane correction.

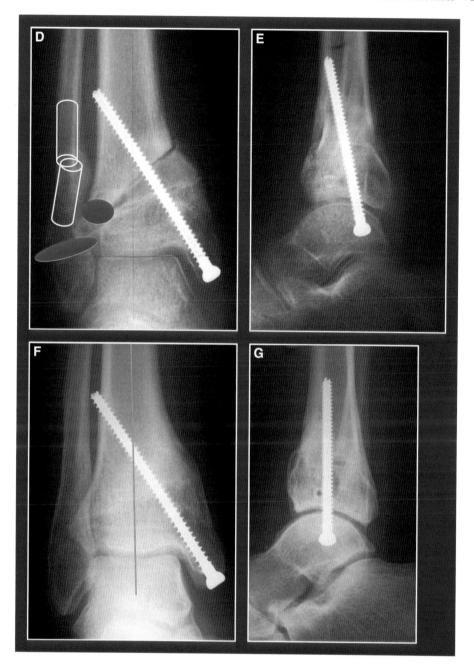

Figure 8-35. *(continued)*

ii. If the distal fibula and lateral distal tibial growth plates are not yet closed, perform epiphysiodesis of both with a drill

iii. Make the tibial incision on the medial surface of the epimetaphysis rather than anteriorly

iv. Expose the tibia subperiosteally as far distal as possible

v. Retract and protect the PT neurovascular bundle

vi. With curved retractors anterior and posterior to the distal metaphysis, make an oblique osteotomy from proximal-medial to distal-lateral starting 3-4 cm proximal to the tip of the medial malleolus and ending at the lateral edge of the growth plate

vii. Open the osteotomy medially, hinging on the lateral periosteum

viii. Insert large tricortical iliac crest bone grafts to fill the space symmetrically from anterior to posterior. Beware not to create a procurvatum or recurvatum deformity

• If a procurvatum or recurvatum deformity exists along with the varus deformity, place the base of the graft(s) more posteromedial or anteromedial to simultaneously correct both planes of deformity.

ix. Insert one to two fully threaded 4.5-mm-diameter cannulated screws retrograde from the tip of the medial malleolus across the osteotomy and graft, capturing the lateral metaphyseal cortex with screw threads

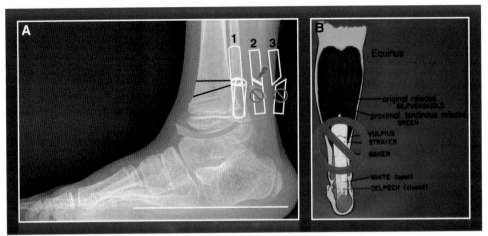

Figure 8-36. A. Lateral x-ray shows the location of the osteotomies of the distal tibia (*black lines*) needed to reorient the ankle joint and create increased dorsiflexion (*green curved arrow*) to eliminate anterior ankle impingement. In this skeletally immature child, guided growth with a screw/plate construct (**see this chapter**) is preferable. This x-ray is used merely for conceptualization of the osteotomy. The distal cut is plantar flexed approximately 10° in relation to the plantar surface of the foot (*yellow line*). The proximal cut is perpendicular to the tibia shaft. A trapezoid of bone is removed, because the apex of the deformity is the tendo-Achilles, not the posterior tibial cortex. The distal fragment is dorsiflexed and *posteriorly translated* (*blue arrow*) to respect the CORA. The anterior cortices of the two fragments should be aligned. The fibula osteotomy should be in the *oblique sagittal plane*, as shown under number *1*, to enable deformity correction of the tibia while maintaining contact between the fibula fragments. The plane of the oblique coronal fibula osteotomy under number *2* would create impingement of the fragments and disallow deformity correction of the tibia. The plane of the oblique coronal fibula osteotomy under number *3* would separate the fragments completely and lead to delayed healing of the fibula. **B.** A reminder that neither the tendo-Achilles nor the gastrocnemius should be lengthened, because that would only increase anterior ankle impingement.

l. ***For correction of anterior ankle impingement in a skeletally*** **mature** *adolescent (Figure 8-36):*

    i. Make sure the fibula osteotomy is in the oblique sagittal plane

    ii. Insert a 0.062″ smooth Steinmann pin retrograde from the medial malleolus stopping short of the intended distal osteotomy site

    iii. Insert a second 0.062″ smooth Steinmann pin retrograde from the anterolateral corner of the epiphysis stopping short of the intended distal osteotomy site (**see Management Principle #20-3, Chapter 4**).

    iv. With narrow Crego retractors surrounding the tibia subperiosteally, perform an osteotomy with a sagittal saw that is 10° plantar flexed in relation to the plantar surface of the foot with the foot held in maximum dorsiflexion

    v. Then perform the second and more proximal osteotomy perpendicular to the shaft (**see Management Principle #20-5, Chapter 4**) such that a trapezoid of bone is removed. The (usually scarred) heel cord is the true CORA, and it will often prevent deformity correction if a simple wedge is removed.

    vi. Bring the osteotomy surfaces into apposition and translate the distal fragment *posteriorly* (**see Management Principle #20-1, Chapter 4**)

    vii. Advance the Steinmann pins retrograde across osteotomy and into the tibial metaphyseal cortices opposite the side of entry. Additional internal fixation can be with anterior staples or a plate and screws.

m. For all types of tibial osteotomies discussed above, close or attempt to close the periosteum over the plate with 2-0 absorbable sutures

n. Approximate the skin edges with interrupted subcutaneous 3-0 absorbable sutures and a running subcuticular 4-0 absorbable suture

o. Apply a short-leg non–weight-bearing fiberglass cast and bivalve it. Overwrap the cast with fiberglass before discharge from the hospital

p. Total cast immobilization is 8-12 weeks, with one or two cast changes and no weight-bearing until at least 6 weeks.

3. <u>Pitfalls</u> (**see Management Principle #20, Chapter 4**)

a. Failure to achieve control of the distal tibial fragment before the osteotomy is performed

b. Failure to make the single cut of a pure rotational tibial osteotomy or the shaft side (2nd) cut of an angular tibial osteotomy perpendicular to the shaft of the tibia

c. Failure to perform a fibula osteotomy

d. Failure to cut the fibula in the proper oblique plane

e. Failure to correct the translational deformity along with the angulation deformity

f. Performing an tendo-Achilles lengthening or gastrocnemius recession

4. <u>Complications</u>

a. Injury to the distal tibial growth plate

    i. *Avoid by* limiting distal subperiosteal exposure to no closer than 1 cm from the physis

b. Delayed or nonunion of the tibia
   i. *Avoid by:*
   • keeping a cool saw blade
   • alternatively, making the osteotomy(s) with drill holes and an osteotome
   • creating good apposition of the osteotomy surfaces and compressing/dynamizing the osteotomy

IV. ARTHRODESES

Hallux Interphalangeal Joint Arthrodesis

1. Indications
   a. As a component part of a Jones transfer of the extensor hallucis longus (EHL) to the 1st MT neck (**see Chapter 7**) for claw deformity of the hallux in a skeletally mature adolescent, *if* tenodesis of the distal stump of the EHL to the EHB is unsuccessful or not possible
      i. Usually performed during the second stage of a two-stage reconstruction for cavovarus deformity with clawing of the hallux (**see Chapter 5**)
   b. Degenerative arthritis of the hallux IP joint.
2. Technique (Figure 8-37)
   a. If this is an isolated procedure, perform a percutaneous tenotomy of the FHL (**see Chapter 7**)
   b. If this procedure is being performed in conjunction with other procedures during the second-stage reconstruction of a cavovarus foot, the FHL was already released in stage 1.
   c. Make a longitudinal incision dorsal to the EHL starting just distal to the hallux interphalangeal joint (avoiding injury to the germinal cells of the toe nail) and

extending proximally to the base of the proximal phalanx or, if performed in conjunction with a Jones transfer, to the base of the 1st MT.
   i. **see Jones transfer of EHL to 1st MT neck, Technique d–g, Chapter 7.**
   d. Make a Z-lengthening type cut in the EHL for later tendon plication.
   e. Release the interphalangeal joint capsule transversely on the dorsal, medial, and lateral surfaces, and elevate the volar capsule off the adjacent ends of the phalanges with a Freer elevator
   f. Using a microsagittal saw, remove the condyles of the proximal phalanx by cutting perpendicular to the dorsal cortex of the bone and to the longitudinal axis of the phalanx.
   g. Sharply elevate the capsule from the proximal end of the distal phalanx to expose the articular surface
   h. Using a microsagittal saw, remove the articular cartilage surface of the distal phalanx perpendicular to the dorsal cortex of the bone
   i. Drill the guide pin for a 4.0- to 4.5-mm cannulated screw antegrade from the center of the cut surface of the distal phalanx out the end of the toe
   j. Cut the proximal end of the pin obliquely to make a point
   k. Bring the cut surfaces of the bones into apposition and drill the guide pin retrograde into the proximal phalanx
   l. Insert a partially threaded 4.0- to 4.5-mm cannulated screw and countersink the head of the screw into the tuft of the distal phalanx
   m. Confirm alignment of the bones and position of the screw with mini-fluoroscopy

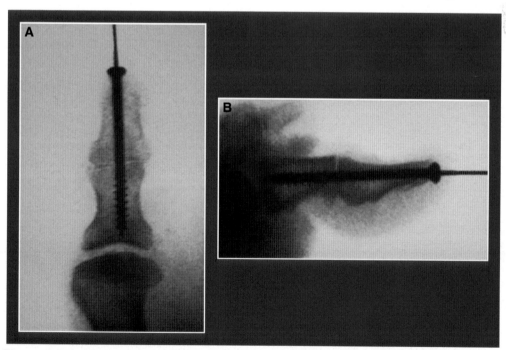

Figure 8-37. **A.** Intraoperative AP x-ray of a hallux interphalangeal joint arthrodesis with a cannulated screw and guide wire in place. There is straight axial alignment of the phalanges. All of the screw threads are in the proximal phalanx which helps with compression at the fusion site. **B.** Intraoperative lateral x-ray shows the ideal position of the phalanges and the screw. The screw head is countersunk in the tuft of the distal phalanx to prevent a painful prominence at the tip of the toe.

n. With the ankle and the hallux MTP joints at neutral dorsiflexion, plicate the overlapping ends of the EHL side-to-side with figure-of-8 2-0 absorbable sutures.
   i. When performed as part of a Jones transfer, tenodese the distal EHL stump to the EHB (**see Jones transfer, Chapter 7**)
o. Approximate the skin edges with interrupted subcutaneous 3-0 absorbable sutures and a running subcuticular 4-0 absorbable suture
p. Complete any other procedures being performed concurrently

3. Pitfalls
   a. Difficulty in finding the proper axial alignment for the screw. Inserting the guide pin antegrade from the cut surface of the distal phalanx and then retrograde into the proximal phalanx diminishes this challenge

4. Complications
   a. Injury to the neurovascular bundles
      i. *Avoid by* staying central with the dissection and maintaining extracapsular retractors
   b. Injury to the germinal cells of the nail plate
      i. *Avoid by* limiting distal dissection to only that required to see the proximal end of the distal phalanx
   c. Pain distal to the screw head resulting in the need to remove it
      i. *Avoid by* countersinking the screw head

Hallux Metatarsophalangeal Joint Arthrodesis

1. Indications
   a. Hallux valgus in a child with cerebral palsy

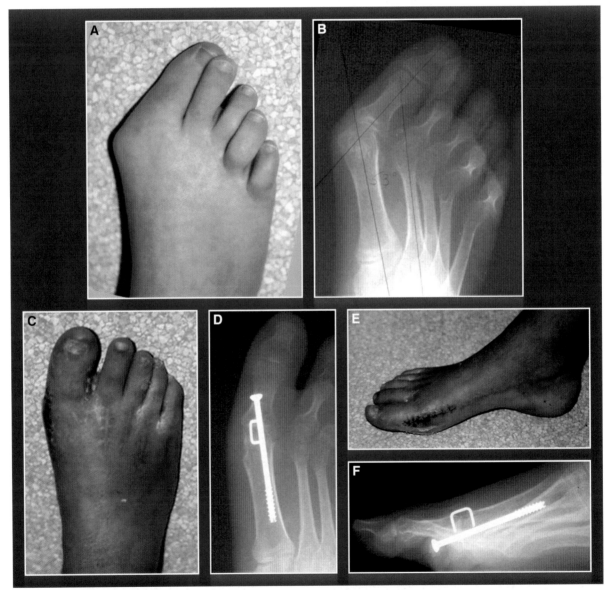

Figure 8-38. **A.** Severe, painful hallux valgus (without metatarsus primus varus or flatfoot) in a teenage girl with cerebral palsy, Gross Motor Function Classification System (GMFCS) level II. **B.** Standing AP x-ray of her foot. **C.** Standing AP photograph of her foot taken 6 weeks postoperatively. **D.** Standing AP x-ray taken 6 months postoperatively. **E.** Standing lateral photograph of her foot at 6 weeks post-op. **F.** Standing lateral x-ray at 6 months.

2. Technique (Figure 8-38)
   a. Correct other foot deformities, which usually include valgus deformity of the hindfoot (**see Calcaneal Lengthening Osteotomy, Chapter 8**), gastrocnemius contracture (**see Gastrocnemius Recession, Chapter 7**), and metatarsus primus varus (**see 1st MT Base Osteotomy, or MC-Medial-OWO, Chapter 8**)
   b. Make a longitudinal incision dorsal to the hallux proximal phalanx and the distal half of the 1st MT
   c. Release or retract the EHL
   d. Incise the 1st MTP joint capsule on the medial, dorsal, and lateral sides
   e. Using a microsagittal saw, resect the proximal articular surface of the proximal phalanx of the hallux perpendicular to the shaft of the bone
   f. Using a microsagittal saw, remove the distal articular cartilage and a portion of the epiphysis of the 1st MT with an osteotomy that is approximately 10° valgus from the long axis of the 1st MT in the frontal plane and angled approximately 15° to 20° extended from the long axis of the 1st MT in the sagittal plane. This will create a 10° hallux valgus angle and 15° to 20° of fixed dorsiflexion at the arthrodesis site of the MTP joint. This assumes an average height longitudinal arch. Less dorsiflexion is required in a flatfoot that is not undergoing reconstruction, and more dorsiflexion is required in a cavus foot that is not undergoing reconstruction.
   g. Fixation can be with crossed smooth Steinmann pins, staples, a mini-fragment plate and screws, or a retrograde large diameter screw inserted from the plantar flair of the proximal phalanx across the fusion site and up the 1st MT medullary cavity.
   h. Approximate the skin edges with interrupted subcutaneous 3-0 absorbable sutures and a running subcuticular 4-0 absorbable suture
   i. Apply a short-leg non–weight-bearing cast
   j. Maintain cast immobilization for at least 6 weeks, based on the other concurrent procedures performed
3. Pitfalls
   a. Failure to correct the other foot deformities concurrently
   b. Failure to create the appropriate dorsiflexion at the arthrodesis site
4. Complications
   a. Wound dehiscence over the plate
      i. *Avoid by* careful tissue handling

Midfoot Wedge Resection/Arthrodesis

1. Indications
   a. Severe, rigid, long-standing cavovarus foot deformity (**see Chapter 5**) in an older adolescent or young adult, as an alternative to a triple arthrodesis
2. Technique (Figure 8-39)
   a. Perform a plantar release (**see Chapter 7**)
   b. Make a longitudinal incision over the dorsum of the midfoot from the ankle to the 3rd MT shaft

   c. For a very severe deformity, it will be easier to use parallel dorsomedial and dorsolateral longitudinal incisions
   d. Isolate and retract the superficial peroneal and sural nerves
   e. Bluntly elevate all soft tissues off the dorsum of the midtarsal bones
   f. Insert a 0.062″ smooth Steinmann pin from medial to lateral through the proximal bodies of the navicular and cuboid perpendicular to the long axis of the hindfoot in the frontal plane
   g. Insert a second 0.062″ smooth Steinmann pin from medial to lateral through the distal bodies of the 3 cuneiform bones and the cuboid perpendicular to the long axis of the forefoot in the frontal plane
   h. Insert a third 0.062″ smooth Steinmann pin from dorsal to plantar in the proximal body of the cuboid perpendicular to the desired plantar surface of the hindfoot
   i. Insert a fourth 0.062″ smooth Steinmann pin from dorsal to plantar in the distal body of the cuboid perpendicular to the desired plantar surface of the forefoot
   j. With retractors dorsal and plantar to the midfoot bones and using a sagittal saw, make one osteotomy immediately proximal to the two anterior pins and a second osteotomy immediately distal to the two posterior pins
   k. Remove the large wedge of bone
   l. Bring the cut surfaces together and rotate the forefoot and hindfoot until the rotational deformities are corrected. The small joints of the midtarsal bones will not align anatomically, but will be sacrificed as an alternative to sacrificing the more important subtalar joint (which takes place in a triple arthrodesis)
   m. Fix the forefoot on the hindfoot with large gauge, smooth, crossed Steinmann pin inserted retrograde and left exposed distally for removal in clinic
   n. Apply a very well-padded short-leg non–weight-bearing fiberglass cast that is immediately bivalved
   o. Overwrap the cast with fiberglass before hospital discharge
   p. Change the cast and remove the wires in clinic at 6 weeks and apply a final partial weight-bearing cast for 4 to 6 weeks
3. Pitfalls
   a. Failure to improve the severe and rigid deformity with a first-stage D-PMR (**see Chapter 7**)
   b. Failure to use the Steinmann pins as guides for the complex bone cuts
4. Complications
   a. PT neurapraxia
      i. *Avoid by* gentle serial stretching casts after the D-PMR and before the wedge resection/arthrodesis in very severe, rigid deformities
   b. Wound edge necrosis
      i. *Avoid by* gentle serial stretching casts after the D-PMR and before the wedge resection/arthrodesis in very severe, rigid deformities

c. Pin tract infection
   i. *Avoid by* relieving skin tension at the insertion site before applying the felt pledget around the pin

Calcaneocuboid Joint Arthrodesis

See earlier in this Chapter.

Subtalar Arthrodesis

1. Indications (**see Management Principle #13, Chapter 4**)
   a. Painful degenerative arthrosis in the talocalcaneal joint associated with severe, rigid, long-standing plano-valgus foot deformity in an older child or adolescent, typically one with an underlying severe neuromuscular disorder. The talonavicular and calcaneocuboid joints should be free of degenerative arthrosis.

2. Technique (Figure 8-40)
   a. Make a modified Ollier incision in a Langer's skin line from the superficial peroneal nerve to the sural nerve half way between the beak of the calcaneus and the tip of the lateral malleolus (Figure 8-17A).
   b. Elevate the soft tissues from the dorsal surface of the anterior calcaneus in the sinus tarsi. Avoid exposure of, or injury to, the capsule of the calcaneocuboid joint

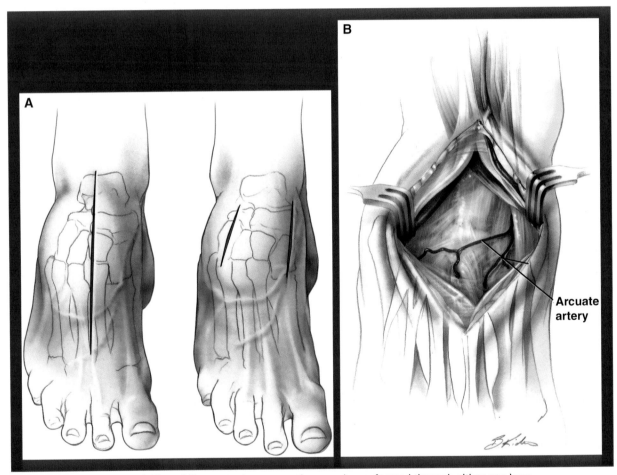

Arcuate artery

Figure 8-39. **A.** The midfoot osteotomy operation may be performed through either one long midline incision or two separate incisions, one over the dorsomedial aspect of the navicular and first cuneiform bone and the second over the cuboid bone in line with the 4th MT. In the severe cavus foot, the single incision makes it difficult to reach the lateral extent of the cuboid bone. The incision must extend from the dorsal aspect of the talar neck distally as far as the middle of the MTs. Through this incision the entire area of the osteotomy can be exposed extraperiosteally without interference from the anterior or PT tendons. It is also easier to see the osteotomy through this single incision. It is important that the operation be preceded by a plantar release. **B.** After the skin and subcutaneous tissues are divided, the interval between the extensor tendons to the second and third toes is developed. The neurovascular bundle lies between the extensor tendons to the second and great toes. In developing this interval, care should be taken to interrupt as few vessels as possible. The arcuate artery coming off the dorsalis pedis artery runs laterally at the level of the tarsal–MT joints. If this is identified, an effort to preserve it should be made.

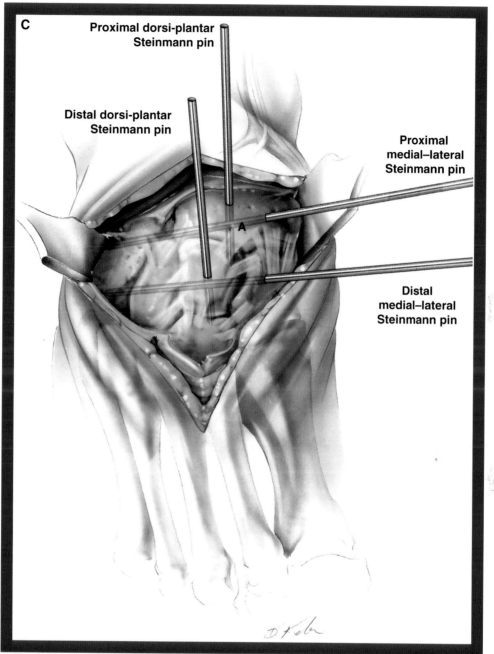

Figure 8-39. *(continued)* **C.** After this interval is developed, the midtarsal bones should be exposed extraperiosteally between Chopart joints proximally and Lisfranc joints distally, while preserving and protecting those joint capsules. Medially, the dissection should go completely around the navicular first cuneiform joint; laterally, it should go completely around the cuboid bone. Most of the cuboid bone should be exposed, but the joints proximal and distal to it do not need to be entered. Steinmann pins can be used as guide wires to mark the proximal and distal limits of the bone wedge that is to be removed. Insert one from medial to lateral parallel with, and immediately distal to, Chopart joints through the navicular and cuboid. Insert another one from dorsal to plantar at the level of this transverse pin perpendicular to the desired longitudinal axis of the hindfoot. Insert a third pin parallel with, and immediately proximal to, Lisfranc joints through the three cuneiforms and the cuboid. A fourth pin is inserted from dorsal to plantar at the level of the third pin perpendicular to the desired longitudinal axis of the forefoot.

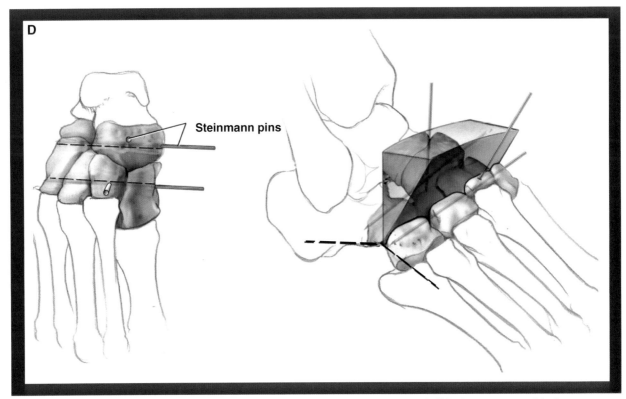

Figure 8-39. *(continued)* **D.** The osteotomy is performed using a large half-inch osteotome, chisel, or sagittal saw. The plantar soft tissues are protected with wide, curved Crego retractors. The proximal cut is made immediately distal to, and parallel with, the plane created by the two proximal guide pins. It passes through the mid-body of the navicular and the proximal end of the cuboid. This cut is estimated to be perpendicular to the hindfoot axis. The distal osteotomy is made immediately proximal to, and parallel with, the plane created by the two distal guide pins. It passes through the mid-body of each of the three cuneiform bones and the distal end of the cuboid. It is made perpendicular to the axis of the forefoot. It is to be noted that unlike the medial half of the osteotomy, the joints on either side of the cuboid bone are not entered. Rather, the wedge is removed entirely from the cuboid bone. To avoid excessive shortening of the foot, the osteotomies should be fashioned so that no gap of bone is present at the plantar apex of the wedge. The osteotomy is closed by elevating the forefoot (**E**).

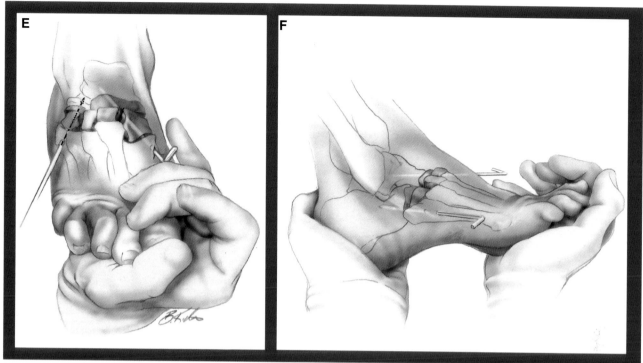

Figure 8-39. *(continued)* (**E**). It is possible to rotate the distal segment, if needed, to correct prona-tion deformity of the fore foot. Often the 1st MT will be more depressed than the others. This can be corrected by supinating the forefoot; however, care should be taken not to produce an unintended malrotation. Much depends on the angulation and flexibility of the hindfoot. The osteotomy can be fixed with either two Steinmann pins or multiple staples. The dorsal surface of the cuneiform bones is usually higher than the navicular, and this may make staple fixation more difficult. Secure fixation with Steinmann pins is not as easy as it may first appear (**F**) as the medial pin may pass too far plan-tarward. The medial pin is inserted first. It must start in the 1st MT at an oblique angle directed dorsally and laterally. This pin should engage the 1st MT, the first cuneiform bone, the navicular, and the talus. The lateral pin is started distal to the flare at the base of the 5th MT and is aimed medially and slightly dorsally, crossing the cuboid bone and entering the calcaneus. The ends of the pins are left protruding outside the skin. A well-padded, non–weight-bearing short-leg cast is applied. The foot is kept elevated for the first few days. The patient is then ambulated with a three-point, non–weight-bearing crutch gait for 6 weeks. After 6 weeks the cast and the pins are removed in the office. A short-leg walking cast is applied, and the patient is permitted partial weight-bearing for an additional 4 to 6 weeks, at which time healing should be complete. (From Mosca VS. The Foot. In: Weinstein S, Flynn J, eds. *Lovell and Winter's Pediatric Orthopaedics.* 7th ed. Philadelphia, PA: Lippincott Williams & Wilkins; 2013.)

c. Partially decorticate the exposed non-articular surfaces of the talus and the calcaneus in the sinus tarsi with a high speed burr

d. Invert the subtalar joint to neutral alignment, and *never* to varus

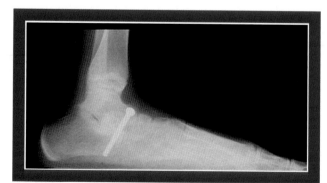

Figure 8-40. Subtalar Arthrodesis.

e. Insert a fully threaded 4.5 mm cannulated screw percutaneously in an oblique trajectory from the antero-dorso-medial head/neck of the talus to the posteroplantar-lateral calcaneus using mini-fluoroscopic guidance

f. Insert and impact morselized cancellous bone graft into the sinus tarsi until the cavity is filled

g. Lengthen the tendo-Achilles or the gastrocnemius tendon (**see Chapter 7**) if contracted, based on the Silfverskiold test (**see Assessment Principle #12, Chapter 3**).

h. Assess the forefoot for structural supination deformity by cupping the heel in one hand, while maintaining neutral ankle dorsiflexion, and visually sighting down the long axis of the foot from toes to heel. If the plane of the metatarsal heads is supinated in relation to the long axis of the tibia or there is dorsal-plantar hypermo-bility of the first metatarsal-medial cuneiform joint, a plantar flexion plantar-based closing wedge osteotomy of the medial cuneiform is needed (**see this Chapter**) (Figure 8-19).

   i. Approximate the skin edges of all incisions with interrupted subcutaneous 3-0 absorbable sutures and a running subcuticular 4-0 absorbable suture

   j. Apply a well-padded short leg fiberglass non-weight-bearing cast and immediately bivalve it to allow for swelling overnight. Obtain final radiographs of the foot in the cast in the recovery room

   k. Over-wrap the cast with fiberglass the following day before hospital discharge

   l. At 6 weeks, the cast is removed to obtain simulated standing AP, lateral, and oblique radiographs of the foot.

      i. An AFO mold is obtained in most cases.

      ii. A below the knee weightbearing cast is applied.

   m. Upon removal of this cast 6 weeks later, final simulated standing AP, lateral, and oblique radiographs of the foot are obtained. The AFO is fitted.

3. Pitfalls

   a. Failure to fully correct the deformity

   b. Failure to identify and concurrently correct rigid forefoot supination deformity

   c. Failure to identify and concurrently correct equinus deformity

4. Complications

   a. Over-correction to varus

      i. *Avoid by* confirming appropriate correction intraoperatively with minifluoroscopy

   b. Non-union

      i. *Avoid by*

        • adequate decortication of the exposed non-articular surfaces of the talus and the calcaneus in the sinus tarsi with a high speed burr

        • complete filling of the sinus tarsi with morselized cancellous bone graft

        • stable fixation with the trans-articular screw

        • adequate immobilization based on post-operative radiographs

   c. Persistent equinus

      i. *Avoid by* lengthening the Achilles or gastrocnemius tendon, based on the Silfverskiold test, and confirming adequacy of ankle dorsiflexion with the knee extended after subtalar joint stabilization

   d. Persistent forefoot supination

      i. *Avoid by* assessing forefoot supination intraoperatively after the subtalar joint has been stabilized and the heel cord has been lengthened. Correct it with a medial cuneiform osteotomy if identified

Triple Arthrodesis

1. Indications (**see Management Principle #13, Chapter 4**)

   a. Painful degenerative arthrosis in the talocalcaneal and talonavicular joints associated with severe, rigid, long-standing cavovarus foot deformity in an older adolescent or young adult

   b. Painful degenerative arthrosis in the talocalcaneal and talonavicular joints associated with severe, rigid, long-standing plano-valgus foot deformity in an older adolescent or young adult, typically one with an underlying severe neuromuscular disorder

2. Technique (Figure 8-41)

   a. Because of intentional and gratifying inexperience with this technique, I am not expert and have no "tricks of the trade" (**see Management Principle #13, Chapter 4**). Therefore, the technique is not discussed in detail, but images and legends from Mosca VS. The Foot. In: Weinstein SL and Flynn JM, editors. *Lovell and Winter's Pediatric Orthopaedics*, 7th ed. Philadelphia, PA: Lippincott Williams & Wilkins; 2013:1441–45 have been borrowed for this chapter.

3. Pitfalls

   a. Failure to fully correct the hindfoot deformity

   b. Failure to identify and concurrently correct rigid forefoot supination or pronation deformity

   c. Failure to identify and concurrently correct equinus deformity

4. Complications

   a. Over-correction to varus in a valgus hindfoot or persistence of varus in a varus hindfoot

      i. *Avoid by* confirming appropriate correction intraoperatively with minifluoroscopy

   b. Non-union

      i. *Avoid by*

        • adequate resection of all articular surfaces and subchondral bone

        • stable fixation with trans-articular screws, staples, wires, etc.

        • adequate immobilization based on post-operative radiographs

   b. Persistent equinus

      i *Avoid by* lengthening the Achilles or gastrocnemius tendon, based on the Silfverskiold test, and confirming adequacy of ankle dorsiflexion with the knee extended after joint stabilizations

   c. Persistent forefoot supination or pronation

      i *Avoid by* assessing forefoot supination or pronation intraoperatively after the joints have been stabilized and the heel cord has been lengthened. Correct it with a medial cuneiform osteotomy if identified

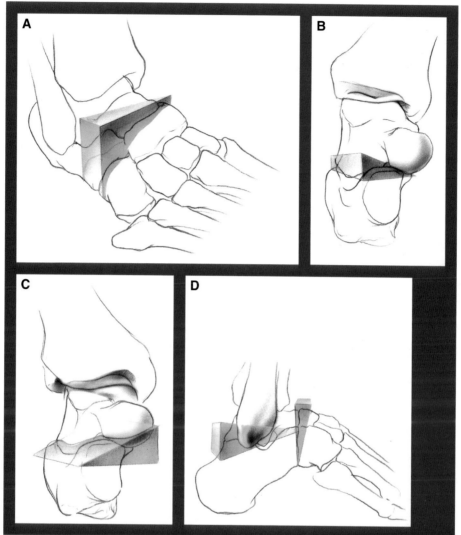

Figure 8-41. Before beginning the triple arthrodesis operation, the surgeon should give some thought and planning regarding the wedges of bone to be removed and, in particular, the amount of bone to be removed. Simplify the cuts to parallel and perpendicular in relation to obvious large bony landmarks. It is not particularly beneficial to preoperatively plan precise wedges with cutouts, since the three-dimensional nature of the deformities makes such planning imprecise. Visualizing the foot at surgery and making the osteotomy cuts to create the wedges, as described in the subsequent discussion, seems much more practical and accurate. The most common deformity for which triple arthrodesis is performed is fixed cavovarus deformity. To correct this deformity, a laterally-based wedge of bone is removed from each of the joints to be resected. Conceptually, two wedges of bone at right angles to each other are removed. The wedge that will allow correction of the forefoot will excise the TN and calcaneocuboid joints. To achieve correction to a neutral position, the distal cut is perpendicular to the long axis of the forefoot and the proximal cut is perpendicular to the longitudinal axis of the calcaneus (A). When these two surfaces are opposed, the forefoot should be straight. To correct the varus of the hindfoot, a laterally based wedge must be removed from the subtalar joint. To correct the heel to a neutral position, the proximal cut from the undersurface of the talus should be perpendicular to the long axis of the tibia (or parallel with the ankle mortise), whereas the distal cut from the superior surface of the calcaneus should be parallel to the bottom of the heel (B). When these two surfaces are apposed, the heel should be in neutral. A triple arthrodesis for fixed valgus deformity is extremely difficult. This is because the medially-based wedges that are created using the espoused principles must be removed from the lateral side (C). This task is simplified if all the joints are widely released by extensive capsulotomies and the interosseous ligament of the subtalar joint is sectioned. A laminar spreader can be used to hold the joints open. Calcaneocavus deformity is the most uncommon indication for triple arthrodesis. In this circumstance a posteriorly based wedge is removed from the subtalar joint, which allows correction of the calcaneus deformity. A dorsal wedge is removed from the TN and calcaneocuboid joints to allow the forefoot to be dorsiflexed (D).

259

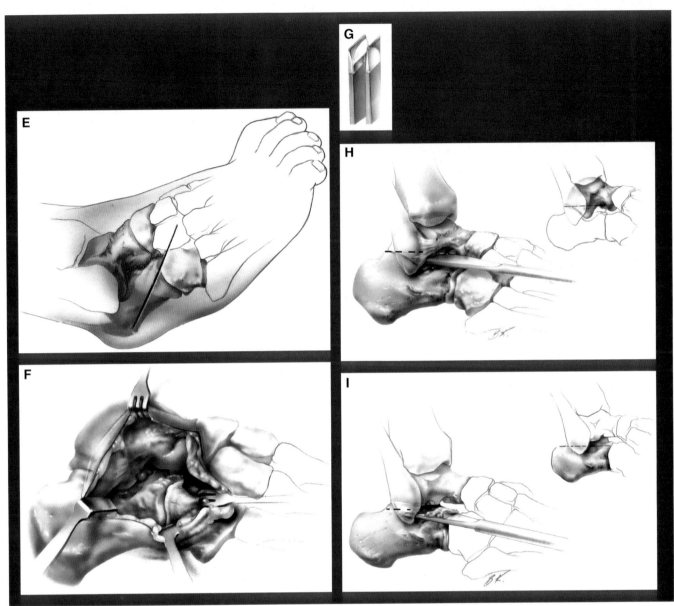

Figure 8-41. *(continued)* A slightly different technique is used for mild deformities. The joint surfaces are simply removed with osteotomes and curettes until there is sufficient resection to gain the desired correction (**E**). The triple arthrodesis operation is illustrated for the most common deformity: cavovarus. The patient is placed on the operating table with a sandbag under the hip on the side to be operated, thus bringing the lateral side of the foot into better position. The incision is a straight lateral incision that crosses the lateral side of the TN joint and the distal end of the calcaneus. It should extend from just medial to the most lateral extensor tendons dorsally to just past the peroneal tendons volarly. There should be no undermining of the skin edges. The superficial peroneal and sural nerves are retracted and protected. After the fascia over the extensor brevis muscle is incised, the proximal insertion of this muscle is identified and the muscle is elevated to expose the lateral capsules of the calcaneocuboid and TN joints. The fibrofatty tissue is removed from the sinus tarsi, exposing the lateral aspect of the subtalar joint (**F**). The TN and calcaneocuboid joint capsules are incised circumferentially, exposing the joint surfaces. It will assist removal of the bone wedges from the subtalar joint if the capsule of the subtalar joint is also nearly circumferentially released. This can be done by sliding a curved periosteal elevator (e.g., a Crego elevator) around the posterior and then medial aspect of the subtalar joint until it rests along the medial side of the joint. At this point, almost the entire capsule of the subtalar joint can be visualized and incised, the interosseous ligament can be divided, and a large bone skid can be used to pry the joint open. This will give the surgeon an excellent view of the two bony surfaces of the subtalar joint that are to be excised. The wedges of bone are now excised. The subtalar joint is resected first. Most of the bone for the correction should be removed from the calcaneus. It is better to use a chisel than an osteotome for these cuts. The chisel, with its flat surface as opposed to the double-beveled surface of an osteotome, is easier to keep on a straight course (**G**). The cut in the bottom of the talus should be parallel with the ankle mortise from lateral to medial (**H**). The cut into the dorsal surface of the calcaneus should be parallel to the bottom of the heel (**I**).

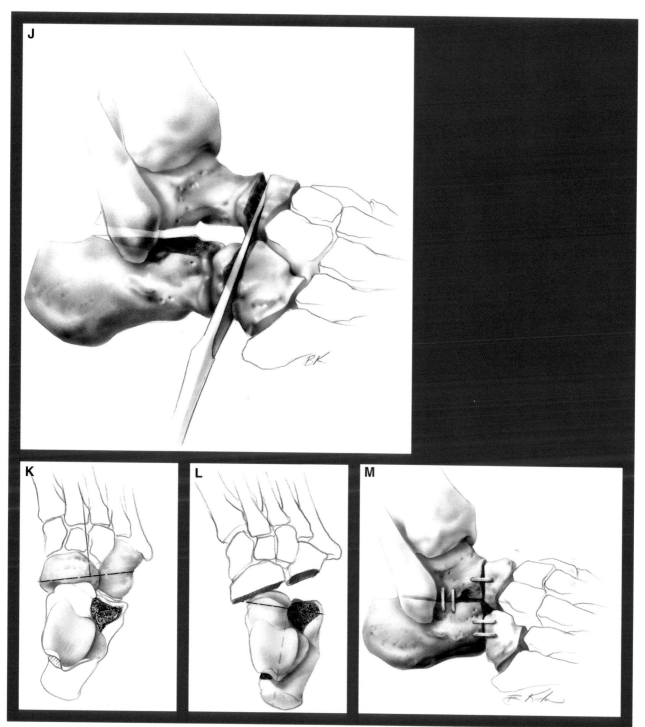

Figure 8-41. *(continued)* It is best to make the most proximal and distal aspects of these cuts first and the middle portion in between them last. This is because the middle part will be the most difficult to remove with remaining capsule attached to the prominent sustentaculum tali and the most worrisome to cut through with the neurovascular bundle in close proximity. If these cuts are made correctly, the heel will be in neutral alignment regarding varus and valgus when the two cut surfaces are apposed. The same principle is used in aligning the forefoot. The cuts in the navicular and the cuboid should be perpendicular to the longitudinal axis of the forefoot (**J, K**), whereas the cuts in the distal talus and calcaneus should be perpendicular to the longitudinal axis of the hindfoot or calcaneus (**L**). When the wedges are removed, the foot is placed in the corrected position and the surfaces are inspected. Good coaptation should be present to ensure prompt healing. Trim additional bone as needed. The external contour of the foot should be inspected to ascertain that the desired three-dimensional alignment of the foot has been achieved. If so, the resected joint surfaces are held together with staples, screws, wires, or combinations of these internal fixation devices. A well-padded short-leg non–weight-bearing cast is applied and bivalved to allow for the expected significant swelling that will occur over the next few days. Radiographs are obtained, and the cast is changed to a weight-bearing cast at 6 weeks. At 12 weeks, healing is usually complete, and no further cast protection is needed (**M**). (From Mosca VS. The Foot. In: Weinstein S, Flynn J, eds. *Lovell and Winter's Pediatric Orthopaedics.* 7th ed. Philadelphia, PA: Lippincott Williams & Wilkins; 2013.)

Bibliography

Accessory Navicular

Chiu NT, Jou IM, Lee BF, et al. Symptomatic and asymptomatic accessory navicular bones: findings of Tc-99m MDP bone scintigraphy. *Clin Radiol.* 2000;55:353.

Geist ES. The accessory scaphoid bone. *J Bone Joint Surg Am.* 1925;7:570.

Grogan DP, Gasser SI, Ogden JA. The painful accessory navicular: a clinical and histopathological study. *Foot Ankle.* 1989;10:164–169.

Kidner F. The pre-hallux (accessory scaphoid) in its relation to flatfoot. *J Bone Joint Surg Am.* 1929;11:831.

Kidner F. The pre-hallux in relation to flatfoot. *JAMA.* 1933;101:1539.

Kiter E, Erduran M, Günal I. Inheritance of the accessory navicular bone. *Arch Orthop Trauma Surg.* 2000;120:582.

Kiter E, Günal I, Karatosun V, et al. The relationship between the tibialis posterior tendon and the accessory navicular. *Ann Anat.* 2000;182:65.

Kopp FJ, Marcus RE. Clinical outcome of surgical treatment of the symptomatic accessory navicular. *Foot Ankle Int.* 2004;25:27.

Shands A. The accessory bones of the foot. *South Med Surg.* 1931;9:326.

Shands AR Jr, Wentz IJ. Congenital anomalies, accessory bones, and osteochondritis in the feet of 850 children. *Surg Clin North Am.* 1953;97:1643–1666.

Sullivan JA, Miller WA. The relationship of the accessory navicular to the development of the flat foot. *Clin Orthop Relat Res.* 1979;144:233–237.

Zadek I, Gold A. The accessory tarsal scaphoid. *J Bone Joint Surg Am.* 1948;30A:957.

Bone Procedures

Abrams RC. Relapsed clubfoot: the early results of an evaluation of Dillwyn Evans' operation. *J Bone Joint Surg Am.* 1969;51:270.

Addison A, Fixsen JA, Lloyd-Roberts GC. A review of the Dillwyn Evans type collateral operation in severe club feet. *J Bone Joint Surg Br.* 1983;65:12.

Adelaar RS, Dannelly EA, Meunier PA, et al. A long-term study of triple arthrodesis in children. *Orthop Clin North Am.* 1976;7:895–908.

Akin O. The treatment of hallux valgus: a new operative procedure and its results. *Med Sentinel.* 1925;33:678.

Anderson AF, Fowler SB. Anterior calcaneal osteotomy for symptomatic juvenile pes planus. *Foot Ankle.* 1984;4:274–283.

Anderson DA, Schoenecker PL, Blair VPI. Combined lateral column shortening and medial column lengthening in the treatment of severe forefoot adductus. *Orthop Trans.* 1991;15:768.

Angus PD, Cowell HR. Triple arthrodesis: a critical long-term review. *J Bone Joint Surg Br.* 1986;68:260–265.

Armstrong G, Carruthers C. Evans elongation of lateral column of the foot for valgus deformity. *J Bone Joint Surg Am.* 1975;57:530.

Aronson J, Nguyen LL, Aronson EA. Early results of the modified Peterson bunion procedure for adolescent hallux valgus. *J Pediatr Orthop.* 2001;21:65.

Austin DW, Leventen EO. A new osteotomy for hallux valgus: a horizontally directed "V" displacement osteotomy of the metatarsal head for hallux valgus and primus varus. *Clin Orthop Relat Res.* 1981;157:25–30.

Azmaipairashvili Z, Riddle EC, Scavina M, et al. Correction of cavovarus foot deformity in Charcot-Marie-Tooth disease. *J Pediatr Orthop.* 2005;25:360–365.

Ball J, Sullivan JA. Treatment of the juvenile bunion by Mitchell osteotomy. *Orthopedics.* 1985;8:1249–1252.

Beischer AD, Brodsky JW, Pollo FE, et al. Functional outcome and gait analysis after triple or double arthrodesis. *Foot Ankle Int.* 1999;20:545–553.

Bennett GL, Weiner DS, Leighley B. Surgical treatment of symptomatic accessory tarsal navicular. *J Pediatr Orthop.* 1990;10:445–449.

Benthien RA, Parks BG, Guyton GP, et al. Lateral column calcaneal lengthening, flexor digitorum longus transfer, and opening wedge medial cuneiform osteotomy for flexible flatfoot: a biomechanical study. *Foot Ankle Int.* 2007;28:70–77.

Berman A, Gartland JJ. Metatarsal osteotomy for the correction of adduction of the fore part of the foot in children. *J Bone Joint Surg Am.* 1971;53:498–506.

Boyd HB. Amputation of the foot with calcaneotibial arthrodesis. *J Bone Joint Surg.* 1939;21:997.

Bradley GW, Coleman SS. Treatment of the calcaneocavus foot deformity. *J Bone Joint Surg Am.* 1981;63:1159.

Butte F. Navicular-cuneiform arthrodesis for flatfoot: an end-result study. *J Bone Joint Surg Am.* 1937;19:496.

Cain TJ, Hyman S. Peroneal spastic flat foot: its treatment by osteotomy of the os calcis. *J Bone Joint Surg Br.* 1978;60-B:527–529.

Caldwell GD. Surgical correction of relaxed flatfoot by the Durham flatfoot plasty. *Clin Orthop Relat Res.* 1953;2:221.

Canale PB, Aronsson DD, Lamont RL, et al. The Mitchell procedure for the treatment of adolescent hallux valgus: a long-term study. *J Bone Joint Surg Am.* 1993;75:1610–1618.

Clark MW, Ambrosia RDD, Ferguson AB. Congenital vertical talus: treatment by open reduction and navicular excision. *J Bone Joint Surg Am.* 1977;59:816–824.

Chambers EFS. An operation for the correction of flexible flat feet of adolescents. *West J Surg Obstet Gynecol.* 1946;54:77–86.

Chambers RB, Cook TM, Cowell HR. Surgical reconstruction for calcaneonavicular coalition: evaluation of function and gait. *J Bone Joint Surg Am*. 1982;64:829–836.

Choi IH, Yang MS, Chung CY, et al. The treatment of recurrent arthrogrypotic club foot in children by the Ilizarov method. A preliminary report. *J Bone Joint Surg Br*. 2001;83:731–737.

Comfort TK, Johnson LO. Resection of symptomatic talocalcaneal coalition. *J Pediatr Orthop*. 1998;18:283–288.

Cowell H. Extensor brevis arthroplasty. *J Bone Joint Surg Am*. 1970;82:820.

Crego CH Jr, Ford LT. An end-result of various operative procedures for correcting flat feet in children. *J Bone Joint Surg Am*. 1952;34-A:183–195.

Davids JR, Valadie AL, Ferguson RL, et al. Surgical management of ankle valgus in children: use of a transphyseal medial malleolar screw. *J Pediatr Orthop*. 1997;17:3–8.

Dedrick D, Kling D. Ray resection in the treatment of macrodactyly of the foot in children. *Orthop Trans*. 1985;9:145.

Dekel S, Weissman S. Osteotomy of the calcaneus and concomitant plantar stripping in children with talipes cavo-varus. *J Bone Joint Surg Br*. 1973;55:802–808.

Dogan A, Albayrak M, Akman YE, et al. The results of calcaneal lengthening osteotomy for the treatment of flexible pes planovalgus and evaluation of alignment of the foot. *Acta Orthop Traumatol Turc*. 2006;40:356–366.

Dollard MD, Marcinko DE, Lazerson A, et al. The Evans calcaneal osteotomy for correction of flexible flatfoot syndrome. *J Foot Surg*. 1984;23:291–301.

Drew AJ. The late results of arthrodesis of the foot. *J Bone Joint Surg Br*. 1951;33-B:496–502.

Duncan JW, Lovell WW. Modified Hoke-Miller flatfoot procedure. *Clin Orthop Relat Res*. 1983;181:24–27.

Dwyer F. Osteotomy of the calcaneum for pes cavus. *J Bone Joint Surg Br*. 1959;41:80–86.

Eilert RE, Jayakumar SS. Boyd and Syme ankle amputations in children. *J Bone Joint Surg*. 1976;58(8):1138.

Evans D. Calcaneo-valgus deformity. *J Bone Joint Surg Br*. 1975;57:270–278.

Evans D. Relapsed club foot. *J Bone Joint Surg Br*. 1961;43:722.

Fitzgerald JAW. Review of long-term results in arthrodesis of the first metatarsophalangeal joint. *J Bone Joint Surg*. 1969;53-B:772.

Fowler SB, Brooks AL, Parrish TF. The cavovarus foot. *J Bone Joint Surg Am*. 1959;41:757.

Gamble JG, Decker S, Abrams RC. Short first ray as a complication of multiple metatarsal osteotomies. *Clin Orthop Relat Res*. 1982;(164):241–244.

Geissele AE, Stanton RP. Surgical treatment of adolescent hallux valgus. *J Pediatr Orthop*. 1990;10:642–648.

Glynn MK, Dunlop JB, Fitzpatrick D. The Mitchell distal metatarsal osteotomy for hallux valgus. *J Bone Joint Surg Br*. 1980;62-B:188–191.

Gonzalez P, Kumar SJ. Calcaneonavicular coalition treated by resection and interposition of the extensor digitorum brevis muscle. *J Bone Joint Surg Am*. 1990;72:71–77.

Gould N. Surgery in advanced Charcot-Marie-Tooth disease. *Foot Ankle*. 1984;4:267–273.

Graham GP, Dent CM. Dillwyn Evans operation for relapsed club foot. Long-term results. *J Bone Joint Surg Br*. 1992;74:445.

Grice DS. An extra-articular arthrodesis of the subastragalar joint for correction of paralytic flat feet in children. *J Bone Joint Surg Am*. 1952;34A:927–940; passim.

Grice DS. Further experience with extra-articular arthrodesis of the subtalar joint. *J Bone Joint Surg Am*. 1955;37-A:246–259; passim.

Grill F, Franke J. The Ilizarov distractor for the correction of relapsed or neglected clubfoot. *J Bone Joint Surg Br*. 1987;69:593–597.

Hall JE, Calvert PT. Lambrinudi triple arthrodesis: a review with particular reference to the technique of operation. *J Pediatr Orthop*. 1987;7:19–24.

Hansson G. Sliding osteotomy for tailor's bunion: brief report. *J Bone Joint Surg*. 1989;71(2):324.

Haraldsson S. Pes plano-valgus staticus juvenilis and its operative treatment. *Acta Orthop Scand*. 1965;35:234–256.

Helal B, Gupta SK, Gojaseni P. Surgery for adolescent hallux valgus. *Acta Orthop Scand*. 1974;45:271–295.

Helal B. Surgery for adolescent hallux valgus. *Clin Orthop Relat Res*. 1981;157:50–63.

Hofmann A, Constine R, McBride G, et al. Osteotomy of the first cuneiform as treatment of residual adduction of the fore part of the foot in club foot. *J Bone Joint Surg Am*. 1984;66:985–990.

Hoke M. An operation for the correction of extremely relaxed flat-feet. *J Bone Joint Surg Am*. 1931;13:773.

Holden D, Siff S, Butler J, et al. Shortening of the first metatarsal as a complication of metatarsal osteotomies. *J Bone Joint Surg Am*. 1984;66:582–587.

Inglis G, Buxton RA, Macnicol MF. Symptomatic calcaneonavicular bars: the results 20 years after surgical excision. *J Bone Joint Surg Br*. 1986;68B:128–131.

Ireland ML, Hoffer M. Triple arthrodesis for children with spastic cerebral palsy. *Dev Med Child Neurol*. 1985;27:623–627.

Jack EA. Naviculo-cuneiform fusion in the treatment of flat foot. *J Bone Joint Surg Br*. 1953;35-B:75–82.

Jahss MH. Tarsometatarsal truncated-wedge arthrodesis for pes cavus and equinovarus deformity of the fore part of the foot. *J Bone Joint Surg Am*. 1980;62:713–722.

Janecki CJ, Wilde AH. Results of phalangectomy of the fifth toe for hammertoe: the Ruiz-Mora procedure. *J Bone Joint Surg Am*. 1976;58:1005–1007.

Japas LM. Surgical treatment of pes cavus by tarsal V-osteotomy. Preliminary report. *J Bone Joint Surg Am*. 1968;50:927–944.

Jones KJ, Feiwell LA, Freedman EL, et al. The effect of chevron osteotomy with lateral capsular release on the blood supply to the first metatarsal head. *J Bone Joint Surg Am*. 1995;77:197–204.

Kling TF, Schmidt TL, Conklin JJ. Open-wedge osteotomies of the first cuneiform for metatarsus adductus. *Orthop Trans*. 1991;15:106.

Koutsogiannis E. Treatment of mobile flat foot by displacement osteotomy of the calcaneus. *J Bone Joint Surg Br*. 1971;53:96–100.

Kucukkaya M, Kabukcuoglu Y, Kuzgun U. Management of the neuromuscular foot deformities with the Ilizarov method. *Foot Ankle Int*. 2002;23:135–141.

Lichtblau S. A medial and lateral release operation for club foot. A preliminary report. *J Bone Joint Surg Am*. 1973;55:1377–1384.

Light TR, Ogden JA. The longitudinal epiphyseal bracket: implications for surgical correction. *J Pediatr Orthop*. 1981;1:299–305.

Lincoln CR, Wood KE, Bugg EI Jr. Metatarsus varus corrected by open wedge osteotomy of the first cuneiform bone. *Orthop Clin North Am*. 1976;7:795–798.

Lord JP. Correction of extreme flat foot. *JAMA*. 1923;81:1502.

Lourenco AF, Dias LS, Zoellick DM, et al. Treatment of residual adduction deformity in clubfoot: the double osteotomy. *J Pediatr Orthop*. 2001;21:713–718.

Luba R, Rosman M. Bunions in children: treatment with a modified Mitchell osteotomy. *J Pediatr Orthop*. 1984;4:44–47.

Luhmann SJ, Schoenecker PL. Symptomatic talocalcaneal coalition resection: indications and results. *J Pediatr Orthop*. 1998;18:748–754.

Macnicol MF, Voutsinas S. Surgical treatment of the symptomatic accessory navicular. *J Bone Joint Surg Br*. 1984;66:218–226.

Mann DC, Hsu JD. Triple arthrodesis in the treatment of fixed cavovarus deformity in adolescent patients with Charcot-Marie-Tooth disease. *Foot Ankle*. 1992;13:1.

Mann RA, Pfeffinger L. Hallux valgus repair: DuVries modified McBride procedure. *Clin Orthop Relat Res*. 1991;272:213–218.

McCall RE, Lillich JS, Harris JR, et al. The Grice extraarticular subtalar arthrodesis: a clinical review. *J Pediatr Orthop*. 1985;5:442–445.

McCormack T, Olney B, Asher M. Talocalcaneal coalition resection: a 10-year follow-up. *J Pediatr Orthop*. 1997;17:13–15.

McDonald MG, Stevens DB. Modified Mitchell bunionectomy for management of adolescent hallux valgus. *Clin Orthop Relat Res*. 1996;332:163.

McHale KA, Lenhart MK. Treatment of residual clubfoot deformity—the "bean-shaped" foot—by opening wedge medial cuneiform osteotomy and closing wedge cuboid osteotomy. Clinical review and cadaver correlations. *J Pediatr Orthop*. 1991;11:374–381.

McKay DW. Dorsal bunions in children. *J Bone Joint Surg Am*. 1983;65:975–980.

Miller GR. The operative treatment of hypermobile flatfeet in the young child. *Clin Orthop Relat Res*. 1977;122:95–101.

Miller O. A plastic flat-foot operation. *J Bone Joint Surg Am*. 1927;9:84.

Mitchell CL, Fleming JL, Allen R, et al. Osteotomy-bunionectomy for hallux valgus. *J Bone Joint Surg Am*. 1958;40:41.

Mitchell GP. Posterior displacement osteotomy of the calcaneus. *J Bone Joint Surg Br*. 1977;59:233.

Mitchell GP, Gibson JMC. Exclusion of calcaneonavicular bar for painful syasmotic flatfoot. *J Bone Joint Surg Br*. l967;49:281–287.

Mosca VS. Skewfoot deformity in children: correction by calcaneal neck lengthening and medial cuneiform opening wedge osteotomies. *J Pediatr Orthop*. 1993;13:807.

Mosca VS. Calcaneal lengthening for valgus deformity of the hindfoot. Results in children who had severe, symptomatic flatfoot and skewfoot. *J Bone Joint Surg Am*. 1995;77:500–512.

Mosca VS. Calcaneal lengthening osteotomy for valgus deformity of the hindfoot. In: Skaggs DL, Tolo VT, eds. *Master Techniques in Orthopaedic Surgery: Pediatrics*. Philadelphia, PA: Lippincott Williams & Wilkins; 2008:263–276.

Mosca VS. Calcaneal lengthening osteotomy for the treatment of hindfoot valgus deformity. In: Weisel S, ed. *Operative Techniques in Orthopaedic Surgery*. Philadelphia, PA: Lippincott Williams & Wilkins; 2010:1608–1618.

Mosca VS, Bevan WR. Talocalcaneal tarsal coalitions and the calcaneal lengthening osteotomy: the role of deformity correction. *J Bone Joint Surg Am*. 2012;94:1584–1594.

Moyes ST, Crawfurd EJ, Aichroth PM. The interposition of extensor digitorum brevis in the resection of calcaneonavicular bars. *J Pediatr Orthop*. 1994;14:387–388.

Mubarak SJ, Brien TJO, Davids JR. Metatarsal epiphyseal bracket: treatment by central physiolysis. *J Pediatr Orthop*. 1993;13:5–8.

Mubarak SJ, Patel PN, Upasani VV, et al. Calcaneonavicular coalition: treatment by excision and fat graft. *J Pediatr Orthop*. 2009;29:418–426.

Mubarak SJ, Van Valin SE. Osteotomies of the foot for cavus deformities in children. *J Pedatr Orthop*. 2009;29:294–299.

Olney BW, Asher MA. Excision of symptomatic coalition of the middle facet of the talocalcaneal joint. *J Bone Joint Surg Am*. 1987;69:539–544.

Penny JN. The neglected clubfoot. *Tech Orthop*. 2005;7:19–24.

Peterson HA. Skewfoot (forefoot adduction with heel valgus). *J Pediatr Orthop*. 1986;6:29–30.

Peterson HA, Newman SR. Adolescent bunion deformity treated with double osteotomy and longitudinal pin fixation of the first ray. *J Pediatr Orthop*. 1993;13:80–84.

Phillips GE. A review of elongation of os calcis for flat feet. *J Bone Joint Surg Br*. 1983;65:15–18.

Prichasuk S, Sinphurmsukskul O. Kidner procedure for symptomatic accessory navicular and its relation to pes planus. *Foot Ankle Int*. 1995;16:500.

Rathjen KE, Mubarak SJ. Calcaneal-cuboid-cuneiform osteotomy for the correction of valgus foot deformities in children. *J Pediatr Orthop*. 1998;18:775–782.

Ray S, Goldberg VM. Surgical treatment of the accessory navicular. *Clin Orthop Relat Res*. 1983;177:61–66.

Robbins H. Naviculectomy for congenital vertical talus. *Bull Hosp Jt Dis*. 1976;37:77.

Ross PM, Lyne ED. The Grice procedure: indications and evaluation of long-term results. *Clin Orthop Relat Res*. 1980;153:194–200.

Saltzman CL, Fehrle MJ, Cooper RR, et al. Triple arthrodesis: twenty-five and forty-four-year average follow-up of the same patients. *J Bone Joint Surg Am*. 1999;81:1391–1402.

Samilson R. Calcaneocavus feet: a plan of management in children. *Orthop Rev*. 1981;10:125.

Sammarco GJ, Taylor R. Cavovarus foot treated with combined calcaneus and metatarsal osteotomies. *Foot Ankle Int*. 2001;22:19–30.

Sangeorzan BJ, Mosca V, Hansen ST Jr. The effect of calcaneal lengthening on relationships among the hindfoot, midfoot, and forefoot. *Foot Ankle*. 1993;14:136–141.

Schaefer D, Hefti F. Combined cuboid/cuneiform osteotomy for correction of residual adductus deformity in idiopathic and secondary club feet. *J Bone Joint Surg Br*. 2000;82:881.

Scott SM, Janes PC, Stevens PM. Grice subtalar arthrodesis followed to skeletal maturity. *J Pediatr Orthop*. 1988;8:176–183.

Scranton PE Jr, Zuckerman JD. Bunion surgery in adolescents: results of surgical treatment. *J Pediatr Orthop*. 1984;4:39–43.

Scranton PE Jr. Treatment of symptomatic talocalcaneal coalition. *J Bone Joint Surg Am*. 1987;69:533–539.

Segev E, Ezra E, Yaniv M, et al. V osteotomy and Ilizarov technique for residual idiopathic or neurogenic clubfeet. *J Orthop Surg*. 2008;16:215–219.

Seymour N. The late results of naviculo-cuneiform fusion. *J Bone Joint Surg Br*. 1967;49:558–559.

Silver CM, Simon SD, Litchman HM. Long term follow-up observations on calcaneal osteotomy. *Clin Orthop Relat Res*. 1974;99:181–187.

Silver D. The operative treatment of hallux valgus. *J Bone Joint Surg*. 1923;5:225–232.

Smith JB, Westin GW. Subtalar extra-articular arthrodesis. *J Bone Joint Surg Am*. 1968;50:1027–1035.

Solly S. Case of double talipes varus in which the cuboid bone was partially removed from the left foot. *Med Chir Trans*. 1857;40:119.

Southwell RB, Sherman FC. Triple arthrodesis: a long-term study with force plate analysis. *Foot Ankle*. 1981;2:15–24.

Sponsel KH. Bunionette correction by metatarsal osteotomy. *Orthop Clin North Am*. 1976;7:809.

Stevens PM, Belle RM. Screw epiphysiodesis for ankle valgus. *J Pediatr Orthop*. 1997;17:9–12.

Stevens PM, Otis S. Ankle valgus and clubfeet. *J Pediatr Orthop*. 1999;19:515–517.

Steytler JC, van der Walt ID. Correction of resistant adduction of the forefoot in congenital club-foot and congenital metatarsus varus by metatarsal osteotomy. *Br J Surg*. 1966;53:558–560.

Swanson AB, Braune HS, Coleman JA. The cavus foot concept of production and treatment by metatarsal osteotomy. *J Bone Joint Surg Am*. 1966;48-A:1019.

Swiontkowski MF, Scranton PE, Hansen S. Tarsal coalitions: long-term results of surgical treatment. *J Pediatr Orthop*. 1983;3:287–292.

Tenuta J, Shelton YA, Miller F. Long-term followup of triple arthrodesis in patients with cerebral palsy. *J Pediatr Orthop*. 1993;13:713–716.

Topoleski TA, Ganel A, Grogan DP. Effect of proximal phalangeal epiphysiodesis in the treatment of macrodactyly. *Foot Ankle Int*. 1997;18:500–503.

Turra S, Santini S, Cagnoni G. Gigantism of the foot: our experience in seven cases. *J Pediatr Orthop*. 1998;18:337–345.

Veitch JM. Evaluation of the Kidner procedure in treatment of symptomatic accessory tarsal scaphoid. *Clin Orthop Relat Res*. 1978;131:210–213.

Viegas GV. Reconstruction of the pediatric flexible planovalgus foot by using an Evans calcaneal osteotomy and augmentative medial split tibialis anterior tendon transfer. *J Foot Ankle Surg*. 2003;42:199–207.

Wallander H, Hansson G, Tjernstrom B. Correction of persistent clubfoot deformities with the Ilizarov external fixator. Experience in 10 previously operated feet followed for 2–5 years. *Acta Orthop Scand*. 1996;67:283–287.

Ward CM, Dolan LA, Bennett DL, et al. Long-term results of reconstruction for treatment of a flexible cavovarus foot in Charcot-Marie-Tooth disease. *J Bone Joint Surg Am*. 2008;90:2631–2642.

Watanabe RS. Metatarsal osteotomy for the cavus foot. *Clin Orthop Relat Res*. 1990;252:217–230.

Wei SY, Sullivan RJ, Davidson RS. Talo-navicular arthrodesis for residual midfoot deformities of a previously corrected clubfoot. *Foot Ankle Int*. 2000;21:482–485.

Wetmore RS, Drennan JC. Long-term results of triple arthrodesis in Charcot-Marie-Tooth disease. *J Bone Joint Surg Am*. 1989;71(3):417–422.

Wicart P, Seringe R. Plantar opening-wedge osteotomy of cuneiform bones combined with selective plantar release and Dwyer osteotomy for pes cavovarus in children. *J Pediatr Orthop*. 2006;26:100–108.

Wilcox PG, Weiner DS. The Akron midtarsal dome osteotomy in the treatment of rigid pes cavus: a preliminary review. *J Pediatr Orthop*. 1985;5:333–338.

Wilde PH, Torode IP, Dickens DR, et al. Resection for symptomatic talocalcaneal coalition. *J Bone Joint Surg Br*. 1994;76:797–801.

Williams PF, Menelaus MB. Triple arthrodesis by inlay grafting: a method suitable for the undeformed or valgus foot. *J Bone Joint Surg Br*. 1977;59B:333–336.

Wilson JN. Oblique displacement osteotomy for hallux valgus. *J Bone Joint Surg Br*. 1963;45:552–556.

Wu WL, Huang PJ, Lin CJ, et al. Lower extremity kinematics and kinetics during level walking and stair climbing in subjects with triple arthrodesis or subtalar fusion. *Gait Posture*. 2005;21:263–270.

Wukich DK, Bowen JR. A long-term study of triple arthrodesis for correction of pes cavovarus in Charcot-Marie-Tooth disease. *J Pediatr Orthop*. 1989;9:433–437.

Yoo WJ, Chung CY, Choi IH, et al. Calcaneal lengthening for the planovalgus foot deformity in children with cerebral palsy. *J Pediatr Orthop*. 2005;25:781–785.

Zeifang F, Breusch SJ, Döderlein L. Evans calcaneal lengthening procedure for spastic flexible flatfoot in 32 patients (46 feet) with a followup of 3 to 9 years. *Foot Ankle Int*. 2006;27:500–507.

Zimmer TJ, Johnson KA, Klassen RA. Treatment of hallux valgus in adolescents by the chevron osteotomy. *Foot Ankle*. 1989;9:190–193.

Cavus Foot

Aktas S, Sussman MD. The radiological analysis of pes cavus deformity in Charcot Marie Tooth disease. *J Pediatr Orthop B*. 2000;9:137–140.

Alexander IJ, Johnson KA. Assessment and management of pes cavus in Charcot-Marie-Tooth disease. *Clin Orthop Relat Res*. 1989;246:273–281.

Brewerton DA, Sandifer PH, Sweetnam DR. "Idiopathic" pes cavus: an investigation into its aetiology. *Br Med J*. 1963;5358:659–661.

Coleman SS, Chesnut WJ. A simple test for hindfoot flexibility in the cavovarus foot. *Clin Orthop Relat Res*. 1977;123:60–62.

Holmes JR, Hansen ST Jr. Foot and ankle manifestations of Charcot-Marie-Tooth disease. *Foot Ankle*. 1993;14:476–486.

Fuller JE, Deluca PA. Acetabular dysplasia and Charcot-Marie-Tooth Disease in a family: a report of four cases. *J Bone Joint Surg Am*. 1995;77:1087–1091.

Levitt RL, Canale ST, Cooke AJ Jr, et al. The role of foot surgery in progressive neuromuscular disorders in children. *J Bone Joint Surg Am*. 1973;55:1396–1410.

Mann RA, Missirian J. Pathophysiology of Charcot-Marie-Tooth disease. *Clin Orthop Relat Res*. 1988;234:221–228.

Meary R. On the measurement of the angle between the talus and the first metatarsal. Symposium: Le Pied Creux Essential. *Rev Chir Orthop*. 1967;53:389.

Mosca VS. The cavus foot [editorial]. *J Pediatr Orthop*. 2001; 21:423–424.

Nagai MK, Chan G, Guille J, et al. Prevalence of Charcot-Marie-Tooth disease in patients who have bilateral cavovarus feet. *J Pediatr Orthop*. 2006;26:438–443.

Olney B. Treatment of the cavus foot: deformity in the pediatric patient with Charcot-Marie-Tooth. *Foot Ankle Clin*. 2000;5:305–315.

Paulos L, Coleman SS, Samuelson KM. Pes cavovarus: review of a surgical approach using selective soft-tissue procedures. *J Bone Joint Surg Am*. 1980;62:942–953.

Price BD, Price CT. A simple demonstration of hindfoot flexibility in the cavovarus foot. *J Pediatr Orthop*. 1997;17:18–19.

Sabir M, Lyttle D. Pathogenesis of pes cavus in Charcot-Marie-Tooth disease. *Clin Orthop Relat Res*. 1983;175:173–178.

Samilson RL, Dillin W. Cavus, cavovarus, and calcaneocavus an update. *Clin Orthop Relat Res*. 1983;177:125–132.

Schwend RM, Drennan JC. Cavus foot deformity in children. *J Am Acad Orthop Surg*. 2003;11:201–211.

Tynan M, Klenerman L, Helliwell T, et al. Investigation of muscle imbalance in the leg in symptomatic forefoot pes cavus: a multidisciplinary study [published erratum appears in *Foot Ankle*. 1993;14(3):179]. *Foot Ankle*. 1992;13:489.

Walker JL, Nelson KR, Heavilon JA, et al. Hip abnormalities in children with Charcot-Marie-Tooth disease. *J Pediatr Orthop*. 1994;14:54–59.

Clubfoot

Bakalis S, Sairam S, Homfray T, et al. Outcome of antenatally diagnosed talipes equinovarus in an unselected obstetric population. *Ultrasound Obstet Gynecol.* 2002;20:226–229.

Beatson TR, Pearson JR. A method of assessing correction in club feet. *J Bone Joint Surg Br.* 1966;48:40–50.

Bensahel H, Catterall A, Dimeglio A. Practical applications in idiopathic clubfoot: a retrospective multicentric study in EPOS. *J Pediatr Orthop.* 1990;10:186.

Bensahel H, Guillaume A, Czukonyi Z, et al. Results of physical therapy for idiopathic clubfoot: a long-term follow-up study. *J Pediatr Orthop.* 1990;10:189–192.

Carroll NC, McMurtry R, Leete SF. The pathoanatomy of congenital clubfoot. *Orthop Clin North Am.* 1978;9:225–232.

Chou DT, Ramachandran M. Prevalence of developmental dysplasia of the hip in children with clubfoot. *J Child orthop.* 2013;7:263–267.

Cooper DM, Dietz FR. Treatment of idiopathic clubfoot: a thirty-year follow-up note. *J Bone Joint Surg Am.* 1995;77:1477–1489.

Coss HS, Hennrikus WL. Parent satisfaction comparing two bandage materials used during serial casting in infants. *Foot Ankle Int.* 1996;17:483–486.

Cowell HR, Wein BK. Genetic aspects of club foot. *J Bone Joint Surg Am.* 1980;62:1381–1384.

Cuevas de Alba C, Guille JT, Bowen JR, et al. Computed tomography for femoral and tibial torsion in children with clubfoot. *Clin Orthop Relat Res.* 1998;353:203–209.

DePuy J, Drennan J. Correction of idiopathic clubfoot: a comparison of results of early versus delayed posteromedial release. *J Pediatr Orthop.* 1989;9:44–48.

Dietz F. The genetics of idiopathic clubfoot. *Clin Orthop Relat Res.* 2002;401:39.

Dimeglio A, Bensahel H, Souchet P, et al. Classification of clubfoot. *J Pediatr Orthop B.* 1995;4:129–136.

Dimeglio A, Bonnet F, Mazeau P, et al. Orthopaedic treatment and passive motion machine: consequences for the surgical treatment of clubfoot. *J Pediatr Orthop B.* 1996;5:173–180.

Dobbs MB, Corley CL, Morcuende JA, et al. Late recurrence of clubfoot deformity: a 45-year followup. *Clin Orthop Relat Res.* 2003;411:188–192.

Dobbs MB, Gordon JE, Walton T, et al. Bleeding complications following percutaneous tendoachilles tenotomy in the treatment of clubfoot deformity. *J Pediatr Orthop.* 2004;24:353.

Dobbs MB, Nunley R, Schoenecker PL. Long-term follow-up of patients with clubfeet treated with extensive soft-tissue release. *J Bone Joint Surg Am.* 2006;88:986–996.

Dobbs MB, Rudzki JR, Purcell DB, et al. Factors predictive of outcome after use of the Ponseti method for treatment of idiopathic clubfeet. *J Bone Joint Surg Am.* 2004;86:22.

Epeldegui T, Delgado E. Acetabulum pedis, part I: talocalcaneonavicular joint socket in normal foot. *J Pediatr Orthop B.* 1995;4:1–10.

Epeldegui T, Delgado E. Acetabulum pedis, part II: talocalcaneonavicular joint socket in clubfoot. *J Pediatr Orthop B.* 1995;4:11–16.

Feldbrin Z, Gilai AN, Ezra E, et al. Muscle imbalance in the aetiology of idiopathic club foot. An electromyographic study. *J Bone Joint Surg Br.* 1995;77:596–601.

Flynn JM, Donohoe M, Mackenzie WG. An independent assessment of two clubfoot-classification systems. *J Pediatr Orthop.* 1998;18:323–327.

Goldner JL, Fitch RD. Classification and evaluation of congenital talipes equinovarus. In: Simons GW, ed. *The Clubfoot.* New York, NY: Springer-Verlag; 1993.

Grayhack J, Zawin J, Shore R, et al. Assessment of calcaneocuboid joint deformity by magnetic resonance imaging in talipes equinovarus. *J Pediatr Orthop B.* 1995;4:36–38.

Haasbeek J, Wright J. A comparison of the long-term results of posterior and comprehensive release in the treatment of clubfoot. *J Pediatr Orthop.* 1997;17:29–35.

Hamel J, Becker W. Sonographic assessment of clubfoot deformity in young children. *J Pediatr Orthop B.* 1996;5:279–286.

Hattori T, Ono Y, Kitakoji T, et al. Effect of the Denis Browne splint in conservative treatment of congenital club foot. *J Pediatr Orthop B.* 2003;12:59–62.

Herzenberg J, Carroll N, Christofersen M, et al. Clubfoot analysis with three-dimensional computer modeling. *J Pediatr Orthop.* 1988;8:257–262.

Herzenberg JE, Radler C, Bor N. Ponseti versus traditional methods of casting for idiopathic clubfoot. *J Pediatr Orthop.* 2002;22:517–521.

Honein MA, Paulozzi LJ, Moore CA. Family history, maternal smoking, and clubfoot: an indication of a gene-environment interaction. *Am J Epidemiol.* 2000;152:658–665.

Howard C, Benson M. Clubfoot: its pathological anatomy. *J Pediatr Orthop.* 1993;13:654–659.

Howlett J, Mosca VS, Bjornson K. The association between idiopathic clubfoot and increased internal hip rotation. *Clin Orthop Relat Res.* 2009;467:1231–1237.

Hutchins PM, Rambicki D, Comacchio L, et al. Tibiofibular torsion in normal and treated clubfoot populations. *J Pediatr Orthop.* 1986;6:452–455.

Ippolito E, Ponseti IV. Congenital club foot in the human fetus: a histological study. *J Bone Joint Surg Am.* 1980;62:8–22.

Irani RN, Sherman MS. The pathological anatomy of idiopathic clubfoot. *Clin Orthop Relat Res.* 1972;84:14–20.

Isaacs H, Handelsman JE, Badenhorst M, et al. The muscles in club foot—a histological, histochemical and electron microscopic study. *J Bone Joint Surg Br.* 1977;59-B:465–472.

Karol LA, Concha MC, Johnston CE II. Gait analysis and muscle strength in children with surgically treated clubfeet. *J Pediatr Orthop.* 1997;17:790–795.

Karol LA, O'Brien SE, Wilson H, et al. Gait analysis in children with severe clubfeet: early results of physiotherapy versus surgical release. *J Pediatr Orthop.* 2005;25:236.

Kite J. *The Clubfoot.* New York, NY: Grune & Stratton; 1964.

Kite JH. Principles involved in the treatment of congenital clubfoot. *J Bone Joint Surg Am.* 2003;85(9):1847; discussion 1847.

Kuhns LR, Koujok K, Hall JM, et al. Ultrasound of the navicular during the simulated Ponseti maneuver. *J Pediatr Orthop.* 2003;23:243–245.

Kuo KN, Jansen LD. Rotatory dorsal subluxation of the navicular: a complication of clubfoot surgery. *J Pediatr Orthop.* 1998;18:770–774.

Laaveg SJ, Ponseti IV. Long-term results of treatment of congenital club foot. *J Bone Joint Surg Am.* 1980;62:23–31.

Lehman W, Atar D, Grant A, et al. Treatment of failed clubfoot surgery. *J Pediatr Orthop.* 1994;3:168–170.

Lehman WB, Mohaideen A, Madan S, et al. A method for the early evaluation of the Ponseti (Iowa) technique for the treatment of idiopathic clubfoot. *J Pediatr Orthop B.* 2003;12:133–140.

Little D, Aiona M. Limb length discrepancy in congenital talipes equinovarus. *Aust N Z J Surg.* 1995;65:409–411.

Lourenco AF, Morcuende JA. Correction of neglected idiopathic club foot by the Ponseti method. *J Bone Joint Surg Br.* 2007;89:378–381.

Lovell WW, Bailey T, Price CT, et al. The nonoperative management of the congenital clubfoot. *Orthop Rev.* 1979;8:113–115.

Mahan ST, Yazdy MM, Kasser JR, Werler MM. It is worthwhile to routinely ultrasound screen children with idiopathic clubfoot for hip dysplasia? *J pediatr Orthop.* 2013;33:847–851.

Malone FD, Marino T, Bianchi DW, et al. Isolated clubfoot diagnosed prenatally: is karyotyping indicated? *Obstet Gynecol.* 2000;95: 437–440.

McKay D. New concept of and approach to clubfoot treatment, Section I: principles and morbid anatomy. *J Pediatr Orthop.* 1982; 2:347–356.

McKay D. New concept of and approach to clubfoot treatment, Section III: Evaluation and results. *J Pediatr Orthop.* 1983;3:141–148.

Morcuende JA, Weinstein S, Dietz F, et al. Plaster cast treatment of clubfoot: the Ponseti method of manipulation and casting. *J Pediatr Orthop B.* 1994;3:161.

Napiontek M. Intraoperative ultrasound for evaluation of reduction in congenital talipes equinovarus. *J Pediatr Orthop B.* 1995;4: 55–57.

Olshan AF, Schroeder JC, Alderman BW, et al. Joint laxity and the risk of clubfoot. *Birth Defects Res A Clin Mol Teratol.* 2003;67:585–590.

Paton RW, Choudry Q. Neonatal foot deformities and their relationship to developmental dysplasia of the hip. *J Bone Joint Surg Br.* 2009;91:655–658.

Pirani S. *A Reliable and Valid method of Assessing the Amount of Deformity in the Congenital Clubfoot.* St. Louis, MO: Pediatric Orthopaedic Society of North America; 2004.

Pirani S, Zeznik L, Hodges D. Magnetic resonance imaging study of the congenital clubfoot treated with the Ponseti method. *J Pediatr Orthop.* 2001;21:719–726.

Ponseti IV. *Congenital Clubfoot: Fundamentals of Treatment.* Oxford: Oxford University Press; 1996.

Ponseti IV. Treatment of congenital club foot. *J Bone Joint Surg Am.* 1992;74:448–454.

Ponseti IV, Smoley EN. Congenital clubfoot: the results of treatment. *J Bone Joint Surg Am.* 1963;45:2261–2275.

Pous JG, Dimeglio A. Neonatal surgery in clubfoot. *Orthop Clin North Am.* 1978;9:233–240.

Rebbeck TR, Dietz FR, Murray JC, et al. A single-gene explanation for the probability of having idiopathic talipes equinovarus. *Am J Hum Genet.* 1993;53:1051–1063.

Richards BS, Faulks S, Rathjen KE, et al. A comparison of two nonoperative methods of idiopathic clubfoot correction: the Ponseti method and the French functional physiotherapy method. *J Bone Joint Surg Am.* 2008;90:2313–2321.

Richards BS, Wilson H, Johnston CE, et al. Nonoperative clubfoot treatment using the French method: comparing clinical outcome with radiographs. In: *Pediatric Orthopaedic Society of North America 2001 Annual Meeting.* Rosemont, IL: Pediatric Orthopaedic Society of North America; 2001:142.

Rijhsinghani A, Yankowitz J, Kanis AB, et al. Antenatal sonographic diagnosis of club foot with particular attention to the implications and outcomes of isolated club foot. *Ultrasound Obstet Gynecol.* 1998;2:103–106.

Ryoppy S, Sairanen H. Neonatal operative treatment of club foot: a preliminary report. *J Bone Joint Surg Br.* 1983;65:320–325.

Scarpa A. *A Memoir on the Congenital Club Feet of Children, and of the Mode of Correcting that Deformity.* Edinburgh: Archibald Constable; 1818:8–15. Translated by Wishart JH. *Clin Orthop Relat Res.* 1994;308:4–7.

Shipp TD, Benacerraf BR. The significance of prenatally identified isolated clubfoot: is amniocentesis indicated? *Am J Obstet Gynecol.* 1998;178:600–602.

Skelly AC, Holt VL, Mosca VS, et al. Talipes equinovarus and maternal smoking: a population-based case-control study in Washington state. *Teratology.* 2002;66:91–100.

Spiegel DA, Loder RT. Leg-length discrepancy and bone age in unilateral idiopathic talipes equinovarus. *J Pediatr Orthop.* 2003;23:246–250.

Staheli LT. *Clubfoot: Ponseti Management.* 3rd ed. Global-HELP Publications, 2009. www.global-help.org.

Tibrewal S, Benson M, Howard C, et al. The Oxford club-foot programme. *J Bone Joint Surg Br.* 1992;74:528–533.

Tillett RL, Fisk NM, Murphy K, et al. Clinical outcome of congenital talipes equinovarus diagnosed antenatally by ultrasound. *J Bone Joint Surg Br.* 2000;82:876–880.

Tolat V, Boothroyd A, Carty H, et al. Ultrasound: a helpful guide in the treatment of congenital talipes equinovarus. *J Pediatr Orthop B.* 1995;4:65–70.

Treadwell MC, Stanitski CL, King M. Prenatal sonographic diagnosis of clubfoot: implications for patient counseling. *J Pediatr Orthop.* 1999;19:8–10.

Van Campenhout A, Molenaers G, Moens P, et al. Does functional treatment of idiopathic clubfoot reduce the indication for surgery? Call for a widely accepted rating system. *J Pediatr Orthop B.* 2001;10:315–318.

Wainwright AM, Auld T, Benson MK, et al. The classification of congenital talipes equinovarus. *J Bone Joint Surg Br.* 2002;84:1020–1024.

Waisbrod H. Congenital club foot: an anatomical study. *J Bone Joint Surg Br.* 1973;55:796–801.

Westberry DE, Davids JR, Pugh LI. Clubfoot and developmental dysplasia of the hip: value of screening hip radiographs in children with clubfoot. *J Pediatr Orthop.* 2003;23:503–507.

Wynne-Davies R. Family studies and the cause of congenital club foot: talipes equinovarus, talipes calcaneo-valgus and metatarsus varus. *J Bone Joint Surg Br.* 1964;46:445–463.

Wynne-Davies R. Genetic and environmental factors in the etiology of talipes equinovarus. *Clin Orthop Relat Res.* 1972;84:9–13.

Congenital Vertical Talus

Aroojis AJ, King MM, Donohoe M, et al. Congenital vertical talus in arthrogryposis and other contractural syndromes. *Clin Orthop Relat Res.* 2005;434:26.

Dobbs MB, Purcell DB, Nunley R, et al. Early results of a new method of treatment for idiopathic congenital vertical talus. *J Bone Joint Surg Am.* 2006;88:1192–1200.

Dobbs MB, Schoenecker PL, Gordon JE. Autosomal dominant transmission of isolated congenital vertical talus. *Iowa Orthop J.* 2002;22:25.

Dodge LD, Ashley RK, Gilbert RJ. Treatment of the congenital vertical talus: a retrospective review of 36 feet with long-term follow-up. *Foot Ankle.* 1987;7:326–332.

Drennan JC, Sharrard WJ. The pathological anatomy of convex pes valgus. *J Bone Joint Surg Br.* 1971;53:455–461.

Duncan RD, Fixsen JA. Congenital convex pes valgus. *J Bone Joint Surg Br.* 1999;81:250–254.

Hamanishi C. Congenital vertical talus: classification with 69 cases and new measurement system. *J Pediatr Orthop.* 1984;4:318–326.

Herndon CH, Heyman CH. Problems in the recognition and treatment of congenital pes valgus. *J Bone Joint Surg Am.* 1963;45:413–429.

Jacobsen ST, Crawford AH. Congenital vertical talus. *J Pediatr Orthop.* 1983;3:306–310.

Kumar SJ, Cowell HR, Ramsey PL. Vertical and oblique talus. *Instr Course Lect.* 1982;31:235–251.

Lamy L, Weissman L. Congenital convex pes valgus. *J Bone Joint Surg Am.* 1939;21:79–91.

Lloyd-Roberts GC, Spence AJ. Congenital vertical talus. *J Bone Joint Surg Br.* 1958;40-B:33–41.

Ogata K, Schoenecker PL, Sheridan J. Congenital vertical talus and its familial occurrence: an analysis of 36 patients. *Clin Orthop Relat Res.* 1979;139:128–132.

Patterson WR, Fitz DA, Smith WS. The pathologic anatomy of congenital convex pes valgus: post mortem study of a newborn infant with bilateral involvement. *J Bone Joint Surg Am.* 1968;50:458–466.

Specht EE. Congenital paralytic vertical talus: an anatomical study. *J Bone Joint Surg Am.* 1975;57:842–847.

Stern HJ, Clark RD, Stroberg AJ, et al. Autosomal dominant transmission of isolated congenital vertical talus. *Clin Genet.* 1989;36:427–430.

Flatfoot

Arangio GA, Chopra V, Voloshin A, et al. A biomechanical analysis of the effect of lateral column lengthening calcaneal osteotomy on the flat foot. *Clin Biomech.* 2007;22:472–477.

Bleck EE, Berzins UJ. Conservative management of pes valgus with plantar flexed talus, flexible. *Clin Orthop Relat Res.* 1977;122:85–94.

Bordin D, De Giorgi G, Mazzocco G, et al. Flat and cavus foot, indexes of obesity and overweight in a population of primary-school children. *Minerva Pediatr.* 2001;53:7–13.

Dowling AM, Stelle JR, Baur LA. Does obesity influence foot structure and plantar pressure patterns in prepubescent children? *Int J Obesity.* 2001;25:845–852.

Driano AN, Staheli L, Staheli LT. Psychosocial development and corrective shoewear use in childhood. *J Pediatr Orthop.* 1998;18:346–349.

DuMontier TA, Falicov A, Mosca V, et al. Calcaneal lengthening: investigation of deformity correction in a flatfoot model. *Foot Ankle Int.* 2005;26:166–170.

Echarri JJ, Forriol F. The development in footprint morphology in 1851 Congolese children from urban and rural areas, and the relationship between this and wearing shoes. *J Ped Orthop.* 2003;12:141–146.

Evans AM, Rome K. A Cochrane review of the evidence for non-surgical interventions for flexible pediatric flat feet. *Eur J Phys Rehabil Med.* 2011;47:69–89.

Garcia-Rodriguez A, Martin-Jimenez F, Carnero-Varo M, et al. Flexible flat feet in children: a real problem? *Pediatrics.* 1999;103:e84.

Giladi M, Milgrom C, Stein M, et al. The low arch: a protective in stress fractures. *Orthop Rev.* 1985;14:81–85.

Gould N, Moreland M, Alvarez R, et al. Development of the child's arch. *Foot Ankle.* 1989;9:241–245.

Harris RI, Beath T. *Army Foot Survey: An Investigation of Foot Ailments in Canadian Soldiers.* Ottawa, ON: National Research Council of Canada; 1947.

Harris RI, Beath T. Hypermobile flatfoot with the short tendo Achillis. *J Bone Joint Surg Am.* 1948;30:116.

Husain ZS, Fallat LM. Biomechanical analysis of Maxwell-Brancheau Arthroereisis implants. *J Foot Ankle Surg.* 2002;41:352–358.

Kuwada GT, Dockery GL. Complications following traumatic incidents with STA-peg procedures. *J Foot Surg.* 1988;27:236.

Lanham RH Jr. Indications and complications of arthroereisis in hypermobile flatfoot. *J Am Podiatr Assoc.* 1979;69:178.

Larsen B, Reimann I, Becker-Andersen H. Congenital calcaneovalgus: with special reference to treatment and its relation to other congenital foot deformities. *Acta Orthop Scand.* 1974;45:145–151.

LeLievre J. Current concepts and correction in the valgus foot. *Clin Orthop Relat Res.* 1970;70:43–55.

Lin CJ, Lai KA, Kuan TS, et al. Correlating factors and clinical significance of flexible flatfoot in preschool children. *J Pediatr Orthop.* 2001;21:378–382.

MacKenzie A, Rome K, Evans AM. The efficacy of nonsurgical interventions for pediatric flexible flat foot: a critical review. *J Pediatr Orthop.* 2012;32(8):830–834.

Miller CD, Laskowski ER, Suman VJ. Effect of corrective rearfoot orthotic devices on ground reaction forces during ambulation. *Mayo Clin Proc.* 1996;71:757–762.

Mosca VS. Flexible flatfoot and skewfoot. In: Drennan JC, ed. *The Child's Foot and Ankle.* New York, NY: Raven Press; 1992:355.

Mosca VS. Calcaneal lengthening for valgus deformity of the hindfoot. Results in children who had severe, symptomatic flatfoot and skewfoot. *J Bone Joint Surg Am.* 1995;77:500–512.

Mosca VS. Flexible flatfoot and skewfoot. *Instr Course Lect.* 1996;45:347–354.

Mosca VS. Flexible flatfoot and skewfoot. In: McCarthy J, Drennan JC, eds. *The Child's Foot and Ankle.* 2nd ed. Philadelphia, PA: Lippincott Williams & Wilkins; 2009:136–159.

Mosca VS. Letter to the JPO editors re: article by Ragab AA, et al. entitled "Implications of subtalar joint anatomic variation in calcaneal lengthening osteotomy" (*J Pediatr Orthop.* 2003;23:79–83). *J Pediatr Orthop.* 2009;29:315–316.

Mosca VS. Flexible flatfoot in children and adolescents. *J Child Orthop.* 2010;4:107–121.

Needleman RL. Current topic review: subtalar arthroereisis for the correction of flexible flatfoot. *Foot Ankle Int.* 2005;26:336–346.

Oeffinger DJ, Pectol RW, Tylkowski CM. Foot pressure and radiographic outcome measures of lateral column lengthening for pes planovalgus deformity. *Gait Posture.* 2000;12:189–195.

Oloff LM, Naylor BL, Jacobs AM. Complications of subtalar arthroereisis. *J Foot Ankle Surg.* 1987;26:136–140.

Park KB, Park HW, Lee KS, et al. Changes in dynamic foot pressure after surgical treatment of valgus deformity of the hindfoot in cerebral palsy. *J Bone Joint Surg Am.* 2008;90:1712–1721.

Penneau K, Lutter LD, Winter RD. Pes planus: radiographic changes with foot orthoses and shoes. *Foot Ankle.* 1982;2:299–303.

Pfeiffer M, Kotz R, Ledl T, et al. Prevalence of flat foot in preschool-aged children. *Pediatrics.* 2006;118:634–639.

Ragab AA, Stewart SL, Cooperman DR. Implications of subtalar joint anatomic variation in calcaneal lengthening osteotomy. *J Pediatr Orthop.* 2003;23:79–83.

Rao UB, Joseph B. The influence of footwear on the prevalence of flat foot. A survey of 2300 children. *J Bone Joint Surg Br.* 1992;74:525–527.

Sachithanandam V, Joseph B. The influence of footwear on the prevalence of flat foot. A survey of 1846 skeletally mature persons. *J Bone Joint Surg Br.* 1995;77:254.

Scranton PE, Goldner JL, Lutter LD, et al. Management of hypermobile flatfoot in the child. *Contemp Orthop.* 1981;3:645–663.

Sim-Fook L, Hodgson AR. A comparison of foot forms among the non-shoe and shoe-wearing Chinese population. *J Bone Joint Surg Am.* 1958;40(5):1058–1062.

Staheli LT, Chew DE, Corbett M. The longitudinal arch: a survey of eight hundred and eighty-two feet in normal children and adults. *J Bone Joint Surg Am*. 1987;69:426–428.

Theologis TN, Gordon C, Benson MK. Heel seats and shoe wear. *J Pediatr Orthop*. 1994;14:760–762.

Vanderwilde R, Staheli LT, Chew DE, et al. Measurements on radiographs of the foot in normal infants and children. *J Bone Joint Surg Am*. 1988;70:407–415.

Wenger DR, Mauldin D, Speck G, et al. Corrective shoes and inserts as treatment for flexible flatfoot in infants and children. *J Bone Joint Surg Am*. 1989;71:800–810.

General/Biomechanics

Basmajian JV, Stecko G. The role of muscles in arch support of the foot. *J Bone Joint Surg Am*. 1963;45:1184–1190.

Close JR, Inman VT, Poor PM, et al. The function of the subtalar joint. *Clin Orthop Relat Res*. 1967;50:159–179.

Cowan DN, Jones BH, Robinson JR. Foot morphologic characteristics and risk of exercise-related injury. *Arch Fam Med*. 1993;2:773–777.

Davids JR, Gibson TW, Ugh LL. Quantitative segmental analysis of weight-bearing radiographs of the foot and ankle for children: normal alignment. *J Pediatr Orthop*. 2005;25:769–776.

Duchenne G. *Physiology of Motion*. Philadelphia, PA: WB Saunders; 1959.

Elftman H. The transverse tarsal joint and its control. *Clin Orthop Relat Res*. 1960;16:41–46.

Hicks JH. The mechanics of the foot, II: the plantar aponeurosis and the arch. *J Anat*. 1954;88:25–39.

Inman VT. *The Joints of the Ankle*. Baltimore, MD: Lippincott Williams & Wilkins; 1976.

Jones RL. The human foot: an experimental study of its muscles and ligaments in the support of the arch. *Am J Anat*. 1941;68:1.

Kanatli U, Yetkin H, Cila E. Footprint and radiographic analysis of the feet. *J Pediatr Orthop*. 2001;21:225–228.

Kaufman KR, Brodine SK, Shaffer RA, et al. The effect of foot structure and range of motion on musculoskeletal overuse injuries. *Am J Sports Med*. 1999;27:585–593.

Kelikian AS. *Sarrafian's Anatomy of the Foot and Ankle*. 3rd ed. Philadelphia, PA: Lippincott Williams & Wilkins; 2011.

Mann R, Inman VT. Phasic activity of intrinsic muscles of the foot. *J Bone Joint Surg Am*. 1964;46:469–481.

Mann RA. Biomechanics of the foot and ankle. In: Mann RA, ed. *Surgery of the Foot*. St. Louis, MO: CV Mosby; 1986:1–30.

Manter JT. Movements of the subtalar and transverse tarsal joints. *Anat Rec*. 1941;80:397–410.

Mosca VS. The child's foot: principles of management [editorial]. *J Pediatr Orthop*. 1998;18:281–282.

Mosca VS. The foot In: Weinstein SL, Flynn JM, editors. *Lovell & Winters Pediatric Orthopaedics*, 7th edition. Philadelphia, PA: Lippincott Williams & Wilkins; 2013:1425–1562.

Paley D. *Principles of Deformity Correction*. Berlin: Springer-Verlag; 2002.

Reimers J, Pedersen B, Brodersen A. Foot deformity and the length of the triceps surae in Danish children between 3 and 17 years old. *J Pediatr Orthop B*. 1995;4:71–73.

Salenius P, Vankka E. The development of the tibiofemoral angle in children. *J Bone Joint Surg Am*. 1975;57:259–261.

Scarpa A. *A Memoir on the Congenital Club Feet of Children, and of the Mode of Correcting that Deformity*. Edinburgh: Archibald Constable; 1818:8–15. Translated by Wishart JH. *Clin Orthop Relat Res*. 1994;308:4–7.

Staheli LT, Chew DE, Corbett M. The longitudinal arch: a survey of eight hundred and eighty-two feet in normal children and adults. *J Bone Joint Surg Am*. 1987;69:426–428.

Staheli LT, Corbett M, Wyss C, et al. Lower-extremity rotational problems in children: normal values to guide management. *J Bone Joint Surg Am*. 1985;67:39–47.

Vanderwilde R, Staheli LT, Chew DE, et al. Measurements on radiographs of the foot in normal infants and children. *J Bone Joint Surg Am*. 1988;70:407–415.

Vining NC, Warme WJ, Mosca VS. Comparison of structural bone autografts and allografts in pediatric foot surgery. *J Pediatr Orthop*. 2012;332(7):719–723.

White WJ. Torsion of the Achilles tendon: its surgical significance. *Arch Surg Am*. 1943;46:784.

Wulker N, Stukenborg C, Savory KM. Hindfoot motion after isolated and combined arthrodeses: measurements in anatomic specimens. *Foot Ankle Int*. 2000;21:921–927.

Wynne-Davies R. Family studies and the cause of congenital clubfoot, talipes equinovarus, talipes calcaneovalgus and metatarsus varus. *J Bone Joint Surg Br*. 1964;46–445.

Wynne-Davies R, Littlejohn A, Gormley J. Aetiology and interrelationship of some common skeletal deformities. (Talipes equinovarus and calcaneovalgus, metatarsus varus, congenital dislocation of the hip, and infantile idiopathic scoliosis). *J Med Genet*. 1982;19:321–328.

Juvenile Hallux Valgus

Antrobus J. The primary deformity in hallux valgus and metatarsus primus varus. *Clin Orthop Relat Res*. 1984;184:251–255.

Bonney G, Macnab I. Hallux valgus and hallux rigidus: a critical survey of operative results. *J Bone Joint Surg Br*. 1952;34-B:366–385.

Coughlin M. Juvenile hallux valgus. In: Coughlin M, Mann R, eds. *Surgery of the Foot and Ankle*. 7th ed. St Louis, MO: Mosby; 1999:270.

Coughlin MJ. Roger A. Mann award. Juvenile hallux valgus: etiology and treatment. *Foot Ankle Int*. 1995;16:682–697.

Durman D. Metatarsus primus varus and hallux valgus. *Arch Surg*. 1957;74:128–135.

Goldner JL. Hallux valgus and hallux flexus associated with cerebral palsy: analysis and treatment. *Clin Orthop Relat Res*. 1981;157:98–104.

Goldner JL, Gaines RW. Adult and juvenile hallux valgus: analysis and treatment. *Orthop Clin North Am*. 1976;7:863–887.

Groiso JA. Juvenile hallux valgus: conservative approach to treatment. *J Bone Joint Surg Am*. 1992;74:1367–1374.

Holstein A. Hallux valgus—an acquired deformity of the foot in cerebral palsy. *Foot Ankle*. 1980;1:33–38.

Inman VT. Hallux valgus: a review of etiologic factors. *Orthop Clin North Am*. 1974;5:59–66.

Jones A. Hallux valgus in the adolescent. *Proc R Soc Med*. 1948:392.

Kalen V, Brecher A. Relationship between adolescent bunions and flatfeet. *Foot Ankle*. 1988;8:331.

Kilmartin TE, Barrington RL, Wallace WA. A controlled prospective trial of a foot orthosis for juvenile hallux valgus. *J Bone Joint Surg Br*. 1994;76:210–214.

Kilmartin TE, Wallace WA. The significance of pes planus in juvenile hallux valgus. *Foot Ankle*. 1992;13:53–56.

Price GF. Metatarsus primus varus: including various clinico-radiologic feautres of the female foot. *Clin Orthop Relat Res*. 1979;145:217–223.

Richardson EG. Complications after hallux valgus surgery. *Instr Course Lect*. 1999;48:331.

Richardson EG, Graves SC, McClure JT. First metatarsal head-shaft angle: a method of determination. *Foot Ankle*. 1993;14:181–185.

Shine IB. Incidence of hallux valgus in a partially shoe-wearing community. *Br Med J*. 1965;5451:1648–1650.

Simmonds FM, Menelaux MB. Hallux valgus in adolescents. *J Bone Joint Surg Br*. 1960;42:761.

Vittetoe DA, Saltzman CL, Krieg JC, et al. Validity and reliability of the first distal metatarsal articular angle. *Foot Ankle Int*. 1994;15:541–547.

Malformations

Ackland MK, Uhthoff HK. Idiopathic localized gigantism: a 26-year follow-up. *J Pediatr Orthop*. 1986;6:618.

Barsky A. Macrodactyly. *J Bone Joint Surg Am*. 1967;49:1255.

Blauth W, Borisch NC. Cleft feet: proposals for a new classification based on roentgenographic morphology. *Clin Orthop Relat Res*. 1990;258:41–48.

Chang CH, Kumar SJ, Riddle EC, et al. Macrodactyly of the foot. *J Bone Joint Surg Am*. 2002;84-A:1189–1194.

Chen SH, Huang SC, Wang JH. Macrodactyly of the feet and hands. *J Formos Med Assoc*. 1997;96:901–907.

DeCosta H, Hunter D. Magnetic resonance imaging in macrodactyly. *Br J Radiol*. 1996;69:1189–1194.

Dennyson WG, Bear JN, Bhoola KD. Macrodactyly in the foot. *J Bone Joint Surg Br*. 1977;59:355–359.

Farmer AW. Congenital hallux varus. *Am J Surg*. 1958;95:274–278.

Grogan DP, Bernstein RM, Habal MB, et al. Congenital lipofibromatosis associated with macrodactyly of the foot. *Foot Ankle*. 1991;12:40–46.

Kalen V, Burwell DS, Omer GE. Macrodactyly of the hands and feet. *J Pediatr Orthop*. 1988;8:311–315.

Mah J, Kasser J, Upton J. The foot in Apert syndrome. *Clin Plast Surg*. 1991;18:391–397.

McElvenny R. Hallux varus. *Q Bull Northwest Univ Med Sch*. 1941;15:277.

McMullen G. Pearson K. One the inheritance of the deformity known as split foot or lobster claw. *Biometrika*. 1913;9:381.

Mills JA, Menelaus MB. Hallux varus. *J Bone Joint Surg Br*. 1989;71:437–440.

Nogami H. Polydactyly and polysyndactyly of the fifth toe. *Clin Orthop Relat Res*. 1986;204:261–265.

Phelps DA, Grogan DP. Polydactyly of the foot. *J Pediatr Orthop*. 1985;5:446–451.

Stiles K, Pickard JS, Hereditary malformations of the hands and feet. *Plast Reconstr Surg*. 1943:627.

Venn-Watson EA. Problems in polydactyly of the foot. *Orthop Clin North Am*. 1976;7:909–927.

Walker JC, Clodius L. The syndromes of cleft lip, cleft palate, and lobsterclaw deformities of hands and feet. *Plast Reconstr Surg*. 963;32:627–636.

Woolf C, Myrianthopoulos N. Polydactyly in American Negroes and Whites. *Am J Hum Genet*. 1973;25:397.

Metatarsus Adductus/Skewfoot

Berg EE. A reappraisal of metatarsus adductus and skewfoot. *J Bone Joint Surg Am*. 1986;68:1185–1196.

Bleck EE. Developmental orthopaedics, III: toddlers. *Dev Med Child Neurol*. 1982;24:533.

Bleck EE. Metatarsus adductus: classification and relationship to outcomes of treatment. *J Pediatr Orthop*. 1983;3:2–9.

Browne RS, Paton DF. Anomalous insertion of the tibialis posterior tendon in congenital metatarsus varus. *J Bone Joint Surg Br*. 1979;61:74–76.

Cappello T, Mosca VS. Metatarsus adductus and skewfoot. *Foot Ankle Clin*. 1998;3:683–700.

Cook DA, Breed AL, Cook T, et al. Observer variability in the radiographic measurement and classification of metatarsus adductus. *J Pediatr Orthop*. 1992;12:86–89.

Farsetti P, Weinstein SL, Ponseti IV. The long-term functional and radiographic outcomes of untreated and non-operatively treated metatarsus adductus. *J Bone Joint Surg Am*. 1994;76:257–265.

Ghali NN, Abberton MJ, Silk FF. The management of metatarsus adductus et supinatus. *J Bone Joint Surg Br*. 1984;66:376–380.

Gruber MA, Lozano JA. Metatarsus varus and developmental dysplasia of the hip: is there a relationship? *Orthop Trans*. 1991;15:336.

Hunziker UA, Largo RH, Duc G. Neonatal metatarsus adductus, joint mobility, axis, and rotation of the lower extremity in preterm and term children 0–5 years of age. *Eur J Pediatr*. 1988;148:19–23.

Jacobs JE. Metatarsus varus and hip dysplasia. *Clin Orthop*. 1960;16:203–213.

Kite JH. Congenital metatarsus varus. *J Bone Joint Surg Am*. 1967;49:388–397.

Kite JH. Congenital metatarsus varus: report of 300 cases. *J Bone Joint Surg Am*. 1950;32(3):500–506.

Kollmer CE, Betz RR, Clancy M, et al. Relationship of congenital hip and foot deformities: a national Shriner's Hospital survey. *Orthop Trans*. 1991:96.

Kumar SJ, MacEwen GD. The incidence of hip dysplasia with metatarsus adductus. *Clin Orthop Relat Res*. 1982;164:234–235.

Lincoln CR, Wood KE, Bugg EI Jr. Metatarsus varus corrected by open wedge osteotomy of the first cuneiform bone. *Orthop Clin North Am*. 1976;7:795.

McCauley J Jr, Lusskin R, Bromley J. Recurrence in congenital metatarsus varus. *J Bone Joint Surg Am*. 1964;46:525–532.

McCormick DW, Blount WP. Metatarsus adductovarus: "skewfoot." *JAMA*. 1949;141:449.

Morcuende JA, Ponseti IV. Congenital metatarsus adductus in early human fetal development: a histologic study. *Clin Orthop Relat Res*. 1996;333:261–266.

Mosca VS. Flexible flatfoot and skewfoot. In: Drennan JC, ed. *The Child's Foot and Ankle*. New York, NY: Raven Press; 1992:355.

Mosca VS. Flexible flatfoot and skewfoot. In: McCarthy J, Drennan JC, eds. *The Child's Foot and Ankle*. 2nd ed. Philadelphia, PA: Lippincott Williams & Wilkins; 2009:136–159.

Mosca VS. Flexible flatfoot and skewfoot. *Instr Course Lect*. 1996;45:347–354.

Peabody CW, Muro F. Congenital metatarsus varus. *J Bone Joint Surg Am*. 1933;15A:171.

Ponseti IV, Becker JR. Congenital metatarsus adductus: the results of treatment. *J Bone Joint Surg Am*. 1966;48:702.

Reimann I, Werner HH. The pathology of congenital metatarsus varus: a post-mortem study of a newborn infant. *Acta Orthop Scand*. 1983;54:847.

Rushforth GF. The natural history of hooked forefoot. *J Bone Joint Surg Br*. 1978;60-B:530–532.

Smith JT, Bleck EE, Gamble JG, et al. Simple method of documenting metatarsus adductus. *J Pediatr Orthop*. 1991;11:679–680.

Thompson SA. Hallux varus and metatarsus varus. *Clin Orthop*. 1960;16:109.

Soft Tissue Procedures

Addante JB, Chin MW, Loomis JC, et al. Subtalar joint arthroereisis with silastic silicone sphere: a retrospective study. *J Foot Surg*. 1992;31:47.

Allen BL Jr. Plantar-advancement skin flap for central ray resections in the foot: description of a technique. *J Pediatr Orthop*. 1997;17:785.

Asirvatham R, Stevens PM. Idiopathic forefoot-adduction deformity: medial capsulotomy and abductor hallucis lengthening for resistant and severe deformities. *J Pediatr Orthop*. 1997;17:496–500.

Atar D, Lehman WB, Grant AD, et al. Revision surgery in clubfeet. *Clin Orthop Relat Res*. 1992;283:223–230.

Barnett RS. Medial/lateral column separation (third street operation) for dorsal talonavicular subluxation. In: Simons G, ed. *The Clubfoot: The Present and a View of the Future*. New York, NY: Springer-Verlag; 1994:268.

Bensahel H, Csukonyi Z, Desgrippes Y, et al. Surgery in residual clubfoot: one-stage medioposterior release "a la carte." *J Pediatr Orthop*. 1987;7:145–148.

Bentzon P. Pes cavus and the m. peroneus longus. *Acta Orthop Scand*. 1933;4:50.

Black PR, Betts RP, Duckworth T, et al. The Viladot implant in flat-footed children. *Foot Ankle Int*. 2000;21:478–481.

Black GB, Grogan DP, Bobechko WP. Butler arthroplasty for correction of the adducted fifth toe: a retrospective study of 36 operations between 1968 and 1982. *J Pediatr Orthop*. 1985;5:439–441.

Bliss DG, Menelaus MB. The results of transfer of the tibialis anterior to the heel in patients who have a myelomeningocele. *J Bone Joint Surg Am*. 1986;68:1258.

Bost FC, Schottstaedt ER, Larsen LJ. Plantar dissection: an operation to release the soft tissues in recurrent or recalcitrant talipes equinovarus. *J Bone Joint Surg*. 1960;42-A:151.

Breusch SJ, Wenz W, Doderlein L. Function after correction of a clawed great toe by a modified Robert Jones transfer. *J Bone Joint Surg Br*. 2000;82:250–254.

Carroll N. Surgical technique for talipes equinovarus. *Oper Tech Orthop*. 1993;3:115.

Carroll NC. Pathoanatomy and surgical treatment of the resistant clubfoot. *Instr Course Lect*. 1988;37:93–106.

Chuinard EG, Baskin M. Claw-foot deformity: treatment by transfer of the long extensors into the metatarsals and fusion of the interphalangeal joints. *J Bone Joint Surg Am*. 1973;55:351–362.

Cockin J. Butler's operation for an over-riding fifth toe. *J Bone Joint Surg Br*. 1968;50:78–81.

Cole WH. The classic *The treatment of claw-foot* by Wallace H. Cole. 1940. *Clin Orthop Relat Res*. 1983;(181):3–6.

Coleman SS, Stelling FH III, Jarrett J. Pathomechanics and treatment of congenital vertical talus. *Clin Orthop Relat Res*. 1970;70:62–72.

Colton CL. The surgical management of congenital vertical talus. *J Bone Joint Surg Br*. 1973;55:566–574.

Crawford AH, Marxen JL, Osterfeld DL. The Cincinnati incision: a comprehensive approach for surgical procedures of the foot and ankle in childhood. *J Bone Joint Surg Am*. 1982;64:1355–1358.

DeBoeck H. Butler's operation for congenital overriding of the fifth toe: retrospective 1–7-year study of 23 cases. *Acta Orthop Scand*. 1993;64:343.

DeRosa G, Stepro D. Results of posteromedial release for the resistant clubfoot. *J Pediatr Orthop*. 1986;6:590–595.

Eilert RE, Jayakumar SS. Boyd and Syme ankle amputations in children. *J Bone Joint Surg*. 1976;58(8):1138.

Ezra E, Hayek S, Gilai AN, et al. Tibialis anterior tendon transfer for residual dynamic supination deformity in treated club feet. *J Pediatr Orthop B*. 2000;9:207–211.

Ferlic RJ, Breed AL, Mann DC, et al. Partial wound closure after surgical correction of equinovarus foot deformity. *J Pediatr Orthop*. 1997;7:486–489.

Frank GR, Johnson WM. The extensor shift procedure in the correction of clawtoe deformities in children. *South Med J*. 1966;59:889.

Garceau GJ. Anterior tibial tendon transfer for recurrent clubfoot. *Clin Orthop Relat Res*. 1972;84:61–65.

Giannini S, Ceccarelli F, Benedetti MG, et al. Surgical treatment of flexible flatfoot in children: a four-year follow-up study. *J Bone Joint Surg Am*. 2001;83(suppl 2, pt 2):73–79.

Giannini S, Girolami M, Ceccarelli F. The surgical treatment of infantile flat foot: a new expanding orthotic implant. *Ital J Orthop Traumatol*. 1985;11:315–322.

Goldner J, Fitch R. Idiopathic congenital talipes equinovarus (clubfoot). In: Jahss M, ed. *Disorders of the Foot and Ankle: Medical and Surgical Management*. 2nd ed. Philadelphia, PA: WB Saunders; 1991:771.

Goldner JL. Congenital talipes equinovarus—fifteen years of surgical treatment. *Curr Pract Orthop Surg*. 1969;4:61–123.

Green WT. Tendon transplantation in rehabilitation. *JAMA*. 1957;163:1235.

Gutierrez PR, Lara MH. Giannini prosthesis for flatfoot. *Foot Ankle Int*. 2005;26:918–926.

Hamer AJ, Stanley D, Smith TW. Surgery for curly toe deformity: a doubleblind, randomised, prospective trial. *J Bone Joint Surg Br*. 1993;75:662–663.

Harris RI. Syme's amputation: the technical details essential for success. *J Bone Joint Surg*. 1956;38-B:614.

Harris RI. The history and development of Syme's amputation. *Artif Limbs*. 1961;6:4.

Heyman CH, Herndon CH, Strong JM. Mobilization of the tarsometatarsal and intermetatarsal joints for the correction of resistant adduction of the fore part of the foot in congenital club-foot or congenital metatarsus varus. *J Bone Joint Surg Am*. 1958;40(2): 299–309; discussion 291–309.

Hibbs R. An operation for "clawfoot." *JAMA*. 1919;73:1583.

Hoffer MM, Baraket G, Koffman M. 10-year follow-up of split anterior tibial tendon transfer in cerebral palsied patients with spastic equinovarus deformity. *J Pediatr Orthop*. 1985;5:432.

Hoffer MM, Reiswig JA, Garrett AM, et al. The split anterior tibial tendon transfer in the treatment of spastic varus hindfoot of childhood. *Orthop Clin North Am*. 1974;5:31.

Hoke M. An operation for stabilizing paralytic feet. *Am J Orthop Surg Am*. 1921;3:494.

Hudson I, Catterall A. Posterolateral release for resistant club foot. *J Bone Joint Surg Br*. 1994;76:281–284.

Kendrick RE, Sharma NK, Hassler WL, et al. Tarsometatarsal mobilization for resistant adduction of the fore part of the foot. A follow-up study. *J Bone Joint Surg Am*. 1970;52:61–70.

Kuo KN, Hennigan SP, Hastings ME. Anterior tibial tendon transfer in residual dynamic clubfoot deformity. *J Pediatr Orthop*. 2001;21:35–41.

Maxwell JR, Carro A, Sun C. Use of the Maxwell-Brancheau arthroereisis implant for the correction of posterior tibial tendon dysfunction. *Clin Podiatr Med Surg*. 1999;16:479–489.

Maxwell JR, Knudson W, Cerniglia M. The MBA arthroereisis implant: early prospective results. In: Vickers NS, Miller SJ, Mahan KT, eds. *Reconstructive Surgery of the Foot and Leg*. Tucker, GA: Podiatry Institute; 1997:256–264.

Mazet R Jr. Syme's amputation: a follow-up study of fifty-one adults and thirty-two children. *J Bone Joint Surg*. 1968;50-A:1549.

Mazzocca AD, Thomson JD, Deluca PA, et al. Comparison of the posterior approach versus the dorsal approach in the treatment of congenital vertical talus. *J Pediatr Orthop*. 2001;21:212–217.

McKay DW. Dorsal bunions in children. *J Bone Joint Surg Am*. 1983;65:975–980.

McKay DW. New concept of and approach to clubfoot treatment, section II: correction of the clubfoot. *J Pediatr Orthop*. 1983;3:10–21.

Miller GM, Hsu JD, Hoffer MM, et al. Posterior tibial tendon transfer: a review of the literature and analysis of 74 procedures. *J Pediatr Orthop*. 1982;2:363.

Mulier T, Dereymaeker G, Fabry G. Jones transfer to the lesser rays in metatarsalgia: technique and long-term follow-up. *Foot Ankle Int*. 1994;15:523–530.

Nelson SC, Haycock DM, Little ER. Flexible flatfoot treatment with arthroereisis: radiographic improvement and child health survey analysis. *J Foot Ankle Surg*. 2004;43:144–155.

Pollard JP, Morrison PJ. Flexor tenotomy in the treatment of curly toes. *Proc R Soc Med*. 1975;68:480–481.

Ross ER, Menelaus MB. Open flexor tenotomy for hammer toes and curly toes in childhood. *J Bone Joint Surg Br*. 1984;66:770–771.

Rosselli P, Reyes R, Medina A, et al. Use of a soft tissue expander before surgical treatment of clubfoot in children and adolescents. *J Pediatr Orthop*. 2005;25:353.

Saxena A, Nguyen A. Preliminary radiographic findings and sizing implications on patients undergoing bioabsorbable subtalar arthroereisis. *J Foot Ankle Surg*. 2007;46:175–180.

Seimon LP. Surgical correction of congenital vertical talus under the age of 2 years. *J Pediatr Orthop*. 1987;7:405–411.

Sherman FC, Westin GW. Plantar release in the correction of deformities of the foot in childhood. *J Bone Joint Surg Am*. 1981;63:1382–1389.

Simons GW. Complete subtalar release in club feet, part I: a preliminary report. *J Bone Joint Surg Am*. 1985;67:1044–1055.

Simons GW. Complete subtalar release in club feet, Part II: comparison with less extensive procedures. *J Bone Joint Surg Am*. 1985;67:1056–1065.

Smith SD, Millar EA. Arthrorisis by means of a subtalar polyethylene peg implant for correction of hindfoot pronation in children. *Clin Orthop Relat*. 1983;(181):15–23.

Stark JG, Johanson JE, Winter RB. The Heyman–Herndon tarsometatarsal capsulotomy for metatarsus adductus: results in 48 feet. *J Pediatr Orthop*. 1987;7:305–310.

Steindler A. Operative treatment of pes cavus. *Surg Gynecol Obstet*. 1917;24:612.

Steindler A. Stripping of the os calcis. *Am J Orthop Surg*. 1920;2:8.

Steindler A. The treatment of pes cavus. *Arch Surg*. 1921;2:325.

Stricker SJ, Rosen E. Early one-stage reconstruction of congenital vertical talus. *Foot Ankle Int*. 1997;18:535–543.

Sumiya N, Onizuka T. Seven years' survey of our new cleft foot repair. *Plast Reconstr Surg*. 1980;65:447–459.

Sweetnam R. Congenital curly toes: an investigation into the value of treatment. *Lancet*. 1958;2:398–400.

Syme, J. Amputation at the ankle joint. *Lond Edin Month J Med Sci*. 1843;3:93.

Taylor RG. The treatment of claw toes by multiple transfers of flexor into extensor tendons. *J Bone Joint Surg Br*. 1951;33:539.

Thompson G, Richardson A, Westin G. Surgical management of resistant congenital talipes equinovarus deformities. *J Bone Joint Surg Am*. 1982;64:652–665.

Turco VJ. Resistant congenital club foot—one-stage posteromedial release with internal fixation. A follow-up report of a fifteen-year experience. *J Bone Joint Surg Am*. 1979;61:805–814.

Turco VJ. Surgical correction of the resistant club foot. One-stage posteromedial release with internal fixation: a preliminary report. *J Bone Joint Surg Am*. 1971;53:477–497.

Tynan MC, Klenerman L. The modified Robert Jones tendon transfer in cases of pes cavus and clawed hallux. *Foot Ankle Int*. 1994;15:68–71.

Verheyden F, Vanlommel E, Van Der Bauwhede J, et al. The sinus tarsi spacer in the operative treatment of flexible flat feet. *Acta Orthop Belg*. 1997;63:305–309.

Viladot A. Surgical treatment of the child's flatfoot. *Clin Orthop Relat Res*. 1992;283:34.

Walker AP, Ghali NN, Silk FF. Congenital vertical talus: the results of staged operative reduction. *J Bone Joint Surg Br*. 1985;67:117–121.

Westin GW, Sakai DN, Wood WL. Congenital longitudinal absence of the fibula: treatment by Syme amputation. Indications and technique. *J Bone Joint Surg*. 1963;47-A:1159.

Wood VE, Peppers TA, Shook J. Cleft-foot closure: a simplified technique and review of the literature. *J Pediatr Orthop*. 1997;17:501–504.

Yoneda B, Carroll N. One-stage surgical management of resistant clubfoot. *J Bone Joint Surg Br*. 1984;66:302.

Zaret DI, Myerson MS. Arthroerisis of the subtalar joint. *Foot Ankle Clin N Am*. 2003;8:605–617.

Tarsal Coalition

Brown RR, Rosenberg ZS, Thornhill BA. The C sign: more specific for flatfoot deformity than subtalar coalition. *Skeletal Radiol*. 2001;30:84–87.

Bunning PSC, Barnett CH. Variations in the talocalcaneal articulations. *J Anat London*. 1963;97:643.

Clarke DM. Multiple tarsal coalitions in the same foot. *J Pediatr Orthop*. 1997;17:777–780.

Conway JJ, Cowell HR. Tarsal coalition: clinical significance and roentgenographic demonstration. *Radiology*. 1969;92:799–811.

Cooperman DR, Janke BE, Gilmore A, et al. A three-dimensional study of calcaneonavicular tarsal coalitions. *J Pediatr Orthop*. 2001;21:648–651.

Deutsch AL, Resnick D, Campbell G. Computed tomography and bone scintigraphy in the evaluation of tarsal coalition. *Radiology*. 1982;144:137–140.

Emery KH, Bisset GS III, Johnson ND, et al. Tarsal coalition: a blinded comparison of MRI and CT. *Pediatr Radiol*. 1998;28:612–616.

Grogan DP, Holt GR, Ogden JA. Talocalcaneal coalition in patients who have fibular hemimelia or proximal femoral focal deficiency: a comparison of the radiographic and pathological findings. *J Bone Joint Surg Am*. 1994;76:1363–1370.

Harris R, Beath T. Etiology of peroneal spastic flatfoot. *J Bone Joint Surg Br*. 1948;30:624.

Herschel H, Ronnen JRV. The occurrence of calcaneonavicular synosteosis in pes valgus contractus. *J Bone Joint Surg Am*. 1950;32A:280–282.

Herzenberg JE, Goldner JL, Martinez S, et al. Computerized tomography of talocalcaneal tarsal coalition: a clinical and anatomic study. *Foot Ankle*. 1986;6:273–288.

Jayakumar S, Cowell HR. Rigid flatfoot. *Clin Orthop Relat Res*. 1977;122:77–84.

Khoshbin A, Law PW, Caspi L, et al. Long-term functional outcomes of resected tarsal coalitions. *Foot Ankle Int*. 2013;34:1370–1375.

Kumai T, Takakura Y, Akiyama K, et al. Histopathologic study of nonosseous tarsal coalition. *Foot Ankle Int*. 1998;19:525–531.

Kumar SJ, Guille JT, Lee MS, et al. Osseous and non-osseous coalition of the middle facet of the talocalcaneal joint. *J Bone Joint Surg Am*. 1992;74:529–535.

Lateur LM, Hoe LRV, Ghillewe KVV, et al. Subtalar coalition: diagnosis with the C sign on lateral radiographs of the ankle. *Radiology*. 1994;193:847–851.

Leonard MA. The inheritance of tarsal coalition and its relationship to spastic flat foot. *J Bone Joint Surg Br*. 1974;56-B:520–526.

Lysack JT, Fenton PV. Variations in calcaneonavicular morphology demonstrated with radiography. *Radiology*. 2004;230:493–497.

Mosca VS. Flexible flatfoot and tarsal coalition. In: Richards B, ed. *Orthopaedic Knowledge Update: Pediatrics*. Rosemont, IL: American Academy of Orthopaedic Surgeons; 1996:211.

Mosca VS, Bevan WR. Talocalcaneal tarsal coalitions and the calcaneal lengthening osteotomy: the role of deformity correction. *J Bone Joint Surg Am*. 2012;94:1584–1594.

Mosier KM, Asher M. Tarsal coalitions and peroneal spastic flat foot. A review. *J Bone Joint Surg Am*. 1984;66:976–984.

Oestreich AE, Mize WA, Crawford AH, et al. The "anteater nose": a direct sign of calcaneonavicular coalition on the lateral radiograph. *J Pediatr Orthop*. 1987;7:709–711.

Simmons EH. Tibialis spastic varus foot with tarsal coalition. *J Bone Joint Surg Br*. 1965;47:533–536.

Slomann W. On coalitio calcaneo-navicularis. *J Orthop Surg*. 1921;3:586.

Spero CR, Simon GS, Tornetta P III. Clubfeet and tarsal coalition. *J Pediatr Orthop*. 1994;14:372–376.

Stormont DM, Peterson HA. The relative incidence of tarsal coalition. *Clin Orthop Relat Res*. 1983;181:28–36.

Stuecker RD, Bennett JT. Tarsal coalition presenting as a pes cavovarus deformity: report of three cases and review of the literature. *Foot Ankle*. 1993;14:540–544.

Takakura Y, Sugimoto K, Tanaka Y, et al. Symptomatic talocalcaneal coalition: its clinical significance and treatment. *Clin Orthop Relat Res*. 1991;(269):249–256.

Taniguchi A, Tanaka Y, Kadono K, et al. C sign for diagnosis of talocalcaneal coalition. *Radiology*. 2003;228:501–505.

Upasani VV, Chambers RC, Mubarak SJ. Analysis of calcaneonavicular coalitions using multi-planar 3-dimensional computed tomography. *J Child Orthop*. 2008;2:301–307.

Wechsler RJ, Schweitzer ME, Deely DM, et al. Tarsal coalition: depiction and characterization with CT and MR imaging. *Radiology*. 1994;193:447–452.

Wray J, Herndon C. Hereditary transmission of congenital coalition of the calcaneus to the navicular. *J Bone Joint Surg Am*. 1963;45:365.

Index

Muscular activity of normal foot, 11–12
Muscular dystrophy, 18
Myelomeningocele, 16–18, 22*f*, 25, 36, 36*f*, 51*f*,
    52*f*, 57, 62–66, 63*f*, 64*f*, 71–73, 71*f*, 118, 165,
    178–180, 214

N

Natural history, of foot deformities, 40
Naviculectomy, 211–214, 213*f*, 214*f*
    for neglected/recurrent/residual CVT, 90*f*, 91
Neglected clubfoot, 73–74, 73*f*, 74*f*
Nonoperative treatment, for foot deformities
    congenital deformities, 42, 42*f*
    malformations, 42
    outcome of, 39–40, 43
Nonsteroidal anti-inflammatory drugs (NSAIDs)
    calcaneonavicular tarsal coalition, 106, 202
    for talocalcaneal tarsal coalition, 103, 205
NSAIDs. *See* Nonsteroidal anti-inflammatory drugs

O

Ollier incision, modified, 137, 137*f*, 217, 219, 219*f*, 254
Open double cut slide tendo-Achilles lengthening,
    146–147, 147–148*f*
Open plantar fasciotomy
    for limited, minimally invasive soft tissue releases for
        clubfoot, 173
    for severe, rigid, resistant arthrogrypotic
        clubfoot, 76
Open tibialis posterior tenotomy
    for severe, rigid, resistant arthrogrypotic
        clubfoot, 76
Open Z-lengthening tendo-Achilles lengthening,
    149–152, 151*f*
Orthotics, 40, 41, 119
    flat, 92
    heel wedge, 83
Osteotomies
    anterior calcaneus closing wedge, 242–244, 243*f*
    anterior calcaneus lateral closing wedge, 45, 46*f*
    calcaneal lengthening, 137, 216–226, 218–226*f*
    cuboid closing wedge, 43, 96, 101, 238–239, 239*f*
    distal tibia, 47–50, 50–54*f*, 247–251, 250*f*
    extension, 247–251
    fibula deformity correction, 47–50, 50–54*f*
    fibula varus, 247–251
    5th metatarsal, 245–246, 245*f*
    1st metatarsal base, 244–245
    1st metatarsal distal, 246–247
    flexion, 247–251
    medial closing wedge, 82

medial cuneiform (dorsiflexion) dorsal-based closing
    wedge, 47, 49*f*, 238
medial cuneiform (plantar flexion) dorsal-based
    opening wedge, 47, 49*f*, 237–238
medial cuneiform (medial) opening wedge, 96,
    230–232, 231–232*f*
medial cuneiform (plantar flexion) plantar-based
    closing wedge, 47, 48*f*, 94, 235–237, 236*f*
medial cuneiform (dorsiflexion) plantar-based
    opening wedge, 46, 48*f*, 232–235, 233–235*f*
medial cuneiform osteotomy, generic,
    229–230, 229*f*
for planovalgus deformity, 45
posterior calcaneus displacement osteotomy, 67, 134,
    163, 226–229, 227–228*f*
for residual bone deformities, 44
rotational, 247–251
valgus, 247–251

P

Pain
    assessment of, 18
    history of, 18
    site identification, 27, 27*f*
Park–Harris line, 84*f*, 196*f*, 248*f*
PCDO. *See* Posterior calcaneus displacement
    osteotomy
Percutaneous tendo-Achilles tenotomy, 139–145,
    140–144*f*, 214
    for congenital clubfoot, 73
    for neglected clubfoot, 74
    for recurrent/persistent clubfoot deformity, 78
    for severe, rigid, resistant arthrogrypotic
        clubfoot, 76
Percutaneous tenotomies of FHL and FDL to
    toes 2-to 5, 138–139, 138*f*, 139*f*, 188
    limited, minimally invasive soft tissue releases for
        clubfoot, 173
    for severe, rigid, resistant arthrogrypotic clubfoot, 76
Peroneus brevis tendon lengthening
    for congenital oblique talus, 90
    with CLO, 219, 220*f*
    for neglected/recurrent/residual CVT, 91
Peroneus longus to peroneus brevis transfer, 58,
    163–165, 164–165*f*
    for cavovarus foot (due to cerebral palsy), 71
    for cavovarus foot, 69
PF. *See* Plantar fasciotomy
PF/KE. *See* Plantar flexion/knee extension
Physical examination, for foot deformities, 18–28
Physical stretching, for foot deformities, 40, 41